Globalization in
Historical Perspective

A National Bureau
of Economic Research
Conference Report

Globalization in Historical Perspective

Edited by **Michael D. Bordo,
Alan M. Taylor, and
Jeffrey G. Williamson**

The University of Chicago Press

Chicago and London

The University of Chicago Press, Chicago 60637
The University of Chicago Press, Ltd., London
© 2003 by the National Bureau of Economic Research
All rights reserved. Published 2003
Paperback edition 2005
Printed in the United States of America
12 11 10 09 08 07 06 05   2 3 4 5
ISBN: 0-226-06598-7 (cloth)
ISBN: 0-226-06600-2 (paperback)

Library of Congress Cataloging-in-Publication Data

Globalization in historical perspective / edited by Michael D. Bordo,
    Alan M. Taylor, and Jeffrey G. Williamson.
        p.   cm. — (National Bureau of Economic Research conference
    report)
        "The papers were presented at a pre-conference at the NBER in
    Cambridge, Massachusetts, on November 16, 2000, and at a final
    conference held at the Four Seasons Biltmore Hotel, Santa Barbara,
    California, on May 3–6, 2001"—Ackn.
    Includes bibliographical references and index.
    ISBN 0-226-06598-7 (cloth : alk. paper)
    1. International economic integration—Congresses.
    2. Globalization—Economic aspects—Congresses.
    3. Globalization—Social aspects.   4. International trade—Social
    aspects.   5. International finance—Congresses.   6. International
    economic relations—Congresses.   I. Bordo, Michael D.   II. Taylor,
    Alan M., 1964–.   III. Williamson, Jeffrey G., 1935–.   IV. National
    Bureau of Economic Research.   V. Series.

    HF1418.5 .G585 2003
    337—dc21
                                                                2002075080

Contents

Acknowledgments

This volume is the result of a National Bureau of Economic Research (NBER) Conference Project. The papers were presented at a preconference at the NBER in Cambridge, Massachusetts, on 16 November 2000, and at a final conference held at the Four Seasons Biltmore Hotel, Santa Barbara, California, on 3–6 May 2001.

The editors would like to thank Martin Feldstein for his encouragement and support of this project since its inception. Furthermore, the organizational efforts of Kirsten Foss Davis and Rob Shannon of the NBER conference department were essential in making the conferences so lively and productive. In addition, we thank Helena Fitz-Patrick of the NBER publications department for skillfully shepherding the papers through the various stages to publication.

Finally, we would like to state publicly what a joy it was to have a hand in bringing together a wonderful group of social scientists for this project. We hope the chapters in the volume give some sense of the excitement generated during the debates we had along the way. It certainly helped clarify our own understanding of globalization, and we hope the same will be true for readers.

Introduction

Michael D. Bordo, Alan M. Taylor, and
Jeffrey G. Williamson

Overview

Modern globalization has been a recognized force around the world for at least three decades. Academic journals, newspapers, television specials, and political discourse are dominated by globalization events, and their impact seems to be ubiquitous. For most it is a good force, but for a very angry minority it appears to be a bad force. One would have thought that the terms of a force so important would be well defined, its impact understood, and its historical evolution appreciated. This hardly seems to be the case, especially concerning the economic dimensions of globalization, and so this collection of essays attempts to fill an important gap.

Defining Terms

We should begin at the beginning. What do economists mean by the term *globalization*? What is included on their agenda when they debate globalization issues? Typically, their agenda is defined by between-country integration in three markets.

First, there are commodity markets. Here, the debate is about the cause of trade, the impact of trade, and the political determinants of trade policy. As for causes, what determines how much is traded between partners? What are the political, geographic, language, and institutional barriers to trade? What have been the relative contributions of more liberal trade policies and

Michael D. Bordo is professor of economics at Rutgers University and a research associate of the National Bureau of Economic Research. Alan M. Taylor is professor of economics at the University of California–Davis and a research associate of the National Bureau of Economic Research. Jeffrey G. Williamson is the Laird Bell Professor of Economics at Harvard University and a research associate of the National Bureau of Economic Research.

transport revolutions to lowering the barriers to trade? How much of the ongoing trade boom is simply due to fast world economic growth since 1950? As for impact, the questions revolve around specialization, structural adjustment, and distribution. Since the whole point of trade is specialization, the key question here is which industries advance and which retreat in the face of foreign competition. Are the trade gains big or small, and how are they manifested by cheaper and better goods for consumers? How do economies make the supply-side adjustment? Who gains and who loses? What happens to resources thrown out of work by the collapse of a domestic industry that cannot withstand the winds of foreign competition, and do they find alternative employment quickly? Do institutions and government policies tend to minimize the losses by transferring some of the gains from the winners to the losers? Finally, what about the political determinants of trade policy? How do constituents communicate to their political representatives, how do politicians interpret that information, and how do they act on it? Under what conditions would one expect political backlash to globalization?

Second, there are labor markets. When migration is open and free, who does the migrating and why? What are the economic and demographic conditions that matter most in source and destination? What impact does the migration have on the sending and receiving economies? Which residents gain and which lose with a rise of foreign immigration and domestic emigration? What happens to migration flows when restricted by policy? And what is the source of the policy restriction? It should be clear that many of the questions raised about trade and commodity market integration apply here to migration and labor market integration. Indeed, how do the two interact? Is trade a substitute for or a complement to migration?

Third, there are capital markets, where the same questions apply that were just posed for labor markets. In addition, however, global capital market integration raises even more questions. Here are some: What causes global capital market crises? Does integration cause contagion between markets, so that one country's irresponsible policies spread more easily to another country, no matter how responsible? Does a globally integrated world economy ensure that capital flows to poor countries? Do borrowing countries then lose their ability to control their economies? Alternatively, is there a "race to the bottom" as countries try to attract more capital by offering tax advantages and eliminating social welfare programs? Do foreign investors then extract all the gains, or do the host countries get their fair share?

These are the issues that define globalization in this volume. We are aware that this definition excludes much that also matters. It ignores the transmission of disease by traders, so it cannot speak to the twenty-first-century AIDS/HIV epidemic sweeping Africa and Asia. Nor can it address the fourteenth-century European plagues that arrived on ships plying the Asia trade, or the destruction of fifteenth- and sixteenth-century native American populations by smallpox, syphilis, and other European diseases. It pays little attention to the transmission of technology, and thus may miss one of the more important determinants of modern economic growth. It ignores any environmental damage thought to be the result of globalization. It fails to value any loss of native language and culture thought to be the result of globalization. We do not assert that these events are unrelated to globalization, or that they are unimportant. We simply think that, as economists, we are better equipped to resolve the other issues first.

History Matters

The essays in this volume take the long view. Globalization is not a new phenomenon. It pays to seek explanations that can account for more than just global events since 1950; they should also explain global events between 1820 and 1914, and even during the three centuries after Columbus and da Gama started their voyages from the Mediterranean. The long view has another value: The impact of globalization simply cannot be assessed over a year, a decade, or even two. Furthermore, if we fear that the violent political reaction to globalization seen recently in Seattle, Ottawa, Gothenberg, and Genoa might cause a political retreat from liberal policy, then it would pay to look carefully at the twenty years or so before World War I. Then, under popular pressure, immigration restrictions were passed eventually by both houses of the United States Congress, and tariffs were on the rise almost everywhere in the economies of the periphery and also in parts of the core. It would also pay to look carefully at the interwar years when the world moved sharply away from openness and toward self-sufficient autarky, with expanded trade protection everywhere, increased barriers to labor and capital mobility, and widespread monetary and financial dysfunction. Presumably, these experiences might speak to the future possibility of another globalization backlash.

The Papers

The essays in this volume fall into three parts. The first asks how the progress of globalization should be measured. Three chapters document the extent of market integration across time and space in goods, labor, and capital markets. The second places this knowledge into a wider context. Two chapters look at the relationship of globalization to the convergent and divergent outcomes that have occurred within and between nations. Divergence having been the more predominant outcome, two more chapters look globally at the nonuniformity of technological efficiency and the agglomerative forces of economic geography. The third part of the book examines the role of the financial sector in globalization. These essays explore world exchange rate regimes, financial development, financial crises, and the architecture of the international financial system.

Part I: The Rise and Fall (and Rise) of Market Integration

Ronald Findlay and Kevin O'Rourke (chap. 1) examine five hundred years of trade in goods markets to assess the state of integration today in light of history. Their focus is on intercontinental commodity trade, for this is the trade that distinguished post-Columbian globalization from earlier epochs, and it is also the source of the most consistent data with which to assess changes over time. Volumes of trade and prices of trade goods can both tell stories about market integration under different auxiliary assumptions, but here each tells a coherent and complementary story. Trade grew slowly from 1500 to 1800, and price gaps between markets remained large. If transport costs did decline then, it was only a little and was likely offset by the mercantilist bent of the imperial trade regimes.

The nineteenth and twentieth centuries represent a marked break with the past, when trade's weight in the world economy scaled new heights and prices converged dramatically, with the process reaching its first crescendo around 1913. On that basis we can date the globalization of trade as a modern phenomenon of the last two centuries, a statement that may seem unremarkable but will stir some controversy among early modern historians. Perhaps the more remarkable finding for economists, however, is the suggestion that, after an interwar hiatus, the postwar reintegration may have brought us to a point where transport cost and tariff barriers together still impede the flow of goods more than they did on the eve of World War I.

Barry R. Chiswick and Timothy J. Hatton (chap. 2) face a lesser challenge in trying to convince us that today's global labor market is less integrated than its pre-1914 predecessor. Drawing on 400 years of global labor market history, they focus on the causes and consequences of migration in five different eras: (a) the migrations of mostly coerced slave and contracted indentured labor between 1600 and 1790; (b) the early free migrations up to 1850; (c) the mass migrations between 1850 and 1913; (d) the cessation of international migrations during the World Wars and in between; and (e) the modern era of "constrained" mass migration since 1945.

Opportunities for improving living standards drive the migration decision. The trick for the analyst, however, is to isolate the economic, social, and demographic fundamentals that underlie those decisions. Chiswick and Hatton identify those fundamentals and then note that changes in the structure of the world economy have radically altered the direction of the flows since 1945: European outflows dwindled, Latin America switched from destination to source, and new emigrants increasingly flowed out of Africa, Asia, and Eastern Europe. The likely complementarity of migration to globalization in goods and factor markets, and the "permissive" slant given to policy during times of rapid wage growth and labor scarcity in the Organization for Economic Cooperation and Development (OECD), may explain the recent resumption of flows on a scale not seen since 1914. Even so, the current efforts by rich receiving countries to stem the tide of low-skilled immigrants—since they pose the greatest threat to domestic inequality—are likely to continue. Given the size of global disparities, however, the OECD is likely to have limited success.

Maurice Obstfeld and Alan M. Taylor (chap. 3) survey the development of international capital mobility since the mid-nineteenth century. They document the long U traced out by the creation of a well-integrated global capital market by 1914, its collapse during the interwar years, and its resurrection since 1970. This description is enhanced by reference to the open-economy "trilemma" faced by policymakers when choosing between capital markets, domestic monetary targets, and exchange rate regimes.

Obstfeld and Taylor examine a wide array of new evidence, including data on gross asset stocks, interest rate arbitrage, real interest differentials, and equity-return differentials. On all measures examined, the degree of international capital mobility appears to follow this U pattern, being high before World War I, low in the Great Depression, and high today. The debate over whether global capital mobility is greater today than it was on the eve of World War I may never be resolved, and no such attempt is made in the chapter. However, the authors do suggest that world capital may have flowed more easily to the poorer countries before 1914 than it does today.

Part II: The Great Divergence, Geography, and Technology

J. Bradford DeLong and Steve Dowrick (chap. 4) examine the relationship between the persistence of global disparities and the rising forces of globalization. Specifically, they examine inequality in technology, capital intensity, and per capita incomes at the national level, a place where enormous gaps have opened up. Although one or another subgroup of economies has from time to time enjoyed convergence in all these dimensions—notably the poorest countries within the OECD—much of the world has remained stubbornly outside the process.

Mapping the "convergence club" over two centuries shows how its membership has changed over time and also how it correlates with the major ups and downs in globalization. The "great divergence" in incomes that began with the uneven spread of industrialization in the nineteenth century has only intensified on a global scale in the last one hundred years, and nations today occupy "the most unequal world ever seen." However, levels and trends tell different stories, and recent positive news, especially from China and India, suggests that more countries are now closing the gap, or climbing on the "escalator of modern economic growth." The explanation of these recent trends is still contested, but the authors conclude that a combination of poverty traps and antigrowth policies held back the poorest countries, and that openness was a positive but by no means uniform brake on between-country inequality.

Peter H. Lindert and Jeffrey G. Williamson (chap. 5) expand the debate over global disparities by adding globalization's impact on within-country inequality. Over the very long run, they find no comparable divergence within countries associated with globalization. At the global level, international productivity disparities tell most of the long-run story. They also show, however, how changing within-country inequality in the short run has had important political influences in the past.

The nineteenth century offers some good examples. In the 1840s, the Anti–Corn Law League found vociferous support from working-class protests starting on the streets of Manchester. For labor-abundant, land-scarce European countries, free trade in that era meant cheaper foodstuffs from overseas, and this acted as an income-equalizing force by raising real wages of the laboring poor while reducing the land rents of the rich aristocracy. Conversely, the trade boom among land-abundant trading partners, like the United States, raised land rents relative to wages, moving income distribution in the opposite direction. By analogy we can expect offsetting movements in within-country inequality in different regions of the world at all times, whether trade is on the rise or not, and this helps us understand the flat within-country inequality trend worldwide and the important cross-country tensions it masks. For both proponents and opponents of globalization, the importance of the inequality question may depend on whether one's egalitarian philosophy stretches beyond one's national border. Since open countries seem to grow faster, and since growth seems to be shared equally among those in poor countries, there is every reason to believe that globalization is good, and good for the poor, too. However, that conclusion is strongest where the definition of global participation is most comprehensive.

Gregory Clark and Robert C. Feenstra (chap. 6) ponder the role of technology in the "great divergence" between nations. Various factors can combine to cause one country's level of productivity to be low relative to another: a low capital intensity, a scarcity of other resource inputs, or a low level of technology. Although capital, both physical and human, has been shown to play a role, the authors place technology at center stage.

Measured by total factor productivity, this factor varies enormously across countries, and explains most of the dispersion in productivity levels. Moreover, under assumptions of an open capital market, technological differences might also endogenously determine equilibrium capital intensities, which will also then be lower. Evidence can be adduced from a variety of sources across the twentieth century to make the case, such as sector studies of textile mills and railroads. More aggregative studies using trade flows to reveal the inherent differences in country-specific factor productivity provide independent confirmation, but whereas these differences are known to exist, their precise channels of operation and underlying sources remain mysterious.

Nicholas Crafts and Anthony J. Venables (chap. 7) examine another possible source of divergence in the world economy, the effect of increasing returns. The new economic geography has turned space into anything but a homogeneous area of evenly spread industries, inputs, outputs, and incomes. Initial conditions, transaction costs, and location matter a great deal in the new economic geography, and the power of cumulative causation can generate persistently unequal outcomes.

The authors use this thinking to explore the first great era of globalization, applying those historical lessons to the present. Looking first at the "Atlantic economy" of the late nineteenth century, they see benefits to explaining the rise of industry in the New World economies, particularly the United States, in this framework. Simple classical competitive models cannot account for the American "overtaking" in industry, which somehow overcame an initial comparative advantage that favored agriculture in 1800 to create a springboard for overall economic superiority in the "American Century" after 1900. However, in a new economic geography model—with monopolistic competition and positive feedback in manufacturing—economic scale and size of market are the keys to "Smithian" growth and agglomeration. This model helps us understand the seeming oddities of changing economic leadership in the short run, and it thus yields deeper insight into patterns of divergence in the long run.

Part III: Financial Institutions, Regimes, and Crises

Peter L. Rousseau and Richard Sylla (chap. 8) explore the links between domestic financial development, domestic growth, and international financial market integration. Historical accounts of the Dutch Republic, England, the United States, France, Germany, and Japan demonstrate that in each case the emergence of a domestic financial system jump-started modern economic growth. Indeed, using a cross-country panel of seventeen countries covering the 1850–1997 period, they uncover a robust correlation between financial factors and economic growth that is consistent with a leading role for finance, and, moreover, these effects were strongest over the eighty years prior to the 1930s.

By identifying roles for both finance and trade in the convergence of interest rates among Atlantic economies in the prewar period, Rousseau and Sylla show that countries with more sophisticated financial systems tended to engage in more trade and appeared to be better integrated with other economies. Their results suggest that both the growth and the increasing globalization of these economies depended on improvements in their financial systems.

Michael D. Bordo and Marc Flandreau (chap. 9) focus on international monetary regimes. They distinguish between the experience of core (advanced countries) and periphery (emerging countries). Before 1914, the core adhered to gold, while the periphery either emulated the core or floated. Some periphery countries were especially vulnerable to financial crises and debt default, in large part because of their extensive external debt obligations denominated in core-country currencies. This left them with the difficult choice of floating but restricting external borrowing or devoting considerable resources to maintaining an extra hard peg. Although advanced countries can successfully float today, emerging countries that are less financially mature are likely to fear floating: To obtain access to foreign capital, they may need a hard peg to core-country currencies.

Thus, the authors emphasize that the key distinction between core and periphery both then and now with respect to the exchange rate choice is financial maturity, making their approach complementary to the growth findings in chapter 9. They then develop their financial maturity hypothesis and present narrative evidence for the pre-1914 period of the different experiences of core and periphery in adhering to the gold standard and offer evidence from the past and present that suggests a strong link between financial maturity and the exchange rate regime.

Larry Neal and Marc Weidenmier (chap. 10) examine the history of financial crisis that accompanied the first phase of international financial integration laid out in chapter 8. Using a newly compiled high frequency database of short-term interest rates in the pre-World War I gold standard decades, the authors explore the interdependencies between financial markets in both the core and the periphery in periods of financial crisis. They interpret evidence of a weaker response of periphery countries to core-country shocks as being consistent with the presence of credit rationing. They test the effects of both increased interdependence that accompanied globalization and contagion that occurs independent of increased interdependence. They find little evidence for contagion in the crisis of 1873, but more in the crises of 1893 and 1907. They attribute this pattern of contagion to the presence of implicit capital controls.

Barry Eichengreen and Harold James (chap. 11) review the history of international monetary and financial reform in two eras of globalization, the late nineteenth century and the late twentieth century, and in the period in between. Their narrative is organized around the hypothesis that a consensus on the need for monetary and financial reform is apt to develop when such reform is seen as essential for the defense of the global trading system. In most periods, the international monetary and financial system evolves in a gradual and decentralized manner, largely in response to market forces. The shift toward greater exchange rate flexibility and capital account convertibility since 1973 is the most recent and therefore most obvious illustration of what is a more general point.

Throughout the period they consider, there has existed an abiding faith in the advantages of trade for economic growth, the principal exception being the 1930s. In contrast, there has never existed a comparable consensus on the benefits of open international capital markets for stability, efficiency, and growth. It follows that disruptions to capital markets that do not also threaten the trading system have had less of a tendency to catalyze reform. They test this hypothesis by confronting it with evidence from major attempts—successful, such as Bretton Woods in 1944, and unsuccessful, such as the London Economic Conference 1933—to reform the international monetary system.

Globalization in Interdisciplinary Perspective: A Panel

Following the papers, a round table on the Costs and Benefits of Globalization convened, chaired by Peter B. Kenen of Princeton University. Experts from different disciplines were invited to focus their attention on the themes raised by the conference papers in terms of the following questions: What are the benefits? What are the costs? Who wins and who loses? And what does the future look like?

The first panelist was Clive Crook, an editor of *The Economist*. Crook considered the possibility that globalization would be reversed by political forces in the advanced countries the way it was after 1914. He expressed concern that popular and political opinion had considerable support for the current crop of protestors. He discussed the fears, imaginary and real, that were capturing the popular imagination to some extent. These included falling real wages for the unskilled, general concern over economic security, and sympathy with the erroneous belief that globalization raises poverty in the Third World and undermines the capacity to pay for the welfare state. According to Crook, the evidence does not support most of these concerns. However, government officials do not generally acknowledge this evidence. Indeed, many have expressed sympathy for such views, offering inappropriate support for the proponents of political backlash.

Gerardo della Paolera, rector of Universidad Torcuato di Tella in Buenos Aires, reflected on the conference from the perspective of Argentina and other countries that are in transition toward opening up to the global trading and financial system. Della Paolera feels that it is crucial to understand the forces producing stop-go in those countries exploiting globalization as they try to catch up on the leaders. Thus, he makes a case for more research on the institutional development and political economy of globalization to understand why reforms became truncated and why such countries are led to import institutions wholesale from more successful countries.

Niall Ferguson, a historian at Jesus College, Oxford, considered some big issues not directly addressed by the conference papers. He argued that although the conference covered the flows of goods, labor, capital, and technology there was no discussion on the flows of knowledge, institutions, culture, and political systems. He stressed the importance of political globalization and its many dimensions, including the crucial role of empires and warfare in eighteenth- and nineteenth-century globalization experience. Ferguson noted that the global spread of democracy in our time has led to political fragmentation, civil wars, and corruption—forces that may act to impede globalization.

Anne O. Krueger, deputy managing director of the International Monetary Fund, reflected on the role of postwar U.S. economic policy in setting the stage for the last two decades of globalization. From World War II onward, policies toward developing countries that led to many successful outcomes were based on a consensus between cold warriors and humanists. This consensus has broken down with the end of the cold war, and Krueger worries about the influence of U.S. spokesmen and spokeswomen on the effectiveness of international financial institutions, nongovernmental organizations, and others who believe that globalization is hurting the poor countries. Krueger also contrasted the pre-1914 globalization era with the present one. For example, she argues that although the success of Germany in the pre-1914 era relied much less on access to the global economy, today's stars, as is illustrated by South Korea, have relied extensively on an open trading system to achieve rapid growth since the 1960s. Also in comparison to the earlier era of globalization, the high rates of per capita growth today in countries like Korea considerably minimized the losses borne by the groups of globalization losers.

Finally, Ronald Rogowski, a political scientist from the University of California, Los Angeles, assessing directly the costs and benefits and identifying the winners and losers. The benefits are global, whereas the costs are local. The key losers in today's advanced countries are unskilled workers. They are affected adversely by technological change, by international trade, by migration, by capital flows to emerging countries, and by their greater exposure to exogenous shocks. According to Rogowski, these are the groups that are increasingly turning to the political system in Europe and America to try to stop the global advance. However, he concludes that globalization in the advanced countries will not be derailed by such forces because median voters are net winners, and policies to compensate the losers will continue to be important.

Rogowski argues that the forces creating a divergence between winners and losers stressed in the conference—local economies of scale, human capital accumulation, technological change—may not be as important as bad institutions and bad policies. The fact that some major less developed countries, like China and India, are changing these policies raises hope for the future.

An Assessment

This book reveals just how much we now know about the globalization process, and it is impressive. It also reveals how much *more* we need to learn about the interaction of politics and economics. The better we understand the political economy of globalization, the better armed we will be to anticipate any future globalization backlash. History need not repeat itself if we understand the mistakes of the past.

Islamic world, stretching from the Atlantic to the Himalayas, and Sung China were the most advanced economic systems of that era with large cities, considerable manufacturing production, and sophisticated monetary and credit systems. Western Europe, except for the Italian cities and Flanders, was a relatively backward agricultural area.

Despite the destruction unleashed during the process of its creation, the establishment of the Mongol Empire in the thirteenth century led to a unification of the Eurasian continent as a result of the "Pax Mongolica" across Central Asia. As Needham (1954) and others have argued, perhaps without sufficient specificity, the Pax Mongolica led to a significant transmission of ideas and techniques, along with an increased volume of goods and people. In addition, however, there was also the transmission of the deadly plague germs that resulted in the demographic catastrophe of the Black Death in the 1340s: This reduced the population of Europe and the Middle East by about a third. The reduced volume of production and trade led economic historians to speak of the centuries of the Renaissance in Europe as a time of economic depression. As several authors have pointed out, however, the plague raised per capita wealth, incomes, and wage-rates, replacing a large but relatively stagnant European economy in 1340 that was already at its Malthusian limits with one that had two-thirds of the population but the same amount of land, capital, and stock of precious metals in coins and bullion. The economic and monetary consequences of the Black Death are worked out by means of a general equilibrium model with endogenous population, capital, and commodity money supply in Findlay and Lundahl (2000). Real wages rise; population slowly recovers, driving real wages slowly down again; and an initial inflationary spike is followed by a long phase of deflation. The model postulates a demand for Eastern luxuries that rises with the higher per capita wealth and income, leading to an increased outflow of precious metals to the East and hence a prolonged monetary contraction. Thus what Day (1978) called the "Great Bullion Famine of the Fifteenth Century" can be explained as a consequence of the Black Death in the previous century. Eventually the model predicts a return to the initial long-run stationary equilibrium that prevailed before the onset of the Black Death, if all underlying behavioral relationships remain unchanged.

As Herlihy (1997) argues, however, the drastically altered circumstances of people's lives would prompt alternatives in attitudes and institutions. The greater scarcity of labor would tend to dissolve feudal ties and stimulate labor-saving innovations, the higher per capita incomes could lead to postponement of the age at marriage in an effort to maintain the higher income levels, and so on. Furthermore, this period of increased incomes and a higher demand for Asian luxury goods coincided with the demise of the Pax Mongolica and its associated overland trade, and a consequent reliance (once more) on traditional Indian Ocean trade routes and monopolistic Egyptian and Venetian intermediaries. Presumably this increased the incentive to find a sea route to Asia. The result of all these changed incentives could well be a more modern society in 1450 than in 1350, one that was ready to venture more readily and further abroad and so usher in a true era of globalization with the Voyages of Discovery linking all the continents by sea.

1.3   World Trade 1500–1780

1.3.1   Introduction

This period opens with the European Voyages of Discovery across the Atlantic and around the Cape of Good Hope to the eastern seas, shortly followed by the crossing of the Pacific and the circumnavigation of the globe. The "globalization" of the world economy in the sense of the linking of markets in the Old and New Worlds that had hitherto been separated thus begins in this period, even if we have to wait until later for evidence of a "big bang" in terms of convergence in world product and factor prices. Thus Flynn and Giraldez (1995) are not necessarily only tongue in cheek when they date the "origin of world trade" to the year 1571 when the city of Manila was founded, directly linking the trade of Europe, Asia, Africa, and the Americas. However, with transport costs still high relative to production costs, long-distance trade was largely confined to commodities with a high ratio of value to weight and bulk, such as spices, silk, silver, and, last but not least, slaves. Nevertheless, the channels were laid along which the volume of world trade could grow later under the influence of technological change, capital accumulation, and population growth.

The most momentous immediate consequence of the discoveries was the injection of large amounts of silver into the circuits of world trade, with the influx into Europe in particular leading to the so-called "price revolution of the sixteenth century." Within Europe the period was marked also by shifts in the locus of what Kindleberger (1996) calls "economic primacy." The Iberian voyages led to a shift away from the earlier commercial dominance of Venice and the Italian cities, since the Cape route broke the monopoly shared by Venice and the rulers of Egypt on the spice trade through the Red Sea. The Portuguese were soon displaced, however, by the rising power of the Dutch, with Amsterdam, the "Venice of the North," displacing the original one and its successor Antwerp. There followed the long struggle between the Dutch and the English East India companies, the "multinational corporations" of that area.

Despite the prominence of European explorers, conquistadors, and merchants during the earlier part of this period it is a profound historical mistake to imagine European dominance of the global economy as dating from soon after the original voyages. Ironically, the phrase "Vasco da Gama Epoch" was coined not by a European but by the nationalist Indian diplomat and historian **K. M.** Panikkar (1953). We must not forget that Constantinople fell to the Ottoman Turks shortly before da Gama was born and that the Safavids and Mughals established their rule in Persia and India before his death, in the first case, and shortly after it, in the second. All three of these formidable "gunpowder empires" were involved in the network of world trade despite being essentially territorial powers, with dependence on imports of silver for their coinage being the most important link. Access to firearms and opportunities for greater revenue through taxing trade were also an important factor in strengthening native kingdoms throughout Southeast Asia and Japan. In the case of Ming China the introduction of the sweet potato, peanuts, and other New World crops led to a substantial increase in agricultural productivity, stimulating population growth and the demand for imported silver and leading in turn to the export of tea, porcelain, and silk (Ho 1959).

1.3.2   Trade after the Voyages of Discovery: Qualitative Trends

One way of thinking about the qualitative evolution of world trade over time is given in Mauro (1961), who presents an intriguing intercontinental matrix for world trade during this period, with the Americas separated into tropical and temperate zones. The Voyages of Discovery, as well as those of Captain Cook, led to the emergence of trade flows between continents where previously there had been none; thus cells in the matrix which had been empty were no longer so. Second, once this had happened the range of goods being traded between continents began to expand, in response to declining transport costs, or shifts in demand and supply in the various regions of the world. The period from 1500 to 1780 was marked by a gradual evolution in the type of goods being traded. Originally the goods concerned were for the most part noncompeting, in the sense that the trade was driven by the availability of commodities in some continents but not in others. Thus, Asia exported spices and silk, while the Americas exported silver. These goods had an extremely high value-to-bulk ratio, the high prices being due to the absence of local substitutes in destination markets. As the period progressed, bulkier commodities began to be shipped. Typically, these commodities (e.g., sugar and raw cotton) were still produced only in particular continents and faced rather imperfect substitutes in destination markets (e.g., honey and wool). The great counterexample was India's exports of cotton textiles, which accounted for more than half of the East India Company's exports to Europe in the 1750s (table 1.1). However, it was really only after the transport revolutions of the nineteenth century that intercontinental trade began in homogeneous bulk commodities, such as wheat, iron, and steel, that could be produced anywhere.

The discovery of the Cape route had an almost immediate impact on Venetian imports of pepper and spices, but the effect was short-lived. Wake (1979, 373) reports that pepper imports declined by 85 percent in 1501 over

Table 1.1   Composition of European Overseas Imports, 1513–1780

A. Imports from Asia to Lisbon, 1513–1610 (% of weight)

	1513–19	1523–31	1547–48	1587–88	1600–03	1608–10
Pepper	80.0	84.0	89.0	68.0	65.0	69.0
Other spices	18.4	15.6	9.6	11.6	16.2	10.9
Indigo	0.0	0.0	0.0	8.4	4.4	7.7
Textiles	0.2	0.0	0.0	10.5	12.2	7.8
Miscellaneous	1.4	0.4	1.4	1.5	2.2	4.6
Total	100.0	100.0	100.0	100.0	100.0	100.0

B. Imports of VOC into Europe, 1619–1780 (% by invoice value)

	1619–21	1648–50	1668–70	1698–1700	1738–40	1778–80
Pepper	56.5	50.4	30.5	11.2	8.1	9.0
Other spices	17.6	17.9	12.1	11.1	6.1	3.1
Textiles	16.1	14.2	36.5	54.7	41.1	49.5
Tea and coffee				4.2	32.2	27.2
Drugs, perfumes, and dye-stuffs	9.8	8.5	5.8	8.3	2.8	1.8
Sugar		6.4	4.2	0.2	3.7	0.6
Saltpeter		2.1	5.1	3.9	2.6	4.4
Metals	0.1	0.5	5.7	5.3	1.1	2.7
Miscellaneous		0.2	0.1	0.4	2.3	1.7
Total	100.0	100.0	100.0	100.0	100.0	100.0

C. Imports of English East India Company into Europe, 1668–1760 (% of invoice value)

	1668–70	1698–1700	1738–40	1758–60
Pepper	25.25	7.02	3.37	4.37
Textiles	56.61	73.98	69.58	53.51
Raw silk	0.6	7.09	10.89	12.27
Tea	0.03	1.13	10.22	25.23
Coffee	0.44	1.93	2.65	
Indigo	4.25	2.82		
Saltpeter	7.67	1.51	1.85	2.97
Miscellaneous	5.15	4.52	1.44	1.65
Total	100.0	100.0	100.0	100.0

the average of the 1490s and spices by 42 percent. Portuguese imports supplied half the European market in 1503–06 and much more a decade later (Wake, 381). However, the Portuguese never succeeded in their ambition to monopolize the pepper and spice trade. As the sixteenth century progressed the Venetians and the overland trade fought back: In 1560 Venice imported 2,000 tons of pepper, more than it had imported in 1496 (Bulbeck et al.

Table 1.1   (continued)

D. *Estimated Annual Sales of Colonial Imports, England and the Netherlands, 1751–54*

	Total Sales (thousands of pesos)	Percentage of Sales	
		From Asia	Of Total
Textiles	6,750	41.7	21.1
Pepper	1,100	6.8	3.4
Tea	2,800	17.3	8.7
Coffee	1,000	6.2	3.1
Spices	1,850	11.4	5.8
Miscellaneous	2,700	16.7	8.4
Total from Asia	16,200	100.0	50.5
		From America	Of Total
Sugar	8,050	50.8	25.1
Tobacco	3,700	23.3	11.5
Miscellaneous	4,100	25.9	12.8
Total from America	15,850	100.0	49.5
Total overseas imports	32,050		100.0

Sources: Prakesh (1998, 36, 115, 120); Steensgaard (1995, 12).

1998, table 3.2, 72–73).[1] Nor did the voyages of discovery lead to an immediate collapse in European pepper prices: Instead, figure 1.1 shows real pepper prices initially rising sharply, as the Portuguese disrupted traditional trade routes, and then rising for a second time in midcentury.[2] They then started to decline, especially during the seventeenth century, which saw the Portuguese displaced by the Dutch and English East India Companies. Imports into Europe increased substantially and prices fell to 30–40 percent below the prices maintained by the Portuguese in the previous century (Wake, 389). Although Venice had successfully competed with the Portuguese during the sixteenth century it could not survive the Anglo-Dutch competition in the first half of the seventeenth century. The annual consumption of pepper in Europe increased from about 3.4 million pounds in

1. Similarly, the new sea routes did *not* lead to the collapse of the traditional caravan trade across central Asia. To be sure, this trade did indeed eventually collapse in the late sixteenth and seventeenth centuries, but this was primarily due to political turmoil along the route. By contrast, caravan trade did prosper in the late seventeenth and eighteenth centuries along a northern route (through southern Siberia and northern Central Asia). This trade was conducted by Russian merchants and took place within Russian territory until the merchants reached China itself (Rossabi 1990).

2. These are the European pepper price series given in Bulbeck et al. (1998, 70), deflated by the average Valencian price level calculated in Hamilton (1934).

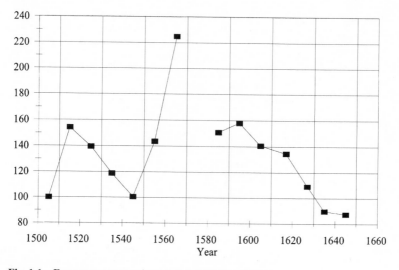

Fig. 1.1   European pepper prices, deflated (1505 = 100)

1611 to 8.6 million in 1688, of which the Dutch supplied 4.00 and the English 3.24 million (Wake, p. 391).

Pepper production and exports from Southeast Asia rose in response to the increased demand not only from Europe but also from China. Bulbeck et al. (1998, table 3.7) indicate total exports from Southeast Asia increasing by a factor of 3.4 from the beginning to the end of the sixteenth century, by a further 50 percent to the end of the seventeenth century, and by 20 percent more to the end of the eighteenth century—about sixfold from 1500–1800. The table also shows that the shares of Europe, China, and "Other Regions" in total exports were stable at roughly one-third each over the entire period, despite considerable fluctuations between decades. Chinese emigrants from the southern provinces engaged in a vigorous expansion of cultivation in Southeast Asia during the eighteenth century, using innovative labor-intensive methods that raised yields per acre substantially.

Table 1.1 presents various estimates of the commodity composition of European imports from 1513 to 1780. European imports from Asia were initially dominated by pepper and other spices (nutmeg, mace, cloves, and cinnamon), but over time the list of commodities being traded widened. Pepper, which accounted for well over half of imports from Asia in the sixteenth century (and initially accounted for more than 80 percent of Portuguese imports: table 1.1, panel A) declined sharply to less than 10 percent of Asian imports by the eighteenth. The Portuguese were importing textiles from Asia by the late sixteenth century; cotton textiles, mainly from India, made up 70 to 80 percent of British East India Company imports after 1660 and were the single most important import commodity for the Dutch as

Table 1.2   **Intercontinental Silver Flows, 1501–1800 (annual average)**

Years	American Production (tons)	European Imports Tons	European Imports % of American Production	European Exports Tons	European Exports % of European Imports	Asian Imports Tons	Asian Imports % of American Production
1501–1525	45	40	88.9				
1526–1550	125	105	84.0				
1551–1575	240	205	85.4				
1575–1600	290	205	70.7			2.4	0.8
1601–1625	340	245	72.1	100	40.8	17	5.0
1626–1650	395	290	73.4	125	43.1	16	4.1
1651–1675	445	330	74.2	130	39.4	6	1.3
1676–1700	500	370	74.0	155	41.9	15	3.0
1701–1725	550	415	75.5	190	45.8	15	2.7
1726–1750	650	500	76.9	210	42.0	15	2.3
1751–1775	820	590	72.0	215	36.4	15	1.8
1776–1800	940	600	63.8	195	32.5	20	2.1

Source: Barrett (1990, tables 7.3, 7.6).

well after 1700 (table 1.1, panels B, C). Tea and coffee were insignificant until they rose sharply around 1700, constituting a quarter of East India Company sales in Europe by the middle of the century. Despite this diversification, however, the Asian trade was still heavily concentrated in just a few items: pepper, fine spices, cotton textiles, tea, and coffee constituted between 80 and 90 percent of imports from Asia throughout the period (Steensgaard 1995, 10).

By the middle of the eighteenth century, total colonial imports by England and the Netherlands combined were valued at 32 million pesos, about equally divided between Asia and the Americas (table 1.1, panel D). Quantification of imports from America is more difficult, since this trade was not dominated by a few large companies for long periods of time, as was the case in Asia (Steensgaard 1995, 11). The most important nonmonetary import was sugar: Total European imports of sugar were 170,000 metric tons by about 1750, ten times the level of the early seventeenth century (Steensgaard, 12). Sugar accounted for roughly 50 percent of Europe's imports from America, with the remainder being evenly divided between tobacco and miscellaneous items.

Initially, however, the most important European import from the New World, in terms of its economic consequences, was silver. Table 1.2 reproduces the data given in Barrett (1990) on flows of silver from the Americas to Europe and Asia, as well as on European exports of silver. American production rose for every quarter century over this period, from an annual average of 45 tons in 1501–25 to 340 tons in 1601–25, 550 tons in 1701–25, and 940 tons in 1776–1800. Europe imported almost 90 percent of this output in the early sixteenth century, but the proportion shipped to Europe fell over time, reflecting increased retention within the Americas: The figure hovered between 70 and 80 percent during most of the period. Some part of silver production in the New World was exported by the Acapulco galleons across the Pacific to Manila. However, the annual average flow was around 15 tons for most of the seventeenth and eighteenth centuries. It was thus relatively insignificant compared to the export of American silver through Europe.

What happened to the silver that Europe imported? Europe's deficit on imports of Indonesian spices; Chinese porcelain, silk, and tea; and Indian cotton textiles was largely paid for by American silver drained from Spain: Exports from Europe rose from 100 tons in 1601–25 to nearly double a century later, after which they flattened out. Calculations by Steensgaard (1995, table 2) clearly show that the Asian trade of the English and Dutch East India companies would have been impossible without access to the bullion supplies of the New World to finance the gap between the invoice value of imports and exports of goods and services (the value of remittances).[3] On the other hand, retention within Europe also rose, from 145 tons in 1601–25 to 225 tons in 1701–25 and over 400 tons in the last quarter of the eighteenth century. Indeed, Europe absorbed an increasing proportion of the American shipments over the period (from around 60 percent at the start of the seventeenth century to almost 70 percent at the end of the eighteenth, despite the widespread allegation that China and India had a supposedly irrational desire to hoard specie unproductively. Since bullion formed the high-powered money of the period, these figures indicate the extent of monetization in Europe and Asia. The impact on Europe of this monetary expansion continues to be a hotly debated issue, and its possible ramifications as far afield as Ottoman Turkey, Mughal India, and Ming China have also been examined. Despite its turbulence, the sixteenth century was almost everywhere an age of monetary, economic, and demographic expansion, while the seventeenth has been associated with a famous crisis (first identified by Hobsbawm 1954) during which growth stagnated and prices fell. Here again the phenomenon was first debated in a European

---

3. Steensgaard presents a calculation of the values of exports, imports, and profits of the two East India companies, expressed as annual averages for the 1740–45 period. Total exports were 6.1 million pesos, while the sales value of imports was 12.8 million pesos, compared with an invoice value of 5.7 million pesos, leaving a gross profit of 7.1 million pesos. Dividends were 1.3 million with 5.8 million left over to cover all costs other than the invoice value of imports. The exports of 6.1 million pesos break down into only 1.2 million for commodity exports, while exports of treasure (mainly silver) were over half the total at 3.6 million, the rest being remittances by merchants and staff of 1.2 million, or 20 percent of the total. The gross profit margin (ratio to invoice value of sales) was huge, at over 125 percent, roughly the same for both companies, while net profits were estimated by Steensgaard at about 13 percent for the English and 10 percent for the Dutch company. These net profit figures indicate that the companies were not in any way exceptionally profitable, contrary to the implication by Wallerstein (1980), for example, that vast profits were extracted by the "core" from the "periphery."

the means for obtaining strategic imports such as naval stores from the Baltic, and Oriental wares such as tea and muslin for re-export to other European markets. In a classic formulation, Viner (1948) pointed out that the "power" of the state (primarily naval) was used to obtain "plenty" through trade, which could be taxed in turn to finance the sources of power. The history of the Anglo-Dutch wars of the seventeenth century and the Anglo-French wars of the eighteenth illustrate the links between commercial and geopolitical factors exemplified by Viner's analysis.

The wars on the continent of Europe involving France, Prussia, and Austria were over territorial acquisition and dynastic aggrandizement. These became intertwined, however, with commercial conflicts in the New World and India, leading some to speak of the Seven Years' War from 1756 to 1763 as the first "world" war. The bonanza opened up by the Iberian voyages of discovery led to a series of sustained conflicts between their predatory successors that was not to be resolved until the triumph of Britain at the end of the Napoleonic Wars. It is only within a framework such as this that we can obtain a proper perspective on the plethora of monopoly rights, navigation acts, bounties, drawbacks, prohibitions, and blockades that constituted trade policy during the Age of Mercantilism. Needless to say, such an attempt, fascinating as it would be, is well beyond the scope of this paper.

1.3.4   Trade after the Voyages of Discovery: Quantitative Trends

O'Rourke and Williamson (2001, table 1) assemble an extensive range of published estimates for particular channels of trade for the past five centuries, and compute growth rates of world trade for each of them. The results show that intercontinental trade grew at 1.26 percent per annum in the sixteenth century, and that growth fell to 0.66 percent per annum in the seventeenth century before rising back to 1.26 percent per annum in the eighteenth century. The growth rate for the entire 1500–1800 period was 1.06 percent per annum. Although this may look small to modern eyes it was certainly well ahead of the growth rate of world population during this period, which increased from 461 million in 1500 to 954 million in 1800, or at a rate of 0.24 percent per annum. While we do not have data it is highly unlikely that intercontinental trade as a whole grew faster than world population for any previous century; in this sense, the post-1500 period does mark a clear break with the past. Similarly, the qualitative evidence assembled above regarding the development of new trade routes, especially across the Atlantic, the growing volume of trade in particular commodities over those routes, and changing patterns of comparative advantage, also suggest that 1500 marked an important turning point in the history of world trade.

Nonetheless, the best measure of international commodity market integration remains international price convergence. Figure 1.2 plots markups for cloves, pepper, and coffee (O'Rourke and Williamson 2000, based on Bulbeck et al. 1998), where markups are defined as the ratio of European to

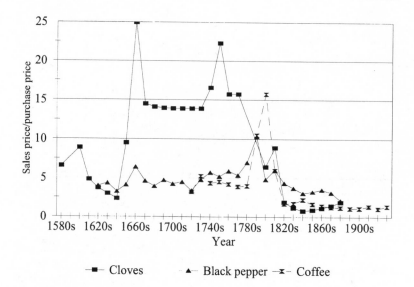

Fig. 1.2   Spice and coffee markups: Amsterdam versus Southeast Asia, 1580–1939

Asian price. The figure shows price convergence for cloves from the 1590s to the 1640s, but it was short-lived, since the spread rose to a 350-year high in the 1660s and maintained that high level during the Vereenigde Oostindische Compagnie (VOC) monopoly and up to the 1770s. The clove price spread fell steeply at the end of the French Wars, and by the 1820s was one-fourteenth of the 1730s level. This low spread was maintained across the nineteenth century. Between the 1620s and the 1730s the pepper price spread remained fairly stable, after which it soared to a 250-year high in the 1790s. By the 1820s, the pepper price spread of the early seventeenth century was recovered, and price convergence continued up to the 1880s, when the series ends. While there was some modest price convergence for coffee during the half century between the 1730s and the 1780s, the French Wars saw a dramatic rise in price spreads. At the war's end, price convergence resumed, so that the coffee price spread in the 1850s was one-sixth of what it had been in the 1750s, and in the 1930s it was one-thirteenth of what it had been in the 1730s. Thus, there is absolutely no evidence of commodity price convergence for these important Dutch imports prior to the nineteenth century. Was English trade in Asia any different than Dutch trade? Apparently not. Figure 1.3 plots the average prices received by the East India Company on its Asian textile sales in Europe, divided by the average prices it paid for those textiles in Asia. Again, there is no sign of declining markups (where markups include all trade costs, as well as any East India Company monopoly profits) over the century between 1664 and 1769. Figure 5 in

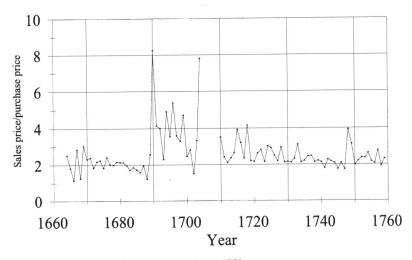

Fig. 1.3   Asian textile trade markups, 1664–1759

O'Rourke and Williamson (2000) reproduces Chaudhuri's markup figures for the East India Company's trade in pepper, saltpeter, tea, raw silk, coffee, and indigo, between about 1660 and 1710. With the possible exception of saltpeter, it would be very hard to establish a convincing case that markups were declining during this fifty-year period.

Of course, these price spreads were not driven solely, or even mainly, by the costs of shipping, but rather, and most importantly, by monopoly, international conflict, and government tariff and nontariff restrictions. For example, for pepper the markup in figure 1.2 was relatively stable at between 3 and 6 over the entire period, reflecting relatively competitive conditions in the pepper market. Where the Dutch were able to secure a monopoly, as with the cloves of the Spice Islands and the cinnamon of Ceylon, this ratio could become enormous, reaching 25 around 1640 for cloves and remaining at about 15 for the next century.[4] Nonetheless, anything that impedes price convergence suppresses trade, and there is no evidence of secular, intercontinental commodity price convergence before the 1820s. Nor have scholars such as Menard (1991) uncovered much evidence of transport revolutions during this period (O'Rourke and Williamson 2000). What, then, drove the unprecedented growth in world trade in the three centuries following Columbus? Outward shifts in export supply and import demand is

---

4. The competition in the seventeenth century between the two great rival companies has been elegantly analyzed in terms of the Brander-Spencer duopoly model of strategic trade policy by Irwin (1991). He demonstrates the advantage of the Dutch institutional form in which the decision makers obtained a share not only of the profit but also of gross revenue.

the answer suggested by O'Rourke and Williamson (2001), who estimate that between 50 and 65 percent of the boom could have been due to European income growth alone.

1.3.5 The Economic Impact of World Trade: Economic Primacy within Europe

Economic geography models typically ask what the impact of international integration is on the relative welfare of core and periphery. One of the most notable features of this period of globalization, however, was a change in the location of the core itself; and such changes were intimately linked with the changing nature of international trade. In the case of Western Europe the discoveries were said to have induced a shift in the main locus of economic activity from the Mediterranean to the Atlantic, as exemplified by the rise of Antwerp, Amsterdam, Seville, Lisbon, and London relative to Venice and Genoa. This makes one think of intercontinental trade as displacing intra-European trade, and therefore illustrating a dramatic early instance of the importance of "globalization." This claim is disputed, however: According to Rapp (1975, 501), "it was the invasion of the Mediterranean, not the exploitation of the Atlantic, that produced the Golden Ages of Amsterdam and London." Production and marketing innovations in English woolen textiles, Dutch improvements in shipping, and a growing dependence of southern Europe on northern grain imports were important factors in shifting economic primacy away from the south to Holland and England before the trade with Asia and the New World grew sufficiently in importance. In the 1660s almost half of London's total exports were to the Mediterranean, compared with only 9 percent to the Americas and 6 percent to Asia (Davis 1962).[5]

The discoveries can be looked upon as creating the prospect for a "new global economy," displacing traditional trade routes and centers. As with the new economy of today it was not clear who the eventual winners were to be. The Portuguese were the pioneers and Spain controlled the territories in the New World, but neither of the Iberian states had the commercial and organizational capacity to fully exploit the opportunities that were opened up. Thus Portugal found it necessary from as early as 1501 to use Antwerp as the emporium through which to dispose of the spices obtained from the East. Antwerp also attracted the woolen cloth of England; silver, copper, and financial capital from South Germany; and many other items of European and colonial trade. The city grew rapidly in population to over 100,000 by the 1560s and could rightly be considered the first truly global emporium, with a range and diversity of commodities vastly exceeding those of

---

5. Subsequently, however, intercontinental trade grew in absolute and relative importance. The share of colonial commodities in the total imports of London rose from practically nil in 1600 to 24 percent in 1660 and to 46 percent of total English imports in 1750.

Venice, Bruges, and other earlier commercial centers. Despite its wealth and splendor, however, Israel (1989) argues that Antwerp was too passive to be a truly dynamic center of world trade, with no active involvement in creating and attracting business toward itself. Its dominance did not last long and the peak was passed before it succumbed to the depredations of the Spanish armies in the last quarter of the sixteenth century. Its entrepreneurs and skilled craftsmen mostly fled to the United Provinces, benefiting the rival that was to supplant it: Amsterdam.

The Dutch golden age is usually taken to begin from about 1590 and lasted until about 1740, with a peak in the second half of the seventeenth century. Maddison (1991, 31) states that Dutch income per head in 1700 was around 50 percent higher than in Britain, with the shares of industry and services in total employment substantially higher. He also cites Gregory King as estimating the Dutch savings rate to be 11 percent in 1688, as compared with 4 percent for Britain and France. The volume of international trade was approximately the same as in Britain, which meant that it was five times as high per capita. How a country whose population never exceeded 2 million during these years could have led the world economy for so long has been a never-ending source of wonder and controversy among historians down to the present day. Geography provides part of the answer: The foundations were laid by taking advantage of location, midway between the Bay of Biscay and the Baltic. Seville and Lisbon and the Baltic ports were too far apart for direct trade between the two terminal points, enabling the Dutch to provide profitable intermediation, carrying salt, wine, and cloth and later silver, spices, and colonial products eastward while bringing Baltic grains, fish, and naval stores to the west. The Dutch share of European shipping tonnage was enormous, well over half during most of the period of their ascendancy. With such a small population this concentration on trade, shipping, and manufacture required reliance on imported grain, most of which was from the Baltic regions. The urban population was over half of the total, with the 57 cities of the seven United Provinces making it one of the most densely populated parts of Europe. The Calvinistic ethic promoted thrift and education, with the lowest interest rates and the highest literacy rates in Europe. The abundance of capital made it possible to maintain an impressive stock of wealth, embodied not only in the large fleet but in the plentiful stocks of an array of commodities that were used to stabilize prices and take advantage of profit opportunities. The grading, sorting, and packaging of goods provided the essential services of a commercial hub.

In comparison with the larger European states the Dutch offset their inferiority in numbers with a concentration on commerce and finance that the others could not match, distracted as they were by dynastic ambitions and other rivalries. While Amsterdam and Holland were undoubtedly the leaders, the other provinces and cities cooperated in their own interest. Unlike

Antwerp, which was a dependency of the Habsburgs, Amsterdam and the United Provinces were fiercely independent, carrying on a long and successful military struggle against their erstwhile Habsburg masters while continuing to trade with them to obtain silver and other necessities for the operation of their global commercial system. War and trade were inseparable in the Age of Mercantilism, and the Dutch excelled at both, particularly at sea.

There has been an ongoing historical controversy about the modernity of the Dutch Republic in the seventeenth century. Identifying modernity with the industrial revolution, writers such as Braudel, Hobsbawm, and Wallerstein have stressed continuities with past patterns of trade and commercial organization, such as Dutch experience with the bulk trade of the Baltic in the case of Braudel, as opposed to any innovative departures. As against this Israel (1989), de Vries and van der Woude (1997), and Steensgaard (1982) have emphasized the originality of the Dutch in creating new institutions and practices to take advantage of the new opportunities opened up by the prospect of intercontinental trade. Steensgaard convincingly demonstrates how the fusion of public and private interests in creating a large and growing fund of "permanent, anonymous capital" that internalized protection costs while maintaining a steady annual dividend of 12.5 percent made the Dutch East India Company of the seventeenth century a truly revolutionary global organization. De Vries and van der Woude are also convincing in entitling their splendid work on the Dutch economy from 1500 to 1815 "The First Modern Economy," since, as they say, "the harbors of the Republic were in direct and continuous contact with Dutch settlements stretching from New Amsterdam and Curacao in the west to Formosa and Nagasaki in the east, and from Smeerenburg on Spitzbergen in the north to Capetown at the southern tip of Africa" (376).

1.3.6 The Economic Impact of World Trade: Trade and the Industrial Revolution

The industrial revolution that got underway in Britain in the late eighteenth century undoubtedly ushered in a new era in the evolution of the world economy, and confirmed the emergence of Britain as the dominant world economic power. As Wrigley (1988) has emphasized, the use of coal and other fossil fuels radically altered the constraints on the world's energy supplies. Until the eighteenth century even major technical innovations in Europe and Asia raised living standards only temporarily, until they were whittled down by induced population growth. Improvements could be made in specialization and the division of labor, and population growth held in check by such factors as the delay of marriages, but ultimately there was always a limit. This is what Wrigley called the "advanced organic economy" that can exhibit only "Smithian" growth, as opposed to the "mineral-based energy economy" that can exhibit "Schumpeterian" growth, continuously raising per capita incomes as a result of incessant technical change, accompanied by a demographic revolution that reduces fertility rates to maintain the higher per capita incomes.

If silver was the main commodity in the Atlantic trade of the seventeenth century there is little doubt that the slave trade and its ramifications dominated that of the eighteenth century. Africa's participation in the world economy, long confined to the almost-legendary "golden trade of the Moors," grew to major proportions with the expansion of sugar, tobacco, and cotton cultivation in the New World on slave plantations. The eighteenth century accounted for about two-thirds of the total transfer of 9–10 million persons over the entire history of the trade from its inception around 1450 to its abolition in the nineteenth century. The last two decades of the eighteenth century in particular saw a surge in slave imports in response to the cotton boom triggered by the onset of the industrial revolution in Britain.

This pattern of relationship in the international trade of the Atlantic gave rise to the celebrated thesis of Eric Williams (1944) that the profits of the slave trade spurred the industrial revolution. This argument was heavily criticized by several prominent historians but sympathetically treated by William A. Darity and Barbara L. Solow, and by Findlay (1990), who provides the relevant references as well as a simple general-equilibrium model of the "triangular trade" among Europe (largely Britain), Africa, and the New World. O'Brien and Engerman (1991) are also somewhat receptive to the Williams thesis, after having been among its most prominent critics in earlier work. For a current review and references, see Morgan (2000).

A more general issue is the question of the role of foreign trade as a whole in relation to the origin and sustainability of the industrial revolution. The growing importance of international trade for the British economy is indicated by the rise in the share of exports in national income from 8.4 percent in 1700 to 14.6 percent in 1760 and 15.7 percent in 1801 (Crafts 1985, table 6.6). Even more interesting is the shift in the geographical distribution of British trade reported by Davis (1962). North America, Africa, and the West Indies took 12 percent of exports and provided 20 percent of retained imports in 1700, with these shares rising to 60 percent of exports and 32 percent of imports.[6] Thus the triangular trade grew faster than total trade, which in turn grew faster than national income. Findlay (1982) considered a model in which a discrete but substantial technical innovation in the export sector is responsible for the initial spurt, rather than an exogenous shift in foreign demand. The apparent deterioration of Britain's terms of trade in the aftermath of the original spurt is consistent with this supply-side explanation; however, it may be that the existence of wide and growing foreign

---

6. Esteban (1997) presents valuable evidence on the rising share of manufactured exports to industrial output in Britain from 1700 to 1851.

markets made it possible for the impulse from technological change in the export sector not to be choked off by too sharp a decline in relative prices.

The triangular trade model in Findlay (1990) also predicts an expansion of demand for raw cotton imports into Britain and of slaves to the Americas as a consequence of the innovation in Manchester in the 1780s. There is abundant evidence for both, together with improvements in the terms of trade for the newly independent United States, where cotton was the main export, and also for the slave-exporting kingdoms on the west coast of Africa. One further interesting aspect of the intercontinental complex was the role of Indian cotton textiles. These were a major import of the East India Company, sold to Britain itself and re-exported to Africa in payment for slaves. Ultimately Lancashire, with its raw cotton imports from the slave plantations of the New World, displaced the long-standing Indian cotton textile industry, leading to the sad fate of the handloom weavers of Bengal. "Globalization" was thus fully at work at the turn of the eighteenth century to the nineteenth century, with both positive and negative consequences in all four continents.

1.4   The French and Napoleonic Wars

The previous sections have documented the growth and maturation of a well-defined global economy encompassing not just Europe and Asia, but Africa and the Americas as well. However, progress toward greater economic integration had been periodically impeded by war, as various European nations struggled for supremacy. This was not a new phenomenon: For example, Menard (1991, 240–43) finds a threefold increase in freight charges on the English-Continental wine trade during the fourteenth century, due to the onset of the Hundred Years' War. Figure 1.2 indicates increases in clove and pepper markups during the 1650s and 1660s, coinciding with the first and second Anglo-Dutch Wars (1652–54 and 1665–67); and the spike in the clove markup during the 1750s coincides with the outbreak of the Seven Years' War (1756–63). Even more noticeable are the increases in markups during the 1790s, coinciding with the outbreak of what have become known as the French and Napoleonic Wars. On 1 February 1793 the French National Convention declared war on Great Britain. The ensuing period of warfare, which lasted almost uninterrupted until 1815, had profound and long-lasting effects on international trade.

Within a month, the convention had prohibited the importation of large classes of British goods, and in October it banned all British manufactured goods; meanwhile, the British side adopted a policy of blockading the coast of France. As Eli Heckscher's (1922) classic account emphasizes, each side was motivated by a mercantilist desire to prevent the other's exporting, and thus acquiring precious metals, rather than by a desire to prevent the other side's importing food or other goods that might be useful to the war effort.[7] In addition, both the French and the British took measures against neutral shipping that transported enemy goods, but trade disruption was to become far more widespread in the aftermath of Napoleon's military victories over Austria in 1805 and Prussia in 1806. In November 1806, his Berlin Decree declared that the British Isles were under blockade (somewhat fancifully, since Britain controlled the seas); he also began applying these restrictions, not just in France, but in vassal states such as Spain, Naples, and Holland. The result was that virtually the entire Continent was now in a state of self-blockade against the exports of Britain, the overwhelmingly dominant industrial power of the time.[8] In November 1807 the British declared that neutral ships could be seized if found to be carrying goods from enemy colonies directly to their mother countries; Napoleon retaliated by declaring that any neutral ship putting into a British port was fair prize, and could be seized. Faced with a situation where neutral ships carrying colonial goods to the Continent were now subject to seizure from either one side or the other, the U.S. government closed its ports in December to belligerent shipping and forbade its own ships to leave these ports.

This Embargo Act was repealed in 1809, and replaced with a Non-Intercourse Act which banned trade only with Britain and France (and which was clearly difficult to enforce, once ships had been given leave to sail to Europe). Russia broke with France in 1810; by 1813 Napoleon was in retreat and the Continental blockade was unraveling in several directions; and the blockade legislation was finally repealed following Napoleon's abdication in 1814. Nonetheless, for over twenty years leading governments had acted so as to severely disrupt international trade, and under the Continental system that disruption had been widespread and rather extreme. Did these measures seriously impede the integration of international commodity markets, or were they so undermined by smuggling, corruption, and fiscally motivated legal exceptions to the general protectionist rule as to have had no significant effect?

The literature on these issues is sparse, and to a large effect relies on qualitative evidence, or quantity data, rather than the price data we really need. In a classic article, Crouzet (1964) drew attention to the disruptive effects of the wars on Continental industry. The sea blockade by the British Royal Navy affected Atlantic-oriented export activities severely: shipbuilding, rope making, sailmaking, sugar refining, and the linen industry all suffered. Industrial activity shifted from the Atlantic seaboard to the interior, as import-substituting industries such as cotton textiles flourished behind the protection from British competition afforded by the Continental system.

---

7. The exception being that food exports were occasionally banned when domestic food supplies were scarce.

8. The only Continental country to hold out was Sweden, which was eventually forced to join the blockade in 1810.

The gains to interior regions such as Alsace were mirrored by the population loss in coastal cities such as Amsterdam, Bordeaux, and Marseilles. Naturally, Continental industries that had prospered under these wartime circumstances were unlikely to favor peacetime moves toward free trade; the effects of the wartime shock were thus to prove quite persistent, with path dependency being induced by the political process.

Frankel (1982) has produced more price-based evidence speaking to the issue of how Jefferson's Embargo Act affected trade and welfare in the United States and Britain during 1808 and early 1809. In 1807, the Liverpool price of cotton was 27.5 percent higher than the Charleston price; in the final two months of the embargo, the Liverpool price was 293.3 percent higher than the Charleston price (Frankel 1982, 307–08). Using prices for a number of key agricultural and industrial commodities, Frankel found that the British terms of trade deteriorated by between 41.9 percent and 49.7 percent during the dispute, while the U.S. terms of trade deteriorated by between 31.6 percent and 32.7 percent (Frankel, 304). The smaller impact on the U.S. economy was largely due to its success in developing import-substituting industries in states such as Pennsylvania. As in the French case, these new industries and their home states would form the basis of a powerful protectionist lobby in the years ahead, yet another example of politically induced hysteresis.

By how much did the wars increase the costs of trade between Britain and the Continent? According to Thomas Tooke, it cost between 30 and 50 shillings per quarter to ship wheat from the Baltic to Britain in 1810, as compared with 4s. 6d. in 1837.[9] Hueckel (1973) has estimated that wartime freight, insurance, and licence costs accounted for between 25 and 40 percent of British wheat prices in 1812, and that over the period 1790–1815, wartime disruption raised the relative price of agricultural commodities in Britain by 28 percent (Hueckel, 369, 389). Not surprisingly, this raised landowners' incomes significantly (Hueckel; Williamson 1984), and equally unsurprisingly, British landowners tried to hold onto those gains after the war by means of strict protection.

It seems as though the Napoleonic Wars not only managed to disrupt the workings of international commodity markets in the years before 1815; in France and the United States the hothouse protection afforded by war created import-substituting industries that would require continuing protection for their survival. The resulting emergence of powerful protectionist constituencies would ensure that the road to free trade in the nineteenth century would not be as universal or as smooth as is sometimes supposed. North-South conflict over tariff policy would be a feature of American politics for decades to come; Crouzet (1964, 588) goes so far as to speculate that the instinctively interventionist French attitude toward protection evi-

9. Cited in Hueckel (1973, 369).

dent at the time he was writing (the early 1960s) might be traced back to these long-run political effects of the Napoleonic Wars.

Moreover, in Britain the Corn Laws survived until 1846. When Europe eventually moved toward freer trade in the late nineteenth century, it was largely as a result of Britain's example; might Britain have liberalized earlier had the Napoleonic Wars not intervened? Such an argument assumes that industrialization (which would have proceeded more rapidly in the absence of the war; Williamson 1984) would have led to the emergence of powerful export interests, which would have eventually triumphed as their political power grew. Would the extension of the franchise-favoring urban interests have predated the 1832 Reform Act, had war not occurred? Alternatively, might landlords have diversified into nonagricultural interests earlier, and been coopted by the free trade side as eventually happened (Schonhardt-Bailey 1991)? Did the Napoleonic Wars delay the advent of free trade in Britain and Europe by as much as several decades? We confess that we do not know the answers to these important questions.

1.5   World Trade 1815–1914

1.5.1   The Worldwide Nineteenth-century Decline in Transport Costs

Although canals also made a significant contribution to commodity market integration (Slaughter 1995), steamships were the most important nineteenth-century innovation in shipping technology.[10] In the first half of the century, steamships were mainly used on rivers, the Great Lakes, and inland seas such as the Baltic and the Mediterranean. A regular transatlantic steam service was inaugurated in 1838, but until 1860 steamers mainly carried high-value goods like passengers and mail, similar to those carried by airplanes today (Cameron 1989, 206). As late as 1874, steamships carried 90 percent of the ginger, 90 percent of the poppyseed, 90 percent of the tea, and 99 percent of the cowhides from Calcutta to Britain, but only 40 percent of the jute cuttings and one-third of the rice (Fletcher 1958, 561).

A series of innovations in subsequent decades helped make steamships more efficient: the screw propeller, the compound engine, steel hulls, bigger size, and shorter turnaround time in port. Another important development was the opening of the Suez Canal on 17 November 1869. Far Eastern trade was still dominated by sail: In the absence of sufficient coaling stations around the coast, the trip around Africa by steamer required carrying too much coal. The compound engine reduced fuel requirements, and the Suez Canal made it possible to pick up coal at Gibraltar, Malta, and Port Said, in addition to halving the distance from London to Bombay. Not only did the Suez Canal make it possible for steamships to compete on Asian routes,

---

10. This section draws heavily on O'Rourke and Williamson (1999, chap. 3).

but it was of no use to sailing ships, which would have to be towed for the roughly 100-mile journey. Before 1869, steam tonnage had never exceeded sail tonnage in British shipyards; in 1870, steam tonnage was over twice as great as sail, and sail tonnage exceeded steam in only two years after that date (Fletcher 1958).

The other major nineteenth-century development in transportation was, of course, the railroad. The Liverpool-Manchester line opened in 1830; early Continental emulators included Belgium, France, and Germany. The growth in railway mileage during the late nineteenth century was phenomenal, particularly in the United States, where trains would play a major role in creating a truly national market. Indeed, transport costs between the American Midwest and East Coast fell even more dramatically than transatlantic transport costs during the late nineteenth century. Drawing on American sources, the British Board of Trade published in 1903 an annual series of transport costs for the wheat trade between Chicago, New York, and Liverpool. It cost 6 shillings and 11 pence to ship a quarter of wheat by lake and rail from Chicago to New York in 1868. The cost using rail alone was 10s. 2d. The cost of shipping a quarter of wheat from New York to Liverpool by steamer was 4s. 7 1/2d.[11] In 1902, these costs had fallen to 1s. 11d, 2s. 11d., and 11 1/2d., respectively. While the percentage decline in transatlantic costs was greater, in absolute terms it was the American railways that did most of the work in reducing price gaps between producer and consumer.[12] In any case, regional price convergence within the United States was dramatic. The wheat price spread between New York City and Iowa fell from 69 to 19 percent from 1870 to 1910, and from 52 to 10 percent between New York City and Wisconsin (Williamson 1974, 259).

The railroad had similar effects elsewhere. Metzer (1974) provided the evidence for Russia, where railway construction took off after the mid-1860s. He finds a clear decline in St. Petersburg-Odessa price gaps for wheat and rye, starting in the 1870s; bilateral grain price differentials declined for a wider sample of nine markets between 1893 and 1913. Corresponding to this price convergence was a growing regional dispersion of wheat and rye production, as regions specialized according to their comparative advantage. Hurd (1975) has documented the predictable consequences of the railroad for Indian food grain prices, as internal transport costs were reduced by about 80 percent. The coefficient of variation of wheat and rice prices across districts fell from over 40 percent in 1870 to well below 20 percent in the decade before World War I; moreover, the coefficient of variation was consistently higher among India's districts without railways than among districts with railways.

What was the impact of these transport innovations on the cost of mov-

---

11. These figures imply that transport costs from Chicago to Liverpool were about 19 percent of the New York wheat price in 1868.
12. Harley's (1980) data tell a similar story.

ing goods between countries? Harley's (1988) index of British ocean freight rates remains relatively constant between 1740 and 1840, before dropping by about 70 percent between 1840 and 1910. The North (1958) freight rate index among American export routes drops by more than 41 percent in real terms between 1870 and 1910. These two indices imply a decline in Atlantic-economy transport costs of about 1.5 percent per annum, or a total of 45 percentage points up to 1913. The transport revolution was not limited to the Atlantic economy: Harlaftis and Kardasis (2000) have shown that the declines in freight rates between 1870 and 1914 were just as dramatic on routes involving Black Sea and Egyptian ports as on those involving Atlantic ports. Meanwhile, the tramp charter rate for shipping rice from Rangoon to Europe, for example, fell from 73.8 to 18.1 percent of the Rangoon price between 1882 and 1914;[13] the freight rate on coal (relative to its export price) between Nagasaki and Shanghai fell by 76 percent between 1880 and 1910; and total factor productivity on Japan's tramp freighter routes serving Asia advanced at 2.5 percent per annum in the thirty years between 1879 and 1909 (Yasuba 1978, tables 1 and 5).

1.5.2   Nineteenth-century Trade Policy: Two Steps Forward, One Step Back

Bairoch (1989, 7) has described European trade policy after Waterloo as "an ocean of protectionism surrounding a few liberal islands."[14] Gradually, however, the demand for trade liberalization in Britain grew, partly under the influence of economists like David Ricardo, partly as a result of the growing power of urban interests, symbolized by the Reform Act of 1832. The proglobalization movement applied to both commodity and factor markets. Skilled workers were allowed to emigrate in 1825, an option that had not been available to them since 1719. A new Corn Law Act in 1828 abandoned import prohibitions for grains, replacing them with a sliding-scale tariff that varied inversely with the domestic price of grain. Various tariffs were reduced again in 1833. Robert Peel allowed the export of machinery in 1842 (banned since 1774), abolished the export tax on wool, and reduced protection on grains and other goods still further. Tariffs were again reduced in 1845. Britain finally made the decisive move toward free trade by repealing the Corn Laws in 1846.

The British example was followed by the rest of Europe, but much more slowly:

> Before 1860 only a few small Continental countries, representing only 4% of Europe's population, had adopted a truly liberal trade policy. These were the Netherlands, Denmark, Portugal and Switzerland, to which we

13. The Asian material that follows (in this section and later) draws on Williamson (2000, 2002).

14. This section draws heavily on O'Rourke and Williamson (1999, chaps. 3, 6), who in turn draw heavily on Bairoch (1989), the standard reference on European trade policy in this period.

may add Sweden and Belgium (but only from 1856–7 onwards), and even these maintained some degree of protection. (Bairoch 1993, 22)

The Cobden Chevalier treaty between France and the United Kingdom was not signed until 23 January 1860, but, although delayed, the signature heralded a decisive shift toward European free trade. The treaty abolished all French import prohibitions, replacing them with ad valorem duties not to exceed 30 percent. Britain reduced wine tariffs by more than 80 percent, admitted many French products duty free, and abolished the export duty on coal. Most importantly, perhaps, the treaty's use of the most-favored-nation (MFN) clause established the principle of nondiscrimination as a corner-stone of European commercial practice. The clause stipulated that each country would automatically extend to the other any trade concessions granted to third parties. Most-favored-nation clauses were inserted into the many bilateral trade treaties that followed in the ensuing years, ensuring that bilateral concessions were generalized to all. France and Belgium signed a treaty in 1861; a Franco-Prussian treaty was signed in 1862; Italy entered the "network of Cobden-Chevalier treaties" in 1863 (Bairoch 1989, 40); Switzerland in 1864; Sweden, Norway, Spain, the Netherlands, and the Hanseatic towns in 1865; and Austria in 1866. By 1877, less than two decades after the Cobden Chevalier treaty and three decades after British Repeal, Germany "had virtually become a free trade country" (Bairoch, 41). Average duties on manufactured products had declined to 9–12 percent on the Continent, a far cry from the 50 percent British tariffs, and numerous prohibitions elsewhere, of the immediate post-Waterloo era (Bairoch, table 3, p. 6, and table 5, p. 42).

Until the 1870s, therefore, European trade policy trends were reinforcing the impact of the transport cost declines outlined earlier. Things would soon change, however. The turning point came in the late 1870s and 1880s, when the impact of cheap New World and Russian grain began to make itself felt in European markets: For example, real British land rents fell by over 50 percent between 1870 and 1913. Almost all of this British decline can be attributed to international commodity market integration (O'Rourke and Williamson 1994); more generally, by the late nineteenth century international trade was having a profound impact on income distribution, lowering the incomes of landowners relative to those of workers throughout Europe (Lindert and Williamson, chap. 5 in this volume). Wherever landed interests were powerful enough, the legislative reaction was predictable. The German turning point came in 1879, when Bismarck protected both agriculture and industry. While the specific tariffs started low, they were raised in 1885, and again in 1887, reaching the equivalent of about 33 percent ad valorem on wheat and 47 percent on rye. In France, tariffs were raised in the 1880s, but the protectionist breakthrough is commonly taken to be 1892 when the Méline tariff was adopted; by 1894, the duty on wheat was equivalent to an ad valorem rate of 32 percent. In Sweden, agricultural protection was reimposed in 1888, and industrial protection was increased in 1892. Italy had been a free trader in the wake of unification, but shortly thereafter it introduced moderate tariffs in 1878, followed by rather more severe tariffs in 1887.

There was thus a common pattern across western Europe of liberalization followed by a reversion to protection, prompted by the distributional effects of the grain invasion. There were exceptions; for example, liberalization was both shorter and less dramatic in Iberia. Other small countries were more liberal in the wake of the grain invasion; Denmark, for example, adhered to agricultural free trade throughout, switching from being a net grain exporter to a net grain importer (to feed its booming animal husbandry).[15] The Netherlands followed a similar path, maintaining free trade throughout the period. Dutch farmers also adopted improved techniques, and developed a strong export trade in animal products, fruit, and vegetables (Tracy 1989, 23). Both Belgium and Switzerland maintained free or nearly free grain imports, although they did impose some duties on animal products, as well as moderate duties on manufactured goods. Most importantly, the United Kingdom also maintained free trade, despite some domestic dissension.

In summary, there was a major retreat from open trade policies in Europe toward the end of the nineteenth century, triggered largely by pressure from landowners. Transport cost declines led to distributional changes, which in turn prompted an attempt by the losers to insulate themselves from the international economy. Moreover, it turns out that countries such as Denmark that retained agricultural free trade were less vulnerable to the agricultural output and land price reductions that globalization implied (O'Rourke 1997). Elsewhere, it seems that globalization undermined itself.

New World landowners benefited from free trade, of course, but this does not mean that New World trade policy was any more liberal. In the United States, those infant industries mentioned earlier that sprang up during the French Wars had formed the basis for a long-standing Northern protariff lobby: Northern victory in the Civil War had predictable consequences for subsequent tariff policy. Tariffs were raised during the war for revenue purposes, but Republican domination of Congress would ensure that they remained exceptionally high for a very long time thereafter.

Canada also protected manufacturing, especially after 1878 when the conservatives were elected on a protectionist platform. In Australia, the Victoria tariff bill of 1865 allowed for maximum ad valorem tariffs of 10 percent, but by 1893, after a succession of tariff increases, the maximum rates stood at 45 percent (Siriwardana 1991, 47). The first federal tariff of

---

15. It did, however, impose tariffs on various manufactured goods: Manufactured textiles faced duties between 20 and 25 percent (Bairoch 1989, 81).

1902 represented a compromise between protectionist Victoria and the other more liberal colonies, but protection was greatly strengthened in 1906 and 1908 (Bairoch 1989, 146–47) and it proved to be remarkably enduring.

While the third quarter of the nineteenth century saw an easing of protection in Latin America, tariffs rose again in the final quarter. Argentina increased tariffs from the 1870s onward (Bairoch 1989, 150–51). By 1913, average tariffs were almost 35 percent in Uruguay, almost 40 percent in Brazil, and over 45 percent in Venezuela (Bulmer-Thomas 1994, 142). It appears that the highest tariff barriers were in the New World, not Europe. The tariffs were directed toward manufactures and they served to favor scarce urban labor and capital while penalizing possession of abundant land.

Late-nineteenth-century trade policy thus offset the impact of transport cost declines in both Europe and the New World. The opposite was the case in Asia, where Japan switched from virtual autarky to free trade in 1858. Other Asian nations—China, Siam, Korea, India, and Indonesia—also followed this liberal path, mostly forced to do so by colonial dominance or gunboat diplomacy. This shift had largely taken place from the 1860s; from then on, commodity price convergence was driven entirely by sharply declining transport costs in Asia without much change in tariffs one way or the other.

1.5.3 Nineteenth-century Commodity Market Integration

What impact did these technological and political developments have on international commodity markets? As we have seen, world trade grew at a little over 1 percent per annum between 1500 and 1800, but it has grown at around 3.5 percent per annum since 1820, with the nineteenth- and twentieth-century growth rates being roughly equal (Maddison 1995). Indeed, the nineteenth-century growth rate was more impressive than the twentieth-, in the sense that world gross domestic product (GDP) growth was twice as high since 1913 as it was between 1820 and 1913: The implication is that trade ratios (e.g., the ratio of merchandise exports to GDP) grew more rapidly during the nineteenth century than they did during the twentieth. Table 1.3 documents the eightfold increase in this ratio worldwide between 1820 and 1913, when merchandise exports accounted for almost 8 percent of world GDP and more than 16 percent of western European GDP.

The nineteenth century marks a dramatic break with the past insofar as intercontinental commodity market integration is concerned, since as we have seen there was little or no intercontinental price convergence prior to 1800. By contrast, figure 1.2 indicated that there was substantial Dutch-Asian price convergence during the nineteenth century, while late-nineteenth-century price convergence more generally has been extensively documented. For example, Liverpool wheat prices exceeded Chicago prices

Table 1.3   **Merchandise Exports as a Share of GDP (%)**

Country	1820	1870	1913	1929	1950	1973	1992	1998
France	1.3	4.9	7.8	8.6	7.6	15.2	22.9	28.7
Germany	n.a.	9.5	16.1	12.8	6.2	23.8	32.6	38.9
The Netherlands	n.a.	17.4	17.3	17.2	12.2	40.7	55.3	61.2
United Kingdom	3.1	12.2	17.5	13.3	11.3	14.0	21.4	25.0
Total Western Europe	n.a.	10.0	16.3	13.3	9.4	20.9	29.7	n.a.
Spain	1.1	3.8	8.1	5.0	3.0	5.0	13.4	23.5
U.S.S.R./Russia	n.a.	n.a.	2.9	1.6	1.3	3.8	5.1	10.6
Australia	n.a.	7.1	12.3	11.2	8.8	11.0	16.9	18.1
Canada	n.a.	12.0	12.2	15.8	13.0	19.9	27.2	n.a.
United States	2.0	2.5	3.7	3.6	3.0	4.9	8.2	10.1
Argentina	n.a.	9.4	6.8	6.1	2.4	2.1	4.3	7.0
Brazil	n.a.	12.2	9.8	6.9	3.9	2.5	4.7	5.4
Mexico	n.a.	3.9	9.1	12.5	3.0	1.9	6.4	10.7
Total Latin America	n.a.	9.0	9.5	9.7	6.2	4.6	6.2	n.a.
China	n.a.	0.7	1.7	1.8	2.6	1.5	2.3	4.9
India	n.a.	2.6	4.6	3.7	2.9	2.0	1.7	2.4
Indonesia	n.a.	0.9	2.2	3.6	3.4	5.1	7.4	9.0
Japan	n.a.	0.2	2.4	3.5	2.2	7.7	12.4	13.4
Korea	0.0	0.0	1.2	4.5	0.7	8.2	17.8	36.3
Taiwan	n.a.	n.a.	2.5	5.2	2.5	10.2	34.4	n.a.
Thailand	n.a.	n.a.	2.5	5.2	2.5	10.2	34.4	n.a.
Total Asia	n.a.	1.3	2.6	2.8	2.3	4.4	7.2	n.a.
World	1.0	4.6	7.9	9.0	5.5	10.5	13.5	17.2

Source: Maddison (1995, 38); these have been updated for some countries using Maddison (2001, 363) and for other countries using the raw export and GDP data given in Maddison (2001), where these produced results consistent with the earlier data series.

Note: n.a. = not available.

by 57.6 percent in 1870, by 17.8 percent in 1895, and by only 15.6 percent in 1913 (O'Rourke and Williamson 1994, based on Harley 1980). London-Cincinnati price differentials for bacon were 92.5 percent in 1870, over 100 in 1880, 92.3 in 1895, and 17.9 in 1913. The Boston-Manchester cotton textile price gap fell from 13.7 percent in 1870 to –3.6 percent in 1913; the Philadelphia-London iron bar price gap fell from 75.0 to 20.6 percent, while the pig iron price gap fell from 85.2 to 19.3 percent, and the copper price gap fell from 32.7 to almost zero; the Boston-London hides price gap fell from 27.7 to 8.7 percent, while the wool price gap fell from 59.1 to 27.9 percent. Commodity price convergence can also be documented for coal, tin, and coffee (O'Rourke and Williamson).

Continental European grain tariffs did succeed in impeding international price convergence (O'Rourke 1997), but O'Rourke and Williamson (1995) document significant price convergence in the British-Swedish case.

Meanwhile, in Asia trade policy strengthened the impact of technological developments.[16] The cotton price spread between Liverpool and Bombay fell from 57 percent in 1873 to 20 percent in 1913, and the jute price spread between London and Calcutta fell from 35 to 4 percent (Collins 1996, table 4). The same events were taking place even farther east, involving Burma and the rest of Southeast Asia: The rice price spread between London and Rangoon fell from 93 to 26 percent in the four decades prior to 1913 (Collins, table 4). Finally, the impact of transport revolutions on commodity price convergence involving the eastern Mediterranean was just as powerful. The average percentage by which Liverpool cotton prices exceeded Alexandria price quotes was as follows: 1824–32, 42.1; 1837–46, 63.2; 1863–67, 40.8; 1882–89, 14.7; 1890–99, 5.3 (Issawi 1966, 447–48). Commodity market integration in the late nineteenth century was both impressive in scale and global in scope; indeed, third world economies were becoming more rapidly integrated with the rest of the world than their Atlantic economy counterparts during this period (Williamson 2002).

1.5.4   Trade in the Late Nineteenth Century: Conclusion

By 1913, international commodity markets were vastly more integrated than they had been in 1750; world trade accounted for a far higher share of world output; and a far broader range of goods, including commodities with a high bulk-to-value ratio, was being transported between continents. These trends, in combination with rapid industrialization in northwest Europe and its overseas offshoots, had a dramatic impact on the worldwide division of labor. By the late nineteenth century there was a stark distinction between industrial and primary producing economies. According to the available figures (given in table 1.4), primary products accounted for between 62 and 64 percent of total world exports in the late nineteenth century; in 1913, food accounted for 27 percent of world exports, agricultural raw materials for 23 percent, and minerals for 14 percent. The United Kingdom and northwest Europe were net importers of primary products and net exporters of manufactured goods. North America still exported primary products, but rapid industrialization there was leading to a more balanced trade in manufactures over time. Meanwhile, Oceania, Latin America, and Africa exported virtually no manufactured goods, and Asian exports were overwhelmingly composed of primary products; for example, according to Lamartine Yates (1959, 250) primary products accounted for more than three-quarters of India's exports in 1913. By contrast, textiles had still accounted for more than half of the English East India Company's exports to Europe in the late 1750s (table 1.1, panel C). By 1811–12 the share of piece-goods in India's exports had declined to 33 percent; the figure was 14 percent just three years later, and only 4 percent in 1850–51. By 1910–11 the

---

16. The remainder of this paragraph draws on O'Rourke and Williamson (2000).

Table 1.4   **World Trade, 1876–80 and 1913 ($ millions)**

Region	1876–80			1913		
	Exports	Imports	Balance	Exports	Imports	Balance
	Primary Products					
United States and Canada	600	330	270	2,101	1,542	559
United Kingdom	117	1,362	−1,245	760	2,596	−1,836
Northwestern Europe	840	1,800	−960	3,064	5,894	−2,830
Other Europe	750	515	235	1,793	1,689	104
Oceania				455	129	326
Latin America				1,531	595	936
Africa				680	307	373
Asia				1,792	949	843
All four	1,413	575	838			
Total	3,720	4,582	−862	12,176	13,701	−1,525
	Manufactures					
United States and Canada	100	190	−90	734	891	−157
United Kingdom	865	225	640	1,751	601	1,150
Northwestern Europe	1,080	450	630	3,318	1,795	1,523
Other Europe	210	330	−120	578	1,133	−555
Oceania				9	370	−361
Latin America				51	879	−828
Africa				26	451	−425
Asia				461	1,247	−786
All four	35	1,285	−1,250			
Total	2,290	2,480	−190	6,928	7,367	−439

Source: Lamartine Yates (1959).

Note: World trade does not balance due to unrecorded trade.

share of cotton goods in exports had increased to 6 percent, but this was dwarfed by the share of raw cotton in exports (17 percent; Chaudhuri 1983, 842, 844). The contrast with the situation 150 years earlier was striking; the impact of this changing division of labor on growth in both the core and periphery would become a major subject of economic debate in the twentieth century, particularly in the periphery. In turn, this would eventually have significant effects on policy in the developing world.

1.6   World Trade 1914–2000

1.6.1   The First World War and Its Aftermath

World War I brought the liberal economic order of the late nineteenth century to an abrupt end: While there were signs of a globalization backlash from the 1870s onward, 1914 clearly marked a dramatic and discontinuous break with the past. Each side attempted to disrupt the other's trade, through blockades or U-boat campaigns; even more serious was the centralized control that even traditionally liberal governments, such as the British, imposed on trade and shipping, with scarce cargo space necessitating that government dictate both the composition of imports through a system of quotas and the allocation of shipping capacity. This was, of course, part of a more general shift toward massive and unprecedented government intervention in the economy, with military expenditure absorbing 38 percent of U.K. national output during 1916–17, and 53 percent of German national output during 1917 (Feinstein, Temin, and Toniolo 1997, 189). In Britain, the McKenna tariff of 1915, designed to save on scarce shipping space, was explicitly protectionist. Moreover, this shift was not reversed after the war: The Key Industries Act of 1919 and the Safeguarding of Industries Act of 1921 introduced additional protection (Kindleberger 1989). These acts did not represent widespread and severe protection—at the beginning of the 1930s, only £13 million worth of imports were subject to these tariffs, compared with the £138 million subject to traditional revenue duties, and a total import bill of £1030 million (Kenwood and Lougheed 1983, 216). Nonetheless, they represented a break with Britain's free-trade past.

Surprisingly, import shares fell only marginally in Britain during the war; it was exports that collapsed (from 20 to 13 percent of GDP) as resources were diverted to the war effort and raw materials for export industries were rationed. In France, the import share rose from 20 percent before the war to 37 percent during it; again, exports fell sharply.[17] Correspondingly, export ratios rose in neutral economies, such as Sweden; in Japan; and in North America, where grain production expanded sharply during the war years to meet Allied demand. It was this reorientation of trade, and the consequent supply responses, that led to some of the most destructive long-term economic consequences of the war: Agricultural oversupply would be a chronic problem contributing to trade tensions after the war. In addition, the absence of European manufactured exports on world markets stimulated the expansion of industrial capacity, above all in the United States and Japan, but also in countries such as India, Australia, and Latin America. Just as excess food supplies would lead to pressures for agricultural protection, so the hothouse stimulation of industrial "war babies" would lead to postwar demands for industrial protection in India, Australia, and Argentina (Kenwood and Lougheed 1983, 185–86; Eichengreen 1994, 88–89). Once again, wartime shocks would have a long-run impact on trade flows and resource allocation, in part because of their impact on policy. To this (by now, traditional) mechanism was added the impact of the emergence of new nation states in Europe (Feinstein, Temin, and Toniolo 1997, 28–32). Although nationalist leaders in today's aspiring nation states, such as Scotland and Quebec, speak of a free-trading future (Alesina and Spolaore

17. Based on Jones and Obstfeld (1997) and Mitchell (1992).

1997), in the early twentieth century independence was typically costly from an economic standpoint, involving the adoption of protectionist policies (Johnson 1965).

The end of war did not imply an end to protection. Subsequent British tariff acts have already been mentioned; quantitative restrictions on trade remained prevalent, particularly in Central and Southeastern Europe, due largely to shortages of food, raw materials, and currency problems; meanwhile, antidumping legislation was introduced in Japan in 1920, and in Australia, New Zealand, the United Kingdom, and the United States in 1921. In 1922 the United States, whose government was once again in Republican hands, passed the Fordney-McCumber tariff act, which substantially raised tariffs (Kindleberger 1989, 162–63; League of Nations 1942, 18; Irwin 1998b, 328). While quantitative restrictions were eventually abolished, these were replaced with high tariffs; for example, average tariffs on industrial products were 28 percent in Yugoslavia, compared with a prewar figure of 18 percent. The corresponding figures for France were 25.8 percent, as compared with 16.3 percent; and for Germany, 19 percent, as compared with 10 percent (Liepmann 1938, cited in Irwin 1993, 105).

The international community was active, but ultimately ineffectual, in calling for liberalization. Appeals for the resumption of free trade were made by the Supreme Economic Council in 1920, by the Genoa Conference in 1922, and by the World Economic Conference in 1927, among others. In its retrospective on the interwar period, the League of Nations itself ruefully acknowledged the paradox that "the international conferences unanimously recommended, and the great majority of Governments repeatedly proclaimed their intention to pursue, policies designed to bring about conditions of 'freer and more equal trade'; yet never before in history were trade barriers raised so rapidly or discrimination so widely practised" (League of Nations 1942, 101). Few if any commentators have dissented from this negative assessment.

The symbol of interwar protection remains the American Smoot-Hawley tariff, whose roots lay in the wartime extension of non-European agricultural supplies mentioned earlier. With the resumption of European supplies, overproduction began to be a chronic problem, and agricultural prices fell—wheat prices, for example, fell sharply from 1925. Continental European protection made the situation of New World suppliers worse; while some exporting governments (the Canadians and Americans) attempted to keep domestic prices high, the Soviet Union's aim of earning sufficient revenues to pay for capital equipment imports led it to export more as prices fell, thus exacerbating the problem (Kindleberger 1973, chap. 4). The fact that Russian peasants' supply curves were upward sloping, unlike that of their government, inevitably led to conflict and widespread suffering (Kindleberger 1989, 184).

Herbert Hoover thus promised U.S. farmers tariff protection, and called a special session of Congress in early 1929 to deliver on his pledge. The Smoot-Hawley tariff, which emerged in mid-1930, protected industry as well as agriculture, and represented a substantial increase in overall protection.[18] Deflation over the course of the next two years would increase average tariffs by an even greater extent (Crucini 1994; Irwin 1998a). In contrast to the nineteenth-century experience, the United States was now sufficiently important that the tariff triggered a wave of tariff increases in countries such as Canada, France, Italy, Spain, and Switzerland (Kindleberger 1989; Jones 1934), although the extent to which the more general rise in tariffs that followed was due to retaliation, as opposed to various domestic causes, remains subject to dispute (Eichengreen 1989; Irwin 1998b). At a minimum, the tariff sent the signal that the United States was not willing to be the unilateral guarantor of open markets that the United Kingdom had been before the war. In any event, the increases were severe: By 1931, average tariffs on foodstuffs had risen to 83 percent in Germany, 53 percent in France, 66 percent in Italy, 60 percent in Austria, and 75 percent in Yugoslavia (Liepmann 1938, cited in Irwin 1993, 105). Even the traditionally free-trading Netherlands abandoned a three-centuries-long tradition of open markets when it intervened to prop up agricultural prices in 1931 (Kindleberger 1989, 178–79).

In 1932 Britain took a decisive move toward protection, establishing 10 percent tariffs on a wide variety of imports; for a few months, little Ireland was one of the only free-trade holdouts in Europe, but later that year it succumbed as Éamon de Valera was elected, and embarked on a wholesale trade war with the United Kingdom. In opting for a policy of import substitution, Ireland was typical of primary producers around the periphery, most notably in Latin America, and as in Latin America the policy seemed initially to be successful in insulating the economy from the worst effects of the Great Depression (Diaz Alejandro 1984; O'Rourke 1991). Certainly, the traditional export-oriented policy seemed no longer to be working: Between 1928–29 and 1932–33, the value of exports fell by over 80 percent in Chile; by 75–80 percent in China; by 70–75 percent in Bolivia, Cuba, Malaya, Peru, and Salvador; by 65–70 percent in thirteen other primary exporters; and by over 50 percent in another twenty-two (Kindleberger 1973, 191).

The Great Depression was of course another major reason for the adoption of severe protection, and not just in the periphery. In France, quotas became widespread during the 1930s, while in Germany the Nazi regime in-

---

18. How substantial depends on how the average tariff is measured. As a share of total imports, tariff revenues in 1931 were around 18 percent, which (as De Long 1998 points out) would have been a low tariff by nineteenth-century standards, and was less than the level attained at the start of the century (De Long, 358; Eichengreen 1989, 16). As a share of dutiable imports, however, tariff revenues were higher in 1931 and 1932 than they had been in 1900, and, Irwin (1998b) claims, the Smoot-Hawley tariffs were "arguably the highest since the Civil War" (327).

stituted totalitarian quantitative controls on foreign trade reminiscent of a war economy. By 1937, 58 percent of French imports were covered by some sort of quantitative restriction, with the corresponding figures for Switzerland, the Netherlands, and Belgium being 52, 26, and 24 percent respectively (Haberler 1943, cited in Irwin 1993, 108). Irwin (1993) makes the point that there was a trade-off between countries' adherence to monetary orthodoxy and their adherence to free trade orthodoxy: The four countries just mentioned stuck rigidly to the gold standard for much of the 1930s, leading to deflation, overvaluation, and balance-of-payments difficulties. Quantitative restrictions were in large measure a response to these difficulties. In Central and Eastern Europe, countries responded to similar problems by following Germany's lead and introducing widespread exchange controls; this "pernicious bilateralism", as Irwin (1993) calls it, combined with the imperial preferences of Britain (established in Ottowa in 1932) and other colonial powers, led to the complete breakdown of the MFN principle of nondiscrimination.

Beginning in 1932, there were several signs that at least some countries were trying to moderate, if not reverse, the increases in protectionism of the previous year or two, although the World Economic Conference of 1933 proved a failure. In 1932 what we now know as the three Benelux countries agreed at Ouchy to start cutting tariffs on each others' exports; this agreement came to nothing as it required other countries, with whom the Ouchy group had MFN relations, to waive their MFN rights, which the United Kingdom refused to do. The Oslo group, comprising the Ouchy three, plus Denmark, Norway, Sweden, and (eventually) Finland, had met in 1930 for discussions on tariff reform, and agreed in The Hague in 1937 to a program of eliminating quotas between member states—on the basis that this would not violate others' MFN rights, which applied only to tariffs. Most importantly, perhaps, the 1932 U.S. presidential election led to the appointment of the strongly pro–free trade Cordell Hull as secretary of state. In 1934, the U.S. Reciprocal Trade Agreements Act delegated authority to the executive to conclude trade agreements, which Hull proceeded to do. By 1939, the United States had signed twenty treaties with countries accounting for 60 percent of its trade, the most important of which was with the United Kingdom—although this last treaty only came into effect in 1939, and was soon overtaken by other events.

One interesting theme that emerges from the literature on interwar trade policy concerns the role of the MFN principle during the period. As mentioned previously, the common perception is that the MFN clause played a crucial role in the years after 1860 in speeding up Europe's shift to free trade, by generalizing concessions that were being made anyway. By contrast, the literature has not been so kind regarding the impact of the clause during the 1920s and 1930s. We have already mentioned the chilling effect that the MFN principle had on the Ouchy group's attempts to promote more rapid regional trade liberalization; more generally, it has long been recognized that once countries are bound together in a web of MFN treaty obligations, and attempt to advance tariff reductions through bilateral deals, a free-rider problem may arise, with all parties waiting to reap the benefits of other parties' agreements. The League of Nations had been a persistent advocate of the principle of nondiscrimination, but was forced to admit in 1942, in its review of trade policy in the 1920s, that

> instead of facilitating, the clause tended to obstruct the reduction of tariffs by means of bilateral or multilateral agreements, owing to the reluctance of governments to make concessions which would be generalized by it. This was the result, mainly, of two causes: first, the refusal of the United States to reduce its own very high tariff by negotiation while claiming to benefit from any tariff reduction negotiated between European countries; secondly, the opposition of certain countries—notably the United Kingdom, the United States and the British Dominions—to derogations from strict MFN practice permitting the conclusion of regional or similar agreements for tariff reduction, the benefits of which would be limited to the participants. (League of Nations 1942, 119)

How to explain this distinction between the experiences of the 1860s and 1870s, and the interwar period? One approach would be to speculate that, in a multicountry situation in which bilateral tariff bargaining might produce multiple equilibria, the introduction of the MFN clause might serve to produce more extreme equilibria, both good and bad. An alternative interpretation of the data is that the 1860s wave of tariff-cutting succeeded because the bilateral MFN treaties were, initially, discriminatory: Once Britain and France had granted each other concessions, the Belgians found themselves at a disadvantage in these markets, and had an incentive to conclude a treaty, and so on. Thus, the MFN treaties of the 1860s in fact constituted an example of what Irwin (1993, 112) calls "progressive" bilateralism, of the sort that Cordell Hull was advocating in the 1930s: In his submission to the 1933 London conference, he proposed that the MFN principle not be invoked to prevent agreements among groups of countries, but suggested that a number of conditions be attached, one of which was that such agreements be "open to the accession of all countries" (Viner 1950, 35).[19]

19. The latter interpretation would lead to a sanguine view of regional trade agreements; on the other hand, some of the *costs* of discrimination identified by recent authors have their echoes in the historical record, too. For example, the argument that in the absence of the MFN principle, countries may be reluctant to reach bilateral agreements on the grounds that their partners may reach subsequent agreements that, "by granting to third countries concessions still greater than those given to themselves, and to which they would have no claim, would render nugatory the concessions which they received" (Viner 1951, 107; Bagwell and Staiger 1999) finds support in the failure of the United States (and Sardinia) to negotiate satisfactory trade agreements while pursuing a conditional MFN policy in the nineteenth century. It was largely as a result of this experience that the United States adopted the unconditional form of the MFN in 1923.

Most-favored-nation status was of course a cornerstone of the postwar General Agreement on Trade and Tariffs (GATT), which has seen a dramatic decline in tariff barriers (see below). The initial rounds continued to cut tariffs on the basis of bilateral agreements that were then multilateralized through the MFN principle to all GATT members. (However, initially it was only the richer countries that were involved: Less developed countries only joined in from the mid-1960s onward.) While the initial Geneva round was a success, other rounds, such as Torquay, were less so, and eventually the GATT shifted to multilateral deal-making, which was to prove such a success in the 1960s (Irwin 1995).

1.6.2 Twentieth-century Transport Costs

Transport costs continued to fall during the twentieth century, but at a slower rate than previously. Isserlis (1938) provides an index of British tramp freight rates from 1869 to 1936. As figure 1.4 shows, between 1869–71 and 1911–13 these freight rates (deflated by the Statist wholesale price index) fell by 22 percentage points, a figure that is reduced by the fact that rates increased sharply in 1911 and 1912; fitted values based on a regression of these deflated rates on time and time-squared show a drop of 34 percent. As expected, the rates increased sharply during the war, remaining abnormally high until 1920. While they continued to fall until 1925, they never attained their prewar levels, and rose thereafter, with the overall trend between 1921 and 1936 being broadly flat (at a level roughly equal to the 1869 level).

In the most careful study to date of post-1945 trends, Hummels (1999)

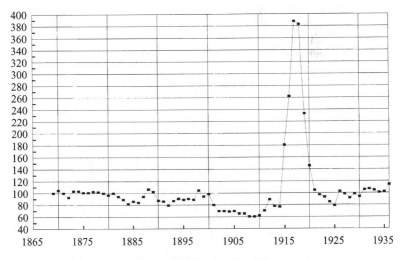

Fig. 1.4   Deflated freight rates, 1869–1914 (1869 = 100)

concludes that ocean freight rates have actually increased over much of the period. An index of liner shipping prices, calculated by the German Ministry of Transport, rises from1954 to 1958, is fairly flat until 1970 (despite the introduction of containers in the 1960s), rises through the 1970s, peaks in 1985, and falls sharply thereafter. Deflated by the German GDP deflator, it never attains its 1960s levels, even as late as 1997; deflated by the U.S. GDP deflator, it only recovers to its 1954 position by 1993. A less representative tramp-shipping index, constructed by the *Norwegian Shipping News,* shows that tramp freight rates were constant or increased between 1952 and 1997, when deflated by a commodity price deflator; when deflated by a U.S. GDP deflator they declined over the period as a whole, but were flat or increased over long subperiods. Moreover, the tramp rates, unlike the liner rates, exclude port costs, which were sharply rising during the period.

On the other hand, it is important to stress that air freight rates have declined dramatically in the 1950s, 1960s, and 1980s, while declining more slowly in the 1990s, and rising in the 1970s. These declines were greatest on North American routes. The result, predictably enough, has been a more than tenfold increase in the ratio of air to ocean shipments in the years since 1962 (Hummels 1999).

1.6.3   Late Twentieth-century Trade Policies

If transport cost declines were much less impressive during the late twentieth century than they were in the late nineteenth, then it follows that trade liberalization probably played a much greater role in commodity market integration in the later period than it did during the former. Table 1.5 gives average tariffs on manufactured products in a number of countries for which data are available back to 1913. It shows clearly the rise in protection during the interwar period, and the decline in tariff barriers since 1950. It also shows that for most of these countries, tariffs are much lower today than in 1913. There are exceptions, of course, notably Britain, as well as certain Asian countries that had a low tariff regime forced upon them by European powers or the United States. Both China and India, for example, have substantially higher tariffs now than in 1913: An extremely important caveat given these countries' populations. As table 1.5 suggests, tariffs are much higher now in developing countries than in rich countries, while the opposite was more true of the late nineteenth century. Table 1.6 gives average tariffs on manufactured goods in Latin America, East Asia, and sub-Saharan Africa during the 1980s and early 1990s: It shows a substantial decline in Latin America, and smaller declines in the other two regions. By the early 1990s, these average tariffs stood at 12.5 percent in Latin America, 17.1 percent in East Asia, and 22.5 percent in sub-Saharan Africa, as compared with figures of 4 or 5 percent for the United States, the European Union, and Japan.

Table 1.5   **Average Tariffs on Manufactured Goods, Selected Countries, 1913–98**

	1913	1931	1950	1980	1998–99
Austria	18	24	18	14.6	n.a.
Belgium	9	14	11	n.a.	n.a.
Denmark	14	—	3	n.a.	n.a.
France	20	30	18	n.a.	n.a.
Germany	13	21	26	n.a.	n.a.
Italy	18	46	25	n.a.	n.a.
The Netherlands	4	—	11	n.a.	n.a.
Spain	41	63	—	8.3	n.a.
Sweden	20	21	9	6.2	n.a.
United Kingdom	0	—	23	n.a.	n.a.
European Union	n.a.	n.a.	n.a.	8.3	4.1
Russia	84	a	a	a	13.4[b]
Switzerland	9	19	—	3.3	3.2[c]
Australia	16	—	—	—	6.0
Canada	26	—	—	—	4.9
Japan	25–30	—	—	9.9	5.5
New Zealand	15–20	—	—	—	4.4
United States	44	48	14	7.0	4.5
Argentina	28	—	—	—	14.0
Brazil	50–70	—	—	—	15.2
Colombia	40–60	—	—	—	11.4
Mexico	40–50	—	—	—	12.6
China	4–5	—	—	—	17.4
India	approx. 5	—	—	—	34.2
Iran	3–4	—	—	—	—
Thailand	2–3	—	—	—	47.2[d]
Turkey	5–10	—	—	—	0.3

Sources: Bairoch (1989, 1993); World Bank's *World Development Indicators* (2000).

Notes: n.a. = not applicable; dash = not available.

[a]Refers to the fact that the USSR ran such a restrictive trade policy that average tariffs were irrelevant.

[b]1997.

[c]1996.

[d]1993.

Table 1.6   **Average Tariffs on Manufactured Goods, DCs, 1980–93**

Region	1980–83	1984–87	1988–90	1991–93
Latin America and the Caribbean	23.6	25.1	22.7	12.5
East Asia	21.6	18.1	18.0	17.1
Sub-Saharan Africa	32.8	23.5	22.5	n.a.

Source: Rodrik (1999).

Note: n.a. = not available.

It is important to remember, of course, that emphasizing industrial tariffs overstates the extent to which industrial countries today have moved toward free trade, since agricultural protection (which triggered the move back toward protection in late-nineteenth-century Europe, as well as the protection of the late 1920s) remains extremely high in many wealthy countries, higher certainly than in 1913. Coppel and Durand (1999) report that protection raises the prices received by farmers by about 60 percent in Japan, 40 percent in the European Union, 15 percent in Canada, and 20 percent in the United States. Moreover, nontariff barriers (or NTBs, such as countervailing and antidumping duties, quotas, voluntary export restraints, production subsidies, and technical barriers to trade) are much more important today than they were in 1913. According to Coppel and Durand (1999, table 2), NTBs became less pervasive in all the major industrial economies between 1988 and 1996, although the use of antidumping measures has become more common, and has been on the increase in the European Union and outside the Organization for Economic Cooperation and Development (OECD). Meanwhile, the average incidence of NTBs on manufactured imports fell in Latin America from 28.4 percent in the mid-1980s to 1.8 percent in the early 1990s; it fell from 23.1 percent to 5.5 percent in East Asia; and it *increased* from 42.7 percent to 45.4 percent in sub-Saharan Africa between 1984–87 and 1988–90 (Rodrik 1999, table 1.3). For all these reasons one cannot automatically assume that average worldwide protection is less severe today than it was in 1913.

Given the increased importance of NTBs, it is difficult to measure long-run trends in the overall stance of trade policy, although in principle, measures such as the trade restrictiveness index (Anderson and Neary 1994) could do precisely this. Nonetheless, the consensus is that the world is becoming more open; for example, according to Sachs and Warner (1995) all regions have become more open in recent decades. However, Africa still lags well behind the rest of the world: As late as 1992, only 30 percent of African countries were judged open by Sachs and Warner, as compared with 86 percent of countries in the Latin American and Caribbean (LAC) region and 67 percent of Asian countries (fig. 1.5).

The reasons for the descent of the interwar economy into protectionism are well understood, and have been touched on above; but what were the fundamentals driving postwar liberalization, and even more importantly, what can explain the different timing of liberalization across regions? The United States liberalized almost immediately; as figure 1.5 (based on Sachs and Warner 1995) suggests, Western Europe waited about fifteen years to liberalize, and when it did, it did so in a rush at the end of the 1950s (although the European Payments Union, European Coal and Steel Community, and the Organization for European Economic Cooperation had been promoting intra-European trade since the beginning of the decade). By contrast, Latin America became progressively more closed from the 1950s

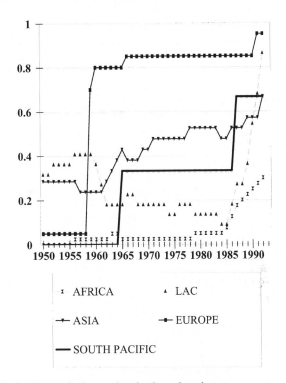

Fig. 1.5   Sachs-Warner indicator, fraction in each region open

onward, only opening in the 1980s (along with New Zealand), a quarter-century after the Europeans—yet another powerful example of path dependence arising from an exogenous shock (in this case, world depression rather than war) and operating through the political process. The former Communist economies only opened during the 1990s; much of Africa still remains closed.

Were ideas or interests responsible for these differences between regions? On the one hand, when countries in Latin America or elsewhere turned to import substitution during the 1930s and 1940s, this created constituencies that now depended on protection, and lobbied for its maintenance; an interest-based explanation would require arguing that for some reason, the protectionist coalitions of capital and labor that characterized Latin America or Australasia were more powerful than similar coalitions that emerged in peripheral European economies, for example. Alternatively, disillusion with the market as a result of the interwar experience led many intellectuals and policymakers to advocate socialism or state-led industrialization, which was inimical to open markets. Bodies such as the United Nations Economic Commission for Latin America were influential in advocating import substitution, and their hostility to free trade was shared by many development economists (Corbo 1992; Krueger 1997). Were these ideas more appealing to developing country elites, and if so, why? If ideas explain postwar protection, then disillusion with those ideas must explain eventual liberalization; and indeed, in countries such as Ireland there was deep disillusionment with import substitution by the late 1950s. Why did it take longer for the failures of that policy to become apparent elsewhere? And what were the roles of the Cold War in explaining OECD liberalization, or of decolonization in explaining sub-Saharan or Indian protection? Although much work has been done on individual countries and regions, we have not yet seen a comprehensive and comparative account that can explain the diversity of the post-1945 experience worldwide.

1.6.4 Commodity Market Integration in the Twentieth Century

What has been the combined impact of the transport cost and trade policy developments documented above? Turning first to the volume of trade, table 1.3 shows that merchandise exports accounted for a smaller share of world GDP in 1950 than they had done in 1913; and that the 1913 levels of openness (on this measure) had not been recouped as late as 1973 in the United Kingdom, Spain, Australia, Latin America, China, India, and Thailand. Indeed, consistent with the average tariff data in table 1.5, they had not been recouped as late as 1992 in much of the developing world, in particular Latin America and India (where they had not even been recouped by 1998).

However, as stressed in the introduction, trade shares may vary because of shifts in export supply or import demand, rather than reflecting changes in international commodity market integration. In addition, the merchandise share of GDP has been shrinking since 1913, which would tend to pull down the share of merchandise exports in GDP, irrespective of globalization trends. As Feenstra (1998), among others, has pointed out, the growth in merchandise trade has been far more impressive relative to merchandise value-added than relative to GDP (although even his table 2, which gives data for advanced countries only, shows Japanese and U.K. ratios lower in 1990 than in 1913). Other, more qualitative criteria, such as the amount of intrafirm trade, associated with outsourcing and what Feenstra calls the "disintegration of production," also clearly demarcate the present era from the period before World War I.

However, on other criteria the contribution of commodity market integration during the twentieth century does not seem so impressive. Baier and Bergstrand (2001) report that income growth explains fully two-thirds of world trade growth between the late 1950s and the late 1980s, leaving only 25 percent to tariff reductions, and a mere 8 percent to transport cost declines. Strikingly, the share of trade growth due to income growth during the late twentieth century is very similar to that during the three centuries following Columbus—a period for which there is little or no evidence of commodity market integration (section 1.3.4). Whether a much larger share of trade growth in the rapidly globalizing nineteenth century was due to commodity market integration is not yet known.

Price gaps for identical commodities in different markets remain the best measure of commodity market integration; yet surprisingly little work has been done collecting such evidence for the twentieth century. Presumably, the post-1945 trade liberalization documented above has swamped any increases in ocean freight rates, and the result has been price convergence; but this remains purely speculative.[20] Of course, documenting price convergence requires laborious work in the archives, ensuring that price quotes are for identical goods in various markets; but if the nineteenth century can yield such evidence for economic historians, then cannot the twentieth century surely do the same?

Finally, what has happened to the composition of trade over the course of the twentieth century? Table 1.7 gives the World Bank's estimates of the shares of primary and manufactured goods in the various regions' exports and imports. Recall that in 1913, primary products had accounted for between 62 and 64 percent of total merchandise exports, with food accounting for 27 percent, agricultural raw materials for 22.7 percent, and minerals for 14 percent. By 1999, the share of primary products in merchandise exports had declined to 18 percent, with the shares of food, agricultural raw materials, and minerals (including fuel) accounting for a mere 8, 2, and 8 percent, respectively, of the total. The impact of third world industrialization comes across clearly from these figures: Manufactures now account for more than half of merchandise exports everywhere, barring the Middle East and North Africa, and sub-Saharan Africa. Even in the case of Africa, however, manufactures are now vastly more important than they were on the eve of World War I (compare with table 1.4).[21]

1.7   Conclusions

There are several themes that have emerged from this survey. The range of goods that have been traded between continents since the Voyages of Dis-

---

20. Indeed, obvious international sources of price data (e.g., the commodity price data to be found in the *World Bank Development Indicators* or the International Monetary Fund's *International Financial Statistics*) reveal no discernable general trend toward commodity price convergence during the past four decades.

21. Table 1.7 also indicates the importance of trade in commercial services, which accounted for 19 percent of total exports (i.e., of merchandise exports plus commercial services exports) worldwide in 1999, and for between 10 and 20 percent of exports from all regions. In 1913, services had accounted for 22 percent of total exports from the United Kingdom; commercial service exports accounted for 27 percent of U.K. exports in 1999. For the United States, the figures were 8 percent in 1913 and 27 percent in 1999 (Mitchell 1988; U.S. Department of Commerce 1975; World Bank 2001).

Table 1.7 Composition of Trade by Region

Region	Food (1)	Ag. Raw Materials (2)	Fuels (3)	Ores and Metals (4)	Primary (5)	Manufactures (6)	Primary (7)	Manufactures (8)	Services (9)
	Percent of Merchandise Exports						Percent of Total Exports		
East Asia and Pacific	7	2	5	2	16	81	14	73	13
Europe and Central Asia	6	3	20	7	36	56	31	48	21
Latin America and Caribbean	24	3	17	6	50	51	44	44	12
Middle East and North Africa	4	1	73	1	79	21	67	18	15
South Asia	16	2	0	2	20	79	16	63	21
Sub-Saharan Africa	15	4	29	14	62	39	55	35	11
High-income	7	2	3	2	14	82	12	68	20
World	8	2	5	3	18	82	15	66	19
	Percent of merchandise imports						Percent of total imports		
East Asia and Pacific	5	3	10	5	23	74	19	63	18
Europe and Central Asia	10	2	7	3	22	67	21	63	16
Latin America and Caribbean	9	2	7	2	20	80	17	69	14
Middle East and North Africa									
South Asia	12	4	18	5	39	56	33	47	21
Sub-Saharan Africa	11	2	10	2	25	71	22	63	15
High-income	8	2	7	3	20	77	17	64	19
World	8	2	7	3	20	76	17	65	18

Source: World Bank's *World Development Indicators* (2001).

Notes: The entry in column (5) is the sum of columns (1) through (4). The sum of columns (1) through (4). The sum of primary and manufactured trade in columns (5) and (6) is less than 100 because of unclassified trade. The data in column (9) are for commercial service exports only. "Total" exports in columns (7) through (9) equals total merchandise exports plus commercial service exports. Columns (7) and (8) are calculated by assuming that total merchandise exports are allocated between the two categories in the same proportion as the figures in columns (5) and (6).

covery has steadily increased over time, and there has been substantial commodity market integration over the period, driven by technology in the nineteenth century and politics in the late twentieth century. However, this trend toward greater market integration was *not* monotonic; it was periodically interrupted by shocks such as wars and world depressions, or by endogenous political responses to the distributional effects of globalization itself. In some periods, politics has reinforced the effects of technology, while in other periods it has offset them. In several cases, severe shocks have had long-run effects on the international integration of commodity markets, as a result of politically induced hysteresis. Finally, we know remarkably little about international commodity market integration during the twentieth century.

References

Abu-Lughod, J. 1989. *Before European hegemony: The world system A.D. 1250–1350.* New York: Oxford University Press.

Alesina, A., and E. Spolaore. 1997. On the number and size of nations. *Quarterly Journal of Economics* 112:1027–56.

Anderson, J. E., and J. P. Neary. 1994. Measuring the restrictiveness of trade policy. *World Bank Economic Review* 8:151–69.

Bagwell, K., and R. W. Staiger. 1999. Multilateral trade negotiations, bilateral opportunism, and the rules of GATT. NBER Working Paper no. 7071. Cambridge, Mass.: National Bureau of Economic Research, April.

Baier, S. L., and J. H. Bergstrand. 2001. The growth of world trade: Tariffs, transport costs, and income similarity. *Journal of International Economics* 53:1–27.

Bairoch, P. 1989. European trade policy, 1815–1914. In *The Cambridge economic history of Europe.* Vol. 8, ed. P. Mathias and S. Pollard, 1–160. Cambridge: Cambridge University Press.

———. 1993. *Economics and world history: Myths and paradoxes.* Chicago: University of Chicago Press.

Baldwin, R. E., and P. Martin. 1999. Two waves of globalization: Superficial similarities, fundamental differences. NBER Working Paper no. 6904. Cambridge, Mass.: National Bureau of Economic Research, January.

Barrett, W. 1990. World bullion flows, 1450–1800. In *The rise of merchant empires: Long-distance trade in the early modern world 1350–1750,* ed. J. Tracy, 224–54. Cambridge: Cambridge University Press.

Bulbeck, D., A. Reid, L. C. Tan, and Y. Wu. 1998. *Southeast Asian exports since the fourteenth century: Cloves, pepper, coffee, and sugar.* Leiden, The Netherlands: KITLV Press.

Bulmer-Thomas, V. 1994. *The economic history of Latin America since independence.* Cambridge: Cambridge University Press.

Cameron, R. 1989. *A concise economic history of the world from paleolithic times to the present.* New York: Oxford University Press.

Chaudhuri, K. N. 1983. Foreign trade and the balance of payments (1757–1947). In *The Cambridge economic history of India.* Vol. 2, c. 1757–c. 1970, ed. D. Kumar, 804–77. Cambridge: Cambridge University Press.

Collins, W. J. 1996. Regional labor markets in British India. Harvard University, Department of Economics. Mimeograph, November.

Coppel, J., and M. Durand. 1999. Trends in market openness. OECD Economics Department Working Paper no. 221. Paris: Organization for Economic Cooperation and Development.

Corbo, V. 1992. *Development strategies and policies in Latin America: A historical perspective.* San Francisco: International Center for Economic Growth.

Crafts, N. F. R. 1985. *British economic growth during the Industrial Revolution.* Oxford: Clarendon Press.

Crouzet, F. 1964. Wars, blockade, and economic change in Europe, 1792–1815. *Journal of Economic History* 24:567–88.

Crucini, M. J. 1994. Sources of variation in real tariff rates: The United States, 1900–1940. *American Economic Review* 84:732–43.

Davis, R. 1962. English foreign trade, 1700–1774. *Economic History Review* 15:285–303.

———. 1966. The rise of protection in England, 1689–1786. *Economic History Review,* 2nd ser., 19:306–17.

Day, J. 1978. The Great Bullion Famine of the fifteenth century. *Past and Present* 79:3–54.

De Long, J. B. 1998. Trade policy and America's standard of living: A historical perspective. In *Imports, exports, and the American worker,* ed. S. M. Collins, 349–88. Washington, D.C.: Brookings Institution.

de Vries, J., and A. van der Woude. 1997. *The first modern economy: Success, failure, and perseverance of the Dutch economy, 1500–1815.* Cambridge: Cambridge University Press.

Diaz Alejandro, C. 1984. Latin America in the 1930s. In *Latin America in the 1930s: The role of the periphery in world crisis,* ed. R. Thorpe, 17–49. London: Macmillan.

Eichengreen, B. 1989. The political economy of the Smoot-Hawley tariff. *Research in Economic History* 12:1–43.

———. 1994. *Golden fetters: The gold standard and the Great Depression 1919–1939.* Oxford: Oxford University Press.

Esteban, J. C. 1997. The rising share of British industrial exports in industrial output, 1700–1851. *Journal of Economic History* 57:879–906.

Feenstra, R. 1998. Integration of trade and disintegration of production in the global economy. *Journal of Economic Perspectives* 12:31–50.

Feinstein, C. H., P. Temin, and G. Toniolo. 1997. *The European economy between the wars.* Oxford: Oxford University Press.

Findlay, R. 1982. Trade and growth in the Industrial Revolution. In *The long view in economics: Essays in honor of W. W. Rostow.* Vol. 1, ed. C. P. Kindleberger and G. Di Tella, 178–88. London: Macmillan.

———. 1990. The triangular trade and the Atlantic economy of the eighteenth century: A simple general-equilibrium model. Princeton Essays in International Finance no. 177. Princeton University, Department of Economics, International Finance Section.

———. 1996. The emergence of the world economy: Towards a historical perspective 1000–1750. Economics Discussion Paper no. 9596–08. New York: Columbia University, April.

Findlay, R., and M. Lundahl. 2000. Towards a factor proportions approach to economic history: Population, precious metals, and prices from the Black Death to the price revolution. Columbia University and Stockholm School of Economics. Manuscript.

Fletcher, M. E. 1958. The Suez Canal and world shipping, 1869–1914. *Journal of Economic History* 18:556–73.

Flynn, D. O., and A. Giraldez. 1995. Born with a "silver spoon": The origin of world trade in 1571. *Journal of World History* 6:201–21.

Frankel, J. A. 1982. The 1808–1809 embargo against Great Britain. *Journal of Economic History* 42:291–307.

Haberler, G. 1943. *Quantitative trade controls: Their causes and nature.* Geneva: League of Nations.

Hamilton, E. J. 1934. *American treasure and the price revolution in Spain, 1501–1650.* Cambridge: Harvard University Press.

Harlaftis, G., and V. Kardasis. 2000. International shipping in the eastern Mediterranean and the Black Sea: Istanbul as a maritime centre, 1870–1910. In *The Mediterranean response to globalization before 1950,* ed. Ş. Pamuk and J. G. Williamson, 233–65. London: Routledge.

Harley, C. K. 1980. Transportation, the world wheat trade, and the Kuznets cycle, 1850–1913. *Explorations in Economic History* 17:218–50.

———. 1988. Ocean freight rates and productivity, 1740–1913: The primacy of mechanical invention reaffirmed. *Journal of Economic History* 48:851–76.

Heckscher, E. F. 1922. *The Continental system: An economic interpretation.* Oxford, U.K.: Clarendon.

Herlihy, D. 1997. *The Black Death and the transformation of the West.* Cambridge: Harvard University Press.

Ho, P. T. 1959. *Studies on the population of China, 1368–1953.* Cambridge: Harvard University Press.

Hobsbawm, E. J. 1954. The general crisis of the European economy in the seventeenth century. *Past and Present* 5:33–53; 6:44–65.

Hueckel, G. 1973. War and the British economy, 1793–1815: A general equilibrium analysis. *Explorations in Economic History* 10:365–96.

Hummels, D. 1999. Have international transportation costs declined? Purdue University, Department of Economics. Mimeograph, September.

Hurd, J. 1975. Railways and the expansion of markets in India, 1861–1921. *Explorations in Economic History* 12:263–88.

Irwin, D. A. 1991. Mercantilism as strategic trade policy: The Anglo-Dutch rivalry for the East India trade. *Journal of Political Economy* 99:1296–1314.

———. 1993. Multilateral and bilateral trade policies in the world trading system: An historical perspective. In *New dimensions in regional integration,* ed. J. de Melo and A. Panagariya, 90–127. Cambridge: Cambridge University Press.

———. 1995. The GATT's contribution to economic recovery in post-war Western Europe. In *Europe's post-war recovery,* ed. B. Eichengreen, 127–50. Cambridge: Cambridge University Press.

———. 1998a. Changes in U.S. tariffs: The role of import prices and commercial policies. *American Economic Review* 88:1015–26.

———. 1998b. From Smoot-Hawley to reciprocal trade agreements: Changing the course of U.S. trade policy in the 1930s. In *The defining moment: The Great Depression and the American economy in the twentieth century,* ed. M. Bordo, C. Goldin, and E. White, 325–52. Chicago: University of Chicago Press.

Israel, J. I. 1989. *Dutch primacy in world trade 1585–1740.* Oxford, U.K.: Clarendon.

Issawi, C. 1966. *The economy of the Middle East 1800–1914.* Chicago: University of Chicago Press.

Isserlis, L. 1938. Tramp shipping cargoes and freights. *Journal of the Royal Statistical Society* 101, pt. 1:304–417.

Iwao, S. 1976. Japanese foreign trade in the sixteenth and seventeenth centuries. *Acta Asiatica* 30:1–18.

Johnson, H. G. 1965. A theoretical model of economic nationalism in new and developing states. *Political Science Quarterly* 80:169–85.

Jones, J. M. 1934. *Tariff retaliation: Repercussions of the Hawley-Smoot bill.* Philadelphia: University of Pennsylvania Press.

Jones, M. T., and M. Obstfeld. 1997. Saving, investment, and gold: A reassessment of historical current account data. NBER Working Paper no. 6103. Cambridge, Mass.: National Bureau of Economic Research, July.

Kenwood, A. G., and A. L. Lougheed. 1983. *The growth of the international economy 1820–1980: An introductory text.* 2nd ed. London: Unwin Hyman.

Kindleberger, C. P. 1973. *The world in depression.* Boston: Little, Brown.

———. 1989. Commercial policy between the wars. In *The Cambridge economic history of Europe.* Vol. 8, ed. P. Mathias and S. Pollard, 161–96. Cambridge: Cambridge University Press.

———. 1996. *World economic primacy 1500–1990.* Oxford: Oxford University Press.

Krueger, A. O. 1997. Trade policy and economic development: How we learn. *American Economic Review* 87:1–22.

Lamartine Yates, P. 1959. *Forty years of foreign trade.* New York: Macmillan.

League of Nations. 1942. *Commercial policy in the interwar period: International proposals and national policies.* Geneva: League of Nations.

Liepmann, H. 1938. *Tariff levels and the economic unity of Europe.* London: Allen and Unwin.

Maddison, A. 1991. *Dynamic forces in capital development.* Oxford: Oxford University Press.

———. 1995. *Monitoring the world economy 1820–1992.* Paris: Organization for Economic Coordination and Development.

———. 2001. *The world economy: A millennial perspective.* Paris: Organization for Economic Cooperation and Development.

Mauro, F. 1961. Towards an "Intercontinental Model": European overseas expansion between 1500 and 1800. *Economic History Review* 14:1–17.

Menard, R. 1991. Transport costs and long-range trade, 1300–1800: Was there a European "transport revolution" in the early modern era? In *Political economy of merchant empires,* ed. J. D. Tracy, 228–75. Cambridge: Cambridge University Press.

Metzer, J. 1974. Railroad development and market integration: The case of tsarist Russia. *Journal of Economic History* 34:529–50.

Mitchell, B. R. 1988. *British historical statistics.* Cambridge: Cambridge University Press.

———. 1992. *International historical statistics: Europe 1750–1988.* 3rd ed. New York: Stockton.

Morgan, K. 2000. *Slavery, Atlantic trade, and the British economy 1660–1800.* Cambridge: Cambridge University Press.

Needham, J. 1954. *Science and civilization in China.* Vol. 1. Cambridge: Cambridge University Press.

North, D. C. 1958. Ocean freight rates and economic development 1750–1913. *Journal of Economic History* 18:538–55.

O'Brien, P. K., and S. L. Engerman. 1991. Exports and the growth of the British economy from the Glorious Revolution to the Peace of Amiens. In *Slavery and the rise of the Atlantic system,* ed. B. L. Solow, 177–209. Cambridge: Cambridge University Press.

O'Rourke, K. H. 1991. Burn everything British but their coal: The Anglo-Irish economic war of the 1930s. *Journal of Economic History* 51:357–66.

———. 1997. The European grain invasion, 1870–1913. *Journal of Economic History* 57:775–801.

O'Rourke, K. H., and J. G. Williamson. 1994. Late nineteenth century Anglo-American factor price convergence: Were Heckscher and Ohlin right? *Journal of Economic History* 54:892–916.

———. 1995. Open economy forces and late nineteenth century Swedish catch-up: A quantitative accounting. *Scandinavian Economic History Review* 43:171–203.

———. 1999. *Globalization and history: The evolution of a nineteenth century Atlantic economy.* Cambridge: MIT Press.

———. 2000. When did globalization begin? NBER Working Paper no. 7632. Cambridge, Mass.: National Bureau of Economic Research, April. Forthcoming, *European Review of Economic History.*

———. 2001. After Columbus: Explaining the global trade boom 1500–1800. NBER Working Paper no. 8186. Cambridge, Mass.: National Bureau of Economic Research, March.

Panikkar, K. M. 1953. *Asia and Western dominance.* London: George Allen.

Parker, G., and L. Smith, eds. 1978. *The general crisis of the seventeenth century.* London: Routledge.

Prakesh, O. 1998. European commercial enterprise in pre-colonial India. In *The new Cambridge economic history of India.* Vol. 5, part 2. Cambridge: Cambridge University Press.

Rapp, R. T. 1975. The unmaking of the Mediterranean trade hegemony. *Journal of Economic History* 35:499–525.

Rodrik, D. 1999. *The new global economy and developing countries: Making openness work.* Washington, D.C.: Overseas Development Council.

Rossabi, M. 1990. The "decline" of the Central Asian caravan trade. In *The rise of the merchant empires: Long-distance trade in the early modern world 1350–1750,* ed. J. D. Tracy, 351–70. Cambridge: Cambridge University Press.

Sachs, J. D., and A. Warner. 1995. Economic reform and the process of global integration. *Brookings Papers on Economic Activity,* Issue no. 1:1–118. Washington, D.C.: Brookings Institution.

Schonhardt-Bailey, C. 1991. Specific factors, capital markets, portfolio diversification, and free trade: Domestic determinants of the repeal of the Corn Laws. *World Politics* 43:545–69.

Siriwardana, A. M. 1991. The impact of tariff protection in the colony of Victoria in the late nineteenth century: A general equilibrium analysis. *Australian Economic History Review* 31:45–65.

Slaughter, M. J} 1995. The antebellum transportation revolution and factor-price convergence. NBER Working Paper no. 5303. Cambridge, Mass.: National Bureau of Economic Research, October.

Steensgaard, N. 1982. The Dutch East India Company as an institutional innovation. In *Dutch capitalism and world capitalism,* ed. M. Aymard, 235–57. Cambridge: Cambridge University Press.

———. 1995. Commodities, bullion, and services in intercontinental transactions before 1750. In *The European discovery of the world and its economic effects on pre-industrial society,* ed. H. Pohl, 9–23. Stuttgart: Franz Steiner Verlag.

Tracy, M. 1989. *Government and agriculture in Western Europe 1880–1988.* 3rd ed. New York: Harvester Wheatsheaf.

U.S. Department of Commerce. 1975. *Historical statistics of the United States: Colonial times to 1970.* Part 2. Washington, D.C.: GPO.

Viner, J. 1948. Power versus plenty as objectives of foreign policy in the seventeenth and eighteenth centuries. *World Politics* 1:1–29.

———. 1950. *The customs union issue.* New York: Carnegie Endowment for International Peace.

————. 1951. *International economics.* Glencoe, Ill.: Free Press.
von Glahn, R. 1996. Myth and reality of China's seventeenth-century monetary crisis. *Journal of Economic History* 56:429–54.
Wake, C. H. H. 1979. The changing pattern of Europe's pepper and spice imports, 1400–1700. *Journal of European Economic History* 8:361–403.
Wallerstein, I. 1980. *The modern world system.* Vol. 2. New York: Wiley.
Williams, E. 1944. *Capitalism and slavery.* Chapel Hill: University of North Carolina Press.
Williamson, J. G. 1974. *Late nineteenth century American development: A general equilibrium history.* Cambridge: Cambridge University Press.
————. 1984. Why was British growth so slow during the Industrial Revolution? *Journal of Economic History* 44:687–712.
————. 2000a. Globalization, factor prices, and living standards in Asia before 1940. In *Asia Pacific dynamism 1500–2000,* ed. A. J. H. Latham and H. Kawakatsu, 13–45. London: Routledge.
————. 2002. Land, labor, and globalization in the pre-industrial third world, 1870–1940. *Journal of Economic History* 62 (1): 55–85.
Wilson, C. H. 1949. Treasure and trade balances: The mercantilist problem. *Economic History Review,* 2nd ser. 2:152–61.
World Bank. 2000. *World development indicators 2001.* Washington, D.C.: World Bank.
Wrigley, E. A. 1988. *Continuity, chance, and change: The character of the Industrial Revolution in England.* Cambridge: Cambridge University Press.
Yasuba, Y. 1978. Freight rates and productivity in ocean transportation for Japan, 1875–1943. *Explorations in Economic History* 15:11–39.

Comment   Douglas A. Irwin

The conference organizers have given Findlay and O'Rourke the "modest" task of examining what we know about commodity market integration— over the past half-millennium! And that is exactly what they do in this wide-ranging and close-to-exhaustive survey of what we know about world trade from 1500 to the present. This informative paper will serve as an excellent introduction for those who are not familiar with this history and the extensive secondary literature that has studied that history in detail. It is difficult to disagree with Findlay and O'Rourke's assessment of various periods, so I will not take much issue with the authors' conclusions. Rather, my comments will focus on some aspects of commodity market integration that the paper has not emphasized, not by way of criticism but more as a reminder to the reader that there are other potentially important features of integration during this period.

The authors confine their focus to intercontinental trade, an understandable choice that conveniently limits the scope of the paper to manageable

Douglas A. Irwin is professor of economics at Dartmouth College and a research associate of the National Bureau of Economic Research.

proportions. But the reader should not conclude that local, national, and regional commodity market integration was unimportant. Quite to the contrary, this trade was quantitatively more important than intercontinental trade, and it would be helpful to have a brief comparison of the relative size of each. Intra-European trade, for example, was quite extensive after 1500. A large literature in economic history examines this thriving trade in raw materials, foodstuffs, and textiles in detail. This trade promoted market integration throughout Europe, and presumably led to gains from specialization.

This intranational and intraregional trade was promoted by the reduction of government trade barriers. The authors discuss the fall (and subsequent rise) in European tariffs after the mid-1840s. But these developments came after a period in which there were dramatic reductions in intranational trade barriers, notably the elimination of the last tolls on intra-French trade in 1790 and the formation of the Zollverein in Germany in 1832.

Intra-European trade also differed from the early intercontinental trade in terms of the commodities exchanged. The authors note that intercontinental trade from 1500 to 1800 was largely confined to goods with a high value-to-bulk ratio, such as spices (pepper and cloves), tea and coffee, and silk. Intra-European trade was much more mundane, consisting of commodities such as grain, animals, wool, timber, and textiles. I suspect that the laboring masses during this period may have been largely unaffected by the exotic intercontinental trade of the day because most of their expenditures were confined to food, clothing, and shelter. Thus, intranational and regional trade may have been more important for European standards of living and economic welfare than trade in the luxury commodities that were consumed mainly by the wealthy. (However, intercontinental trade in slaves and in silver had a more pervasive economic effect in Europe: the former for altering production patterns in the New World, and the latter for having real as well as monetary effects, as Findlay and Lundahl 2000 point out).

Thus, while the authors have justifiably chosen to restrict their focus on intercontinental trade, we should remember that intranational (as well as international with a region) trade was also a powerful force throughout this period.

Aside from that major point, a few smaller details deserve comment. The authors rightly stress that price convergence is the best measure of market integration. But, as I am sure they would agree, this should not be the sole metric of interest. The best evidence on price gaps is from the 1850 to 1913 period, and here O'Rourke and Williamson (1999) have presented evidence showing a great deal of price convergence. In the early modern period from 1500 to 1800, however, the authors point out that there is little evidence of commodity price convergence. (Figure 1.1 of the paper makes this point.) But the lack of price convergence could be an unimportant piece of evidence in relation to the fact that trade existed at all. Ideally, one would like to compare autarky prices and traded prices, and not simply examine whether traded prices have converged. Thus, figure 1.1 shows that the markups on spices were stuck at roughly a factor of 5 throughout the seventeenth century. But if the price gap had been a factor of 50 prior to the introduction of trade, then the movement from 50 to 5 would constitute massive convergence and the lack of subsequent convergence would be second order. (The problem, of course, is that autarky or pretrade prices are virtually impossible to come by.) In the post-1950 period, unfortunately, comparing prices on similar goods is difficult because trade is dominated by manufactured goods, whose different product characteristics and terms of sale make the exercise hazardous.

The reader should also be reminded that quantitative magnitudes do not always correspond to economic importance. In terms of the quantity of trade, spices dominated exchange between Europe and Asia. Although quantitatively small, trade in other goods, such as those that embody new technology, may have been of key importance. As work by Elhanan Helpman, Jonathan Eaton, and others has pointed out, trade in capital goods, in tools, and in "new" goods can have important and lasting productivity effects. As a good example, the paper mentions that the introduction of the sweet potato in Asia brought about widespread productivity improvements in agriculture. The introduction of gunpowder from Asia to Europe does not feature in the trade statistics, but also had explosive repercussions. If Paul Romer is right, then the welfare effect of introducing new goods and product innovations is also much larger than standard gains from reductions of tariffs on existing trade in goods.

Finally, the authors tantalize us by posing a major question at the end of the paper that they do not answer, namely, what drives policy liberalization and why different regions liberalize at different times. The authors' speculation on this point, in light of their review of 500 years of trade, would be quite interesting. For example, the Napoleonic War and World War I were followed by periods of protection (for the new industries stimulated by disruption of trade due to the war), whereas World War II was followed by a concerted effort to eliminate trade barriers. What accounts for the difference? A political-economy explanation for the timing of liberalization would be quite interesting to explore, and could perhaps be the subject of a future conference.

References

Findlay, R., and M. Lundahl. 2000. Towards a factor proportions approach to economic history: Population, precious metals, and prices from the Black Death to the price revolution. Columbia University and Trinity College, Dublin. Manuscript.
O'Rourke, K. H., and J. G. Williamson. 1999. Globalization and history: The evolution of a nineteenth century Atlantic economy. Cambridge: MIT Press.

2

International Migration and the Integration of Labor Markets

Barry R. Chiswick and Timothy J. Hatton

2.1 Introduction

Globalization in the labor market is qualitatively different from globalization of goods or asset markets. With international migration, the factor of production (labor services) crosses national boundaries embodied in individuals. As a result, trading in goods and services and capital flows are fundamentally different from trading in labor services (people). In Adam Smith's words, "man is of all sorts of luggage the most difficult to be transported." Nevertheless, international migration does respond strongly to market signals, either legally, when the policy environment allows, or illegally, when there are artificial barriers to mobility. International migration alters the labor supply and the demographic characteristics of both the sending and the receiving countries. Moreover, it influences economic growth, patterns of trade, income distribution, and the distribution of political power within and between countries.

In this paper we shall illustrate that the globalization of world markets has been of prime economic importance in the two key eras: the age of mass migration, which rose to a crescendo between 1850 and 1913, and the era of "constrained" mass migration of the last fifty years. The focus is on intercontinental migrations: from Europe to the New World and from parts of Asia to other areas around the globe in the late nineteenth and early twen-

Barry R. Chiswick is UIC Distinguished Professor and head of the Department of Economics at the University of Illinois at Chicago. Timothy J. Hatton is professor of economics at the University of Essex.

We appreciate the many helpful comments we received on earlier drafts from the organizers and participants in this NBER project. We are particularly grateful to Riccardo Faini and Jeffrey Williamson for constructive suggestions. We are, however, solely responsible for any errors of omission or commission.

tieth centuries, and primarily from the third world to the first world and the Persian Gulf in the late twentieth century. We begin (in section 2.2) by mapping out the different eras of international migration and labor mobility over the last four centuries. In the following section (section 2.3) we examine the underlying forces that drove mass migration in the two eras of globalization. Perhaps even more important are the effects of migration on sending and receiving countries and the impact of these economic effects on what has been dubbed the "policy backlash" (section 2.4). Although the fundamentals driving international migration were similar in the two periods, the nature, direction, and consequences of the flows reflect changes in the structure and integration of the international economy. The effects of international migration are conditioned both by structural changes in the world economy and by changes in policy regimes. In turn, the policy regimes have evolved in response to changing economic structures, political developments, and migration itself (section 2.5). This paper concludes with an overview of migration flows and policy in the past, and with speculation about the future (section 2.6).

2.2 International Migration in Different Economic Eras

2.2.1 Contracts and Coercion, 1600–1790

The discovery of the Americas stimulated a steady stream of migrants (voluntary and involuntary) from Europe and Africa. But these streams were a mere trickle compared to what came later. At first the conditions were harsh and the economic returns were too low in relation to the costs to make mass migration feasible. High transport costs and the risks (both financial and to life itself) and uncertainties involved ensured that only the richest and the most intrepid could bear the cost. Although the migrations of religious groups and other pioneers gradually increased, their numbers were dwarfed by those who came under contract or coercion. By the end of the eighteenth century something like eight million had journeyed to the New World, but largely as slaves from Africa (about 7 million) and convicts from Great Britain, or indentured servants from western Europe, whose migration was financed by others (see Lovejoy 1983, 478, 496). Coercion and contracts were the chief means through which the New World recruited its labor force during this period.

It is estimated that about 700,000 Europeans migrated to North America and the Caribbean between 1650 and 1780, more than half to the mainland colonies. Of these, between one-half and two-thirds came under contracts of indentured servitude (Galenson 1981, 17; Engerman 1986, 271). Around 1650 a passage to America would have cost about £6, or about five months' wages for an agricultural laborer in southern England (Eltis 1983, 258). Indentured servitude evolved in response to this overwhelming wealth constraint, a high ratio of costs to income, little accumulated wealth, and weak capital markets. Under this system servants were given free passage to the colonies and then, on arrival, sold (at an average price of about £8) to merchants or farmers.[1] But by the end of the eighteenth century fixed-period contract servitude for Europeans was in decline, partly because of diminishing European supply, but more importantly because of the expansion of another form of recruitment: slavery.

The sharp rise in slave imports from the late seventeenth century, first to the West Indies and then to the mainland colonies of the Chesapeake and South Carolina prevented the implicit wages of indentured servants from rising (i.e., prevented the contract length from falling) and slowed the growth in numbers (Grubb 1992, 196). The slave trade continued to grow in the eighteenth century, particularly to the cotton- and tobacco-growing colonies and states on the mainland of North America and to the sugar-growing colonies of the Caribbean.

The abolition of the slave trade to the United States in 1807, the emancipation of slaves in the northern United States, and the emancipation in the British colonies in 1834 ended these forced migrations, although slavery itself lasted longer. The decline in the supply of slave labor led to a revival of contract labor for work on plantations and in mines, this time primarily from China and India, to Southeast Asia, Africa, the Indian Ocean and Pacific Islands, the Caribbean, and North and South America, which lasted in some cases until the start of World War I (Engerman 1986). Although the numbers of these nineteenth-century contract laborers to the New World, as well as coerced convicts to Australia, were insignificant in comparison with the movement of free migrants, contract labor migration remained the dominant form of labor migration from the sending regions in Asia.

2.2.2   The Rise of Pioneer Free Settlers, 1790–1850

The intercontinental flow of free settlers, from northwest Europe to the New World, which was slow at first, gathered pace in the early nineteenth century. In the United States the inflows outnumbered slaves by the end of the eighteenth century, but elsewhere the transition came later. For the Americas as a whole it was not until the 1830s that the decadal flow of free migrants exceeded that of African slaves (table 2.1). And according to Eltis (1983, 255) it was not until the 1880s that the cumulative sum of European immigration overtook that of coerced labor from Africa. In Australia, too,

---

1. The sale price covered the shipping cost, and the comparison of this price with the present value of the servant's expected productivity over and above maintenance determined the length of bound labor—usually between four and seven years—after which the servant was freed. According to one historian of indentured servitude, "Although the institutional arrangements of the indenture system were different from those surrounding the immigration of free Europeans to colonial America, the same is not necessarily true of the servants' motives. Though some of the hardships they faced may have been different, the potential rewards were much the same for servants as for other European immigrants" (Galenson 1981, 113).

Table 2.1   Free and Coerced Migration, 1790s to 1840s (thousands per annum)

	1790s	1800s	1810s	1820s	1830s	1840s
Americas						
Slaves	—	—	—	60.25	56.34	44.51
Free migrants	—	—	—	15.38	67.07	178.53
% free	—	—	—	20.2	54.3	80.0
Australia						
Convicts	0.49	0.43	1.70	3.23	5.00	3.37
Free settlers	0.02	0.05	0.08	1.03	5.72	14.09
% free	3.4	10.4	4.5	24.1	53.4	80.7

Sources: Americas: Eltis (1983, 256); Australia: free immigration from Berlin (1994, 22); convicts from Shaw (1966, 363–68).

Note: Dashes indicate data are not available.

coerced labor declined as the proportion of free settlers outnumbered the flow of convicts from the 1830s, although the absolute numbers are tiny compared with those in North America.

In North and South America, as well as Australia, free settlers began to arrive in ever larger numbers. Although some fled wars or sought better democratic rights and religious freedom, the vast majority were attracted by growing prosperity and by the prospect of becoming landowners or tenant farmers. These migrants traveled in family groups, often with the intention of starting or joining new communities at the New World's frontier.[2] These groups were often led by farmers, craftsmen, and artisans, and they originated chiefly in northwest Europe. It is estimated that three-quarters of the English and Welsh, two-thirds of the Dutch, and two-thirds of those from Osnabrück and Baden who migrated to the United States in the 1830s were in family groups and one-third of them were children under fifteen (Erickson 1994, 143).

Migrants to Australia needed even greater incentives, and in order to attract free migrants a policy of assisted emigration was begun in 1834. Some migrants were given free passage, either under the government scheme or under a bounty system that provided incentives for existing settlers to bring new settlers to the Australian colonies.[3] In South America, too, the longer journey times and more arduous conditions, which prolonged coerced and

2. Erickson (1994, 19–50) found that English migrants preferred Wisconsin, Illinois, Michigan, and Iowa to Massachusetts or Connecticut and that even those from industrial or urban backgrounds were attracted to farming and often bought unimproved land.

3. Under the scale issued in 1837 the bounties were £36 for a man and wife, £18 for an unmarried male or female, £10 for a child aged eight to fourteen, and £5 for a child aged one to seven (Madgwick 1937, 154). For the adults, certain age limits applied. The individual sponsoring the migrant usually paid travel and settlement costs from the bounty received. Under the government scheme, emigration agents recruited prospective migrants for free passages. It is estimated that about 40 percent of all free migrants between 1848 and 1872 were government assisted.

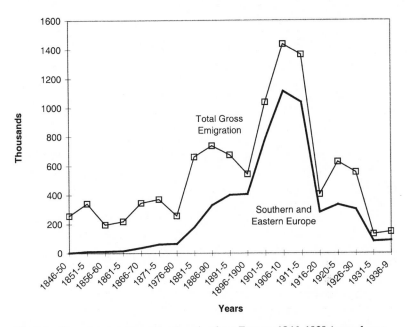

Fig. 2.1   Gross intercontinental emigration from Europe, 1846–1939 (annual averages)

contract labor, delayed the onset of free migration. Incentives in the form of free passages were used to encourage the flow of free settlers.

2.2.3   The Age of Mass Migration from Europe, 1850–1913

It was not until after the middle of the nineteenth century that mass migration can really be said to have taken hold. The figures for (gross) intercontinental emigration from Europe are plotted as five-year averages in figure 2.1. In the first three decades after 1846 the numbers averaged around 300,000 per annum, doubling in the following two decades and exceeding one million per annum by the turn of the century. The first wave of the late 1840s was associated with famine and revolution in Europe, and the second wave with the shift in ocean transport from sail to steam. The nominal cost of passage on the North Atlantic route remained roughly constant (Keeling 1999), although it declined relative to average wages. Moreover, the transition from sail to steam cut typical transit times from five weeks in the 1840s to twelve days by 1913 and to nine days by the late 1960s.[4]

---

4. The data for contract prices for government-assisted passages to Australia also suggest little downward trend in nominal prices between the late 1840s and the early 1880s. But voyage times fell by 10 percent, and mortality fell by 80 percent (McDonald and Shlomowitz 1990, 1991).

In the first half of the nineteenth century the dominant source of migrants was the British Isles. These were joined from the 1840s by a stream of emigrants from Germany, followed, after 1870, by a rising tide from Scandinavia and elsewhere in northwestern Europe. Emigration surged from southern and eastern Europe from the 1880s. It came first from Italy and parts of the Austro-Hungarian empire, and then from Poland, Russia, Spain, and Portugal. As figure 2.1 shows, these migrants from southern and eastern Europe, the so-called "new immigrants," account for most of the surge in numbers from the 1880s. About 60 percent of all European emigrants went to the United States. However, from the 1870s significant flows developed—largely from Italy, Spain, and Portugal—to South America, principally Brazil and Argentina, that is, from Romance language origins to Romance language destinations.[5]

The characteristics of the emigrants also changed. It was no longer a "family" migration. The mass migrants were typically young and single, and about two-thirds of them were male. More than three-quarters of the immigrants entering the United States between 1868 and 1913 were aged sixteen to forty at a time when 42 percent of the U.S. population was in this age group. Among men emigrating from England and Wales, only one in nine traveled with other family members, compared with more than half in the 1830s (Erickson 1994, 143).[6] The migrants from any one country were increasingly urban but remained largely unskilled. Nevertheless, European migrants as a whole remained largely rural in origin as the sources shifted toward the less developed southern and eastern Europe.

These outflows generated flows of return migrants, small at first (perhaps 10 percent of the outflow), but rising by the turn of the century to about 30 percent of the outflow. The extent of the return migration varied sharply by country of origin, motive for migrating, whether it was family based, and economic conditions in the destination and origin. The return migration rates were very high for some groups, for example, Italian and Greek immigrants, and very low for other groups, such as eastern European and Russian Jews, who viewed themselves as refugees and, more than other groups, migrated in a family context. In the absence of a social safety net in the destinations, the return flows were greater when the destinations were experiencing a recession. The return migrants, those returning often after only a few years, were a sign of the growing globalization of labor, in part due to

5. The surge of immigrants to Brazil from the 1880s owes much to the combination of the abolition of slavery and the introduction of free passages (Leff 1982, 60). As was often the case elsewhere, subsidies to immigration were financed by export taxes, in the Brazilian case export taxes on coffee. This intensified the linkage between immigration and international trade.

6. The change in the demographic characteristics of the migrants may well have reflected the change in where they were to settle in the destination. With urbanization and the rise of industrial job opportunities, urban areas replaced farming areas as the primary destination. Although accompanying wives and children may have been an asset for an immigrant intending to become a farmer, they may have been perceived as a liability among those anticipating urban industrial work.

the steamship's lowering the cost—measured in money, time, and danger—of oceanic travel. The return migrants often brought back to their home countries skills, information, and capital acquired in the New World.

Although the discussion of the nineteenth century and pre–World War I intercontinental migration has focused on the emigration of Europeans to the New World, large-scale migrations were taking place in other parts of the world. There were substantial movements within Europe itself, including the Irish moving to Great Britain and eastern Europeans moving to western Europe, sometimes merely sojourning before embarking for the New World and sometimes remaining permanently. There was migration to southern Africa from Europe (first by the Dutch, then by the British), South Asia, and East Africa. Asians, particularly from India, China, and Japan, were also on the move, most often as contract laborers, to East Africa, Southeast Asia, the Pacific Islands, the Caribbean region, and the West Coast of North America.

2.2.4   Asian Emigration, Nineteenth and Early Twentieth Centuries

The increased globalization of the political system through the spread of European colonization in the nineteenth century to Asia, Africa, and the Pacific and Indian Ocean islands resulted in increased intercontinental trade, with sugar, rubber, jute, tin, and other primary products being produced in the colonies, much of it for export to Europe and North America. The establishment of colonial plantation agriculture and mining, and the development of transportation and communication, increased the demand for low-cost pliant labor. In the absence of slavery, colonial governments and business enterprises sought fresh sources and instruments to attract the labor for these activities. The new source became Asia, and in particular India, China, and Japan. The new instrument was a return to an earlier means of financing migration—indentured servitude or contract labor.

Asia offered a large supply of low-cost unskilled labor, but even with the cost of international migration lower in the nineteenth century than in earlier centuries, Asian laborers were too poor to finance the move. Indentured servitude or contract labor was introduced both to finance the migration and to provide the information networks to match workers to jobs. The contracts (for Indian workers) were typically of five years' duration. At the expiration of the contract some of the workers had accumulated the resources to return home. The poverty that drove them to become indentured servants remained, however, and for India, so too did the repressive caste system. Most indentured servants (perhaps three-quarters in many times and places) remained where they were, acquiring some land, working part time in the plantations for wages, or migrating to urban areas. As a result, Asian communities began developing in East Africa and southern Africa, North America, Latin America, and Oceania, and nonindigenous Asian communities developed in Southeast Asia.

One of the largest of these intercontinental indentured servant migrations was from India. Thiara (1995) reports that in the eighty years of the formal indentured servant system (1830 to 1916) over one million Indians were transported overseas to further the British goal of empire building and, indirectly, the globalization of the economy. Over one-half million Indian indentured servants went to Mauritius, and another half million went to the Caribbean (primarily the south Caribbean, Trinidad, British Guiana, and Surinam), with smaller numbers going to Fiji in the Pacific Ocean, Natal in southern Africa, and East Africa (Thiara 1995; Vertovec 1995). Another group of Indian international migrants were the Sikhs who were recruited into the British India Army after the 1857 Punjab Mutiny (Tatla 1995). Sikhs were considered by the British to be a "martial race," and many served in the British Army in Sikh units and were posted in various parts of the Empire, often remaining when their tour of duty ended. Others served in British police and military units in various parts of the British Empire.

China was another major source of Asian labor, with indentured servitude contracts being most prevalent from the 1840s to the 1920s. In addition to the poverty and demographic pressures prevalent in India, China experienced far more political turmoil. The indentured servant system was less formalized in China than in India, and in addition to the indentured servant contract for a fixed period, a "credit-ticket system" was used in which the loan of the ticket money was to be repaid. Although the Chinese government's official position was to oppose emigration, its political weakness prevented it from enforcing its will (Hui 1995). The Chinese indentured servants were to be found in many sectors, including Malay tin mines, Cuban sugar plantations, and railroad construction in the United States. When the contracts ended, some returned to China, while others remained, forming the nucleus of the emerging Chinese communities (Chinatowns) in Southeast Asia, the Caribbean, and North and South America.

Japan, too, was a source of emigrant labor, with somewhat fewer than one million emigrants from the mid-nineteenth century to the early 1930s (Shimpo 1995). Labor-recruiting agents and the labor contract system were used. The Japanese workers went to Hawaii and the mainland United States, as well as to South America, primarily Peru and Brazil, as indentured servants or as recruited free immigrants.

Competition between Asian laborers and white workers, particularly in California, led to the first restrictions on immigration to the United States based on country of origin. The Chinese Exclusion Act of 1882, and its subsequent amendments, barred Chinese laborers from entering the United States. With the annexation of Hawaii by the United States in 1898 and with the 1908 "gentleman's agreement" between the governments of Japan and the United States, the emigration of Japanese workers to the United States ended. Legislation in 1917 created the "Asiatic Barred Zone," which effectively prohibited the migration to the United States of persons from Asia (including the non-Asian-born descendants of Asians), with the exception of the Asian Middle East.

In other regions the demand for indentured servants declined as changes in technology reduced the demand for unskilled labor in plantation agriculture and as small-scale farms owned by freed indentured workers and their descendants produced the crops. The disruption of the world economy in the two world wars and the Great Depression further disrupted international migration from less developed to other less developed regions. Post–World War II movements for independence among the colonies in Asia, Africa, and Oceania reduced the political acceptability of low-skilled foreign workers with ethnicities different from those of the indigenous populations.

The colonial-inspired Asian migration to various corners of the globe had long-term economic and political consequences. The presence of Asians provided a substitute for, or competitors for, indigenous labor. Tensions between the Asian indentured servants and their descendants on the one hand, and the indigenous populations on the other hand, persisted throughout the migration period but were held in check by the colonial powers. With the transition to independence after WWII came violent conflicts among ethnic groups. Conflicts between Indian-origin and African peoples in East Africa, between the Indian-origin and native Fijians, and between the Chinese and native Malays and Indonesians, among other conflicts, have harmed their economic development and ended this form of mass migration. Thus, a consequence of the post-WWII independence movements that resulted in the demise of European overseas empires, in particular the British Empire, was the decline in international migration and the globalization of labor markets within the third world.

2.2.5 War, Depression, and Restriction, 1914–45

Mass migration fell sharply as war and depression halted the globalization trend and immigration policies entered a new age of restriction. In the United States, the quotas enacted in 1921 and 1924 favored the countries of northwestern Europe and bit deepest into emigration from southern and eastern Europe (fig. 2.1).[7] Although the quotas were binding in the 1920s on new immigrant nationalities, a number of old immigrant nationalities fell below the quotas. In the Depression of the 1930s, with few exceptions, even new immigrant nationalities fell below quota (Gemery 1994, 180).[8] Emigration restrictions, introduced by some countries, such as the Soviet Union, also limited opportunities for international migration.

---

7. Although immigrants from the new source countries were four-fifths of U.S. immigrants in 1910–14, they were allocated only one-fifth of the quota enacted in 1924 (and implemented in 1929) (Kirk 1946, 84).

8. This was not always due to a lack of interest in migrating to the United States. Administrative rules were used by the U.S. authorities in the 1930s to restrict the immigration of German Jews.

Immigration to other destination countries fell less sharply as compared with the pre–World War I period. The share of the United States in intercontinental emigration from Europe was 51 percent in 1921–25, and 32 percent (of a much smaller total) in 1931–35, in part because of the U.S. limits on immigration. Some southern European migrants were diverted to Brazil and Argentina, the latter receiving 3 million in the 1920s, although as many as 2 million returned. But emigration from everywhere in Europe fell in the 1920s, with the exception of Poland and other eastern European countries. And apart from Jewish emigration from Germany, the economic maelstrom of the 1930s completed the process of deglobalization of the international labor market. Indeed, in some years during the Depression of the 1930s the return migration to Europe exceeded immigration, resulting in a negative net migration rate to the United States.

2.2.6 Constrained Mass Migration, 1946–2000

The post-WWII period has seen a dramatic decline in the costs of travel as a result of the shift from sea to air travel. It also has seen a decline in the cost of information and communication that has also lowered the cost of international migration. After the population dislocations following the Second World War, intercontinental migration resumed, initially on a pattern similar to before the First World War. The breaking of family ties that often characterized pre-WWI immigration has become less relevant in the post-WWII period. Yet the flow of migrants has been partially controlled by immigration policies introduced in the major receiving countries earlier in the century. Immigration policies changed sharply in the 1960s in the United States, Canada, and Oceania, with a shift away from quotas that favored immigrants from northwest Europe.

As figure 2.2 shows, total immigration to North America and Oceania rose gradually to one million per annum in the 1990s. Although the absolute numbers are similar to those in the age of mass migration about a century earlier, relative to destination country populations they are much smaller. Thus the annual immigration rate to the United States fell from 11.6 immigrants per thousand population in the first decade of the twentieth century to 0.4 immigrants per thousand population in the 1940s, rising again to 4.0 immigrants per thousand population in the 1990s. The proportion of foreign-born in the population was 15 percent in 1910, falling to a low of 4.7 percent in 1970, then, with the growing postwar immigration, increasing to 8 percent in 1990 and 10 percent in 2000.[9] Although the immigration rate is lower than at its peak in the first decade of the twentieth century, its contribution to population and labor force growth is similar because the rate of natural increase has also declined.

---

9. The proportion of the foreign-born in the population is influenced not only by immigration inflows but also by "exits," whether through remigration or through death.

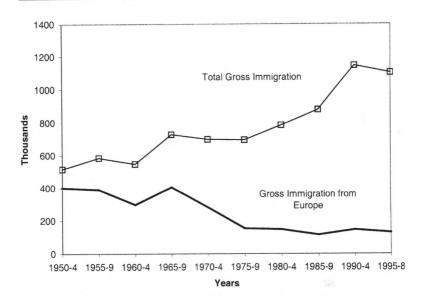

Fig. 2.2   Gross immigration to the United States, Canada, Australia, and New Zealand: 1950–54 to 1995–98 (annual averages)

There were three key structural changes in the pattern of intercontinental migration. The first was the decline in Europe as a source of emigrants and the rise of Asia as a source of emigrants. As figure 2.2 shows, European emigration to North America and Oceania declined from the 400,000 in the early 1950s to less than 100,000 per annum in the early 1990s. In part this reflects a resurgence of migration within Europe. Thus, for example, the share of emigrants from Portugal moving within Europe rose from 1.5 percent in 1950–54 to 57.1 percent in 1970–74 (United Nations [UN] 1979). Migration within Europe (including Turkey) grew rapidly in the early postwar years through "guest-worker" systems, particularly in Germany, where, by 1973 one in nine workers was foreign born. For Western Europe as a whole, foreign nationals increased from 1.3 percent of the population in 1950 to 4.5 percent in 1990. Including the foreign-born who had become naturalized would double this figure (Stalker 1994, 189–90).

In more recent decades Western and southern Europe has become a destination for immigrants from Asia, the Middle East, and Africa, and since the demise of the Soviet Union in the 1990s Western Europe has experienced migration from Eastern Europe and the former Soviet Union. As a result, net immigration to the European Union (EU) rose from 200,000 per annum in the 1980s to over a million in 1989–93, falling again to 640,000 per annum in 1994–98. Thus, in terms of inflows, the EU has now surpassed the United States, and by more if illegal immigration is included.

Table 2.2   Region of Origin of Immigrants, by Decade of Immigration, 1921–98 (%)

Decade of Immigration	Europe or Canada[a]	Mexico	Other Latin America	Asia	Africa	Total	Number (thousands)
1991–98[b]	17.6	25.5	22.3	31.0	3.7	100.0	7,582
1981–90[c]	13.1	22.6	24.6	37.3	2.4	100.0	7,338
1971–80	22.5	14.3	26.1	35.3	1.8	100.0	4,493
1961–70	47.0	13.7	25.6	12.9	0.9	100.0	3,322
1951–60	68.7	11.9	12.7	6.1	0.6	100.0	2,515
1941–50	78.0	5.9	11.8	3.6	0.7	100.0	1,035
1931–40	86.8	4.2	5.5	3.1	0.3	100.0	528
1921–30	82.7	11.2	3.2	2.7	0.2	100.0	4,107

Source: Statistical Yearbook of the Immigration and Naturalization Service, 1998, tables 2 and 4.
Note: Detail may not add to total due to rounding.
[a]Includes Australia, New Zealand, and Oceania.
[b]Eight years. Includes over 1.3 million former illegal aliens receiving permanent resident alien status in 1991 and over 200,000 in 1992–97 under the Immigration Reform and Control Act of 1986.
[c]Includes nearly 1.4 million former illegal aliens receiving permanent resident alien status in 1989 and 1990 under the Immigration Reform and Control Act of 1986.

The second key structural change was the transformation of Latin America from a destination to a source region, the mirror image of Europe's (and Japan's) transformation from a source to a destination. Between 1960 and 1980 the stock of immigrants in Latin America and the Caribbean who were born outside the region fell from 3.7 million to 3.0 million, while Latin Americans and Caribbeans residing outside the region increased from 1.9 million to 4.8 million. The changing sources of immigrants to the United States are particularly instructive (table 2.2). Whereas more than four out of five immigrants even as late as the early post-WWII years came from Europe and Canada, in recent years less than one in five come from there. About half now come from Latin America, nearly equally split between Mexico and the rest of Latin America and the Caribbean.

The third key structural change for the countries of overseas settlement during the postwar period was the increase in immigration from Asia, from negligible numbers to a large flow, and the beginnings of immigration from Africa (table 2.2). The Asian migrants come from India, Pakistan, China, Korea, the Philippines, and Vietnam, among other places. The pattern of Asian immigration was also observed in Europe, with the addition of African and Middle Eastern immigrants. Among five main European destination countries, immigration from developing countries rose from 97,000 in 1975–79 to 225,000 in 1990–93.[10] For Germany alone, between 1975–79 and 1990–93 immigration from northern Africa and western Asia rose from

10. United Nations 1998, 32–33. The five countries are Belgium, Germany, the Netherlands, Sweden, and the United Kingdom.

20,000 to 67,000 per annum, while that from sub-Saharan Africa rose from a mere 1,200 to 22,000 per annum.

2.2.7 Contract Workers in the Persian Gulf, Post-1970

In the post-WWII period a major current of international migration emerged around the Persian Gulf. The development of oil production and exports in the countries bordering the Persian Gulf, particularly the thinly populated Arab countries such as Saudi Arabia, Kuwait, Bahrain, and the United Arab Emirates, led to a large increase in the demand for foreign workers in the construction, trade, and low-skilled service industries, as well as for more highly educated foreign workers, such as teachers, engineers, and doctors. Initially this demand for imported labor was satisfied by temporary contract workers from nearby parts of the Arab world—Egyptians, Palestinians, and Yemenis, among others.

After the formation of the Organization of Petroleum Exporting Countries (OPEC), the redistribution of price-setting powers for crude oil from the Western-owned oil companies to the exporting countries, the continuing increase in world demand for oil, and the 1973–74 oil embargo, crude oil prices reached unprecedented heights. The revenues from exported oil from the Arab states that were members of OPEC increased from less than $200 billion in 1971–75 to over $600 billion in 1976–80 (Abella 1995, 418).

The result was an extraordinary increase in the demand for foreign workers. Although workers from other Arab states continued to move to the Persian Gulf as contract workers, they were soon far outnumbered by millions of temporary workers from nearly all parts of Asia—south, southeast, and east Asia—with the sources moving eastward over time.[11] The annual flow of Asian workers to the Middle East increased from less than 100,000 in 1975 to nearly one million in 1991. The share from Pakistan and India decreased from 97 percent in 1974 to 36 percent in 1991, and the share from Southeast and east Asia and from Bangladesh and Sri Lanka increased to 42 percent and 22 percent, respectively, in 1991. By 1990 the stock of Asian workers had grown to about 400,000 in Kuwait, to nearly one-half million in the United Arab Emirates, to over 1.5 million in Saudi Arabia, and to over 3.5 million in the entire Gulf region (Abella 1995).

The Asian workers came under short-term contracts (generally only one to two years). Private agencies were established in the sending countries, but some governments (e.g., South Korea and the Philippines) were actively promoting contracts for their construction companies and workers. The sources also shifted. Contract workers from South Korea reached a peak in 1982 of nearly 200,000 and then declined sharply, whereas those from the Indian subcontinent and Indonesia followed a rising trend (UN 2000, 62, 110).

---

11. For studies of the impact of this labor migration on the sending countries in Asia, see Amjad (1989).

The initial shift from Arab to Asian labor arose in part because of their lower labor costs, but also because the receiving countries wanted foreign workers that would not settle permanently and who would be less of a demographic, cultural, and political threat to the indigenous population than other Arabs, who were more difficult to segregate while in the country and to repatriate. The "eastward" movement in Asia of the sources of migrant workers was an attempt to diversify their origins to prevent any one group from dominating. For the sending countries, of course, the arrangement provided benefits in the form of higher-wage jobs for many of their nationals, contracts for their construction firms, and substantial foreign exchange in the form of remittances and repatriated wages and profits (Amjad 1989).

As a result of the Iraqi invasion of Kuwait in 1990 and the resulting Persian Gulf War (1991), many Arab workers (particularly Palestinians and Yemenis whose leaders sided with Iraq) left or were expelled from the Arab Persian Gulf states. Primarily for political reasons, the reliance on Asian as distinct from Arab workers has since increased even further.

2.3   What Drives Mass Migrations?

2.3.1   Explaining Migration Streams

Mass migrations are driven by economic incentives, and numerous studies testify to that fact. The era of mass migration before the First World War, when international migration was relatively unfettered by restrictions, is a good time to examine the forces that determined patterns of migration. The bias toward certain emigrant characteristics reflects the economic calculus underlying their migration (Chiswick 2000). Although the young and single might be more adventurous and enterprising, and had fewer ties (investments) specific to their origin and hence a lower cost of migration, they also had the most to gain from the move. By emigrating as young adults, they were able to reap the gains over most of their working lives while minimizing the costs of earnings forgone during passage, job search, and adjustment in the destination. By moving as single adults they were also able to minimize the direct costs of the move. Unskilled emigrants also had little technology- or country-specific human capital invested and hence stood to lose few of the economic returns from such acquired skills. The transoceanic migrations from Europe also sought to minimize the loss of language capital, with migrants to South America more likely to come from Romance language countries, whereas those from the British Isles favored North America.

What accounts for fluctuations in migration streams? Since the pioneering study of Jerome (1926), there have been many studies aimed at identifying the economic forces determining the uneven flow of migrants from Old World origins to New World destinations. The older literature was preoccupied with measuring the influence of "push" forces in the origin countries versus "pull" forces in the destination, and with the relative significance of variables representing job opportunities (as measured by indexes of production or employment) versus real wage rates.[12] More recent studies have used an economic decision-making framework in which potential emigrants compare expected future streams of income at home and abroad. Following Todaro (1969), expected income depends on the wage rate and the probability that the migrant will find a job. Because migrants are risk averse and because greater uncertainty attaches to the probability of employment (especially in the destination) than to the wage rate, and because of greater cyclical fluctuation in employment among new immigrants than among natives, employment outcomes take a greater weight in the timing of migration decision.[13]

Strong empirical support for this approach has been obtained for annual time series emigration rates for a number of European countries in the late nineteenth century (Hatton and Williamson 1998, ch. 4). The results indicate that wage rates *and* employment rates, both at home *and* in the destination, all help explain the year-to-year variations in emigration rates. Employment rates had a powerful effect, particularly those in the destination. The fact that short-run emigration rates are so volatile, and correspond so closely to booms and slumps, may seem surprising at first sight. Given that migration decisions are based on comparing future expected lifetime earnings, one might expect that short-run changes, quickly reversed, would have little effect on this long-run comparison. The volatility can be explained by the option value of waiting. Although the net present value of migration today may be positive, it might be higher next year if conditions in the destination are expected to improve.[14] Moreover, when migrants are constrained by limited wealth, the resources to finance the migration and adjustment may be very sensitive to short-run factors. Hence, even where the *decision* to become a migrant is based on long-run country differences in employment and wages, the *timing* of the actual move is closely correlated with cyclical fluctuations in source and destination countries.

Whereas unemployment rates were a powerful short-run determinant of emigration, the long-run trends are determined more by changes in the

12. The literature up to the 1970s was critically reviewed by Gould (1979), who pointed to the lack of consistency in the results of different studies.

13. This model is derived in Hatton (1995). A case can also be made for stronger real wage effects in the destination than the origin. A dollar increase in the wage in the destination has income and substitution effects that encourage migration, whereas a dollar decrease in the wage in the origin has a substitution effect that favors migration but an income effect that discourages it.

14. The option value of waiting is also incorporated in the equation dynamics (Hatton 1995). Simulations that abstract from cyclical effects and equation dynamics reduce the coefficient of variation of predicted emigration rates for Sweden, Norway, and Denmark by between one-half and two-thirds (Hatton and Williamson 1998, 73).

wage ratio. For emigration from the United Kingdom, a permanent increase of 10 percent in the ratio of foreign to home real wages would increase the gross emigration rate by 1.9 per thousand in the long run and the net emigration rate by 1.4 per thousand. The overseas real wage was 69 percent higher than the home wage on average over the period, and the present value of the wage gains far exceeded the costs of passage.[15] In part this reflects the costs of location-specific human capital including job-related skills and labor market information. It also reflects the compensating differential needed to offset the psychic cost of separation from family, friends, and community.

Consistent with this, the other most important variable explaining emigration rates is the stock of previous emigrants living in the destination. The migrant stock captures the chain migration effect where friends and relatives who have previously migrated generate new migration by lowering the costs and uncertainty of migration.[16] This proves to be a very powerful effect, and it explains much of the long-run persistence in emigration streams. In Italy, for example, cumulative previous emigration helps to explain why emigrants from the north continued to migrate to South America despite a substantial wage differential favoring North America. Thus the shift in the composition of Italian migration to North America occurred only gradually between the 1870s and 1913 (Hatton and Williamson 1998, ch. 6).

2.3.2 Long-Run Trends in Migration, 1850–1913

What explains why some countries produced few emigrants and some produced many? And why did emigration rise for some countries and decline for others? Table 2.3 illustrates the wide range of experience for European countries for decade average gross emigration rates in the age of mass migration. The highest rates were for Ireland, averaging twelve per thousand between 1850 and 1913. Norway and Sweden had rates approaching five per thousand from 1870 to 1913, whereas those from Germany and Belgium were under two per thousand, and that for France was close to zero. These emigration rates also display different trends. Emigration from

---

15. This is a weighted average of real unskilled wage rates in the United States, Canada, and Australia relative to the real unskilled wage rate in the United Kingdom. The estimates imply that, holding other variables constant, a wage gap of 27 percent would just eliminate net emigration.

16. Consider a destination country D that has no immigrants from the origin country Y. The first immigrant from Y to D may be indifferent among a set of equally attractive destinations within country D. If one destination is chosen, say at random, that destination becomes more attractive than others in D for future arrivals from country Y. The original settler's presence provides lower-cost information and ethnic-specific goods and reduces information uncertainty. Future migrants from Y to D are no longer indifferent among the alternative destinations in D. The formation of immigrant enclaves is a nearly universal characteristic of mass immigration flows and is not necessarily a sign of "clannishness" but rather a response to economic incentives and opportunities (Chiswick and Miller 2001).

Table 2.3   **Gross Emigration Rates from European Countries, 1850–1913**
                     (emigrants per 1,000 population per annum, decade averages)

	1850–59	1860–69	1870–79	1880–89	1890–99	1900–13
Belgium	1.90	2.22	2.03	2.18	1.96	2.32
Denmark	—	—	1.97	3.74	2.60	2.80
France	—	0.12	0.16	0.29	0.18	0.15
Germany	1.80	1.61	1.35	2.91	1.18	0.43
Great Britain	4.83	2.47	3.87	5.71	3.92	7.08
Ireland	18.99	15.16	11.28	16.04	9.70	7.93
Italy	—	—	4.29	6.09	8.65	17.97
The Netherlands	0.50	1.67	2.66	4.06	4.62	5.36
Norway	—	—	4.33	10.16	4.56	7.15
Portugal	—	—	2.91	3.79	5.04	5.67
Spain	—	—	—	3.91	4.63	6.70
Sweden	0.51	2.52	2.96	8.25	5.32	2.93

Source: Hatton and Williamson (1998, 33).

Notes: These figures are for gross emigration, drawn largely from Ferenczi and Willcox (1929). Where possible, the figures include emigration to other countries within Europe. Unfortunately, data on return migration are limited. Dashes indicate data are not available.

Ireland declined from the 1860s, and from Germany and Norway it declined from the 1880s. Almost at the same time, emigration rates from Italy and Spain began a steep ascent, a trend halted only by the outbreak of war in Europe.

Various theories have been offered to explain this wide range of experience. Different studies have stressed the effects of demographic forces, relative income incentives, structural change, poverty, and backwardness in agriculture and the spread of information about emigration opportunities, among other things (Lowell 1987, ch. 2). Recently assembled data for internationally comparable real wage rates make it possible to include real wage ratios between source and destination countries to explain the emigration rates displayed in table 2.3. Real wage ratios alone, however, have only a weak inverse correlation (–0.20) with gross emigration rates. Other variables must be included that systematically shifted the emigration function. One of these is the growth in the population in the emigration age group, as measured by natural increase twenty years earlier. This captures the hypothesis first put forward by Easterlin (1961) that the demographic transition in Europe drove emigration. Another variable is the share of the labor force in agriculture, reflecting structural change—a variable that the literature suggests could have conflicting effects. One argument has it that growing population pressure on limited landholdings generated emigration. Alternatively, it has been argued that rural populations were less internationally mobile than urban populations, which have often already been uprooted from their rural origins. Finally, as noted earlier, the effects of friends and relatives' providing information, supplying prepaid tickets, reducing the costs of job search, and lowering the cost of ethnic goods are reflected in the emigrant stock (per thousand of the population of the source country).

These variables have been included in an econometric analysis of the emigration rates in table 2.3 (Hatton and Williamson 1998, ch. 3). The result implies that a 10 percent rise in the destination to source wage ratio generates a rise in the emigration rate of 1.3 per thousand population in the origin, when controlling for the lagged dependent variable, among other variables. In the long run the share of the labor force in agriculture has a weak negative effect, suggesting that, on balance, agricultural populations were less mobile internationally than urban populations. By contrast, the lagged natural increase in the population has a powerful effect, with emigration increasing by about half of all births in excess of the number needed for a stable population. It should be noted also that this was not the result of a labor force boom pushing down the wage rate, since this effect is already taken into account through the wage ratio. Rather, it was a direct demographic spillover into emigration, which prevents an even sharper fall in the origin wage rate. Finally, controlling for the lagged emigration rate, the migrant stock abroad gives an effect that implies that for each thousand previous migrants, a further twenty were pulled abroad each year.[17]

One important fact that theories of emigration must explain is this: During the onset of modern economic growth in Europe, national emigration rates often rose, gradually at first, reached a peak, and then declined. This "life cycle" of emigration has been identified for a number of European countries prior to World War I. The influences just examined can help explain this pattern. Figure 2.3 presents a stylized picture of the European emigration cycle based on (quadratic) trends in the explanatory variables and the (long-run) coefficients of the emigration equation.[18] Rising incomes that relaxed the "wealth constraint" provided resources to finance migration. Demographic growth, a declining share of the labor force in agriculture, and the consequent growth of the stock of previous emigrants together increased emigration by about four per thousand in the upswing of the emigration cycle. But the narrowing wage gap, as real wages in Europe converged on those of the New World, had a countervailing effect. Eventually the peak was passed as continuing real wage convergence overcame the weakening effects of industrialization, demographic boom, and the migrant stock.

These results are confined to western Europe, and they exclude eastern

17. This effect is much smaller than that typically obtained from estimation on annual time series. When one uses decade average data, a part of the friends and relatives effect will be picked up by the lagged dependant variable, because recent emigrants are likely to be the most important.

18. The trends in the explanatory variables were obtained by regressing each of them on a variable that gives a numerical value to the stage of the emigration cycle for each country (and its square). For further details, see Hatton and Williamson (1998, 47–49).

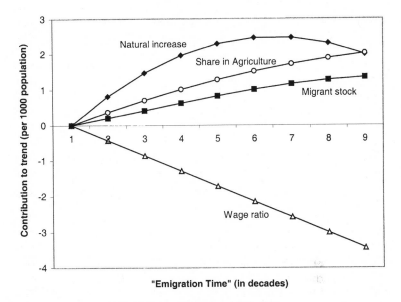

Fig. 2.3   The fundamentals driving emigration, 1850–1913

European latecomers to mass migration. In these least-developed countries and regions, despite the large incentive to emigrate, those who had the most to gain were simply too poor to finance the move. Thus, some growth in wages and income was a precondition for eastern Europe to enter into mass migration—an effect that has also been used to explain the late surge in emigration from Italy (Faini and Venturini 1994). On average, across western Europe, the poverty constraint was not important because there was no additional positive effect for the home real wage. Once a migration flow became established, the help of friends and relatives who had previously emigrated served to attenuate the poverty constraint. This would help explain why emigration could be so high from a country like Ireland and so low (at least until the end of the nineteenth century) from the south of Italy, an equally poor region. In the Irish case, the great famine of the 1840s effectively ejected a million Irish migrants, who formed a substantial migrant stock, particularly in the United States. With the poverty constraint substantially attenuated, emigration from Ireland was large in the 1850s and 1860s but decreased as real wages in Ireland rose relative to those abroad. By contrast, in Italy, emigration increased as growing incomes at home *and* the growing migrant stock together gradually eased the poverty constraint.

2.3.3   Trends in Migration Since 1950

It seems likely that the same factors that drove mass migration in the late nineteenth and early twentieth centuries can help explain the changing

Table 2.4   Growth of Emigration Age Group on Four Continents, 1955–95

	1955	1965	1975	1985	1995
Growth in previous five years of population aged 20–29 (%)					
Europe	3.1	–3.2	14.0	1.9	–3.7
Latin America plus Caribbean	11.1	12.3	19.9	15.5	8.5
Asia	10.6	4.8	21.4	13.1	9.0
Africa	11.6	10.4	14.4	17.0	14.3
Population aged 20–29/population aged 20–64 (%)					
Europe	28.5	25.6	27.1	26.8	24.1
Latin America plus Caribbean	35.0	34.9	37.2	37.8	35.6
Asia	34.4	32.8	35.3	35.5	34.7
Africa	37.0	36.1	37.4	38.7	38.6

Source: Calculated from United Nations (1999, various tables).

composition of contemporary international migration. The dramatic convergence of income and earnings in Europe, especially southern Europe, during the so-called golden age from 1950 to 1973 helps explain the sharp drop in the share of European migrants to the New World (figure 2.2, table 2.2). The rise in immigration from Asia coincides with the beginnings of the "Asian miracle" of economic growth and the fall after 1975–84 in Asian growth rates. As table 2.4 shows, the growth of the emigrating age cohorts in these regions also contributed to the swings in the composition of migration. In Europe and in Asia, the growth of population aged twenty to twenty-nine slowed after 1975 (UN 2000, 61). By contrast, in Africa the population in this age group continued to surge—a fact that clearly influenced inter-African migration (Hatton and Williamson 2001).

Of course, since the Second World War immigration has been heavily constrained by quotas and other regulations. Thus, migration pressures cannot be so clearly observed, and trends in the sources of immigration may largely reflect immigration policy. The end of country quotas for Europe based on national origin and the end of the virtual ban on Asian immigration in North America and Oceania in the 1960s broke the preexisting link between allocated quotas and nineteenth-century European immigration, and opened the door to immigration from Asia (see further below). Subsequent legislation further altered the country composition of the quotas and altered the rules governing employment-based immigration.

Where these constraints were absent, economic influences clearly shaped the pattern of immigration. Jasso, Rosenzweig, and Smith (2000) analyzed those obtaining immigrant visas as husbands of United States citizens by country of origin, because spouses of U.S. citizens are not subject to numerical restriction. They found that, for the years 1972 to 1990, per capita income in the origin country had a negative effect on the number admitted, whereas origin country education had a positive effect (219). For Australia, Cobb-Clark and Connolly (1997) examined an ex ante measure of immigration: the applications for skilled immigration visas.[19] They too found that real gross domestic product (GDP) ratios as well as relative unemployment rates between home and destination countries determined the flow of applicants.

Economic forces also explain ex post (policy constrained) outcomes. In their study of postwar immigration into Germany (1964–88), Karras and Chiswick (1999) demonstrate that immigration was determined by short-term cyclical phenomena, as measured by unemployment rates, and by long-term factors as measured by incomes per capita, in both Germany and the sending countries. The lagged net migration rate, representing chain migration effects, was also highly statistically significant and important. For the United States and Canada, Kamemera, Oguledo, and Davis (2000) find evidence that incomes, unemployment, population and a variety of other economic variables influenced rates of immigration across source countries and through time. Other evidence points to the immigrant stock as the most important single determinant of the country composition of U.S. immigration (Yang 1995, 119). This reflects the fact that, since 1965, kinship to a U.S. citizen or resident alien is the single most important channel of entry.

The famines and revolutions that caused spurts of migration in the nineteenth century also have postwar parallels. In Africa civil wars typically displaced sixty-four per thousand of the population per year across international borders, whereas government crises, coups d'etat, and guerilla warfare had somewhat smaller effects (Hatton and Williamson 2001, 11). Some political upheavals have generated large flows to the developed world. The fall of Saigon in April 1975 produced a large-scale exodus of refugees from Vietnam, Laos, and Cambodia to the United States, and twenty-years later the disintegration of Yugoslavia generated large flows to the EU. Yet the number seeking asylum in developed countries is also influenced by economic factors. Applications to Germany for asylum in 1984–95 from seventeen third world countries were influenced by relative incomes and by the existing migrant stock, as well as by terror and armed conflict (Rotte, Vogler, and Zimmermann 1997). Interestingly, they also responded to economic conditions and asylum policies in France, suggesting that even asylum seekers compared alternative destinations.

Given that the same variables influenced international migration flows before 1914 and after 1950, how different are the magnitudes of the effects? There are really two questions here. First, are the unconstrained effects the same now as then? Second, how much difference does policy make? Net emigration from African countries, largely across the porous borders within Africa, provides one benchmark (Hatton and Williamson 2001). Estimates on panel data from the 1970s to 1995 indicate that a 10 percent rise in the ratio of foreign to home wages increased net out-migration by 0.9 per thou-

---

19. Of course, applications will be influenced by the anticipated outcome and hence by immigration policy.

sand as compared with 1.3 per thousand in late nineteenth-century Europe. The demographic effects, although not directly comparable, are just as powerful as they were in late nineteenth-century Europe. Thus, one piece of evidence suggests that the relevant elasticities for unconstrained emigration have not changed much between the two eras.

The effects of immigration policy in attenuating economic effects can be illustrated by comparing estimates for emigrants from the United Kingdom since 1975, when they faced immigration controls, with those for 1870–1913 (Hatton 2001; Hatton and Williamson 1998, 65). The "friends and relatives" effect operates even more powerfully now than in the late nineteenth century because it has been reinforced by family reunification policies. Each thousand of the migrant stock generates between 50 and 100 percent more new migrants per year in the postwar period as compared with the period before 1914.[20] By contrast, the effect of source-country unemployment is between one-fifth and one-third as large, and relative income between one-tenth and one-fifth, in the recent period as they were before 1914. Thus the impact of immigration policy is to act as a filter that enhances immigrant stock effects and mutes wage and employment effects on international migration.

Such orders of magnitude are at best a very rough approximation of the effect of policy. Nevertheless, they suggest that liberalizing barriers to migration would dramatically alter the demographic landscape, partly because of the increase in responsiveness to incentives and partly because of the magnitude of those incentives. In the late nineteenth century, New World real wages were double those in western Europe; today real wages in the first world are five to ten times those in the third world. Conservative estimates of the effect of expanding the EU to include the ten central and Eastern European accession candidate countries (with income levels 40 percent of those in the EU) suggest a westward movement of 3 million people into the existing fifteen EU countries within fifteen years (Bauer and Zimmermann 1999). Liberalizing immigration from the third world is likely to produce much larger effects, both relatively and absolutely, effects that would cumulate as rising immigrant stocks in the destination and rising real wages at home relaxed the poverty constraint.

2.3.4   Illegal Immigration

As a result of immigration policy, the demand for visas by potential immigrants exceeds the supply made available by the immigrant-receiving countries. The result has been queues for visas of increasingly length in the immigrant-receiving countries, such as the United States, that ration, in part, by queuing, and a growing population of illegal aliens in the developed

---

20. Because of differences in model specification, the coefficients estimated for the two periods are not strictly comparable. In particular, the pre-1914 model includes lags whereas the post-1974 model does not. The range of magnitudes reflects the difference between using short-run and long-run coefficients from the pre-1914 estimates.

immigrant-receiving countries.[21] The illegal aliens include persons for whom the cost of obtaining a legal visa is very high, for whom it is not possible to obtain a visa, or who are jumping ahead in the queue. Whereas some of the host countries experiencing large illegal immigration are New World countries of overseas settlement, such as Australia, the United States and Canada, others are traditional countries of emigration that in recent decades have been experiencing pressures for in-migration, such as Western Europe and Japan (Organization for Economic Cooperation and Development [OECD] 2000; Weiner and Hanami 1998).

The illegal workers, for various reasons, tend to be very low-skilled (Chiswick 2001). This arises only in small part from the tilting of legal immigration opportunities in favor of highly skilled applicants. More important has been the increase in wealth and information that facilitate illegal migration even among low-skilled workers in the developing countries of Latin America, Asia, and Africa, and the greater difficulty high-skilled workers would have relative to those of low-skilled workers in masking their illegal status and in securing and maintaining employment comparable to their skill level. Low-skilled jobs are less likely to require licenses, certifications, and other documentation that might reveal one's legal status. The issue of the transferability of skills acquired in the origin is far more relevant for skilled workers than for those with few, if any, skills. Illegal aliens are less likely to bring dependent family members with them, because this would increase the probability that their illegal status would be detected. As a result, they are more likely to move back and forth between the origin and destination. For skilled workers there is a cost to this in the form of location-specific skills depreciating when they are in the other location, whereas for workers with perfectly internationally transferable skills or, more likely, without skills, this depreciation does not occur. If illegal alien workers are largely confined to low-skilled jobs in the destinations, the wage differential between the origin and destination is much larger for low-skilled than for high-skilled potential illegal migrants.

The policy response has been threefold (OECD 2000; Chiswick 2001). One has been to increase border enforcement. Although this has reduced what would otherwise be the flow of illegal alien workers, the borders have been porous. Even island nations, such as the United Kingdom and Japan, have discovered that liberal democracies cannot seal their borders. A second response has been to improve the effectiveness of interior enforcement, mainly by imposing penalties on the employers of illegal aliens. Although employer sanctions have been adopted in many countries, including the United States (in the 1986 Immigration Reform and Control Act), they have been at most weakly enforced, as have other instruments intended to en-

21. During the earlier era of mass migration, with few restrictions on entry prior to WWI, illegal immigration was not a significant issue. The first significant illegal aliens in the United States were of Chinese origin in the 1880s, because they were the first group to be excluded by law (1882).

force immigration law away from the borders. The third response has been to convert illegal workers into legal workers through amnesties. Many of the countries receiving illegal aliens have regularized their status, often in a series of amnesties.

The United States had the largest amnesty program. Under the provisions of the two amnesty programs in the 1986 Immigration Reform and Control Act, nearly three million individuals received legal status, primarily low-skilled workers from Latin America and their family members (Chiswick 1988). Although the combination of amnesty and employer sanctions was supposed to "wipe the slate clean" (amnesty) and "keep it clean" (sanctions), illegal immigration to the United States has continued unabated, and it is estimated that there are again about five to seven million illegal aliens, primarily low-skilled workers, living in the United States. In the late 1990s, the very tight labor market, the growing size of the illegal alien population, and the difficulty that private-sector labor unions have had in maintaining their membership base have resulted in a call from many quarters in both major political parties for another amnesty. The political pressure for another large amnesty diminished with the slow-down in the economy in 2001 and the terrorist attack by aliens in September of that year.

High-income liberal democracies are in a quandary. They offer wage opportunities that are high by the standards of the sending countries. The increase in wealth in the origin countries, the lower cost of transportation and communication—and hence the lower cost of information about alternative destinations and the ease of staying in contact with the origin—and the emergence of new immigrant enclaves have spurred incentives for low-skilled migration. Legal barriers are introduced in part to protect low-skilled native workers from this competition in the labor market, as well as in the markets for public income transfers and low-cost housing. Yet these legal barriers, including employer sanctions, are not fully effective. Liberal democracies will not adopt the draconian measures that would be needed to prevent illegal migration or discourage its permanence once it occurs. Because of the negative externalities and social problems associated with a population living and working at the margins of or outside the law, amnesties are introduced. However, rather than "wiping the slate clean," amnesties do not address the causes of the growth of the illegal alien population, but they do encourage others to become illegal migrants, because amnesties once instituted offer the prospect of future amnesties.

2.4 The Immigrant Impact

2.4.1 Real Wage Convergence in the Age of Mass Migration

One of the most important questions both in the pre-WWI era and in the post-WWII era is the effect of immigration on the earnings and incomes of nonmigrants, in both destination and source countries. International labor mobility, as well as the mobility of capital and tradable goods, should tend to bring about a convergence across countries in real wage rates for workers of a given level of skill in the absence of other factors that generate divergent wages. Purchasing power parity–adjusted unskilled real wage rates for Old World and New World countries show that real wage rates did indeed converge. Between 1870 and 1913 the coefficient of variation across seventeen countries fell from 0.50 to 0.43: Among the same seventeen countries it fell from 0.45 in 1950 to 0.33 in 1987.[22] The conjecture that mass migration played a part is strengthened by the fact that most of the convergence in the late nineteenth century is accounted for by the erosion of real wage gaps between the Old and New worlds, rather than among Old World countries or among New World countries. New World wage rates were higher than those in the Old World: by 136 percent in 1870, by 100 percent in 1895, and by 87 percent in 1910. In real wage terms the Old World caught up quite a bit with the New World.

Convergence was modest between Great Britain and the United States. Real wages in the United States were higher than those in Britain: by 67 percent in 1870, 50 percent in 1890, and 54 percent in 1913 (O'Rourke, Williamson, and Hatton 1994, 208). The contribution of international migration to Anglo-American real wage convergence has been analyzed using computable general equilibrium (CGE) models for the two economies calibrated for 1910. These models contain three output sectors, tradable manufacturing and agriculture and non-tradable services, and three inputs: labor and capital, which are mobile across sectors, and land, which is specific to agriculture. Under a counterfactual of no immigration to the United States and no emigration from Great Britain from 1870 to 1910, the real wage would have been 34 percent higher in the former and 13 percent lower in the latter. In the absence of the mass migrations the Anglo-American wage gap would have doubled between 1870 and 1913 rather than falling by one-fifth; instead of convergence there would have been divergence (Hatton and Williamson 1998, 213–6).[23]

The impacts were even greater elsewhere in the Atlantic economy.

---

22. The countries included are, in the Old World, Belgium, Denmark, France, Germany, Great Britain, Ireland, Italy, the Netherlands, Norway, Portugal, Spain, and Sweden; and in the New World, Argentina, Australia, Brazil, Canada, and the United States.

23. This counterfactual assumes that capital stocks in the two countries would have been those actually observed. As a result of the reallocation of labor, the return on capital would have been 24 percent lower in the United States and 13 percent higher in Britain in 1913 under the no-migration counterfactual. If, instead, the international capital market is assumed to be perfectly arbitraged, then less capital would have followed labor from the Old World to the New. As a result, under the counterfactual, wages in Britain would fall by only 6 percent and those in the United States would rise by only 9 percent. Under the no-migration assumption, the U.S.-U.K. real wage ratio would have increased from 1.67 in 1870 to 1.89 in 1913 with capital mobility, as compared with 2.47 in 1913 with no capital mobility. Hence, there would still have been divergence in Anglo-American real wages.

Among receiving countries, such as Argentina and Australia, the labor-force–augmenting effects of immigration were larger than in the United States. And in Europe labor force losses were proportionately largest for Ireland, Italy, and Sweden. In Ireland, postfamine emigration reduced the population by a third between 1851 and 1911; in the absence of emigration it would have risen by between 50 percent and 120 percent. Even on the lower counterfactual labor force increase, a CGE model for Ireland indicates that agricultural wages would have been lower by 16 percent and nonagricultural wages would have been lower by 19 percent. Two-thirds of Ireland's catch-up on real wages in Great Britain was due to mass emigration. In the absence of emigration, the shift out of agriculture would have been less rapid and the shift from tillage to pasture within agriculture less marked (Boyer, Hatton, and O'Rourke 1994, 235).

Between 1870 and 1914 the Scandinavian countries and even Italy underwent significant real wage catch-up on Great Britain and the United States. In Scandinavia real unskilled wages grew twice as fast as those in the New World and well above the European average. In Scandinavia, emigration accounted for only a part of this spectacular catch-up; one-fifth for Sweden and Denmark and nearly one-half for Norway. Other forces, such as industrialization, trade, education, and capital formation, accounted for the rest (O'Rourke and Williamson 1997). In Spain and Portugal, by contrast, the failure of industrialization led to real wage divergence despite the effects of emigration in the other direction. Yet for the Atlantic economy as a whole Taylor and Williamson (1997) find that, in the absence of mass migrations, the international dispersion of real wage rates would have dramatically increased. Instead of falling by 9 percent, the gap between New and Old World real wage rates would have increased by 167 percent.

Real unskilled wage rates were not the only factor prices that converged in the late nineteenth century, nor was migration the only source of convergence. As labor was transferred from the Old World to the New, land prices (and rents) boomed in the New World and stagnated in the Old. The integration of global commodity markets also contributed: A dramatic decline in ocean freight rates and overland rates led to a trade boom. The New World exported land- and resource-intensive goods and imported labor-intensive goods just as the Heckscher and Ohlin model of international trade would have predicted. For this reason, too, the wage rental ratio fell in the New World and rose in the Old World, with clearly identifiable consequences for trends in inequality. As we shall see, slow growth in real wages and rising inequality in the Americas and Oceania contributed to what Williamson (1998) has called the "globalization backlash" in the form of rising barriers to both trade and migration.

2.4.2 Labor Market Impacts in the Postwar Period

In the post–Second World War period, rising concern about immigration has been accompanied by a proliferation of studies aimed at measuring the labor market impact of immigration, particularly in the United States. The presumptions have been the same as those that have guided research for the epoch just discussed. That is, the increase in labor supply brought by immigration should reduce the earnings of factors that are close substitutes for immigrants, such as native-born labor, and it should raise the incomes of co-operating (complementary) factors, such as capital, land, and—if the immigrants are unskilled—skilled labor.[24] But the typical findings have been very different.

It is said that immigration policy is made at the national level, but the direct impacts are largely felt in a small number of local areas. Thus, a characteristic of immigrants in the major immigrant-receiving countries is a very high degree of immigrant and ethnic geographic concentration. For example, there was a very high degree of geographic concentration within the United States among the foreign-born at the turn of the twentieth century, just as there was a century later. In 1998, 9.9 percent of the population of the United States was foreign born. Of the foreign-born, 71 percent lived in only six states, with 30 percent in California (24 percent of the state's population), 14 percent in New York (20 percent), 9 percent in Florida (16 percent), 9 percent in Texas (12 percent), 4.5 percent in Illinois (9.9 percent), and 4.5 percent in New Jersey (15 percent). The geographic concentration of the foreign-born is even more intense when data are analyzed on a county basis (Chiswick and Sullivan 1995). In the United States in 1990, 8 percent of the population was foreign born. Among the 3,145 counties, in 1,521 counties (48.4 percent) the proportion foreign born was 1 percent or less; in 1,464 counties (46.6 percent) it was 1–8 percent; in another 109 counties (3.5 percent) it was 8–16 percent; and in only 47 counties (1.5 percent) it was 16–45 percent (Chiswick and Sullivan 1995). Dade County, Florida, had the record of 45 percent of its population foreign born.

Not surprisingly, numerous studies have attempted to isolate the effects of immigration on wage rates or wage changes by exploiting this cross section's variation. Of the many studies, most find almost no effect of the percentage of foreign-born on native-born wages (Greenwood and McDowell 1994; Borjas 1994). The largest effects found suggest that a 14 percent increase in the share of foreign-born reduced the wage of low-skilled native-born workers by less than 1 percent (Altonji and Card 1991). Even this seems surprisingly small. But the total effect of immigrants on the economy would be the same as the local impact only if local areas were (relatively) closed economies. The mobility of labor, goods, and capital across regions and localities within a destination country will produce a tendency toward price equalization that would preclude observing a relationship between immigration and wages and prices across local areas (Chiswick 1993).

There is abundant evidence that the settlement patterns of immigrants

---

24. For models of the impact of immigration on the destination labor market, see Chiswick, Chiswick, and Karras (1992) and Chiswick (1980, 1998).

depend on economic incentives. A number of studies have examined the intended destinations of immigrants arriving in the United States and Canada at the turn of the century (Dunlevy 1978; Green and Green 1993; Dunlevy and Saba 1992) and in more recent decades (Bartel 1989; Bartel and Koch 1991). They find that immigrants systematically migrated toward states with relatively high earnings. This responsiveness to economic incentives would tend to undermine any negative correlation between earnings and the concentration of immigrants. But immigrants were guided by other influences as well, settling first in ports of entry and in areas with a larger stock of previous immigrants from the same country of origin. As a result, the geographic distribution of immigrants then and now differs significantly from that of the native-born.

The skewed distribution of immigrant settlement influences internal migration among the native-born. An interesting "natural experiment" was the Mariel boatlift in 1980, which brought an influx of 45,000 Cubans into Miami, equivalent to 7 percent of the Miami labor force. Card (1990) found that this influx had almost no long-run effect on the size of the city's labor force or on the wages of competing groups of whites, blacks, and other Hispanics because of the mobility response of the native-born and previous immigrants. Filer (1992) examined native-born migration patterns across 272 localities in 1975–80. He found that, after controlling for local labor market characteristics, an influx of foreign-born workers crowded out native workers one for one.[25] There is also evidence along these lines for late nineteenth-century America. In the states comprising the northern quarter of the country (New England, the mid-Atlantic, and the east-north-central regions), changes in the number of immigrants across census years between 1880 and 1910 displaced the native-born either by generating westward outmigration or by averting internal in-migration.[26] Every additional 100 immigrants to the northeastern states displaced an estimated forty of the native-born population (Hatton and Williamson 1998, 168).

This discussion suggests that markets do respond to the impacts of immigrants and that the impacts are mitigated in the immigrant-receiving areas and are disseminated throughout the economy. Although immigrants may be geographically concentrated, their impacts are distributed throughout the economy, even to regions or sectors where there are no immigrants. It also suggests that an analysis of the impact of immigrants in an advanced industrial economy should focus on their effects on economywide factor proportions. In advanced industrial economies it also requires the explicit recognition of the heterogeneity of labor, in particular, the distinction between high-skilled and low-skilled labor.

25. Findings like these have been contested, most recently by Card and Di Nardo (2000).
26. The large internal migration of blacks from the rural south to the urban northern and western cities had to await both low urban unemployment in the destinations and low immigration from Europe.

The relative supplies of high-skilled and low-skilled native workers and immigrants differ over time, as does the definition of what constitutes a skilled worker. In an economy with two types of labor—say, high-skilled or professional workers and low-skilled nonprofessional workers—and a third factor, capital, the impact of immigration becomes more complex. If different types of labor are not strong substitutes for each other in production, the immigration of one type of labor can not only affect its wages, but also affect in an opposite direction the wages of complementary types of labor (Chiswick 1980, 1982; Chiswick, Chiswick, and Karras 1992). The immigration of low-skilled workers (e.g., Mexican laborers into the United States or Turkish laborers into Germany) would tend to depress the wages of all low-skilled workers in the destination but raise the wages of the complementary factors, including high-skilled workers and capital. This would increase wage differentials by skill and earnings inequality. On the other hand, the immigration of high-skilled workers (e.g., South Asian computer programmers into the OECD countries) would tend to lower the wages of high-skilled workers but raise the returns to low-skilled workers and the return to capital.

An interesting "natural experiment" with regard to the impact on relative wages of exogenous immigration that differed sharply by skill level in different periods in the context of a three-factor model is offered by Israel. There was a relatively large scale immigration of Jews from the 1930s through the 1960s into the Jewish economy of Mandatory Palestine/Israel that was primarily exogenous to the wages in the destination and was large relative to the destination economy.[27] These migrants were refugees and displaced persons, whose choice of destination was motivated by religious and ideological factors, as well as constraints on alternative destinations. Relative to the size of the preexisting Jewish economy in Mandatory Palestine, during the 1930s there was a large Jewish refugee flow with professional and other high levels of skill from Germany and central Europe into a capital-poor economy. The result was a decline in the relative wages of skilled workers, a decline in the rate of return from skill, and a very small earnings inequality. Following independence (May 1948), Israel experienced a relatively even larger influx of refugees as Holocaust survivors (whose skills and health had depreciated) and primarily very low skilled Jewish refugees from Arab countries in North Africa and the Middle East, from Morocco to Yemen. The large immigration of low-skilled workers depressed the relative wages of low-skilled workers, increased the rate of return from schooling, and increased earnings inequality (Chiswick 1974, 97–101). More recently, starting in 1989, there was a large exogenous influx of relatively high skilled Jewish refugees into Israel from the various parts of the former Soviet Union, referred to collectively as Russian Jews. This inflow increased the Israeli

27. For a more detailed analysis see Chiswick (1974, 97–101) and the references therein.

population by 7 percent in two years (1990 and 1991) and by 12 percent in the first half of the 1990s (Friedberg 2001). The previous upward trend in real wages halted in the early 1990s as the Israeli labor market absorbed the increased labor supply, but returned later in the decade. Although a large proportion of the Russian Jewish immigrants were in high-skilled jobs in the former Soviet Union, it took time for them to learn Hebrew and for some to transform their preimmigration skills into high levels of skill relevant for the Israeli labor market, and for others, particularly older immigrants, this transformation did not and may never take place. Thus, by the late 1990s, although some were able to join the high-skilled ranks in the labor force, others remained in lower skilled jobs. The Russian Jewish immigrants helped fuel the growth in Israel's high-technology sector ("Silicon Wadi") during the 1990s, but because of their wide distribution across skill levels relevant for the Israeli economy, they had mixed effects on the relative wages in skilled occupations.

Economists have been slow to recognize that effects such as these must be measured at the economywide level. One recent study based on economywide factor proportions estimates that about half of the increase in the wage gap between those with less than and those with more than twelve years of education in the United States from 1979 to 1995 was due to immigration (Borjas, Freeman, and Katz 1997, 53). Between the mid-1890s and World War I the wage gap between the skilled and the unskilled also grew, and this has been associated with the flood of "new" immigrants. But the evidence suggests that it owed more to unbalanced derived demand growth favoring skilled workers than to unskilled immigration (Williamson and Lindert 1980, 208–9, 236).

2.4.3   Adjusting to Migration

Economists have taken a long detour over assessing the effects of immigration on labor markets. Most of the work has focused on the United States, and there has been little consideration of the impacts on sending countries in the second era of globalization. Nevertheless, two things are clear. First, in both sending and in receiving countries there have been both gainers and losers from migration. Thus, migration's main direct effects have been on the relative scarcity of factors, on relative factor prices and on income distribution. Second, those effects have been different in the two eras of mass migration. Among immigrant-receiving developed economies the foreign-born are a smaller share of the population now than they were in 1913, so their effects should be smaller. Adjustments in other markets, however, could also have attenuated or enhanced the impacts differently across the two periods.

One development is the integration of capital markets examined in this volume by Obstfeld and Taylor (ch. 3). Before 1914 capital and labor flowed in the same direction in the Atlantic economy: from the Old World to the New. Immigrant-induced growth in New World labor supply drove up the return to capital and generated capital inflows, whereas the opposite occurred in the Old World. As a result the marginal product of labor fell less in the New World and rose less in the Old World than it would have in the absence of capital market integration. In the computable general equilibrium framework, with perfect capital mobility and no international migration since 1870, the U.S. real wage in 1910 would have been 9.2 percent higher than it actually was; capital would have retreated to Europe. As noted earlier, with no capital mobility the real wage would have been 34 percent higher in 1910, a big difference. For Great Britain, perfect capital mobility cuts the effect of emigration on the real wage by half, and for the Atlantic economy as a whole, by three-quarters (Taylor and Williamson 1997, 47).

In the late nineteenth century, the endogenous flows of international capital did not completely offset the effect of migration on wage rates. The main reason is because of the importance of land, fixed in supply and specific to one sector: agriculture. Thus, one reason immigration impacts are smaller now than a century ago is that agriculture and other land-intensive sectors are now a much smaller part of developed economies. In the United States the share of the labor force in agriculture and mining fell from 43 percent in 1890 to 3 percent in 1990, in Germany it fell from 44 percent to 4 percent, and in Great Britain it fell from 22 percent to 3 percent.

What about trade in goods and services? In the Hekscher-Ohlin model, trade between countries reflects their factor endowments and is therefore a potential substitute for migration. In a frictionless, perfectly competitive environment, migration-induced changes in relative labor intensities could alter trade patterns and, through Rybczynski effects, leave factor prices unaltered. If such effects mattered, we should see trade and migration moving in opposite directions: Migration should make endowments more similar across countries and thus reduce the basis for trade. But the crude correlation suggests it did not. Migration and trade both expanded after 1850, as they did again after 1950 (see Findlay and O'Rourke, ch. 1 in this volume). An analysis of the determinants of trade volumes in the Atlantic economy in the (relatively) free trade era before 1913 suggests that migration was not an important influence (Collins, O'Rourke, and Williamson 1999). It seems likely, however, that the effects on trade were overwhelmed by other forces that drove both trade *and* migration.

Alternatively, relative factor proportions could have determined the direction of technical change. If endogenous biases in technical change responded to cross-country differences in factor intensities, then these would push in the same direction as migration by augmenting the scarce factor. Rather inconclusive debates point to labor-saving innovation in mid-nineteenth-century America and to skill-saving technical changes in the late nineteenth century, with neutral or opposite effects in the Old World. By contrast, there is widespread agreement that skill-biased technical change has widened the wage distribution in Great Britain and the United

States since the 1960s. Here, the debates are about the ultimate causes, the permanence, and the magnitude of the effects of skill-biased technical change, rather than about its general direction.[28] Whether endogenous or not, relative biases in technology probably compounded the effects of migration on factor rewards in both eras.

What about endogenous changes in the composition of migration itself? In both mass migration eras there have been important streams of human capital incorporated in workers who were highly skilled by the standards of the day. In the eighteenth century the migration of European artisans was frequently subsidized to bring high levels of skill to North America. These artisans substituted for the importation of the products that they would have produced in Europe and exported. With the Industrial Revolution occurring in Europe in the nineteenth century, the new version of high-level manpower, skilled industrial workers, flowed from Europe to the countries of overseas settlement to advance the development of industry in North America and elsewhere. From 1820 to 1910 "entrepreneurs" were a higher proportion of the foreign-born than of the native-born, although that difference was declining (Ferrie and Mokyr 1994, 130).

With the development of science and technology in North America, home-grown human capital provided much of the highly skilled manpower. Skilled workers came as refugees, especially from Germany and other parts of Europe in the 1930s and 1940s, while others formed part of normal migrant flows, following the usual incentives. Recent evidence for the United Kingdom suggests that the increase since the 1970s in the returns to skill, as reflected in the widening income distribution, increased the skill content of immigration (Hatton 2001). But this was in the presence of skill-selective immigration policies. In the late nineteenth century and in the late twentieth century the incentive effects of returns to skill on the composition of migration have often been swamped as low-skill countries have entered into the upswing of their emigration cycles.

A more important influence on the skill composition of migration is the immigration policies of major receiving countries. Although the 1965 amendments to U.S. immigration law emphasized "kinship" to a U.S. citizen or resident alien for rationing admissions, they explicitly included a small skilled-professional-worker category. Canada, Australia, and New Zealand placed far greater emphasis on the applicants' skills in the rationing of immigration visas. In the late 1980s, but especially in the 1990s, changes in U.S. immigration policy widened the scope for the admission of

---

28. Consider the useful distinction between "worker (task-performing) efficiency" and "allocative (decision-making) efficiency." Technological change that is neutral with respect to high and low levels of worker efficiency will initially appear to be skill biased because workers with more human capital also have greater allocative efficiency and are better able to quickly and efficiently exploit the new technology. Whether the observed skill bias in the new computer-related technology is permanent or temporary will depend on whether it only appears to be so because of the temporary advantages of those with greater allocative efficiency.

skilled workers as permanent resident aliens (as in the Immigration Act of 1990) and by creating and expanding a series of "temporary worker" programs for high-level manpower. Temporary worker categories were created or expanded for registered nurses (H1-A and H1-C visas), trainees (work experience for highly skilled workers; H3 visas), workers with extraordinary ability (O visas), and athletes and entertainers (P visas); and under the umbrella of the North American Free Trade Agreement, an exchange program was established for high-skilled workers, primarily between the United States and Canada. The best known of these temporary worker programs is the H1-B visa, for workers with "specialty occupations" admitted on the basis of professional education, skills, or equivalent experience. The H1-B visas have been used primarily in the high-technology and higher education industries, upon employers' satisfying the U.S. Department of Labor that after making a good faith effort the employer has found no qualified worker with a legal right to work in the United States who is available for and willing to take the job at prevailing wages.[29] The United States is not unique in the inflow of high-skilled workers from other developed (OECD) countries and from the developing countries, particularly Asia. Many of the other developed OECD countries are also importing high-technology workers from each other and from the developing countries.[30] Whether they are admitted as temporary or permanent workers, the duration of their stay is likely to be determined by their own wishes, rather than the initial intent of their host countries. Among high-technology workers in particular, because of the rapid spread of information and the industry's use of English as the lingua franca, there appears to be emerging a single worldwide labor market in the developed countries, regardless of the worker's country of origin.

2.5   The Political Economy of Immigration Control

2.5.1   Rising Barriers

Early in the age of mass migration, controls on migration were either absent or largely ineffective. But as the numbers mounted toward the end of the nineteenth century, receiving countries became increasingly concerned

29. The entrants under the temporary visa program for workers and trainees (H's, O's, and P's), as well as the professional workers who enter under the North American Free Trade Agreement (NAFTA) increased from less than 75,000 in 1985 to over 430,000 in 1998, and the numbers have grown since then. Their accompanying spouses and children increased from over 12,600 in 1985 to nearly 105,000 in 1998. Thus, in 1998 these "temporary" migrants totaled over 535,000 individuals, rivaling the 660,477 persons admitted as "lawful permanent resident aliens" (legal immigrants) in the same year.

30. In the decade of the 1990s, following the collapse of the Soviet Union in 1989, approximately one million Soviet Jews and their family members emigrated to Israel, raising the population to six million. This was an unusually high-skilled mass migration, dominated by doctors, engineers, and computer specialists. In addition to depressing the relative wages of highly skilled workers, the influx spurred the development of "Silicon Wadi," the Israeli high-technology sector.

with controlling the flow. The door to immigrants was closed gradually in stages rather than being slammed shut, as is sometimes supposed. The shift away from pro-immigration policies began in New World countries with the regulation of shipping companies and emigration agents, the banning of contract labor, and the banning of those who were likely to become "public charges" or were considered undesirable because of their race or origin. The positive inducements to immigration offered by some countries also began to diminish. Argentina abandoned its subsidies in 1890, as did Chile in 1891. From the 1880s, Australia and New Zealand progressively reduced their levels of assistance, policies that were revived briefly with subsidies from the British government under the Empire Settlement Act of 1922.

In the United States, the Chinese were excluded by an act of 1882 and the Japanese by a "gentlemen's agreement" in 1908; all Asians (other than those from the Middle East) were excluded under the "Asiatic Barred Zone" in 1917. After several attempts at legislation, the United States introduced a literacy test, in any language, in 1917, although illiterate relatives (spouse and children) of a literate admitted immigrant were also given visas. This was followed by quotas based on national origins in 1921 and 1924, aimed against immigrants from southern and eastern Europe.[31] A literacy test was introduced in Natal in 1897 and was followed by similar tests introduced in Australia (the so-called "white Australia policy," 1901), New Zealand (1907), and Canada (1910).[32] Similar patterns of escalating restrictions were adopted in South Africa and Brazil, culminating in quota systems in 1930 and 1934, respectively. Even the British dominions adopted severe restrictions limiting immigration from Britain: Australia in 1930, New Zealand in 1931, and Canada in 1932.

Post-WWII immigration policies are even more heterogeneous, but for major receiving areas, they can be classified into four, often overlapping, regimes. The first of these is the guestworker systems of the early postwar years. The best known is that of Germany, where wartime forced labor was replaced first by inflows of ethnic Germans displaced from territories lost in the east and then, through a series of bilateral agreements, with guestworkers from southern Europe and Turkey.[33] Between 1960 and 1973, when recruitment was abruptly stopped, about a million a year were recruited. Less

31. The quotas established in 1921 restricted the annual number of immigrants to the number from each country recorded in the 1910 census. Those enacted in 1924 (effective in 1929) allowed 2 percent of the number of each nationality present in the 1890 census, which predates much of the surge of emigration from southern and eastern Europe.

32. The white Australia policy involved a dictation test (as in Natal) in which the prospective immigrant was required to write out a dictated passage in a European language chosen by the immigration officer. In practice this meant English, so that the white Australia policy was really a British Australia policy. On this and other regulations, see Daniels (1995).

33. Initially, seasonal workers were recruited from Italy; subsequently, agreements were signed with Greece (1960), Spain (1960), Turkey (1961), Portugal (1961), and Yugoslavia (1968). For a recent study of the guestworker experience, see Herbert and Hunn (2000, 189).

well known and on a smaller scale were guestworker programs in France, Belgium, and the Netherlands, all of which were abruptly halted as a result of the oil price increase and recession in 1974. In the New World, too, there was active recruitment of low-skilled temporary migrants. Under the Bracero Program in the United States (1942–64), initiated during the tight labor market during WWII, workers were recruited, chiefly from Mexico, and mainly to work in agriculture, under short-term contracts. And, as we have seen, new guestworker streams became established in the Persian Gulf.

Second, there was a dramatic shift in the major immigrant-receiving countries from systems based on national origins to worldwide quotas. In the United States, prior to 1965, 70 percent of the Eastern Hemisphere quota was allocated to the United Kingdom, Ireland, and Germany. The 1965 Amendments to the Immigration and Nationality Act broke the link between allocated quotas and past immigration, ended the virtual ban on immigration from Asia, and introduced a quota for the Western Hemisphere.[34] Similarly, preferences for British, Irish, and other northern European immigrants were abolished in Canada in 1962. In Australia the "white Australia policy" was abandoned, gradually in the 1960s, and then decisively in 1973, although in New Zealand it had to wait until 1987.

It is not likely to be mere coincidence that the three major English-speaking countries of overseas settlement abandoned their pro–northwest European immigration policies at about the same time. High rates of economic growth in these countries and the decline in emigration from Europe due to the tight labor markets in Western Europe were important factors. The growing civil rights movement in the United States was also in sharp contrast to the openly racist "national origins" quota system still in effect since the 1920s. However, another aspect of globalization may have been important. Much of Africa and Asia was gaining independence from the former colonial powers of Western Europe. Clearly racist immigration policies in the United States, Canada, and Australia did not sit well with the newly independent countries that were to become increasingly important trading partners and neutrals or participants in the Cold War with communism.[35]

---

34. The system introduced in 1965 allowed an annual limit of 20,000 for immigrants for each Eastern Hemisphere country, up to a total of 170,000, and a numerical limit of 120,000 visas per year for the Western Hemisphere. In 1976 the same overall country quota and system of preferences was extended to immigrants from the Western Hemisphere, and the two hemispheric ceilings were combined into a worldwide quota. Immediate relatives of the U.S. citizens (e.g., the spouse, minor children, and parents) were not subject to numerical limit and were not charged to the quotas. Legislation enacted in 1990 modified the latter system by limiting some of the kinship visas (in particular the sibling category) the larger the number of immediate relatives admitted.

35. In the United States, the 1965 amendments replaced the "national origins" quota system with a system largely based on kinship to a U.S. citizen or permanent resident alien. The intention was to replace an obviously racist system with one that would appear racially neutral but would largely replicate the countries of origin of the immigrants who came to the United

Third, humanitarian considerations were given an important role. The widening in the range of source-country refugee admissions was often followed by policies that strengthened rights of immigration through family reunification. These were underpinned by a growing body of international agreements through organizations, such as the UN and the International Labor Organization (ILO), aimed at protecting human rights.[36] Humanitarian agreements such as the 1951 Geneva Convention on Refugees, to which a growing number of countries subscribed, also opened the door from the 1980s to an increasing number of asylum seekers.[37] In most countries of Western Europe, North America, and Australia, where primary immigration was limited by quotas or caps on work permits, some categories of family reunification and refugee admissions were unlimited in principle, subject to the relevant conditions.

In addition, a number of countries gave amnesties to illegal immigrants, notably France (1981–82), Argentina (1984), Italy (1977–78), and the United States (1986; Stalker 1994, 152), with a further wave among EU countries in the 1990s. At the same time, however, they began to tighten up on the conditions for family reunification and on the generosity toward asylum seekers and illegal immigrants. In Europe, countries like France and Germany revised their domestic laws and ordinances, and the EU's summit meetings in Dublin (1990) and Tampere (1999) sought mechanisms to regulate the flow of asylum seekers. Several countries, including the United States (1986), introduced sanctions against employers who knowingly hired illegal aliens. The enforcement of these penalties on employers has, however, been very weak.

Finally, as we have seen, OECD countries have sought to allocate the diminishing share of visas going to primary immigrants increasingly on the basis of skills. A skills component was introduced into the Canadian points

---

States in the previous decades (Daniels and Graham 2001, 43–44 and 147–48). For a variety of reasons this was not to be the case, and Mexican and Asian immigrants, rather than European immigrants, have become the largest beneficiaries of the kinship visas (Chiswick and Sullivan 1995).

36. The UN *Declaration of Human Rights* (1948) and the *International Convention on the Elimination of All Forms of Racial Discrimination* (1965) were followed by other agreements encouraging the protection of refugees and affirming the primacy of the family. From the 1960s a series of ILO conventions provided for equal treatment of nonnationals. Although not all countries subscribed to these, a number of regional associations such as the EU, Mercosur (South America), NAFTA (North America), and the Economic Community of West African States (ECOWAS) enunciated rights for migrant workers. On these and other agreements, see UN (1998, 71–76).

37. For example, in the postwar period the United States provided for the admissions of refugees from Communist countries and certain parts of the Middle East, but not from elsewhere. Under the Refugee Act of 1980, however, the United States abandoned its largely "communist country only" policy and adopted the UN language of defining refugees as persons with a "well-founded fear of persecution" for political, religious, ethnic, or several other reasons, regardless of the communist orientation of the regime in the origin. The result was an increase in the range of source countries and refugee admissions.

system in 1967, which was later given more weight. Australia and New Zealand also shifted further toward selecting on the basis of education and experience and away from specific occupations (see Winklemann 2000). These systems award points for education, experience, language skills, and being in a prime age group, and they also include categories for business migrants bringing capital or intending to start a business. Almost alone among the developed countries, the United States sharply increased its employment-related immigrant visas in 1990, more than doubling what had been a small skill-based employment visa program. Although a Canadian-style point system was seriously considered by Congress in the late 1980s, rather than causing a move to a point system, the 1990 Immigration Act retained the U.S. employer-petition, job-specific (job-targeting) method of rationing skill-based visas. Cumbersome administrative procedures (which require that employers demonstrate to the U.S. Department of Labor that there is no qualified person with a legal right to work in the United States willing to take the job at prevailing wages) have limited the use of the employment-based visas, and the quotas have not been filled.

2.5.2 Explaining Policy Regimes

Dramatic shifts in policy and differences among countries have often been explained on a purely ad hoc basis, but a literature has developed that tries to systematically account for policy formation. Interest-group politics link immigration policy outcomes with the actual or perceived effects of immigration, past or prospective, on different interest groups or constituencies. If those who stand to gain are politically powerful, then immigration policy should be less restrictive than if the losers wield the most political muscle. It does not follow from this that economic determinism is the only thing that matters. Politics also matter, and in several different ways. First, shifts in the political balance, either through the adoption of democratic institutions or through the extension of the franchise, could tip the balance in favor of immigration control. This, together with the weakening of landed interests and the growing influence of labor, particularly unskilled labor since the mid-nineteenth century, should have shifted the political balance against immigration, as it did in the early twentieth century. Second, since economic interests may not be the only ones that drive immigration policy, attitudes to immigration and racial prejudice may matter independently. Third, ethnic politics may be important, where members of an ethnic group seek to encourage the immigration of those who will add to the group's size and power. Fourth, political elites may be captured by particular interest groups, or they may be sufficiently strong (or impervious) to pursue strategic aims independently of their political mandate. The bottom line is that the same economic changes may translate into different policy outcomes across countries and over time.

To explore the economic correlates further, Timmer and Williamson

(1998) constructed an index of immigration policy openness for six countries between 1870 and 1930. They explain declining openness by variables representing the gains (or losses) from immigration for different interest groups. For Argentina, Brazil, Canada, and the United States the ratio of unskilled wage rates to GDP per capita was associated with more open immigration policies. The resulting mass migration, by increasing the return on nonlabor assets, and shifting New World income distributions away from labor, contributed to the policy backlash that began in the late nineteenth century. The backlash also depended on the volume and composition of immigration itself. In Argentina and Australia, with relatively homogeneous immigration streams, it was the rising share of foreign-born that mattered; in Canada and the United States, where immigrant origins were more diverse, it was immigration from low-wage countries that differed in ethnicity and religion from earlier immigrants and the native population that helped close the door (Timmer and Williamson 1998, 752).

The effects identified by Timmer and Williamson (1998) also seem relevant to the partial reopening of the immigration door in the early postwar period—but in reverse. The rapid growth of real wages, narrowing income distributions, diminishing skill differentials, and falling foreign-born shares should all have eased the pressure for restriction. This was reflected in broadening access to previously excluded groups. European recruitment policies of the 1960s, the United States Immigration Amendments of 1965, and Australia's abandonment of its British-only policy were each preceded by a slowdown in the most desired source of immigrants. Thus, Germany turned to southern Europe after the Berlin Wall went up; the United States changed its policy as economic growth, demographic decline, and the barriers to emigration from the countries controlled by the Soviet Union stanched the flow of Europeans; and Australia dismantled its British-only policy as the numbers fell short of the 1 percent target.

Macroeconomic conditions also matter. If, at times of high unemployment, immigrants simply add to the unemployed pool or displace natives, then no one benefits and some lose. All groups then have an interest in tightening immigration policy. Shughart, Tollinson, and Kimenyi (1986) found that unemployment was a key determinant of policy restrictiveness in the United States since the turn of the century, as reflected in either deportations or required departures relative to the immigrant flow. Money (1999, ch. 2) found unemployment to be the key explanator of restrictiveness in OECD countries since the 1960s. Casual empiricism also supports these findings. Sharp increases in restrictiveness took place in Australia and Canada in the early 1930s, and the abrupt ending of guestworker policies in Europe in 1974 surely owes much to deteriorating economic conditions. In postwar Australia, the unemployment rate has been found to be the single most important determinant of the annually announced targets for immigrant intake (Wooden et al. 1994, 304).[38]

2.5.3 Political Interest Groups and Coalitions

Globalization forces can explain why the immigration door to the New World began to close in the late nineteenth century. That is, they help explain *changes* in immigration openness, but not necessarily the *level* of restriction prior to the 1930s. After all, these globalizing forces can be observed from the middle of the nineteenth century. In economies where labor was the source of income for the many, and capital and land were concentrated among the few, one might have expected the door to close earlier and more firmly. One reason is that the democratic franchise was often limited to male owners of property. Another is that agricultural or manufacturing interests often formed powerful political coalitions. A third reason is that opposition to immigration was balanced by wider national interests (Foremen-Peck 1992).

In countries like Argentina and Brazil, landowners and planters were the dominant forces behind immigration policy. In the case of Brazil, the plantation economy was supplied by slave labor until midcentury, but, under external pressure, slave imports ceased in 1852 and slavery was eventually abolished in 1888. With the prospect of rapidly increasing labor costs, the São Paulo coffee planters used their political influence over the government of São Paulo and over the central government to lobby successfully for the provision of free passage for immigrants from southern Europe.[39] As a result, profits of the *fazendeiro* were enhanced, although the gains to workers "appear to have been negative" (Leff 1982, 68). But with the growth of manufacturing and urban expansion from the turn of the century, the planters' power to promote mass migration waned and finally evaporated.

By contrast, Canada and Australia were characterized by more representative government, by ongoing imperial ties, and above all by developmental states. Both countries were thinly populated and both adopted nation-building policies that involved encouraging immigration but re-

38. As in other countries, such as Canada, changes in immigration targets have often been the subject of administrative control rather than requiring legislation as in the United States. However, even in the United States administrative rules barring persons who were likely to become a public charge were tightened in the 1930s (and more stringently invoked to reduce the immigration of German Jews), and the requirements for labor certification for the employment-based visas in the post-WWII period have a countercyclical effect.

39. Between 1885 and 1913 £11 million was spent in subsidies to secure this labor supply. Leff (1982, 61) argues that providing free passages was more profitable to planters than paying higher wages to attract more migrants. There are also reasons why planters would have preferred government subsidies to private subsidies, even though government revenues came mainly from the coffee sector. One is that the implied pooling overcomes the free-rider problem, that is, the problem of tying the migrant to the employer who financed the move. Another is that some proportion of the costs would be borne by other taxpayers.

stricting it to (relatively homogeneous) northern Europeans. In Canada the National Policy from 1872 aimed both to populate the prairies through immigration and to industrialize through tariff protection. In Australia, where agriculture was relatively more important, where landholding was more concentrated, and where (as in new South Wales) the squatters were a powerful interest group, policy was more pro-immigration. But the foundation of the Australian Federation in 1901 diluted these interests and led to the more restrictionist white Australia policy.

In Europe, policy toward *emigration* also varied, although attempts to restrict emigration in countries such as Belgium, Italy, and Switzerland were largely ineffective. Where landed interests were most powerful, such as in Russia, emigration was illegal and the law was more strongly enforced. In labor-abundant Great Britain, the declining influence of landed interests in the early nineteenth century and the development of the Empire ensured a strongly pro-emigration policy. And the rising influence of labor in the late nineteenth century saw the introduction of the first restrictions on immigration in 1905.

Although the pre-1930 policies of most countries would seem to fit into a loose political economy framework, some observers see the United States as an exception, at least before 1917. Limited imperial and nation-building imperatives (post–Civil War), a wide democratic franchise, a burgeoning industrial/urban sector, and widespread opposition to mounting immigrant flows would seem to predict rising barriers to immigration. The myth, if not the reality, of the westward movement of the frontier and of cheap land provided scope for more immigrants, at least until the close of the nineteenth century, as did the expanding industrial and mining sectors of the economy.[40] The rise of nativism in the pre–Civil War period resulted in individual disqualifiers, that is, immigration restrictions against "socially undesirable" individuals, including those who were criminals, immoral, or likely to become a public charge. In the postbellum period, nativist sentiment emerged again but was successful only in restricting the immigration of Chinese laborers and, later, other Asian workers. On the whole, however, the door remained open for Europeans until the 1920s.

In 1897, the U.S. Congress came within two votes of introducing the literacy test, but legislation was delayed for a further twenty years. Goldin (1994) set out to explain why. She found that in the House of Representatives votes in favor of the literacy test in 1915 were positively associated, across cities, with falling wage rates, with population density, and with the proportion of immigrants in the population. Thus, globalization forces

---

40. Foreman-Peck (1992) speculated that American exceptionalism could be explained by the fact that most immigrants were unskilled and that unskilled immigrant labor might be a complementary factor to native-born skilled labor. However, his production function estimates for U.S. manufacturing in the 1890s indicated that native- and foreign-born labor were not complements—so the anomaly remains.

were at work, but they were mediated by interest-group politics. With the high unemployment of the 1890s, the alignment of nativist and labor interests generated almost enough votes to get the literacy test passed into law. As prosperity returned, employers returned to a strong pro-immigration stance. But now the South became more anti-immigration, partly to protect its strength in Congress. Finally, the weakening of the urban pro-immigrant vote, driven by rising isolationism stimulated by World War I, ensured sufficient support to pass the literacy test into law in 1917. The literacy test, however, was literacy in any language. It was thought that this would advantage potential immigrants from the more literate countries of northwestern Europe and disadvantage immigrants from the less literate southern European and eastern European origins.

Thus, in what should, on the face of it, have been a strongly pro-labor country, immigration restriction had to wait for an alignment of different interest groups with sufficient political muscle. Restrictionist policy became firmly entrenched when, with the concern over the resurgence of immigration from Europe in the post-WWI period, the national origins quota system was introduced in 1921 and reinforced in 1924. Immigration from the more highly skilled countries of the "older" immigrant sources (northwestern Europe) were favored, whereas immigration from the less developed and less skilled "newer" immigrant sources (southern and eastern Europe) was sharply curtailed.

2.5.4   The Public Opinion Puzzle

With the flourishing of democracy in the postwar period, policy should better reflect the balance of individual preferences. But here lies a puzzle: In democratic countries, public opinion in recent decades has been far more anti-immigrant than has public policy. A UN survey of government attitudes toward immigration records that 8 percent of developed country governments in 1976 considered immigration levels to be too high. This rose rapidly in the 1980s to reach 29 percent in 1995 (UN 1998, 71). But this still stands in sharp contrast with public opinion polls, which regularly find that two-thirds of the population would prefer less immigration. Studies of individual countries report that governments have consistently ignored widespread clamor for less immigration. This leads to two questions: What drives public opinion, and why is it not reflected in policy?

Recently a literature has emerged that analyzes public opinion polls to gain greater understanding of the motives lying behind anti-immigration sentiment. Economic self-interest is the most obvious motive, and this can be related either to the individual's own circumstances or to the tax implications of immigrant's use of public services. Second, some analysts argue that marginal groups are likely to identify with immigrants. Third, there is "contact theory," which essentially suggests that greater familiarity with immigrants reduces racism (although it could go the other way). A fourth factor is ethnic-group politics. Members of individual ethnic or immigrant groups favoring the immigration of members of their own group formed political coalitions with other such groups to favor more general pro-immigration policies.

One study for the United States in the 1980s found limited support for economic self-interest as reflected in being unemployed, being poor, suffering declining finances, or working as a manual laborer. But low-wage ethnic groups such as blacks and Hispanics were found to be less anti-immigration, and those living in high-immigrant-density areas more pro-immigration—a finding that supports marginality and contact motives (Fetzer 2000, 95–107). Similar analyses for France indicated that cultural threats were uppermost, whereas for Germany economic threats—for example, being poor or a manual laborer—were stronger. In both countries geographic concentrations of immigrants generated greater anti-immigration sentiment (Fetzer 2000, 131–39).

The most consistent results, from these and other studies, are that the more educated are always less anti-immigrant, and that attitudes toward immigrants vary with their legal status (e.g., legal or illegal) or ethnicity (country of origin). These findings are supported in an analysis of British social attitudes for 1983–90 by Dustmann and Preston (2001). They identify components of anti-immigrant sentiment arising from racism, concerns about cultural conflict, concerns about jobs, and concerns about the costs of welfare services. These in turn are related to the characteristics of individuals in the survey. They find prejudice against West Indian and Asian immigrants to be very strong, especially among the lowest education group. Concerns about immigrant welfare use are stronger among those higher up the income distribution. These results suggest a reason why the "classical" interest-group results are hard to observe in the data for overall attitudes to immigration where there is a redistributive welfare state. Those lower in the income distribution are less concerned about competition for jobs and welfare funds but are more racist, whereas those higher up are less racist but more concerned about the welfare burden.[41]

A recent study of the attitudes of Australian-born adults toward immigrants and ethnic minorities provides additional insight into these issues (Chiswick and Miller 1999). The analysis found that native-born Australians did not view the ethnic or racial background of immigrants as important if the immigrants were committed to Australia (89 percent), but they had negative reactions if "ethnic groups kept their own culture" (76 percent). They supported government subsidies for immigrants to learn English and to learn of government programs (94 percent), but many op-

---

41. For the United States, Scheve and Slaughter (2001) find a clear negative relationship between education or skill level and anti-immigrant sentiment. Differences between the United States and European countries may reflect the relative size of the welfare state.

posed public money for ethnic groups to teach their origin language and culture to their children (47 percent). Negative attitudes toward immigration arise among those born in Australia from a view that multiculturalism is the basis of Australia's immigration policy (86 percent). The immigrants in the survey, on the other hand, had far more favorable attitudes toward their maintaining their own culture, toward public subsidies for this, and toward multiculturalism. The study also found that immigrants from non-English-speaking countries who had more positive attitudes toward becoming Australian were more fluent and literate in English. Thus, Australians are more favorably disposed toward immigrants who want to be "Australians" culturally, and immigrants who are more favorably disposed toward becoming Australian have a more successful adjustment.

2.5.5 Public Opinion and Public Policy

One problem with such cross-sectional analyses is that they do not necessarily capture the forces that underlie *changes* in attitudes, which might be more relevant for public policy. Changes in real incomes, income distributions, the intensity of unemployment, racism, defense or strategic concerns, or media hype will not be reflected in static cross sections. Alternatively, it has been argued that the rise of an educated elite, beholden to, but not locked into, landed or capitalist interests has damped or even eliminated the impact of changes in opinion on policy. Thus, a recent study of postwar immigration policy in Great Britain concludes that "throughout the post-war period British policymakers were, taken as a whole, more liberal than the public to which they owed their office" (Hansen 2000, vi). Nevertheless, it is clear that governments have responded to rising or falling anti-immigrant public opinion but that the effects of public opinion have operated imperfectly, with a lag, and its influence in electoral politics has varied across time and place.

In Australia the proportion of adults saying that too many immigrants were being admitted rose from a mere 16 percent in 1961 to 68 percent in 1988. Betts (1988) argues that the lack of policy response in the face of such seismic changes in attitudes was due to the rise of the educated (and largely public-sector) elite. However, the steep increase in Australian anti-immigrant sentiment came between 1968 and 1972, and it was followed by sharp cuts in the immigration target by the incoming Whitlam government. Although immigration was not a central policy issue in the election campaign, it nevertheless played a key role at the margin in the Labour Party's election victory (Money 1999, 192).

Shifts in policy are not always reflected by changes in the ruling party—either because other issues dominate or because policies toward immigration do not follow party lines. Thus, anti-immigration opinion increased in Great Britain during the 1960s, but it had little influence in the elections because most voters failed to see a difference between the political parties

(Studlar 1978). Rather, both parties shifted their policies to a more anti-immigrant stance. In the 1970s the rise of strongly anti-immigrant minority parties shifted immigration controls up the agenda in majority party platforms. Thus, the presence of Jean Marie Le Pen's Front National influenced the debate in the French presidential election of 1974, and the rise of the National Front in Great Britain influenced Margaret Thatcher's stance on immigration in the parliamentary election of 1979.

Although immigration policies do respond to swings in public opinion, one might still argue (as Betts does for Australia) that they are not tight enough to reflect the widespread desire for less (often zero) immigration. This is in part because the bulk of immigrants to the developed world in the 1980s and 1990s were admitted through family reunification schemes or as refugees. To some degree this reflects humanitarian policies that are embodied in international treaties. But it also reflects the fact that reunification and refugee admissions command far more popular support than does primary immigration and, least of all, illegal immigration. Thus, seemingly tough policies toward some (illegals and spurious asylum-seekers) and generous policies toward others (reunification and refugees) largely reflect differences in popular opinion toward these different groups. At the same time, such policies often imply loss of administrative control over the total numbers admitted.

In the United States, attitudes toward immigration restriction cut across the conventional liberal (Democratic) and conservative (Republican) party lines. Pro-immigration policies are generally favored by conservative business and fruit-and-vegetable agricultural interests, as well as by liberal civil libertarians and members of recent immigrant and ethnic groups. Pro-immigration policies are generally opposed by other conservative (nativist) groups, blue-collar workers, and union officials, as well as by some population control and environmentalist groups. With a declining trade union base in the private sector and an increasing share of its membership of recent immigrant origin, the leadership of the unions, particularly those involving low-skilled workers in internationally footloose industries, has been advocating a more pro-immigration position in the very tight labor market of the late 1990s. It remains to be seen whether the adoption of these new union attitudes will be reversed with a softening of the labor market.

The United States is seen as something of an exception in the late twentieth century, just as it was in the late nineteenth. Some observers see the pro-immigration bias embodied in immigration reforms since the 1965 amendments as drawing its strength from the platforms of well-organized religious, ethnic, and civil rights groups (DeLaet 2000). A left-right coalition of these groups and employers' organizations provided support for the 1990 Immigration Act, which significantly raised the overall immigration quota despite opposition of the general public. Employer groups supported an increase in employment-based visas, whereas ethnic and civil rights groups supported an increase in family-based migrants (Lee 1998, 102–03). This coalition dominated the weaker and less united interest groups, including labor unions and conservative anti-immigrant groups, such as the Federation for American Immigration Reform (FAIR). Thus, just as one interest group coalition pushed the door closed in the early twentieth century, another propped it open wider in the late twentieth century.

2.6   Conclusions: Migration and Policy

2.6.1   Migration and Globalization in the Long Run

Immigration policy clearly has responded to globalizing forces since the age of mass migration began in the middle of the nineteenth century. At the end of the nineteenth century barriers were rising as labor became more abundant in the New World, real wage growth slowed, and income distributions widened. But the door was closed slowly and with a lag, as a result of nation building, unrepresentative politics, or interest group dynamics. Wars and the interwar depression intensified the process of restriction in the short term, a process that was reversed as stability returned in the early post-WWII period. In the early post-WWII years, narrowing income distributions and rapid wage growth provided permissive conditions for a return to a more open immigration policy in Europe and the New World. But from the 1970s, a rising demand for migration was accompanied by slower real wage growth and widening income distributions. Anti-immigration sentiment increased rapidly, and in some countries this was reflected in policy tightening aimed against labor migrants.

During the nineteenth and early twentieth centuries the colonial empires of the European powers furthered a dimension of globalization. Skilled workers (administrators, engineers, doctors, etc.), primarily from the colonial powers, were brought to the dependencies, but much larger numbers of unskilled workers from Asia, primarily from India and China, were brought to other less developed areas to work on the plantations and in the mines. This dimension of the globalization of labor markets had largely ended by World War I. Wars and the Depression interrupted the flow. The post-WWII demise of these empires due to independence movements in Asia and Africa precluded its resuming.

The indirect effects of globalization have also been important. In the late nineteenth century, capital chased labor across the Atlantic to the resource-abundant New World. Although this raised the rental rates on land, the free flow of capital attenuated the diminishing returns to labor. In the absence of globalization in the capital market, it is likely that immigration controls would have come earlier. When the global capital market did implode in the interwar period, barriers rose more rapidly—even before the Great Depression. After the Second World War, as natural resource endowments became less important and as globalization returned to the capital market, the effects of migration on real wages and income distributions diminished. Globalizing capital markets, by attenuating the wage impacts of migration, helped to underpin liberalizing immigration policies up the mid-1970s and to dampen the immigration backlash in the following decades.

The integration of goods markets also influenced the shape of immigration policy. In the late nineteenth century declining transport costs eased relative factor scarcities and promoted wage convergence in the Atlantic economy. It was reflected in the invasion of New World agricultural goods into the Old World and of Old World manufactures into the New World. Although trade effects reduced the overall demand for labor in the Old World, they increased the *relative* demand for unskilled labor. And in the New World trade effects increased the *relative* demand for skilled labor. In the United States, at least, the McKinley and Dingley tariffs of 1890 and 1897, respectively, were aimed at protecting skilled labor by raising tariffs on a wide variety of manufactured and semimanufactured goods to protect American industry and labor from foreign competition. Had they not done so then perhaps barriers to immigration would have risen earlier, especially considering the protracted depression of the 1890s.

From the 1970s the globalization of trade lowered the returns to low-skilled labor in the first world and raised them in the labor-abundant third world. Trade hurt low-skilled workers in the first world relative to the skilled. Immigration simply added to the glut of low-skilled workers in the developed economies that was being created by trade and technical change. It is no surprise, then, that moves to restrict immigration since the early 1970s have been aimed principally at stemming the inflow of low-skilled workers—family unification policies notwithstanding.

2.6.2 The Future of Immigration Policy

The trend toward the integration and globalization of labor, product, and capital markets observed over the past few centuries is likely to continue. The decrease in the cost of information, communication, and transportation will encourage this development. The emergence of the poorer countries from the poverty trap will provide the resources to finance international migration, as will the emigrant remittances of kinsmen already in the high-income destinations. The continued pace of economic growth in the developed (OECD) countries will draw immigrants. The advanced economies will experience a high level of immigrant supply from the less developed countries in Latin America, Asia, and Africa. Yet these immigrants are entering technologically advanced economies in which there is a growing demand for high-skilled workers but shrinking relative employment opportunities for lower skilled workers. In this way the first decade of the twenty-first century differs from the first decade of the twentieth century. At that time there were still expanding opportunities for low-skilled workers in the industrial, mining, and agricultural sectors of the growing economies of overseas settlement.

Yet declining relative wages for low-skilled immigrant workers in the developed countries will still exceed the rising relative wages these workers are likely to receive in their less developed countries of origin. This will tend to bring about a greater convergence of wages by skill level across the globe. The wages of the high-skilled and the wages of the low-skilled will show less variance across international borders, but because of a steepening skill differential they will show perhaps even greater inequality in earnings within countries. This greater inequality and continued international migration is likely to be exacerbated by a substantially lower-than-replacement fertility rate in the economically advanced countries.

The current period differs from the earlier period in another dimension as well: There is now a much greater role for income distribution in the social welfare function. To a greater or lesser extent all of the developed economies have evolved into modern welfare states. This is evident from the much greater share of national income devoted to governmental income transfers to low-income groups in various forms—welfare payments, child allowances, unemployment compensation, health benefits, and old age assistance. This means that the widening of inequality (compared to what it would be otherwise as a result of low-skilled immigrants) plays a more prominent role in public policy. The result of increased low-skilled immigration and continued shrinking of job opportunities for low-skilled workers in the advanced economies as a result of the globalization of trade and technological change will mean increasing shares of national income transferred by the government to the low-skilled and poor native-born and immigrant populations.

The result will be a continuation of a process that we are already witnessing. Over the last few decades, the immigrant-receiving countries have been giving greater preference to high-skilled immigrants and have made the legal immigration of low-skilled workers that much more difficult. This has been done in the face of pressure for more "humanitarian visas" issued on the basis of a refugee status or a family relationship to someone already in the destination. Through the issuance of permanent visas or through temporary visas (e.g., the U.S. H1-B program), allocated on the basis of the worker's skill or occupation-specific employer petitions, high-skilled immigration can be expected to continue to grow.

A tightening of visa standards and numbers for kinship visas is also likely. The tightening of visa requirements for low-skilled workers will increase the supply of low-skilled illegal alien workers. Liberal democracies find it increasingly difficult to limit illegal immigration. Globalization is bringing about the reduction in barriers to mobility across countries. For example, the free movement of the citizens of the EU across member states makes it that much more difficult to limit the cross-border movement of immigrant workers, whether legal or illegal, in their country of initial settlement. Free trade agreements even across countries with sharply different levels of economic development seem to bring forth arguments for less stringent restrictions on the mobility of people (e.g., the United States and Mexico in NAFTA). International tourism and family visits to relatives in developed economies expand with globalization, facilitating illegal employment after a legal entry. Border enforcement is of limited value when a liberal democracy shares a border with a less developed country, but the increase in illegal immigration in Japan suggests it is no longer possible, if it ever was, for even an island nation to seal its border from illegal entries (Weiner and Hanami 1998). Enforcement of immigration law in the interior of a liberal democracy, including the use of national identity cards and employer sanctions, comes into conflict with the growing appreciation for civil liberties and efforts to reduce regulatory burdens and the intrusiveness of the state.

The likely result will be a menu of policies. Public policy in the high-income countries will favor the migration of skilled workers of all sorts. Efforts to reduce family-based immigration will meet with only limited political success. Where they do not already exist, employer sanctions and national identity cards may be introduced to stem the tide of illegal aliens, but they will not be used effectively. Because draconian measures will not be used, the growing low-skilled illegal alien population will be beneficiaries of periodic amnesties.[42] Until such time as there is substantial convergence in the incomes of workers of the same level of skill in the origin and destination countries (as was the case between Western Europe and North America), legal and illegal immigration pressures from the poorer to the wealthier nations will build up. Immigration restrictions may slow the numbers and shape the characteristics of the legal migrants, but the globalization and the integration of labor markets will continue well into the twenty-first century.

References

Abella, Manolo I. 1995. Asian migrant and contract workers in the Middle East. In *The Cambridge survey of world migration*, ed. Robin Cohen, 418–23. Cambridge: Cambridge University Press.
Altonji, Joseph G., and David Card. 1991. The effects of immigration on the labor

---

42. Shortly after this paragraph was first written, the Bush administration proposed an amnesty for several million illegal aliens from Mexico. Political pressures were exerted to expand it to all illegal aliens regardless of country of birth. The slowdown in the economy and reactions to the terrorist attacks in September 2001 by aliens, many of whom were in an illegal status, are likely to delay if not prevent this broad amnesty.

market outcomes of less-skilled natives. In *Immigration, trade, and the labor market*, ed. J. M. Abowd and R. B. Freeman, 201–34. Chicago: University of Chicago Press.

Amjad, Rashid, ed. 1989. *To the Gulf and back: Studies on the economic impact of Asian labour migration*. New Delhi, India: ILO Asian Employment Programme.

Bartel, Ann P. 1989. Where do the new immigrants live? *Journal of Labor Economics* 7 (October): 371–91.

Bartel, Ann P., and Marianne J. Koch. 1991. Internal migration of U.S. immigrants. In *Immigration, trade, and the labor market*, ed. John M. Abowd and Richard B. Freeman, 121–34. Chicago: University of Chicago Press.

Bauer, Thomas, and Klaus F. Zimmerman. 1999. Assessment of possible migration pressure and its labour market impact following EU enlargement to Central and Eastern Europe. IZA Research Report no. 3. Bonn, Germany: IZA.

Betts, Katherine. 1988. *Ideology and migration: Australia 1976 to 1987*. Melbourne: Melbourne University Press.

Borjas, George J. 1994. The economics of immigration. *Journal of Economic Literature* 32 (4): 1667–717.

Borjas, George J., Richard B. Freeman, and Lawrence F. Katz. 1997. How much do immigration and trade affect labor market outcomes? *Brookings Papers on Economic Activity*, Issue no. 1:1–67.

Boyer, George R., Timothy J. Hatton, and Kevin H. O'Rourke. 1994. The impact of emigration on real wages in Ireland, 1850–1914. In *Migration and the international labor market, 1850–1949*, ed. Timothy J. Hatton and Jeffrey G. Williamson, 221–39. London: Routledge.

Butlin, Noel G. 1994. *Forming a colonial economy: Australia 1810–1850*. Cambridge: Cambridge University Press.

Card, David. 1990. The impact of the Mariel boatlift on the Miami labor market. *Industrial and Labor Relations Review* 43 (2): 245–57.

Card, David, and John Di Nardo. 2000. Do immigrant inflows lead to native outflows? *American Economic Review* 90:360–67.

Chiswick, Barry R. 1974. *Income equality: Regional analyzes within a human capital framework*. New York: National Bureau of Economic Research.

———. 1980. *An analysis of the economic progress and impact of immigrants*. Washington, D.C.: U.S. Department of Labor, Employment and Training Administration, National Technical Information Service.

———. 1982. The impact of immigration on the level and distribution of economic well-being. In *The gateway: U.S. immigration issues and policies*, ed. Barry R. Chiswick, 289–313. Washington, D.C.: American Enterprise Institute.

———. 1988. Illegal immigration and immigration control. *Journal of Economic Perspectives* 3 (August): 101–15.

———. 1993. Review of *Immigration and the work force: Economic consequences for the United States and source areas*, by George J. Borjas and Richard Freeman. *Journal of Economic Literature* 31 (June): 910–11.

———. 1998. The economic consequences of immigration: Application to the United States and Japan. In *Temporary workers or future citizens? Japanese and U.S. migration policies*, ed. Myron Weiner and Tadashi Hanami, 177–208. New York: New York University Press.

———. 2000. Are immigrants favorably self-selected? An economic analysis. In *Migration theory: Talking across disciplines*, ed. Caroline D. Brettell and James F. Hollifield, 61–76. New York: Routledge.

———. 2001. The economics of illegal migration for the host economy. In *International migration into the twenty-first century*, ed. M. A. B. Siddique, 74–85. London: Edward Elgar.

Chiswick, Barry R., and Paul W. Miller. 1999. Immigration, language, and multiculturalism in Australia. *Australian Economic Review* 32 (4): 369–85.
———. 2001. Do enclaves matter for immigrant adjustment? University of Illinois at Chicago, Department of Economics. Photocopy.
Chiswick, Barry R., and Teresa A. Sullivan. 1995. The new immigrants. In *State of the union: America in the 1990s.* Vol. 2, *Social trends,* ed. R. Farley, 211–70. New York: Russell Sage.
Chiswick, Carmel U., Barry R. Chiswick, and Georgios Karras. 1992. The impact of immigrants on the macroeconomy. *Carnegie-Rochester Conference Series on Public Policy* 37 (4): 279–316.
Cobb-Clark, Deborah A., and Marie D. Connolly. 1997. The worldwide market for skilled migrants: Can Australia compete? *International Migration Review* 31 (3): 670–93.
Collins, William, Kevin H. O'Rourke, and Jeffrey G. Williamson. 1999. Were trade and factor mobility substitutes in history? In *Migration: The controversies and the evidence,* ed. Riccardo Faini, Jaime De Melo, and Klaus Zimmermann, 227–60. Cambridge: Cambridge University Press.
Daniels, Roger. 1995. The growth of restrictive immigration policy in the colonies of settlement. In *The Cambridge survey of world migration,* ed. Robin Cohen, 39–46. Cambridge: Cambridge University Press.
Daniels, Roger, and Otis L. Graham. 2001. *Debating American immigration: 1882–present.* Lanham, Md.: Rowman and Littlefield.
DeLaet, Debra L. 2000. *U.S. immigration policy in an age of rights.* Westport, Conn.: Praeger.
Dunlevy, James A. 1978. Economic opportunity and the responses of new and old immigrants in the United States. *Journal of Economic History* 38 (4): 901–17.
Dunlevy, James A., and R. P. Saba. 1992. The role of nationality-specific characteristics on the settlement patterns of late-nineteenth century European immigrants. *Explorations in Economic History* 29 (2): 228–49.
Dustmann, Christian, and Ian Preston. 2001. Racial and economic factors in attitudes toward immigration. University College, London, Department of Economics. Photocopy.
Easterlin, Richard. 1961. Influences in European overseas emigration before World War I. *Economic Development and Cultural Change* 9 (April): 33–51.
Eltis, David. 1983. Free and coerced transatlantic migrations: Some comparisons. *American Historical Review* 88 (2): 251–80.
Engerman, Stanley L. 1986. Servants to slaves to servants: Contract labor and European expansion. In *Colonialism and migration: Indentured labor before and after slavery,* ed. E. van den Boogaart and P. C. Emmer, 263–94. Dordrecht, The Netherlands: Martinus Nijhof.
Erickson, Charlotte. 1994. *Leaving England: Essays on British emigration in the nineteenth century.* Ithaca, N.Y.: Cornell University Press.
Faini, Riccardo, and Alessandra Venturini. 1994. Italian emigration in the pre-war period. In *Migration and the international labor market, 1850–1939,* ed. Timothy J. Hatton and Jeffrey G. Williamson, 72–90. London: Routledge.
Ferenczi, Imre, and Walter F. Willcox. 1929. *International migrations.* Vol. 1. New York: National Bureau of Economic Research.
Ferrie, Joseph P., and Joel Mokyr. 1994. Immigration and entrepreneurship in the nineteenth century U.S. In *Economic aspects of international migration,* ed. Herbert Geirsch, 115–38. Berlin: Springer-Verlag.
Fetzer, Joel S. 2000. *Public attitudes toward immigration in the United States, France, and Germany.* Cambridge: Cambridge University Press.

Filer, Randall K. 1992. The effect of immigrant arrivals on migratory patterns of native workers. In *Immigration and the workforce: Economic consequences for the United States and source areas*, ed. George J. Borjas and Richard B. Freeman, 245–70. Chicago: University of Chicago Press.

Foreman-Peck, James. 1992. A political economy of international migration, 1815–1914. *Manchester School of Economics and Social Studies* 60 (4): 359–76.

Friedberg, Rachel M. 2001. The impact of mass migration on the Israeli labor market. *Quarterly Journal of Economics* 105 (1): 1373–408.

Galenson, David W. 1981. *White servitude in Colonial America*. Cambridge: Cambridge University Press.

Gemery, Henry A. 1994. Immigrants and emigrants: International migration and the U.S. labor market in the Great Depression. In *Migration and the international labor market, 1850–1939*, ed. Timothy J. Hatton and Jeffrey G. Williamson. London: Routledge.

Goldin, Claudia. 1994. The political economy of immigration restriction in the United States. In *The regulated economy: A historical approach to political economy*, ed. Claudia Goldin and G. D. Libecap, 223–58. Chicago: University of Chicago Press.

Gould, John D. 1979. European intercontinental emigration, 1815–1914: Patterns and causes. *Journal of European Economic History* 8 (3): 593–679.

Green, Alan G., and David A. Green. 1993. Balanced growth and the geographical distribution of European immigrant arrivals to Canada, 1900–12. *Explorations in Economic History* 30 (1): 31–59.

Greenwood, Michael J., and John M. McDowell. 1994. The national labor market consequences of U.S. immigration. In *Economic aspects of international migration*, ed. Herbert Giersch, 155–94. Berlin: Springer-Verlag.

Grubb, Farley. 1992. The long-run trend in the value of European immigrant servants: New measurements and interpretations. *Research in Economic History* 14:167–241.

Hansen, Randall. 2000. *Citizenship and immigration in postwar Britain*. Oxford: Oxford University Press.

Hatton, Timothy J. 1995. A model of U.K. emigration, 1870–1913. *Review of Economics and Statistics* 77 (3): 407–15.

———. 2001. Why has U.K. net emigration increased? University of Essex, Department of Economics. Unpublished manuscript.

Hatton, Timothy J., and Jeffrey G. Williamson. 1998. *The age of mass migration: Causes and economic effects*. New York: Oxford University Press.

———. 2001. Demographic and economic pressure on emigration out of Africa. NBER Working Paper no. 8124. Cambridge, Mass.: National Bureau of Economic Research.

Herbert, Ulrich, and Karin Hunn. 2000. Guest workers and policy on guest workers in the Federal Republic: From the beginning of recruitment in 1955 until its halt in 1973. In *The miracle years: A cultural history of West Germany*, ed. Hanna Schissler, 180–208. Princeton, N.J.: Princeton University Press.

Hu-De Hart, Evelyn. 1995. The Chinese of Peru, Cuba, and Mexico. In *The Cambridge survey of world migration*, ed. Robin Cohen, 220–22. Cambridge: Cambridge University Press.

Hui, Ong Jin. 1995. Chinese indentured labor: Coolies and colonies. In *The Cambridge survey of world migration*, ed. Robin Cohen, 51–57. Cambridge: Cambridge University Press.

Jasso, Guillermina, Mark R. Rosenzweig, and Mark R. Smith. 2000. The changing skill of new immigrants to the United States: Recent trends and their determinants. In *Issues in the economics of immigration*, ed. George J. Borjas, 185–226. Chicago: National Bureau of Economic Research.

Jerome, Harry. 1926. *Migration and business cycles*. New York: National Bureau of Economic Research.

Kamemera, David, Victor I. Oguledo, and Bobby Davis. 2000. A gravity model analysis of international migration to North America. *Applied Economics* 32 (13): 1745–55.

Karras, Georgios, and Carmel U. Chiswick. 1999. Macroeconomic determinants of migration: The case of Germany, 1964–1988. *International Migration* 37 (4): 657–77.

Keeling, Drew. 1999. The transport revolution and transatlantic migration, 1850–1914. *Research in Economic History* 19:39–74.

Kirk, Dudley. 1946. *Europe's population in the interwar years*. Geneva: League of Nations.

Lee, Kenneth K. 1998. *Huddled masses, muddled laws: Why contemporary immigration policy fails to reflect public opinion*. Westport, Conn.: Praeger.

Leff, Nathaniel H. 1982. *Underdevelopment and development in Brazil*. Vol. 1, *Economic structure and change, 1822–1947*. London: George Allen and Unwin.

Lovejoy, Paul E. 1983. The volume of the Atlantic slave trade: A synthesis. *Journal of African History* 23 (4): 473–501.

Lowell, Bryant L. 1987. *Scandinavian exodus: Demography and social development of nineteenth-century rural communities*. Boulder, Colo.: Westview.

Madgwick, R. B. 1937. *Immigration into eastern Australia, 1788–1851*. London: Longmans Green.

McDonald, J., and Ralph Shlomowitz. 1990. Mortality on immigrant voyages to Australia. *Explorations in Economic History* 27 (1): 84–113.

———. 1991. Passenger fares on sailing vessels to Australia in the nineteenth century. *Explorations in Economic History* 28 (2): 192–208.

Money, Jeannette. 1999. *Fences and neighbors: The political geography of immigration control*. Ithaca, N.Y.: Cornell University Press.

Organization for Economic Cooperation and Development (OECD). 2000. *Combating the illegal employment of foreign workers*. Paris: OECD.

O'Rourke, Kevin H., and Jeffrey G. Williamson. 1997. Around the European periphery 1870–1913: Globalization, schooling, and growth. *European Review of Economic History* 1 (2): 153–90.

O'Rourke, Kevin H., Jeffrey G. Williamson, and Timothy J. Hatton. 1994. Mass migration, commodity market integration, and real wage convergence: The late nineteenth century Atlantic economy. In *Migration and the international labor market, 1850–1939*, ed. T. J. Hatton and J. G. Williamson, 203–20. London: Routledge.

Rotte, Ralph, Michael M. Vogler, and Klaus F. Zimmermann. 1997. South-north refugee migration: Lessons for development co-operation. *Review of Development Economics* 1 (1): 99–115.

Scheve, Kenneth F., and Matthew J. Slaughter. 2001. Labor market competition and individual preferences over immigration policy. *Review of Economics and Statistics* 83:133–45.

Shaw, Alan G. L. 1966. *Convicts and the colonies*. Melbourne: Melbourne University Press.

Shimpo, Mitsuru. 1995. Indentured migrants from Japan. In *The Cambridge survey of world migration*, ed. Robin Cohen, 48–50. Cambridge: Cambridge University Press.

Shughart, William F., Robert D. Tollinson, and Mwangi S. Kimenyi. 1986. The political economy of immigration restrictions. *Yale Journal on Regulation* 4 (1): 79–97.

Stalker, Peter. 1994. *The work of strangers: A survey of international labor migration.* Geneva: International Labor Organization.

Studlar, Dudley T. 1978. Policy voting in Britain: The colored immigration issue in the 1964, 1966, and 1970 general elections. *American Political Science Review* 72 (1): 46–64.

Tatla, Darshan Singh. 1995. Sikh free and military migration during the colonial period. In *The Cambridge survey of world migration*, ed. Robin Cohen, 69–73. Cambridge: Cambridge University Press.

Taylor, Alan M., and Jeffrey G. Williamson. 1997. Convergence in the age of mass migration. *European Review of Economic History* 1 (1): 27–63.

Thiara, Ravinder K. 1995. Indian indentured workers in Mauritius, Natal, and Fiji. In *The Cambridge survey of world migration*, ed. Robin Cohen, 63–68. Cambridge: Cambridge University Press.

Timmer, Ashley S., and Jeffrey G. Williamson. 1998. Immigration policy prior to the 1930s: Labor markets, policy interactions, and globalization backlash. *Population and Development Review* 24 (4): 739–71.

Todaro, Michael P. 1969. A model of labor migration and urban unemployment in less developed countries. *American Economic Review* 59 (1): 138–48.

Twaddle, Michael. 1995. The settlement of South Asians in East Africa. In *The Cambridge survey of world migration*, ed. Robin Cohen, 74–76. Cambridge: Cambridge University Press.

United Nations (UN). 1979. *Trends and characteristics of international migration since 1950.* New York: UN.

———. 1998. *World population monitoring 1997: International migration and development.* New York: UN.

———. 1999. *World population prospects: The 1998 revision.* Washington, D.C.: UN.

———. 2000. *World migration report.* New York: UN International Organization for Migration.

U.S. Immigration and Naturalization Service. 2000. *Statistical yearbook of the Immigration and Naturalization Service, 1998.* Washington, D.C.: GPO.

Vertovec, Steven. 1995. Indian indentured migration to the Caribbean. In *The Cambridge survey of world migration*, ed. Robin Cohen, 57–62. Cambridge: Cambridge University Press.

Weiner, Myron, and Tadashi Hanami, eds. 1998. *Temporary workers or future citizens? Japanese and U.S. migration policies.* New York: New York University Press.

Williamson, Jeffrey G. 1998. Globalization, labor markets, and policy backlash in the past. *Journal of Economic Perspectives* 12 (4): 51–72.

Williamson, Jeffrey G., and Peter H. Lindert. 1980. *American inequality: A macroeconomic history.* New York: Academic Press.

Winklemann, Rainer. 2000. Immigration policies and their impact: The case of New Zealand and Australia. IZA Discussion Paper no. 169. Bonn, Germany: IZA–Institute for the Study of Labor.

Wooden, Mark, Robert Holton, Graeme Hugo, and Judith Sloan. 1994. *Australian immigration: A survey of the issues.* Canberra, Australia: Australian Government Printing Service.

Yang, Philip Q. 1995. *Post-1965 immigration to the United States: Structural determinants.* Westport, Conn.: Praeger.

Comment   Riccardo Faini

Migration is a controversial and divisive issue. By taking a broad historical perspective, Barry R. Chiswick and Timothy J. Hatton are able to cast new light on an old debate. Their paper covers a lot of ground. It provides the reader with a fascinating overview of the main trends in international migration starting back in the seventeenth century; it offers an in-depth discussion of the determinants of mass migration; it then takes a close look at the impact of migration; and finally it assesses the role of political economy factors in shaping policies toward migration.

The main messages of the paper can be summarized as follows. First, migration is quite responsive to basic economic incentives. This is best seen in the nineteenth century, before immigration policies took a restrictive turn, thereby muting the impact of wage and employment conditions. Second, the labor market impact of migration comes mainly through its effects on economywide factor endowments. Third, given the growing emphasis in host countries on income distribution considerations, the restrictive stance toward unskilled migration is likely to continue.

The first point is well taken, although the explanatory power of wage and employment conditions should not be overestimated (as the authors themselves acknowledge when they emphasize other factors, such as financial constraints, demography, and chain effects). It is true, for instance, that the migration transition in southern Europe during the second half of the twentieth century owes much to the catching-up process with respect to the rest of the continent. However, although there was some wage convergence, it was at best incomplete. Moreover, while wage converged, unemployment diverged. Given that, as shown by Hatton (1995), migration should respond more to unemployment differentials than to wage differentials, we would have expected emigration from southern Europe to rise rather than falling. To understand why it did not we need to look at additional factors, such as the levels of unemployment and income (rather than simply their differentials). High unemployment rates in receiving countries may well discourage migration, even if unemployment differentials are unchanged. Similarly, if income rises at home, potential migrants may be increasingly unwilling to suffer the emotional and cultural shocks associated with migration, even if the wage differential with the host country remains unchanged. Finally, additional factors emphasized in the so-called new migration literature may also have a role to play. For instance, there is some evidence that the desire for risk diversification has been a significant motive for emigration from backward economies, where insurance markets are relatively underdevel-

Riccardo Faini is professor of economics at the University of Brescia. Currently, he is on leave at the Ministry of Economy in Italy.

oped. There are good a priori reasons to believe that it may have played a similar role in affecting intercontinental migration flows in the nineteenth century.

The second point, namely that the economic impact of migration works through its effects on relative factor endowments, is also well taken. Under the reasonable assumption that migrants have less overall capital than natives, income will fall, in a static model, and growth will slow down, at least temporarily, in a dynamic model. However, we should not overlook one basic fact, namely that the welfare impact of immigration is not the same as its growth and income effect. This is better seen in a static Barry-Soligo model, where gross domestic product (GDP) per capita definitely falls after immigration of capital poor workers, but natives' welfare unambiguously increases. The fall in GDP is explained by the fact that immigrants are relatively poor (they have little or no capital) and therefore drive down average income in the host country. Natives gain, however, because the fall in wages is more than offset by higher returns to capital. Further immigration is even more beneficial to natives, since it drives down the wage of previous migrants. Borjas (1995) has also noticed that the welfare impact of immigration is a decreasing function of the wage elasticity of labor demand. If wages do not fall—say, because labor demand is infinitely elastic—the welfare impact is nil. There is a trade-off, therefore, between the welfare and the distributional impact: For the former to be large, we also need the latter to be large.

The third part of the paper deals with the political economy of immigration. The authors highlight one puzzle, which is that "in democratic countries public opinion in recent years has been far more anti-immigration than public policy." This may be true, but the fact is that by and large immigration policies have become significantly more restrictive in the twentieth century, after the First World War, than in the previous period. Interestingly enough, this shift is mirrored by an opposite shift in the policy stance toward trade that used to be quite restrictive in the nineteenth century and was significantly liberalized after the Second World War. There is therefore an additional and equally surprising puzzle, namely the substantial asymmetries in the policy stance on goods trade and migration. In the traditional trade model, these aspects—and one could add capital flows as well—are all substitutes. Limiting one flow is ineffective if the other flow is unrestricted. Are voters in democratic countries therefore so myopic that they do not realize that restrictions on immigration are negated by the liberal stance on trade policies and capital flows? The typical answer of the profession is that the relationships among migration, capital mobility, and trade are complex and model dependent. However, we can be somewhat more exhaustive and note some factors that may plausibly explain why the stance toward migration is more restrictive than that on trade. First, migration is likely to be significantly less reversible than goods trade. Whereas factor services embodied in imports can be easily stopped through temporary protection measures, expelling migrants on purely economic reasons is unacceptable to most. Second, immigrants may compete with natives in the non-traded-goods sector in a way that imports do not. In both cases, we would still be left with the task of explaining why in the nineteenth century migration policy was more liberal than trade policy. Clearly, this is an area with substantial scope for additional research.

To conclude, Chiswick and Hatton highlight two major differences between the first and the most recent globalization episodes, namely the much diminished demand for unskilled workers and the more significant role for income distribution considerations in receiving countries. There is, however, a third major difference, which has to do with the impact of migration flows in sending countries. Although this latter aspect is somewhat neglected by the authors, they can hardly be blamed for such an omission, given that even the *Handbook of Population Economics* says very little on this issue. However, the truth is that although migration flows played a key role in fostering convergence between the Old and the New worlds until 1913, this is no longer the case in the current globalization phase. The fact that immigration policy is increasingly geared to limit unskilled immigration and favor skilled immigration has indeed far-reaching implications for sending countries. First, unskilled labor flows are no longer there to foster convergence as they did quite successfully in the nineteenth century and in the 1960s in Europe. Second, immigration policy in receiving countries will aggravate the brain drain and its related negative effects on the sending country. There is also some evidence (Faini 2002) that skilled migrants have a lower propensity to remit home, most likely because they tend to migrate permanently and bring along their family. Overall, sending countries therefore lose on all three counts, the more limited role of unskilled migration, the decline in human capital attendant on skilled emigration, and the dearth of remittances flows. There is still a long way to go to the globalization of labor markets.

References

Borjas, George. 1995. The economic benefits from immigration. *Journal of Economic Perspectives* (Spring): 3–22.
Faini, Riccardo. 2002. Development, trade, and migration. *Revue d'Economie et du développement* (forthcoming).
Hatton, Timothy. 1995. A model of U.K. emigration, 1875–1913. *Review of Economics and Statistics* 77 (3): 407–15.

3   Globalization and Capital Markets

Maurice Obstfeld and Alan M. Taylor

3.1   Global Capital Markets: Overview and Origins

At the turn of the twenty-first century, the merits of international financial integration are under more forceful attack than at any time since the 1940s. Even mainstream academic proponents of free multilateral commodity trade, such as Bhagwati, argue that the risks of global financial integration outweigh the benefits it affords. Critics from the left such as Eatwell, more skeptical even of the case for free trade on current account, suggest that since the 1960s "free international capital flows" have been "associated with a deterioration in economic efficiency (as measured by growth and unemployment)" (Eatwell 1997, 2).[1]

The resurgence of concerns over international financial integration is understandable in light of the financial crises in Latin America in 1994–95,

Maurice Obstfeld is the Class of 1958 Professor of Economics at the University of California–Berkeley and a research associate of the National Bureau of Economic Research. Alan M. Taylor is professor of economics at the University of California–Davis and a research associate of the National Bureau of Economic Research.

Jay Shambaugh, Julian di Giovanni, and Miguel Fuentes provided superb research assistance. For assistance with data we thank Luis Bértola, Michael Bordo, Guillermo Bózzoli, Charles Calomiris, Gregory Clark, Niall Ferguson, Stephen Haber, Ian McLean, Satyen Mehta, Chris Meissner, Leandro Prados de la Escosura, Jamie Reis, Gail Triner, Michael Twomey, and Tarik Yousef. For editorial suggestions we thank Michael Bordo. We received helpful comments from our discussant Richard Portes; from Marc Flandreau and other conference participants at Santa Barbara; from Michael Jansson, Lawrence Officer, and Rolf vom Dorp; and from participants in seminars at Stanford Graduate School of Business, the University of Southern California, the University of Oregon, the University of California–San Diego, the Bank of Japan, King's College, Cambridge, and Universidad Argentina de la Empresa, Buenos Aires. Obstfeld acknowledges the financial support of the National Science Foundation, through a grant administered by the National Bureau of Economic Research.

1. See Bhagwati (1998) and Eatwell. For a skeptical perspective on the future prospects of economic integration in general, see Rodrik (2000).

East Asia and Russia in 1997–98, and Argentina in 2001–02. Proponents of free trade in tangible goods have long recognized that its net benefits to countries typically are distributed unevenly, creating domestic winners and losers. But recent international financial crises have submerged entire economies and threatened their trading partners, inflicting losses all around. International financial transactions rely intrinsically on the expectation that counterparties will fulfill future contractual commitments; they therefore place confidence and possibly volatile expectations at center stage.[2] These same factors are present in purely domestic financial trades, of course; but oversight, adjudication, and enforcement all are orders of magnitude more difficult among sovereign nations with distinct national currencies than within a single national jurisdiction. Moreover, there is no natural world lender of last resort, so international crises are intrinsically harder to head off and contain. Factors other than the threat of crises, such as the power of capital markets to constrain domestically oriented economic policies, also have sparked concerns over greater financial openness.

The ebb and flow of international capital since the nineteenth century illustrates recurring difficulties, as well as the alternative perspectives from which policymakers have tried to confront them. The subsequent sections of this paper are devoted to documenting these vicissitudes quantitatively and explaining them. Economic theory and economic history together can provide useful insights into events of the past and deliver relevant lessons for today. We argue that theories of how international capital mobility has evolved must be understood within the framework of the basic policy trilemma constraining an open economy's choice of monetary regime.

3.1.1   The Emergence of World Capital Markets

Prior to the nineteenth century, the geographical scope for international finance was relatively limited compared to what was to come. Italian banks of the Renaissance financed trade and government around the Mediterranean, and as trade expanded within Europe, financial innovations spread farther north through the letters of credit developed at the Champagne Fairs and the new banks in North Sea ports such as Bruges and Antwerp. Later, London and Amsterdam became the key centers, and their currencies and financial instruments were the principal focus of market players. As the industrial revolution gathered force and radiated out from Great Britain, the importance of international financial markets became more apparent in both the public and private spheres.[3]

In due course, the scope for such trades extended to other centers that developed the markets and institutions capable of supporting international financial transactions, and whose governments were not hostile to such de-

2. The vast majority of commodity trades also involve an element of intertemporal exchange, via deferred or advance payment for goods, but the unwinding of the resulting cross-border obligations tends to be predictable.
3. See Cameron (1993); Neal (1990, 2000); Oppers (1993); Brezis (1995).

velopments. In the eastern United States, a broad range of centers including Boston, Philadelphia, and Baltimore gave way to what became the dominant center of national and international finance, New York. By the late nineteenth century, both France and Germany had developed sophisticated and expanding international markets, well integrated into the networks of global finance. Elsewhere in Europe and the New World similar markets began from an embryonic stage, and eventually financial trading spread to places as far afield as Melbourne and Buenos Aires.[4]

As we shall discuss later, after 1870 these developments were to progress even further. With the world starting to converge on the gold standard as a monetary system, and with technological developments in shipping (e.g., steamships' replacing sail; the Panama Canal) and communications (the telegraph, transoceanic cables), the first global marketplace in capital, as well as in goods and labor, took shape in an era of undisputed liberalism and virtual laissez-faire.

Within finance, the technological and institutional developments were many: the use of modern communications to transmit prices; the development of a very broad array of private debt and equity instruments, and the widening scope for insurance activities; the expanding role of government bond markets internationally; and the more widespread use of forward and futures contracts, and derivative securities. By 1900, the use of such instruments permeated the major economic centers of dozens of countries around the world, stretching from Europe, east and west, north and south, to the Americas, Asia, and Africa. The key currencies and instruments were known everywhere, and formed the basis for an expanding world commercial network, whose rise was equally meteoric. Bills of exchange, bond finance, equity issues, foreign direct investments, and many other types of transactions were by then quite common among the core countries, and among a growing number of nations at the periphery.

Aside from haute finance, more and more day-to-day activities came into the orbit of finance via the growth and development of banking systems in many countries, offering checking and saving accounts as time passed. This in turn raised the question of whether banking supervision would be done by the banks themselves or the government authorities, with solutions including free banking and "wildcat" banks (as in the United States), and changing over time to include supervisory functions as part of a broader central monetary authority, the central bank. From what was once an esoteric sector of the economy, the financial sector grew locally and globally to touch an ever-expanding range of activity.[5]

---

4. On the United States see Davis (1965) and Sylla (1975, 1998). On Europe see Kindleberger (1984). For a comprehensive discussion of the historical and institutional developments in some key countries where international financial markets made an impact at this time—the United Kingdom, the United States, Australia, Argentina, and Canada—see Davis and Gallman (2001). On comparative financial deepening and sophistication see Goldsmith (1985).
5. On financial development, see chapter 8, by Rousseau and Sylla, in this volume.

Thus, the scope for capital markets to do good—or do harm—loomed larger as time went by. As an ever-greater part of national and international economies became monetized and sensitive to financial markets, agents in all spheres—public and private, labor and capital, domestic and foreign— were affected. Who stood to gain or lose? What policies would emerge as government objectives evolved? Would global capital markets proceed unfettered or not? From the turn of the twentieth century, the unfolding history of the international capital market has been of enormous import. At various times the market has shaped the course of national and international economic development and swayed political interests in all manner of directions. In terms of distribution and equality, it has made winners and losers, although so often is the process misunderstood that the winners and losers are often unclear, at the national and the global level. An aim of this paper is to tell the history of what became a truly *global* capital market on the eve of the twentieth century, and explore how it has influenced the course of events ever since.

3.1.2 Stylized Facts for the Nineteenth and Twentieth Centuries

Notwithstanding the undisputed record of technological advancement and economic growth over the long run, we must reject the temptations of a simple linear history as we examine international capital markets and their evolution. It has not been a record of ever-more-perfectly functioning markets with ever-lower transaction costs and ever-expanding scope. The mid-twentieth century, on the contrary, was marked by an enormous reaction against markets, international as well as domestic, and against financial markets in particular.[6] Muted echoes of these same themes could be heard once again at the end of the twentieth century.

What do we already know about the evolution of global capital mobility in the last century or more? Very few previous studies exist for the entire period and covering a sufficiently comprehensive cross-section of countries; but many authors have focused on individual countries and particular epochs, and from their work we can piece together a working set of hypotheses that might be termed the conventional wisdom concerning the evolution of international capital mobility in the post-1870 era. The story comes in four parts, and not coincidentally these echo the division of the twentieth century into distinct international monetary regimes.[7]

The first period runs up to 1914. After 1870 an increasing share of the world economy came into the orbit of the classical gold standard, and a global capital market centered on London. By 1880, quite a few countries were on gold, and by 1900 a large number. This fixed exchange rate system

---

6. See Polanyi (1944).
7. On this division of history see, in particular, Eichengreen (1996). Earlier surveys of the progress of financial market globalization since the nineteenth century include Obstfeld and Taylor (1998), Bordo, Eichengreen, and Kim (1999), and Flandreau and Rivière (1999).

was for most countries a stable and credible regime, and functioned as a disciplining or commitment device. Accordingly, interest rates across countries tended to converge, and capital flows surged. Many peripheral countries, not to mention the New World offshoots of western Europe, took part in an increasingly globalized economy in not only the capital market, but also the goods and labor markets.[8]

In the second period, from 1914 to 1945, this global economy was destroyed. Two world wars and a Great Depression accompanied a rise in nationalism and increasingly noncooperative economic policymaking. With gold-standard credibility broken by World War I, monetary policy became subject to domestic political goals, first as a way to help finance wartime deficits. Later, monetary policy was a tool to engineer beggar-thy-neighbor devaluations under floating rates. As a guard against currency crises and to protect gold, capital controls became widespread. The world economy went from globalized to almost autarkic in the space of a few decades. Capital flows were minimal, international investment was regarded with suspicion, and international prices and interest rates fell completely out of synchronization. Global capital (along with finance in general) was demonized, and seen as a principal cause of the world depression of the 1930s.[9]

In the third period, the Bretton Woods era (1945–71), an attempt to rebuild the global economy took shape. Trade flows began a remarkable expansion, and economic growth began its most rapid spurt in history worldwide. Yet fears formed in the interwar period concerning global capital were not easily dispelled. The International Monetary Fund (IMF) initially sanctioned capital controls as a means to prevent currency crises and runs, and this lent some autonomy to governments by providing more power to activist monetary policy. For twenty years, this prevailing philosophy held firm; and although capital markets recovered, they did so slowly. But by the late 1960s global capital could not be held back so easily, and its workings eventually broke the compromise that had sustained the fixed exchange rate system.[10]

In the fourth and final period, the post–Bretton Woods floating-rate era, a different trend has been evident. Although fixed-rate regimes were reluctantly given up, and although some countries still attempt to maintain or create such regimes anew, the years from the 1970s to the 1990s have been characterized by a seeming increase in capital mobility. Generally speaking,

8. On the gold standard regime and late-nineteenth-century capital markets see, inter alia, Eichengreen (1996); Eichengreen and Flandreau (1996); Bordo and Kydland (1995); Bordo and Rockoff (1996); Edelstein (1982). On this first era of globalization in goods and factor markets see Sachs and Warner (1995); Williamson (1996); O'Rourke and Williamson (1999); and chapters 1 (by Findlay and O'Rourke) and 2 (by Chiswick and Hatton) in this volume.

9. See Eichengreen (1992, 1996) and Temin (1989). In labor markets migrations collapsed and in goods markets trade barriers multiplied (Kindleberger 1986, 1989; Williamson 1995; James 2001).

10. On Bretton Woods see, for example, Bordo and Eichengreen (1993); Eichengreen (1996).

industrial-country governments no longer needed capital controls as a tool to help preserve a fixed exchange rate peg, since the peg was gone. As a floating rate could accommodate market developments, controls could be lifted. This was encouraging to the flow of capital in all countries. In peripheral countries, economic reforms reduced the transactions costs and risks of foreign investment, and capital flows grew there, too—at least until the crises of the later 1990s reminded investors of the fragility of the fixed-rate regimes that tended to persist in the developing world. Increasingly, the smaller peripheral countries that desire fixed exchange rates seek credibly to give up domestic monetary policy autonomy through currency boards or even dollarization, whereas larger developing countries such as Mexico, Chile, and Brazil have opted for exchange rate flexibility coupled with inflation targeting.

In the 1990s, the term *globalization* has became a catch-all to describe the phenomenon of an increasingly integrated and interdependent world economy, one that exhibits supposedly free flows of goods, services, and capital, albeit not of labor. Yet for all the hype, economic history suggests we be a little cautious in assessing how amazing this development really is. We will show that a period of impressive global integration has been witnessed before, at least for capital markets—at the turn of the twentieth century, just about a hundred years ago. Of course, that earlier epoch of globalization did not endure. As the above discussion suggests, if we were roughly to sketch out the implied movements in capital mobility, we would chart an upswing from 1880 to 1914; this would be followed by a collapse to 1945, although perhaps with a minor recovery during the brief reconstruction of the gold standard in the 1920s, between the autarky of World War I and the Depression; we would then think of a gradual rise in mobility after 1945, becoming faster after the demise of Bretton Woods in the early 1970s.

For illustrative purposes, let us make the tenuous assumption that international capital mobility or global capital market integration *could* be measured on a single parameter. Suppose we could plot that parameter over time for the last century or so. We would then expect to see a time path something like figure 3.1, where the vertical axis carries the mobility or integration measure. It is reasonable, given the specific histories of various subperiods or certain countries, as contained in numerous fragments of the historical literature, to speak of capital mobility increasing or decreasing at the times we have noted. Thus, the overall U-shaped trend line indicated by the figure is probably correct.

However, without further quantification the usefulness of the stylized view remains unclear. For one thing, we do not know if it accords with empirical measures of capital mobility. Moreover, even if we know the direction of changes in the mobility of capital at various times, we cannot measure the extent of those changes. Without such evidence, we cannot assess whether the U-shaped trend path is complete: That is, have we now reached

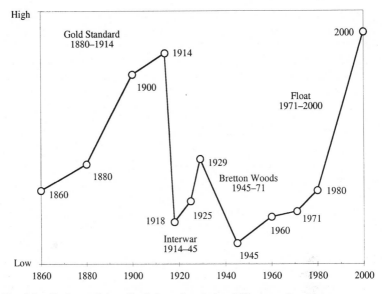

Fig. 3.1   Conjecture? A stylized view of capital mobility in modern history
Source: Introspection.

a degree of capital mobility that is above, or still below, that seen in the years before 1914? To address these questions requires more formal empirical testing, and that is one of the motivations for the quantitative analysis that follows.

3.1.3   The Trilemma: Capital Mobility, the Exchange Rate, and Monetary Policy

We seek in this paper not only to offer evidence in support of the stylized view of global capital market evolution, but also to provide an organizing framework for understanding that evolution and the forces that shaped the international economy of the late nineteenth and twentieth centuries. Given the stylized description, we must address the following question: What explains the long stretch of high capital mobility that prevailed before 1914, the subsequent breakdown in the interwar period, and the very slow postwar reconstruction of the world financial system? The answer is tied up with one of the central and most visible areas in which openness to the world capital market constrains government power: the choice of an exchange rate regime.[11]

The *macroeconomic policy trilemma* for open economies (also known as

11. This section draws on Obstfeld and Taylor (1998), who invoked the term "trilemma," and Obstfeld (1998).

the *inconsistent trinity* proposition) follows from a basic fact: An open capital market deprives a country's government of the ability simultaneously to target its exchange rate and to use monetary policy in pursuit of other economic objectives. The trilemma arises because a macroeconomic policy regime can include, at most, two elements of the inconsistent trinity of three policy goals:

1. full freedom of cross-border capital movements
2. a fixed exchange rate
3. an independent monetary policy oriented toward domestic objectives

If capital movements are prohibited, in the case where element (1) is ruled out, a country on a fixed exchange rate can break ranks with foreign interest rates and thereby run an independent monetary policy. Similarly, a floating exchange rate, in the case where element (2) is ruled out, reconciles freedom of international capital movements with monetary-policy effectiveness (at least when some nominal domestic prices are sticky). But monetary policy is powerless to achieve domestic goals when the exchange rate is fixed and capital movements free, the case where element (3) is ruled out, since intervention in support of the exchange parity then entails capital flows that exactly offset any monetary-policy action threatening to alter domestic interest rates.[12]

Our central proposition is that secular movements in the scope of international lending and borrowing may be understood in terms of this trilemma. Capital mobility has prevailed and expanded under circumstances of widespread political support either for an exchange-rate-subordinated monetary regime (e.g., the gold standard), or for a monetary regime geared mainly toward domestic objectives at the expense of exchange rate stability (e.g., the recent float). The middle ground in which countries attempt simultaneously to hit exchange rate targets and domestic policy goals has, almost as a logical consequence, entailed exchange controls or other harsh constraints on international transactions.

It is this conflict among rival policy choices, the trilemma, that informs our discussion of the historical evolution of world capital markets in the

---

12. The choice between fixed and floating exchange rates should not be viewed as dichotomous; nor should it be assumed that the choice of a floating-rate regime necessarily leads to a useful degree of monetary policy flexibility. In reality, the degree of exchange rate flexibility lies on a continuum, with exchange rate target zones, crawling pegs, crawling zones, and managed floats of various other kinds residing between the extremes of irrevocably fixed and freely floating. The greater the attention given to the exchange rate, the more constrained monetary policy is in pursuing other objectives. Indeed, the notion of a "free" float is an abstraction with little empirical content, as few governments are willing to set monetary policy without some consideration of its exchange rate effects. Even under a free float, autonomy could be compromised. If floating exchange rates are subject to persistent speculative shocks unrelated to economic fundamentals, and if policymakers are concerned to counter these movements, then monetary control will be compromised.

pages that follow, and helps make sense of the ebb and flow of capital mobility in the long run and in the broader political-economy context.

Of course, the trilemma is only a proximate explanation, in the sense that deeper sociopolitical forces explain the relative dominance of some policy targets over others. Cohen (1996, 274–75) usefully distinguishes four potential categories of explanation concerning the evolution of international financial integration. We paraphrase his categories by distinguishing explanations based upon

1. technological innovation, including resulting increases in market competition;
2. policy competition among governments seeking to advance "state interest," somehow defined;
3. domestic politics, including partisan rivalry and interest-group lobbying;
4. ideology and advances in economic knowledge.

We view explanations based on technology as secondary for the period of interest to us (starting in the latter part of the nineteenth century), as it follows the deployment of transoceanic cable technology.[13] The precise definition of *state interest* may well reflect the domestic political power structure, so explanations of classes (2) and (3) need not be disjoint. Yet there may be situations in which there is a broad domestic consensus regarding certain policies as in the national interest. Similarly, ideology and the state of knowledge can determine the policies that states pursue in seeking a given perceived national interest. As will become clear in what follows, we regard explanations along the lines of (2) and especially (3) as the "deep factors" behind movements in international financial integration, with a supporting role for (4) as well.[14] The central role of the trilemma is to constrain the choice set within which the deep factors play their roles.

3.1.4   A Brief Narrative

The broad trends and cycles in the world capital market that we will document reflect changing responses to the fundamental trilemma. Before 1914, each of the world's major economies pegged its currency's price in terms of gold, and thus, implicitly, maintained a fixed rate of exchange against every other major country's currency. Financial interests ruled the world of the classical gold standard and financial orthodoxy saw no alter-

13. We recognize, however, that technology- or policy-driven changes in the extent of goods-market integration might affect some measures of financial integration, as in the analysis of Obstfeld and Rogoff (2000).

14. Rajan and Zingales (2001) place interest-group politics at center stage in their theory of domestic financial market liberalization. They find a U-shaped evolution of domestic financial evolution reminiscent of the pattern for international integration that we document in this paper. While they seem to view international capital mobility as basically exogenous to the process of domestic liberalization, we would view the two as jointly determined by the deeper factors.

native mode of sound finance.[15] Thus, the gold standard system met the trilemma by opting for fixed exchange rates and capital mobility, sometimes at the expense of domestic macroeconomic health. Between 1891 and 1897, for example, the U.S. Treasury put the country through a harsh deflation in the face of persistent speculation on the dollar's departure from gold. These policies were hotly debated; the Populist movement agitated forcefully against gold, but lost.[16]

The balance of political power began to shift only with the First World War, which brought a sea change in the social contract underlying the industrial democracies. For a sample of industrial countries, figure 3.2 shows the Polity IV coding for "institutional democracy" as it evolved over the period bracketing the First World War (the coding ranges from 0 to 11; see Marshall and Jaggers n.d. for details). Other than for the United States (which has a constant score of 10 throughout the sample period, and is omitted from the figure) there is clear evidence of a discrete increase in political openness in the decade or so after 1918.[17] Organized labor emerged as a political power, a counterweight to the interests of capital, as seen in the British labor unrest of the 1920s, which culminated in a general strike. Great Britain's return to gold in 1925 led the way to a restored international gold standard and a limited resurgence of international finance, but weaknesses in the rebuilt system helped propagate a global depression after the 1929 U.S. downturn.

Following (and in some cases anticipating) Great Britain's example, many countries abandoned the gold standard in the early 1930s and depreciated their currencies; many also resorted to trade and capital controls in order to manage independently their exchange rates and domestic policies. Those countries in the "gold bloc," which stubbornly clung to gold through the mid-1930s, showed the steepest output and price-level declines. James's (2001, 189–97) account of French policymakers' vacillation between controls and devaluation well illustrates the interaction between political pressures and the trilemma. Eventually, in the 1930s, all countries jettisoned rigid exchange rate targets and open capital markets in favor of domestic macroeconomic goals.[18]

---

15. See Bordo and Schwartz (1984); Eichengreen (1996).

16. Frieden's (1997) econometric evidence shows how financial interests promoted U.S. adherence to gold, whereas those who would have gained from currency depreciation favored silver. A similar debate over the monetary regime arose in Germany, where Prussian agriculture estate owners lobbied for relaxing the restraints of the gold standard (but were much more successful at getting tariff protection). See Gerschenkron (1943, 57n. 62).

17. The variable is composed of separate codings for the "competitiveness of political participation," the "openness and competitiveness of executive recruitment," and "constraints on the chief executive." We do not plot the variable during periods of political interruption or transition. These data are comparable to the Polity III source used to construct the index of global democratization presented by Niall Ferguson in the panel discussion that concludes this volume.

18. See Eichengreen and Sachs (1985); Temin (1989); Eichengreen (1992); Bernanke and Carey (1996); Obstfeld and Taylor (1998).

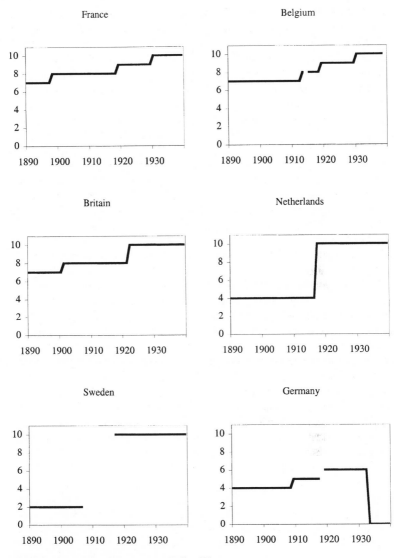

Fig. 3.2   Institutional democracy, Polity IV scores
Source: Marshall and Jaggers (n.d.).

These decisions reflected the shift in political power solidified by the First World War. They also signaled the beginnings of a new consensus on the role of economic policy that would endure through the inflationary 1970s. As an immediate consequence, however, the Great Depression discredited gold-standard orthodoxy and brought Keynesian ideas about macroeconomic management to the fore. It also made financial markets and financial practitioners unpopular. Their supposed excesses and attachment to gold became identified in the public mind as causes of the economic calamity. In the United States, the New Deal brought a Jacksonian hostility toward eastern (read: New York) high finance back to Washington. Financial markets were more closely regulated, and the Federal Reserve was brought under heavier Treasury influence. Similar reactions occurred in other countries.

Changed attitudes toward financial activities and economic management underlay the new postwar economic order negotiated at Bretton Woods, New Hampshire, in July 1944. Forty-four allied countries set up a system based on fixed, but adjustable, exchange parities, in the belief that floating exchange rates would exhibit instability and damage international trade. At the center of the system was the IMF. The IMF's prime function was as a source of hard-currency loans to governments that might otherwise have to put their economies temporarily into recession to maintain a fixed exchange rate. Countries experiencing permanent balance-of-payments problems had the option of realigning their currencies, subject to IMF approval.[19]

Importantly, the IMF's founders viewed its lending capability as primarily a substitute for, not a complement to, private capital inflows. Interwar experience had given the latter a reputation as unreliable at best and, at worst, as a dangerous source of disturbances. Broad, encompassing controls over private capital movement, perfected in wartime, were expected to continue. The IMF's Articles of Agreement explicitly empowered countries to impose new capital controls. Articles VIII and XIV of the IMF agreement did demand that countries' currencies eventually be made convertible—in effect, freely saleable to the issuing central bank, at the official exchange parity, for dollars or gold. But this privilege was to be extended only if the country's currency had been earned through current account transactions. Convertibility on capital account, as opposed to current-account convertibility, was not viewed as mandatory or desirable.

Unfortunately, a wide extent even of current-account convertibility took many years to achieve, and even then it was often restricted to nonresidents. In the interim, countries resorted to bilateral trade deals that required balanced or nearly balanced trade between every pair of trading partners. If France had an export surplus with Great Britain, and Great Britain a surplus with Germany, then Great Britain could not use its excess deutsche marks to obtain dollars with which to pay France. Germany had very few dollars and guarded them jealously for critical imports from the Americas. Instead, each country would try to divert import demand toward countries with high demand for its goods, and to direct its exports toward countries whose goods were favored domestically.

19. On the Bretton Woods system, see Bordo and Eichengreen (1993).

Convertibility gridlock in Europe and its dependencies was ended through a regional multilateral clearing scheme, the European Payments Union (EPU). The clearing scheme was set up in 1950 and some countries reached de facto convertibility by mid-decade. But it was not until 27 December 1958 that Europe officially embraced convertibility and ended the EPU. Although most European countries still chose to retain extensive capital controls (Germany being the main exception), the return to convertibility, important as it was in promoting multilateral trade growth, also increased the opportunities for disguised capital movements. These might take the form, for example, of misinvoicing, or of accelerated or delayed merchandise payments. Buoyant growth encouraged some countries in further financial liberalization, although the United States, worried about its gold losses, raised progressively higher barriers to capital outflow over the 1960s. Eventually, the Bretton Woods system's very successes hastened its collapse by resurrecting the trilemma.[20]

Key countries in the system, notably the United States (fearful of slower growth) and Germany (fearful of higher inflation), proved unwilling to accept the domestic policy implications of maintaining fixed rates. Even the limited capital mobility of the early 1970s proved sufficient to allow furious speculative attacks on the major currencies, and after vain attempts to restore fixed dollar exchange rates, the industrial countries retreated to floating rates early in 1973. Although viewed at the time as a temporary emergency measure, the floating-dollar-rate regime is still with us thirty years later.

Floating exchange rates have allowed the explosion in international financial markets experienced over the same three decades. Freed from one element of the trilemma—fixed exchange rates—countries have been able to open their capital markets while still retaining the flexibility to deploy monetary policy in pursuit of national objectives. No doubt the experience gained after the inflationary 1970s in anchoring monetary policy to avoid price instability has helped to promote ongoing financial integration. Perhaps for the first time in history, countries have learned how to keep inflation in check under fiat monies and floating exchange rates.

There are several potentially valid reasons, however, for countries to still fix their exchange rates—for example, to keep a better lid on inflation or to counter exchange-rate instability due to financial market shocks. Such arguments may find particular resonance, of course, in developing countries. However, few countries that have tried to fix have succeeded for long; eventually, exchange rate stability tends to come into conflict with other policy objectives, the capital markets catch on to the government's predicament, and a crisis adds enough economic pain to make the authorities give in. In recent years only a very few major countries have observed the discipline of

20. See Triffin (1957); Einzig (1968); Bordo and Eichengreen (2001).

fixed exchange rates for at least five years, and most of those were rather special cases.[21]

The European Union members that maintained mutually fixed rates prior to January 1999 were aided by market confidence in their own planned solution to the trilemma, a near-term currency merger. Developing countries have generally not fared so well. Even Hong Kong, which operates a currency board supposedly subordinated to maintaining the Hong Kong–U.S. dollar peg, suffered repeated speculative attacks in the Asian crisis period. Another currency-board experiment, Argentina, held to its 1:1 dollar exchange rate from April 1991 for a remarkable stint of more than ten years. To accomplish that feat, the country relied on IMF and private credit and, despite episodes of growth, endured levels of unemployment higher than many countries could tolerate. It suffered especially acutely after Brazil moved to a float in January 1999. Three years later Argentina's political and economic arrangements disintegrated in the face of external default (December 2001) and currency collapse (January–February 2002).

For most larger countries, the trend toward greater financial openness has been accompanied—inevitably, we would argue—by a declining reliance on pegged exchange rates in favor of greater exchange rate flexibility. Some countries have opted for a different solution, however, adopting extreme straitjackets for monetary policy in order to peg an exchange rate. If monetary policy is geared toward domestic considerations, capital mobility or the exchange rate target must go. If, instead, fixed exchange rates and integration into the global capital market are the primary desiderata, monetary policy must be subjugated to those ends.

The details of this argument require a book-length discourse (Obstfeld and Taylor 2003), which allows a full survey of the empirical evidence and the historical record, but we can already pinpoint the key turning points (see table 3.1). The Great Depression stands as the watershed here, in that it was caused by an ill-advised subordination of monetary policy to an exchange rate constraint (the gold standard), which led to a chaotic time of troubles in which countries experimented, typically noncooperatively, with alternative modes of addressing the fundamental trilemma. Interwar experience, in turn, discredited the gold standard and led to a new and fairly universal policy consensus. The new consensus shaped the more cooperative postwar international economic order fashioned by Harry Dexter White and John Maynard Keynes, but implanted within that order the seeds of its own eventual destruction a quarter-century later. The global financial nexus that has evolved since then rests on a solution to the basic open-economy trilemma quite different than that envisioned by Keynes or White—one that allows considerable freedom for capital movements and gives the major currency areas freedom to pursue internal goals, but largely leaves their mutual exchange rates as the equilibrating residual.

---

21. See Obstfeld and Rogoff (1995).

Table 3.1   **The Trilemma and Major Phases of Capital Mobility**

Era	Sacrifices Countries Choose to Resolve Trilemma			Notes
	Activist Policies	Capital Mobility	Fixed Exchange Rate	
Gold standard	Most	Few	Few	Broad consensus
Interwar (when off gold)	Few	Several	Most	Capital controls, especially in Central Europe and Latin America
Bretton Woods	Few	Most	Few	Broad consensus
Float	Few	Few	Many	Some consensus, except currency boards, dollarization, etc.

3.1.5 Summary

As always, we have to consider the potential costs and benefits of international capital mobility for the national participants. Clearly, the ability to lend or borrow represents, trivially, a loosening of constraints relative to a perfectly closed economy. In this dimension, at least, open trade in financial markets offers unambiguous gains relative to a closed economy. Such trades permit insurance and the smoothing of shocks, and allow capital to seek out its highest rewards, implying the usual gains-from-trade results.

However, in other ways, international financial mobility raises concerns, particularly for policymakers attached to certain policy goals that may be inconsistent with the free flow of capital across international boundaries. In addition, the risks of financial and balance-of-payments crises—some of them self-fulfilling crises unrelated to "fundamentals"—may represent further obstacles to the adoption of free capital markets.

Although these are very much contemporary issues in world capital markets, the questions they raise can be traced back to the very founding of international financial markets centuries ago during the Renaissance. Then, too, advanced forms of financial asset trades developed very quickly, sometimes as a response to Church-imposed constraints such as usury proscriptions. Financial innovation was subject to suspicion from various quarters, both public and private. Thus, calls for the regulation and restriction of financial market activity have been with us since the earliest days.

Despite these fears, by the late nineteenth century a succession of technological breakthroughs, and a gradual institutional evolution, had positioned many nations in a newly forming international capital market. This network of nations embraced modern financial instruments and operated virtually free of controls on the part of governments. Under the gold standard monetary regime, this flourishing global market for capital reached at least a local peak in the decades just prior to World War I.

The subsequent history of the twentieth century showed that this seemingly linear path toward ever more technological progress and institutional sophistication in a liberal world order could indeed be upset. Two global wars and a depression led the world down an autarkic path. Conflicting policy goals and democratic tensions often put the interests of global capital at a low premium relative to other objectives. Activist governments appealed to capital controls to sidestep the discipline of external markets, invoking monetary policy as a tool of macroeconomic control.

These events demonstrate the power of the macroeconomic policy trilemma to account for many of the ups and downs in global capital market evolution in the twentieth century. In the next section, we match up these stylized facts with details from the quantitative and institutional record, so as to better document the course of events. It is a remarkable history without which today's economic, financial, political, and institutional landscape cannot be fully understood.

3.2   Evidence

In theory and practice, the extent of international capital mobility can have profound implications for the operation of individual and global economies. With respect to theory, the applicability of various classes of macroeconomic models rests on many assumptions, and not the least important of these are axioms linked to the closure of the model in the capital market. The predictions of a theory and its usefulness for policy debates can revolve critically on this part of the structure.

The importance of these issues for policy is not surprising at all, and a moment's reflection on practical aspects of macroeconomic policy choice underscores the impact that capital mobility can have on the efficacy of various interventions: Trivially, if capital is perfectly mobile, this dooms to failure any attempts to manipulate local asset prices to make them deviate from global prices, including the most critical macroeconomic asset price, the interest rate. Thus, the feasibility and relevance of key policy actions cannot be judged, absent some informed position on the extent to which local economic conditions are in any way separable from global conditions. This means an empirical measure of market integration is implicitly, although rarely explicitly, a necessary adjunct to any policy discussion. Although recent globalization trends have brought this issue to the fore, this paper shows how the experience of longer-run macroeconomic history can clarify and inform these debates.

In attacking the problem of measuring market integration, economists have no universally recognized criterion to turn to. For example, imagine the simple expedient of examining price differentials: Prices would be identical in two identical neighboring economies, being determined in each by the identical structures of tastes, technologies, and endowments; but if the two markets were physically separated by an infinitely high transaction-cost barrier one could hardly describe them as being integrated in a single market, as the equality of prices was merely a chance event. Or consider looking at the size of flows between two markets as a gauge of mobility; this is an equally flawed criterion, for suppose we now destroyed the barrier between the two economies just mentioned, and reduced transaction costs to zero. We would then truly have a single integrated market, but because, on either side of the barrier, prices were identical in autarky, there would be no incentive for any good or factor to move after the barrier disappeared.

Thus, convergence of prices and movements of goods are not unambiguous indicators of market integration. One could run through any number of other putative criteria for market integration, examining perhaps the levels or correlations of prices or quantities, and find essentially the same kind of weakness: All such tests may be able to evaluate market integration, but only as a joint hypothesis test where some auxiliary assumptions are needed to make the test meaningful.

Given this impasse, a historical study such as the present paper is potentially valuable in two respects. First, we can use a very large array of data sources covering different aspects of international capital mobility over the last 100 years or more. Without being wedded to a single criterion, we can attempt to make inferences about the path of global capital mobility with a battery of tests, using both quantity and price criteria of various kinds. As long as important caveats are kept in mind about each method, especially the auxiliary assumptions required for meaningful inference, we can essay a broad-based approach to the evidence. Should the different methods all lead to a similar conclusion we would be in a stronger position than if we simply relied on a single test.

Historical work offers a second benefit in that it provides a natural set of benchmarks for our understanding of today's situation. In addition to the many competing tests for capital mobility, we also face the problem that almost every test is usually a matter of degree, of interpreting a parameter or a measure of dispersion or some other variable or coefficient. We face the typical empirical conundrums (how big is big? or how fast is fast?) in placing an absolute meaning on these measures.

A historical perspective allows a more nuanced view, and places all such inferences in a relative context: When we say that a parameter for capital mobility is big, this is easier to interpret if we can say that by this we mean bigger than a decade or a century ago. The historical focus of this paper will be directed at addressing just such concerns.[22] We examine the broadest range of data over the last 100-plus years to see what has happened to the degree of capital mobility in a cross-section of countries.[23]

---

22. But note that, again, auxiliary assumptions will be necessary, and the caveats will be considered along the way; for example, what if neighboring economies became exogenously more or less identical over time, but no more or less integrated in terms of transaction costs?

23. Given the limitations of the data, we will frequently be restricted to looking at between a dozen and twenty countries for which long-run macroeconomic statistics are available, and this sample will be dominated by today's developed countries, including most of the Organization for Economic Cooperation and Development (OECD) countries. However, we also have long data series for some developing countries such as Argentina, Brazil, and Mexico; and in some criteria, such as our opening look at the evolution of the stock of foreign investments, we can examine a much broader sample.

The empirical work begins by looking at quantity data, focusing on changes in the stocks of foreign capital over a century or more.[24] Subsequent empirical sketches focus on price-based criteria for capital market integration, looking at nominal interest arbitrage, real interest rate convergence, and equity returns.

3.2.1   Gross Stocks of Foreign Capital

In this section we examine the extant data on foreign capital stocks to get some sense of the evolution of the global market. We seek some measure of the size of foreign investment globally that is appropriately scaled and consistent over time.

Although the concept is simple, the measurement is not. Perhaps the simplest measure of the activity in the global capital market is obtained by looking at the total stock of overseas investment at a point in time. Suppose that the total asset stock in country or region i, owned by country or region j, at time t is A_{ijt}. Included in here is the domestically owned capital stock A_{ijt}. Of interest are two concepts: What assets of country j reside overseas, and what liabilities of country i are held overseas?

A relatively easy hurdle to surmount concerns normalization of the data; foreign investment stocks are commonly measured at a point in time in current nominal terms, in most cases U.S. dollars. Obviously, the growth of both the national and international economies might be associated with an increase in such a nominal quantity, as would any long-run inflation. These trends would have nothing to do with market integration per se. To overcome this problem, we elected to normalize foreign capital at each point in time by some measure of the size of the world economy, dividing through by a denominator in the form of a nominal size index.

A seemingly ideal denominator, given that the numerator is the stock of foreign-owned capital, would probably be the total stock of capital, whether financial or real. The problem with using financial capital measures is that they have greatly multiplied over the long run as financial development has expanded the number of balance sheets in the economy, thanks to the rise of numerous financial intermediaries.[25] This trend, in principle, could happen at any point in time without any underlying change in the extent of foreign asset holdings. The problem with using real capital stocks is that data construction is fraught with difficulty.[26]

---

24. Elsewhere we have examined flows of foreign capital, and more refined quantity criteria using the correlations of saving and investment over the long run (Obstfeld and Taylor 1998, 2003).

25. See Goldsmith (1985).

26. Only a few countries have reliable data from which to estimate capital stocks. Most of these estimates are accurate only at benchmark censuses, and in between census dates they rely on combinations of interpolation and estimation based on investment-flow data and depreciation assumptions. Most of these estimates are calculated in real (constant price) rather than nominal (current price) terms, which makes them incommensurate with the nominally mea-

Given these problems we chose a simpler and more readily available measure of the size of an economy, namely the level of output Y measured in current prices in a common currency unit.[27] Over short horizons, unless the capital-output ratio were to move dramatically, the ratio of foreign capital to output should be adequate as a proxy measure of the penetration of foreign capital in any economy. Over the long run, difficulties might arise if the capital-output ratio has changed significantly over time—but we have little firm evidence to suggest that it has.[28] Thus, as a result of these long-run data constraints, our analysis focuses on capital-to-GDP ratios of the forms

(1)   Foreign Assets-to-GDP Ratio$_{it}$ $= \sum_{j \neq i} \frac{A_{jit}}{Y_{it}}$ and

(2)   Foreign Liabilities-to-GDP Ratio$_{it}$ $= \sum_{j \neq i} \frac{A_{ijt}}{Y_{it}}$.

However, even with the concept established, measurement is still problematic in the case of the numerator. It is in fact very difficult to discover the extent of foreign capital in an economy using both contemporary and historical data. For example, the IMF has always reported balance-of-payments flow transactions in its *International Financial Statistics*. It is straightforward for most of the recent postwar period to discover the annual flows of equity, debt, or other forms of capital account transactions from these accounts. Conversely, it was only in 1997 that the IMF began reporting the corresponding stock data, namely, the international investment position of each country. These data are also more sparse, beginning in 1980 for fewer than a dozen countries, and expanding to about thirty countries by the mid-1990s.

The paucity of data is understandable, since the collection burden for these data is much more significant: Knowing the size of a bond issue in a single year reveals the flow transaction size; knowing the implications for future stocks requires, for example, tracking each debt and equity item and its fluctuating market value over time, and maintaining an aggregate of these data. The stock data are not simply a temporal aggregate of flows: The

sured foreign capital data. At the end of the day, we would be unlikely to find more than a handful of countries for which this technique would be feasible for the entire twentieth century, and certainly nothing like global coverage would be possible even for recent years.

27. For the GDP data we rely on Maddison's (1995) constant price 1990 U.S. dollar estimates of output for the period from 1820. These figures are then "reflated" using a U.S. price deflator to obtain estimates of nominal U.S. dollar "world" GDP at each benchmark date. This approach is crude, since, in particular, it relies on a purchasing power parity assumption. Ideally we would want historical series on nominal GDP and exchange rates, to estimate a common (U.S. dollar) GDP figure at various historical dates.

28. But for exactly the reasons just mentioned, since we have no capital stock data for many countries, it is hard to form a sample of capital-output ratios to see how these differ across time and space. The conventional wisdom is that the capital-output ratio ranges from three to four for most countries, although perhaps lower in capital-scarce developing countries.

stock value depends on past flows; capital gains and losses; any retirements of principal or buybacks of equity; defaults and reschedulings; and a host of other factors. Not surprisingly, accurate data of this type are hard to assemble.[29] Just as the IMF has had difficulty doing so, so too have economic historians. Looking back over the nineteenth and twentieth centuries an exhaustive search across many different sources yields only a handful of benchmark years in which estimates have been made, an effort that draws on the work of dozens of scholars in official institutions and numerous other individual efforts.[30]

It is based on these efforts that we can put together a fragmentary, but still potentially illuminating, historical description in table 3.2 and figure 3.3. Displayed here are nominal foreign investment and output data for major countries and regions, grouped according to assets and liabilities. Many cells are empty because data are unavailable, but where possible, summary data have been derived to illustrate the ratio of foreign capital to output, and the share of various countries in foreign investment activity.

What do the data show? On the asset side it is immediately apparent that for all of the nineteenth century, and until the interwar period, the British were rightly termed the "bankers to the world"; at its peak, the British share of total global foreign investment was almost 80 percent. This is far above the recent U.S. share of global foreign assets, a mere 22 percent in 1995, and still higher than the maximum U.S. share of 50 percent circa 1960. The only rivals to the British in the early nineteenth century were the Dutch, who according to these figures held perhaps 30 percent of global assets in 1825. This comes as no surprise given what we know of Amsterdam's early preeminence as the first global financial center before London's rise to dominance in the eighteenth and nineteenth centuries. By the late nineteenth century both Paris and Berlin had also emerged as major financial centers, and, as their economies grew and industrialized, French and German holdings of foreign capital rose significantly, each eclipsing the Dutch position.

In this era the United States was a debtor rather than a creditor nation, and was only starting to emerge as a major lender and foreign asset holder after 1900. European borrowing from the United States in World War I then suddenly made the United States a big creditor. This came at a time when she was ready, if not altogether willing, to assume the mantle of "banker to the world," following Great Britain's abdication of this position under the burden of war and recovery in the 1910s and 1920s.[31] But the dislocations of the interwar years were to postpone the United States' rise as a foreign creditor,

29. An important new source, however, is Lane and Milesi-Ferretti (2001). See below.
30. See, for example, Paish (1914), Feis (1931), Lewis (1938), Rippy (1959), Woodruff (1967), and Twomey (2000). Twomey, following Feinstein (1990), favors the estimates of Paish and the other aforementioned authors, versus the downward revisions to pre-1914 British overseas investment proposed by Platt (1986).
31. This Anglo-American transfer of hegemonic power is discussed by Kindleberger (1986) and by Bordo, Edelstein, and Rockoff (1999). Gallarotti (1995) challenges the view that Great Britain acted as a monetary hegemon up to 1914.

Table 3.2 Foreign Capital Stocks

	1825	1855	1870	1900	1914	1930	1938	1945	1960	1971	1980	1985	1990	1995
Assets														
United Kingdom	0.5[a]	0.7[a]	4.9[a]	12.1[a]	19.5[a]	18.2[a]	22.9[c]	14.2[a]	26.4[a]	—	551[d]	857[d]	1,760[d]	2,490[d]
France	0.1[a]	—	2.5[a]	5.2[a]	8.6[a]	3.5[a]	3.9[e]	—	—	—	268[d]	428[d]	736[d]	1,100[d]
Germany	—	—	—	4.8[a]	6.7[a]	1.1[a]	0.7[e]	—	1.2[a]	—	247[d]	342[d]	1,100[d]	1,670[d]
The Netherlands	0.3[a]	0.2[a]	0.3[a]	1.1[a]	1.2[a]	2.3[a]	4.8[c]	3.7[a]	27.6[a]	—	99[d]	178[d]	418[d]	712[d]
United States	0.0[a]	0.0[a]	0.0[a]	0.5[a]	2.5[a]	14.7[a]	11.5[a]	15.3[a]	63.6[a]	—	775[d]	1,300[d]	2,180[d]	3,350[d]
Canada				0.1[a]	0.2[a]	1.3[a]	1.9[e]			—	92[d]	129[d]	227[d]	302[d]
Japan							1.2[c]			—	160[d]	437[d]	1,860[d]	2,720[d]
Other Europe							4.6[c]			—	503[d]	715[d]	1,777[d]	2,855[d]
Other							6.0[c]	2.0[a]	5.9[a]	—	94[d]	123[d]	214[d]	337[d]
All	0.9[a]	0.9[a]	7.7[a]	23.8[a]	38.7[a]	41.1[a]	52.8[c]	35.2[a]	147.7[a]	4,733[b]	2,800[d]	4,508[d]	10,272[d]	15,536[d]
World GDP			111[b]	128[b]	221[b]	491[b]	491[b]	722[b]	1,942[b]		11,118[e]	12,455[e]	21,141[e]	25,110[e]
Sample GDP			16[f]	43[f]	76[f]	149[f]	182[f]	273[f]	671[f]		7,806[d]	9,705[d]	17,250[d]	21,956[d]
Sample size			4[f]	7[f]	7[f]	7[f]	7[f]	7[f]	7[f]		25[d]	25[d]	25[d]	25[d]
Assets/sample GDP			0.47	0.55	0.51	0.28	0.26	0.12	0.18		0.36	0.46	0.60	0.71
Assets/world GDP			0.07	0.19	0.18	0.08	0.11	0.05	0.06		0.25	0.36	0.49	0.62
United Kingdom/all	0.56	0.78	0.64	0.51	0.50	0.44	0.43	0.40	0.21		0.20	0.19	0.17	0.16
United States/all	0.00	0.00	0.00	0.02	0.06	0.36	0.22	0.43	0.51		0.28	0.29	0.21	0.22
Liabilities														
Europe				5.4[a]	12.0[a]		10.3[a]		7.6[a]		1,457[d]	2,248[d]	5,405[d]	8,592[d]
North America				2.6[a]	11.1[a]		13.7[a]		12.5a		684[d]	1,412[d]	2,830[d]	4,681[d]
Australia and New Zealand				1.6[a]	2.0[a]		4.5[a]		2.2[a]		71[d]	118[d]	216[d]	318[d]
Japan				0.1[a]	1.0[a]		0.6[a]		0.3[a]		147[d]	307[d]	1,530[d]	1,970[d]
Latin America				2.9[g]	8.9[g]		11.3[g]		9.2[a]	57[g]	250[g]	—	505[g]	768[g]

(continued)

Table 3.2 (continued)

	1825	1855	1870	1900	1914	1930	1938	1945	1960	1971	1980	1985	1990	1995
Asia (exc. Japan)	—	—	—	2.4[g]	6.8[g]	—	10.6[g]	—	2.7[a]	29[a]	129[g]	—	524[g]	960[g]
Africa	—	—	—	3.0[g]	4.1[g]	—	4.0[g]	—	2.2[a]	19[a]	124[g]	—	306[g]	353[g]
Developing countries	—	—	—	6.0[g]	13.0[g]	—	25.9[g]	—	14.1[a]	107[g]	506[g]	—	1,338[g]	2,086[g]
All	—	—	—	18.0[a]	45.5[a]	—	55.0[a]	—	39.9[a]	—	3,368[c,f]	—	12,655[c,f]	19,728[c,f]
World GDP	—	—	111[b]	128[b]	221[b]	491[b]	491[b]	722[b]	1,942[b]	4,733[b]	11,118[e]	12,455[e]	21,141[e]	25,110[e]
Sample GDP	—	—	—	—	—	—	—	—	—	—	9,508[d]	—	19,294[d]	25,043[d]
Sample size	—	—	—	—	—	—	—	—	—	—	65[e,f]	—	65[e,f]	65[e,f]
Liabilities/sample GDP	—	—	—	—	—	—	—	—	—	—	0.35	—	0.66	0.79
Liabilities/world GDP	—	—	—	0.14	0.21	—	0.11	—	0.02	—	0.30	—	0.60	0.79
Developing countries/all	—	—	—	0.33	0.29	—	0.47	—	0.35	—	0.15	—	0.11	0.11

Note: Units for foreign investment and GDP are billions of current U.S. dollars.

[a] From Woodruff (1967, 150–59).
[b] From Lewis (1945, 292–97).
[c] From Maddison (1995); sample of 199 countries; 1990 U.S. dollars converted to current dollars using U.S. GDP deflator; some interpolation.
[d] Excludes "Other Europe" and "Other"; GDP data from Mitchell (1992, 1993, 1995), Maddison (1995, 2001), and unpublished data from Michael Bordo.
[e] From Twomey (1998; unpublished worksheets).
[f] From IMF (1997). Up to twenty-six countries, fixed sample, trend interpolation on missing data.
[g] From World Bank (1994).

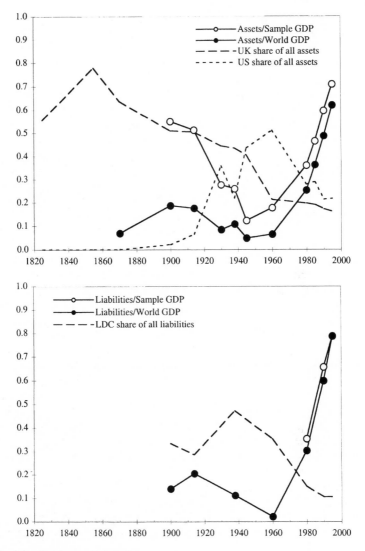

Fig. 3.3   Foreign capital stocks
Source: Table 3.2.

and New York's pivotal role as a financial center. After 1945, however, the United States decisively surpassed Great Britain as the major international asset holder, a position that has never since been challenged.[32]

32. Of course, this is the gross foreign investment position, not the net position. The United States is also now the world's number-one debtor nation, in both gross and net terms, having become a net debtor for the first time since the First World War in the late 1980s.

How big were nineteenth century holdings of foreign assets? In 1870 we estimate that foreign assets were just 7 percent of world gross domestic product (GDP), but this figure rose quickly, to just below 20 percent in the years 1900–14 at the zenith of the classical gold standard. During the interwar period, the collapse was swift, and foreign assets were only 8 percent of world output by 1930, 11 percent in 1938, and just 5 percent in 1945. Since this low point, the ratio has climbed, to 6 percent in 1960, 25 percent in 1980, and then climbing dramatically to 62 percent in 1995. Thus, the 1900–14 ratio of foreign investment to output in the world economy was not equaled again until 1980, but has now been approximately tripled.

An alternative measure recognizes the incompleteness of the data sources: For many countries we have no information on foreign investments at all, so a zero has been placed in the numerator, although that country's output has been included in the denominator as part of the world GDP estimate. This is an unfortunate aspect of our estimation procedure, and makes the above ratio likely an underestimate, or lower bound, for the true ratio of foreign assets to output. One way to correct this is to include in the denominator only the countries for which we actually have data on foreign investment in the numerator.[33] This procedure yields an estimate we term the ratio of foreign assets to sample GDP. This is likely an overestimate, or upper bound, for the true ratio, largely because in historical data, if not in contemporary sources, attention in the collection of foreign investment data has usually focused on the principal players, that is, the countries that have significant foreign asset holdings.[34]

Given all these concerns, does the ratio to sample GDP evolve in a very different way? No, but the recent upswing is not as pronounced using this alternative measure. The two ratios are very close after 1980. But before 1945 they are quite far apart: From 1870 to 1914, the sample of seven countries has a foreign asset to GDP ratio of over 50 percent, far above the world figure of 7 to 20 percent. By this measure we only surpassed the 1914 ratio as recently as 1990, and narrowly even then.

Clearly, these seven major creditors were exceptionally internationally diversified in the late nineteenth century in a way that no group of countries is today. By this reckoning, in countries like today's United States, we still have yet to see a return to the extremely high degree of international port-

33. That sample of countries is much less than the entire world, as we have noted. Until 1960, it includes only the seven major creditor countries noted in table 3.2; after 1980, we rely on the IMF sample from which we can identify up to thirty countries with foreign investment and GDP data.

34. That is, we are probably restricted in these samples to countries with individually high ratios of foreign assets to GDP. For example, in the rest of Europe circa 1914, we would be unlikely to find countries with portfolios as diversified internationally as those of the British, French, Germans, and Dutch. If we included those other countries it would probably bring our estimated ratio down. However, in the 1980s and 1990s IMF data, the problem is much less severe since we observe many more countries, and both large and small asset holders.

folio diversification seen in, say, Great Britain in the 1900–14 period, a historical finding that places in historical perspective the ongoing international diversification puzzle.[35]

Is the picture similar for liabilities as well as assets? Essentially, yes. The data are much more fragmentary here, with none in the nineteenth century, when the information for the key creditor nations was perhaps simpler to collect than data for a multitude of debtors. Even so, we have some estimates running from 1900 to the present at a few key dates. The ratio of liabilities to world GDP follows a path very much like that of the asset ratio, which is reassuring: They are each approximations built from different data sources at certain time points, although, in principle, they should be equal. Again, the ratio reaches a local maximum in 1914 of 21 percent, collapsing in the interwar period to 11 percent in 1938, and just 2 percent in 1960. By 1980 it had exceeded the 1914 level and stood at 30 percent. By 1995, the ratio was 79 percent.

To summarize, data on gross international asset positions seem broadly consistent with the idea of a U shape in the evolution of international capital mobility since the late nineteenth century, although it is less clear how we should compare the degree of diversification attained by some countries then with today's apparently significant, albeit declining, home bias in foreign asset holdings. Figuring whether too much or too little diversification existed at any point must remain conjectural, and conclusions would hinge on a calibrated and estimated portfolio model applied historically. This is certainly an object for future research. However, unless the global economy has dramatically changed in terms of the risk-return profile of assets and their global distribution, we have no prior reason to expect the efficient degree of diversification to have changed. For the present we can just say that, unless such a massive change did occur in the 1914–45 period, and unless it was then promptly reversed in the 1945–90 period, we cannot explain the time path of foreign capital stocks seen in table 3.2 and figure 3.3 except as a result of a dramatic decline in capital mobility in the interwar period, and a very slow recovery of capital mobility thereafter.

There is another important dimension of international asset stock data that we have not yet discussed: the evolution of net stocks, that is, the behavior of longer term development flows, as distinct from diversification flows. The literature on the Feldstein-Horioka (1980) paradox alerts us to the possibility that gross flows are orders of magnitude above net flows. We postpone discussion of that issue until later.

3.2.2   Real Interest Rate Convergence

A fundamental property of fully integrated international capital markets is that investors are indifferent on the margin between any two activities to

---

35. On the international diversification puzzle see Lewis (1999).

which they allocate capital, regardless of national location. International real interest rate equality would hold in the long run in a world where capital moves freely across borders and technological diffusion tends to drive a convergence process for national production possibilities.[36]

One basic indication of internationally integrated financial markets therefore would be the statistical stationarity of long-term real interest differentials. We investigate this property using long-term real interest rate data constructed from the Global Financial Data database. For a nominal interest rate i_t we use the monthly series on long-term government bond yields, which applies to bonds of maturities of seven years or longer. For inflation $\pi_t = (P_{t+12} - P_t)/P_t$ we use the ex post twelve-month forward rate of change of the consumer price index. The ex post real interest rate is then calculated as $r_t = i_t - \pi_t$, and for now we make the standard assumption that this is equal to the ex ante real rate plus a white-noise stationary forecast error. We focus on real long-term bond yields because these are most directly related to financing costs for capital investments, and hence to the expected marginal yield on investment. It is the latter variable we would like to be able to measure directly in order to evaluate the international mobility of capital.[37]

We consider three countries in our sample, relative to the United States as a base country. They are Great Britain, France, and Germany. We should note that the series are as consistent as they can be given the changing types of domestic bonds issued by the various countries over the last century, although maturities do change at several points for some countries. There are a few exceptions, such as the British consol, which has a continuous time series. We also note that prior to 1914 most countries have only annual price indices, meaning that our derived inflation series will also consist of annual observations, the exceptions being the United States and Great Britain. For the other two countries, we construct monthly series of ex post real interest rates by matching monthly nominal interest rates within a year t with the realized inflation rate between years $t + 1$ and t. Of course, in measuring long-term real interest rates, we would like to proxy long-term inflation expectations, but that cannot be done reliably. Thus we follow earlier empirical studies in utilizing a relatively short-horizon inflation measure notwithstanding the longer term of the corresponding nominal interest rates.

The real interest rate differential for three countries is shown in figure 3.4. This differential is calculated as $\tilde{r}_t = r_t - r_{US,t}$. This is the first time real inter-

---

36. We focus on long-term real interest rates here because these rates are most closely linked to the cost of long-lived capital, because the slow mean reversion in real exchange rates makes it difficult to discern expected exchange rate changes in short-term data, and because risk premia can be reduced over long horizons if long-run purchasing power parity holds.

37. For recent data, there is substantial evidence that international real interest rate differentials on short-term bonds are I(0); see, for example, Meese and Rogoff (1988) and Edison and Melick (1999).

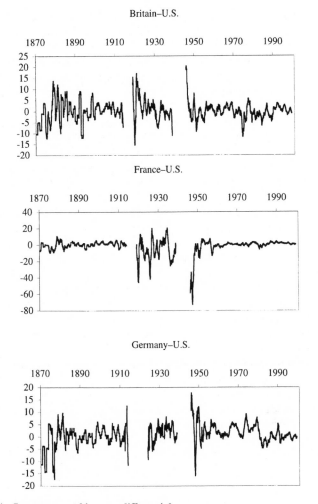

Fig. 3.4   Long-term real interest differentials

Notes: See text. The differential is calculated relative to the United States as $\tilde{r}_t = r_t - r_{US,t}$.

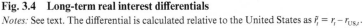

est rates over more than a century have been analyzed for this set of countries at such high frequency, so it is of interest to start by evaluating some general features of the data. The most striking impression conveyed by the figure is that differentials have varied widely over time, but have stayed relatively close to a zero mean. That is, the series appears to have been stationary over the very long run, and even in shorter subperiods.

The figures also reveal some of the changing coherence of real interest rates in the subperiods. To avoid noisy data from nonmarket periods, the wartime years (1914–18, 1939–45) have been omitted, as has the German hyperinflation period (1919–23). Again we can focus on the four different subperiods that correspond to the four different monetary regimes: the gold standard (1890–1914), the interwar period (1921–38), Bretton Woods and the brief transitional period prior to generalized floating (1951–73), and the float (1974–2000).[38]

Allowing for the annual inflation data used before 1914, we can see that real interest differentials became somewhat more volatile in the interwar period, with a larger variance (this is less obvious in the German case because the hyperinflation period has been omitted). There is a decline in this volatility after 1950, and perhaps very little change between the pre-1974 period and the float. The latter observation may seem surprising, except that it is consistent with observations that, aside from nominal and real exchange rate volatility, there is little difference in the behavior of macro fundamentals between fixed and floating rate regimes, at least for developed countries (e.g., Baxter and Stockman 1989).

With no real interest rate divergence apparent, these figures provide prima facie evidence that real interest rates in developed countries have been cointegrated over time, where the differentials between countries appear stationary. A formal test of this hypothesis appears in table 3.3, where we apply two stationarity tests to the data for the period as a whole, as well as in various subperiods. The first test is the traditional augmented Dickey-Fuller (ADF) unit root test, and the second is the Dickey-Fuller generalized least squares (DFGLSu) test, one of a family of enhanced point-optimal and asymptotically efficient unit root tests recently proposed.[39] This table also reports a broader set of tests for the recent float, for an expanded sample including the Group of Seven (G7) plus the Netherlands, for comparison with the contemporary literature.

Where the null is rejected at the 1 percent level, the results show conclusively that the real interest differential has no unit root over the long run. Changes in the variances of series over time, of the kind evident in the preceding figures, may distort unit root tests (Hamori and Tokihisa 1997). However, the hypothesis of a unit root can be rejected in almost all cases at the 1 percent level in all periods except for the recent float. With respect to the recent float, the evidence against a unit root is stronger over the second

38. For the purpose of the present empirical analysis we begin our floating-rate period in early 1974 to be consistent with other empirical literature on the real interest rate–real exchange rate nexus. However, most historians would place the end of the Bretton Woods system in August 1971, the month the U.S. official gold window was shut.

39. See Elliott, Rothenberg, and Stock (1996) and Elliott (1999). We use the DFGLSu test from the latter, which allows for the initial observation to be drawn from the unconditional mean of the series. The RATS code for this procedure is available online at [http://www.estima.com].

Table 3.3 **Stationarity Tests: Long-Term Real Interest Differentials**

	Starting Date	Ending Date	ADF	DFGLSu
		A. Historical epochs		
Great Britain	1890:1	2000:7	−4.30***	−5.54***
France	1890:1	2000:7	−6.05***	−6.36***
Germany	1890:1	2000:7	−4.64***	−5.14***
Great Britain	1890:1	1913:12	−1.38	−3.44***
France	1890:1	1913:12	−3.18**	−4.36***
Germany	1890:1	1913:12	−3.86***	−3.70***
Great Britain	1921:1	1938:12	−3.59***	−4.01***
France	1921:1	1938:12	−2.39	−4.31***
Germany	1921:1	1938:12	−2.42	−2.84**
Great Britain	1951:1	1973:2	−5.09***	−5.37***
France	1951:1	1973:2	−3.81***	−3.34***
Germany	1951:1	1973:2	−3.32**	−3.51***
		B. Recent float		
Great Britain	1974:2	2000:8	−2.42	−3.75***
The Netherlands	1974:2	2000:8	−2.75*	−2.57*
France	1974:2	2000:8	−2.70*	−2.52*
Germany	1974:2	2000:8	−2.82*	−2.73*
Italy	1974:2	2000:8	−2.52	−2.87**
Japan	1974:2	2000:8	−2.20	−2.52*
Canada	1974:2	2000:8	−3.71***	−3.15**
Great Britain	1974:2	1986:3	−2.61*	−2.82**
The Netherlands	1974:2	1986:3	−1.28	−1.19
France	1974:2	1986:3	−2.21	−1.77
Germany	1974:2	1986:3	−1.77	−1.64
Italy	1974:2	1986:3	−2.56	−2.89**
Japan	1974:2	1986:3	−1.50	−1.72
Canada	1974:2	1986:3	−1.92	−1.93
Great Britain	1986:4	2000:7	−2.01	−2.62*
The Netherlands	1986:4	2000:7	−2.61*	−2.37
France	1986:4	2000:7	−2.25	−2.50*
Germany	1986:4	2000:7	−3.34**	−2.83**
Italy	1986:4	2000:7	−2.54	−2.55*
Japan	1986:4	2000:7	−2.43	−2.55*
Canada	1986:4	2000:7	−0.86	−2.28

Notes: See text. ADF is the augmented Dickey Fuller *t*-statistic; DFGLSu is the Dickey-Fuller generalized least-squares test (the test of Elliott 1999). The critical values are, respectively, (−3.43, −2.86, −2.57) for the ADF test, and (−3.28, −2.73, −2.46) for the DFGLSu test. Lag selection was via the Lagrange multiplier criterion with a maximum of twelve lags.
***Significant at the 1 percent level.
**Significant at the 5 percent level.
*Significant at the 10 percent level.

subperiod (1986–2000) than over the first (1974–86). The above findings refer to the more powerful DFGLSu test, which rejects the null more frequently than the standard ADF test.

This indication of a stationary long-term real interest differential, especially insofar as it applies to the recent period of floating industrial-country exchange rates, contradicts much of the empirical literature produced through the mid-1990s. Why do we find more evidence of stationarity than earlier researchers, such as Meese and Rogoff (1988) and Edison and Pauls (1993)? We note that previous authors had shorter samples and used tests of relatively low power, such as the ADF test.

Indeed, our data and methods are consistent with earlier findings: If we switch to the Meese-Rogoff sample of February 1974 to March 1986, and use the ADF test as they did, then we replicate their conclusions exactly (as shown in the penultimate panel of the table). Even if we switch to the DFGLSu test on the same data, we can reject the null in only two out of seven cases. The results for the post-1986 sample show similar problems, even though for the post-1974 period as a whole we can always reject the null[40] at the 10 percent level or higher.

These findings, which are supportive of stationarity in recent long-term real interest differentials, are consistent with another strand in the literature that finds support for international real interest rate equalization at longer horizons (Fujii and Chinn 2000). We conclude that earlier analyses of recent data were hampered by the low power of unit root tests on samples of small span.[41]

3.2.3 Exchange-risk-free Nominal Interest Parity

Perhaps the most unambiguous indicator of capital mobility is the relationship between interest rates on identical assets located in different finan-

---

40. Edison and Melick (1999, 97) find mixed results on the stationarity of Canadian, German, and Japanese long-term real interest differentials against the United States, but nonetheless base their econometric analysis of real interest parity on the assumption that all real interest differentials are stationary.

41. A more stringent test would examine the validity of long-term real interest parity. A focus on long-term real rather than nominal interest parity seems preferable because with mean reverting real exchange rates, it is easier to proxy long-run expected real exchange rates than the corresponding nominal exchange rates. Meese and Rogoff (1988) rejected a version of real interest parity based on the maintained assumption of an underlying sticky-price exchange rate model. More supportive is the recent long-run panel cointegration study by MacDonald and Nagayasu (2000) of fourteen OECD countries relative to the United States. The statistical methodology of that work, however, assumes that long-term real interest differentials are nonstationary. Chortareas and Driver (2001) implement a similar approach using a seventeen-country panel of OECD countries versus the United States; their conclusions are similar to those of MacDonald and Nagayasu. Chortareas and Driver report mixed results for tests on the stationarity of long-term real interest differentials. One issue pervading all of the work in this area is the effect of alternative proxies for long-term inflation expectations. The proxies that are chosen often differ across authors, affecting some results. A systematic discussion of these differences lies beyond the scope of this paper.

cial centers.[42,43] The great advantage of comparing onshore and offshore interest rates such as these is that relative rates of return are not affected by pure currency risk. For much of the period we study here, a direct onshore-offshore comparison is impossible. However, the existence of forward exchange instruments allows us to construct roughly equivalent measures of the return to currency-risk-free international arbitrage operations.

Using monthly data on forward exchange rates, spot rates, and nominal interest rates for 1921 to the latter half of 2001, we assess the degree of international financial-market integration by calculating the return to covered interest arbitrage between financial centers. For example, a London resident could earn the gross sterling interest rate $1 + i_t^*$ on a London loan of one pound sterling. Alternatively, he or she could invest the same currency unit in New York, simultaneously covering the exchange risk by selling dollars forward. The investor would do this in three steps: Buy e_t dollars in the spot exchange market (where e_t is the spot price of sterling in dollar terms); next, invest the proceeds for a total of $e_t(1 + i_t)$, where i_t is the nominal dollar interest rate; and finally, sell that sum of dollars forward for $e_t(1 + i_t)/f_t$ in sterling (where f_t, the forward exchange rate, is the price of forward sterling in terms of forward dollars). The net gain from borrowing in London and investing in New York,

$$(3) \qquad \frac{e_t}{f_t}(1 + i_t) - (1 + i_t^*),$$

is zero when capital mobility is perfect and the interest rates and forward rate are free of default risk. The left-hand side of the preceding expression represents a price of present pounds sterling in terms of future pounds sterling (i.e., of pounds dated t in terms of pounds dated $t + 1$), but it can be viewed as the relative price prevailing in the New York market, that is, as a kind of offshore interest rate. Thus, our test, in effect, examines the equality of the onshore sterling interest rate i^* with the offshore New York rate so defined. We perform a similar calculation for German mark interest differentials between London (considered as the offshore center) and Germany (onshore), thereby gauging the difference between implicit mark interest rates in London and the rates prevailing near the same time in Germany.

For pre-1920 data, we examine a related but distinct measure based on current New York prices of sterling for (two-months) future delivery, as in Obstfeld and Taylor (1998). The parallel Germany-London arbitrage calculation before 1920, corresponding to the preceding New York-London

---

42. See the discussion in Obstfeld (1995), for example.
43. This section draws heavily on Obstfeld and Taylor (1998) for the case of Great Britain, but adds new data on Germany for comparison. After our 1998 paper was published, we became aware of a similar 1889–1909 U.S.-U.K. interest rate comparison contained in Calomiris and Hubbard (1996).

comparison, is based on London prices for German marks to be delivered three months in the future. Forward exchange contracts of the kind common after 1920 were not prevalent before then (except in some exceptional financial centers; see Einzig 1937), so we instead base our pre-1920 comparison of onshore and offshore interest rates on the most widely traded instrument, one for which prices were regularly quoted in the major financial centers' markets, the long bill of exchange. Long bills could be used to cover the exchange risk that might otherwise be involved in interest-rate arbitrage.[44]

To see how such a transaction would work, let b_t denote the date-t dollar price in New York of £1 deliverable in London after sixty days, and e_t the spot New York price of sterling.[45] One way to purchase a future pound deliverable in London would be through a straight sterling loan, at price $1/(1 + i_t^*)$, where i_t^* is the London sixty-day discount rate. An alternative would be to purchase in New York a bill on London, at a price in terms of current sterling of b_t/e_t. With perfect and costless international arbitrage, these two prices of £1 to be delivered in London in the future should be the same.

Perkins (1978) observed that the series $(e/b) - 1$ defines the sterling interest rate in American financial markets, that is, the offshore sterling rate in the United States. This series may be compared with the London rate i^*, as we did in our 1998 paper, to gauge the degree of cross-border financial integration; that is, we calculate the differential

$$\frac{e_t}{b_t} - (1 + i_t^*)$$

before 1920.

Perkins's (1978) primary aim was to modify earlier series of dollar-sterling spot rates derived by Davis and Hughes (1960), who applied U.S. rather than U.K. interest rates to the dollar prices of long sterling bills in order to infer a series of sight exchange rates. Perkins argued that the sight bill rate should be derived by multiplying the (lower) long bill rate by a sterling, not a dollar, interest factor, and subsequent scholars have followed him; see, for example, the judgment of Officer (1996, 69). From a theoretical point of view, the verdict is clear: The relative price of current and future sterling defines a sterling nominal interest rate, in the present case, the offshore New York rate that we compare to London rates.

The upper panel of figure 3.5 is based on monthly differences between sterling rates in New York and in London from 1870 to 2001, where we simply splice together the 1870–1919 numbers based on time bill rates with

---

44. Margraff (1908, 37) speaks explicitly of the need to cover interest arbitrage through the exchange market.
45. In fact, such bills were payable after sixty-three days due to a legal grace period of three days, an institutional fact we account for in the calculations below (Haupt 1894, 429).

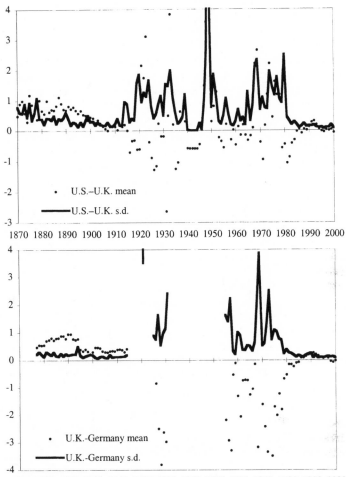

Fig. 3.5   Exchange-risk-free nominal interest differentials since 1870: *A*, U.S.-U.K.; *B*, U.K.-Germany

Sources: See text.

Notes: Annual samples of monthly data, percent per annum.

the subsequently available covered interest differentials. Differential returns are calculated as annual rates of accrual.[46]

46. The U.S.-U.K. comparison is based on the data described in Obstfeld and Taylor (1998, 361n. 7), with the following amendments. From January 1975 to August 2001, the London sterling interest rate *i* is the three-month bank bill middle rate, from Datastream. From January 1981 to August 2001, the New York dollar interest rate *i* is the discount rate on ninety-day bankers' acceptances, from Datastream. Finally, from January 1981 to August 2001 spot and

The figure broadly supports other indicators of the evolution of capital mobility. Differentials are relatively small and steady under the pre-1914 gold standard, but start to open up during World War I. They stay quite large in the early 1920s. Differentials diminish briefly in the late 1920s, but widen sharply in the early 1930s. There are some big arbitrage gaps in the late 1940s through the mid-1950s—including a sharp spike in volatility at the time of the 1956 Suez crisis.[47] But these shrink starting in the late 1950s and early 1960s, only to open up again in the late 1960s as sterling's 1967 devaluation initiates a period of foreign exchange turmoil, culminating in the unraveling of the Bretton Woods system in the early 1970s. Interest differentials have become small once again since the disappearance of U.K. capital controls around 1980. The differentials appear even smaller now than before 1914.[48]

Indeed, for the 1870–1914 data we observe a tendency, quite systematic albeit declining over time, for New York sterling rates to exceed London

---

three-month forward dollar-sterling exchange rates come from Datastream. All of these new data are end-of-month observations.

For the U.K.-German comparison, data are monthly averages up until January 1981 and end of month thereafter, as follows. *Exchange rates*: From October 1877 to July 1914 we use the month-average spot Mark-sterling exchange rate from the National Bureau of Economic Research (NBER) macrohistory database, series 14106. London sterling prices for three-month bills on Berlin are "money" rates taken from the "Course of Exchange" table in *The Economist*. From January 1921 to September 1931 we average the weekly spot and three-month forward exchange rates listed by Einzig (1937). From May 1955 to December 1980, spot exchange rates are from *The Economist* through 1957 and thereafter from Datastream. Forward exchange rates are from the London *Times* (May 1955–October 1958), from *The Economist* subsequently through 1964, then from the London *Times* through 1975, and, finally, starting January 1976, from Datastream. *U.K. three-month interest rate*: Open market three-month discount rate, NBER series 13016, through September 1931. Data from 1955 to 1974 come from the Federal Reserve banking database (and are similar to the well-known Capie-Webber series). Starting in January 1975 we use the U.K. interbank (money market) three-month middle rate of interest. *German three-month interest rate*: From October 1877 through September 1931, where observations are available, we use the Berlin private open market discount rate for prime bankers' acceptances given as NBER series 13018. The German three-month money market rate for 1955–59 is an average of monthly high and low rates taken from *Monthly Report of the Deutsche Bundesbank* and thereafter, through end-1980, comes from the IMF's *International Financial Statistics*. Subsequent data are from Datastream, the three-month "dead middle" money market rate.

47. See Klug and Smith (1999) for a fascinating empirical study of the Suez crisis. The paper includes a discussion of daily covered arbitrage differentials from 1 June 1956 to 31 January 1957.

48. We alert the reader to several potential problems with our calculations and data. First, as we have already stressed above and indeed stressed quite clearly in Obstfeld and Taylor (1998), the two measures of market integration that we calculate refer to different arbitrage possibilities before and after 1920. Second, some forward transactions appear at different maturities in our data set. Third, most data are observed at or near end-of-month, but some data are averages of weekly numbers. Averaging has the effect of dampening measured volatility. Fourth, data from World War II reflect rigidly administered prices and have no capital mobility implications. Fifth, the data used are not closely aligned for time of day (and even differ as to day in some cases), so that some deviations from parity may be exaggerated. The purpose of the exercise, however, is merely to convey a broad sense of the trend in integration, not to pursue a detailed hunt for small arbitrage possibilities.

rates. In arguing in favor of a sterling discount rate for valuing long sterling bills traded in the United States, Perkins (1978) demonstrated a tendency for the implicit offshore sterling interest rate $(e/b) - 1$ to converge toward bank rate toward the end of the nineteenth century (see his fig. 2, p. 399). Our figure 3.5, however, compares the New York offshore sterling interest rate with the London money-market rate of discount, which tended to be somewhat below bank rate. Were we to use bank rate as the London interest rate in the figure, much of the pre-1914 gap would be eliminated. Given that the U.S. data consist of prices of high-quality paper (such as bank bills), however, comparisons with bank rate are probably inappropriate. As Spalding (1915, 49) observes: "Bank Rate, as is well known, is usually higher than market rate; therefore if ordinary trade bills are remitted [to London] from [abroad], to find the long exchange, interest will be calculated at our Bank Rate, as trade paper is not considered such a good security as bank bills."[49] Officer (1996, 69) concurs, although on different grounds: "Whereas the Bank Rate was set by the Bank of England, the money-market rate was a true competitive price. . . . The money-market rate of discount is the better measure."

If it is impermissible to compare the sterling interest rate in New York with bank rate in London, how, then, can we explain the systematic positive interest gap in favor of New York before 1914? Much if not all of the gap can be explained as an artifact of the procedure we have used to extract the offshore interest rate from the observations on sight and time bill prices.

Continuing our focus on the New York–London comparison of sterling interest rates, we notice that the published money-market discount rate for London is quoted as a "pure" relative price of future in terms of present sterling. In contrast, as practitioners' textbooks of the period make amply clear, in determining the price to be paid for a long bill of exchange on London, purchasers would factor in not only the spot exchange rate and the London market discount rate, but, in addition, commissions, profit margins, and, importantly, the stamp duty (0.05 percent of the bill's face value) payable to the British government. These factors made bill prices lower than they would have been if they simply were equal to the spot exchange rate discounted by the pure New York sterling rate of interest.

Margraff (1908, 121) estimates that for a ninety-day bill, the total of such factors amounted to 0.125 percent of face value. For a sixty-day bill, that charge would represent about 75 basis points in annualized form; Escher (1918, 81–82), published a decade later, cites a very slightly smaller number. By subtracting that "tax" from the pre-1914 differentials plotted in the top of figure 3.5, we see that the apparent average excess return in New York disappears.

Indeed, the average return becomes negative for 1890–1914, so that 75

---

49. See also the summary table in Margraff (1908, 112).

basis points in additional costs may well be an overestimate for the entire prewar period. Suggestive of declining costs is the tendency shown in the figure for the average bias to decline over time. Perkins (1978, 400–01) argues that U.S. foreign exchange dealers of the period were able to exploit market power to inflate their commissions. Certainly such market power declined through 1914 as markets evolved, and Officer's (1996, 75) data on brokers' commissions supports this view.[50] Of course, a process of market integration increases competition and drives commissions down. Thus, leaving aside the portion due to the stamp tax, the size of the New York–London discrepancy is to some degree a reflection of financial market segmentation and its secular decline evidence of a process of progressive integration.

The lower panel of figure 3.5 shows the difference between the implicit mark interest rate in London and the one prevailing in Germany. Again, the U-shaped evolution of capital mobility is evident over our entire sample period. Before 1914, the former, offshore, rate is calculated on the basis of ninety-day prime bills of exchange on Berlin traded in London. The results are remarkably consistent with those for New York–London.

In particular, we again observe a systematic but secularly declining excess return in London prior to 1914. The explanation is essentially the same as in the New York–London comparison above. Germany levied a stamp duty on bills at the same rate as Britain's (0.05 percent; see Haupt 1894, 164, or Margraff 1908, 133). Margraff's estimates of concomitant costs suggest that for a ninety-day bill on Berlin, about 40 basis points should be subtracted from the annualized sight bill premium $4 \times ([e/b] - 1)$ to ascertain the true London mark rate of interest. On the assumption that some costs decline over time, with 40 basis points an average for the prewar period as whole, that cost adjustment brings the offshore and onshore mark rates roughly into line.[51]

While the cost and tax considerations we have described potentially eliminate the pre-1914 upward bias in our estimated series of offshore interest rates, other financial transaction costs would, as usual, create no-arbitrage bands around the point of onshore-offshore interest rate equality. One way to evaluate the evolution of capital mobility through time would be to estimate over different eras what Einzig (1937, 25) calls "transfer points," that is, the minimum return differential necessary to induce arbitrage operations. Keynes and Einzig agreed that during the interwar period, at least a 50 basis point covered differential would be needed to induce arbitrage.

50. Country-risk-type arguments cannot easily rationalize the pre-1920 interest differential in favor of New York, as we pointed out earlier in Obstfeld and Taylor (1998, 361n. 6). The reason is that both of the two transactions we compare entail future payment in the same place, London. This is not the case in the post-1920 covered interest arbitrage calculations.

51. Flandreau and Rivière (1999) focus on a London-Paris comparison for 1900–14. Their results are entirely consistent with the data that we show in figure 3.5, including a systematic excess of the London franc interest rate over that in Paris. Their rationale for the differential is apparently different from ours, although they do not include details of their derivation.

That is, they suggested a no-arbitrage band of ±50 basis points. Applying nonlinear estimation techniques including a threshold autoregression (TAR) methodology to weekly interwar data on dollar-sterling covered return differentials, Peel and Taylor (2002) confirm that a no-arbitrage band close to ±50 basis points did appear to prevail, as Keynes and Einzig claimed. Only outside this range did arbitrage forces push spot and forward exchange rates toward conformity with the band.

A detailed investigation is beyond the scope of this paper, but a first pass at the data using the TAR methodology of Obstfeld and Taylor (1997) is suggestive. For the dollar-sterling exchange between June 1925 and June 1931, we calculate a band of inaction of ±60 basis points, very close to the Peel-Taylor estimate given that we are using coarser, monthly data. For the corresponding interwar sterling-mark exchange our estimated band is ±91 basis points wide. On 1880–1914 differentials, in contrast, we find (after subtracting a constant mean differential) bands of only ±19 basis points for New York–London and ±35 basis points for London-Berlin. By way of comparison, Clinton (1988) suggests that covered interest differentials in the mid-1980s needed to reach just ±6 basis points to become economically significant. Balke and Wohar (1998) produce an estimate 50 percent higher for the 1974–93 period. We suspect that a more careful analysis of pre-1914 differentials, one taking account of the upward trend in market integration, would reduce our estimated transaction cost bands for the early twentieth century. Accordingly, the degree of integration among core money markets achieved under the classical gold standard must be judged as truly impressive compared to conditions over the following half-century or more.

The Great Depression, perhaps as part of a much broader interwar phase of disintegration, therefore stands out as an event that transformed the world capital market and left interest arbitrage differentials higher and more volatile than ever before.

3.2.4   Equity Returns

It is interesting to ask whether the long-run evidence on the U shape of capital market integration extends to other criteria, and other markets such as equities. Over the long run, global equity markets have evolved at a very different rate than global bond markets, for example. Government bonds from core countries have generally traded in financial centers in the last 100 years, but for long spans of time, emerging-market debt was very difficult to place in the private sector, and most went through multilateral intermediaries. Similarly, international trade in equities, although quiescent in the middle of the century, grew substantially in core countries after the lifting of capital controls in the 1970s and 1980s, and by the 1990s several emerging equity markets were involved as well.

Does quantitative evidence exist to verify this narrative? Quantity data are harder to find at a disaggregated level. Breaking down foreign investment into its components is an enormous historical task, and few have attempted it in the quest for long-run comparable series across many countries (but see Twomey 2000). We will not attempt to press further here. Instead, we will examine price evidence to see what changing patterns of equity returns might tell us about globalization.

There is certainly some debate about the indicators of equity returns in the long run and what they tell us about globalization. Jorion and Goetzmann (1999) find that most of the world's stock markets have exhibited fairly low real returns over the long run in the last century, around 1 percent, with the exception of the United States, which has yielded around 4 percent annually since 1921. These figures caution that U.S. exceptionalism might extend to stock market returns also, and cast doubt on the general, global truth of the equity premium puzzle. The authors also note that survivorship bias likely afflicts the United States and many other markets in the core countries for which data exist. In many emerging markets, stock prices have fluctuated wildly and many series break down at critical historical junctures and during wars, limiting our ability to compare like with like.

In this section we take a fresh look at long-run equity returns using data similar to those employed by Jorion and Goetzmann (1999), the Global Financial Data source. We ask two questions not addressed by previous authors: To what extent have stock returns (measured in a common currency, the U.S. dollar) diverged or converged over time, and to what extent have the time series correlations of returns across countries changed over time? We then consider what the answers may have to say about globalization.

Figure 3.6 shows summary statistics for a sample of up to twenty-two country stock price indices based on annual U.S. dollar-denominated returns since 1880.[52] The bottom chart indicates that the sample size diminishes markedly prior to 1950, evidence of the survivorship problem. We usually have twenty countries in the sample after that date, but in the interwar period the sample size is about a dozen, and before 1920 between five and ten. A wide line traces out the sample size for a limited set of core countries, the G7. For this group there is a more consistent sample size over time, although only three series before 1920.

The middle panel shows the standard deviation of returns across time, calculated for a centered moving window of ten-year length and encompassing the largest sample possible.[53] Again, the thin line is the full sample, the wide line the G7. As a description of the coherence of the returns in G7 equity markets this figure is strikingly consistent with the U-shape hypothesis and the underlying arbitrage arguments. Returns showed relatively little dispersion prior to 1914, but larger gaps opened up in the interwar period. This dispersion reached a peak around 1945 or 1950, but has been

52. Since dividend data are not available for the entire sample, the calculated returns are based on equity price changes only.
53. Specifically, we plot ten-year averages of the cross-sectional standard deviations of returns.

Correlations (10 Year Window)

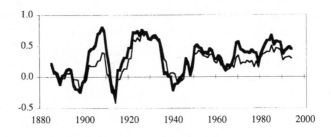

S.d. (10 Year Window)

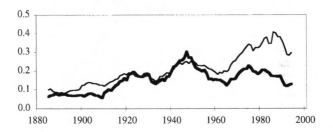

Sample Size

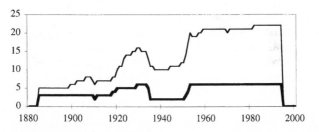

Fig. 3.6   Equity returns in U.S. dollars for the G7 and up to twenty-two global stock markets, 1880–2000

Source: Global Financial Data.

falling since, with a minor reversal in the late 1960s but convergence again after 1980, roughly when G7 capital controls loosened. The picture for the full sample is a little less clear, since the sample size is not consistent. We do not know how much of the long-run increase in dispersion, for example, is due to an increase in the sample size over time; for example, the addition in recent years of more volatile emerging markets might be expected to raise the variance. But for the post-1950 period, when the sample is stable, the trends are quite similar to those in the G7, although the returns are much less coherent than for the G7 in the 1970s and 1980s, a period in which capital controls were much tighter in the periphery than in the core. It is also apparent that in the 1990s, the emerging markets have seen a much larger decline in dispersion, at a time when economic reforms generally reduced barriers to capital mobility, and emerging market portfolio investment grew rapidly.

Finally, the top panel explores a second measure of coherence of stock prices across countries, based on the average correlation of annual dollar returns with that on the U.S. market, again calculated for a centered moving window of ten-year length and encompassing the largest sample possible, and where the thin line is the average for the full sample and the wide line for the G7. The correlations show clear disconnects between markets during times of well-known autarky, such as the two world wars. Periods of high correlation also appear more recently and before 1914 (although only just before). Although the noisiness of the correlations is quite large, this much, at least, is consistent with the U-shape story. What is not consistent with the story is the large spike in cross-country correlations in the 1920s and 1930s. Why should this be so, in what was an era of supposedly fairly low capital mobility?

One answer has been provided already by Eichengreen and Sachs (1985, fig. 5), who show that the interwar patterns may simply reflect common shocks associated with going on and off the gold standard. To follow their example, consider the 1929 to 1935 period. Countries that stayed on gold like France and Germany did endured a brutal downturn in prices and output, whereas countries that devalued did not. This has been empirically verified for wider samples such as Latin America (Campa 1990). It is consistent with monetary explanations of recovery that build on both the debt-deflation logic of Fisher and the expected-real-interest-rate channel emphasized by Mundell, not to mention the conventional Keynesian transmission mechanism (Temin 1989; Romer 1992; Eichengreen 1992; Bernanke and Carey 1996).

What did this mean for stock markets? In a world of nonneutral money, devaluers would be able to drive up Tobin's q by restoring positive investment expectations. Eichengreen and Sachs (1985) found a statistically significant correlation between the change in q and the change in the exchange rate (relative to gold parity) in a sample of nine countries from 1929 to 1935. We replicate and extend their analysis in figure 3.7. This figure shows that the correlation holds true in a wider sample of eighteen countries.

These results imply that we must therefore be cautious about interpreting an increased correlation among markets as evidence of globalization per se. Instead, certain high correlations might simply be a result of common shocks among a group of countries, in this case countries experiencing, and

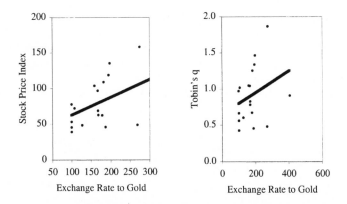

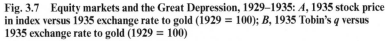

Fig. 3.7   Equity markets and the Great Depression, 1929–1935: *A*, **1935 stock price in index versus 1935 exchange rate to gold (1929 = 100);** *B*, **1935 Tobin's** *q* **versus 1935 exchange rate to gold (1929 = 100)**
Sources: Global Financial Data; Obstfeld and Taylor (2003).

then reacting to, the biggest single macroeconomic shock of the twentieth century. This caveat is well known. For example, a recent article in *The Economist* (Economics Focus, "Dancing in Step," 24 March 2001) reports that in the 1990s global stock market correlations have risen to even higher levels than in the late 1980s (as high as 0.8 in year 2000, although at what frequency is not mentioned).[54] This came after a decline in correlations in the early 1990s, but "the long term trend is upward." Overall, the article concludes, this is consistent with increased globalization pressures, but certain large shocks, like the recent crises in Asia, might also have also been associated with higher correlations via contagion channels. As the article notes, "stock markets tend to be more correlated at times of high volatility in share prices; during calmer periods, correlations tend to be weaker." Similar reasoning, of course, could pertain to the roaring twenties and the bust of the thirties.[55]

3.2.5   Summary

Many studies of market integration have focused on a single kind of criterion. This approach seems unreasonably restrictive to us, since the interpretation of such narrow criteria must necessarily rest upon untested auxiliary assumptions. By contrast, we see no reason to dismiss any useful information, in either price or quantity form, especially given the paucity of

54. On these correlations see also Gourinchas and Rey (2001) and IMF (2001, 76).
55. The definition of *contagion* is controversial: Contagion may entail a structural intensification of spillovers in crisis periods. As Forbes and Rigobon (2000) stress, however, higher return volatility itself can mechanically raise cross-border return correlations even in the absence of any underlying structural change, and it may be misleading to view this as a contagion effect.

historical data in certain quarters. Thus, we have opted for a broad battery of tests to try to cut down the possible set of explanations that could account for the empirical record, and so, by a process of elimination, work toward a set on controlled conjectures concerning the evolution of the global capital market.

The preceding section succinctly conveys the benefits we think this kind of approach can deliver. Our quantity-based tests delivered a certain set of stylized facts, and the price-based tests another set of facts. Combining the two, and introducing evidence on convergence and divergence in other economic phenomena such as living standards and demography, we claim there is overwhelming support for the notion that the major long-run changes in the degree of global capital mobility have taken the form of changes in the impediments to capital flows, rather than any encouragement or discouragement to flows arising from structural shifts within the economies themselves. That is not to discount the fact that such changes have occurred, and are no doubt important at the margin; but it is an assertion that the virtual disappearance of foreign capital flows and stocks in midcentury, and the explosion in price differentials, can be explained only by an appeal to changes in arbitrage possibilities as permitted by two major constraining factors in capital market operations: technology and national economic policies.

From this point, it is a short step to the conclusion that a full accounting of the phenomena at hand must rest on a detailed political and institutional history. Clearly, technology is a poor candidate for the explanation of the twentieth-century collapse of capital mobility. In the 1920s and 1930s, the prevailing financial technologies were not suddenly forgotten by market participants: Indeed some technologies, such as futures markets for foreign exchange, came to fruition in those decades. Technological evolution was not smooth and linear, but as we have already noted, was at least unidirectional, and, absent any other impediments, would have implied an uninterrupted progress toward an ever more tightly connected global marketplace.

Such was not allowed to happen, of course. Rather, the shifting forces of national economic policies, as influenced by the prevailing economic theories of the day, loomed large during and after the watershed event of the twentieth century, the economic and political crisis of the Great Depression. Understanding the macroeconomic and international economic history of the last century in these terms, and the changes it wrought for the operation of the global capital market, is a long and complex story, a narrative that properly accompanies the empirical record presented in this paper, and we take up some of the political economy dimensions of that story in the section that follows.

3.3 Political Economy

We have thus far amassed evidence that international capital mobility has experienced two major swings over the course of the twentieth century:

a pronounced decline during the interwar years and a recovery in the later postwar years. The timing is hard to pin down precisely, and, indeed, surely varied by country and by the type of capital movements being considered.

Taking this as given, we now must ask why capital mobility followed this path, and what corroborative evidence we can assemble to buttress an account of these events that incorporates the forces of political economy. We start first with the downturn in capital mobility after 1914.

3.3.1   The Downturn

The conventional macrohistorical account of the collapse of capital mobility after 1914 focuses on the trilemma, as we have noted, (Eichengreen 1996; Obstfeld and Taylor 1998). The literature suggests that the major political economy forces at work during this period were increasing pressure for macroeconomic activism, particularly from newly or better-enfranchised groups such as the working classes. If fixed exchange rates were to be maintained, then capital mobility would have to be compromised, at least on some occasions. Maintenance of capital mobility instead would preclude an exchange rate target. Either option would raise uncertainty for investors.

It is believed that prior to 1914, gold standard orthodoxy had been a sine qua non for access to global capital markets on favorable terms. A first study by Bordo and Rockoff (1996) found that adherence to gold standard rules acted as a "seal of approval" for sovereign debt. Gold standard countries had lower country risk, measured by the bond spread in London over the British consol.[56] Accordingly, evidence of a new political dynamic after 1914 might be seen in a changing relationship between country risk and gold after the gold standard was reconstituted starting in 1925. With the rules of the game in question after World War I, investors might have doubted whether the announcement of a gold standard commitment alone would signal credibility. In addition, public solvency indicators, such as debt-GDP ratios, or inflation, might be seen as having a bigger impact on international bond spreads under the reconstituted gold standard than before. Do such doubts manifest themselves in the data?

There is no uniform and comprehensive study of bond spreads across these two eras that would allow us definitively to answer this question, but a second study by Bordo, Edelstein, and Rockoff (1999) came to a conclusion that was surprising, even by the authors' own admission. Looking solely at 1920s bonds they found continued evidence that the gold standard remained a seal of approval, lowering bond spreads significantly, at least when a country stuck to its prewar parity. Devaluers were not so lucky with their bond spreads, since for them, the impact of being on gold was small

---

56. Clemens and Williamson (2000), however, find no statistically significant gold standard effect on the shares of British capital flows to various foreign recipients during 1870–1913. It remains to reconcile the apparently conflicting message of the price and quantity data.

and statistically insignificant. Such a conclusion challenged the conventional wisdom that the interwar gold standard was a pale and less credible shadow of its predecessor.

These are two pioneering studies but, for comparative work across regimes, they are not ideal. Unfortunately, they cannot be merged together into a consistent picture because of differences in the methods and data employed. The former study looked at long-term government bonds in the secondary market, and examined their yield to maturity; the latter examined new issues and their yield at the moment of flotation only. The former study therefore had complete time series, whereas the latter had a small sample that was often interrupted by missing data in years when no issues took place—a not uncommon event in the 1920s, and one that could raise a potential sample-selection issue. Finally, the former studied prices in London, the latter prices in New York, a switch that could be defended as the hegemonic center of global capital markets shifted across the Atlantic around this time, and one that allowed the use of Cleona Lewis' (1938) data on new issues for the 1920s.

To overcome the differences between these studies, we reexamine the question of what determined bond spreads in the pre-1914 and interwar years using a much larger database that allows us to view a consistent set of data for a larger sample of countries from 1870 to 1940. In the Global Financial Data source and other primary sources we found the yields to maturity of government bonds traded in London for this entire period, and we focus on more than twenty countries, some in the core and some in the periphery, to see how their country risk evolved. This allows us to focus on the same market and the same type of risk measure across both eras. To isolate the effects of default risk, our spreads over London are exclusively for bonds denominated in gold or in sterling.

Figure 3.8 offers an overview of the data. The mean bond spread for the core and periphery subsamples is presented in the top and bottom panels, respectively, and each is surrounded by a measure of dispersion, a band equal to ±2 standard deviations. The units are percentage points and the scales are deliberately the same on the two charts.[57]

57. Country risk is calculated as the spread between the country's long bond, denominated in hard currency or gold (the external London bond), and the British consol. The core and empire countries are Australia, Canada, Denmark, Germany, India, New Zealand, Norway, South Africa, Sweden, and the United States. The periphery countries are Argentina, Austria (or Austria-Hungary, before World War I), Brazil, Chile, Egypt, Finland, Greece, Hungary (after World War I), India, Italy, Japan, Mexico, Portugal, Spain, Turkey, and Uruguay. There are occasional missing data, due to the fact that bonds are recorded by Global Financial Data (GFD) in domestic currency (paper) only or are not recorded at all. Notable gaps are Argentina (1935–40), Austria (1933–40), Chile (1934–40), Denmark (1870–1918), Finland (1870–1910), Greece (1927–40), Mexico (1933–40), Sweden (1933–40), Uruguay (1934–40), and several countries around the time of World War I (1914–18). We supplement the GFD source as follows: For Argentina we use improved data from della Paolera (1988) and Nakamura and Zarazaga (2003). For the United States (1870–1914) we follow Bordo and Rockoff

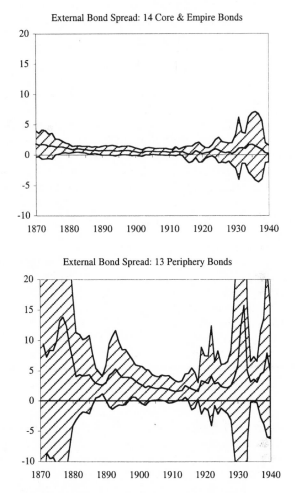

External Bond Spread: 14 Core & Empire Bonds

External Bond Spread: 13 Periphery Bonds

Fig. 3.8   London bond spreads, core and periphery, 1870–1940
Source: Global Financial Data
Notes: See footnote 57.

The differences between the two subsamples are very striking: The core had much smaller country risk than the periphery, as expected. Core countries

(1996), who use Calmoiris' adjusted gold rate, since at this time government bonds bore silver risk. For interwar Belgium, Denmark, Finland, France, Italy, Norway, Portugal, Sweden, Turkey, and Uruguay, GFD does not report gold or sterling bonds, so we collected new inter-war-yield data on London sterling or gold bonds from *Investor's Monthly Manual, The Times, The Wall Street Journal,* and *The Economist.* For further details see Obstfeld and Taylor (forthcoming).

usually had interest rates within 1 or 2 percentage points of Great Britain's. The periphery could have spreads as large as 10 percentage points, which was tantamount to having a bond in default in many cases. But the figures also show some similarities, once we normalize for this scale difference: Both core and periphery experienced a convergence in bond spreads up to 1914, and then a good deal of volatility in the interwar years, when spreads widened.

The gradual convergence of bond spreads warns us that a simple static "on and off" gold indicator is unlikely to capture the full dynamics of evolving country risk in this period. Intuitively, these figures hint at high levels of persistence or serial correlation in bond spreads, and it is easy to imagine why. Bond spreads are a function of reputation, which, in capital markets as in any other repeated game, cannot be built overnight. Instead, there is an "I know what you did last summer" effect: One's reputation in the previous period is likely to have substantial explanatory power in deciding one's reputation today. Beyond this, levels of public indebtedness were relevant for at least some countries. A general concern is that macroeconomic variables correlated with gold standard adherence might be responsible for the apparent pre-1914 benefits of going on gold, or might mask such benefits after the First World War. Before the war, countries on gold may have had more disciplined fiscal policies, lower public debt, and hence more favorable treatment by the bond markets. On the other hand, perhaps countries that inflated away their public debts in the early or mid-1920s would have been unlikely to rejoin gold at parity, making high public debts and a return to gold at prewar parity positively correlated variables. In these circumstances, omitting macrocontrols could lead us to overestimate the prewar benefit of gold standard adherence and underestimate the postwar benefit of returning to gold at the prewar par.[58]

Following Bordo and Rockoff (1996), we investigate the relationship between the dependent variable country risk, measured by the bond spread over London, $\text{SPREAD}_{it} = \text{YIELD}_{it} - \text{YIELD}_{\text{UK},t}$, and selected macroeconomic policy variables that could play a role for country i and time t. One such variable is gold standard adherence, measured by two dummy variables: GSPAR_{it}, which takes the value 1 if on date t country i is on gold at

58. Flandreau, Le Cacheux, and Zumer (1998) argue that a major factor driving the evident convergence of bond spreads after the early 1890s and through 1914 is worldwide inflation resulting from gold discoveries, a factor that caused both an unexpected reduction in countries' ratios of public debt to nominal GDP and a more widespread adherence to the gold standard. For the pre-1914 period, Flandreau, Le Cacheux, and Zumer investigate borrowing spreads over London using an all-European country sample different from that of Bordo and Rockoff (1996) and an econometric specification encompassing the public debt ratio to GDP as well as gold standard adherence. They report benefits from gold standard adherence on the order of 35–55 basis points. They also find a positive effect of public debt on borrowing spreads. (Bordo and Rockoff included the public deficit in their estimating equation but found little effect.) It is possible in principle that some of the benefits ascribed by Bordo and Rockoff to gold standard adherence before 1914 can be accounted for by a tendency of association with more moderate real public debt levels, a point that provides a strong rationale for including the debt as an explanatory variable.

the 1913 parity, and $GSDEV_{it}$, which takes the value 1 if the country is on gold at a devalued parity after 1913. Monetary policy reputation is proxied by the lagged inflation rate, $INFL_{i,t-1}$. As a final macroexplanatory variable, we examine the effects of lagged public debt levels, measured by the ratio of debt to output, $PUBDGDP_{i,t-1}$. We also include country fixed effects to capture constant but unmeasured political, economic, institutional, or geographic features of individual countries (e.g., location on the periphery).

Like Bordo and Rockoff (1996), we also find it necessary to account for global interest rate shocks that affect spreads in all markets in a given year. To do this, following the logic of the "international capital asset pricing model," we include (with a country-specific slope, or β) a measure of market risk in the form of $SPREAD_{W,t} = YIELD_{WORLD,t} - YIELD_{UK,t}$, where this term is the (1913 GDP-weighted) average world spread on the "safe rate" (London) for the countries in the sample at time t.[59,60]

Using pooled annual data for a large sample of countries, the basic regression equation is then of the form

(4) $\quad\quad SPREAD_{it} = \alpha_i + \beta_i SPREAD_{W,t} + \gamma X_{it} + u_{it}$

where

$$X_{it} = \begin{pmatrix} GSPAR_{it} \\ GSDEV_{it} \\ PUBDGDP_{i,t-1} \\ INFL_{i,t-1} \end{pmatrix}$$

59. We experimented with other ways to control for time-specific asset market shifts, such as simple time dummies, but the results appear robust.

60. Bond spread series as described in footnote 57.

Gold standard adherence data are from Meissner (2001) and Obstfeld and Taylor (forthcoming), available for all countries in all years. Other variables are available for only a subset of years and countries, and this restricts the sample in our econometric tests accordingly.

Central-government public debt data (mostly starting in 1880) come from Bordo and Jonung (1996) for a sample of fourteen countries consisting of Belgium, Canada, Denmark, Finland, France, Germany, Italy, Japan, the Netherlands (starting 1900), Norway, Sweden, Switzerland (starting 1913), the United Kingdom, and the United States. For those countries, the same source has data on nominal GDP. After 1914, we augment our other public debt data with the total central government debts reported by United Nations (1948); and we use the nominal GDP figures from Obstfeld and Taylor (2003) or GFD. Additional sources for debt were as follows. Argentina: della Paolera (1988). Australia: Barnard (1987). Austria-Hungary: Niall Ferguson, based on data collected by Marc Flandreau (unpublished). Brazil: IBGE (1990) and Levy (1995). Chile: Mamalakis (1978–89). Egypt: Niall Ferguson, based on Crouchley (1938). India: Reserve Bank of India (1954). New Zealand: Lloyd Prichard (1970). Portugal: Valério (2001). Spain: Barciela and Carreras (1989). Turkey: Tezel (1986). Uruguay: unpublished data from Reto Bertoni, kindly provided by Luis Bértola, and based on the official data from *Anuarios Estadísticos*. Debts relative to nominal GDP were calculated using nominal GDP data from Mitchell (1992, 1993, 1995), collated or augmented by Bordo and Schwarz (1997) and GFD, interpolated or supplemented by other sources as follows. Argentina: della Paolera and Ortiz (1995). Austria-Hungary: Niall Ferguson, based on data collected by Marc Flandreau (unpublished). Egypt: Yousef (forthcoming). France: Jones and Obstfeld (2001). India: Goldsmith (1983). New Zealand: Hawke (1975) and Lineham (1968). Portugal: Nunes, Mata, and Valério (1989). Spain: Prados (2002). Uruguay: Bértola (1998) and Bertino and Tajam (2000).

Table 3.4   Country Risk and the Gold Standard, 1870–1913

	OLS	AR1
N	563	546
Adjusted R^2	0.68	0.84
Mean of dependent variable	1.72	1.70
Standard error of dependent variable	1.52	1.51
Standard error of estimate	0.86	0.60
Durbin-Watson statistic	0.59	1.37
GS	−0.39 (0.16)	−0.50 (0.19)
PUBDGDP($t − 1$)	−0.05 (0.14)	0.06 (0.22)
INFL($t − 1$)	0.69 (0.48)	0.75 (0.03)
ρ	—	0.75 (0.03)

Sources: See text and footnotes 57 and 60.
Notes: The dependent variable is SPREAD as in figure 3.8. Standard errors appear in parentheses. Country fixed effects (α_j) and betas (β_j) are not reported. The seventeen countries in the unbalanced panel are Argentina, Australia, Austria-Hungary, Brazil, Canada, Chile, Egypt, India, Italy, Japan, New Zealand, Norway, Portugal, Spain, Sweden, the United States, and Uruguay. There are some missing data. In the AR1 model a common autoregressive parameter ρ applies to all countries.

is the vector of explanatory variables. (We also tried interacting debt and inflation with a dummy variable equal to 1 for the periphery countries, not including regions of the British Empire, to capture the possibly different risk treatment of established versus emerging markets, but the results were insignificant and are therefore not reported.)[61] The main question we ask is whether 1914 was a watershed—that is, if the interwar gold standard differed from its predecessor. Accordingly, we investigate this relationship on prewar (1870–1913) and interwar (1925–31) samples.

In tables 3.4 and 3.5 we report results for the prewar (1870–1913, using December yields) and interwar (1925–31, using June yields) periods. Since

We also tried using deficit-to-GDP ratios, following Bordo and Rockoff (1996), but, like them, we found deficit ratios to be statistically insignificant in preliminary testing.

Inflation data are based on consumer (or GDP) price indices taken from Obstfeld and Taylor (2003), Bordo and Schwarz (1997), and GFD, supplemented by other sources above or as follows. Argentina: Irigoin (2000); Cortés Conde (1989); and from della Paolera and Ortiz (1995). Austria-Hungary: Schulze (2000). Chile: Braun et al. (2000). Egypt: Yousef (forthcoming). India: Goldsmith (1983). New Zealand: an implicit deflator of GDP, based on nominal GDP as above, and real GDP from Maddison (1995). Portugal: Nunes, Mata, and Valério (1989).

We are unable to make our pre-1914 analysis of spread-debt relationships comparable with that of Flandreau, Le Cacheux, and Zumer (1998), as their data set, which comprises a different country sample than ours, has not been made available. Besides apparently covering the countries in our prewar sample, excluding Argentina, Australia, New Zealand, and the United States, Flandreau and colleagues' sample adds public debt data for Switzerland and some additional "European peripheral" countries. Judging from the 1892 data from Haupt (1894) graphed by Dornbusch (1998), the European peripheral countries had significant public debts relative to GDP.

61. The core and empire countries are Australia, Belgium, Canada, Denmark, France, Germany, India, the Netherlands, New Zealand, Norway, South Africa, Sweden, Switzerland, and the United States. The periphery countries are Argentina, Austria, Brazil, Chile, Finland, Greece, Hungary, Italy, Japan, Mexico, Portugal, Spain, and Uruguay. See figure 3.8.

Table 3.5   **Country Risk and the Gold Standard, 1925–31**

	OLS	AR(1)
N	160	137
Adjusted R^2	0.92	0.93
Mean of dependent variable	0.94	0.88
Standard error of dependent variable	1.21	1.15
Standard error of estimate	0.34	0.31
Durbin-Watson statistic	1.79	1.87
GSPAR	−0.31 (0.12)	−0.25 (0.11)
GSDEV	−0.60 (0.18)	−0.52 (0.17)
PUBDGDP($t-1$)	1.24 (0.44)	1.64 (0.44)
INFL($t-1$)	0.14 (0.08)	0.00 (0.12)
ρ	—	0.37 (0.05)

Sources: See table 3.4.

Notes: GSPAR denotes gold standard restored at the 1913 parity; GSDEV denotes gold standard restored at a devalued parity. The twenty-three countries in the unbalanced panel are Argentina, Australia, Austria, Belgium, Brazil, Canada, Chile, Denmark, Egypt, Finland, France, Germany, Hungary, India, Italy, Japan, New Zealand, Norway, Portugal, South Africa, Sweden, the United States and Uruguay.

we are focusing on spreads against London, and we implicitly treat London as a benchmark of what is a safe yield under gold standard credibility, we omit all other interwar years in our sample. Column (1) shows the ordinary least squares (OLS) results, while column (2) adds an autoregression (AR1) correction since we find evidence of high serial correlation in column (1).[62]

Being on gold appears statistically significant before 1914, subtracting about 50 basis points from the spread over London. But being on gold at the 1913 parity appears to be only about half as valuable for the interwar years 1925–31.

Public debt and inflation are seen to have had effects that were quantitatively small and of low statistical significance in the prewar period. The prewar autoregressive parameter is quite high, 0.75, suggesting that during the classical gold standard period countries could rely on some reputational persistence to help them maintain credibility in the capital market. Before 1914, then, classical gold standard adherence alone seems to have been sufficient to warrant the market "seal of approval."[63,64]

62. Using mid-year data interwar expands the time dimension to seven years, since June 1925 follows British resumption and June 1931 precedes British suspension of the gold standard. For the prewar period, the Durbin-Watson statistics for the uncorrected equations are very low. The AR1 model was also used by Bordo and Rockoff (1996). Flandreau, Le Cacheux, and Zumer (1998) add additional controls, the export-to-output ratio and output per capita, which appear to soak up some serial correlation.

63. According to our AR(1) estimate, for example, a debt-GDP ratio of 100 percent, assuming linearity, would raise the cost of foreign borrowing by only 6 basis points per year. Evidently, markets believed that prewar gold standard countries would take the steps needed to make good on their debts.

64. Flandreau, Le Cacheux, and Zumer (1998, 145) conclude that before 1914, "countries had to plunge quite deep into debt before they started feeling the pain." Core countries gener-

It is important to note that this pattern does not hold for the interwar period. For that era, the market seems to have been more discerning in its scrutiny of *all* borrowers' public debt data (although inflation remains unimportant). In these samples we also find somewhat weaker evidence of reputational persistence (as measured by the autoregressive parameter of 0.37), perhaps further evidence of the fragile credibility associated with the interwar gold standard where markets seemed to discount reputation.

Our estimates suggest that an interwar increase in public debt equivalent to 10 percentage points of GDP could raise spreads by 12 to 16 basis points. By this measure, the sensitivity of bond spreads to debt was much larger after the war than before.

These findings may help us to understand why many policymakers in the 1920s and 1930s so feared the market response to unbalanced public budgets, notwithstanding the countercyclical case for fiscal expansion (James 2001). In this period, being on gold was not, in itself, enough to soothe markets.

A noteworthy finding in the 1925–31 results of table 3.5 is that returning to gold at a devalued parity is estimated to have fully twice the beneficial effect of returning at prewar parity, very much contrary to the Bordo-Edelstein-Rockoff empirical result. This finding supports the theoretical view of Drazen and Masson (1994) that policymakers may hurt rather than enhance their credibility through policies that appear tough in the short term but are too draconian to be sustained for long. It also shows that interwar markets could forgive the expropriation of prior bondholders, provided the current economic fundamentals looked sustainable.

One concern about the results of table 3.5 is that they may conflate the benefits countries gained when they returned to gold with the spread effects of the dire circumstances in which countries left gold (never to return) prior to Great Britain's own departure in September 1931. Our on-gold dummy captures the complement of the set of all dates on which a country was on gold. Thus, we may overstate the case for gold by viewing the effects of the gathering Great Depression simply as a market response to gold abandonment.

To address such an overstatement we add a third dummy, GSOFF, which takes a value of 1 for years in which a country was off gold following a prior interwar resumption. Table 3.6 reports the results of estimation. In these regressions, the effect of returning to gold at par is wiped out, whereas the effect of returning at devalued parity, although smaller than in table 3.5 (around 40 basis points now), remains significant. Being forced off of gold raised spreads by 50–60 basis points, and the effect is highly significant.

---

ally had public debt levels at which, according to the authors, "markets did not inflict massive punishments." Unlike in our sample, as we have noted, those authors do find that debt raised spreads before 1914.

Table 3.6   Country Risk and the Gold Standard, 1925–31

	OLS	AR(1)
N	160	137
Adjusted R^2	0.93	0.93
Mean of dependent variable	0.94	0.88
Standard error of dependent variable	1.21	1.15
Standard error of estimate	0.33	0.30
Durbin-Watson statistic	1.77	1.71
GSPAR	−0.02 (0.15)	0.04 (0.13)
GSDEV	−0.45 (0.18)	−0.37 (0.17)
GSOFF	0.53 (0.17)	0.58 (0.17)
PUBDGDP($t-1$)	1.08 (0.43)	1.41 (0.42)
INFL($t-1$)	0.14 (0.08)	0.04 (0.10)
ρ	—	0.40 (0.05)

Sources: See table 3.5.
Notes: GSOFF denotes gold standard suspension after interwar resumption.

These results are not surprising. Primary exporting countries such as Argentina, Australia, and Uruguay returned to gold at par only to be forced off in 1929–30 amid sharply higher external borrowing costs. The significant negative coefficient on GSPAR in table 3.5 mainly reflects the fact that these countries enjoyed lower external borrowing costs before the onset of the Depression. (For the same reason, estimating over the truncated period 1925–30 attenuates the effect of GSPAR.) Both the Drazen-Masson effect and the importance of public debt remain, however, in table 3.6, so these may be regarded as robust features of the interwar capital market.

In Obstfeld and Taylor (forthcoming), we explore a different specification, but our main conclusions do not change very much. Accounts of the Great Depression (such as Kindleberger 1986) emphasize the role of adverse terms of trade shocks in forcing primary exporters to leave gold prior to Great Britain's own 1931 departure. Thus, we add the terms of trade as an explanatory variable in our equation but omit GSOFF. We also allow for the spread effects of countries' default statuses. The most notable change from the preceding results is a decline in the prewar "good housekeeping" effect to roughly −25 basis points, an estimate that remains highly statistically significant. The terms of trade are a significant determinant of spreads between the wars but not prior to 1914.

To recapitulate: Unlike Bordo, Edelstein, and Rockoff (1999), we find very different behavior of bond spreads in relation to the gold standard over the interwar period 1925–31 as compared to the pre-1914 period. This may be ascribed mainly to differences in concept (use of around-secondary-market bond yields in London versus new issues in New York) and differences in macroeconomic control variables (government debt rather than deficit). Of these features in our empirical approach, the first, at least, seems necessary if we are to make comparisons on an equal footing with Bordo and Rockoff (1996).

Before 1914, we find that the gold standard did indeed confer a "seal of approval," with macrofundamentals such as public debt and inflation mattering little. For the interwar period, a return to gold after devaluation (as in the case of France) seemed more credible, notwithstanding the arguments that led Great Britain and other countries to return to gold at par; indeed, returning at par yielded small benefits at best. Moreover, for core and periphery countries alike, high public debts were punished, suggesting that policymakers' room for maneuver was further curtailed.

Our results both on the drop in spreads associated with going on gold, and on markets' differential response to public debt prewar versus interwar, suggest that the interwar gold standard was indeed seen as different and less credible than its pre-1914 predecessor. It remains fully to reconcile these results with findings such as those of Hallwood, MacDonald, and Marsh (1996) that indicate a highly credible gold standard during the late 1920s, at least in the short term. Perhaps the bond markets adopted a longer perspective under which protracted adherence to unchanging gold parities seemed less probable than short-term adherence.

3.3.2   The Upturn

After the immediate post–World War II dislocations, the world economy began to reconstitute its severed linkages, a process both promoting and promoted by the return of some degree of durable prosperity and peace. Postwar policymakers, through the IMF, successive multilateral trade liberalization rounds, current account currency convertibility, and other measures, successfully promoted growing world trade. By the late 1960s, the very success of these initiatives in forging trading linkages among countries simultaneously made capital flows across borders ever more difficult to contain. As a result, the trilemma reemerged with full force, and on a global scale, in the early 1970s. The Bretton Woods system, initially designed for a world of tightly controlled capital movements, blew apart. The major industrial countries retreated to floating exchange rates.

While initially viewed as a temporary expedient, floating rates have remained a durable feature of the international financial landscape. Floating rates helped reconcile the social demand for domestic macroeconomic stabilization with the interest of the business community for open markets in goods and assets. Some episodes of exchange rate misalignment have prompted calls for renewed protection and even capital account restrictions. Some of these calls have been accommodated, but usually not in the form of across-the-board restrictions on international transactions.

Other forces have also helped to promote liberalization. In Europe, the political and economic rationales for a large single market have prompted ongoing financial liberalization; at the same time, the political (and, some argue, economic) imperative of stable exchange rates has pushed toward the logical conclusion of a single currency, the euro. Other regions, likewise, have opted for fixed exchange rates, either by some form of ultrahard peg or outright dollarization, in either case bending to the trilemma by giving up monetary policy autonomy.

Since the late 1980s, the drive toward capital account liberalization in the developing world is probably the most striking pattern in the evolution of global capital markets. Clearly one element has been the widespread failure in the periphery of populist policies adopted in the 1980s and earlier. Reactions to those failures gave free-market ideologies a greater influence. On a larger scale, the collapse of the Soviet empire in the late 1980s also highlighted the advantages of the capitalist model. The resulting decline in Cold War tensions certainly held out the promise of greater fluidity in private international capital. Whether exchange rates float or are fixed, there is much greater openness to private financial flows on the periphery than in the 1980s. In part a reflection of U.S. business interests, American administrations have pushed developing economies to liberalize on capital account; in some cases, liberalization ran far ahead of domestic financial systems' absorptive capacities, and clashed with national exchange rate policies. The resulting contradictions helped spark the developing-country currency crises of the latter 1990s. To attract productive capital from the industrial world remains a prime goal on the periphery, however, and that requires market-oriented reforms, stable macropolicies, and transparency in governance and legal systems.

There is, however, one critical dimension in which pre-1914 international capital flows differ sharply in nature from what we see today, with important implications for the periphery; to see this we return to the distinction between net and gross international asset stocks. A cursory glance at the data reveals that this problem is very serious in recent decades but was relatively unimportant in the pre-1914 era of globalization. The reason is simple: In the late nineteenth century the principal flows were long-term investment capital, and virtually unidirectional at that. There was one notable exception, the United States, where both inflows and outflows were large. But in most cases key creditor nations, principally Great Britain but also France and Germany, engaged in the financing of other countries' capital accumulation, and in doing so, developed enormous one-way positions in their portfolios.

For example, circa 1914 the scale of Argentine assets in Great Britain's portfolio was very large, but the converse holding of British assets by Argentines was trivial by comparison. Thus, the nineteenth century was an era of one-way asset shifts, leading to great portfolio diversification by the principal creditor-outflow nations like Great Britain, but relatively little diversification by the debtor-inflow nations. To a first approximation, the gross asset and liability positions were very close to net in that distant era. The 1980s and 1990s are obviously very different: For example, the United States became in this period the world's largest net debtor nation. While accounting for the biggest national stock of gross foreign liabilities, however, the United States also held the largest stock of gross foreign assets.

Our earlier discussion of the gross stock data, and our inferences concerning the recovery of foreign assets and liabilities in the world economy after 1980, therefore need considerable modification to take into account this problem. Indeed, it is a significant problem for all of the countries concerned: The ranking of countries by foreign assets in the IMF data is very highly correlated with the ranking by foreign liabilities. Countries such as Great Britain, Japan, Canada, Germany, and the Netherlands are all big holders of both foreign assets and liabilities. Strikingly, when we net out the data the result is that, since 1980, the net foreign asset position (or liability) positions in the world economy have remained very low indeed, as indicated by figure 3.9. Unlike the gross stocks, the net stocks have increased little, and if we trust the asset data rather more (arguably more of the net asset data are collected in richer industrial countries with better accounting methods), then the picture is one of relative decline in the size of net foreign capital stocks relative to GDP.

Thus, for all the suggestion that we have returned to the pre-1914 type of global capital market, here is one major qualitative difference between then and now. Today's foreign asset distribution is much more about asset swap-

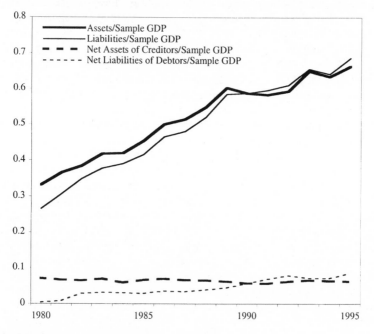

Fig. 3.9   Foreign capital stocks: Net versus gross
Source: IMF.

ping by rich countries—diversification—than it is about the accumulation of large one-way positions—a critical component of the development process in poorer countries in standard textbook treatments. It is therefore more about hedging and risk sharing than it is about long-term finance and the mediation of saving supply and investment demand between countries. In the latter sense, we have never come close to recapturing the heady times of the pre-1914 era, when a creditor like Great Britain could persist for years in satisfying half of its accumulation of assets with foreign capital, or a debtor like Argentina could similarly go on for years generating liabilities of which one-half were taken up by foreigners. Instead, still to a very great extent today, a country's net wealth will depend, for accumulation, on the provision of financing from domestic rather than foreign sources (Feldstein and Horioka 1980).

An interesting, and closely related, insight also follows from looking at the share of less developed countries (LDCs) in global liabilities. This is now at an all-time low. In 1900, LDCs in Asia, Latin America, and Africa accounted for 33 percent of global liabilities; in the 1990s, only 11 percent (fig. 3.3). The global capital market of the nineteenth century centered on Europe, especially London, extended relatively more credit to LDCs than does today's global capital market. Is this surprising? There are various interpretations for this observation. One is that capital markets are biased now, or were biased in the past; for example, did Great Britain, as an imperial power, favor LDCs within her orbit with finance? Or, today, does the global capital market fail in the sense that there are insufficient capital flows to LDCs, and an excess of flows among developed countries? These are hard claims to prove, as market failure could be a cause, as could a host of other factors including institutions and policies affecting the marginal product of capital in different locations. Of course, this result just follows from the fact that many of the top asset holders also figure in the top liability holders, and most of them are developed OECD countries.

Figure 3.10 illustrates both the periphery's need to draw on industrial country savings, and an important dimension in which the globalization of capital markets remains behind the level attained under the classical gold standard. In the last great era of globalization, the most striking characteristic is that foreign capital had its biggest impact (relative to receiving region GDP) in capital-scarce poor countries, although it also moved to some richer countries. The richer countries were the settler economies where capital was attracted by abundant land, and the poor countries were places where capital was attracted by abundant labor.[65]

Globalized capital markets are back, but with a difference: Capital transactions seem to be mostly a rich-rich affair, a process of "diversification finance" rather than "development finance." The high-impact creditor-

65. On the broad distribution of foreign capital then, see Twomey (2000).

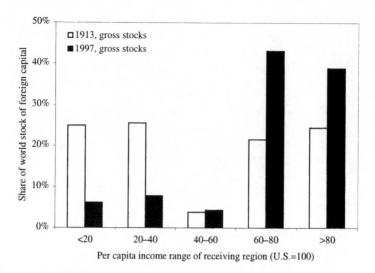

Fig. 3.10   Did capital flow to poor countries? 1913 versus 1997

Sources: The 1913 stock data are from Woodruff (1967) and Royal Institute of International Affairs (1937); incomes are from Maddison (1995). The 1997 data are from Lane and Milesi-Ferretti (2001), based on the stocks of inward direct investment and portfolio equity liabilities.

debtor country pairs involved are more rich-rich than rich-poor, and today's foreign investment in the poorest developing countries lags far behind the levels attained at the start of the last century. In other words, we see again the paradox noted by Lucas (1990), of capital failing to flow to capital-poor countries, places where we would presume the marginal product of capital to be very high. The figure may also understate the failure in some ways: A century ago, world income and productivity levels were far less divergent than they are today, so it is all the more remarkable that so much capital was directed to countries at or below the 20 percent and 40 percent income levels (relative to the United States). Today, a much larger fraction of the world's output and population is located in such low-productivity regions, but a much smaller share of global foreign investment reaches them.[66]

As we have noted, capital is discouraged from entering poorer countries by a host of factors, and some of these were less relevant a century ago. Capital controls persist in many regions. The risks of investment may be perceived differently after a century of exchange risks, expropriations, and defaults. Domestic policies that distort prices, especially of investment goods, may result in returns too low to attract any capital. These conditions make

66. See Clemens and Williamson (2000) for a detailed analysis of the determinants of British capital export before 1914.

a difficult situation much worse. Poorer countries must draw on foreign capital to a greater extent than they do at present if they are to achieve an acceptable growth in living standards. This is a fundamental reason that reform and liberalization in the developing world, despite the setbacks of the late 1990s, are likely to continue, albeit hopefully with due regard to the painful lessons learned in the recent past.

References

Balke, N. S., and M. E. Wohar. 1998. Nonlinear dynamics and covered interest rate parity. *Empirical Economics* 23:535–59.

Barciela, C., and A. Carreras. 1989. *Estadisticas historicas de España: Siglos XIX–XX* (Spanish historical statistics: Nineteenth and twentieth centuries). Madrid: Fundación Banco Exterior.

Barnard, A. 1987. Government finance. In *Australians: Historical statistics,* ed. W. Vamplew, 254–85. Broadway, New South Wales: Fairfax, Syme, and Weldon.

Baxter, M., and A. C. Stockman. 1989. Business cycles and the exchange-rate regime: Some international evidence. *Journal of Monetary Economics* 23 (May): 377–400.

Bernanke, B. S., and K. Carey. 1996. Nominal wage stickiness and aggregate supply in the Great Depression. *Quarterly Journal of Economics* 111 (August): 853–83.

Bertino, M., and H. Tajam. 2000. El PBI de Uruguay 1900–55. Montevideo.

Bértola, L. 1998. El PBI uruguayo 1870–1936 y otras estimaciones (Uruguayan GDP 1870–1936 and other estimations). Montevideo: Facultad de Ciencias Sociales. Mimeograph.

Bhagwati, J. N. 1998. The capital myth. *Foreign Affairs* 77 (May-June): 7–12).

Bordo, M. D., M. Edelstein, and H. Rockoff. 1999. Was adherence to the gold standard a "Good Housekeeping Seal of Approval" during the interwar period? NBER Working Paper no. 7186. Cambridge, Mass.: National Bureau of Economic Research, June.

Bordo, M. D., and B. Eichengreen, eds. 1993. *A retrospective on the Bretton Woods system: Lessons for international monetary reform.* Chicago: University of Chicago Press.

———. 2001. The rise and fall of a barbarous relic: The role of gold in the international monetary system. In *Money, capital mobility, and trade: Essays in honor of Robert A. Mundell,* ed. R. Dornbusch, M. Obstfeld, and G. Calvo, 53–121. Cambridge, Mass.: MIT Press.

Bordo, M. D., B. Eichengreen, and J. Kim. 1999. Was there really an earlier period of international financial integration comparable to today? In *The implications of the globalization of world financial markets,* ed. S. Lee, 27–75. Seoul: Bank of Korea.

Bordo, M. D., and L. Jonung. 1996. Monetary regimes, inflation, and monetary reform: An essay in honor of Axel Leijonhufvud. In *Inflation, institutions, and information: Essays in honor of Axel Leijonhufvud,* ed. D. Vaz and K. Velupillai, 157–244. London: Macmillan.

Bordo, M. D., and F. E. Kydland. 1995. The gold standard as a rule: An essay in exploration. *Explorations in Economic History* 32:423–64.

Bordo, M. D., and H. Rockoff. 1996. The gold standard as a "Good Housekeeping Seal of Approval." *Journal of Economic History* 56 (June): 389–428.

Bordo, M. D., and A. J. Schwartz. 1997. Monetary policy regimes and economic performance: The historical record. NBER Working Paper no. 6201. Cambridge, Mass.: National Bureau of Economic Research, September.

———. Eds. 1984. *A retrospective on the classical gold standard, 1821–1931.* Chicago: University of Chicago Press.

Braun, J., M. Braun, I. Briones, J. Díaz, R. Lüders, and G. Wagner. 2000. Economia Chilena 1810–1995: Estadísticas históricas (The Chilean economy 1810–1995: Historical statistics). Documento de Trabajo no. 187. Pontificia Universidad Católica de Chile, Instituto de Economia, January.

Brezis, E. S. 1995. Foreign capital flows in the century of Britain's industrial revolution: New estimates, controlled conjectures. *Economic History Review* 48 (February): 46–67.

Calomiris, C. W., and R. G. Hubbard. 1996. International adjustment under the classical gold standard: Evidence for the United States and Britain, 1879–1914. In *Modern perspectives on the gold standard,* ed. T. Bayoumi, B. Eichengreen, and M. P. Taylor, 189–217. Cambridge: Cambridge University Press.

Cameron, R. E. 1993. *A concise economic history of the world: From paleolithic times to the present.* New York: Oxford University Press.

Campa J. M. 1990. Exchange rates and economic recovery in the 1930s: An extension to Latin America. *Journal of Economic History* 50 (September): 677–82.

Chortareas, G. E., and R. L. Driver. 2001. PPP and the real exchange rate–real interest rate differential puzzle revisited: Evidence from non-stationary panel data. London: Bank of England. Photocopy, June.

Clemens, M., and J. G. Williamson. 2000. Where did British foreign capital go? Fundamentals, failures, and the Lucas paradox 1870–1913. NBER Working Paper no. 8028. Cambridge, Mass.: National Bureau of Economic Research, December.

Clinton, K. J. 1988. Transactions costs and covered interest arbitrage: Theory and evidence. *Journal of Political Economy* 96 (April): 358–70.

Cohen, B. J. 1996. Phoenix risen: The resurrection of global finance. *World Politics* 48:268–96.

Cortés Conde, R. 1989. *Dinero, deuda y crisis: evolución fiscal y monetaria en la Argentina, 1862–90.* Buenos Aires: Editorial Sudamericana.

Crouchley, A. E. 1938. *The economic development of modern Egypt.* London: Longmans Green.

Davis, L. E. 1965. The investment market, 1870–1914: The evolution of a national market. *Journal of Economic History* 25:355–99.

Davis, L. E., and R. E. Gallman. 2001. *Evolving financial markets and international capital flows: Britain, the Americas, and Australia, 1865–1914.* Japan-U.S. Center Sanwa Monographs on International Financial Markets. Cambridge: Cambridge University Press.

Davis, L. E., and J. R. T. Hughes. 1960. A Dollar-Sterling Exchange, 1803–1895. *Economic History Review* 13 (August): 52–78.

della Paolera, G. 1988. How the Argentine economy performed during the international gold standard: A reexamination. Ph.D. diss. University of Chicago.

della Paolera, G., and J. Ortiz. 1995. Dinero, intermediación financiera y nivel de actividad en 110 años de historia económica Argentina (Money, financial intermediation, and level of activity in 110 years of Argentine economic history). Documentos de Trabajo no. 36. Universidad Torcuato Di Tella, December.

Dornbusch, R. 1998. Discussion. *Economic Policy* 26 (April): 149–52.

Drazen, A., and P. R. Masson. 1994. Credibility of policies versus credibility of policymakers. *Quarterly Journal of Economics* 109 (August): 735–54.

Eatwell, J. 1997. *International financial liberalization: The impact on world develop-*

ment. United Nations Development Program Discussion Paper no. 12. New York: United Nations.

Edelstein, M. 1982. *Overseas investment in the age of high imperialism.* New York: Columbia University Press.

Edison, H. J., and W. R. Melick. 1999. Alternative approaches to real exchange rates and real interest rates: Three up and three down. *International Journal of Finance and Economics* 4:93–111.

Edison, H. J., and B. D. Pauls. 1993. A re-assessment of the relationship between real exchange rates and real interest rates: 1974–1990. *Journal of Monetary Economics* 31 (April): 165–87.

Eichengreen, B. J. 1992. *Golden fetters: The gold standard and the Great Depression, 1919–1939.* Oxford: Oxford University Press.

———. 1996. *Globalizing capital: A history of the international monetary system.* Princeton, N.J.: Princeton University Press.

Eichengreen, B. J., and M. Flandreau. 1996. The geography of the gold standard. In *Currency convertibility: The gold standard and beyond,* ed. J. Braga de Macedo, B. J. Eichengreen, and J. Reis, 113–43. London: Routledge.

Eichengreen, B. J., and J. Sachs. 1985. Exchange rates and economic recovery in the 1930s. *Journal of Economic History* 45 (December): 925–46.

Einzig, P. 1937. *The theory of forward exchange.* London: Macmillan.

———. 1968. *Leads and lags: The main cause of devaluation.* London: Macmillan.

Elliott, G. 1999. Efficient tests for a unit root when the initial observation is drawn from its unconditional distribution. *International Economic Review* 40 (August): 767–83.

Elliott, G., T. J. Rothenberg, and J. H. Stock. 1996. Efficient tests for an autoregressive unit root. *Econometrica* 64:813–36.

Escher, F. 1918. *Elements of foreign exchange.* 8th ed. New York: Bankers Publishing Company.

Feinstein, C. K. 1990. Britain's overseas investments in 1913. *Economic History Review* 43 (May): 288–96.

Feldstein, M., and C. Horioka. 1980. Domestic savings and international capital flows. *Economic Journal* 90 (June): 314–29.

Feis, H. 1931. *Europe, the world's banker, 1870–1914: An account of European foreign investment and the connection of world finance with diplomacy before the war.* New Haven, Conn.: Yale University Press.

Flandreau, M., J. Le Cacheux, and F. Zumer. 1998. Stability without a pact? Lessons from the European gold standard, 1880–1914. *Economic Policy* 26 (April): 115–62.

Flandreau, M., and C. Rivière. 1999. La grande "retransformation"? L'intégration financière internationale et contrôles de capitaux, 1880–1996 (The great "retransformation"? International financial integration and capital controls, 1880–1996). *Économie Internationale* 78:11–58.

Forbes, K., and R. Rigobon. 2000. Contagion in Latin America: Definitions, measurement, and policy implications. NBER Working Paper no. 7885. Cambridge, Mass.: National Bureau of Economic Research, September.

Frieden, J. A. 1997. Monetary populism in nineteenth-century America: An open economy interpretation. *Journal of Economic History* 57 (June): 367–95.

Fujii, E., and M. Chinn. 2000. Fin de siècle real interest parity. NBER Working Paper no. 7880. Cambridge, Mass.: National Bureau of Economic Research, September.

Gallarotti, G. M. 1995. *The anatomy of an international monetary regime: The classical gold standard 1880–1914.* New York: Oxford University Press.

Gerschenkron, A. 1943. *Bread and democracy in Germany.* Berkeley and Los Angeles: University of California Press.

Goldsmith, R. W. 1983. *The financial development of India, 1860–1977.* New Haven, Conn.: Yale University Press.

———. 1985. *Comparative national balance sheets: A study of twenty countries, 1688–1978.* Chicago: University of Chicago Press.

Gourinchas, P. O., and H. Rey. 2001. Stocks and monies. Princeton University. Unpublished manuscript.

Hallwood, C. P., R. MacDonald, and I. W. Marsh. 1996. Credibility and fundamentals: Were the classical and interwar gold standards well-behaved target zones? In *Modern perspectives on the gold standard,* ed. T. Bayoumi, B. Eichengreen, and M. P. Taylor, 129–61. Cambridge: Cambridge University Press.

Hamori, S., and A. Tokihisa. 1997. Testing for a unit root in the presence of a variance shift. *Economics Letters* 57:245–53.

Haupt, O. 1894. *Arbitrages et parités* (Arbitrage and parities). 8th ed. Paris: Librairie Truchy.

Hawke, G. R. 1975. Income estimation from monetary data: Further explorations. *Review of Income and Wealth* 21:301–07.

IBGE (Fundação Instituto Brasileiro de Geografia e Estatística). 1990. *Estatísticas históricas do Brasil: séries econômicas, demográficas e sociais de 1550 a 1988* (Historical statistics of Brazil: Economic, demographic, and social statistics from 1550 to 1988). Rio de Janeiro: IBGE.

International Monetary Fund. 1997. *International financial statistics.* Washington, D.C.: September.

———. 2001. *World economic outlook.* Washington, D.C.: IMF, October.

Irigoin, M. A. 2000. Finance, politics, and economics in Buenos Aires 1820s–1860s: The political economy of currency stabilization. Ph.D. diss., London School of Economics.

James, H. 2001. *The end of globalization: Lessons from the Great Depression.* Cambridge: Harvard University Press.

Jones, M. T., and M. Obstfeld. 2001. Saving and investment under the gold standard. In *Money, capital mobility, and trade: Essays in honor of Robert A. Mundell,* ed. G. Calvo, R. Dornbusch, and M. Obstfeld, 303–63. Cambridge: MIT Press.

Jorion P., and W. N. Goetzmann. 1999. Global stock markets in the twentieth century. *Journal of Finance* 54 (June): 953–80.

Kindleberger, C. P. 1984. *A financial history of Western Europe.* London: George Allen and Unwin.

———. 1986. *The world in depression, 1929–1939.* Rev. ed. Berkeley: University of California Press.

———. 1989. Commercial policy between the wars. In *The Cambridge economic history of Europe,* ed. P. Mathias and S. Pollard. Cambridge: Cambridge University Press.

Klug, A., and G. W. Smith. 1999. Suez and sterling, 1956. *Explorations in Economic History* 36 (July): 181–203.

Lane, P., and G.-M. Milesi-Ferretti. 2001. The external wealth of nations: Measures of foreign assets and liabilities for industrial and developing countries. *Journal of International Economics* 55 (December): 243–62.

Levy, M. B. 1995. The Brazilian public debt: Domestic and foreign, 1824–1913. In *The public debt in Latin America in historical perspective,* ed. R. Liehr, 209–54. Frankfurt am Main: Vervuert.

Lewis, C. 1938. *America's stake in international investments.* Washington, D.C.: Brookings Institution.

————. 1945. *Debtor and creditor countries: 1938, 1944.* Washington, D.C.: The Brookings Institution.

Lewis, K. K. 1999. Trying to explain home bias in equities and consumption. *Journal of Economic Literature* 37 (June): 571–608.

Lineham, B. T. 1968. New Zealand's gross domestic product, 1918–38. *New Zealand Economic Papers* 2:16.

Lloyd Prichard, M. F. 1970. *An economic history of New Zealand to 1939.* Auckland: Collins.

Lucas, R. E., Jr. 1990. Why doesn't capital flow from rich to poor countries? *American Economic Review* 80 (May): 92–96.

MacDonald, R., and J. Nagayasu. 2000. The long-run relationship between real exchange rates and real interest rate differentials: A panel study. *IMF Staff Papers* 47 (November): 116–28.

Maddison, A. 1995. *Monitoring the world economy.* Paris: Organization for Economic Cooperation and Development.

————. 2001. *The world economy: A millennial perspective.* Development Centre Studies. Paris: Organization for Economic Cooperation and Development.

Mamalakis, M. J. 1978–89. *Historical statistics of Chile,* 6 vols. Westport, Conn.: Greenwood Press.

Margraff, A. W. 1908. *International exchange: Its terms, parts, operations, and scope.* 3rd ed. Chicago: Privately printed.

Marshall, M. G., and K. Jaggers. N.d. *Polity IV project: Political regime characteristics and transitions, 1800–1999. Dataset Users' Manual.* College Park: University of Maryland, Center for International Development and Conflict Management.

Meese, R. A., and K. Rogoff. 1988. Was it real? The exchange rate–interest differential relation over the modern floating-rate period. *Journal of Finance* 43 (February): 933–48.

Meissner, C. 2001. A new world order: Explaining the emergence of the classical gold standard. University of California–Berkeley. Photocopy.

Mitchell, B. R. 1992. *International historical statistics: Europe, 1750–1988.* New York: Stockton Press.

————. 1993. *International historical statistics: The Americas, 1750–1988.* New York: Stockton Press.

————. 1995. *International historical statistics: Africa, Asia, and Oceania, 1750–1988.* New York: Stockton Press.

Nakamura, L. I., and C. E. J. M. Zarazaga. 2003. Banking and finance, 1900–35. In *Argentina: Essays in the new economic history,* ed. G. della Paolera and A. M. Taylor. Cambridge: Cambridge University Press. Forthcoming.

Neal, L. 1990. *The rise of financial capitalism: International capital markets in the Age of Reason.* Cambridge: Cambridge University Press.

————. 2000. How it all began: The monetary and financial architecture of Europe during the first global capital markets, 1648–1815. *Financial History Review* 7 (October): 117–40.

Nunes, A. B., E. Mata, and N. Valério. 1989. Portuguese economic growth 1833–1985. *Journal of European Economic History* 18:291–330.

Obstfeld, M. 1995. International capital mobility in the 1990s. In *Understanding interdependence: The macroeconomics of the open economy,* ed. P. B. Kenen, 201–61. Princeton, N.J.: Princeton University Press.

————. 1998. The global capital market: Benefactor or menace? *Journal of Economic Perspectives* 12 (Fall): 9–30.

Obstfeld, M., and K. Rogoff. 1995. The mirage of fixed exchange rates. *Journal of Economic Perspectives* 9 (Fall): 73–96.

————. 2000. The six major puzzles in international macroeconomics: Is there a common cause? In *NBER macroeconomics annual 2000*, ed. B. S. Bernanke and K. Rogoff, 339–90. Cambridge: MIT Press.

Obstfeld, M., and A. M. Taylor. 1997. Nonlinear aspects of goods-market arbitrage and adjustment: Heckscher's commodity points revisited. *Journal of the Japanese and International Economies* 11 (December): 441–79.

————. 1998. The Great Depression as a watershed: International capital mobility in the long run. In *The defining moment: The Great Depression and the American economy in the twentieth century*, ed. M. D. Bordo, C. D. Goldin, and E. N. White, 353–402. Chicago: University of Chicago Press.

————. 2003. *Global capital markets: Integration, crisis, and growth.* Japan-U.S. Center Sanwa Monographs on International Financial Markets. Cambridge: Cambridge University Press. Forthcoming.

————. Forthcoming. Sovereign risk, credibility, and the gold standard: 1870–1913 versus 1925–31. *Economic Journal.*

Officer, L. H. 1996. *Between the dollar-sterling gold points: Exchange rates, parity, and market behavior.* Cambridge: Cambridge University Press.

Oppers, S. E. 1993. The interest rate effect of Dutch money in eighteenth-century Britain. *Journal of Economic History* 53 (March): 25–43.

O'Rourke, K. H., and J. G. Williamson. 1999. *Globalization and history: The evolution of a nineteenth-century Atlantic economy.* Cambridge: MIT Press.

Paish, G. 1914. Export of capital and the cost of living. *The Statist* (Supplement, 14 February): i–viii.

Peel, D. A., and M. P. Taylor. 2002. Covered interest rate arbitrage in the inter-war period and the Keynes-Einzig conjecture. *Journal of Money, Credit, and Banking* 34 (February): 51–75.

Perkins, E. H. 1978. Foreign interest rates in American financial markets: A revised series of dollar-sterling exchange rates, 1835–1900. *Journal of Economic History* 38 (June): 392–417.

Platt, D. C. M. 1986. *Britain's investment overseas on the eve of the First World War: The use and abuse of numbers.* New York: St. Martin's.

Polanyi, K. 1944. *The great transformation.* New York: Rinehart.

Prados de la Escosura, L. 2002. El progreso económico de España, 1850–2000 (Spain's economic progress, 1850–2000). Madrid: Universidad Carlos III. Photocopy.

Rajan, R. G., and L. Zingales. 2001. The great reversals: The politics of financial development in the twentieth century. University of Chicago, Graduate School of Business. Photocopy.

Reserve Bank of India. 1954. *Banking and monetary statistics of India.* Bombay: Reserve Bank of India.

Rippy, J. F. 1959. *British investments in Latin America, 1822–1949: A case study in the operations of private enterprise in retarded regions.* Minneapolis: University of Minnesota Press.

Rodrik, D. 2000. How far will international economic integration go? *Journal of Economic Perspectives* 14 (Winter): 177–86.

Romer, C. D. 1992. What ended the Great Depression? *Journal of Economic History* 52 (December): 757–84.

Royal Institute of International Affairs. 1937. *The problem of international investment.* London: Oxford University Press.

Sachs, J. D., and A. Warner. 1995. Economic reform and the process of global integration. *Brookings Papers on Economic Activity,* Issue no. 1:1–118. Washington, D.C.: Brookings Institution.

Schulze, M.-S. 2000. Patterns of growth and stagnation in the late 19th century Habsburg economy. *European Review of Economic History* 4:311–40.

Spalding, W. F. 1915. *Foreign exchange and foreign bills in theory and practice.* London: Sir Isaac Pitman and Sons.

Sylla, R. E. 1975. *The American capital market, 1846–1914: A study of the effects of public policy on economic development.* New York: Arno.

———. 1998. U.S. securities markets and the banking system, 1790–1840. *Federal Reserve Bank of St. Louis Review* 80 (3): 83–98.

Temin, P. 1989. *Lessons from the Great Depression.* Cambridge: MIT Press.

Tezel, Y. S. 1986. *Cumhuriyet döneminin iktisadi tarihi, 1923–50.* 2nd ed. Ankara: Yurt Yayınları.

Triffin, R. 1957. *Europe and the money muddle: From bilateralism to near-convertibility, 1947–1956.* New Haven, Conn.: Yale University Press.

Twomey, M. J. 1998. Patterns of foreign investment in Latin America in the twentieth century. In *Latin America and the world economy since 1800,* ed. J. H. Coatsworth and A. M. Taylor. Cambridge: Harvard University Press.

———. 2000. *A century of foreign investment in the third world.* London: Routledge.

United Nations. 1948. *Public debt 1914–1946.* Lake Success, N.Y.: United Nations Publications.

Valério, N., ed. 2001. *Estatísticas históricas portuguesas* (Portuguese historical statistics). Lisbon: Instituto Nacional de Estatística.

Williamson, J. G. 1995. The evolution of global labor markets since 1830: Background evidence and hypotheses. *Explorations in Economic History* 32 (April): 141–96.

———. 1996. Globalization, convergence, and history. *Journal of Economic History* 56 (June): 277–306.

Woodruff, W. 1967. *Impact of Western man: A study of Europe's role in the world economy 1750–1960.* New York: St. Martin's.

World Bank. 1994. World data 1994: World Bank indicators on CD-ROM. Washington, D.C.: World Bank.

Yousef, T. Forthcoming. Egypt's growth performance under economic liberalism, 1885–1945: A reassessment using new GDP estimates. *Review of Income and Wealth.*

Comment   Richard Portes

The key assertion of this paper is that the extent of globalization or integration of capital markets since the second half of the nineteenth century has followed a clear pattern: a remarkable rise of capital market globalization from (say) 1860 to 1914, then a sharp fall in World War I, followed by a trough lasting over fifty years, then a strong new upsurge to the present day. The paper offers a hypothesis to explain this pattern: the "trilemma" and national policy responses to it. A subsidiary theme is the shift from cap-

Richard Portes is professor of economics at the London Business School, president of the Centre for Economic Policy Research, and a research associate of the National Bureau of Economic Research.

ital flows as development finance in the first period of globalization to capital flows as portfolio diversification across industrial countries in the second globalization era.

There is no attempt to test the trilemma hypothesis, even to confront it with alternatives. The main effort is to assemble wide-ranging evidence that the pattern itself was very general and observable in both quantities (cross-border capital flows) and prices (interest rates, equity returns).

There are alternative drivers of capital mobility that may suggest at least some qualifications to the trilemma hypothesis. It is not clear whether some are consistent with the historically observed oscillation that is documented here, nor whether they are truly exogenous, as the trilemma-based forces could claim to be.

Consider first information and communications technology (ICT). Many regard that as the primary force behind the global integration of capital markets in the past two decades. One could say this recent ICT revolution has only one parallel historically, the invention of the telegraph and then the telephone pre-1914—with no such impetus in the interwar period, but on the other hand, no breakdown of the technology either. So that might get us somewhere in explaining the two waves of globalization, but it does not have anything to say about the interwar trough. The same could be said of financial market technology itself—there was a remarkable development of financial instruments in the first wave of globalization, and again in the past two decades, but of course no "technological regress" that could be responsible for the interwar period.

The enforcement of international contracts is essential for financial integration. Pre-1914, this was ensured by imperial structures and gunboat diplomacy. They offered a political and legal framework sufficient to support development finance from rich to poor countries and the accumulation of large net foreign asset positions in unreliable environments. That framework disintegrated in the First World War, and only from the late 1960s onward did we get adequate substitutes: the Paris Club, the London Club, IMF conditionality, and overall U.S. geopolitical hegemony that often exerted pressure on debtors to meet their contractual obligations.

International financial instability—in particular, volatility and wide swings in exchange rates—is a deterrent to financial integration. Indeed, many would say that the first era of globalization was underpinned by the gold standard and British hegemony. Yet although the dollar peg, gold exchange standard established at Bretton Woods was instrumental in maintaining monetary discipline and low inflation, and American hegemony replaced the British role, the period 1945–70 nevertheless did not see a major advance in international financial integration. Financial globalization took off again after the Bretton Woods exchange rate mechanism broke down. And in view of the crises of 1982, 1995, 1997, and 1998, it is hard to see the IMF as the guarantor of stability. This may help, however, to explain why the major cross-border financial flows have been between advanced countries rather than between them and the emerging market countries.

We might regard the globalization of production and of financial institutions as a partly exogenous driver of cross-border financial flows. The imperialist system played this role pre-1914, and in recent decades it has been the large multinational firms that invest abroad and develop extensive outsourcing that also requires financial support. There were "global" investment banks such as Rothschilds and Barings pre-1914. They played a significant role in the sovereign lending boom of the 1920s, too, but only in the past decade or two have we seen real financial power accrue to Goldman Sachs and the other "bulge-bracket" banks. Again, there is some relation to the historically observed pattern of financial globalization, but perhaps not a dominant explanation.

A final hypothesis presents itself: that current accounts—or savings-investment imbalances—are the primary drivers of capital accounts. The interwar trough for financial globalization corresponds to a period in which current account surpluses and deficits were severely constrained by major disturbances to international trade.

We see, therefore, that there is a wide variety of alternatives to the authors' fundamental hypothesis. The observed pattern could have been driven by exogenous common shocks rather than common national policy responses to the trilemma. In that case, the appropriate structural break came in 1930, rather than in World War I, and the trough is also not as long-lasting—say, until the late 1950s. There is evidence that international capital markets did reopen substantially in the 1920s, with a buildup of sovereign debt that came crashing down in the defaults of 1931–33. Again, restrictions on capital movements started to break down immediately after the restoration of current account convertibility at the end of the 1950s, and it was the growing capital flows of the 1960s that led to the breakdown of the Bretton Woods exchange rate regime.

None of this in any way diminishes the tremendous achievement of the authors in developing the empirical record of financial globalization. There are many new and important stylized facts that they establish in this paper. The wealth of data, analysis, and interpretations gives a discussant ample opportunity to find interesting questions, and I shall offer only a short list of those that intrigued me.

First, the asset stock data of table 3.2 show that net holdings were close to gross holdings pre-1914, whereas net are now much lower than gross. The authors interpret this as a shift from development finance to portfolio diversification, and overall I find this convincing and illuminating. But we know that this is not so true of foreign direct investment or bank lending as it is of portfolio flows. Moreover, home bias is still very strong—is that consistent with the story? There are also some quite substantial discrepancies between total assets and total liabilities (e.g., 1960, where they differ by a factor of 3). And it would be good to get the authors' views on why the U.K. share of total assets stayed so stable (indeed, so high) from 1960 to 1990, while the U.S. share fell by three-fifths to a level only slightly above that of Great Britain.

The discussion in the text now resolves two puzzles that appear from the covered interest parity data (see fig. 3.4): the apparently systematic positive interest rate gap in favor of New York pre-1914, and the surprisingly large size of the pre-1914 differentials. In fact, they conclude, there was an extraordinarily high degree of integration among the core money markets pre-1914, and I find this convincing.

I am less convinced by the results of tables 3.4 and 3.5 on real interest parity. For example, in table 3.4, with their preferred filter (linear detrend), the Great Britain "band of inaction" widens monotonically from 1890 to 1974. All bands but that of France are much wider post-1973 than in the interwar period. Can we really believe that transaction frictions were greater? Why should the bands be explained entirely by frictions in goods trade—do capital market frictions not also impair the ability to arbitrage in a way that hinders real exchange rate convergence? I therefore find it hard to give great weight to table 3.5.

Interesting questions arise from the discussion of equity and bond returns. Gross equity portfolio flows did not become important until the late 1980s and are still less than cross-border bond flows. I would therefore not expect convincing evidence of "coherence of the returns in G7 equity markets" over a long historical period, nor of the U-shape hypothesis. And no matter how long I look at figure 3.5 and read the corresponding passage in the text, I do not in fact see it. The rationale given by figure 3.6 (an extension of the analysis in Eichengreen and Sachs 1985) is also not convincing: If one removes one or at most two outliers, the upward-sloping line in the right-hand panel becomes vertical. For bonds, again, the U-shape claimed by the authors in figure 3.7 does not seem obvious to me.

I conclude with a few additional problems for the trilemma story. First, the authors suggest that World War I brought political pressures for demand management, hence for independent national monetary policies, hence for restrictions on capital flows—this was the common national policy response conditioned by the trilemma. But in fact, capital mobility rose substantially in the 1920s, with the boom in sovereign lending. Second, they say that it was a common national policy choice (again, a response to the trilemma) to move away from the Bretton Woods exchange rate regime. I can accept this as a characterization of the half-hearted, ultimately unsuccessful attempts to put the system back together again in 1973–76. But I agree with the authors that it is not an explanation for the breakdown of the system—that, as they say, was due to rising capital mobility. Finally, how does 1930–45 fit in the trilemma scheme? Most countries went off gold to float their exchange rates, but at the same time capital controls multiplied.

The problem was in fact the debt defaults of 1931–33, then the approach of war.

All this makes me eager to read the authors' forthcoming book, which will expand on these and other issues in the historical development of capital markets.

Reference

Eichengreen, B. J., and J. Sachs. 1985. Exchange rates and economic recovery in the 1930s. *Journal of Economic History* 45 (December): 925–46.

II

The Great Divergence, Geography, and Technology

4   Globalization and Convergence

Steve Dowrick and J. Bradford DeLong

4.1   Introduction

We see "globalization" everywhere. The nineteenth century saw falls in the costs of transporting goods across oceans that made large-scale intercontinental trade in staples rather than just curiosities and luxuries possible for the first time in human history (see O'Rourke and Williamson 1998; Findlay and O'Rourke, ch. 1 in this volume). It also saw mass flows of capital and mass migration on an extraordinary scale (see Lewis 1978). The second half of the twentieth century saw a further advance in international economic integration. It is hard to argue today that there is any dimension—trade, communication, intellectual property, ideas, capital flows, the scope of entrepreneurial control—save that of mass migration in which we today are less "globalized" than our predecessors at the end of World War I.

By contrast, we do not see "convergence" everywhere. We certainly see convergence at some times and in some places. We see it in the sample of Organization for Economic Cooperation and Development (OECD) economies after World War II (see Dowrick and Nguyen 1989). We see it in East Asia after 1960 (see World Bank 1994). We believe we see the rapid growth in real incomes and productivity levels, the rapid adoption and adaptation of industrial-core technologies, and the shifts in economic struc-

Steve Dowrick is professor of economics at Australian National University. J. Bradford De-Long is professor of economics at the University of California–Berkeley and a research associate of the National Bureau of Economic Research.

We would like to thank Michael Bordo, Barry Chiswick, Greg Clark, Nick Crafts, Barry Eichengreen, Niall Ferguson, Tim Hatton, Chad Jones, Joel Mokyr, Kevin O'Rourke, Richard Portes, Lant Pritchett, Peter Rousseau, Andrei Shleifer, Jean-Philippe Stijns, Alan Taylor, Robert Waldmann, Steven Weber, Jeffrey Williamson, and others for helpful discussions and comments.

ture that are the hallmarks of the process of convergence to world leading-edge economies in China and in India today (see Sachs 2000). During the interwar period, there were signs that economies as diverse as Soviet Russia, colonial Ghana, and Argentina were closing the gap that separated them from the world's industrial core. But these examples of successful convergence have been much more the exception than the rule. Looking at the world as a whole, what convergence there has been has been limited in geography and in time. The rule has been, instead, "divergence, big time" (see Pritchett 1997).

Baumol and Wolff (1988) set out the idea that it would be fruitful to analyze the pattern of world economic growth in terms of membership in a "convergence club." Their insight was that it would be fruitful to distinguish between those economies in which the forces that economists would expect to be generating convergence were strong enough to overwhelm counter-pressures, and those economies in which economists' expectations were not coming to pass. Lucas (2000) showed that such a framework with the assumption of a once-and-for-all switch for an economy's joining the convergence club could account in a stylized fashion for much of the global experience of the past two centuries.

In this paper we seek to push Baumol and Wolff's insight as far as we can. We do not believe that we can put forward a convincing causal analysis of why economies join (and leave) the convergence club. We restrict ourselves much more to description—description of geographic patterns and of correlations between measures of globalization and the power of forces making for convergence.

Our conclusions are four tentative theses about the extent of convergence and the relationship of convergence to globalization:

- The first era of globalization—the knitting together of the world economy into a single unit in which staples could be profitably traded across oceans in the years before World War I—was essential in spreading the possibility of convergence beyond the narrow North Atlantic. Successful economic growth and industrial development in what Lewis (1978) called the temperate economies of European settlement was possible only because of this degree of economic integration (see O'Rourke and Williamson 1998).
- However, outside the charmed circle made up of the western European economies plus the temperate economies of European settlement, the first era of globalization in 1870–1914 did not bring convergence. It brought much structural change and economic integration—the rubber plant to Malaya, the tea plant to Ceylon, the coffee bean to Brazil. It brought large-scale migration—workers from China to Java, from India to South Africa, from Japan to Peru. But the relative gap in income and productivity and the gap in industrial structure vis-à-vis the industrial core of the world economy continued to widen.

- During the interwar era of globalization retreat, there were signs that the world's convergence club was significantly expanding. Pieces of coastal Africa, much of Latin America, and the Stalin-ruled Soviet Union appeared to be closing the relative gap that separated their economies from those of the world's industrial core.
- The post–World War II period has brought an expansion in the size but also a shift in the location of the world's convergence club. First, the OECD economies—as they were defined in the 1980s—have effectively completed the process of convergence. Second, there is the East Asian miracle, which has seen the fastest-growing economies anywhere, any time. Third, successful post-1980 development in China and India has put countries that together amount for two-fifths of the world's population "solidly on the escalator to modernity," in Lawrence Summers's (1994) phrase. However, these episodes of successful economic growth and convergence have been counterbalanced by many economies' loss of their membership in the world's convergence club. Consider the stagnation of late-Communist and post-Communist economies, the disappointment of post-WWII growth in much of Latin America, especially in the southern cone, and the extreme disappointment of Africa's postcolonial economic performance.

If correct, these theses seem to immediately raise three large questions. First, why the limited extent of convergence under the first globalized economy in the decades before 1914? The integrating world economy was powerful enough to move tens of millions of people across oceans and shape crop and livestock patterns in Java, central Brazil, and Ceylon as well as on the pampas and in the outback. Yet it was not strong enough to induce convergence outside the narrow charmed circle. Second, why did the area subject to convergence enlarge in the interwar period, when by and large the forces of globalization have been in retreat? Third, what were the forces behind the change in the shape of the convergence club after World War II? However, the narratives and analyses we provide do not provide convincing answers to these questions.

4.2   Joining and Leaving the Convergence Club

4.2.1   Economists' Expectations

Some thirty years ago, geopoliticians and commentators spoke often of the countries of the globe as divided into three "worlds": first, second, and third. To be of the third world was to try to play off the United States against the Soviet Union (and hopefully receive large amounts of aid from both). To be of the third world was to stress the differences between one's own polity and economy and those of the industrial core grouped around the North Atlantic. To be of the third world was to be—relatively—poor.

Today the Communist second world is gone, but the term *third world* is still useful. It underscores the differences—the sharp economic divergence in living standards and productivity levels—in the world today. To use the more common "developed" and "developing" nomenclature for groups of countries is to suggest that differences are narrowing, that countries are converging. However, this is not the case—at least not for most of the post-WWII period. Those economies that were relatively rich at the start of the twentieth century have by and large seen their material wealth and prosperity explode. Those nations and economies that were relatively poor have grown richer too, but for the most part much more slowly. And the relative gulf between rich and poor economies has grown steadily.

That the pattern of economic growth over the twentieth century is one of striking *divergence* is surprising to economists, for economists expect *convergence*. World trade, migration, and flows of capital should all work to take resources and consumption goods from where they are cheap to where they are dear. As they travel with increasing speed and increasing volume as transportation and communication costs fall, these commodity and factor-of-production flows should erode the differences in productivity and living standards between continents and between national economies.

Moreover, most of the edge in standards of living and productivity levels held by the industrial core is no one's private property, but instead the common intellectual and scientific heritage of humankind. Here every poor economy has an excellent opportunity to catch up with the rich by adopting and adapting from this open storehouse of modern machine technology. Yet economists' expectations have, throughout the past century, been disappointed, whether the expectations were those of John Stuart Mill that the spread of democracy, literacy, and markets would develop the world; or of Karl Marx that the British millowners' building of a network of railroads across India would backfire and have long-run consequences the millowners had never envisioned.

We can view this particular glass either as half empty or as half full. It is half empty in that we live today in the most unequal world (at least in terms of the divergence in the relative lifetime income prospects of children born into different economies) ever seen. It is half full in that most of the world has already made the transition to sustained economic growth. Most people today live in economies that, while far poorer than the leading-edge postindustrial nations of the world's economic core, have successfully climbed onto the escalator of modern economic growth.

4.2.2   The Idea of the Convergence Club

Why have economists been disappointed in their expectation that economic forces—international trade, international migration, international investment, and technology transfer—will gradually smooth out the enormous gaps in productivity levels, real incomes, and living standards around the world?

Back in 1988, William Baumol and Edward Wolff proposed that we begin thinking about this problem by examining the membership over time of the convergence club, which they defined as that set of economies where the forces of technology transfer, increased international trade and investment, and the spread of education were powerful enough to drive productivity levels and industrial structures to (or at least toward) those of the industrial core. Baumol and Wolff believed that examining how it is that economies enter and fall out of this convergence club should reveal clues to what are the particular economic, political, and institutional blockages that keep convergence the exception in the world today, and not the rule.[1]

Steve Dowrick and Duc-Tho Nguyen were the first to powerfully argue that the countries that belonged to the OECD had converged over the course of the post-WWII period (see Dowrick and Nguyen 1989). Convergence *could* work powerfully if circumstances and institutions were sufficiently favorable. In the case of the OECD after World War II, the set of countries that converged by and large shared a common social-democratic political setup, a common mixed-economy market-oriented economic setup, and a commitment to cutting back on protectionist barriers and to an open world economy.[2] But the set of OECD economies were not the only ones that belonged to the world's convergence club in the post-WWII period. Before we can begin to answer Baumol and Wolff's question and analyze the relationship of globalization and convergence, we need to map the size of the world's convergence club.

4.2.3   Mapping the Convergence Club

The task, therefore, is to examine the evolution of the world's convergence club over time by taking snapshots of its membership during four different eras over the past two centuries: 1820–70, 1870–1913, 1913–50, and 1950–2000. Moreover, it is important to be somewhat sophisticated in how we define *convergence*. When growth macroeconomists use the word *convergence*, they tend to think of a reduction in the variance of the distribution of output per worker levels (or total factor productivity levels, or real wage levels) across countries, or possibly of an erosion over time of initial edges or deficits in relative productivity vis-à-vis other national economies. But for a historically oriented economist, *convergence* means something somewhat different. It means the assimilation of countries outside northwest Europe of the institutions, technologies, and productivity levels currently in use in northwest Europe and in the rest of the industrial core. What you are converging to is thus a moving target.

Moreover, it is as much a structural and organizational target as a target indicated by levels of gross domestic product (GDP) per worker. The World

---

1. There is in this notion of a convergence club an implicit (and largely valid) critique of one-size-fits-all cookie-cutter growth regressions that search for one common law of motion to apply to the whole world, as found in, for example, DeLong (1988).
2. Or so DeLong and Eichengreen (1994) argued.

Bank reports that Saudi Arabia and the Persian Gulf Emirates certainly have levels of GDP per worker and standards of living equivalent to those of Western Europe. Yet we would not want to claim that they have converged to the industrial core. Before World War II there were periods of as long as a generation during which Argentine or Australian productivity levels were falling relative to those of the industrial core, either because of declining terms of trade or because of prolonged drought (see Butlin 1970). However, throughout such periods the Argentine and Australian economies were building up their industrial sectors and raising their economies' educational levels. In economic structure they were thus converging to the industrial core, even if they were losing relative ground in terms of standards of living and value of output per worker (see Diaz-Alejandro 1970).

So our definition of which economies are in the convergence club over a time period is not merely those countries in which GDP per capita as a proportion of the North Atlantic level rose over the time period in question. It looks at the extent of industrial development and structural change as well.

4.2.4   The Convergence Club, 1820–70

By 1820 the British industrial revolution was in full swing. The steam engine was nearly a century old. The automated textile mill was no longer a novelty. The long-distance railroad was on the horizon. As the pace of structural change and industrial development accelerated in Great Britain, its technologies began to diffuse elsewhere, to the continent of Europe and overseas to North America.

As Sidney Pollard (1981, 45–46) put it, the process of diffusion

> found no insuperable obstacles in [spreading to continental Europe]. . . .
> The regions of Europe differed, however, very greatly in their preparedness. . . . There was . . . an "inner" Europe . . . closest . . . to the social and economic structure . . . in Britain. Surrounding that core . . . other areas
> . . . less prepared. . . . Moreover, this conquest did not proceed indefinitely outward. . . . [T]here came a line where the process stopped, sometimes for generations, and, in some cases, until today. Beyond it . . . only scattered outposts, too weak to affect much the surrounding country. . . .

As time passed, the process of diffusion gathered force and the size of the convergence club grew.

In the beginning the convergence club was very small. Between 1820 and 1870 it was, as Pollard (1981) notes, limited to Great Britain itself, Belgium, and the northeastern United States. Industrialization had begun to spread elsewhere, to Canada, to the rest of the United States, to the Netherlands, to Germany, to Switzerland, to what is now Austria, to what is now the Czech Republic, and to France. However, all of these economies found themselves further from Great Britain in industrial structure in 1870 than they had been back in 1820.[3]

3. See Pollard (1981), Maddison (1994), and Landes (1969).

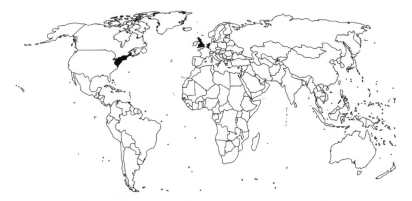

Fig. 4.1   The world's "convergence club" ca. 1850
Note: Solid black: economies that are members of the "convergence club."

Note that here the focus on industrial structure rather than economy-wide productivity or labor productivity makes the biggest difference. The labor-scarce U.S. west and Canada certainly had higher real wages than Great Britain by the end of this period, as did labor-scarce Australia and New Zealand. The Netherlands was in all probability more prosperous in overall terms than Great Britain in 1820, and even in 1870 the productivity and living standard gap was relatively small.[4] But on an industrial-structure and an industrial-technology definition of convergence, the primary product-producing economies, even the richest ones like Canada, do not belong in the convergence club before 1870. They are rich primary-sector-based economies, not industrializing economies. And the Netherlands, also, is not yet an industrializing economy: It is still a rich mercantile economy. To the extent that one takes industrialization as the key measure of modernity or development in the middle and late nineteenth century, the mid-nineteenth-century convergence club (see fig. 4.1) was very small indeed.[5]

4.2.5   The Convergence Club, 1870–1914

Between 1870 and 1914 the convergence club expands considerably. What Arthur Lewis called the countries of temperate European settlement—Canada, the western United States, Australia, and New Zealand,

4. Indeed, the most parsimonious hypothesis explaining the slow industrialization of the Netherlands in the mid-nineteenth century is that Dutch workers had more productive and profitable things to do than work in the dark satanic mills and forges of the early industrial revolution. You can get coal to Amsterdam almost as cheaply as to Brussels, but real wages were much lower in the second than in the first; hence, that is where the mills were located. See Mokyr (1976).

5. It is, of course, debatable whether one should focus so exclusively on machines, factories, and manufacturing, and give the development of those sectors priority over wealth as defined by output per worker.

plus Argentina, Chile, Uruguay, and perhaps South Africa—clearly belong to the convergence club (see Lewis 1978). They are rich and are experiencing (for the most part) rapid income growth. But they are also making use of industrial technology, building up their materials-processing and factor sectors, and becoming industrial economies. Australia started the period as the sheep-raising equivalent of the Organization of Petroleum Exporting Countries (OPEC) of the late nineteenth century, but by the beginning of World War I it was clearly well on the way to being a successfully industrializing economy. Argentina before World War I had a large and rapidly growing portion of its labor force employed in railroads and in food processing. By 1913 Buenos Aires ranked in the top twenty world cities in terms of telephones per capita.

The successful spread of the convergence club to include the economies of temperate European settlement is an achievement of the first, 1870–1914, era of globalization. The coming of the steamship and the telegraph made the transoceanic shipment of staple commodities economically feasible for the first time in human history. However, ocean transport was not so cheap as to make it economically efficient to do all materials and food processing in the industrial core of northwest Europe and the northeast United States. Buenos Aires, Melbourne, Santiago, Toronto, and San Francisco became manufacturing as well as trade and distribution centers. And the ease of transport and communication brought about by this first late-nineteenth-century global economy made the technology transfer to enable this "rich peripheral" industrialization feasible.

In this period also the Industrial Revolution, and thus the convergence club, spread to include nearly all the countries of inner Europe: Belgium, the Netherlands, France, Germany, Switzerland, Spain (but probably not yet Portugal), Italy (even if surely not its south), Austria, what is now Hungary, what is now the Czech Republic, Denmark, Norway, Sweden, Finland, and Ireland (see Pollard 1981). Beyond that line, however, the convergence club did not extend, in spite of small and weak enclaves of industrialization. With one exception, the relative gap in per capita productivity and industrial structure between the industrial core and economies like Russia, Turkey, Egypt, and the rest was wider in 1914 than it had been in 1870. That one exception was Japan (see Ohkawa and Rosovsky 1973).

The failure of the tropical primary-product-producing regions to join the convergence club in the 1870–1914 period marks the limited scale of this first era of globalization. International trade, international investment, international migration, and international conquest profoundly affected economic, social, and political structures throughout the world. The British Empire brought the rubber plant to Malaysia. British investors financed the movement of indentured workers south from China to Malaysia to work the plantations to produce the rubber to satisfy demand back in the world economy's core. The British Empire brought the tea plant from China to

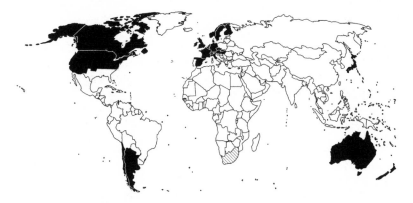

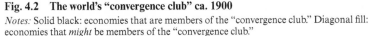

Fig. 4.2   The world's "convergence club" ca. 1900

Notes: Solid black: economies that are members of the "convergence club." Diagonal fill: economies that *might* be members of the "convergence club."

Ceylon. British investors financed the movement of Tamils from India across the strait to work the plantations to produce the tea to satisfy demand from the British actual and would-be middle classes. But these did *not* trigger any rapid growth in real wages. They did not trigger any acceleration in productivity growth or industrialization. They did not trigger any rapid growth in factory employment, or any convergence to the world's economic core (see Lewis 1978).

The convergence club remained of limited size, not touching continental Asia at all, and barely touching Africa and Latin America (see fig. 4.2).[6]

4.2.6   The Convergence Club, 1914–50

The enormous physical destruction wrought by two world wars, coupled with the enormous economic destruction of the Great Depression, makes it difficult to discern trends between 1914 and 1950. By 1950 the gap in productivity and living standards between Japan and the United States was larger than it had been in 1914. But does this mean that Japan had fallen further behind in technology and industrial structure? Perhaps, but perhaps not: It depends whether you take the as your benchmark the industrial structure of still war-ravaged Japan in 1950, or the level and quality of the technologies being installed in the rebuilding Japan, which were much

6. W. Arthur Lewis (1978) argued that it was the particular position of China and India in the Malthusian cycle at the end of the nineteenth century that gave rise to this peculiar wage increase–less, structural change–less form of development and growth, that whatever increases in demand for labor in the tropical periphery were produced by the first era of globalization were overwhelmed by the elastic supply of potential migrant labor from China and India. But an equally valid way to look at it is not that migrant labor supply from China and India was remarkably large, but that the amount of increased trade between tropical periphery and industrial core was relatively small.

closer to world best practice in 1950 than in 1914 and which by the 1970s would have world-leading productivity levels in some industries (see Patrick and Rosovsky 1976).

We argue, once again, for the second definition—we want to compare relative technology, industrial structure, and productivity gaps in 1914 to what they would have been in 1950 had postwar reconstruction been completed. Thus, from our perspective, Japan and its inner empire of Korea and Taiwan definitely belong in the convergence club over the extended interwar period from 1914 to 1950 (see fig. 4.3). During this interwar period the southern United States joins the convergence club. Its long economic decline relative to the industrial core comes to an end in this period (see Wright 1978). The Soviet Union joins as well. Stalinist industrialization was a disaster for human life, social welfare, and economic efficiency, but it was a powerful motor of industrialization. Elsewhere in Europe, however, there was little expansion in the convergence club.

However, the convergence club did expand outside of Europe. In Latin America, Venezuela, Peru, and Brazil appear to have joined. Brazilian real GDP per capita appears to have more than doubled in the years 1913–50 (see Maddison 2001). Because of the discovery and exploitation of oil, Venezuelan GDP per capita grew more than sixfold.

In Africa, Ghana, the Ivory Coast, Kenya, Tanzania, Nigeria, and perhaps other regions appear to make progress (see Hopkins 1973). French North Africa—Morocco, Algeria, and Tunisia—closed some of the relative gap between themselves and Western Europe (see Dumont 1966). Per capita income in such economies appears to grow as rapidly as in the industrial core. There are signs of, if not widespread industrialization, at least widespread integration of plantation and smallholder agriculture into the

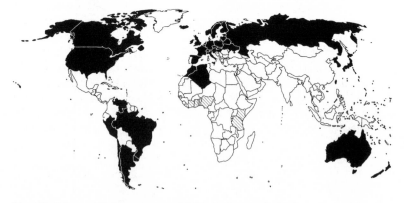

Fig. 4.3   The world's "convergence club" in the interwar period
Notes: Solid black: economies that are members of the "convergence club." Diagonal fill: economies that *might* be members of the "convergence club."

world economy. Whether this is sufficient structural change to qualify for full-fledged membership in the convergence club is debatable.

An optimist—a John Stuart Mill, say, looking for knowledge, education, trade, and markets to bring the whole world together in a march to a liberal utopia[7]—might have looked at the world in 1950 and been relatively optimistic. Naziism had been defeated. Communism was a bloody and authoritarian form of economic growth, but it might well become less bloody and less authoritarian over time. And elsewhere the convergence club was clearly growing, even if it was growing less rapidly than one would wish.

4.2.7   The Convergence Club, 1950–2000

However, the next period—the period between 1950 and 2000, which we have just lived through—has brought surprises. The convergence club both expanded and contracted massively, as for the first time many economies joined and, also for the first time ever, many economies dropped out. In Latin America, countries like Venezuela, Peru, Argentina, Chile, and Uruguay exhibited stunning relative economic declines over the last half century. Argentine relative income levels had declined during 1913 to 1950, as the value of primary products fell, but its industrial structure had converged toward industrial-core norms. But between 1950 and 2000 the sectoral distribution of the labor force froze, and Argentinians lost a third of their relative income vis-à-vis the industrial core.

Coastal West Africa fell out of the convergence club (if it had ever belonged in the first place); coastal East Africa fell out as well (if it, too, had ever belonged). South Africa did not maintain modern economic growth fast enough to close the gap with the industrial core over the second half of the twentieth century, and educational and industrial structure gaps vis-à-vis Western Europe grew substantially. Purchasing power parity–concept GDP per capita in South Africa was perhaps a quarter of that in the industrial core in 1950, and is less than a sixth of that in the industrial core today.[8]

Moreover, the countries of French North Africa fell out of the convergence club: Morocco, Tunisia, and Algeria are today further behind France in relative material productivity and industrial structure than they were in 1950. The former Soviet Union dropped its membership in the convergence club as well. First came the stagnation that began in the mid-1970s as the ability of the centrally planned system to deliver even its own kind of limited, resource- and capital-intensive economic growth eroded and effectively ended in the 1970s. Then came the collapse of economic activity in the 1990s that followed the end of communism.

This shrinkage of the convergence club during what was an era of ex-

---

7. See Mill (1848).
8. Neighboring Botswana, however, has been one of the fastest-growing economies in the world.

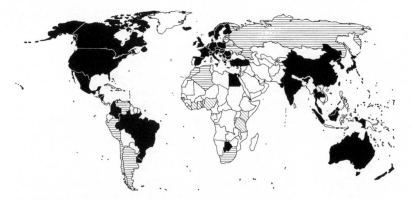

Fig. 4.4   The world's "convergence club" in recent years

Notes: Solid black: economies that are members of the "convergence club." Vertical fill: economies that *might* be members of the "convergence club." Horizontal fill: economies that used to belong to the convergence club, but have fallen out. Diagonal fill: economies that *might* have once belonged, but that have fallen out.

panded international trade and massive moves toward an open world economy is remarkable, and very much counter to economists' perhaps naïve expectations. In each case the driving factors may have been political. Agronomist Rene Dumont warned at the very beginning of African decolonization that the postcolonial governments were following policies that destructively taxed agriculture and enriched relatively parasitic urban elites (see Dumont 1966). The work of Robert Bates two decades later suggested that little had changed (see Bates 1981).

Diaz-Alejandro (1970) and DeLong and Eichengreen (1994) argued that the failure of the southern cone of South America in economic development after World War II was largely a political failure. And the (largely political) failure of the Soviet Union to live up to its potential both before and after its disintegration is well known. If correct, this would suggest that all the potential for international economic contact and technology transfer cannot survive bad economic policies. It would, however, beg the question of why such bad economic policies were so likely to be adopted by so many countries in the half-century after World War II.

As these economies fell out of the convergence club, other economies joined (see fig. 4.4). The East Asian miracle took hold: Japan, South Korea, Taiwan, Hong Kong, Singapore, Thailand, Malaysia, Indonesia (after 1965), and China (after 1978) clearly belong to the convergence club. Only the unreformed socialist governments of Burma, Cambodia, Laos, and Vietnam keep them from joining the rest of east and Southeast Asia.[9] In the Balkans, Yugoslavia, Romania, and Bulgaria join the convergence club:

9. However, the Philippines and Papua New Guinea go their own way as well.

Once again centrally planned economies succeed in growth at a particular stage of early industrialization, albeit at a large human cost. In the eastern Mediterranean, Greece, Turkey, Israel, and Egypt are now in the convergence club. In Latin America, Colombia and Mexico join. After 1980, India begins not only to grow economically but to narrow the gap in aggregate productivity and industrial structure (see Sachs et al. 2000).

In the first (1870–1914) era of globalization its implications for the size of the convergence club were clear. Globalization forces were sufficient to pull the temperate economies of European settlement into the convergence club, but insufficient to pull any other regions into the club even though they had powerful effects on economic structure. In the second (1950–2000) era of globalization, the implications of globalization for the size of the convergence club are less clear. Why has it been such a friend to East Asia but not to Latin America? Why has the eastern Mediterranean done so well and the southwestern Mediterranean so badly? What explains the economic collapse of Africa relative to the high hopes of the decolonization era and to the 1914–50 interwar period?

4.3 Debating Convergence while Incomes Diverge

4.3.1 Is "Conditional Convergence" Meaningful?

Recent debates on growth theory have contrasted the convergence predictions of the neoclassical growth models of Swan (1956) and Solow (1956) with predictions of potential nonconvergence from the newer models of endogenous technological progress of Romer (1990) and Aghion and Howitt (1998). Most of this debate has been in the context of closed economy modelling. The standard neoclassical assumption of diminishing returns to investment implies that each economy converges to its own steady-state level of labor productivity. Higher rates of saving and lower rates of population growth will raise the long-run level of income, but not its growth rate. Long-run growth is simply the world's rate of technical progress.

In this framework, empirical studies of short-run growth are predicted to find conditional convergence if they control for factor accumulation. A negative partial correlation between growth and initial income is confirmation of convergence toward steady state. (In the terms of modern time series econometrics, it is evidence of cointegration between income levels and the country-specific determinants of steady state.) Even when this negative partial correlation is observed on cross-country data, it has no implications for convergence across countries. Thus, studies such as Mankiw, Romer, and Weil (1992) can find strong conditional convergence, at a rate of around 2 or 3 percent per year, on postwar data covering both industrialized and unindustrialized economies.

Over recent years, the use of panel data and higher levels of econometric sophistication (or sophistry?) have produced ever-increasing estimates of the magnitude of the conditional convergence coefficient. The annual rate of global convergence since 1960 is estimated to be around 10 percent both by Islam (1995) and by Caselli, Esquivel, and Lefort (1996), whereas Lee, Pesaran, and Smith (1998) suggest that the true figure is closer to 30 percent.[10] This focus on conditional convergence has tended to obscure the fact that, across the globe, income levels have actually been diverging rather than converging over the past forty years.[11]

Perhaps the foremost advocate of the position that there has been or is "convergence" in the world over the past fifty years and today is Harvard economist Robert Barro (1996). His work finds "strong support [for] the general notion of conditional convergence"—that is, that if other things are held equal then there is a strong tendency for countries to converge toward a common level of total factor productivity, a common level of labor productivity, and a common standard of living.

In Barro's view, strong and powerful forces are pushing countries together. His regressions show that, on average, a country with the same value of the other right-hand-side variables closes between 2.5 and 4.5 percent of the log gap between it and the world's industrial leaders each year. This means that even a country as poor as Mozambique could—if it attained the same values for the other right-hand-side variables—close half the (log) gap between its level of productivity and that of the United States in sixteen to twenty-nine years, and in such an eyeblink of historical time become as rich and productive as Thailand or Panama or Lithuania is today.

The joker in the deck, of course, is the assumption that other things—the other right-hand-side variables in Barro's regression—could be made equal. Barro's other right-hand-side variables include an index of democracy, an index of the rule of law, government noninvestment spending as a share of GDP, life expectancy, the male secondary-school attendance rate, and the fertility rate. And a moment's thought will convince anyone that these other right-hand-side variables could never be brought to the mean values found in the industrial core of the world economy in any country that has not already attained the productivity level and socioeconomic structure found in the industrial core.

First and most important, consider the fertility rate. At extremely low levels of income per capita—levels lower than found anywhere else in the world today save in exceptional years—there is a positive Malthusian

---

10. In this last case, the use of annual time series data and dummy variables for country-specific exogenous technical progress may have resulted in the convergence coefficient capturing the average frequency of the business cycle.

11. We need to qualify this statement as referring to an unweighted measure of global income dispersion. When population weights are applied, there is evidence of some decrease in global income inequality—but this depends entirely on the rapid growth of average real income in China over the past twenty years and in India over the past fifteen years.

causal relationship running from income to fertility. But once one passes over this Malthusian peak, there is a strong negative causal relationship running from income to fertility. In richer countries access to birth control is easier, and birth control means that those who did not wish to have more children could exercise their choice. Life expectancies are longer in richer countries, so parents no longer need to birth four sons to be reasonably sure that one will survive into middle age. Starting in eighteenth-century France and continuing in every single country we have observed since, as the resources and educational level of the average household rise, fertility falls.

The same argument applies to life expectancy and to educational levels as well. These are things that are at least as much results of wealth and productivity as causes of it. It is not possible to consistently imagine a counterfactual world in which a poor country like Mozambique could have a secondary-school enrolment rate and a life expectancy as high as those of the industrial core.

For the third group of his right-hand-side variables, the "government group" made up of the rule-of-law index, the democratization index, and government noninvestment spending as a share of GDP, Barro has more of a point. States that tax heavily and do not spend the proceeds on public investments, states too weak to enforce the rule of law or control the corruption of their functionaries, and states that rest not on the consent of the governed but on the bayonets of soldiers and the whispers of informers destroy economic growth. But here, as well, the cause-and-effect links run both ways. Richer countries with larger tax bases afford governments more resources that they can use to enforce the rule of law and control the corruption of their own functionaries. In richer countries the rewards from concentrating activity on the positive-sum game of production are greater relative to the rewards of grasping for a redistribution of rents from the export trade.

For these reasons we find demonstrations of convergence conditional on fertility, life expectancy, education, and even on the structure and effectiveness of government to be of dubious value. A claim that convergence is a powerful and active force in the world today but is masked by other factors suggests that there is an alternative, counterfactual set of political and economic arrangements in which that convergence would come to the forefront and be clearly visible. Yet we can see no way of bringing the poor-country values of Barro's other right-hand-side variables to their rich-country means that does not presuppose that full economic development has already been successfully accomplished.

This argument applies even more strongly to convergence regressions, like those of DeLong and Summers (1991), that include measures of investment in their list of right-hand-side variables. A poor country will face a high relative price of the capital equipment it needs to acquire in order to turn its savings into productive additions to its capital stock. This should come as no surprise. The world's most industrialized and prosperous economies are the most industrialized and prosperous because they have attained very high levels of manufacturing productivity: Their productivity advantage in unskilled service industries is much lower than in capital- and technology-intensive manufactured goods. The higher relative price of machinery in developing countries means that poor countries get less investment—a smaller share of total investment in real GDP—out of any given effort at saving some fixed share of their incomes.

4.3.2 Development Traps, Conditional Convergence, and Absolute Divergence

So the coexistence of actual divergence and conditional convergence reflects the observation that some of the "conditioning" variables in the standard convergence regressions are distributed in such a way as to promote divergence—in particular, faster population growth and lower rates of investment in poorer countries. In autarkic models, this implies the existence of a development trap or poverty trap: A population living close to subsistence is unable to mobilize the surplus required for substantial domestic investment;[12] they will typically face high prices for imported capital goods; they may well be caught in a prisoner's dilemma whereby each family substitutes quantity of children for quality of human capital investment (schooling) in attempting to maximize family welfare, running afoul of diminishing returns to labor in the aggregate.

A related explanation for the limited range of convergence over the past century and a half is put forward by Richard Easterlin (1981), who attributes limited convergence to a lack of formal education throughout much of the world. As Easterlin puts it, the diffusion of modern economic growth has depended principally on the diffusion of knowledge about the productive technologies developed during and since the Industrial Revolution, and this knowledge cannot diffuse to populations that have not acquired the traits and motivations produced by formal schooling. Political conditions and ideological influences played the biggest role in restricting the spread of formal education before World War II. But Easterlin looks forward to a world in which formal education is universal, hence in which the blockages to convergence have vanished.

Perhaps the most interesting contribution to this literature over the past several decades has been that of Gregory Clark (1987), who suggests that the chief obstacle to convergence was not the inability to transfer technology to relatively poor economies, but the relative inefficiency of labor. Clark studies the state of cotton mills worldwide around 1900 and finds that the technologies of automated cotton-spinning had indeed been suc-

---

12. Ben-David (1997) models exactly such a development trap by introducing the notion of subsistence consumption into the neoclassical exogenous growth model.

cessfully transferred all around the world: There were cotton mills not just in Manchester and Lowell, but also in Tokyo, Shanghai, and Bombay, all using the same technology and all equipped with machinery from the same spinning-machine manufacturers in New England or in Lancashire. Yet, according to Clark, labor productivity in factories equipped with the same machines varied by a factor of ten-to-one worldwide, neatly offsetting the ten-to-one variation in real wages worldwide and so making the profitability of cotton-spinning mills approximately equal no matter where they were located.

Clark points out that given the enormous gaps in real wages, something like an equivalent gap in labor productivity was essential if competition were not to rapidly eliminate the cotton-spinning industry from large chunks of the globe. Capital costs were much the same worldwide: Factories did use common sources of machines. Raw material costs varied, but not grossly worldwide. Labor costs were the overwhelming bulk of total costs. Thus, unless labor productivity varied directly and proportionately with the real wage, a cotton-spinning mill in a low-wage economy would have an overwhelming cost advantage. And competition would lead to an international division of labor in which such low-wage economies dominated the worldwide industry of a good as easily and cheaply tradable as cotton thread.

Clark (1987) has been an extremely influential and disturbing paper for the decade and a half since it was first written. But its striking results may be due to some peculiarity of the cotton-spinning industry, rather than with the general nature of modern economic growth. Consider: In order for Clark to do his comparisons of productivity levels in one industry across the whole world, he needs to find an industry that is not heavily concentrated in one particular region or among one particular slice of the world income distribution. Thus, he needs to find an industry in which it is profitable to locate in a country no matter what that country's level of real wages—in which it is profitable to locate in Manchester, Milan, or Mobile as well as in Mumbai.

When will it be profitable to locate an industry in a country no matter what that country's relative level of real wages? It will be profitable if and only if labor productivity in that industry is proportional to the local real wage. Thus, Clark's major conclusion—that in the cotton-spinning industry at the turn of the last century there were extraordinary variations in labor productivity that were roughly proportional to the local real wage—could have been arrived at without any of his calculations just by observing that there were cotton-spinning mills in Mumbai and also in Manchester.

But how common are industries like the cotton-spinning industry? How much of the world's industry is of this character, in which labor productivity is proportional to the local real wage? We know that it is not the case today in toy manufacture: Mattel just closed down its last U.S. toy-manufacturing plant. We know that it is not the case in steel: U.S. producers and unions continue to demand protection against steel makers in Brazil and Korea lest large chunks of their industry vanish. We know that it is not the case in microprocessor manufacture or (Bangalore aside) software design. We know that it is not the case in grain agriculture.

There are some industries in which labor productivity worldwide is roughly proportional to the local real wage. There are more industries in which it is not: Either labor productivity varies less than the real wage (and the industry tends to be concentrated in at least some relatively poor countries), or labor productivity varies more than the real wage (and the industry tends to be concentrated in the richest and most technologically capable economies). We are going to have to learn lessons from many more industries than just the cotton mills before we can understand why the whole world is not developed.

Our picture of world development is one in which some economic forces push in the direction of convergence while other forces are divergent. Globalization is typically presumed to reinforce the convergent trend—through the flow of capital toward capital-poor economies, through trade-induced factor price equalization, and through international knowledge spillovers. Why might globalization have failed to produce convergence over the past fifty years?

Lucas (1990) suggests that human capital complementarity may block the capital channel. The marginal product of capital in a capital-poor country may well be much higher than that in the United States, other things being equal. But typically those other things are not equal: in particular, the availability of the skilled labor required to operate and adapt a new technology. When physical and human capital are complementary, the problems of moral hazard in human capital investment explain the failure of international capital markets to invest in the capital-poor economies.

Similar problems are likely to impede the international transfer of technology, as is argued by Abramovitz (1986), who cites a lack of social capability as the major obstacle preventing the technologically backward from absorbing the technological developments of the advanced economies. This hypothesis is supported by Benhabib and Spiegel (1994), who find evidence that the growth rate of total factor productivity depends on the national stock of human capital.

4.3.3 Openness and Convergence

An alternative explanation for the failure of globalization to bring about convergence comes from Sachs and Warner (1995). They have constructed an index of openness for the twenty-year period 1970–89, in which the index takes the value of 1 for an open economy but a value of zero if the economy was closed according to at least one of the following five criteria:

1. Tariff rates averaging over 40 percent
2. Nontariff barriers covering at least 40 percent of imports
3. A socialist economic system
4. A state monopoly of major exports
5. A black market premium of 20 percent or more on foreign currency

They find evidence for the period 1970–89 of strong convergence in per capita GDP among the group of countries classified as open, but no convergence among the closed economies. The average growth premium for opening an economy is estimated to be a massive 2.5 percentage points on annual growth.

Sachs and Warner (1995) argue that globalization has indeed promoted both growth and convergence (i.e., faster growth for poorer countries), but only to those countries that allow relatively free movement of goods and capital. In other words, those countries that have failed to catch up have usually failed to jump on the globalization bandwagon.

The Sachs and Warner (1995) evidence has been criticized by Rodriguez and Rodrik (1999). They find that the crucial components of the Sachs-Warner index are the measures of export monopoly and black market premiums. These variables identify all but one of the sub-Saharan economies in Africa plus a group of largely Latin American economies with major macroeconomic and political difficulties. Rodriguez and Rodrik conclude that "The [Sachs-Warner] measure is so correlated with plausible groupings of alternative explanatory variables . . . that it is risky to draw strong inferences about the effect of openness on growth" (24).

We turn in the next section to an empirical examination of the robustness of the Sachs-Warner result. We investigate whether their result holds for the most recent decades, noting the contrary finding by Kevin O'Rourke (2000) for the beginning of the last century.

4.4   Evidence on Openness and Convergence, 1960–98

Descriptive statistics are given in table 4.1 for real GDP per capita (RGDP) for 109 countries in 1960, 1980, and 1998,[13] using the Penn World Tables 5.6a[14] and World Bank estimates of real GDP growth in the 1990s. We also report real GDP per member of the workforce (RGDPW) and real GDP per capita as adjusted by Summers and Heston (1991) for changes in

---

13. To reduce the influence of asynchronous business cycles, the data labeled 1960 are actually five-year averages for the period 1960–64; similarly, we give 1978–82 averages as 1980, 1988–92 as 1990, and 1994–98 as 1998.

14. We have identified some problems with the Penn World Tables data on population and real GDP growth for 1960 and 1970 for a number of countries such as Nigeria. This should not be a problem for the study reported here because the data mistakes appear to cancel out over the period 1960–80.

Table 4.1   Breakdown of σ-Divergence 1960–98, Countries Ranked by 1960 Relative Real GDP Levels (in 1985$)

	Real GDP Per Capita			Real GDP Per Worker			Real GDP Per Capita Terms-of-Trade Adjusted		
	1960	1980	1998	1960	1980	1990	1960	1980	1990
Whole sample: 1960–80									
Mean	2,454	4,170	5,544	4,079	6,629	6,971	1,631	2,628	2,831
Annual growth rate		0.025	0.010		0.027	0.005		0.027	0.007
Var (log)	0.815	1.004	1.347	0.955	1.047	1.156	0.815	1.015	1.209
Change in var (log)		+0.189	+0.343		+0.092	+0.109		+0.200	+0.194
Change in var, population weighted		+0.097	-0.158		-0.002	-0.035		+0.084	-0.081
Rich sample: Y60 > $5,000: N = 19									
Mean	7,117	11,475	14,788	17,168	25,588	28,182	6,906	11,365	13,127
Annual growth rate		0.027	0.015		0.022	0.010		0.028	0.014
Var (log)	0.042	0.023	0.064	0.049	0.016	0.032	0.050	0.025	0.066
Change		-0.019	+0.041		-0.033	-0.016		-0.025	+0.041
Middle sample: $1,500 < Y60 < $5,000: N = 35									
Mean	2,434	4,579	6,398	6,478	11,393	11,551	2,314	4,201	4,410
Annual growth rate		0.032	0.013		0.031	0.001		0.033	0.005
Var (log)	0.008	0.035	0.466	0.009	0.048	0.270	0.007	0.034	0.419
Change		+0.027	+0.431		+0.039	+0.222		+0.027	+0.385
Poor sample: Y60 < $1,500: N = 55									
Mean	855	1,385	1,808	1,850	2,945	3,027	793	1,176	1,219
Annual growth rate		0.021	0.006		0.026	0.003		0.022	0.004
Var (log)	0.187	0.329	0.622	0.323	0.495	0.575	0.198	0.347	0.451

the terms of trade (RGDPTT). This terms-of-trade adjustment gives a better measure of changes in average welfare than the fixed-price measure. These latter two measures are available only up until 1992.

Dispersion is measured by the variance of the logarithm. Other measures of dispersion are often used, particularly in welfare analysis, but the log variance is particularly useful in that it can be directly related to the regression analysis of growth rates. In the fifth row of table 4.1 we report changes in population-weighted variances for the whole sample (a measure appropriate to analysis of inequality across individuals), but for the rest of our analysis we adopt a positivist approach to hypothesis testing and treat each country's performance over a period as a single, equally weighted observational unit.

All three measures show increasing dispersion. We have divided the sample of 109 countries into three groups, depending on whether 1960 RGDP was above or below I$1,500 or I$5,000 (measured in constant international prices with the international dollar [I$] normalized to the purchasing power of the U.S. dollar in 1985). Divergence has occurred within each group, except for the richest nineteen countries between 1960 and 1980. But the principal cause of divergence has been the failure of the poorest to match the growth of the more developed.

Between 1960 and 1980, the middle-income countries grew fastest, at 3.2 percent per year, followed by the rich at 2.7 percent and the poorest at 2.1 percent. Over the subsequent two decades growth rates slowed for all groups, with a meager 0.6 percent per year for the fifty-five poorest economies.

It is this falling-behind of the poorest countries, in a period of increasing globalization, that we investigate. From table 4.2 we can see that the fifty-five poorest countries in 1960 are characterized, relative to the richer groups, by high prices of investment goods and low rates of real investment, by low levels of education, by high population growth, low values of openness on the Sachs-Warner (S&W) index, low ratios of trade to GDP, and low growth of the working-age population relative to total population. These discrepancies are exaggerated if we examine the thirty-five slowest growers within the poor group.

The regressions reported in table 4.3 replicate some of the analysis carried out by Sachs and Warner (1995). We use the S&W distinction between open and closed economies for the period 1960–80 to construct a dummy variable equal to 1 for countries they deemed to be open for the period 1970–89. This restricts our sample to ninety-six countries. Since we are also examining growth over the period 1980–98, we extend the S&W classification to our later period, reclassifying countries as open if S&W report that they have been open for a significant number of years since 1980; table 4.3 gives the details of our classifications. This enables us to check whether the S&W results carry over to the 1990s—in particular for the twenty-four

Table 4.2   **Average Characteristics of Country Income Groups**

	Rich	Middle	Poor	Slowest Growers
Real GDP per capita ($)				
1960	7,117	2,466	855	800
1980	11,475	4,579	1,385	978
1990	13,416	5,365	1,555	878
1990	14,788	6,398	1,808	885
RGDP growth rate				
(annual average)				
1960–80	0.027	0.032	0.021	0.007
1980–98	0.015	0.013	0.006	−0.007
Proportion African	0.00	0.14	0.62	0.81
Proportion OECD	0.89	0.17	0.00	0.00
Proportion open				
(extended Sachs-Warner)				
1960–80	0.83	0.39	0.12	0.03
1980–98	0.88	0.75	0.32	0.22
(Imports + Exports)/GDP				
1960–80	0.62	0.70	0.51	0.47
1980–98	0.71	0.85	0.62	0.54
Adjusted trade share				
1960–80	0.01	−0.10	−0.22	−0.28
1980–98	0.20	0.17	0.10	−0.02
Real investment/GDP share				
1960–80	0.26	0.20	0.11	0.08
1980–98	0.23	0.17	0.11	0.07
Relative price of investment				
goods				
1960–80	1.02	1.35	2.37	2.89
1980–98	0.93	1.39	2.48	2.99
Average years of schooling				
1960–80	4.7	3.8	2.4	2.0
1980–98	6.2	5.2	3.6	3.1
Population growth rate				
(annual average)				
1960–80	0.010	0.020	0.025	0.026
1980–98	0.007	0.016	0.024	0.027
Growth of workforce/				
population				
1960–80	0.005	0.002	−0.003	−0.005
1980–98	0.005	0.005	0.002	0.000

Sources: Penn World Tables 5.6 at [http://pwt.econ.upenn.edu/home.html] for trade share, investment share and price, and workforce/population up to 1992. World Bank (2000) for real GDP and population. Sachs and Warner (1995) for open (for adjustments, see our table 4.3). Barro and Lee (1993) and [http://www.nber.org/data/] for schooling, taken as average years of schooling in the adult population over the first decade.

Notes: The "rich" group is composed of nineteen countries with real GDP per capita 1960–64 averaging above I$5,000; the "poor" group comprises fifty-five countries with RGDP 1960–64 averaging below I$1,500. The "middle" group comprises the remaining forty-five countries. The "slow growers" are the thirty-five slowest-growing countries (1960–98) within the "poor" group.

Table 4.3   **Extension of the Sachs-Warner Classifications**

Benin	Open since 1990
Botswana	Open since 1979
Chile	Open since 1976
Colombia	Open since 1986
Costa Rica	Open since 1986
El Salvador	Open since 1989
Gambia	Reform 1985
Ghana	Open since 1985
Guatemala	Open since 1988
Guyana	Open since 1988
Israel	Open since 1985
Mali	Open since 1988
Mexico	Open since 1986
Morocco	Open since 1984
New Zealand	Open since 1986
Paraguay	Open since 1989
The Philippines	Open since 1988
Sri Lanka	Open since 1991
Tunisia	Open since 1989
Turkey	Open since 1989
Uganda	Open since 1988
Uruguay	Open since 1990

Note: These countries, classified as closed by Sachs and Warner (1995) for the period 1970–89, are ranked as open for the period 1980–98 based on the comment in their table 14.

poor and middle-income countries that have only recently opened their economies.

Regression 1 in table 4.4 confirms the S&W result that open economies grew substantially and significantly faster than closed economies over the period 1960–80. Our estimate of a 2.0 percentage point growth premium is only slightly lower than the S&W estimates for 1970–89. By any standards, it is a huge premium—implying that twenty years of openness lifts per capita GDP by a cumulative 50 percent.

When we interact openness with initial income, regression 2 indicates that the growth premium for openness tends to be higher for poorer countries—averaging 3.4 percentage points compared with 1.0 points for rich countries. This confirms the S&W finding that openness promoted convergence over the period 1960–80. The differences in growth rates for open and closed economies are illustrated in figure 4.5, where the solid trend-line represents the predicted growth rate from a regression on a cubic polynomial in log income.

Controlling for openness, these regressions show no evidence of conditional convergence. Indeed, the beta coefficients are positive: Conditional on openness, there were additional factors slowing the growth of the poorest relative to the richest countries. Regression 3 confirms that the usual sus-

Table 4.4   Regressions Relating Convergence and Openness

A. Variables Averaged Over 1960–80

	N	Log y0	S&W Open	S&W Open × log y0	Investment	Population Growth	Workforce-Population Ratio Growth	Adjusted R²	Standard Error of Estimate
1	96	-0.0014** (0.7)	0.020 (4.9)					0.208	.017
2	96	0.0026** (1.0)	0.108 (3.3)	-1.10** (-2.8)				0.247	.016
3	96	-0.004** (-1.5)	0.077 (2.1)	-0.8 (-1.8)	0.078 (2.9)	0.09 (0.4)	0.68** (2.1)	0.347	.015

B. Variables Averaged Over 1980–98

	N	Log y0	S&W Open	Trade Open × log y0	School	School × log y0	Investment	Population Growth	Workforce-Population Ratio Growth	Adjusted R²	Standard Error of Estimate
4	96	0.004** (2.1)	0.013** (28)**							0.174	
5	96	0.003 (1.3)	0.010** (2.3)	0.23** (4.3)						0.286	
6	96	-.008** (-2.6)	0.005^S&W (1.2)	0.17** (2.9)			0.104** (2.7)	-0.80** (-3.3)	0.43 (1.2)	0.451	0.016
7	70	0.006 (1.8)	0.014** (2.6)	0.25** (3.9)	0.012** (2.2)	-0.14** (-2.2)				0.341	.019
8	70	-.007 (-1.4)	0.009 (1.8)	0.15 (1.1)	0.007 (-1.0)	-0.08 (2.2)**	0.118** (-2.1)**	-0.70** (1.1)	0.57	0.495	0.017

Notes: log y0 is the natural logarithm of real GDP per capita at the beginning of the period (Penn World Tables 5.6a). When used in interactive terms, it is divided by 100. "S&W open" is the extended Sachs and Warner dummy variable for openness. "Trade open" is the residual from regressing log (trade share in GDP) on log (population) for the full pooled sample with 218 observations. Regressions using investment are estimated using two-stage least squares (2SLS) with beginning of period investment and investment price as instruments. The dependent variable is the annual growth rate of real GDP per capita, measured at 1995 local prices. White's heteroskedasticity-adjusted *t*-statistics are reported in parentheses. Workforce-Population ratio denotes the ratio of the workforce to total population, as derived from the Penn World Tables.

**Statistically significant at the 5 percent level.

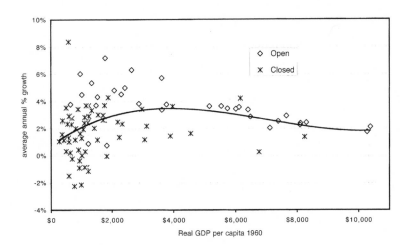

Fig. 4.5   **Relative growth rates and initial income levels of "open" and "closed" economies, 1960–80**

pects were involved. Multiplying the regression coefficients by the differences in sample means from table 4.2, we find that investment rates and demographic differences accounted for 1.3 percentage points of slower growth for the poor countries, relative to the group of rich countries.

Taking account of factor accumulation and of the differential effects of openness, we now find some weak evidence of conditional convergence. This should be interpreted as conditional convergence in multifactor productivity, proceeding at a slow rate of only 0.4 percent per year, possibly resulting from international technology transfer. Because the regression is controlling for trade effects, any such technology spillovers are not operating through trade.

We have followed Benhabib and Spiegel (1994) by adding a variable measuring the level of schooling in the adult population, and by adding the product of schooling with initial income. Neither variable adds significant explanatory power.

We perform similar analysis to explain growth between 1980 and 1998 (see regressions 4–8 in part B of table 4.4). Openness appears to deliver a smaller growth premium than that of the previous twenty years, although 1.3 percentage points is still a very substantial addition to annual growth rates. The positive sign on the interactive term, introduced in regressions 5–8, suggests that poorer countries benefit less from openness than do rich countries. This is the opposite of the S&W finding, which we confirmed for the earlier period 1960–80. The differences in growth rates for open and closed economies are illustrated in figure 4.6.

When we use the S&W measure of openness in the interactive term, we

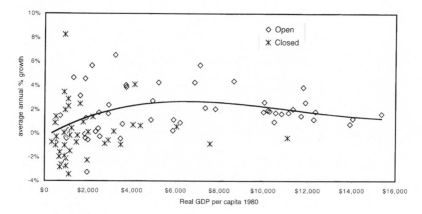

Fig. 4.6   Relative growth rates and initial income levels of "open" and "closed" economies, 1980–98

find that neither of the variables is statistically significant. In the reported regressions 5–8, in order to reduce multicollinearity, we have used instead a direct measure of trade openness, not the S&W variable, in the interactive term. This measure, based on the observation that countries with small populations tend to engage in more international trade than do more populous nations, consists of the residuals from an ordinary least squares (OLS) regression that explains half of the observed variation in trade shares over the pooled sample

$$\text{Log}\left(\frac{\text{exports} + \text{imports}}{\text{GDP}}\right) = 6.23 - 0.25 \log(\text{population});$$

$$N = 218, R^2 = 0.498.$$

Regression 6 adds in control variables for investment and demography. We calculate that, for the period 1980–98, the lower rate of capital deepening in the poorer countries now explains 2.2 points of slower growth, relative to the group of rich countries. Conditional convergence is statistically significant once we control for factor accumulation. The coefficient of –0.008 on the initial income term in regression 6 implies that, over the period 1980–98, the technology gap between countries was eroded at a rate approaching 1 percent per year.

The seventh regression reported in part B of table 4.4 includes the School and School × log (initial income) variables. These were found to be insignificant for the earlier period, but they add significant explanatory power in explaining growth over this later period. The sign pattern, positive on School and negative on School × log(initial income), confirms the Benhabib and Spiegel (1994) finding that a high level of initial human capital does promote growth, especially when initial income is low. It also provides some support for the Abramovitz (1986) hypothesis that successful technology transfer requires a certain level of social capability—although it is puzzling that the schooling variables are not significant when the investment and demographic variables are added in regression 8.

A summary of our empirical findings runs as follows:

- The failure of the world's poorest countries to catch up to the income levels of the richest countries over the past four decades is attributable to the poverty-trap conditions of subsistence income, low saving and investment, low levels of education, and high fertility.
- Openness to the world economy does appear to provide a significant boost to growth, but it does not necessarily promote convergence. A large number of the poorer countries have opened their economies since 1980. But it is precisely during this period that the benefits of openness appear to have diminished.

4.5 Conclusion

Our historical narrative makes it clear that globalization of the economy does not necessarily imply global convergence. Periods of expansion of transport and trade and flows of capital and migrants have marked the development of a club of convergent economies, but countries outside the club have fallen behind in relative terms even in eras of strong growth. Moreover, over the past two decades many countries have fallen behind, not just relatively but absolutely, in terms of both income levels and structural development.

The fact that the news has been very good for India and China over the past few decades has created a sharp division between the average experience of countries (in which divergence continues to be the rule, and in fact to accelerate) and the average experience of people (in which, for the first time in centuries, there are signs of *unconditional* convergence). It is also apparent that failure to join the convergence club is not just a consequence of a country's turning its back on the global economy and sheltering behind tariff barriers and capital controls. During the high years of the great Keynesian boom after World War II, openness to the world economy does appear to have been a magic bullet making for convergence, and those countries that closed their economies, whether in the southern cone of Latin America or in postindependence Africa, suffered enormous penalties. But things appear to have been somewhat different in other eras. At the beginning of the twentieth century, it is hard to see openness to trade and migration as promoting convergence outside a small charmed circle—a point that was made by Lewis (1978) a generation ago. And at the end of the twentieth century, the growth benefits of opening up appear substantially lower than in the twentieth century's third quarter.

It remains an open question whether the growth benefits of openness have really declined in recent decades, or whether an early turn to openness is correlated with other growth-promoting factors omitted from standard cross-country studies.

In either case, there is little reason to be confident that opening doors to the world economy will guarantee a place at the high table. Poor countries remain poor, and so the purchase of investment goods from overseas that embody technology and assist in technology transfer remains expensive, and finding the resources to support mass education remains difficult. Last, the world's poorest countries have still not successfully completed their demographic transitions—and the failure to have shifted to a regime of low population growth puts pressure on resources and capital accumulation that will in all likelihood continue to sharpen the jaws of the poverty trap.

References

Abramovitz, Moses. 1986. Catching up, forging ahead, and falling behind. *Journal of Economic History* 46:385–406.

Aghion, Philippe, and Peter Howitt. 1998. *Endogenous growth theory.* Cambridge: MIT Press.

Barro, Robert. 1996. *Determinants of economic growth.* Cambridge: MIT Press.

Barro, Robert J., and J. W. Lee. 1993. International comparisons of educational attainment. *Journal of Monetary Economics* 32 (3): 363–94.

Bates, Robert. 1981. *Markets and states in tropical Africa.* Berkeley, Calif.: University of California Press.

Baumol, William J., and Edward N. Wolff. 1988. Productivity growth, convergence, and welfare: Reply. *American Economic Review* 78 (5): 1155–59.

Ben-David, David. 1997. Convergence clubs and subsistence economies. NBER Working Paper no. 6267. Cambridge, Mass.: National Bureau of Economic Research.

Benhabib, Jess, and Mark Spiegel. 1994. The role of human capital in economic development: Evidence from aggregate cross-country data. *Journal of Monetary Economics* 34 (2): 143–73.

Butlin, Noel. 1970. Some perspectives of Australian economic development 1890–1965. In *Australian economic development in the twentieth century,* ed. C. Forster, Sydney: Australasian Publishing Co.

Caselli, Francesco, Gerardo Esquivel, and Fernando Lefort. 1996. Reopening the convergence debate: A new look at cross-country growth empirics. *Journal of Economic Growth* 1 (September): 363–89.

Clark, Gregory. 1987. Why isn't the whole world developed? Lessons from the cotton mills. *Journal of Economic History* 47 (1): 141–74.

DeLong, J. Bradford. 1988. Productivity growth, convergence, and welfare: Comment. *American Economic Review* 78 (5):

DeLong, J. Bradford, and Barry Eichengreen. 1994. The Marshall plan: History's most successful structural adjustment programme. In *Postwar economic reconstruction and lessons for the East today,* ed. W. N. Rüdiger Dornbusch and Richard Layard, 189–230. Cambridge: MIT Press.

DeLong, J. Bradford, and Lawrence H. Summers. 1991. Equipment investment and economic growth. *Quarterly Journal of Economics* 106 (2): 445–502.

Diaz-Alejandro, Carlos. 1970. *Essays on the economic history of the Argentine Republic.* New Haven: Yale University Press.

Dowrick, Steve, and Duc Tho Nguyen. 1989. OECD comparative economic growth 1950–85: Catch-up and convergence. *American Economic Review* 79 (5): 1010–30.

Dumont, Rene. 1966. *False start in Africa.* New York: Praeger.

Easterlin, Richard. 1981. Why isn't the whole world developed? *Journal of Economic History* 41 (1): 1–19.

Hopkins, A. G. 1973. *An economic history of West Africa.* London: Longman.

Islam, Nazrul. 1995. Growth empirics: A panel data approach. *Quarterly Journal of Economics* 110 (4): 1127–70.

Landes, David S. 1969. *The unbound Prometheus.* Cambridge: Cambridge University Press.

Lee, Kevin, M. Hashem Pesaran, and Ron Smith. 1998. Comment on "Growth empirics: A panel data approach." *Quarterly Journal of Economics* 113 (1): 319–23.

Lewis, W. Arthur. 1978. *The evolution of the international economic order.* Princeton, N.J.: Princeton University Press.

Lucas, Robert E., Jr. 1990. Why doesn't capital flow from rich to poor countries? *American Economic Review* 80 (2): 92–96.

———. 2000. Some macroeconomics for the twenty-first century. *Journal of Economic Perspectives* 14 (1): 159–68.

Maddison, Angus. 1994. *Monitoring the world economy.* Paris: Organization for Economic Cooperation and Development.

———. 2001. *The world economy in millennial perspective.* Paris: Organization for Economic Cooperation and Development.

Mankiw, N. Gregory, David Romer, and David N. Weil. 1992. A contribution to the empirics of economic growth. *Quarterly Journal of Economics* 107 (2): 407–37.

Mill, John Stuart. 1848. *Principles of political economy.* London: W. J. Ashley.

Mokyr, Joel. 1976. *Industrialization in the Low Countries.* New Haven: Yale University.

Ohkawa, Kazushi, and Henry Rosovsky. 1973. *Japanese economic growth.* Palo Alto, Calif.: Stanford University Press.

O'Rourke, Kevin H. 2000. Tariffs and growth in the late nineteenth century. *Economic Journal* 110 (463): 456–83.

O'Rourke, Kevin H., and Jeffrey G. Williamson. 1998. *Globalization and history: The evolution of the nineteenth-century Atlantic economy.* Cambridge: MIT Press.

Patrick, Hugh, and Henry Rosovsky. 1976. *Asia's new giant: How Japan's economy works.* Washington, D.C.: Brookings Institution.

Pollard, Sidney. 1981. *Peaceful conquest: The industrialization of Europe, 1760–1970.* Oxford: Oxford University Press.

Pritchett, Lant. 1997. Divergence, big time. *Journal of Economic Perspectives* 11 (3): 3–17.

Rodriguez, Francisco, and Dani Rodrik. 1999. Trade policy and economic growth: A skeptic's guide to the cross-national evidence. NBER Working Paper no. 7081. Cambridge, Mass.: National Bureau of Economic Research.

Romer, Paul M. 1990. Endogenous technological change. *Journal of Political Economy* 98 (5): S1971–S1102.

Sachs, Jeffrey D., and Andrew M. Warner. 1995. Economic reform and the process of global integration. *Brookings Papers on Economic Activity*, Issue no. 1:1–95.
Sachs, Jeffrey, Ashutosh Varshney, and Narupam Bajpai, eds. 2000. *India in the era of economic reforms*. Oxford: Oxford University Press.
Solow, Robert M. 1956. A contribution to the theory of economic growth. *Quarterly Journal of Economics* 70 (1): 65–94.
Summers, Robert, and Alan Heston. 1991. Penn World Table (mark 5): An expanded set of international comparisons, 1950–1988. *Quarterly Journal of Economics* 106 (2): 327–68.
Swan, Trevor W. 1956. Economic growth and capital accumulation. *Economic Record* 32 (November): 334–61.
World Bank. 1994. *The East Asian miracle*. Washington, D.C.: World Bank.
———. 2000. *World tables*. Baltimore: Johns Hopkins University Press.
Wright, Gavin. 1978. *The political economy of the cotton South*. New York: Norton.

Comment   Charles I. Jones

I greatly enjoyed the opportunity to read and think about this interesting paper. Its main contribution is to raise a number of important and fascinating questions related to globalization and convergence. This is a valuable contribution, and it provokes the reader to speculate about possible answers. In this, I found the paper to be a great success: It drew me in and got me thinking.

The main puzzle described in the paper involves changes in the relationship between globalization and convergence over time. It appears to be the case that countries that have taken their place at the global table in the second half of the twentieth century have grown faster than those that have not, and countries that have opened their economies have exhibited some convergence. The exact magnitude of this growth gain is uncertain, and the effects may have weakened toward the end of the century (as Dowrick and DeLong argue), but this is a point that is not greatly disputed.[1] On the other hand, as Dowrick and DeLong point out, globalization and convergence did not go hand in hand during the first era of globalization in the years before World War I. Rather, convergence was limited to a narrow charmed circle of countries consisting of some western and middle European countries and their more temperate colonies.

In many ways, this is surprising. Factors of production, including both capital and labor, as well as technologies for production were shifted around the globe because of this globalization. Yet the effects on incomes outside of the charmed circle are argued to be small. As the authors explain,

Charles I. Jones is associate professor of economics at the University of California–Berkeley and a research associate of the National Bureau of Economic Research.

1. Of course, Rodriguez and Rodrik (2000) represent an important exception.

The British Empire brought the rubber plant to Malaysia. British investors financed the movement of indentured workers south from China to Malaysia to work the plantations to produce the rubber to satisfy demand back in the world economy's core. The British Empire brought the tea plant from China to Ceylon. British investors financed the movement of Tamils from India across the strait to work the plantations to produce the tea to satisfy demand from the British actual and would-be middle classes. But these did *not* trigger any rapid growth in real wages. They did not trigger any acceleration in productivity growth or industrialization. They did not trigger any rapid growth in factory employment, or any convergence to the world's economic core.

Why the difference between the two eras? And in particular, why did globalization in the first era not trigger rapid growth and convergence? In my discussion, I will comment on each of these eras and make an effort to suggest one possible resolution to the puzzle.

Let me begin with some remarks on globalization and convergence during the second half of the twentieth century. Until recently, I was under the impression that the absolute divergence in output per worker across countries that characterizes most of history had largely been halted, at least since 1970 or so. Although it is well known that there has not been any convergence in output per worker for the world as a whole, my impression was that the divergence had largely stopped.[2]

In fact, as Dowrick and DeLong document in table 4.1 of the paper, this absolute divergence largely continued throughout the second half of the twentieth century. This is especially apparent in the per capita GDP data, as shown in figure 4C.1. The data here are from the Penn World Tables through 1992 and from the World Bank until 1997.

According to this figure, the standard deviation of the log of GDP per capita across 109 countries shows a steady increase. In 1960, this standard deviation was about 0.9 and by 1997 it had risen to more than 1.2. To interpret these numbers, recall that if countries were normally distributed, then 4 standard deviations would span about 95 percent of the countries. This suggests that the ratio of the second-richest country in the sample to the second-poorest country would be a factor of $e^{4 \cdot 0.9} \approx 36$ in 1960 and would rise to $e^{4 \cdot 1.2} \approx 122$ in 1997. These numbers turn out to be off just a little: The ratio of GDP per capita in the richest country to that in the poorest country was 39 in 1960 and 112 in 1997.

To avoid an undue influence from outliers, figure 4C.1 also plots the ratio of incomes between the fifth-richest and fifth-poorest countries over time. This ratio rises from about 20 in 1960 to nearly 30 in 1990 and then rises quite sharply to more than 40 by 1997.

---

2. In my defense, if one looks at GDP per worker using the Summers-Heston (1991) data up until the late 1980s, this is the impression one gets.

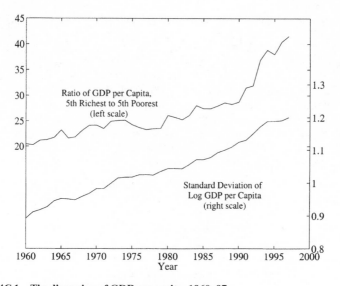

Fig. 4C.1   The dispersion of GDP per capita, 1960–97

Source: Author's calculations using the extension of the Penn World Tables created by Easterly and Yu (2000). One hundred nine countries are represented.

To what extent are these changes influenced by globalization? Figure 4C.2 provides another look at changes in the dispersion of per capita GDP, this time splitting countries into two groups, "open" and "closed." The open countries are those that were classified by Sachs and Warner (1995) as being open for at least half of the years during the period 1950–94.[3]

Among countries classified as open, income dispersion generally decreased over the 1960–97 period, with the bulk of the decline coming by 1970. Among countries classified as closed, dispersion increased slightly, again with the bulk of the change coming before 1970. However it is the "between" rather than the "within" evidence that is perhaps most informative with respect to globalization and convergence. First, the dispersion among the open countries is substantially less than the dispersion among the closed countries. The open countries are richer and less dispersed than the closed countries. Finally, between these two groups of countries, however, income dispersion increased substantially between 1960 and 1997, with the ratio of median incomes rising from 3 in 1960 to 8 by 1997.

Dowrick and DeLong document a related point, which is that the effects of openness on growth seem to have weakened after 1980 relative to before. One might reach a similar conclusion from this figure, but it is unclear if this

3. The actual openness data used are those from Hall and Jones (1999) and include some imputed values.

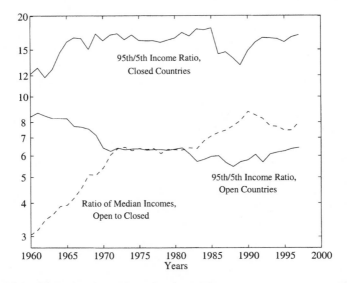

Fig. 4C.2   Dispersion: Open versus closed countries

Source: Author's calculations using the extension of the Penn World Tables created by Easterly and Yu (2000). Thirty-three countries are classified as open, and 76 are classified as closed.

conclusion is warranted. As time has passed, a larger number of countries have opened their economies, but the classification in the figure is held constant. Some of the weakening of the effects of openness apparent in the figure, then, could be an artifact of this classification.

In this most recent era, then, globalization and convergence appear to be linked. The tentative evidence presented here is not nearly persuasive, but there is a large literature on this question and Dowrick and DeLong themselves bring new evidence to bear.

What, then, about the first era of globalization? An aspect of the quotation at the beginning of my comment that strikes me as quite provocative is the claim that globalization did not have a substantial impact on the countries outside of the charmed circle, in what we might call the "poor periphery." The lack of global convergence during this first era could occur as growth rates increased in the charmed circle but remained unchanged and lower in the poor periphery. Alternatively, globalization could have raised growth rates in all countries that took part, but it could have raised them disproportionately in the charmed circle. In fact, I'd like to suggest that something closer to this second alternative may have been going on.

Consider the following possible scenario. In the charmed circle, industrialization was well under way, and these economies had already reached their take-off stage by 1870; globalization then increased growth even fur-

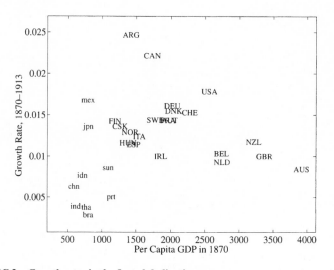

Fig. 4C.3   Growth rates in the first globalization era

Note: Upper-case letters indicate countries in the "charmed circle," and lower-case letters indicate countries in the "poor periphery." *Source:* Author's calculations using Maddison (1995).

ther. In the poor periphery, globalization began the take-off process and led these countries closer to industrialization. It is possible that globalization itself did promote convergence around the world, but the continued industrialization of the charmed circle kept their growth rates rising. By imagining two S-shaped take-off curves, one can easily see how something like this is possible: Divergence results simply because the charmed circle took off sooner and has reached the steep part of its S curve. I will show the empirical version of these S-shaped curves in figure 4C.4.

Some evidence for the rapid growth and convergence within the charmed circle and the lack of rapid growth outside of this circle can be seen in figure 4C.3. This figure plots per capita GDP growth between 1870 and 1913 against the initial level of per capita GDP in 1870. The uppercase letters correspond to the countries in the charmed circle, and the lowercase letters represent other countries for which Maddison (1995) reports data. The charmed circle consists of richer countries that generally exhibit faster growth than the other countries of the world. In addition, one can see the suggestive negative relationship between growth rates and initial income levels for these charmed countries, whereas the countries in the poor periphery lie to the southwest of this growth frontier.

However, it would not be correct to think that the countries outside of the charmed circle experienced no growth. Mexico exhibited the fastest growth of the poor periphery, with growth faster than that in most of the charmed countries, as it more than doubled its per capita GDP between 1870 and

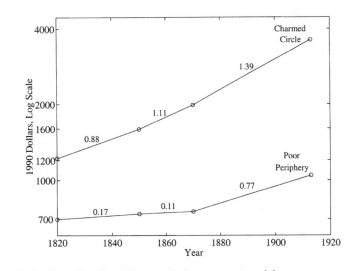

Fig. 4C.4   Per capita GDP: Charmed circle versus poor periphery

Note: The two series plotted represent the typical experience for countries in the charmed circle and the poor periphery. See figure 4C.1 for the countries in these two groups. The numbers above each line segment represent average annual growth rates. *Source:* Author's calculations using Maddison (1995).

1913. Even China and India exhibited substantial growth, with incomes rising by more than 30 percent in the former country and nearly 20 percent in the latter.

Was this growth in the poor periphery a continuation of a previous trend, or did it represent a change, perhaps associated with globalization? Figure 4C.4 sheds light on this question by plotting the level of GDP per capita for a typical charmed country and a typical country in the periphery.[4]

An important fact apparent in this figure is that growth rates in the poor periphery were substantially higher in the first era of globalization (1870–1913) than they were over the preceding half century. To take Maddison's data at face value, average GDP per capita increased from about $750 in 1870 to more than $1,000 by 1913. Although it is true that this era of globalization witnessed a divergence of incomes between the countries in the charmed circle and those outside, this does not mean that globalization brought no benefits to the periphery, or even that it was not a force working to promote convergence. A relevant question is the counterfactual: What would have happened to the poor periphery in the absence of globalization? It would be quite surprising if the substantial flows of capital, labor, and

---

4. By *typical*, we mean the following. The level in 1870 is equal to the unweighted average of the per capita GDPs in the two sets of countries. Values in previous and subsequent years are computed using the unweighted average growth rate of the countries for which data are available in each sample relative to 1870.

technology across countries did not have a significant impact on the periphery. Figure 4C.4 suggests that the impact may have been large. Perhaps globalization raised growth rates throughout the world, and perhaps the divergence between the charmed circle and the poor periphery would have been even greater in the absence of globalization.

References

Easterly, William, and Hairong Yu. 2000. Global development network growth database. Available at [http://www.worldbank.org/research/growth/GDNdata.htm].

Hall, Robert E., and Charles I. Jones. 1999. Why do some countries produce so much more output per worker than others? *Quarterly Journal of Economics* 114 (February): 83–116.

Maddison, Angus. 1995. *Monitoring the world economy 1820–1992.* Paris: Organization for Economic Cooperation and Development.

Rodriguez, Francisco, and Dani Rodrik. 2000. Trade policy and economic growth: A skeptic's guide to the cross-national evidence. In *NBER macroeconomics annual,* ed. Ben Bernanke and Kenneth S. Rogoff, 261–338. Cambridge: MIT Press.

Sachs, Jeffrey D., and Andrew Warner. 1995. Economic reform and the process of global integration. *Brookings Papers on Economic Activity,* Issue no. 1: 1–95. Washington, D.C.: Brookings Institution.

Summers, Robert, and Alan Heston. 1991. Penn World Table (mark 5): An expanded set of international comparisons, 1950–1988. *Quarterly Journal of Economics* 106 (2): 327–68.

5

Does Globalization Make the World More Unequal?

Peter H. Lindert and Jeffrey G. Williamson

5.1 Overview

The world economy has become far more unequal over the last two centuries. Within-country income inequality has risen and fallen episodically. It has often risen in developing countries, although not always. It has fallen in the developed and industrialized countries, although this trend has recently reversed in some parts of the Organization for Economic Cooperation and Development (OECD). Thus, there is no ubiquitous trend in within-country inequality over the past two centuries. It follows that virtually all the observed rise in world income inequality has been driven by widening gaps between nations, and almost none of it has been driven by widening gaps within nations. Meanwhile, the world economy has become much more integrated. If correlation meant causation, these facts would imply that globalization has raised inequality between all nations but that it has not raised inequality within nations.

This essay argues that the likely impact of globalization on world inequality has been very different from what these simple correlations suggest. Globalization probably mitigated the steep rise in income gaps between nations. The nations that gained the most from globalization are

Peter H. Lindert is professor of economics at the University of California, Davis. Jeffrey G. Williamson is the Laird Bell Professor of Economics at Harvard University and a research associate of the National Bureau of Economic Research.

The authors thank François Bourguignon and Christian Morrisson for the chance to use prepublication estimates from their ongoing work on global inequalities. They also acknowledge with thanks the detailed comments of Alan Taylor on earlier drafts, discussions with David Dollar and Andy Warner, and comments made by participants at the NBER Globalization in Historical Perspective conference. Williamson gratefully acknowledges the financial support of the National Science Foundation SES-0001362.

those poor ones that changed their policies to exploit it, whereas the ones that gained the least did not. The effect of globalization on inequality within nations has gone both ways, and not according to any simple correlation between the observed trends, or, for that matter, according to any simple theory.

The economic history of inequality suggests the following five conclusions about the influence of globalization:

1. The dramatic widening of income gaps between nations has probably been reduced, not raised, by the globalization of commodity and factor markets, at least for those countries that integrated into the world economy.

2. Within labor-abundant countries before 1914, opening up to international trade and to international factor movements lowered inequality, a powerful effect when and where emigration was massive.

3. Within labor-scarce countries, opening up to international trade and to international factor movements raised inequality, a powerful effect before 1914 where immigration was massive. Globalization also raised inequality in the postwar OECD, but it was not the main source of widening, partly because immigration was not massive either.

4. All international and intranational effects considered, more globalization has meant less world inequality.

5. World incomes would still be unequal under complete global integration, as they are in any large integrated national economy. But they would be less unequal in a fully integrated world economy than in one fully segmented.

This essay will reach these five conclusions by exploring four dimensions: the components of world inequality, the sources of globalization, the degree to which individual nations actually globalized, and the historical time period.

The two key *components of world inequality*—inequality between country average incomes, and inequality within countries—must be treated separately. Inequality between nations calls for attention to the determinants of per capita incomes. Inequality within countries calls for attention to the determinants of factor prices and their link to the size distribution of income. Even more importantly, international and intranational inequalities have very different implications for policy responses, and thus they demand separate attention. Changing world inequality induced by a changing distribution of population between countries also has different implications for policy, especially if induced by world migration. Finally, which components of world inequality matter most depends on whether observers care as much about the rest of the world as they care about their own citizens. This essay takes the global stance, but we warn again that national policies derive from national attitudes toward intranational globalization effects.

Different *sources of globalization* have different impacts on inequality. Political debate over globalization implicitly poses an alternative in which liberal policy is replaced by barriers to trade and factor migration. Yet globalization in the past has been driven mostly by forces unrelated to policy, such as productivity improvements, rising potential gains from specialization, and transport revolutions, each of which may have very different implications for the distribution of world income compared with policy changes. Even when history offers examples of globalization due to more liberal policies, it matters who did the liberalizing.

Identical globalization events had very different effects on *participants and non-participants*. What globalization does to the inequality among participating countries is quite different from what it does to inequality among *all* nations. Controlling for other forces, we find clear signs of income convergence among countries that integrate more fully into the world economy, but divergence between these active participants and those who remain insulated from global markets. Among those participating in global markets, the already advanced countries, the regions of new settlement (European and otherwise), and the rest all experienced different effects: The gains from trade differed, the contribution of across-border factor flows differed, and the impact on their income distributions differed.

The historical record is divided into four distinctly *different epochs*: the pre-industrial years prior to the 1820s; the long nineteenth century from the 1820s to World War I; the two world wars and the unstable years in between; and the second half of the twentieth century. The first was a long preglobalization epoch in which factor flows were slight and long-distance trade was monopolized and mostly limited to luxuries. The second and fourth epochs contained worldwide surges in global integration. The third epoch witnessed a ubiquitous retreat from globalization into economic autarky.

5.2 Global Divergence Is Far Older than Globalization

To understand the long-run movements in world inequality and globalization, it is useful to begin by standing at the 1820s[1] watershed to survey the earlier and later trends from that vantage point.

From the 1820s onwards, there are better data on world inequality and world market integration. These data document some key facts. *Fact number 1* is that all recent estimates find a dramatic income divergence around the globe over the past two centuries. Furthermore, they all show that this

1. The 1820s represent a dating compromise. The decade is adopted in part to coincide with the peacetime recovery from the Napoleonic Wars on the Continent and an agricultural depression (i.e., structural adjustment) in Great Britain. The decade also serves as a link to Maddison's (1995) estimates for 1820 in his study of the world economy. Most important, however, the decade is consistent with the evidence put forth by O'Rourke and Williamson (2000) showing that international commodity price convergence did not start until then, and that a powerful and epochal move toward liberal policy (e.g., dismantling mercantilism) was manifested during that decade as well, at least in Great Britain.

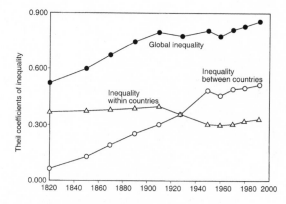

Fig. 5.1   Global inequality of individual incomes, 1820–1992
Source: Bourguignon and Morrisson (2002).
Notes: The "countries" here consist of fifteen single countries with abundant data and large populations, plus eighteen other country groups. The eighteen groups were aggregates of geographical neighbors having similar levels of GDP per capita, as estimated by Maddison (1995).

divergence has been driven almost entirely by the rise of between-nation inequality, not by any rise in inequality within nations (Berry, Bourguignon, and Morrisson, 1983, 1991; Maddison 1995; Pritchett 1997; Prados de la Escosura, 2000; Bourguignon and Morrisson 2002; Ward 2000).[2] This evidence is summarized in figure 5.1. *Fact number 2* is that, since the 1820s, there has also been an impressive worldwide increase in commodity and factor market integration, despite the temporary and disastrous retreat during the world wars and the troubled era in between (Williamson 1995, 1996; Bordo, Eichengreen, and Irwin, 1999; O'Rourke and Williamson 1999). This evidence is summarized in table 5.1.

The centuries before 1820 offer two additional stylized facts. *Fact number 3* is that income gaps almost certainly widened from 1600 or even earlier. As best we can judge from indicators of real wages, real land rents, returns to capital, and the occasional direct tax returns in the more literate countries, the early modern "great divergence" was true in all dimensions—globally *and* between European nations *and* within European nations. At the global level, real wages in England and Holland pulled away from the rest of the world in the late seventeenth and eighteenth century (van Zanden 1999; Pomeranz 2000; Allen 2000, 2001). Furthermore, the landed, merchant, and protomanufacturing classes of England, Holland, and France pulled

---

2. The rise in global income inequality from 1820 to 1950 illustrated in figure 5.1 has not been debated, but there is some disagreement about the experience since 1950. Although the Bourguignon and Morrisson (2002) data in figure 5.1 have the increase in global inequality and inequality between nations decelerating after 1950, the data in Melchior, Telle, and Wiig (2000) actually have the inequality between countries falling after 1960. We shall have more to say about this epochal regime switch later.

Table 5.1 Epochal Shifts in Globalization Since 1820

Epoch	Intercontinental Commodity Market Integration[a]		Migration and World Labor Markets[b]		Integration of World Capital Markets[c]
	Change in Price Gaps between Continents	Why They Changed	How the Migrant Shares Changed in the Receiving Countries	Why They Changed	What Happened to Integration (Feldstein-Horioka Slope Coefficient)
1820–1914	Price gaps cut by 81%	72% due to cheaper transport, 28% due to pre-1870 tariff cuts	Migrant shares rise	Passenger transport cost slashed, push and pull (Immigration policies remain neutral)	60% progress from complete segmentation toward market integration
1914–1950	Gaps double in width, back to 1870 level	Due to new trade barriers only	Migrant shares fall	Restrictive immigration policies	Revert to complete market segmentation
1950–2000, especially since 1970	Price gaps cut by 76%, now lower than in 1914	74% due to policies freeing trade, 26% due to cheaper transport	Migrant shares rise	Transport costs drop, push and pull again (No net change in immigration policies)	Again 60% progress from complete segmentation toward market integration
Overall 1820–2000	Price gaps cut by 92%	18% due to policies, 82% due to cheaper transport	No clear change in U.S. migrant shares, but rises elsewhere	Policy restrictions, offsetting transport improvements	60% progress from complete segmentation toward market integration

[a]From Williamson (1990, 2002); O'Rourke and Williamson (1999). In these calculations, the transport cost component is the nonpolicy residual. However, most of this residual was in fact due to transport improvements.

[b]Migration policy index from Timmer and Williamson (1998); U.S. foreign-born shares from U.S. Department of Commerce (1975, part I, p. 8 and pp. 117–118) and Chiswick and Hatton (table 2.4 of ch. 2 in this volume).

[c]From Taylor (1999, table 3). For supporting evidence on international capital flows as a share of lenders' GDP, see Obstfeld and Taylor (1998, 359).

far ahead of everyone—their compatriots, the rest of Europe, and probably any nation in the world—between the sixteenth and the eighteenth centuries. This divergence was even greater in real than in nominal terms, because luxuries became much cheaper relative to staples (van Zanden 1995; Hoffman et al. 2002; Pamuk 2000). Although we still lack estimates or even guesstimates on the world distribution of income between 1500 and 1820, the bits and pieces we do have suggest that global inequality must have risen significantly in this pre-industrial era.

Fact number 4 is that there was no great march toward globalization after the 1490s and the voyages of de Gama and Columbus, despite the rhetoric about an early modern "world system." Granted, the early voyages made spice price markups a little less astronomical than in the days when the Arabs and Venetians monopolized long-distance trade. Yet there was no further progress toward price convergence in spices or any other long-distance tradable in the three centuries from the early and mid-1500s to the 1820s (O'Rourke and Williamson 2000, 2002; Findlay and O'Rourke, ch. 1 in this volume). Intercontinental trade remained effectively monopolized, and huge price markups between exporting and importing ports were maintained even in the face of improving transport technology.[3] Furthermore, most of the traded commodities were noncompeting. That is, they were not produced at home and thus did not displace some competing domestic industry. In addition, these traded consumption goods were luxuries out of reach of the vast majority of each trading country's population. In short, pre-1820 trade had only a trivial impact on living standards of anyone but the very rich.[4] Finally, the migration of people and capital was only a trickle before the 1820s. True globalization began only after the 1820s.

These four facts imply the following conflict: Although global divergence has been, to use Pritchett's (1997) phrase, "big time" for at least 400 years, globalization has been a fact of life for only about 150 (from about 1820, but omitting the autarkic retreat in 1914–45). This conflict certainly raises initial doubts about the common premise that rising world integration is responsible for rising world inequality.[5]

3. Although the existence of multilateral trade helped harmonize price movements within Europe (Jacks 2000), price gaps remained wide, even for grains, which were the most traded goods in a highly segmented Europe. See Abel (1973, 315, and tables 1 and 2) on the geography of wheat prices in grams of silver. At the local level, overland transport costs were typically higher than in the international sea trade, causing large markups over short distances. Another factor holding up grain trade integration between 1765 and the 1820s was the combination of the peacetime Corn Laws and the wartime Continental blockade.

4. For all the trade involving silver, its ability to buy grains or textiles remained far greater in Asia or even Eastern Europe than in the Americas, where the silver was mined, or in Western Europe. See O'Rourke and Williamson (2000) and Allen (2000) on Asia versus Europe, and Braudel and Spooner (1966), Allen (2001), and van Zanden (1999) on silver prices within Europe.

5. It should be added that, with the exception of sixteenth-century Spain, the countries that pulled ahead between 1500 and 1820 did not do so on the basis of their gains from overseas trade and empire, as quantitative studies have shown (e.g., Eltis and Engerman 2000).

5.3 The First Globalization Boom, 1820–1914

Table 5.1 sketches the integration of world commodity and factor markets during the first great globalization boom and contrasts it with antiglobal trends after the start of World War I. Regarding trade and commodity markets, the liberal dismantling of mercantilism and the worldwide transport revolution worked together to produce truly global markets across the nineteenth century. Almost three-quarters of the commodity price convergence was due to declining transport costs, and a little more than a quarter was due to the liberal policy switch.[6] Although the decline in transport costs continued throughout the century, there was an antiglobalization policy reaction only after 1870, and it was nowhere near big enough to cause a return to the 1820 levels of economic isolation. Mass migration remained free, although immigrant subsidies had evaporated by the end of the century. As European investors came to believe in strong growth prospects overseas, global capital markets also became steadily more integrated, reaching levels in 1913 that may not yet have been regained even today. On all three fronts these pre-1914 globalization achievements were subsequently reversed, and then renewed after 1950.

5.3.1 Which Nations Gained Most from Trade? Terms-of-Trade Clues

Terms-of-trade movements might offer some clues regarding who gains most from trade, and a literature at least two centuries old has offered opinions about whose terms of trade should improve most and why.[7] Classical economists thought the relative price of primary products should rise given an inelastic supply of land and natural resources. This classical conventional wisdom took a revisionist U-turn in the 1950s when Hans Singer and Raoul Prebisch argued that the terms of trade had deteriorated for poor countries in the periphery, exporting primary products, while they had improved for rich countries in the center, exporting industrial products.

The terms of trade can be influenced by a decline in transport costs, in which case everybody's terms of trade can improve. They can also be influenced by policy and by other events, such as intercommodity differences in productivity growth rates, demand elasticities, and factor supply responses. Since transport costs declined sharply in the century following 1820, this is one likely source that served to raise everybody's terms of trade. Furthermore, and as we shall see in a moment, rich countries like Great Britain took a terms-of-trade hit when they switched to free trade by midcentury, an event that must have raised the terms of trade in the poor, nonindustrial periphery even more. But in some parts of the periphery, especially before the 1870s, other factors were at work that mattered even more.

6. The relative contribution of the liberal policy switch between the 1770s and the 1820s, associated with rejecting mercantilism, was, of course, far bigger.
7. See the survey in Diakosavvas and Scandizzo (1991) or Hadass and Williamson (2001).

Probably the greatest nineteenth-century globalization shock did not involve transport revolutions at all. It happened in Asia, and it happened shortly before 1870. Under the persuasion of American gunships, Japan switched from virtual autarky to free trade in 1858. It is hard to imagine a more dramatic switch from closed to open trade policy. In the fifteen years following 1858, Japan's foreign trade rose seventy times, from virtually nil to 7 percent of national income (Huber 1971). The prices of exportables soared, rising toward world market levels. The prices of importables slumped, falling toward world market levels. One researcher estimates that, as a consequence, Japan's terms of trade rose by a factor of 3.5 between 1858 and the early 1870s (Huber 1971). Another thinks the rise was even bigger, a factor of 4.9 between 1857 and 1875 (Yasuba 1996). Whichever estimate one accepts, the combination of declining transport costs and a dramatic switch from autarky to free trade unleashed a powerful terms-of-trade gain for Japan.

Other Asian nations followed this liberal path, most forced to do so by colonial dominance or gunboat diplomacy. Thus, China signed a treaty in 1842 opening her ports to trade and adopting a 5 percent ad valorem tariff limit. Siam adopted a 3 percent tariff limit in 1855. Korea emerged from its autarkic "hermit kingdom" a little later (with the Treaty of Kangwha in 1876), undergoing market integration with Japan long before colonial status became formalized in 1910. India went the way of British free trade in 1846, and Indonesia mimicked Dutch liberalism. In short, and whether they liked it or not, prior to 1870 the most important part of the periphery underwent tremendous improvements in their terms of trade by this policy switch, and it was reinforced by declining transport costs worldwide.

For the years after 1870, we have good evidence documenting terms-of-trade movements the world around (Williamson 2002, table 2). Contrary to the assertions of Prebisch and Singer, not only did the terms of trade improve for the poor periphery[8] up to World War I, but they improved a lot more than they did in Europe. Over the four decades prior to World War I, the terms of trade rose by only 2 percent in the European center, by almost 10 percent in East Asia, and by more than 21 percent in the rest of the third world.

These pre–World War I terms-of-trade clues seem to imply that globalization favored the poor periphery more than it did the center, and thus that globalization contained leveling forces. The inference may be false.

Over the short run, positive and quasi-permanent terms-of-trade shocks of foreign origin will always (ceteris paribus) raise a nation's purchasing power, and the empirical issue is only how much. If the export sector was

8. In the study cited (Williamson 2002), the poor periphery sample includes Burma, Egypt, India, Japan, Korea, Taiwan, and Thailand. The rich (New World) periphery sample includes Argentina, Australia, Canada, the United States, and Uruguay. The Europe center sample includes Great Britain, Denmark, France, Germany, Ireland, Spain, and Sweden.

one-fifth of gross domestic product (GDP; a very large share by the standards of that time), and if the terms of trade improved by 5 percent over a decade (a pretty big relative price shock, as we have seen), then the purchasing power of GDP would have been raised by about 0.1 percentage points a year, a pretty small bang even if the country was growing at only 1 or 2 percent per annum.

Over the long run a positive terms-of-trade shock in primary-product-producing countries could reinforce comparative advantage, pull resources into the export sector from other activities, and cause deindustrialization. To the extent that industrialization is the prime carrier of capital-deepening and technological change, then economists like Hans Singer are right to caution that positive external price shocks for primary producers may actually lower growth rates in the long run. As far as we know, nobody has yet tried to decompose the short-run and long-run components of terms-of-trade shocks like these. But there has been a recent effort to explore the possibility that a positive change in the terms of trade could have had a negative long-run effect around the periphery.[9]

5.3.2 Trade Expansion and the Within-Country Distribution of Income

The standard Stolper-Samuelson prediction is that free trade increases incomes for the abundant factor and reduces incomes for the scarce factor. Protection has the opposite effect, and what holds for trade policy also holds for transport costs. In a simple world where labor works the land, and where each country takes world commodity prices as given, any move toward the globalization of commodity markets through trade and commodity price convergence should favor incomes of the laboring poor in the poorest trading partners where labor is abundant and land is scarce. Conversely, it should favor incomes of the landed rich in the richest trading partners where labor is scarce and land is abundant. But suppose there are more factors of production than just land and labor, and suppose some countries have an impact on their terms of trade. What then? History offers plenty of competing examples.

---

9. Hadass and Williamson (2001). Adding terms-of-trade variables to empirical growth models in the tradition of Robert Barro, Jeffrey Sachs, and many others (Barro and Sala-i-Martin 1995; Sachs and Warner 1995), and estimating for a panel of nineteen countries between 1870 and 1940, yields the result that an improvement in terms of trade augmented growth in the center. That is, the coefficient on terms-of-trade growth in the center is positive and significant in a GDP per capita growth regression. However, the same positive terms-of-trade shock was growth-reducing in the periphery. It appears that the short-run gain from an improving terms of trade was overwhelmed by a long-run loss attributed to deindustrialization in the periphery; in the center, in contrast, the short-run gain was reinforced by a long-run gain attributed to industrialization. Thus, it looks like terms-of-trade shocks before World War I were serving to augment the growing gap between rich and poor nations, with globalization adding to divergence. However, terms-of-trade shocks were rarely big enough to change GDP per capita growth rates by more than 5 or 10 percent (e.g., from 2 to 2.1 or 2.2 percent per annum).

Great Britain's nineteenth-century free-trade leadership, especially its famous Corn Law repeal in 1846, offers a good illustration of how the effects of liberalization depend on its sources, and how the effects of globalization can be egalitarian both at the world level and within the liberalizing advanced country. Was this a redistribution toward the British rich and away from the British poor, as well as from the rest of the world, as some of today's rhetoric would insist? No, the most likely redistributive effects were just the opposite. The big gainers from this leading-country trade liberalization were British laborers and the rest of the world, while the clear losers were British landlords, the world's richest group. How much the rest of the world gained (and whether British capitalists gained at all) depended on foreign-trade elasticities and induced terms-of-trade effects, assessments that pitted David Ricardo against Robert Torrens. But since these terms-of-trade effects were probably quite significant for what then was called "the workshop of the world," Great Britain must have distributed considerable gains to the rest of the world as well as to her own workers. British labor gained because Great Britain was a food-importing country (thus agriculture was a small employer)[10] and unskilled labor was used much less intensively in import-competing production than was land.[11] British nineteenth-century experience offers a very different example than does the United States today, as we shall see below. Thus, history offers two enormously important historical cases in which leading-country trade liberalization had completely different effects: whereas British liberalization in the nineteenth century was unambiguously egalitarian at both the national and global level, American liberalization in the twentieth century was not.

There are even better data for exploiting the factor-price approach to the globalization and inequality connection after 1870, but while we examine these data remember that international factor migration joined trade as an important force affecting intranational inequality in the late nineteenth century. Two kinds of evidence offer hints about inequality trends within countries participating in the global economy (Williamson 1997). One uses trends in the ratio of farm rents per acre to unskilled wages (r/w, in figs. 5.2 and 5.4).[12] The rent-wage ratio might be thought of as a measure of how

10. O'Rourke (1997) has shown that labor would not have gained from free trade on much of the continent because, among other things, agriculture was a much bigger employer, so that the employment effects (the nominal wage) dominated the consumption effects (the cost of living).

11. See Irwin (1988, 1991) and Williamson (1990). The effects on specific factor-income groups within Great Britain are inferred from a computable general-equilibrium model, one that is outfitted with parameters from nineteenth-century Great Britain, and one that is broadly consistent with observed movements in relative factor prices. The effects on Great Britain's terms of trade are estimated econometrically from British time series data.

12. The sources for figures 5.2–5.5 are O'Rourke, Taylor, and Williamson (1996) and Williamson (2002). For expositional convenience, this section examines factor-price ratios as if they were being affected by commodity trade alone, even though the same factor-price movements were affected strongly by the international factor flows to which we will turn next. This

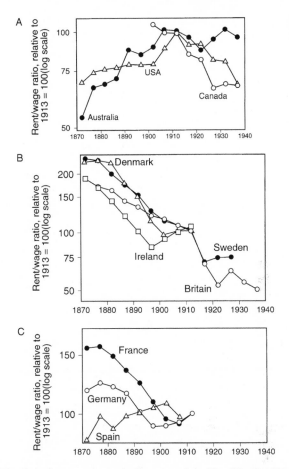

Fig. 5.2   Trends in the rent-wage ratio, Europe and the New World, 1870–1939: *A,*
Initially land-abundant countries; *B,* **Land-scarce free-trade countries;** *C,* **Land-**
scarce countries protecting grain farmers after 1875
Source: See note 12.

many days' labor it would take to pay the rent on a hectare of farmland. It
is a relative factor price whose trends determined inequality movements in

---

expositional assumption seems harmless since econometric analysis confirms that *both* trade
and factor flows contributed to the movements documented in figures 5.2–5.5 (O'Rourke, Taylor, and Williamson). We should note that the land "rents" are in fact indexes of farmland purchase prices, not rents, in the case of Australia, Punjab, Sweden, Thailand, and the United
States. The ratio of land purchase value to rental value could have drifted upward due to reduction in nominal interest rates. For these countries, the rise in the ratio of land value to wages
could overstate (understate) the rise (decline) in the rent-wage ratio to the extent that interest
rates were falling.

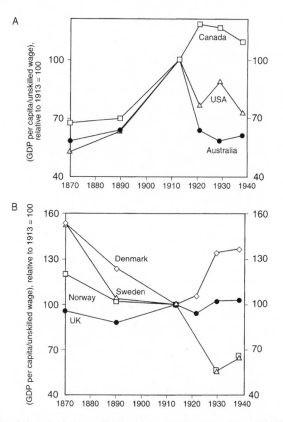

**Fig. 5.3   Trends in a crude inequality indicator, Old and New World, 1870–1939: *A,*
Initially land-abundant countries; *B,* Land-scarce free-trade countries**
Source: See note 12.

a world where the agricultural sector was big and where land was a critical
component of total wealth. It tells us how the typical landlord at the top of
the distribution did relative to the typical unskilled (landless) worker near
the bottom. The other inequality clue from factor prices uses trends in the
ratio of GDP per worker to the unskilled wage rate (v/w, in figs. 5.3 and 5.5).
These tell us how far the recipient of the average income was pulling ahead
of the typical unskilled worker near the bottom.[13] We now have this evidence for the Atlantic economy. Figure 5.3 plots trends in y/w, and it is certainly consistent with the conventional globalization prediction. Inequality

13. Our references to "top," "middle," and "bottom" do not mean that the landlords, average income earners, and unskilled workers occupied fixed percentile positions on the income
spectrum. This assumption would be convenient here, but the data do not allow it.

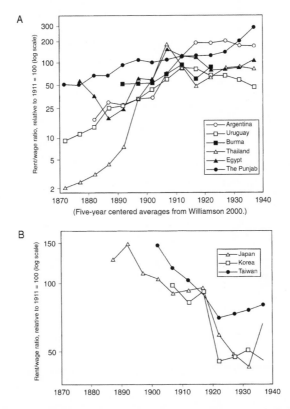

Fig. 5.4   Third world trends in rent-wage ratios, 1870–1939: *A*, Initially land-abundant countries; *B*, Land-scarce countries
Source: See note 12.

should have been rising in labor-scarce and land-abundant countries either due to the trade boom raising incomes of the abundant factor (e.g., land, augmenting incomes of those at the top) or due to a mass immigration lowering unskilled wages (e.g., unskilled labor, eroding incomes of those near the bottom).

A strong link between inequality trends and initial endowment stands out in figures 5.2–5.5, and this link bears the clear imprint of a globalization effect. Our first glimpse of the link comes from the contrasting trends for land-abundant North America and Australia versus land-scarce Europe in figure 5.2. In North America and Australia, where land was initially abundant, rents rose relative to unskilled wages before World War I, although not for the deglobalizing interwar period. The same was true of the initially land-abundant countries of Latin America and Asia, as shown in figure 5.4. By contrast, where land was initially scarce, as in Europe, Japan, Korea,

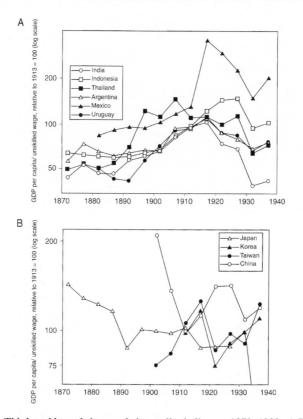

Fig. 5.5 **Third world trends in a crude inequality indicator, 1870–1939:** *A,* **Initially land-abundant countries;** *B,* **Land-scarce countries**
Source: See note 12.

and Taiwan, the rent-wage ratio declined before 1914. Although many factors were at work, globalization must have played the key role in accounting for the sharply contrasting trends between land-abundant and land-scarce countries, and between globalizing prewar and deglobalizing interwar periods. We cannot imagine another causal force that by itself could explain these sharp contrasts in trend between countries and periods, especially in those where industrialization forces were quiet.

Trends within Europe also betray an important distributional role for globalization. Note in figure 5.2 that those who faced the onslaught of cheap foreign grain after 1870, but decided not to impose high tariffs on the invading grains (Great Britain, Ireland, Denmark, and Sweden), recorded the biggest loss on rental income for landlords and the biggest gain for workers. Those who protected their landlords and farmers against cheap foreign grain after 1875 (France, Germany, and Spain) generally recorded a smaller decline in land rents relative to unskilled wage rates.

Inequality should have been falling in labor-abundant and land-scarce European countries, again due to trade booms and mass emigration. That happened in Scandinavia and Italy. Portugal and Spain did not share these egalitarian trends, but Iberia was well known for its unwillingness to play the globalization game. The European industrial leaders fell in the middle, just as we would predict. They were, after all, industrial and thus had smaller agricultural sectors. Land was a smaller component of total wealth in these industrial leaders, and improved incomes for (abundant) capital, whose capitalist owners were located near the top of the income distribution, at least partially offset the diminished incomes from land, whose owners tended to be at the top of the income distribution.

Evidence supporting these rent-wage ratio inferences come from the behavior of the second crude inequality indicator (y/w) in figures 5.3 and 5.5. It rose in the land-abundant countries during the prewar globalization boom. It declined in the land-scarce countries (with the possible exception of East Asia between the 1890s and World War I).

The inequality-globalization connection in the nineteenth century can be summarized this way: Globalization seems to have had an inegalitarian effect in (initially) land-abundant countries, a force raising inequality by rewarding landowners more than workers; and globalization seems to have had an egalitarian effect in (initially) land-scarce countries, especially in those that stuck with free trade and resisted pleas for protection. These two effects might appear at first glance to cancel each other out when aggregating up to the Atlantic economy as a whole. But a longer look tips the scales in favor of net egalitarian effects when we note that European landlords at the top of the Atlantic income distribution lost the most, while European unskilled workers at the bottom gained the most. A lot of the rest was simply New World "churning" in the middle.

5.3.3 The Impact of Factor Migration on Between-Country Income Gaps

Mass Migration and Convergence

Real wages and living standards converged among the currently industrialized OECD countries between 1850 and World War I. The convergence was driven primarily by the erosion of the gap between the New World and the Old. In addition, many poor European countries were catching up with the industrial leaders. How much of this convergence was due to mass migration?[14] Although Barry R. Chiswick and Timothy J. Hatton discuss this question in chapter 2 in this volume, we must treat the issue here too.

Table 5.2 assesses the labor force impact of these migrations on each of seventeen countries in the Atlantic economy in 1910. The impact varied greatly. Among receiving countries, Argentina's labor force was augmented

14. This section draws heavily on O'Rourke and Williamson (1999, 160–66).

Table 5.2   Mass Migration and Convergence in the Atlantic Economy, 1870–1910

	Persons		Labor Force		Impact of Migration (%)		
	Adjusted Net Migration Rate, 1870–1910	Adjusted Cumulative Population Impact (%), 1910	Adjusted Net Migration Rate, 1870–1910	Adjusted Cumulative Labor Force Impact (%), 1910	On Real Wages, 1870–1910	On GDP per Capita, 1870–1910	On GDP per Worker, 1870–1910
Argentina	11.74	60	15.50	86	-21.5	-8.2	-21.0
Australia	6.61	30	8.73	42	-14.6	-6.8	-14.4
Belgium	1.67	7	2.20	9	-4.4	-3.1	-5.1
Brazil	0.74	3	0.98	4	-2.3	-0.5	-1.5
Canada	6.92	32	9.14	44	-15.6	-7.6	-15.5
Denmark	-2.78	-11	-3.67	-14	7.6	3.7	7.4
France	-0.10	0	-0.13	-1	1.4	0.2	0.3
Germany	-0.73	-3	-0.96	-4	2.4	1.3	2.2
Great Britain	-2.25	-9	-2.97	-11	5.6	2.8	5.8
Ireland	-11.24	-36	-14.84	-45	31.9	n.a.	n.a.
Italy	-9.25	-31	-12.21	-39	28.2	14.2	28.6
The Netherlands	-0.59	-2	-0.78	-3	2.7	1.1	1.9
Norway	-5.25	-19	-6.93	-24	9.7	3.1	10.4
Portugal	-1.06	-4	-1.40	-5	4.3	0.0	0.0
Spain	-1.16	-5	-1.53	-6	5.9	0.0	0.0
Sweden	-4.20	-15	-5.55	-20	7.5	2.5	8.2
United States	4.03	17	5.31	24	-8.1	-3.3	-8.1
New World	6.01	29	7.93	40	-12.4	-5.3	-12.1
Old World	-3.08	-11	-4.06	-13	8.6	2.3	5.4
Actual change in dispersion, 17 countries					-28%	-18%	-29%
Change in dispersion with no migration (1870–1913)					7%	-9%	-9%
Implied contribution of migration to dispersion					-35%	-9%	-20%

Source: Taylor and Williamson (1997, tables 3, 4); O'Rourke and Williamson (1999, table 8.1).

Note: Migration rates per thousand per annum. Minus denotes emigration. n.a. = not applicable.

most by immigration (86 percent), Brazil's the least (4 percent), and the United States in between (24 percent), the latter below the New World average of 40 percent. Among sending countries, Ireland's labor force was diminished most by emigration (45 percent), France the least (1 percent), and Great Britain in between (11 percent), the latter just a little below the Old World average of 13 percent. At the same time, real wage dispersion in the Atlantic economy declined between 1870 and 1910 by 28 percent, GDP per capita dispersion by 18 percent, and GDP per-worker dispersion by 29 percent (table 5.2, bottom). What contribution did the mass migration make to that measured convergence? To answer this question, we ask another: What would have been the measured convergence had there been no mass migration?

Migration affects long-run equilibrium output and wages by influencing aggregate labor supply. Taylor and Williamson (1997) estimate labor demand elasticities econometrically and use these results to assess the wage impact of changing labor supply by country. They also estimated the impact of migration on GDP per capita and GDP per worker. The last three columns of table 5.2 present their results.

Table 5.2 accords with intuition. In the absence of the mass migrations, wages and labor productivity would have been a lot higher in the New World and a lot lower in the Old. In the absence of the mass migrations, income per capita would typically (but not always) have been a bit higher in the New World and typically (but not always) a bit lower in the Old World. Not surprisingly, the biggest counterfactual impact is reported for those countries that experienced the biggest migrations. Emigration raised Irish wages by 32 percent, Italian by 28 percent, and Norwegian by 10 percent. Immigration lowered Argentine wages by 22 percent, Australian by 15 percent, Canadian by 16 percent, and American by 8 percent.

This partial equilibrium assessment of migration's impact is higher than a general equilibrium assessment would be. After all, it ignores trade responses and changes in output mix, both of which would have muted the impact of migration. It also ignores global capital market responses, although this latter shortcoming will be repaired in a moment. Whether an overstatement or not, table 5.2 certainly lends strong support to the hypothesis that mass migration made an important contribution to late-nineteenth-century convergence. In the absence of the mass migrations, real wage dispersion would have *increased* by 7 percent, rather than decreasing by 28 percent, as in fact it did (table 5.2, bottom panel). Gross domestic product per-worker dispersion would have decreased by only 9 percent, rather than by 29 percent, as in fact it did. GDP per capita dispersion would also have decreased by only 9 percent, rather than by 18 percent as in fact it did. Wage gaps between New World and Old in fact declined from 108 to 85 percent, but in the absence of the mass migrations they would have *risen* to 128 percent in 1910.

Using results like those in table 5.2, Taylor and Williamson (1997) conclude that for 1870–1910 migration can account for all of the real wage convergence, about two-thirds of the GDP-per-worker convergence, and perhaps one-half of the GDP per capita convergence.[15]

The relative insensitivity of GDP per capita convergence to migration is a result of countervailing effects. Mass migration self-selected young adults. Thus, high migrant labor participation rates amplified the impact of migration on real wages and GDP per worker, but the effect on GDP per capita was muted. Why? For wages and GDP per worker, migration has a bigger impact the bigger its labor content. In the case of GDP per capita, things are less clear because there are two offsetting forces at work. Population emigration reverses diminishing returns, yielding a positive impact on output per capita; but selectivity assures that emigration will also take away a disproportionate share of the labor force, lowering output via labor supply losses, yielding a negative impact on output per capita.[16] The latter effect dominated in the late-nineteenth-century Atlantic economy, so muted GDP per capita effects are no surprise. Based on table 5.2, we can conclude that four decades of migration never lowered New World GDP per capita by more than 9 percent anywhere in the New World, and by as little as 3 percent in the United States, in contrast with per-worker impacts of 21 and 8 percent, respectively.[17] Similar reasoning applies to the Old World: Swedish emigration after 1870 may have raised wages in 1910 by about 8 percent, but it served to raise Sweden's GDP per capita by only 3 percent.

Mass Migration and Global Inequality

An important extra effect of the great migration on global inequality has been omitted from the accounting so far. Table 5.2 was constructed to show the effect of migration on convergence in per capita and per-worker aver-

15. The contributions of mass migration to convergence in the full sample and within the New and Old World differ, the intraregional effects being smaller. Furthermore, in two New World countries, Argentina and Brazil, global convergence would have been *greater* in the absence of mass migration. The fact that the Atlantic labor market was segmented should account for this otherwise bizarre result. Immigrant flows were not efficiently distributed everywhere, because barriers to entry limited destination choices for many southern Europeans, a point central to discussions of Latin American economic performance (Diaz-Alejandro 1970; Hatton and Williamson 1998, chaps. 2, 3, 6, and 10). Thus, migrants did not always obey some simple market-wage calculus; kept out of the best high-wage destinations, or having alternative cultural preferences, many went to the "wrong" countries. The South-South flows from Italy, Spain, and Portugal to Brazil and Argentina were a strong force for local (Latin), not global (Atlantic), convergence. Furthermore, while barriers to exit were virtually absent in most of the Old World, policy in the New World (like assisted passage) still played a part in violating any simple market-wage calculus.

16. This argument assumes that immigrant remittances—while substantial—were nowhere near large enough to erase the first-order "perverse" effect on GDP per capita.

17. This labor-supply compensation effect operated in addition to the usual human-capital transfer influences invoked to describe the net benefit to the United States of the immigrants received before WWI (Neal and Uselding 1972).

ages between countries; it was not constructed to show the impact of migration on income distribution within the Atlantic economy as a whole. To do so, we need to add on the large income gains accruing to the 60 million Europeans who moved overseas. Typically, they came from countries whose average real wages and average GDP per worker were perhaps only half of those in the receiving countries. These migrant gains were an important part of their net equalizing effect on world incomes, and even on "world" income distribution among the seventeen countries in table 5.2.

Capital Flow Responses?

Using ceteris paribus assumptions, we earlier concluded that mass migration accounted for all of the real wage convergence observed in the Atlantic economy between 1870 and 1910. But other things were not constant. There were other powerful proconvergence and anticonvergence forces at work, capital accumulation being one of them. We know that capital accumulation was rapid in the New World, so much so that the rate of capital deepening was faster in the United States than in any of its European competitors (Wright 1990; Wolff 1991), and the same was probably true of other rich New World countries. Thus, the mass migrations may have been at least partially offset by capital accumulation, and a large part of that capital widening was being carried by international capital flows that reached magnitudes unsurpassed before or since, as Obstfeld and Taylor show in chapter 3 in this volume. The evidence on the role of global capital market responses to migration is very tentative, but Taylor and Williamson (1997, tables 4–6a) make exactly this kind of adjustment. They implement the zero-net-migration counterfactual in a model where the labor supply shocks generate capital inflows or outflows in order to maintain a constant rate of return on capital in each country (e.g., perfect global capital market integration). The capital-chasing-labor offsets are very large. Whereas mass migration explained all of the observed real wage convergence using the model without capital chasing labor, it explains about 70 percent of the convergence using the model with capital chasing labor, leaving only about 30 percent to other forces. The findings for labor productivity are similar.

Capital Flows, Convergence, and the Lucas Paradox

Although it is true that capital markets were at least as well integrated globally prior to World War I as they are today, capital flows were mainly an anticonvergence force. This apparently counterintuitive statement is, of course, inconsistent with a simple theory predicting that capital should flow from rich countries (presumably capital abundant) to poor countries (presumably capital scarce). It did not. Just as Lucas (1990) reported for the late twentieth century, Clemens and Williamson (2000) find that capital inflows and GDP per capita were *positively* correlated between 1870 and 1913. The so-called Lucas paradox was alive and well a century ago, and it is explained by the fact that capital chased after abundant natural resources, youthful populations, and human-capital abundance. Thus, capital flows were an anticonvergence force. They drifted toward rich, not poor, countries; they raised wages and labor productivity in the resource-abundant New World; and, with the exception of Scandinavia, their exit from Europe lowered wages and labor productivity in that resource-scarce part of the world.

5.3.4   Summing Up: Nineteenth-Century Convergence Forces in a Diverging World

Among the main participants in the nineteenth-century economy, globalization had offsetting effects. Within rich, land-abundant New World countries, more trade and more immigration augmented inequality. Within poor, primary-product-exporting third world countries, they did the same. Within poor, land-scarce, participating Old World countries, more trade and more emigration reduced inequality. As for income gaps between countries, migration had an equalizing effect, one that was somewhat offset by the fact that capital flowed to rich New World countries. Freer trade might also have had an egalitarian effect, benefiting the poorer new participants like Japan the most, although it may not have favored peripheral counties that were led into deindustrialization. Overall, prewar globalization looks like a force equalizing average incomes between the participating countries, but with mixed effects on inequality within participating countries.

If globalization had mixed effects that probably tilted a bit toward global equalization among the countries involved, why does world income inequality rise so much in figure 5.1? One answer, of course, is that average national incomes were driven apart by more fundamental forces, such as inequalities in schooling, secure property rights, and government quality. Another answer is that there were no mass migrations between poor periphery and rich center.[18] A third answer is that many countries remained detached from the global economy by choice (e.g., Iberia) or by distance (e.g., much of inland Africa, Asia, and Latin America).

5.4   Retreat from Globalization 1914–50: Raising New Policy Barriers

As table 5.1 documents, the globalized world that fell apart after 1914 was not rebuilt during the interwar decades. Indeed, what distinguishes the interwar period is that globalization was dismantled solely by government policy. Governments imposed trade and factor market barriers where there were none before, and some even blocked communications. The interwar period was *not* marked by some disappearance of the previous nonpolicy sources of globalization. The big productivity gains in transportation and

---

18. There was, of course, mass migration *within* the poor periphery, even though economic historians have paid little attention to it.

communications did not evaporate. Nor was there any collapse in world population growth—only new policy barriers imposed on poor populations that restricted their ability to flee miserable conditions for something better. The pace of technological progress may have slowed down, but, more importantly, the appearance of new disincentives reduced investment in the diffusion of modern technology around the world. In short, the interwar retreat from globalization was carried by antiglobal economic policies.

To judge what effect these antiglobal policies had on global inequality, let us begin with the overall trend in world inequality and then look at the role of policy in shaping that trend. Our expectations are to find symmetry between the pre-1914 and interwar periods. Thus, we expect to find the following: a convergence slowdown in the deglobalizing Atlantic economy (and perhaps even an acceleration in the rising trend in inequality gaps worldwide); an easement in the inequality forces operating within rich, labor-scarce economies; and an easement of the egalitarian forces operating within poor, labor-scarce economies.

5.4.1 Between-Country Income Gaps 1914–50

Figure 5.1 documents an interwar acceleration in the rising trend toward inequality between countries. In fact, over the almost two centuries documented by Bourguignon and Morrisson in that figure, there was no period when divergence between countries was more "big time." We do not yet know how much of this should be attributed to the Great Depression, two world wars, antiglobal policies, and other forces. However, there is plenty of evidence documenting that convergence stopped in the Atlantic economy before 1929 (Williamson 1996), when deglobalization was having an inegalitarian influence independent of war and depression. Migration barriers definitely widened international income gaps, and new barriers to trade and capital flows probably added to those widening gaps.

5.4.2 Within-Country Inequality Trends 1914–50

Figure 5.1 also shows that within-country inequality took a sharp nose dive between 1910 and 1950. This change is the most dramatic regime switch documented in the figure. While poor, labor-abundant OECD countries lost their pre-1914 egalitarian trends—some actually drifting toward greater inequality—the industrial European countries continued their egalitarian drift, and the rich, labor-scarce New World countries underwent egalitarian trends that were then called "revolutionary" (Lindert and Williamson 1985; Williamson 1997; Lindert 2000; Bourguignon and Morrisson 2002). True, deglobalization can hardly account for all of this worldwide within-country inequality nose dive; after all, those high pre–World War I within-country inequality levels were never recovered when globalization was reclaimed by the end of the twentieth century. The new barriers to migration must have raised inequality within sending countries and lowered it in receiving countries,[19] reversing the prewar effects. Since the impact of new trade barriers on interwar within-country inequality has not yet been assessed, the overall effect of 1914–50 deglobalization on worldwide within-country inequality will have to await future research.

5.5   Back on Track: The Second Globalization Boom

Globalization by any definition resumed after World War II. It has differed from pre-1914 globalization in several ways.[20] Factor migrations have been less impressive by most measures. The foreign-born are a smaller share of the total population than they were in the main Western Hemisphere receiving nations in 1913 (table 5.1), and capital exports were a smaller percentage of GDP in the postwar United States (0.5 percent in 1960–73 and 1.2 percent in 1989–96; Obstfeld and Taylor 1998, table 11.1) than they were in prewar Great Britain (4.6 percent in 1890–1913). On the other hand, trade barriers are probably lower today than they were in 1913. These differences are tied to policy changes in one dominant nation, the United States, which has switched from a protectionist welcoming immigrants to a free trader restricting immigration. Another difference has already been revealed in figure 5.1: The postwar world started out much more unequal than the world of 1820 or 1870, and international income gaps, not income gaps within countries, now dominate the global inequality of living standards.

5.5.1   International Gaps Again: An Epochal Turning Point?

While the issues are elaborated in far greater detail by J. Bradford DeLong and Steve Dowrick in chapter 4 of this volume, we need to review here what has happened to between-country income gaps since 1950. Figure 5.1 uses data from Bourguignon and Morrisson (2002) to document what looks like a mid-twentieth-century turning point in their between-country inequality index, which slows its rise after 1950. However, the Bourguignon and Morrisson long-period database contains only fifteen countries. Using postwar purchasing-power-parity data for a much bigger sample of 115, Melchior, Telle, and Wiig (2000, 14) actually document a *decline* in their between-country inequality index in the second half of the twentieth century. The authors show stability in between-country inequality up to the late 1970s, followed by convergence centered on the early 1980s and early 1990s. Four other recent studies find the same fall in between-country inequality

19. This, after all, was one central motivation for the legislation that finally brought quotas to North America in the 1920s, after heated public debate over a quarter of a century (Goldin 1994; Timmer and Williamson 1998).
20. See Baldwin and Martin 1999; Bordo, Eichengreen, and Irwin 1999; Findlay and O'Rourke, ch. 1 in this volume; Chiswick and Hatton, ch. 2 in this volume; and section 5.3 in this chapter.

after the early 1960s (Schultz 1998; Firebaugh 1999; Boltho and Toniolo 1999; Radetzki and Jonsson 2000).[21] Among these five recent studies, perhaps most useful in identifying an epochal regime switch is that of Boltho and Toniolo (1999, plotted in Bourguinon and Morrisson, 2002, diagram 2.4, p. 16), who show a rise in between-country inequality in the 1940s, rough stability over the next three decades, and a significant fall after 1980, significant enough to make their between-country inequality index drop well below its 1950 level.

Did the postwar switch from autarky to global integration contribute to this epochal change in the evolution of international gaps in average incomes? Here we seek the answer focusing on trade, returning later to factor migration.

5.5.2 Trade and Postwar Between-Country Inequality

Conventional thinking presumes that liberalizing trade should have benefited third world countries more than it benefited leading industrial countries. The reasoning is the same as that already introduced when we surveyed pre-1914 experience. First, liberalizing trade should have a bigger effect on the terms of trade of the country joining the larger integrated world economy than on countries already integrated. Second, the more a country's terms of trade are changed, the bigger the gain in national income.[22]

In one simple respect, the gains from postwar liberalization should have been greater among the high-income OECD countries than among poorer countries as a whole. The postwar trade that was liberalized the most was in fact intra-OECD trade, not trade between the OECD and the rest. From the very beginning in the 1940s, the General Agreement on Tariffs and Trade (GATT) explicitly excused low-income countries from the need to dismantle their import barriers and exchange controls. This permission probably lowered their national incomes, but it was consistent with the dominant protectionist and antiglobal ideology prevailing in emerging nations at that time. Thus, the succeeding rounds of liberalization under GATT, from the Dillon and Kennedy Rounds through the Uruguay Round, brought freer trade and higher incomes mainly to OECD members. We emphasize again

21. They all use purchasing power parity data for which the fall is far clearer. Indeed, it disappears in studies that use income data in U.S. dollars (Melchior, Telle, and Wiig 2000, diagram 2.4, p. 16). See also Dowrick and DeLong, chap. 4 in this volume.

22. As we noted for the 1820–1913 era, poor-country gains from trade depend on whether expanding before 1914 may have induced deindustrialization in poorer countries. Did the same happen after World War II? Probably not. After all, industrial manufactures have been a rapidly rising share of third world output and exports. For example, for all "developing" (third world) countries, manufactures rose from only 17.4 percent of commodity exports in 1970 to 64.3 percent by 1994 (United Nations Conference on Trade and Development 1988 and 1997). Enough of the third world is now labor-abundant and natural-resource-scarce so that the growth of trade has helped it industrialize. The classic image of third world specialization in primary products is becoming obsolete.

that these facts do not show that globalization favors rich participants. Rather, globalization favors all participants who liberalize, especially those who are newly industrializing, and penalizes those who choose not to liberalize, leaving them behind.

The abundant literature on trade liberalization in the third world is, unfortunately, limited to analysis of the effects of one country's liberalization on *its own* income and ignores effects on the rest of the world. This limitation may be innocuous for small countries, but it is a serious omission for the giants. Thus, we have only assessments of China's liberalization on China, not of China's liberalization on the world. The same is true of the United States, the European Union, the Russian Federation, and other giants. Still, this literature does yield fairly firm conclusions about whether liberalizing countries gain from freer trade.

Four kinds of studies have tried to judge the gains from freer trade, or the losses from more protection, in the developing countries. Led by a large National Bureau of Economic Research (NBER) project on trade and exchange-control regimes in the 1960s and 1970s, economists explored the sectoral connections between protection and growth in fourteen developing countries. To quantify the overall effects of complicated trade regimes, the authors resorted to classic partial-equilibrium calculations of deadweight costs.[23] They concluded that the barriers imposed significant costs on Argentina, Chile, Colombia, Egypt, Ghana, India, Israel, Mexico, Pakistan, the Philippines, South Korea, Taiwan, and Turkey.[24] By themselves, these standard welfare calculations are vulnerable to the charge of assuming, not proving, that trade barriers were bad for these developing countries. Such calculations assume that all the relevant effects are captured by measures of consumer and producer surplus, without allowing protection any chance to lower long-run cost curves, as it is assumed to do in the traditional infant-industry case, and to foster industrialization and thus growth, as in those modern growth models where industry is the carrier of technological change and capital deepening. Thus, it would be fair to demand more proof than that offered by the comparative static calculations of the 1960s and 1970s.

A second kind of evidence consists of cross-country growth studies that contrast the growth performance of relatively open and closed economies. The World Bank conducted such studies for forty-one countries in the periods before and after the first oil shock. Table 5.3 extends this coverage through 1992. The correlation between trade openness and growth seems clear enough in this demonstration, but the correlation is vulnerable to two criticisms. First, assigning countries to trade policy categories is always tricky, since it is hard to measure overall openness. Second, and much more importantly, it is hard to isolate the effect of trade policies alone, since other

23. Bhagwati and Krueger (1973–76). See also Balassa (1971) and Papageorgiou, Michaely, and Choksi (1991).
24. Only in Malaysia did the import barriers yield a slight gain, and that was because of favorable terms-of-trade effects.

Table 5.3   Trade Policy Orientation and Growth Rates in the Third World, 1963–92

	Average Annual Growth Rates of GDP Per Capita (%)		
Orientation	1963–73	1973–85	1980–92
Strongly open to trade	6.9	5.9	6.4
Moderately open	4.9	1.6	2.3
Moderately antitrade	4.0	1.7	–0.2
Strongly antitrade	1.6	–0.1	–0.4

Sources: World Bank (1987, 78–94), with further growth data from World Bank 1994.
Notes: In all periods the three strongly open economies were Hong Kong, South Korea, and Singapore. The identities of the strongly antitrade countries changed over time. In 1963–73, they consisted of Argentina, Bangladesh, Burundi, Chile, the Dominican Republic, Ethiopia, Ghana, India, Pakistan, Peru, Sri Lanka, Sudan, Tanzania, Turkey, Uruguay, and Zambia. For the two overlapping later periods the strongly antitrade group consisted of the previous sixteen plus Bolivia, Madagascar, and Nigeria, but minus Chile, Pakistan, Sri Lanka, Turkey, and Uruguay. For the identities of the moderate-policy groups, see World Bank (1987, 78–94).

policies are usually changing at the same time. Liberalism typically comes as a package. Thus, countries that liberalized their trade also liberalized their domestic factor markets, liberalized their domestic commodity markets, and set up better property-rights enforcement.[25] The appearance of these non-trade policies may deserve more credit for raising income than the simultaneous appearance of more liberal trade policies.

A third kind of evidence comes from event studies. Here the strategy is to focus on periods when trade policy changed the most so as to see its effect on growth. For example, Krueger (1983, 1984) looked at trade-opening moments in South Korea around 1960, Brazil and Colombia around 1965, and Tunisia around 1970. Growth improved after liberalization in all four cases (Krueger 1983, 1984). More recently, Dollar and Kraay (2000b) examined the reforms and trade liberalizations of sixteen countries in the 1980s and 1990s, finding, once again, the positive correlation between freer trade and faster growth. Here, too, critics could argue that the reform episodes changed more than just participation in the global economy, so that an independent trade effect has not been isolated.

Finally, recent studies have used multivariate econometric analysis in an attempt to resolve the doubts left by simpler historical correlations. The number of national experiences analyzed statistically now numbers in the hundreds (Edwards 1992, 1993; Dollar 1992; Dollar and Kraay 2000a, b.) Even with several other variables held constant, those studies show that freer trade policies tend to have a positive effect on growth, although one cannot statistically reject a zero effect in many of the tests. These econometric studies have raised the scientific standard of inquiry about the effects

25. This was true, for example, in Great Britain, where the 1846 repeal of the Corn Laws was immersed in a deluge of domestic liberal reform.

of trade policy, although critics are free to raise their standards too, retaining doubts about omitted variables, simultaneity, and details of the error term in each econometric equation. And economic historians might argue that it depends on when a country goes global: Are its trading partners liberalizing too? Are its competitors liberalizing? Is the liberalizing country ready for industrialization, accumulation, and human capital deepening, or will it be driven instead up some primary-product-producing dead end? It might be argued that conditions were less auspicious for third world liberalization in 1870–1914 or 1914–60 than since 1960, or, as we shall see, in the 1980s and 1990s compared with the 1960s and 1970s.

The doubts that each individual study might raise threaten to block our view of the overall forest of evidence. Even though no one study can establish that trade openness has unambiguously helped the representative third world economy, the preponderance of evidence does seem to support this conclusion. One way to see the whole forest more clearly is to consider two sets, one almost empty and one completely empty. The almost-empty set consists of all statistical studies showing that protection helps third world economic growth or that liberalization harms it. The set would have been completely empty had not Bairoch (1972, 1989) and O'Rourke (2000) both found that protectionist countries grew *faster* before 1914. Thus, their findings suggest a paradox: Although the protection-growth correlation was negative after 1950, it was positive before 1914. True, Bairoch and O'Rourke did not evaluate third world countries, since their samples included only a few members of the Atlantic economy club. However, they get support from Clemens and Williamson (2001), who have recently shown that the positive protection-growth pre-1914 paradox holds for a much bigger world sample, and even holds through the late 1920s, but the correlation is far weaker and often negative for the European and the third world periphery. Clemens and Williamson also show how the world trade environment accounts for the pre-1914 versus post-1950 contrast. The negative (positive) correlation between openness (protection) and growth before 1914 is also consistent with the recent finding by Hadass and Williamson (2001) that terms-of-trade improvements associated with globalization reduced long-run income growth between 1870 and 1940 in the periphery while raising it in the center. The fact that this set is almost but not completely empty raises a challenge; observers will have to deal with the historical paradox in future work.

The second, and this time empty, set contains those countries that chose to be less open to trade and factor flows in the 1990s than in the 1960s and rose in the global living-standard ranks at the same time. As far as we can tell, there are no antiglobal victories to report for the postwar third world.[26]

---

26. Going back further to 1928 would, however, capture the Soviet Union, a country that took off while deglobalizing. Emerging nations in Asia, Africa, and Latin America certainly saw this as an antiglobal victory, but Stalin might have done far better had he stayed open.

We infer that this is because freer trade stimulates growth in the third world today, regardless of its effects before 1940.[27]

Timing matters, and, in retrospect, we think we can detect a hidden source of East Asian super-growth by appealing to it. Other countries may have given the East Asians their chance by failing to compete in labor-intensive manufacturing export markets and make market reforms, long before the 1980s. Thus, the original Four Tigers—Singapore, South Korea, Taiwan, and Hong Kong—probably owe much of their export-led success in the 1960s and 1970s to the protectionist and illiberal domestic policies of mainland China, North Korea, Vietnam, Burma, Bangladesh, India, and Pakistan. In the 1980s a newly opened China began to catch up, perhaps partly because India and the others remained so antitrade.[28]

Trade and Inequality within Postwar Third World Countries

Although removing barriers to trade may raise per capita income in developing countries, what does it do to inequality within them? The simple Stolper-Samuelson model, as we have noted, would predict that freer trade would be egalitarian for these countries, since it allows those abundant in unskilled labor to shift toward unskilled-labor-intensive production, raising unskilled wages relative to skilled wages and returns on property. Has this been true?

The effect of globalization on inequality within third world countries is just as hard to chart for the postwar era as it is for the pre-1914 era. The postwar data are still sparse, and they are available for only a few countries. Fortunately, we can get a good idea of the overall effect on within-country inequality just by following the experience of a few giants neglected by the literature, but we start with the smaller countries that have been studied in far greater detail.

Some Latin and Asian Experience. The recent literature on globalization and inequality within developing countries since the 1960s has a pretty narrow focus. It has concentrated on nine countries—six Latins (Argentina, Chile, Colombia, Costa Rica, Mexico, and Uruguay) and three East Asians (Korea, Singapore, and Taiwan). In order to test the Stolper-Samuelson prediction, the recent literature has dwelt on the pay gaps between skilled and unskilled workers.

This recent assessment of the globalization and inequality connection in

27. As economic historians, we want to know whether what is true now was true a century ago, and if not, why not. Has a shift toward benefiting from trade been due to a century of faster population growth in the third world, which has shifted its comparative advantage toward labor-intensive manufactures and away from resource-intensive primary products? To what extent is this shift just a reflection of the opening up of labor-abundant and resource-scarce Japan, Korea, and China to world trade? These issues are on the research agenda.

28. The experiences of Thailand, Malaysia, and Indonesia are consistent with this conjecture because these three countries were intermediate in all respects—in both the levels and the rates of change in their trade barriers and their incomes.

developing countries diverges sharply between regions and epochs. Wage gaps seemed to fall when the three Asian tigers liberalized in the 1960s and early 1970s. Yet wage gaps generally widened when the six Latin American countries liberalized after the late 1970s (Wood 1994, 1997, 1998; Feenstra and Hanson 1997; Robbins 1997; Robbins and Gindling 1999; Hanson and Harrison 1999). Why the difference?

As Wood (1997) has rightly pointed out, historical context was important, since other things were not equal during these liberalizations. The clearest example in which a Latin wage widening appears to refute the egalitarian Stolper-Samuelson prediction was the Mexican liberalization under Salinas in 1985–90. Yet this liberalization move coincided with the major entry of China and other Asian exporters into world markets. Thus, Mexico faced intense new competition from less skill-intensive manufactures in all export markets.[29] Furthermore, blue-collar wage rates were already higher in Mexico than in many Asian countries, suggesting that the widening of Mexican pay gaps in 1985–90 actually fits the Stolper-Samuelson prediction because at that point Mexico was a *high*-wage country in the relevant world export markets.

Historical context could also explain why trade liberalization coincided with wage widening in the five other Latin countries, and why it coincided with wage narrowing in East Asia in the 1960s and early 1970s. Again, timing matters. Competition from other low-wage countries was far less intense when the Asian tigers pulled down their barriers in the 1960s and early 1970s compared with the late 1970s and early 1980s when the Latin Americans opened up. In addition, trade liberalization in Argentina 1976–82 was accompanied by union-busting and an easing of minimum-wage controls. The same policies were carried out with an even firmer hand in Pinochet's Chile 1974–79, another documented case of wage widening coinciding with trade liberalization. In these cases, at least, wages may have widened for reasons other than the liberalization of international trade and foreign investment.

The Experience of the Giants. Past evidence on the wage-inequality and trade-liberalization connection in developing countries has been decidedly mixed.[30] But even if the findings from the usually studied developing countries were not mixed, they could not have had much of an impact on global inequalities. After all, the half-dozen Latin countries, plus the three Asian tigers, are tiny relative to four huge countries that have undergone even larger policy shocks. Specifically, the literature has focused on nine countries

---

29. It might also be relevant to point out that Mexico's own import liberalization brought much greater tariff reductions on low-skill manufactures than on high-skill manufactures.

30. One other indicator, however, may tip the scale toward the belief that globalization widens pay gaps in developing countries: Latin American employees of multinational firms and international joint ventures receive higher wages, with or without adjustment for skills and other factors (Aitken, Harrison, and Lipsey 1996; Pavcnik 2000).

that together had less than 200 million people in 1980, whereas China by itself had 980 million, India 687 million, Indonesia 148 million, and Russia 139 million. All four of these giants recorded widening income gaps after their economies liberalized. The widening did not start in China until after 1984, because the initial reforms were rural and agricultural and therefore had an egalitarian effect. After the reforms reached the urban-industrial sector in 1984, China's income gaps widened (Griffin and Zhao 1993, especially p. 61; Atinc 1997; World Bank 1993–2000/1; Chowdhury, Harvie, and Levy 2000). India's inequality has risen since liberalization started in the early 1990s. Indonesian incomes became increasingly concentrated in the top decile from the 1970s to the 1990s, although this probably owed more to the Suharto regime's ownership of the new oil wealth than to any conventional trade-liberalization effect. Russian inequalities soared after the collapse of the Soviet regime in 1991 (Flemming and Micklewright 2000).

Income widening in these four giants dominates global trends in intranational inequalities,[31] but how much was due to liberal trade policy and globalization? Probably very little. Indeed, much of the inequality surge during their liberalization experiments seems linked to the fact that the opening to trade and foreign investment was incomplete. That is, the rise in inequality appears to have been based on the exclusion of much of the population from the benefits of globalization.

China, where the gains since 1984 have been heavily concentrated in the coastal cities and provinces (Griffin and Zhao 1993; Atinc 1997), offers a good example. Migration from the hinterland to the cities was pretty much prohibited before the mid-1990s. Those that were able to participate in the new, globally linked economy prospered faster than ever before, while the rest in the hinterland were left behind, or at least enjoyed less economic success. China's inequality had risen to American levels by 1995 (a Gini of .406), but the pronounced surge in inequality from 1984 to 1995 was dominated by the rise in urban-rural and coastal-hinterland gaps, not by widening gaps within any given locale. This pattern suggests that China's inequality has been raised by differential access to the benefits of the new economy, not by widening gaps among those who participate in it, or among those who do not.[32]

---

31. The giants also dominate trends in between-country inequality. Much of the fall in the between-country inequality index offered by Melchior, Telle, and Wiig (2000, 15) is due to the fact that the populations in Japan and the United States are getting relatively fewer and less rich, while those in China and India are getting richer and more populous.

32. In Russia, the benefits were also skewed toward those who were able to participate in the reforms and internationalization, although for a different reason. The handing over of state trading prerogatives and physical assets to a few oligarchs contributed to one of the greatest inequality surges in history (Flemming and Micklewright 2000). Similarly, the assets of the Suharto family and its cronies in Indonesia tended to be concentrated in the expanding trade sector. More comprehensive and competitive access to the international economy might have brought a more egalitarian result in each of these cases.

Multinationals, Sweatshops, and Children. One theme that has dominated recent news coverage about global interactions and global inequality is the imagined association of multinational enterprise with harsh "sweatshop" labor conditions and the use of child labor in the third world. The imagery is familiar: Pakistani boys sew soccer balls, Chinese women make Kathie Lee wardrobe items, and Indonesians make Nike running shoes, all far into the night. Do such interactions widen the income gaps between rich and poor countries? Do they benefit only the multinational firms that employ cheap third world labor?[33]

Two issues of global concern overlap here. One is the extent to which employers violate International Labor Organization (ILO) codes and labor standards regarding fair labor contracts and exploit both adults and children. The other is whether the employment of third world children is at the expense of their schooling, their best investment for the long run. Both are legitimate concerns. The first calls for international and national monitoring to enforce legal codes, although the codes themselves have been vague, perhaps necessarily so (Brown 2001). The second calls for pressure on governments to supply tax-based schooling, as all industrialized countries did when launching primary education in the nineteenth century (Lindert 2001). Both are complex issues, and the relevant theory and evidence are still just emerging (U.S. Department of Labor, Bureau of International Affairs 1995–2000; Basu 1999).

As far as one can tell from partial evidence, however, neither of these potential evils is connected with globalization. The employment of children or other unskilled labor by multinational firms probably reduces those wide income gaps between countries. After all, there is no positive correlation between nonagricultural international exchange and the use of child labor—either over time, or across countries, or across sectors of any economy. During the globalizing half-century since 1950, the rates of work by children under fifteen have been declining in every ILO country, and school enrollment rates have been rising (Brown 2001). The rates of work and nonschooling are lowest in the most internationally involved countries. The most visible recent case of a country's suddenly joining the international economy is China, where the rate of decline in child labor has been faster since 1980 than in the rest of the third world, and faster than it was previously under Chairman Mao. And across sectors of China's economy, the highly publicized manufacturing-export sector has a rate of child employment that is well below the national average. The multinationals hire more skilled, and more schooled, labor than the national average.

---

33. For a typical recent presentation of prima facie evidence of labor abuse involving manufacturing exports from the Third World, see Bernstein, Shari, and Malkin (2000). For a longer presentation of the imagery, see Greider (1997). The social reform literature on child labor in British cities during the first industrial revolution reads pretty much the same way, but some say abuse was minor (Nardinelli 1990) whereas others say it was major (Tuttle 1999).

Would a ban on the use of child labor in globally connected activities send third world children back to school? As Basu (1999) has pointed out, a ban targeted at child labor in manufacturing export sectors would probably send children back to agriculture, where they work the most and attend school the least. It is difficult to see how future third world generations would catch up with the high-income world any faster if there were bans on the export of manufactures that use child labor. Where third world paths to school and faster income growth seem blocked, they are not blocked by employment opportunities in the modern export sector. Instead, they are blocked by the lack of national political resolve to raise tax support for schools.

What Role for Globalization in OECD Wage Inequality since the 1970s?

The best-documented and most heatedly debated experience linking globalization with inequality is the recent OECD wage widening, especially within the United States and the United Kingdom. An enormous amount of recent research now gives us a pretty clear idea of the share of rising inequality that should be attributed to an increase in international integration.

How Wage Gaps Moved. The trend toward wider wage gaps in America and Great Britain was unmistakable in the 1980s and early 1990s, as illustrated in figure 5.6. It showed up in ratios of the 90th percentile full-time wage to the 50th or 10th percentile full-time wage, either for men or for women. In the United States, a rise also took place in the full-time pay ratios of college graduates to high school graduates, and in the pay ratio of nonproduction employees to production employees. The widening has been severe enough

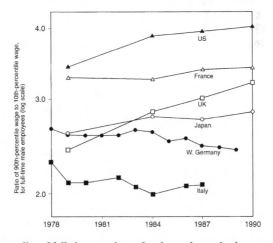

Fig. 5.6   **Inequality of full-time earnings of male employees in six countries, 1978–90**

that lower-skilled groups had no gain, and probably a slight loss, in real pay over the whole quarter-century 1973–98, despite a healthy growth of real earnings for the labor force as a whole.[34]

Other OECD countries probably also experienced pay widening across the 1980s, although different measures tell different stories. Sticking with full-time labor earnings, one cannot find much widening at all for France or Japan, and none for Germany or Italy, as in figure 5.6. Yet income measures that take work hours and unemployment into account reveal some widening even in those cases. A recent OECD study surveyed the inequality of disposable household income from the mid-1970s to the mid-1990s (Burniaux et al. 1998, tables 2.1, 2.2, and 3.1–4.9). Between the mid-1970s and the mid-1980s, the Americans and British were alone in having a clear rise in inequality. From the mid-1980s to the mid-1990s, however, twenty out of twenty-one OECD countries had a noticeable rise in inequality. Furthermore, the main source of rising income inequality after the mid-1980s was the widening of labor earnings. The fact that labor earnings became more unequal in most OECD countries, when *full-time* labor earnings did not, suggests that many countries took their inequality in the form of more unemployment and hours reduction, a well-documented tendency for Western Europe in those years.

What Widened American Wage Gaps? The recent American wage widening has generated an energetic search for its sources, and they are of two sorts. First, there are aspects of globalization: the rise in unskilled worker immigration rates, due to rising foreign immigrant supply or a liberalization of U.S. immigration policy (or both). Increased competition from imports that use unskilled labor more intensively than the rest of the economy must be added to the immigration impact. This increased competition is due to foreign supply improvements, including that carried by U.S. outsourcing; international transportation improvements; and trade-liberalizing policies. Second, there are those sources apparently unrelated to globalization, including a slowdown in the growth of labor-force skills; a weakening of labor unions, which have long lobbied for flatter pay scales; and biased technological change that cuts the demand for unskilled workers relative to skilled workers.

Most contributions to the debate have had a narrower focus than the previous summary would suggest. They have retreated to judging a "trade versus technology" contest, ignoring the possible roles of unions, immigration, and skills or schooling supply.[35] Some agree with Wood (1994, 1998) that

---

34. The assertion about absolute living standards awaits the results of debate about exaggerated measurement of cost-of-living increases over the same period in the United States (Boskin et al. 1998).

35. For a survey of the whole literature up through 1996, see Cline (1997, especially table 2.3 and the surrounding text). For a more up-to-date survey, with deeper coverage of certain econometric issues, see the volume edited by Feenstra (2000), particularly the editor's introduction and the contributions by Slaughter (2000) and Harrigan (2000) in that volume.

trade is to blame for much of the observed wage widening. Others reject this conclusion, arguing that most or all of the widening is due to a shift in technology that has been strongly biased in favor of higher-skill occupational groups (Lawrence and Slaughter 1993; Berman, Bound, and Griliches 1994). Most estimates tend to resemble the guess by Feenstra and Hanson (1999) that perhaps 15–33 percent of the rising inequality is due to trade competition, including outsourcing.

Nonspecialists observing this debate need to pay close attention to how the participants deal with a fundamental endogeneity issue. Are globalization and technology change independent, or does one drive the other? Those inclined to absolve globalization point out that the rise of imports, and the decline of import-competing jobs, is often a by-product of healthy growth, both in the OECD and the third world exporters. To these participants, technological change drives globalization. Two examples taken from the debate illustrate the opposing view. Feenstra and Hanson (1999) argue that skill-saving technological bias within the United States is a by-product of the global communications revolution that allows better monitoring of foreign production and just-in-time inventory delivery from abroad. Thus, Lawrence (2000) argues that rising import competition deserves credit for much of America's technological progress. To these participants, globalization drives technological change.

The boldest attempt at an overall quantitative accounting of these potential sources is the appraisal by Cline (1997). Cline's interpretation of his estimates differs from ours. Cline blames globalization less than do most writers on the subject, and he emerges with a huge 58 percent unexplained residual. In a summary table (1997, table 5.1), Cline suggests that about half of this residual was due to skill-biased technological change, and the resulting 29 percent technology effect is bigger than any globalization effect. However, there is a second way to read Cline's table. His nonglobalization sources appear to almost balance out ($1.58 \times .65 = 1.03$, or only 3 percentage points), whereas his globalization forces could explain almost all the wage-gap widening (16 out of 18 percentage points). The proper question, typically left unasked, is how the period 1973–93 differed from the one that preceded it, 1953–73. If the other sources added up to pretty much the same impact in the first two-decade period, then it would be the *change* in globalization forces between the two periods that mattered.

Broader Perspectives. Although the recent exploration of the determinants of American wage inequality has established fairly firm results, the debate is still too narrow to judge the full impact of globalization on inequality within the industrial OECD. Several extensions are needed before the evidence can be said to have dealt with the big questions that sparked the debate. One extension would be in the direction of more evidence, whereas another would be in the direction of more comprehensive measures.

Regarding the use of more evidence, note that the literature has thrown away information by confining itself to the era of widening wage gaps since about 1980. After all, when the world economy became increasingly integrated in the century or two before 1980, technology also had its factor biases, and the mismatch between technological bias and skills growth kept shifting (Williamson and Lindert 1980; Goldin and Katz 1999, 2000). Why the inequality booms and busts in America over the past century or two? Any attempt to distill the effects of globalization on inequality needs to answer that question. Furthermore, the literature is dominated excessively by American experience, so we need more economic histories to right the balance. After all, while recent inequality rose just as steeply in Great Britain, the steepness of the rise varied a great deal across the OECD.[36] Why?

Confining our view to employee earnings has also denied us extra perspective on both the scope and the source of the rise in inequality. What happened to self-employment income, property income, profits, and executive compensation?[37]

Regarding the use of measurement, note that any force that creates more within-country inequality is automatically blunted today—at least in the OECD, a point that is rarely noted in the inequality debate. Any rise in household net disposable post-fisc income inequality will always be less than the rise in gross nominal pre-fisc income inequality. Tax-and-transfer systems guarantee this result in the OECD. Any damage to the earnings of low-skilled workers is partially offset by their lower tax payments and higher transfer receipts, like unemployment compensation or family assistance. This broadening of income concept therefore serves to shrink any apparent impact of globalization on the inequality of living standards.[38]

Does globalization destroy these automatic stabilizers by undermining

36. Several contributions in the Freeman-Katz volume (1995) do compare explanations of inequality in the United States versus other countries. However, the focus is on the technology-skill demand-inequality connection, with almost no attention to possible globalization-skill demand-inequality connections.

37. Granted, Burniaux and coauthors (1998) did report changes in overall income inequality for several OECD countries, but they did not attempt to assess competing explanations. One tantalizing clue that some stories at the top of the income range have been overlooked comes from recent international comparisons of the compensation of chief executive officers (CEOs; Crystal 1993; Abowd and Bognanno 1995). The level of CEO compensation is far higher in the United States than in other countries, not only in real purchasing power but also in ratio of their pay to that of ordinary production workers. Did the fact that this CEO pay advantage rose from the late 1980s to the early 1990s have anything to do with outsourcing, direct foreign investment, and other dimensions of globalization? The link is certainly not obvious. International differences in CEO compensation seem to be unrelated to performance, since U.S. firms under attack from foreign competition maintained much higher CEO compensation than did their successful foreign competitors. This puzzle should be linked to the competing theories of the determinants of intranational inequality in the OECD.

38. Although this statement certainly applies today, it did not apply to the first globalization boom before World War I, when such safety nets were not yet in place. Similarly, it will not apply to any emerging nations where modern safety nets are not yet in place.

taxes and social transfer programs? In a world where businesses and skilled personnel can flee taxes they dislike, there is the well-known danger of a "race to the bottom," in which governments compete for internationally mobile factors by cutting tax rates and therefore cutting social spending. As Rodrik (1997) has stressed, however, the relationship between a country's vulnerability to international markets and the size of its tax-based social programs is *positive*, not negative, as a race to the bottom would imply. Thus, countries with greater vulnerability to global market changes have higher taxes, more social spending, and broader safety nets. Although there may be other reasons for this positive raw correlation between openness and social programs, there is no apparent tendency for globalization to undermine the safety nets.

Postwar International Investment: How Inegalitarian Could It Be?

The fear that globalization is widening world gaps between rich and poor stems in part from the belief that investors in the rich countries are reaping all the gains from international investment in the poor countries. These fears cannot be allayed solely by reference to competitive-market models, since these fears come from those who do not believe such models. As an alternative demonstration, we can show that the size of such investment income—interest, dividends, repatriated profits, royalties, and fees—is much too small to account for the global inequalities we observe.

Two pessimistic assumptions will set an upper bound on the extent to which returns on international investment could have widened world inequality. First, suppose nobody else in the world gains from these investments, so that these rich investors and patent holders are able to collect *all* of the returns on them, thus increasing their shares of world income and world inequality. Alternatively, suppose international investment is a zero-sum game, so that the amounts gained by the rich international investors are matched by an equal *loss* to somebody in the host countries.

Table 5.4 shows that earnings on international investments and technology could not be big enough to explain the global inequalities we see, regardless of which extreme assumption one chooses. There are three parts: The top one (part A) shows what is to be explained, the rise in the share of the world's income held by the rich, from 1820 and from 1970; the middle (part B) assesses the role of returns on international investment under those two assumptions. The extreme assumption that only the richest are affected (discussed in part C) leads to the conclusion that investments by five leading investor countries (Germany, Japan, the Netherlands, the United Kingdom, and the United States) in all foreign countries (part B, columns [1] and [2]) have not been big enough to explain even a third of the rise in world inequality since 1970. The extreme assumption that the host countries actually lose as much as the international investors gain does not magnify the

Table 5.4   Worst-case Globalization: Overestimates of the Impact of International
                    Investments on Global Income Inequality

A. Net changes up to 1992, as percent of world income

	Since 1820	Since 1970
Top 5% of world incomes	+3.8	+1.6
Top 10% of world incomes	+10.3	+2.5
Top 20% of world incomes	+15.6	+2.4

B. Private investment incomes, as percent of world income

	On Investments in All Foreign Countries		On Investment in Third World Countries	
	Since 1820	Since 1970	Since 1820	Since 1970
U.S. investments only	0.42	0.18	0.13	0.03
Rough estimate for five leading investor countries	1.72	0.50		

C. Maximum impacts on global inequality?

Contrast the historical inequality-related income shifts to be explained (part A, above) with these incomes involved in international investments up to 1992 (part B). Assuming that international investment benefits only the investors and that nobody loses income would suggest using columns (1) and (2) in part B as gains within the top 5 percent of the world income ranks. However, assuming this implies little pessimism about investment globalization, since nobody is hurt.

Using the zero-sum assumption that the investments hurt the host countries as much as they help investors would cancel most of the effect on inequality, since the host countries are usually as rich as the investing countries. Applying this pessimistic zero-sum assumption only to columns (3) and (4), the third world investment, gives tiny effects like those shown for the U.S. investments.

Sources: The changes in top-group shares of world income are from Bourguignon and Morrisson (2002, table 1). The changes in U.S. private investment income in foreign countries, including royalties and fees, are from U.S. Bureau of Economic Analysis, *Survey of Current Business,* various issues. The rough estimate for five leading countries magnifies the U.S. factor incomes by the relative total (not just private investment) factor-income earnings given by IMF, *International Financial Statistics Yearbook,* for the five leading countries chosen here: Germany, Japan, the Netherlands, the United Kingdom, and the United States.

modest effect on inequality, but rather reduces it. The reason is that the host countries are typically as rich as the investors' home countries. In fact, the world's largest net borrower since 1980 has been the United States. The zero-sum assumption therefore actually yields *less* impact on global inequality than the nobody-is-hurt-abroad assumption, since the supposed losses accrue to people near the top of the world income distribution. The net effect on global inequality in this case must be practically zero. To sustain pessimism, critics might want our zero-sum assumption to apply only to investments in the third world, where they are exploitative enough to be zero-sum for the world. Yet, as table 5.4 (part B) shows for American investments in the third world, these magnitudes are tiny in relation to global income and tiny in relation to the net changes to be explained in the top panel. Even if the impact of other leading investing countries is added, the basic point remains: International investment cannot account for much of the observed global inequalities in our modern world, even under extreme assumptions.

5.6   Adding Up the Effects of Globalization

5.6.1   Sources of World Inequality 1500–2000: The Big Picture

Some patterns have emerged through the complexity of history that suggest a tentative answer to the question posed by this essay's title: Does globalization make the world more unequal? The patterns cluster around two observations. One is that the gainers from globalization were never all rich and the losers were never all poor, or vice versa. The other is that participants in globalization pulled ahead of nonparticipants. This was true both for excluded or nonparticipating groups within countries as well as for excluded or nonparticipating countries.

How these patterns emerge from five centuries of diverging world incomes and a shorter period of globalization is summarized in table 5.5. The overall trends to be explained are those introduced in figure 5.1. World income inequality has risen since 1820, and probably since the sixteenth century. Most of that increased world inequality took the form of a rise in income gaps between nations, not of a rise in within-country inequality. However, the gaps between nations were not widened by participation in globalization. As for the visible inequalities within countries, the effects differed by region and by historical era. Before World War I, globalization raised inequality within the United States and other New World countries, but it had the opposite effect in those European countries that were committed to trade and sent out emigrants. After World War II, globalization once again widened inequality within the United States and perhaps other OECD countries. Globalization may also have raised inequality in the newly trading and industrializing countries, such as the Asian tigers, China, Mexico, and Brazil. Yet the rising inequality in these countries was not evident among persons and households in the newly trading regions and sectors. Rather, it took the form of widening gaps between them and the less prosperous, nonparticipating regions. The poorest regions and the poorest countries were probably not hurt by globalization; they just failed to be part of it. Where the nonparticipants were actively excluded, the policies yielding that inegalitarian result can hardly be called liberal, but globalization cannot be made to take the blame.

Table 5.5   Summary of Globalization's Effects on World Inequality

		Inequality between Nations		Inequality within Nations	
Epoch	Global Inequality Trend	Trend	Effects of Globalization	Trend	Effects of Globalization
1500–1820	Rising inequality	Rising inequality	No clear net effect	Rising inequality (Western Europe)	No clear net effect
1820–1914	Rising inequality	Rising inequality	Participants gain on nonparticipating countries. Among participants, migration reduced inequality more than capital flows raised it. Freer trade may have reduced inequality, with exceptions.	No clear trend	Globalization raised inequality in the New World, reduced it in participating Old World nations.
1914–1950	No clear inequality trend	Rising inequality	Retreat from globalization widened the gaps between nations.	Falling inequality (in OECD)	No clear net effect
1950–2000, especially since 1970	Slightly rising inequality	Slightly rising inequality	Globalized trade and migration narrowed the gaps among participants. Nonparticipants fell further behind.	Slightly rising inequality (in OECD)	Globalization raised inequality within OECD countries. In other countries, nonparticipating regions fell behind.
Overall 1820–2000	Rising inequality	Rising inequality	Globalized trade and migration narrowed the gaps among participants. Nonparticipants fell further behind.	No clear trend	No clear net effect

5.6.2   How Unequal Would a Fully Integrated World Economy Be?

What if we had a huge world economy, even bigger than the world economy back at the mid-twentieth century,[39] with a unified currency and only negligible barriers to trade, migration, and capital movements? Would such an economy be more unequal than the world of today?

We have good examples today of huge integrated economies, at least as big as the world economy in 1950. One obvious example is the United States. Japan is another, and the European Union is moving toward becoming the third giant integrated economy. How unequal are incomes within these already globalized economies? Less unequal than in today's only partly globalized world economy, where the Gini coefficient of inequality in income per capita at international (purchasing power parity) prices in 1992 was .663.[40] The Gini for the more integrated U.S. economy, by contrast, was only .408 in 1997, and that for Japan was only .249. There is nothing inherently less egalitarian about a large integrated economy compared with our barrier-filled world.

One might still fear that a truly globalized world would have vast regions with inferior education and chaotic legal institutions, so that the future globalized world would be more unequal than the United States or the European Union today. If so, then the source of that inequality would be poor government and nondemocracy in those lagging countries, not globalization.

References

Abel, Wilhelm. 1973. *Crises agraires en Europe, XIIIe–Xxe siècle*. A translation of the 1966 edition of *Agrarkrisen und Agrarkonjunktur*. Paris: Flammarion.

Abowd, John M., and Michael L. Bognanno. 1995. International differences in executive and managerial compensation. In *Differences and changes in wage structures*, ed. Richard B. Freeman and Lawrence F. Katz, 25–66. Chicago: University of Chicago Press.

Aitken, Brian, Ann Harrison, and Robert E. Lipsey. 1996. Wages and foreign ownership: A comparative study of Mexico, Venezuela, and the United States. *Journal of International Economics* 40 (May): 345–71.

Allen, Robert C. 2000. Real wages in Europe and India 1595. Paper presented at the Conference on Asian and European Pre-Industrial Living Standards, 1–5 August, Arild, Sweden.

Allen, Robert C. 2001. The great divergence: Wages and prices from the Middle Ages to the First World War. *Explorations in Economic History*. 38 (October): 411–47.

39. And thus one that would satisfy any plausible size condition necessary to achieve scale economies.

40. Bourguignon and Morrisson (2002, tables 1 and 3). Milanovic (1999) gives a similar estimate for 1993 with an alternative set of household survey data.

Atinc, Tamar Manuelyan. 1997. *Sharing rising incomes: Disparities in China.* Washington: World Bank.

Bairoch, Paul. 1972. Free trade and European economic development in the nineteenth century. *European Economic Review* 3 (November): 211–45.

———. 1989. European trade policy, 1815–1914. In *The Cambridge economic history of Europe.* Vol. 8, ed. P. Mathias and S. Pollard, 1–190. Cambridge: Cambridge University Press.

Balassa, Bela. 1971. *The structure of protection in developing countries.* Baltimore: Johns Hopkins University Press.

Baldwin, Richard, and Philippe Martin. 1999. Two waves of globalization: Superficial similarities, fundamental differences. NBER Working Paper no. 6904. Cambridge, Mass.: National Bureau of Economic Research, January.

Barro, Robert J., and Xavier Sala-i-Martin. 1995. *Economic growth.* New York: McGraw Hill.

Basu, Kaushik. 1999. Child labor: Cause, consequence, and cure, with remarks on international labor standards. *Journal of Economic Literature* 37 (September): 1083–119.

Berman, Eli, John Bound, and Zvi Griliches. 1994. Changes in the demand for skilled labor within U.S. manufacturing: Evidence from the Annual Survey of Manufactures. *Quarterly Journal of Economics* 109 (May): 367–98.

Bernstein, Aaron, Michael Shari, and Elisabeth Malkin. 2000. A world of sweatshops. *Business Week*, 6 November, pp. 84–86.

Berry, Albert, François Bourguignon, and Christian Morrisson. 1983. Changes in the world distribution of income between 1950 and 1977. *Economic Journal* 93 (June): 331–50.

———. 1991. Global economic inequality and its trends since 1950. In *Economic inequality and poverty: International perspectives*, ed. Lars Osberg, 60–91. Armonk, N.Y.: Sharpe.

Bhagwati, Jagdish, and Anne O. Krueger, eds. 1973–1976. *Foreign trade regimes and economic development.* Multiple vols. New York: Columbia University Press.

Boltho, Andrea, and Gianni Toniolo. 1999. The assessment: The twentieth century—achievements, failures, lessons. *Oxford Review of Economic Policy* 15 (4): 1–17.

Bordo, Michael, Barry Eichengreen, and Douglas A. Irwin. 1999. Is globalization today really different than globalization a hundred years ago? NBER Working Paper no. 7195. Cambridge, Mass.: National Bureau of Economic Research, June.

Boskin, Michael, Ellen R. Dulberger, Robert J. Gorden, Zvi Griliches, and Dale W. Jorgenson. 1998. Consumer prices, the consumer price index, and the cost of living. *Journal of Economic Perspectives* 12 (Winter): 3–26.

Bourguignon, François, and Christian Morrisson. 1990. Income distribution, development, and foreign trade. *European Economic Review* 34 (September): 1113–32.

———. 2002. The size distribution of income among world citizens: 1820–1990. *American Economic Review* 92 (September): 727–44.

Braudel, Fernand P., and Frank C. Spooner. 1966. Prices in Europe from 1450 to 1750. In *Cambridge economic history of Europe.* Vol. 4: *Sixteenth and seventeenth centuries*, ed. Edwin E. Rich and Charles H. Wilson, 374–486. Cambridge: Cambridge University Press.

Brown, Drusilla K. 2001. Labor standards: Where do they belong on the international trade agenda? *Journal of Economic Perspectives* 15 (3): 89–112.

Burniaux, Jean-Marc, Thai-Thanh Dang, Douglas Fore, Michael Forster, Marco Mira d'Ercole, and Howard Oxley. 1998. Income distribution and poverty in selected OECD countries. OECD Economics Department Working Paper no. 189. Paris: Organization for Economic Cooperation and Development, March.

Chowdhury, Khorshed, Charles Harvie, and Amnon Levy. 2000. Regional income inequality in China. In *Contemporary developments and issues in China's economic transition*, ed. Charles Harvie, 238–61. New York: St. Martin's.

Clemens, Michael, and Jeffrey G. Williamson. 2000. Where did British foreign capital go? Fundamentals, failures, and the Lucas paradox 1870–1913. NBER Working Paper no. 8028. Cambridge, Mass.: National Bureau of Economic Research, December.

———. 2001. A tariff-growth paradox? Protection's impact the world around 1875–1997. NBER Working Paper no. 8459. Cambridge, Mass.: National Bureau of Economic Research, September.

Cline, William R. 1997. *Trade and income distribution*. Washington, D.C.: Institute for International Economics.

Crystal, Graef. 1993. *In search of excess: The overcompensation of the American executive*. 2nd ed. New York: Norton.

Diakosavvas, Dimitris, and Pasquale L. Scandizzo. 1991. Trends in the terms of trade of primary commodities, 1900–1982: The controversy and its origin. *Economic Development and Cultural Change* 39 (January): 231–64.

Diaz-Alejandro, Carlos. 1970. *Essays on the economic history of the Argentine Republic*. New Haven, Conn.: Yale University Press.

Dollar, David. 1992. Outward-oriented developing economies really do grow more rapidly: Evidence from 95 LDCs, 1976–1985. *Economic Development and Cultural Change* 40 (April): 523–44.

Dollar, David, and Aart Kraay. 2000a. Growth *is* good for the poor. World Bank. Manuscript, March.

———. 2000b. Trade, growth, and poverty. World Bank. Manuscript, October.

Edwards, Sebastian. 1992. Trade orientation, distortions, and growth in developing countries. *Journal of Development Economics* 39 (July): 31–57.

———. 1993. Openness, trade liberalization, and growth in developing countries. *Journal of Economic Literature* 31 (September): 1358–94.

Eltis, David, and Stanley L. Engerman. 2000. The importance of slavery and the slave trade to industrializing Britain. *Journal of Economic History* 60 (March): 123–44.

Feenstra, Robert C., ed. 2000. *The impact of international trade on wages*. Chicago: University of Chicago Press.

Feenstra, Robert C., and Gordon H. Hanson. 1997. Foreign direct investment and relative wages: Evidence from Mexico's maquiladoras. *Journal of International Economics* 48 (2): 301–20.

———. 1999. The impact of outsourcing and high-technology capital on wages: Estimates for the United States, 1979–1990. *Quarterly Journal of Economics* 114 (August): 907–40.

Firebaugh, G. 1999. Empirics of world income inequality. *American Journal of Sociology* 104 (6): 1597–630.

Flemming, John S., and John Micklewright. 2000. Income distribution, economic systems, and transition. In *Handbook of income distribution*. Vol. 1, ed. Anthony Atkinson and François Bourguignon, 843–917. Amsterdam: Elsevier Science.

Freeman, Richard B., and Lawrence F. Katz, eds. 1995. *Differences and changes in wage structures*. Chicago: University of Chicago Press.

Goldin, Claudia. 1994. The political economy of immigration restriction in the United States, 1890 to 1921. In *The regulated economy: A historical approach to political economy*, ed. Claudia Goldin and Gary D. Libecap, 223–57. Chicago: University of Chicago Press.

Goldin, Claudia, and Lawrence F. Katz. 1999. The returns to skill in the United States across the twentieth century. NBER Working Paper no. 7126. Cambridge, Mass.: National Bureau of Economic Research, May.

———. 2001. Decreasing (and then increasing) inequality in America: A tale of two half centuries. In *The causes and consequences of increasing inequality*, ed. Finis Welch, 37–82. Chicago: University of Chicago Press.

Greider, William. 1997. *One world, ready or not: The manic logic of global capitalism.* New York: Simon and Schuster.

Griffin, Keith, and Renwei Zhao, eds. 1993. *The distribution of income in China.* New York: St. Martin's.

Hadass, Yael, and Jeffrey G. Williamson. 2001. Terms of trade shocks and economic performance 1870–1940: Prebisch and Singer revisited. NBER Working Paper no. 8188. Cambridge, Mass.: National Bureau of Economic Research, March.

Hanson, Gordon, and Ann Harrison. 1999. Trade liberalization and wage inequality in Mexico. *Industrial and Labor Relations Review* 52 (January): 271–88.

Harrigan, James. 2000. International trade and American wages in general equilibrium, 1967–1995. In *The impact of international trade on wages*, ed. Robert C. Feenstra, 171–95. Chicago: University of Chicago Press.

Hatton, Timothy J., and Jeffrey G. Williamson. 1998. *The age of mass migration.* Oxford: Oxford University Press.

Hoffman, Philip T., David Jacks, Patricia A. Levin, and Peter H. Lindert. 2002. Real inequality in Western Europe since 1500. *Journal of Economic History* 62 (June): 322–55.

Huber, J. Richard 1971. Effects on prices of Japan's entry into world commerce after 1858. *Journal of Political Economy* 79 (May–June): 614–28.

Irwin, Douglas A. 1988. Welfare effects of British free trade: Debate and evidence from the 1840s. *Journal of Political Economy* 96 (December): 1142–64.

———. 1991. Was Britain immiserized during the Industrial Revolution? *Explorations in Economic History* 28 (January): 121–24.

Jacks, David. 2000. Market integration in the North and Baltic seas, 1500–1800. Working Papers in Economic History no. 55/00. London School of Economics, April.

Krueger, Anne O. 1983. The effects of trade strategies on growth. *Finance and Development* 20 (June): 6–8.

———. 1984. Trade policies in developing countries. In *Handbook of international economics.* Vol. 1, ed. Ronald Jones and Peter Kenan, 519–69. Amsterdam: North-Holland.

Lawrence, Robert Z. 2000. Does a kick in the pants get you going, or does it just hurt? The impact of international competition on technological change in U.S. manufacturing. In *The impact of international trade on wages, ed.* Robert C. Feenstra, 197–225. Chicago: University of Chicago Press.

Lawrence, Robert Z., and Matthew J. Slaughter. 1993. International trade and American wages in the 1980s: Giant sucking sound or small hiccup? *Brookings Papers in Economic Analysis, Microeconomics,* 2:161–226.

Lindert, Peter H. 2000. Three centuries of inequality in Britain and America. In *Handbook of income distribution.* Vol. 1, ed. Anthony B. Atkinson and François Bourguignon, 167–216. Amsterdam: Elsevier Science.

———. 2001. Democracy, decentralization, and mass schooling before 1914. Agricultural History Center Working Paper no. 104. University of California–Davis, February.

Lindert, Peter H., and Jeffrey G. Williamson. 1985. Growth, equality, and history. *Explorations in Economic History* 22 (October): 341–77.

Lucas, Robert. 1990. Why doesn't capital flow from rich to poor countries? *American Economic Review* 80 (May): 92–96.

Maddison, Angus. 1995. *Monitoring the world economy, 1820–1992.* Paris: Organization for Economic Cooperation and Development.

Melchior, Arne, Kjetil Telle, and Henrik Wiig. 2000. Globalization and inequality: World income distribution and living standards, 1960–1998. Studies on Foreign Policy Issues, Report 6B. Oslo: Royal Norwegian Ministry of Foreign Affairs, October.

Milanovic, Branko. 1999. True world income distribution, 1988 and 1993: First calculation based on household surveys alone. World Bank. Manuscript, October.

Nardinelli, Clark. 1990. *Child labor and the Industrial Revolution.* Bloomington: Indiana University Press.

Neal, Larry, and Paul Uselding. 1972. Immigration: A neglected source of American economic growth: 1790–1912. *Oxford Economic Papers* 24 (March): 68–88.

Obstfeld, Maurice, and Alan M. Taylor. 1998. The Great Depression as a watershed: International capital mobility over the long run. In *The defining moment: The Great Depression and the American economy in the twentieth century,* ed. Michael D. Bordo, Claudia Goldin, and Eugene N. White, 353–402. Chicago: University of Chicago Press.

O'Rourke, Kevin H. 1997. The European grain invasion, 1870–1913. *Journal of Economic History* 57 (December): 775–801.

———. 2000. Tariffs and growth in the late nineteenth century. *Economic Journal* 110 (April): 456–83.

O'Rourke, Kevin H., Alan M. Taylor, and Jeffrey G. Williamson. 1996. Factor price convergence in the late nineteenth century. *International Economic Review* 37 (August): 499–530.

O'Rourke, Kevin H., and Jeffrey G. Williamson. 1999. *Globalization and history.* Cambridge: MIT Press.

———. 2000. When did globalization begin? NBER Working Paper no. 7632. Cambridge, Mass.: National Bureau of Economic Research, April.

———. 2002. After Columbus: Explaining Europe's overseas trade boom, 1500–1800. *Journal of Economic History* 62 (June): 417–56.

Pamuk, Sevket. 2000. *Five hundred years of prices and wages in Istanbul and other cities.* Ankara, Republic of Turkey: State Institute of Statistics.

Papageorgiou, Demetris, Michael Michaely, and Armeane M. Choksi, eds. 1991. *Liberalizing foreign trade.* Oxford, U.K.: Basil Blackwell.

Pavcnik, Nina. 2000. What explains skill upgrading in less developed countries? NBER Working Paper no. 7846. Cambridge, Mass.: National Bureau of Economic Research, August.

Pomeranz, Kenneth. 2000. *The great divergence: China, Europe, and the making of the modern world economy.* Princeton: Princeton University Press.

Prados de la Escosura, Leandro. 2000. International comparisons of real product, 1820–1990: An alternative data set. *Explorations in Economic History* 37 (January): 1–41.

Pritchett, Lant. 1997. Divergence, big time. *Journal of Economic Perspectives* 11 (Summer): 3–18.

Radetzki, M., and B. Jonsson. 2000. The twentieth century—The century of increasing income gaps. But how reliable are the numbers? *Ekonomisk Debatt* 1:43–58.

Robbins, Donald J. 1997. Trade and wages in Colombia. *Estudios de Economia* 24 (June): 47–83.

Robbins, Donald J., and Tim H. Gindling. 1999. Trade liberalization and the relative wages for more-skilled workers in Costa Rica. *Review of Development Economics* 3 (June): 140–54.

Rodrik, Dani. 1997. *Has globalization gone too far?* Washington, D.C.: Institute for International Economics.

Sachs, Jeffrey D., and Andrew Warner. 1995. Economic reform and the process of global integration. *Brookings Papers on Economic Activity*, Issue no. 1:1–118. Washington, D.C.: Brookings Institution.

Schultz, T. Paul 1998. Inequality in the distribution of personal income in the world: How is it changing and why? *Journal of Population Economics* 11:307–44.

Slaughter, Matthew. 2000. What are the results of product-price studies and what can we learn from their differences? In *The impact of international trade on wages*, ed. Robert C. Feenstra, 129–69. Chicago: University of Chicago Press.

Taylor, Alan M. 1999. International capital mobility in history: The saving-investment relationship. NBER Working Paper no. 5743. Cambridge, Mass.: National Bureau of Economic Research, September.

Taylor, Alan M., and Jeffrey G. Williamson. 1997. Convergence in the age of mass migration. *European Review of Economic History* 1 (April): 27–63.

Timmer, Ashley, and Jeffrey G. Williamson. 1998. Immigration policy prior to the 1930s: Labor markets, policy interactions, and globalization backlash. *Population and Development Review* 24 (December): 739–71.

Tuttle, Carolyn. 1999. *Hard at work in factories and mines: The economics of child labor during the British Industrial Revolution.* Boulder, Col.: Westview Press.

United Nations Conference on Trade and Development. 1988. *Handbook of international trade and development statistics 1987.* New York: United Nations.

———. 1997. *Handbook of international trade and development statistics 1995.* New York: United Nations.

U.S. Department of Commerce. 1975. *Historical statistics of the United States.* Part 1. Washington, D.C.: U.S. Bureau of the Census.

U.S. Department of Labor, Bureau of International Affairs. 1995–2000. *By the sweat and toil of children.* Six vols. Available at [http://dol/ilab/media/reports/iclp/sweat/], October 2000.

van Zanden, Jan Luiten. 1995. Tracing the beginning of the Kuznets curve: Western Europe during the early modern period. *Economic History Review* 48 (November): 643–64.

———. 1999. Wages and the standard of living in Europe, 1500–1800. *European Review of Economic History* 3 (August): 175–98.

Ward, Marianne H. 2000. Re-estimating growth and convergence for developed economies: 1870–1990. Ph.D. diss. University of Miami–Coral Gables.

Williamson, Jeffrey G. 1990. The impact of the Corn Laws just prior to repeal. *Explorations in Economic History* 27 (April): 123–56.

———. 1995. The evolution of global labor markets since 1830: Background evidence and hypotheses. *Explorations in Economic History* 32 (April): 141–96.

———. 1996. Globalization, convergence, and history. *Journal of Economic History* 56 (June): 277–306.

———. 1997. Globalization and inequality: Past and present. *World Bank Research Observer* 12 (August): 117–35.

———. 2002. Land, labor, and globalization in the third world, 1870–1940. *Journal of Economic History* 62 (March): 55–85.

Williamson, Jeffrey G., and Peter H. Lindert. 1980. *American inequality: A macroeconomic history.* New York: Academic Press.

Wolff, Edward N. 1991. Capital formation and productivity convergence over the long term. *American Economic Review* 81 (June): 565–79.

Wood, Adrian. 1994. *North-south trade, employment, and inequality.* Oxford, U.K.: Clarendon Press.

————. 1997. Openness and wage inequality in developing countries: The Latin American challenge to East Asian conventional wisdom. *World Bank Economic Review* 11 (January): 33–57.

————. 1998. Globalisation and the rise in labour market inequalities. *Economic Journal* 108 (September): 1463–82.

World Bank. 1983–2001. *World development report.* Washington: Oxford University Press.

Wright, Gavin. 1990. The origins of American industrial success, 1879–1940. *American Economic Review* 80 (September): 651–68.

Yasuba, Yasukichi. 1996. Did Japan ever suffer from a shortage of natural resources before World War II? *Journal of Economic History* 56 (September): 543–60.

Comment   Lant Pritchett

I would be a fool to attempt to summarize what is a masterful review and summary of the literature on the relationship between globalization and inequality, both within and across countries. So, I will limit myself to five comments that both place the existing paper in context and poke around some of the puzzles that current events and attitudes raise.

First, I think too much too soon is being made of the relationship between trade liberalization and inequality. Some have suggested that the rise in inequality (and increase in skill differentials in labor markets) in some countries undergoing trade liberalization both contradicts the standard model and, more fundamentally, challenges the desirability of liberalization.

Suppose the wage profile of educational attainment (which is the usual proxy for "skill differentials") represents two effects. One is that educated people have more skills. The other is that educated people are more likely to adapt quickly and are more likely to be Schumpeterian entrepreneurs who reallocate factors across uses in the face of disequilibrium.

Suppose there is a liberalization between a human-capital-rich and a human-capital-poor country that represents a substantial shift for the human-capital-poor country. Then there will be two effects on inequality. In both countries the returns to entrepreneurship will rise, which, if this is positively associated with education, will steepen the wage-education attainment profile. This disequilibrium effect should emerge and then gradually go away as the economy settles down to its new steady state. According to the standard, simple theory the factor abundance effect should work in different directions—raising skill premiums in the skill-rich country and lowering the skill premiums in the skill-poor country.

Lant Pritchett is a lecturer in public policy at the John F. Kennedy School of Government.

In the skill-rich country these effects are in the same direction so there is an unambiguous increase in inequality. In the skill-poor country these effects work in opposite directions so that, depending on their relative magnitudes, inequality could rise, stay the same, or fall in the short to medium run. Until we have sufficiently ruled out these "adjustment to disequilibria" effects on relative wages I would hesitate to say not only that factor abundance theories have been rejected by the data, but that the factor abundance stories have even been challenged by the data.

Second, the question of globalization and inequality across countries is often driven by the fact that some of the "nonglobalizers" had extraordinarily poor performance. This actually raises something of a puzzle as the "Harberger triangle" effects are typically too small by an order of magnitude to explain the 2 percentage point per annum growth deficit maintained over thirty or more years implied by the growth rates of the nonglobalizers.

I think the reconciliation will come in the structure of the instruments that the General Agreement on Tariffs and Trade (GATT) allowed developing countries to use. I have examined in detail five different developing countries' trade restrictions, and in four of those countries the restrictions were based on a system of three categories of licenses for imports plus a system for licensing foreign exchange (that would come and go). Imports were classified into three groups: (a) freely importable, (b) banned, or (c) imported with a license. This requirement of licensing acted as neither a tariff nor a quota. That is, unlike some types of import rationing in the United States, this type of licensing scheme did not specify a given quantity of men's cotton pants or tons of sugar. Rather, they were discretionary licenses based on a criterion that granted substantial discretion (e.g., whether they were "in the national economic interest").

This meant that the licenses could be made specific not only to the import type but also to the use to which the import was to be put and even to the particular importer (so that public-sector firms could be preferred over private-sector ones, established firms over start-ups—which could not demonstrate "need"—or bribe payers over non–bribe payers). This aspect of the discretionary specificity meant that the usual market clearing conditions for estimating production or welfare losses from restricting imports did not apply. That is, in order to estimate a Harberger triangle from reducing import quantities by 10 percent one needs to assume that the lowest valued users (in the consumer surplus sense) were those rationed out. However with discretionary and specific import licenses this need not be the case as high-value private users could be rationed out in favor of low-value, public-sector firms. Without either perfect bribery or perfect resale market (which did not exist in the cases I studied), the Harberger triangle was replaced by a series of rectangles and the "second order-ness" of production losses from import restrictions could not be guaranteed.

What does this mean for the current paper? One cannot really compare the growth effects of being "protectionist" or a "nonglobalizer" across historical epochs because the instruments used and the intensity with which they were used vary so widely. In the pre-WWII era there were primarily tariff-based restrictions (and most "developing" countries were colonies). In the post-WWII system, developing countries entered the GATT in such a way that more or less exempted them wholesale from any discipline on the instruments used to provide import protection (or the intensity of the use of these instruments). So, while the developed countries moved toward exclusive use of tariffs (except, of course, for obvious exceptions such as multifiber arrangements) the developing countries used primarily nontariff barriers. This use of nontariff barriers, explicitly allowed to cope with the balance of payments, combined with the system of "fixed" exchange rates with periodic revaluations to produce the worst of all worlds. Foreign exchange "shortages" from overvalued exchange rates were met with the use of discretionary import licenses specific to both use and importer—and these have the potential to do almost unlimited economic damage. So I would argue that being a "protectionist" country in the 1970s and 80s has almost no comparison to the "protectionism" of the 1920s and 30s.

Third, what is it about inequality that is so worrisome? Is it inequality across countries? Is it inequality within one('s own) country? Is it increases in the volatility of individual incomes (even if cross-sectional inequality does not increase)? More specifically, if the Seattle-Quebec protester crowd were to read and understand this paper, would they stop their antiglobalization agitation? In part, that depends on what one thinks the protestors are agitated about. I approach this question with a pinch of Bob Dylan's "Senators, Congressmen throughout the land, don't criticize what you can't understand," as I do not really understand what it is that gets the protestors in the streets.

Here are four conjectures, however, each of which might lead to different reactions:

1. U.S. labor unions: concerns about declining real wages in the United States, both directly through changes in factor abundance and indirectly via capital mobility effects that have reallocated economic power (and sharing of rents) between labor and capital.

2. Nongovernmental organizations (NGOs): concerns about inequality across nations, particularly the performance of the poorest.

3. Fear of falling: concerns about the increase in volatility caused by increasing linkages so that white-collar middle managers can lose their jobs because of financial crises in Russia.

4. Hiding costs: concerns that globalization makes it harder to maintain high levels of social transfers as the costs of measures to transfer resources from consumer to certain groups of producers (e.g., farmers in Europe) is made politically more transparent by freer trade.

I think this paper should reassure the NGO crowd. I do not think there is anything in the evidence to suggest that globalization per se or participation in globalization has been bad for raising levels of income in the poorest countries.

However, after devoting all of my professional life to the problems of poor countries, I am not convinced that concern about poorer countries is large enough to generate any political pressure. I personally suspect that the other three motivations are behind the Seattle antiglobalization movement.

Fourth, there are three puzzles and one possible, partial solution, with respect to reconciling the literature on globalization with individual country experience. That is, if we imagine that globalization is the process of leading to deeper integration of financial, goods, and labor markets, then variation in the size of countries should provide some indications about the likely direction and magnitudes of globalization impacts. First, it is not the case that larger countries (whether with respect to population or land size), which have larger markets with or without globalization, have on average substantially higher levels of income. The countries in the world with more than 100 million people are (in order of population size) China, India, the United States, Indonesia, Brazil, the Russian Federation, Pakistan, Bangladesh, Japan, and Nigeria. This is obviously not compelling, as size of market depends on outward orientation as well as on intrinsic size, but large-scale effects in the level of income do not leap off the page. Second, in terms of inequality it is also not clear there is any relationship between inequality and country size, although here the question for globalization is whether regions that are not integrated as a single country would have lower inequality if they were. Finally, one fact that I am very puzzled by is the very weak forces for convergence even within regions of many developing countries. Even with urban-rural and cross-regional migration, inequality in per capita incomes has not decreased in Brazil, India, or China. It seems within countries there should be rapid and absolute convergence.

The one possible resolution of the size puzzle is that what matters for the gains from scale is the size of the market over which one can reliably contract—as that determines investments in the concentration of production and in specialization of assets. If, however, the legal and political systems contain substantial uncertainty about the appropriability of future profit streams, then the true size of the market over which a producer can reliably contract could be orders of magnitude different—even for the same size market because all future flows are so highly discounted.

Fifth, a final issue in globalization and inequality is that counteracting the globalizing forces is a huge increase in the numbers of nation-states. That is, the post-WWII period has seen an increase from maybe 50 completely independent, internationally sovereign states to more than 200. I am currently working with Ricardo Hausmann on a project in which we estimate the growth and income effects of this increasing division of the economic space into units that have their own trade policies (not matter how outwardly oriented), their own currency, their own contract enforcement, and their own restrictions on labor mobility.

All in all, this is a wonderful paper as it both informs with new facts and provokes with new thoughts.

6

Technology in the Great Divergence

Gregory Clark and Robert C. Feenstra

6.1 Introduction

In the late nineteenth century, at the same time that transport and communication costs were declining across the world, there occurred what has recently been dubbed by Ken Pomeranz "The Great Divergence" (2000). Per capita incomes across the world seemingly diverged by much more in 1910 than in 1800, and more in 1990 than in 1910—this despite the voluminous literature on exogenous growth that has stressed the convergence of economies, or, to be more precise, "conditional" convergence. The convergence doctrine holds that economies that are below their steady state should grow more quickly as they converge to the steady state. This approach allows for differences in the steady-state level of per capita income, but its emphasis on convergence has hidden the fact that there has been *divergence* in the absolute levels of income per capita. This has been recently emphasized by Easterly and Levine (2000), who further argue that the divergence of incomes is better explained by appealing to technology differences than by factor accumulation.

In this paper, we examine the changes in per capita income and productivity from 1800 to modern times, and show four things:

1. There has been increasing inequality in incomes per capita across countries since 1800 despite substantial improvements in the mobility of goods, capital, and technology.

2. The source of this divergence was increasing differences in the efficiency or total factor productivity (TFP) of economies.

Gregory Clark is professor of economics at the University of California–Davis. Robert C. Feenstra is professor of economics at the University of California–Davis and a research associate of the National Bureau of Economic Research.

3. These differences in efficiency were not due to the inability of poor countries to *get access* to the new technologies of the Industrial Revolution. Instead, differences in the efficiency of *use* of new technologies explain both low levels of income in poor countries and the slow adoption of Western technology.

4. The pattern of trade from the late nineteenth century between the poor and the rich economies should in principle reveal whether the problem of the poor economies was peculiarly a problem of employing labor effectively.

Results for the first two observations are described in section 6.2, and these are quite consistent with the results of Pomeranz (2000) and of Easterly and Levine (2000). The third observation—that the poor countries had *access* to new technologies—is dealt with in section 6.3. We show that at the same time that incomes were diverging, the ease of technological transmission between countries was increasing because of improvements in transportation, and political and organizational changes. By the late nineteenth century poor countries had access to the same repertoire of equipment, generally imported from the United Kingdom, as the rich. The problem, as we demonstrate in section 6.4 for the case of railways, was inefficiency in the *use* of this new technology in poor countries, even when the direction, planning, and supervision were done by Western experts. Thus, the world was diverging in an era of ever more rapid communication and cheaper transportation, mainly because of mysterious differences in the efficiency of use of technology across countries.

In the last sections of the paper we develop an analytical method that in principle should allow us to say more about the source of these production inefficiencies in poor countries, an area where economists have made little progress. Some have argued that the key is poor management in the low-income countries, and an inability to absorb best-practice technology from the advanced economies because of low levels of education, externalities, or learning by doing. There is just a generalized inefficiency in poor countries. But others, including one of the authors (Clark 1987; Wolcott and Clark 1999), have argued that the problem lies in the poor performance of production workers in low-wage countries and not in management, which in much of the world in the late nineteenth century was relatively easily imported. For ease of reference we call the first hypothesis on efficiency differences *generalized inefficiencies.* The second we refer to as *labor inefficiencies,* or, more generally, *factor-specific inefficiencies.*

Testing which of these possible explanations is correct is not easy. Without knowledge of the parameters of the production function for each industry, how can we say whether the observed inefficiency of the poorer countries stemmed from labor problems or from generalized inefficiencies? Here we make use of results from international trade theory, in particular

Trefler (1993, 1995), to test whether the efficiency differences across countries circa 1910 were of the generalized sort that could come from management or technology absorption problems, as opposed to specific problems in the use of labor. Under this approach we make use of the observed trade patterns of countries to infer the underlying productivities of factors.

Some evidence on the patterns of trade, in historical and modern times, is summarized in section 6.5. We show, for example, that India, at least as of 1910, was a net exporter of land-intensive commodities, which is quite puzzling. This fact can perhaps be explained, however, if its efficiency of land exceeded that of labor. We show in section 6.6 that the factor-content equations from the Heckscher-Ohlin-Vanek (HOV) model allow us to place some bounds on the relative efficiency of factors across countries, so that the trade data can be reconciled. In section 6.7 we explore this issue empirically using the sign pattern of trade, circa 1910 and 1990. Conclusions and directions for further research are given in section 6.8.

6.2   Incomes Per Capita

As noted above, recent research by Pomeranz and others suggests that in 1800 differences in income per capita were modest around the world. In part this result is unsurprising. In a Malthusian world of slow technological advance, living standards themselves reveal nothing about an economy's level of technology or its direction. Thus, the Europeans who visited Tahiti in the eighteenth century were astonished by two things (in addition to the islands' sexual mores)—the stone-age technology of the inhabitants, who so prized iron that they would trade a pig for one nail, and the ease and abundance in which they were living. But that abundance was purchased by a high rate of infanticide, which ensured a small number of surviving children per couple and consequently good material conditions. Tahiti was not a candidate for an industrial revolution, no matter how well fed its inhabitants.

The claim for the sophistication of Chinese and Japanese technology in the eighteenth century lies more properly with their ability to maintain more people per square mile at a high living standard than any European economy could. The low level of Tahitian technology in the late eighteenth century is evident in Tahiti's capacity to support only 14 people per square mile as opposed to England's 166.[1] Japan was supporting about 226 people per square mile from 1721 to 1846, and the coastal regions of China also attained even higher population densities: in 1787 Jiangsu had an incredible 875 people per square mile. It may be objected that these densities were based on paddy rice cultivation, an option not open to most of Europe. But

1. These population figures for Tahiti come from the years 1800 to 1820, when there may already have been some population losses from contact with Europeans. See Oliver (1974).

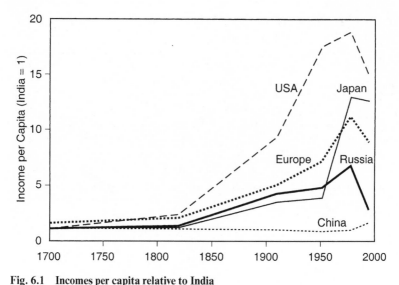

Fig. 6.1   Incomes per capita relative to India

Sources: 1700, 1820, Maddison (1989); 1910, Prados de la Escosura (2000) and Maddison (1989); 1952, 1978, and 1992, Penn World Tables.

even in the wheat regions of Shantung and Hopei, Chinese population densities in 1787 were more than double those of England and France. China had pushed preindustrial organic technology much further by 1800 than anywhere in Europe. The West was clearly behind.

Yet by 1910 the situation had reversed itself, and incomes per capita began to diverge sharply between an advanced group of economies and an underdeveloped world whose most important members were India and China. Figure 6.1 portrays this divergence, showing income per capita in the United States, Japan, Europe, Russia, and China relative to India in 1700, 1820, 1910, 1952, 1978, and 1992. Table 6.1 shows the income per capita of a variety of countries relative to India in 1910, using in part new data assembled by Prados de la Escosura (2000). Income relative to India from the Penn World Tables in 1990 is also shown. In 1910 India and China seem to have been the poorest countries in the world, and income per capita varied by a factor of about 9 to 1 around the world. By 1990 the income in some sub-Saharan Africa countries was no higher than in India in 1910, and incomes per capita by then varied by a factor of about 30 to 1 around the world.

Why did income per capita decline in poor countries such as India and China relative to the advanced economies such as the United States since 1800? We argue that the overwhelming cause was a decline in the efficiency of utilization of technology in these countries relative to the more successful economies such as those of Great Britain and the United States. Conventional estimates report that about one-third of the difference in incomes

Table 6.1   Income Per Capita, 1910 and 1990

Country	GDP per Capita Relative to India		Calculated Efficiency (TFP)		
	1910 (1)	1990 (2)	1910: $\alpha = 0.33, \gamma = 0$ (3)	1990: $\alpha = 0.33, \gamma = 0.1$ (4)	1990: $\alpha = 0.50, \gamma = 0$ (5)
United States	9.4	14.3	3.9	4.4	2.7
Australia	9.2	11.4	2.9	3.5	2.1
Canada	9.1	13.6	3.6	3.8	2.3
Great Britain	8.0	10.5	4.4	3.8	2.5
New Zealand	7.9	8.9	3.1	—	—
Argentina	7.6	3.7	4.0	2.3	1.7
France	7.2	11.0	3.9	3.6	2.2
Germany	7.0	11.6	4.2	3.4	2.1
Sweden	6.0	11.7	3.6	3.3	2.0
Italy	4.9	9.9	3.1	3.8	2.4
Spain	4.8	7.6	2.8	3.4	2.2
Ireland	4.8	7.5	2.9	—	—
Finland	4.6	11.1	2.8	3.0	1.7
Russia	4.2	—	2.2	—	—
Portugal	3.7	5.9	2.5	2.8	2.1
Japan	3.5	11.3	2.8	2.7	1.6
Ottoman Empire	3.3	3.0	2.0	—	—
The Philippines	2.4	1.3	1.8	—	—
Thailand	1.6	2.8	1.3	1.5	1.3
Korea	1.5	5.3	1.5	2.4	1.6
Indonesia	1.3	1.6	1.2	—	—
China	—	1.0	—	—	—
Zimbabwe	—	0.9	—	0.6	0.5
Zambia	—	0.5	—	0.7	0.8

Sources: Prados de la Escosura (2000); Penn World Tables (PWT 5.6).

Notes: TFP in column (3) is computed assuming full capital mobility between countries, according to equation (5). TFP in columns (4) and (5) is computed from equation (1'). Dashes indicate data are not available.

per capita between countries comes from capital (conventionally measured), and the rest from efficiency (TFP) differences.[2] But this assumes that differences in capital per worker across countries, which are very highly correlated with differences in income per capita and measured TFP since World War II, were exogenous. In a world where capital can flow between economies, capital/worker should be regarded as an endogenous variable, and it would itself *respond to* differences in the country productivity levels.

6.2.1 Perfect Capital Mobility

As a first approximation, we believe that the rental cost of capital was effectively equalized across rich and poor countries by international capital

2. See, for example, Easterly and Levine (2000).

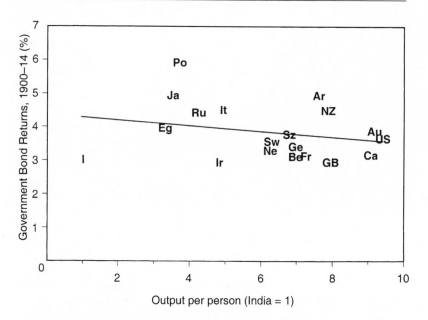

Fig. 6.2   Government bond returns, 1900–1914

Sources: Table 6.1. India and New Zealand: Edelstein (1982). Great Britain, Ireland, United States, France, Germany, Belgium, the Netherlands, Canada, Italy, and Switzerland: Homer and Sylla (1996). Argentina, Egypt, Japan, Russia, Sweden, Portugal, and Australia (sterling bonds in London): Mauro, Sussman, and Yafeh (2001).

Notes: Output per person is measured as an index with India set equal to 1. For the United States, municipal bonds yields were used. Egyptian income per person was asumed the same as the Ottoman Empire. Irish returns were assumed the same as British returns. Indian and New Zealand returns are from 1870–1913. The symbols used are as follows: Au (Australia), Ar (Argentina), Be (Belgium), Ca (Canada), Eg (Egypt), Fr (France), Ge (Germany), GB (Great Britain), I (India), Ir (Ireland), It (Italy), Ja (Japan), Ne (the Netherlands), NZ (New Zealand), Po (Portugal), Ru (Russia), Sw (Sweden), Sz (Switzerland), and US (United States of America).

movements by the late nineteenth century. Figure 6.2, for example, shows rates of return on government bonds in nineteen countries at a variety of income levels in 1900–1914 as a function of the relative level of output per capita in each country in 1910. There was variation in the rates of return on these various government bonds in the range of about 2 to 1. But, importantly, this variation had little correlation with the income level of the country. Indeed, if we regress government bond rates in 1900–1914 on output per capita though the slope coefficient is negative it is statistically insignificantly different from zero: Rates of return on government bonds seem uncorrelated with income.

We can also get rates of return on private borrowing by looking at returns on railway debentures. Railways were the biggest private borrowers in the international capital markets in the late nineteenth century, and their capital needs were so great that if they were able to borrow at international rates

Table 6.2   Rates of Return on Railway Debentures, 1870–1913

Country or Region	Relative Output Per Capita (India = 1)	Rate of Return (%)
United States	9.4	6.03
Canada	9.1	4.99
United Kingdom	7.9	3.74
Argentina	7.6	5.13
Brazil	—	5.10
Western Europe	6.1	5.28
Eastern Europe	4.1	5.33
British India	1.0	3.65

Source: Table 1 in Edelstein (1982, 125).
Note: Dash indicates data are not available.

of return it would help equalize rates of return across all assets in domestic capital markets. Table 6.2 shows the realized rates of return earned by investors in railway debentures in the London capital market between 1870 and 1913. Again, there are variations across countries. But, importantly for our purposes, this variation shows no correlation with output per person. Indeed, India, one of the poorest economies in the world, had among the lowest railway interest costs because the Indian government guaranteed the bonds of the railways as a way of promoting infrastructure investment. This rough equalization of returns to poor and rich countries was achieved by significant capital flows into these countries. By 1914 Egypt, the Ottoman Empire, Argentina, Brazil, Mexico, and Peru had all attracted at least £10 per head of foreign investment (Pamuk 1987).

In a world of rapid capital mobility, how should we calculate TFP? Suppose as an approximation that the production function is Cobb-Douglas so that

$$(1) \qquad Y_i = A_i K_i^\alpha L_i^\beta T_i^\gamma,$$

where T_i denotes land and A_i the efficiency (TFP) of country i. Choose units so that A_i, K_i, Y_i, and T_i are 1 in India. Taking capital stocks as exogenous, the income per capita of other economies relative to India would be

$$(2) \qquad \frac{Y_i}{L_i} = A_i \left(\frac{K_i}{L_i}\right)^\alpha \left(\frac{T_i}{L_i}\right)^\gamma.$$

The rental on capital can be computed by differentiating equation (1). Taking this derivative and assuming the same rental on capital in all countries, then capital per worker in country i relative to India would be[3]

---

3. The derivative of equation (1) with respect to K_i can be expressed as $R_i = \alpha A_i (K_i/L_i)^{(\alpha-1)}(T_i/L_i)^\gamma$. Dividing this entire expression by the same equation for India, which is assumed to have the *same* rental R_i, we therefore obtain $1 = A_i(K_i/L_i)^{(\alpha-1)}(T_i/L_i)^\gamma$, where all variables are now expressed relative to India. Then equation (3) follows directly.

(3)
$$\frac{K_i}{L_i} = A_i^{1/(1-\alpha)}\left(\frac{T_i}{L_i}\right)^{\gamma/(1-\alpha)}.$$

The amount of capital employed would thus depend on the level of efficiency of the economy. The more efficient an economy, the more capital it would attract, which would have a second round effect in increasing income per person. Substituting equation (3) into equation (2), we obtain the following expression for output per capita:

(4)
$$\frac{Y_i}{L_i} = (A_i)^{1/(1-\alpha)}\left(\frac{T_i}{L_i}\right)^{\gamma/(1-\alpha)}.$$

Notice that the right-hand sides of equations (3) and (4) are identical, so that capital/worker and output/worker are equal with capital endogenous and rates of return equalized across countries. It follows from equation (4) that we can calculate relative efficiencies in the world economy circa 1910 as

(5)
$$A_i = \left(\frac{Y_i}{L_i}\right)^{1-\alpha}\left(\frac{T_i}{L_i}\right)^{-\gamma}.$$

Thus, in this case we can calculate relative TFP for each country relative to India from just the relative outputs per capita and the relative amount of land per person. Since the share of land in national income, γ, has become very small in recent years, equation (4) suggests that the sole significant cause of differences in income per capita between India and the United States and other advanced economies is differences in TFP.

6.2.2   Evidence from 1910

Even without reliable data on capital stocks across countries, we can calculate TFP from equation (5) if there is mobile capital. Column (3) of table 6.1 and figure 6.3 show the implied TFP of the various countries in the world in 1910 for which we have data, relative to India, assuming the share of capital in national income was 0.33 and that of land was 0.1. Differences in the land endowment per person were great enough that even assuming land had only a 10 percent share in output we seem to be overcorrecting for the effect of land on income per capita. Thus there is no reason to believe that the efficiency of the U.S., Canadian, or Australian economies was really below that of Great Britain in 1910. What we also see is that in a world of free-flowing capital, modest differences in the efficiencies of economies get translated into much bigger differences in income, through generation of additional savings by higher income and the movement of capital to the high-efficiency areas.

The assumption that capital invested was constant per unit of gross domestic product (GDP) might be regarded as unreasonable for 1910. Perhaps then capital was not so mobile as now, so that poorer economies typically

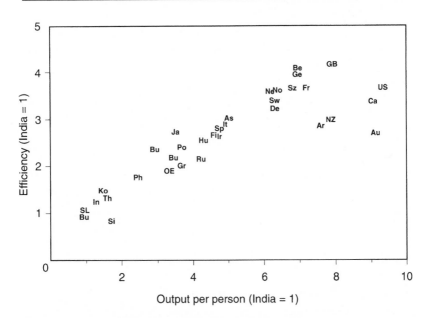

Fig. 6.3   Calculated differences in efficiency (TFP) circa 1910

Notes: Output per person is measured as an index with India set equal to 1. Efficiency is measured as an index with India again set to 1. The country symbols are as follows: A (Austria), Au (Australia), Ar (Argentina), Be (Belgium), Bu (Burma), Ca (Canada), De (Denmark), Fi (Finland), Fr (France), Ge (Germany), GB (Great Britain), Gr (Greece), Hu (Hungary), I (India), In (Indonesia), Ir (Ireland), It (Italy), Ja (Japan), Ko (Korea), Ne (the Netherlands), NZ (New Zealand), OE (Ottoman Empire), Ph (the Philippines), Po (Portugal), Ru (Russia), SL (Sri Lanka), Sp (Spain), Sw (Sweden), Sz (Switzerland), Th (Thailand), and US (United States).

had smaller stocks of capital relative to output and higher returns on capital. This proposition is difficult to test, but one partial measure is afforded by the amount of railway line per unit of GDP observed. Railways were huge sinks of capital in the late nineteenth century and a popular vehicle for foreign investment. If capital was really scarce in the poor countries, then along with other investments the stock of rail line per unit of income should be smaller the lower the income level per person. Figure 6.4 shows railway line per unit of income as an index versus GDP per capita for a variety of countries in 1910. If we were to exclude the low-population-density settler colonies of North America, Argentina, and Australasia, we would find that poor countries had as many miles of railway line per unit of GDP as rich countries.

6.2.3   Evidence from 1990

The assumption here that capital will be proportional to output finds support in the international economy of the 1990s. Using a sample of coun-

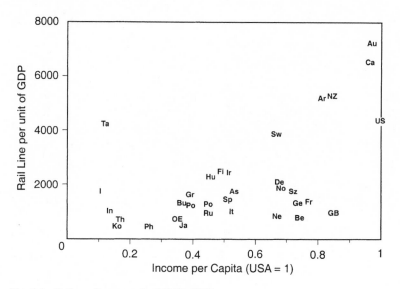

Fig. 6.4   Railway line per unit of GDP, 1910

Note: Country symbols are as in figure 6.3.

tries including those in table 6.1 for 1990, figure 6.5 shows capita per worker versus GDP per worker, with both measured relative to India. Recall from equations (3) and (4) that these should be equal with full capital mobility, and from figure 6.4, capital is clearly closely proportional to output. Regressing the log of capital per worker on the log of GDP per capita on all countries of the Penn World Tables (PWT) for which capital is available for 1990, we find

$$\ln\!\left(\frac{\text{capital}}{\text{worker}}\right) = \underset{(0.11)}{-0.01} + \underset{(0.07)}{1.32}\ln\!\left(\frac{\text{GDP}}{\text{worker}}\right), \qquad N = 60,\ R^2 = 0.85.$$

The coefficient on ln(GDP/worker) is somewhat higher than unity, but still seems consistent with the hypothesis that capital is roughly proportionate to output, as implied by full capital mobility with Cobb-Douglas production functions across countries.

How important are efficiency differences in explaining income differences in 1990? For the 1990 data, since land rents are so small a share of income by then, we ignore these. Since PWT does not provide us with data on the share of national income received by labor and capital, in order to estimate α, we rewrite equation (1) as $\ln(Y_i/L_i) = \ln A_i + \alpha \ln(K_i/L_i)$, and regress real GDP per worker on real capital stock per worker. Running this regression over all countries and years for which data are available in PWT, 1965–90, and including fixed effects for countries, we obtain $\alpha = 0.50$ (stan-

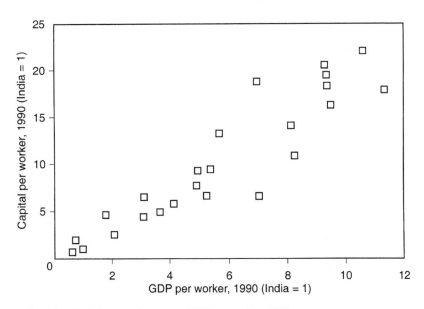

Fig. 6.5   Capital per worker versus GDP per worker, 1990
Source: Penn World Tables (5.6).

dard error = 0.01). Performing the same regression in first differences, which still include fixed effects for countries, we obtain α = 0.34 (s.e. = 0.04). Thus, the interval [0.33, 0.5] gives an adequate range for the share of national income going to capital, and this is quite consistent with our priors for the capital share across various countries. In the final columns of table 6.1 we report the calculation of TFP using these values of α and the formula

$$(1')\qquad\qquad \mathrm{TFP}_i = A_i = \frac{(Y_i/L_i)}{(K_i/L_i)^\alpha},$$

where all variables are measured relative to those in India.

In figure 6.6, we graph real GDP per capita against TFP, using the intermediate value of α = 0.4. There is quite clearly a strong positive relationship between these measures of technology and income for the sample of countries we have used. We saw above that capital per worker and GDP per worker are also closely linked. When GDP per capita is regressed against both these variables for 1990, we obtain

$$\ln(\text{GDP per capita}) = -0.02 + 1.06\ln(\text{TFP}) + 0.43\ln\!\left(\frac{\text{capital}}{\text{worker}}\right),$$
$$\phantom{\ln(\text{GDP per capita}) = }(0.04)\ \ (0.07)\qquad\quad (0.03)$$

$$N = 60,\ R^2 = 0.96.$$

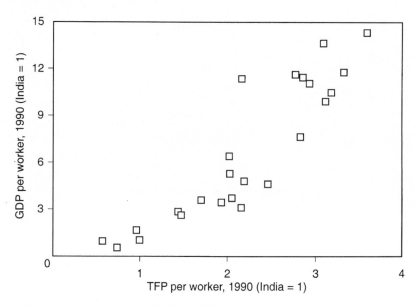

Fig. 6.6   GDP per capita versus TFP, 1990
Source: Penn World Tables (5.6).

From this regression, it appears that both TFP and capital are important determinants of national income. The relative contributions of each in explaining GDP per capita can be computed by expressing this regression in terms of variances:

$$\text{var(GDP per capita)} = 1.06^2 \text{ var(TFP)} + 0.43^2 \text{ var}\left(\frac{\text{capital}}{\text{worker}}\right)$$

$$+ 0.91 \text{ cov} + \text{var(error)},$$

where all variables are expressed in logs, and the covariance is between TFP and capital/worker. Using the sample values for these variances, we find that TFP explains one-quarter of the variance in GDP per capita, and capital/worker explains one-third of this variation, but the *covariance* between TFP and capital/worker explains nearly 40 percent of this variation! This reinforces our argument that capital/worker should be regarded as an endogenous variable, itself *responding to* differences in the level of productivity across countries.

We can test for the endogeneity of capital by using equation (3), while ignoring land ($\gamma = 0$). Running this regression for 1990, we obtain

$$\ln\left(\frac{\text{capital}}{\text{worker}}\right) = 0.55 + 1.86 \ln(\text{TFP}), \qquad N = 60, R^2 = 0.46.$$
$$\qquad\qquad (0.21)\;\;(0.27)$$

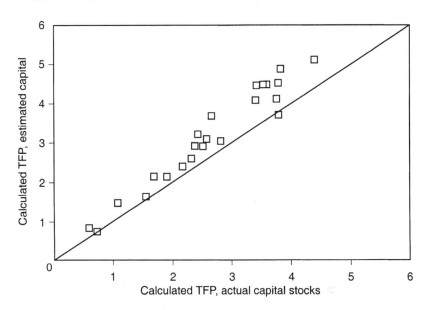

Fig. 6.7   TFP calculated with and without capital stock information, 1990
Note: TFP calculated using $\alpha = 0.33$.

The implied capital share is $\alpha = 1 - (1/1.86) = 0.46$, which is quite close to the value $\alpha = 0.4$ used to construct TFP in this regression. That is, the hypothesis of perfect capital mobility, with equalization of rentals across countries, receives some support from the coefficient on ln(TFP) in this regression. However, the fact that the constant term is significantly different from zero indicates that *full* capital mobility, with Cobb-Douglas production functions across countries, does not appear to hold.

If capital is indeed mobile, then we should really take the regression above, explaining capital/worker, and substitute this into the previous regression, explaining GDP per capital. In other words, let us treat TFP as the only underlying determinant of income, and use this to obtain

$$\ln(\text{GDP per capita}) = 0.21 + 1.85 \ln(\text{TFP}), \qquad N = 60, R^2 = 0.79.$$
$$\qquad\qquad\qquad\;\;\; (0.10)\;\; (0.13)$$

According to these estimates, TFP has a *magnified* impact on income per capita, with an elasticity of 1.85, via its direct effect and its induced effect on capital flows. This is exactly what we expect from equation (4).

As a final check for 1990, we can compute TFP according to equation (3), without using data on capital stocks but assuming full capital mobility. Then, as shown in figure 6.7, we find a very close correlation between TFP calculated using the capital stock information, and TFP calculated assuming that capital per worker is proportional to GDP per worker. The observations mostly lie above the 45-degree line because India has a relatively small capital stock, and output per worker and capital per worker are both measured relative to India. The correlation coefficient between the two measures is 0.96. Thus, by 1990 it seems plausible to regard TFP as the primary driver of differences in income per capita across countries, with capital playing a secondary and derivative role.

6.2.4   Imperfect Capital Mobility

Above we assumed perfect capital mobility. Since there likely were and are frictions in international capital markets, let us consider whether our conclusion that income differences were driven by TFP differences has to be weakened once we allow for imperfect capital mobility, and therefore differences in the rental on capital across countries. To see how differences in the rental cost of capital modify our analysis, again compute the rental on capital by differentiating equation (1). Allowing this to differ across countries, and expressing all variables in country i relative to India, we obtain[4]

$$(3') \qquad \frac{K_i}{L_i} = \left(\frac{A_i}{R_i}\right)^{1/(1-\alpha)}\left(\frac{T_i}{L_i}\right)^{\gamma/(1-\alpha)}.$$

Thus, the amount of capital employed will vary inversely with its rental, which now appears on the right of equation (3'). Substituting equation (3') into equation (2), we obtain the following expression for output per capita:

$$(4') \qquad \frac{Y_i}{L_i} = (R_i)^{-\alpha/(1-\alpha)}(A_i)^{1/(1-\alpha)}\left(\frac{T_i}{L_i}\right)^{\gamma/(1-\alpha)}.$$

Comparing equations (3') and (4'), we see that capital/worker and output/worker differ by exactly the rental term, so that

$$(5') \qquad \frac{K_i}{L_i} = \frac{(Y_i/L_i)}{R_i}.$$

Countries with lower rentals will attract more capital. Note that relative TFP (with $\gamma = 0$) can still be calculated as in equation (1'). The rental of capital is, of course, the product of the rate of return on capital in each country and the purchase price of capital goods. The evidence we have on the purchase price of capital goods for 1910 is the cost of fully equipped cotton spinning and weaving mills per spindle. This is a reasonably good general index of the cost of capital goods in these countries because cotton mills generally embodied imported machinery and power plants combined with local construction of the buildings. We also saw above little sign

---

4. From note 3, the rental on capital is $R_i = \alpha A_i(K_i/L_i)^{(\alpha-1)}(T_i/L_i)^{\gamma}$. Now divide this by the same equation for India and express all variables relative to India, to obtain, $R_i = A_i(K_i/L_i)^{(\alpha-1)}(T_i/L_i)^{\gamma}$. Then equation (3') follows directly.

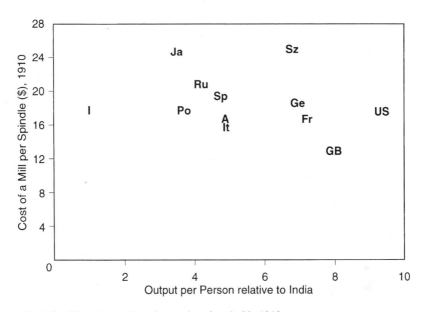

Fig. 6.8   The estimated purchase price of capital in 1910

Sources: Table 6.1 and Clark (1987).

Notes: Output per person is measured as an index with India set equal to 1. The symbols used are as follows: A (Austria), Fr (France), Ge (Germany), GB (Great Britain), I (India), It (Italy), Ja (Japan), Po (Portugal), Ru (Russia), Sp (Spain), Sz (Switzerland), and US (United States).

that rates of return on capital correlated with output per person in 1900–14. Thus the purchase price of capital goods in 1910 should be a reasonably good estimator of the rental cost of capital. Figure 6.8 shows these measures of capital costs relative to output per person in 1910. There is no strong sign in the pre–World War I international economy of any link between rental costs of capital and output per capita. Thus, at least for this period we do not need to worry about restricted capital mobility very much.

The PWT do report significant differences in the purchase prices of capital goods across countries in the post–World War II period, however. For the data in 1990, we can repeat some of our earlier regressions allowing for the effect of capital rental differences. Data on the price of investment goods are taken from the benchmark surveys for the PWT, as described in Jones (1994) and also used in De Long and Summers (1991).[5] Several types of capital goods are available, and we use here the overall price of investment goods. The rental on investment goods is, of course, the interest rate

5. These data are available at [http://emlab.berkeley.edu/users/chad/RelPrice.asc].

times its purchase price. For these years we do not have information on interest rates by country. However, provided that interest rates (and depreciation rates) do not vary with output per capita, we can use the purchase price of investment goods as a proxy for its rental in our estimations.

Regressing the log of capital per worker on the log of GDP per capita and also the log of the rental, we obtain

$$\ln\left(\frac{capital}{worker}\right) = 0.17 + 1.16\ln\left(\frac{GDP}{worker}\right) - 0.47\ln(rental),$$

$$(0.11)\ \ (0.08) \qquad\qquad\qquad (0.23)$$

$$N = 52,\ R^2 = 0.89.$$

The sample used here is on all countries of the PWT for which capital stocks are available for 1990, and we also have the price of investment goods in 1980 reported in Jones (1994). The coefficient on $\ln(GDP/worker)$ is reduced by inclusion of the rental, so that it becomes closer to unity. The rental itself has a negative coefficient, as predicted from (5′), but less than unity; given the measurement error that is present in using the purchase price of investment goods rather than their rental, it is not surprising that this coefficient is biased toward zero.

Computing TFP according to equation (1′) using the value of $\alpha = 0.4$, we can treat this and the rental price of investment goods as the underlying determinants of income, and run equation (4′) to obtain

$$\ln(GDP\ per\ capita) = 0.27 + 1.65\ln(TFP) - 0.67\ln(rental),$$

$$(0.08)\ \ (0.12) \qquad\qquad (0.18)$$

$$N = 52,\ R^2 = 0.87.$$

Once again, we find that TFP has a *magnified* impact on income per capita, with an elasticity of 1.65, via its direct effect and its induced effect on capital allocation. The relative contributions of TFP versus the rental in explaining GDP per capita can be decomposed from this regression according to

$$var(GDP\ per\ capita) = 1.65^2\ var(TFP) + 0.67^2\ var(rental)$$

$$- 2.21\ cov + var(error),$$

where the covariance is between TFP and the rental on investment goods. Using the sample values for these variances, we find that TFP explains fully two-thirds of the variance in GDP per capita, whereas the rental only explains 5 percent of this variation, with the *covariance* between TFP and the rental explaining another 16 percent of this variation. This, including the rental on capital across countries, does not change our conclusion that TFP is the driving force behind differences in GDP per capita, with capital/worker *responding to* differences in the level of productivity.

Where do these differences in productivity come from? Some recent authors have argued that geography or climate (Sachs 2001), or institutions (Acemoglu, Johnson, and Robinson 2001), or social capital (Jones and Hall 1999) plays an important role. We do not dispute that these may be important, but our approach is different. Rather than looking for some external cause for countries to differ in their efficiency levels, we will instead look internally at productivity itself, and ask whether the cross-country variation in TFP should be attributed to the *access* to or to the *use of* technologies.

6.3   Access to Technology

We see that the increased disparity in income per capita across the world stemmed largely from an increased disparity in the efficiency of economies, the amount of output produced per unit of input. The next thing we show is that little of this disparity stemmed from differences in *access* to technology. Economic growth since the Industrial Revolution has been largely based on an expansion of knowledge. The fact that the Industrial Revolution came from an increase in knowledge, rather than from capital accumulation or from the exploitation of natural resources, seemed to imply that it would spread with great rapidity to other parts of the world, for although developing new knowledge is an arduous task, copying innovations is much easier. Also, although some of the new technology eventually was very sophisticated, some of it was relatively simple, or required little technical expertise to operate. Thus, artificial fertilizers in the late nineteenth century, and new strains of crops in the twentieth, for example, which dramatically boosted agricultural yields, were both relatively simple technologies for poor countries to adopt. Further, given the possibilities of specialization in international trade, the poorer countries did not need to acquire all the new Western technology. They could instead adopt the simplest and most easily transferable techniques, and import products embodying more sophisticated processes from the more economically advanced countries. In textiles, for example, spinning coarse yarn was much easier technically than spinning fine yarn. Countries such as India could thus specialize in coarse yarn, and import finer cloth.

Further, there were a series of interrelated technical, organizational, and political developments in the nineteenth century that made technological transmission much easier. The important technological changes were the improvements in transport through the development of railways, steamships, the Suez and (later) Panama canals, and the telegraph. The organizational change was the development of specialized machine-building firms in Great Britain and later the United States. The political changes were the extension of European colonial empires to large parts of Africa and Asia, and the political developments within European countries. By the eve of World War I the first great globalization of the world economy was complete. Political and economic developments in the twentieth century disrupted that earlier globalization, but even by 1914 it was clear that differences in the efficiency of economies could not be attributed just to differences in the type of technology employed.

6.3.1 Transport and Communication

In the course of the nineteenth century, land transportation, even in the poorest countries, was revolutionized by the spread of railways. Table 6.3 shows the miles of railroad completed in selected countries by 1850, 1890, and 1910. The great expansion of the rail network in the late nineteenth century, even in very poor and underdeveloped countries such as Russia and India, improved communication between the coast and the interior immensely (remember, the circumference of the earth is only 26,000 miles). Railroad development was associated with imperialism. Thus, independent countries such as China had little railway development before 1914.

Ocean transport was similarly revolutionized in this period by the development of the steamboat. In the 1830s and 1840s, although steamships were faster and more punctual than sailing ships, they were used only for the most valuable and urgent cargo, such as mail, because of their very high coal consumption. The huge amount of coal that had to be carried limited the amount of cargo they could hold on transoceanic voyages. To sail from Bombay to Aden in 1830 the *Hugh Lindsay* "had to fill its hold and cabins and pile its decks with coal, barely leaving enough room for the crew and the mail" (Headrick 1988, 24). The liner *Britannia* in the 1840s required 640 tons of coal to cross the Atlantic with 225 tons of cargo. Thus, even in the 1850s steam power was used only for perishable and high-value cargoes.

But in the 1850s and 1860s four innovations lowered the cost of steam transport. These were the screw propeller, iron hulls (iron-hulled boats were 30–40 percent lighter and gave 15 percent more cargo capacity for a given amount of steam power), compound engines that were much more fuel efficient, and surface condensers (previously steamboats had to use seawater to make steam, which produced corrosion and fouling of the engine). These last two innovations greatly reduced the coal consumption of engines per horsepower per hour. In the 1830s it took 4 kg of coal to produce 1 hp-hour, but by 1881 the quantity was down to 0.8 kg. This directly reduced costs, but since it also allowed ships to carry less coal and more cargo there was a further reduction in costs. Real ocean freight costs fell by nearly 35 percent

Table 6.3		Railway Mileage Completed				
Year	Britain	United States	Germany	France	Russia	India
1850	6,088	9,021	3,639	1,811	311	0
1890	17,291	208,152	26,638	20,679	19,012	16,918
1910	19,999	351,767	38,034	25,156	41,373	32,789

from 1870 to 1910. In 1906, for example, it cost 8 shillings to carry a ton of cotton goods by rail the thirty miles from Manchester to Liverpool, but only 30 s. to ship those goods the 7,250 miles from Liverpool to Bombay. This cost of shipping cotton cloth was less than 1 percent of the cost of the goods. By the late nineteenth century industrial locations with good water access that were on well-established shipping routes—Bombay, Calcutta, Madras, Shanghai, Hong Kong—could get access to all the industrial inputs of Great Britain at costs not very much higher than many British firms. In part this was because, since Great Britain's exports were mainly manufactures with high value per unit volume, there was excess shipping capacity on the leg out from Great Britain, making the transport of industrial machinery and parts to underdeveloped countries such as India relatively cheap.

While freight costs fell, these technical advances also increased the speed of travel across the oceans. The fastest P&O (Peninsular and Oriental Steam Navigation Company) liner in 1842, the *Hindustan,* had a speed of 10 knots per hour. By 1912 P&O's fastest boat, the *Maloja,* could do 18 knots. The speed of travel across oceans was further enhanced by the opening of the great canals, the Suez canal in 1869 and the Panama canal in 1914. The Suez canal alone saved 41 percent of the distance on the journey from London to Bombay and 32 percent of the distance on the journey from London to Shanghai. Thus, although in the 1840s it took sailing ships from five to eight very uncomfortable months to get to India, by 1912 in principal the journey could be done in fifteen days.

The last of the important technical innovations in the late nineteenth century was the development of the telegraph. For the poorest countries of Africa and the East the key development was the invention of submarine cables for the telegraph. In the 1840s if an Indian firm bought British textile machinery and ran into problems with it, it would take the firm at best ten months to receive any return communication from the machine builders. In 1851 the first submarine telegraph cable was laid between France and England. By 1865 India was linked to Great Britain by a telegraph system partly over land that could transmit messages in twenty-four hours, and in 1866 a successful transatlantic telegraph service had been established. Thus, by 1866 orders and instructions could be communicated halfway across the world in days.

These changes together made the world a much smaller place in the late nineteenth century than it had been earlier. Information could travel much faster. We know, for example, that the average time it took news to travel from Rome to Cairo in the first three centuries A.D., when Egypt was a province of the Roman Empire, was about one mile per hour. As late as the early eighteenth century it had taken four days to send letters 200 miles within Great Britain. With the telegraph, rail, and steamship it was possible to send information across the world in much less time. The steamship and railroad also made travel faster and much more reliable for people and goods. And the development of the steamship made the cost of reaching far-flung places quite low as long as they had good access to ocean navigation. The technological basis for the export of Industrial Revolution technologies to almost any country in the world thus seemed to have been completed by the last quarter of the nineteenth century.

6.3.2   Organizational Changes

In the early nineteenth century a specialized machine-building sector developed within the Lancashire cotton industry. These machinery firms, some of which (such as Platt) were exporting at least 50 percent of their production as early as 1845–70, had an important role in exporting textile technology. These capital goods firms were able to provide a complete package of services to prospective foreign entrants to the textile industry, which included technical information, machinery, construction expertise, and managers and skilled operatives. By 1913 the six largest machine producers employed over 30,000 workers (Bruland 1989, 5, 6, 34). These firms reduced the risks to foreign entrepreneurs by such practices as giving them machines on a trial basis and undertaking to supply skilled workers to train the local labor force. As a result, firms like Platt sold all around the world. Table 6.4 shows the number of orders for ring-spinning frames Platt took (each order typically involved numbers of machines) for a sample of nine years in each of the periods 1890–1914 and 1915–1934. Indeed, for ring frames England was a small share of Platt's market throughout these years.

Similar capital goods exporters developed in the rail sectors, and later in the United States in the boot and shoe industry. British construction crews completed railways in many foreign countries under the captainship of such flamboyant entrepreneurs as Lord Brassey. The reason again for the overseas exodus was in part the saturation of the rail market within Great Britain by the 1870s after the boom years of railway construction. By 1875, in a boom lasting just forty-five years, 71 percent of all the railway line ever constructed in Great Britain was completed. Thereafter the major markets for British contractors and engine constructors were overseas. India, for example, got most of its railway equipment from Great Britain, and the Indian railway mileage by 1910 was significantly greater than the British, as table 6.3 has shown.

6.3.3   Political Developments

A number of political developments should have speeded up the export of technology in the nineteenth century. The most important of these was the expansion of the European colonial territories. By 1900 the European powers controlled as colonies 35 percent of the land surface of the world, even excluding from this reckoning Asiatic Russia. Thus, of a world area of 57.7 million square miles Europe itself constitutes only 3.8 million square

Table 6.4   **Platt Ring Frame Orders by Country, 1890–1934**

Country	Sales, 1890–1914 (9 years)	Sales, 1914–36 (9 years)
Austria	4	0
Belgium	17	15
Brazil	95	43
Canada	15	17
China	5	64
Czechoslovakia	14	10
Egypt	0	5
England	110	74
Finland	1	0
France	41	31
Germany	47	6
Guatemala	1	1
Hungary	0	4
India	66	132
Italy	69	29
Japan	66	117
Mexico	75	7
The Netherlands	7	2
Nicaragua	2	0
Peru	7	0
Poland	41	8
Portugal	8	0
Russia	131	23
Spain	95	35
Sweden	3	0
Switzerland	3	0
Turkey	0	6
United States	2	0
West Africa	0	2

Source: Lancashire Record Office.

miles, but by 1900 its dependencies covered 19.8 million square miles. The British Empire was the largest, covering 9.0 million square miles; the French had 4.6 million, the Netherlands 2.0 million, and Germany 1.2 million.

Even many countries formally outside of the control of European powers were forced to cede trading privileges and special rights to Europeans. Thus, China was forced in the course of the nineteenth century to cede various treaty ports, such as Shanghai. The political control by countries such as Great Britain of so much of the world allowed entrepreneurs to export machinery and techniques to low-wage areas with little risk of expropriation. Thus the great increase in the scope and effectiveness of British political power in the course of the nineteenth century made it easier to export capital from Great Britain to support new textile industries. Most of the Indian subcontinent and Burma was brought under British administrative control in 1858, and Egypt fell to Britain in 1882. In 1842 the British secured Hong Kong from China, and in 1858 they achieved a concession in Shanghai. These were all localities with very low wage rates and easy access to major sea routes. The joint effect of these technological and political developments was to create by 1900 an expanded British economy spanning the globe. British policy within its empire was to eliminate barriers to trade and to allow economic activity to proceed wherever the market deemed most profitable. In India, for example, despite protests from local interests the British insisted on a free trade policy between Great Britain and India. Any manufacturer who set up a cotton mill in Bombay was assured of access to the British market on the same terms as British mills.

The nature of British imperialism also ensured that no country was restrained from the development of industry up until 1917 by the absence of a local market of sufficient size. Because of the British policy of free trade pursued in the nineteenth century, Great Britain itself and most British dependencies were open to imports with no tariff or else a low tariff for revenue purposes only. The large Indian market, which took a large share of English textile production, for example, was open on the same terms to all foreign producers. There was a 3.5 percent revenue tariff on imports, but a countervailing tax was applied to local Indian mills at the insistence of Manchester manufacturers. The Chinese textile market, at the insistence of the imperial powers, was also protected by a 5 percent ad valorem revenue tariff.

6.4   Efficiency in the Use of Technology

Although railways, cotton mills, and other advanced technologies spread rapidly around the world by the late nineteenth century as a result of the above factors, the efficiency with which this technology was used differed greatly across countries. It was this inefficiency in use that in practice limited the spread of new production technologies. We illustrate this using the example of the railroads, but an equivalent story can be told for cotton textiles (Clark 1987; Wolcott and Clark 1999).

Output in each country is measured as a weighted sum of the number of tons of freight hauled, the ton-miles of freight, and passenger-miles of passengers. Both tons of freight and ton-miles were used because the average length of haul varied greatly and the fixed costs in hauling freight from loading and unloading were substantial compared to the costs of hauling goods another ton-mile.[6] Freight output was thus estimated as (tons $\times$ \$0.285 + ton-miles $\times$ \$0.0066). The quality of passenger service varied greatly, which

---

6. From freight revenues across countries we estimate that the cost of freight hauling a ton of freight x miles in the United States in 1914 in \$(0.285 + 0.0066z).

Table 6.5   Railroad Operating Efficiency circa 1914

Country	Year	Output per Worker ($)	Output per Track Mile ($)	Efficiency (United States = 1)	Miles per Locomotive per Year
Australia	1914	691	4,421	0.41	24,243
Austria	1912	567	9,677	0.61	16,934
Belgium	1912	959	10,332	0.78	18,282
Canada	1914	1,400	5,487	0.62	25,175
China	1916	389	5,495	0.37	30,408
Denmark	1914	709	6,669	0.53	15,006
France	1911	772	7,451	0.59	22,926
Germany	1913	857	11,826	0.81	25,746
Hungary	1912	653	5,443	0.45	—
India	1914	297	4,208	0.28	—
Japan	1914	507	6,488	0.46	27,196
The Netherlands	1912	812	6,982	0.57	32,330
Romania	1913	489	6,738	0.46	23,340
Siam	1914	389	2,128	0.21	17,592
Sweden	1912	739	3,288	0.35	22,442
Switzerland	1913	577	6,831	0.49	—
United Kingdom	1912	898	9,457	0.72	25,854
United States	1914	1,743	10,565	1.00	26,092

Sources: Boag (1912); Bureau of Railway Economics (1915); various national railway statistics.
Note: Our method means that output per worker is measured in the same prices everywhere. Dashes indicate data are not available.

shows up in the revenue generated per passenger-mile. For India, for example, this was 2.4¢ per mile for first class and 0.4¢ for fourth class. We thus adjusted passenger-miles by assuming first class was equivalent everywhere and weighting passenger-miles in other classes according to the relative revenue generated per passenger-mile. This weighted passenger-mile figure was multiplied by $0.023, the average revenue per passenger mile for first class. Table 6.5 shows the implied output per worker and output per track mile in dollars. On this measure, output per worker in the United States in 1914 was six times output per worker in India, even though India was using an equivalent technology.

Since Indian rail equipment was mostly imported from Great Britain, a better comparison might be with the United Kingdom. U.K. output per worker was three times output per worker in India. Figure 6.9 shows output per worker on the railways circa 1914 in the countries for which we can get data, versus real GDP per capita for the same countries in 1910. This low output per worker in the poorer countries has little to do with capital/labor substitution in response to lower wages. One measure of the intensity of capital utilization is the number of miles locomotives were driven per year. This varies much less across countries and is uncorrelated with the level of income of the country. As column (5) of table 6.5 shows, the overall effi-

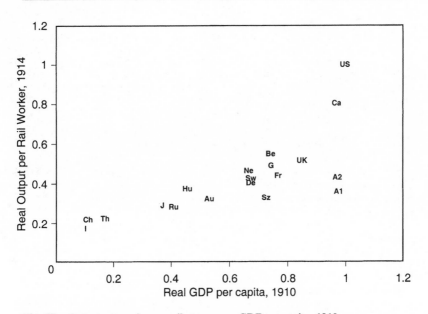

Fig. 6.9   Output per worker on railways versus GDP per capita, 1910

Note: A1 is New South Wales; A2 is South Australia. Otherwise country codes are as in previous figures. Output is measured relative to the U.S., set at 1.

ciency of the rail systems of these countries also varies greatly. The efficiency of the Indian rail system was only 28 percent of that of the U.S. system and 39 percent of that in the United Kingdom. These differences in the efficiency of operation of the rail system between countries like India and the United States and United Kingdom are almost as great as the differences in calculated TFP for these economies as a whole.

Note that the Indian rail system, for example, had extensive British expertise in its operation. In 1910 the Indian railroads employed 7,207 "Europeans" (mainly British) and 8,862 "Eurasians" (principally Anglo-Indians), who occupied almost all the supervisory and skilled positions. Indian locomotive drivers were employed only after 1900, and even as late as 1910 many of the locomotive drivers were British (Morris and Dudley 1975, 202–04; Headrick 1988, 322).

The problem of operating Western technology efficiently in poor countries like India was the main barrier to the spread of this technology. Table 6.6, for example, shows the gross profit rates of Bombay cotton mills by quinquennia from 1905–09 to 1935–39, as well as the size of the Bombay industry and the output per worker in Bombay as an index with 1905–09 set at 100. As can be seen, profits were never great, but the industry grew substantially in the era of modest profits up to 1924. Thereafter, however, profits collapsed (as a result of Japanese competition), and the Bombay indus-

Table 6.6   The Bombay Industry, 1907–38

Year	Gross Profit Rate on Fixed Capital	Size of the Bombay Industry (millions of spindle-equivalents)	Output per Worker in Bombay (index)	Output per Worker in Japan (index)
1905–09	0.06	3.09	100	100
1910–14	0.05	3.43	103	115
1915–19	0.07	3.68	99	135
1920–24	0.08	4.05	94	132
1925–29	−0.00	4.49	91	180
1930–34	0.00	4.40	104	249
1935–39	0.02	3.91	106	281

Source: Wolcott and Clark (1999).
Note: Profits and output per worker were calculable only for the mills listed in the *Investor's India Year-book* (various years).

try soon began to contract. The last column shows what was happening to output per worker in Japan, where, with the same machinery as in India (in both cases purchased from England), output per worker increased greatly.

Thus, the crucial variable in explaining the success or failure of economies in the years 1800–2000 seems to be the efficiency of the production process within the economy. And the differences in the ability to employ technology seemingly got larger over time between rich and poor countries.

6.5   Trade Patterns and the Sources of Inefficiency

Despite the importance of TFP differences, we have very little idea what generates them. We now consider using the pattern of trade to determine whether these TFP differences specifically adhered to labor in poor countries, or lay in some wider managerial failure.

The dominance of Great Britain and its free trade ideology in much of the world circa 1910 meant that trade barriers were low for the countries with the majority of world population in 1910—India (including modern Pakistan, Bangladesh, and Burma), China, Great Britain, Ireland, Egypt, Nigeria, and South Africa. However, the trade patterns for the factors of production within this relatively open world market were often not what we might expect. In particular, the densely populated countries of the East— India, China, and Egypt (counting the cultivable land)—seem to have been net exporters of land and net importers of labor. Table 6.7, for example, shows British India's commodity trade in 1912. The only manufactured good that India exported any quantity of was jute sacking. In the case of cotton the raw material content of India's exports of raw cotton about equaled in value the raw material value of India's imports. Thus India effectively exported its raw cotton to Great Britain to be manufactured there, paying for this with the export of other raw materials. The effective net raw

Table 6.7   The Commodity Trade of British India, 1912–13 (in $ millions)

Commodity	Imports	Exports	Net Exports
Grain, pulse, and flour	0.42	195.64	195.21
Jute, raw	0.00	87.76	87.76
Cotton—raw	7.21	91.20	83.99
Seeds	0.00	73.68	73.68
Hides and skins	0.71	53.11	52.40
Tea	0.23	43.13	42.90
Opium	0.00	36.41	36.41
Oils	16.94	2.78	−14.15
Sugar	46.33	0.00	−46.33
Other raw materials	34.20	64.79	30.58
All raw materials	106.04	648.50	542.46
Cotton—piece goods	195.73	39.58	−156.15
Metals	50.30	3.48	−46.81
Railway plant	20.77	0.00	−20.77
Hardware	17.57	0.00	−17.57
Jute—piece goods	0.00	74.20	74.20
Other manufactures	108.88	5.99	−102.90
All manufactures	393.25	123.26	−270.00

Source: U.S. Department of Commerce, Bureau of Foreign and Domestic Commerce (1915).

material export of India in 1912 was about $460 million. With Indian GDP measured in U.S. prices at about $11.5 billion this implies that exports of raw materials were about 4 percent of Indian GDP. Why was densely populated India poor and agricultural in 1912, as opposed to being poor and industrial?

If we look at the pattern of exports and imports in the cotton industry internationally around 1910 we see other possible anomalies in the pattern of trade. Table 6.8 shows, for example, the flow of manufactured cotton goods internationally. Cotton was the major manufacture in world trade at this time because of its low transport cost relative to price and the existence of a market for yarn and cloth across countries at all income levels. That Argentina, Australia, Canada, and Brazil were net importers of manufactured cotton goods (even though Brazil was a major producer of raw cotton) is entirely expected given that these were land-rich countries. But the substantial importing of cotton goods by densely populated British India, China, and Egypt (all substantial producers of raw cotton) is on the face of it rather puzzling. We turn next to a possible explanation from trade theory for this puzzle.

6.6   The Factor-Content Model

As noted in the introduction, Trefler (1993, 1995) has shown how various forms of generalized versus factor-specific technology differences across countries can be introduced into the HOV model. Such technology differences may help to explain why India was an exporter of land-intensive

Table 6.8   World Trade in Cotton Textiles, 1910 (in $ millions)

	All Cotton Goods	Cotton Yarn	Grey Cloth	Colored Cloth
All Net Exporters				
United Kingdom	453.2	83.4	99.8	270.0
Japan	26.2	22.3	4.6	–0.7
Italy	23.9	4.2	2.9	16.8
France	23.4	–2.7	4.3	21.9
Germany	15.0	–11.3	–2.7	28.9
United States	8.5	–3.5	8.3	3.6
Spain	5.9	0.0		(5.9)
Austria-Hungary	3.4	–4.1	0.2	7.3
The Netherlands	3.2	–13.8	7.5	9.5
Russia	2.7	–4.4		(7.2)
Major Importers				
British India	–100.1	17.8	–53.1	–64.8
China	–80.9	–40.8	–10.6	–29.5
Argentina	–28.6	–2.7	–0.9	–25.0
Australia	–24.8	–2.0	–1.2	–21.6
Ottoman Empire	–19.7	–1.1	–7.4	–11.2
Egypt	–18.2	–1.4		(–16.8)
Canada	–11.6	–1.9	–0.8	–8.8
Brazil	–11.1	–2.5	0.0	–8.6

Source: U.S. House of Representatives (1912, vol. 1, appendix A, 212–18).
Notes: Other large net importers were Romania (–9.9), Chile (–9.3), Algeria (–9.2), British South Africa (–7.7), Venezuela (–4.3), and Bulgaria (–4.3). Numbers in parentheses are those where gray and colored cloth is given together.

goods at the turn of the century. Although this fact is consistent with the sheer size of the Indian subcontinent, it seems inconsistent with her very large population. One resolution of this puzzle would be that each worker in India is less productive than those abroad, so the *effective* population there is smaller than otherwise.

The HOV model expresses trade in terms of the factor content of exports and imports—that is, the amounts of labor, capital, land, and so on embodied in the goods that are traded. That is, the factor content of trade for country c is defined as $F_c \equiv AT_c$, where

- $T_c = Y_c - D_c$ is the ($N \times 1$) vector of net exports of goods $i = 1, \dots, N$ for country c, where Y_c is production and D_c is consumption;
- $A = [a_{ki}]$ is a ($M \times N$) matrix giving the amount of primary factor $k = 1, \dots, M$ used to produce one unit of production in industry $i = 1, \dots, N$. (This matrix should include the primary factors used both directly and indirectly).[7]

7. If D denotes the ($K \times N$) matrix giving the *direct* requirements of primary factors to produce one unit of output in each industry, and B is the ($N \times N$) input-output matrix for the country, then the total primary factor requirements are computed as $A = D(I - B)^{-1}$.

Focusing on the case in which labor, capital, and land are the primary factors, then $\mathbf{F}_c = (F_{Lc}, F_{Kc}, F_{Tc})$ will have three elements, giving the net exports of these factors for country c. Notice that we have not included a subscript on the matrix $\mathbf{A}$, and because it is difficult to obtain the primary factors requirement for many countries, the convention has been to use $\mathbf{A}$ for a *base* country—say, the United Kingdom. At the same time, we allow for a general pattern of factor-specific productivity differences across countries, so that factor k used in country c has productivity π_{kc}, where these are measured *relative to* the productivity in the base country.

Consistent with the measurement of $\mathbf{F}_c$ using the technology of the base country, Trefler (1995) extends the HOV model to show how the factor-content of trade is related to the *effective* endowments labor, capital, and land, where these are measured in efficiency units π_{kc}. That is, letting $\pi_{Lc}L_c$, $\pi_{Kc}K_c$, $\pi_{Tc}T_c$ denote the effective endowments of the factors in country c, the HOV model predicts that

(6A)
$$F_{Lc} = \pi_{Lc}L_c - s_c \sum_{j=0}^{C}\pi_{Lj}L_j$$

(6B)
$$F_{Kc} = \pi_{Kc}K_c - s_c \sum_{j=0}^{C}\pi_{Kj}K_j$$

(6C)
$$F_{Tc} = \pi_{Tc}T_c - s_c \sum_{j=0}^{C}\pi_{Tj}T_j$$

where $s_c \equiv Y_c/\sum_{j=0}^{C}Y_j$ denotes the share of country c's GDP in world GDP.[8]

To interpret these equations, equation (6A) states that country c will be a net exporter of labor services, $F_{Lc} > 0$, if its effective endowment of labor, $\pi_{Lc}L_c$, *exceeds* its GDP share s_c times the world effective endowment of labor, $\sum_{j=0}^{C}\pi_{Lj}L_j$. Put simply, if country c is abundant in labor (with $\pi_{Lc}L_c/\sum_{j=0}^{C}\pi_{Lj}L_j > s_c$), then it will be a net exporter of labor. A similar interpretation holds for the other factors.

Let us now return to the puzzle: Why was India a net exporter of land-intensive products around the turn of the century? We interpret this statement to mean that if the full factor content calculation were done, India would be found to be a net exporter of land, so that $F_{Tc} > 0$. In addition, we expect that India would be found to be a net importer of either capital, $F_{Kc} < 0$, or labor, $F_{Lc} < 0$. Thus, for India we would write equations (6A)–(6C) as

(7A)
$$\pi_{Lc}L_c - s_c \sum_{j=0}^{C}\pi_{Lj}L_j < 0, \text{ or}$$

(7B)
$$\pi_{Kc}K_c - s_c \sum_{j=0}^{C}\pi_{Kj}K_j < 0, \text{ and}$$

8. More precisely, s_c denotes the share of country c's consumption in world consumption, but this will equal its share of world GDP if trade is balanced for country c.

(7C) $$\pi_{Tc}T_c - s_c\sum_{j=0}^{C}\pi_{Tj}T_j > 0.$$

Depending on whether inequality (7A) or (7B) holds, these taken together with (7C) imply that

(8) $$\frac{\pi_{Lc}L_c}{\sum_{j=0}^{C}\pi_{Lj}L_j} < s_c < \frac{\pi_{Tc}T_c}{\sum_{j=0}^{C}\pi_{Tj}T_j}, \text{ or } \frac{\pi_{Kc}K_c}{\sum_{j=0}^{C}\pi_{Kj}K_j} < s_c < \frac{\pi_{Tc}T_c}{\sum_{j=0}^{C}\pi_{Tj}T_j}.$$

From the second inequality in each set, the effective land endowment of India, relative to the world, must be *at least as large* as its GDP share in order for it to be a net exporter of land. Data on actual endowments of land, and GDPs, will therefore allow us to make some conclusion about the effective productivity of land, along with capital and labor.

We see that just the *sign pattern* of the factor-content of trade is enough to place some bounds on the factor-specific productivity differences in India.[9] To simplify these inequalities, consider the corresponding equations for the United Kingdom (labeled b). We expect that if the full factor-content calculation were done, the United Kingdom would be found to be a net importer of land, so that $F_{Tb} < 0$, and a net exporter of either capital, $F_{Kb} > 0$, or labor, $F_{Lb} > 0$. That is, these inequalities are just the reverse as obtained for India. Recalling that the efficiency of each factor is normalized at unity for the United Kingdom, then we also obtain the reverse inequalities as in equation (8),

(9) $$\frac{L_b}{\sum_{j=0}^{C}\pi_{Lj}L_j} > s_b > \frac{T_b}{\sum_{j=0}^{C}\pi_{Tj}T_j}, \text{ or } \frac{K_b}{\sum_{j=0}^{C}\pi_{Kj}K_j} > s_b > \frac{T_b}{\sum_{j=0}^{C}\pi_{Tj}T}.$$

Now, dividing equation (8) by equation (9), we obtain the final equations,

(10) $$\frac{\pi_{Lc}L_c}{L_b} < \frac{s_c}{s_b} < \frac{\pi_{Tc}T_c}{T_b} \text{ or } \frac{\pi_{Kc}K_c}{K_b} < \frac{s_c}{s_b} < \frac{\pi_{Tc}T_c}{T_b}.$$

To interpret the first set of inequalities, if India is a net importer of labor and exporter of land (and conversely for the United Kingdom), then (a) the relative efficiency of land in India π_{Tc} must be *at least as high as* $(s_c/T_c)/(s_b/T_b)$, that is, their relative shares of GDP compared to land; (b) the relative efficiency of labor in India π_{Lc} *cannot exceed* $(s_c/L_c)/(s_b/L_b)$, that is, their relative shares of GDP compared to labor. Taken together, we conclude that the *efficiency of land relative to labor* in India, π_{Tc}/π_{Lc}, must be *at least as high as* $(L_c/T_c)/(L_b/T_b)$, which is simply (population/acre) in India versus the United Kingdom.

In the next section, we will apply these inequalities to estimate the relative productivity of labor and land in 1910 and 1990. Before turning to these results, it might be useful to contrast the HOV approach with the single-

9. Brecher and Choudhri (1982) also make use of the sign pattern of U.S. trade in 1947 (when it exported both labor and capital) to draw some conclusions.

sector Cobb-Douglas function used earlier in the paper. With the single sector, we were assuming that TFP varied across countries and acted as a driving force behind capital mobility. We ignored the contribution of land to total GDP in modern times. Once we introduce trade data, however, it becomes quite relevant to incorporate trade in agricultural goods, and the amount of land embodied in trade. In our calculations below, we will focus on the labor and land content of trade, while ignoring capital embodied in trade. Thus, we do not need to take any stand on the extent of capital flows between countries, and how this responds to productivity. Rather, we will simply treat the labor and land endowments as exogenous across countries, although differing in their productivities, and use their endowments combined with the factor contents of trade to infer the factor productivities.

6.7   Evidence from the Sign Pattern of Trade

To illustrate these calculations, some data on population, land area, GDP, and their ratios are shown in table 6.9 for 1910 and in table 6.10 for 1990. These are all measured relative to world totals. For example, the figure of 0.36 for GDP/population in India for 1910 indicates that India has 36 percent of the world average GDP per capita. Surprisingly, this number remained much the same in 1990 (dropping just slightly to 0.34), although this finding relies on the fact that we are using the purchasing power parity (PPP)–adjusted GDP values from the PWT. Prices are so low in India that its GDP is 3.5 times higher in the PWT for 1990 than obtained from World Bank data, which convert its nominal GDP to dollars with current exchange rates. In contrast to the roughly constant value for India, most European nations have increased their level of real GDP per capita relative to the world, in some cases nearly doubling their world share. This is consistent with the divergence in income levels described in section 6.2, of course. We also report GDP relative to crop acreage, or crop plus pasture, and these show a mixed pattern between 1910 and 1990—increasing for some European nations relative to the world, but falling for others.

To use these data to estimate the productivity of factors, we focus on India relative to some comparison countries. Choosing the United Kingdom as the initial comparison, we use the first set of inequalities in equation (10). Then their ratio of per capita GDP is shown in the column marked (1) in table 6.11, which provides an *upper bound* to the efficiency of labor in India relative to the United Kingdom. The value of 0.13 indicates that an Indian worker is *less than* 13 percent as productive as his counterpart in the United Kingdom.[10] The ratios of GDP to crop land or crop plus pasture are shown in columns (2) and (3), and provide *lower bounds* to the efficiency of land in

10. Rather than using total population in tables 6.9 and 6.10, we should actually use estimates of the workforce.

Table 6.9 Data on Population, Land, and GDP, circa 1910

Country or Area	Share of Population	Share of Crop Area	Share of Crop + Pasture	Share of GDP	GDP ÷ Population (1)	GDP ÷ Crop (2)	GDP ÷ (Crop + Pasture) (3)
India	0.169	0.114	0.044	0.061	0.36	0.54	1.40
China	0.312	0.079	0.074	0.116	0.37	1.47	1.57
United Kingdom	0.023	0.005	0.005	0.064	2.82	12.57	12.86
Rest of Europe	0.197	0.104	0.054	0.360	1.83	3.45	6.67
Austria	0.004	0.001	0.001	0.007	1.77	5.13	6.22
Belgium	0.004	0.001	0.000	0.010	2.47	14.31	23.04
Bulgaria	0.002	0.003	0.001	0.003	1.23	0.96	2.53
Denmark	0.002	0.002	0.001	0.003	2.25	1.73	4.27
Finland	0.002	0.002	0.001	0.003	1.63	1.43	3.59
France	0.022	0.015	0.009	0.056	2.56	3.63	6.26
Germany	0.036	0.010	0.005	0.089	2.46	8.91	16.56
Greece	0.001	0.003	0.002	0.002	1.30	0.75	0.85
Hungary	0.004	0.004	0.002	0.006	1.53	1.57	3.50
Ireland	0.002	0.001	0.001	0.004	1.71	4.09	3.41
Italy	0.019	0.011	0.005	0.034	1.75	2.97	6.26
The Netherlands	0.003	0.001	0.001	0.007	2.22	9.54	12.18
Norway	0.001	0.001	0.000	0.003	2.27	5.02	11.36
Portugal	0.003	0.003	0.001	0.004	1.31	1.47	4.10
Spain	0.011	0.015	0.006	0.019	1.70	1.27	3.34
Sweden	0.003	0.003	0.001	0.007	2.23	2.60	6.13
Switzerland	0.002	0.000	0.001	0.005	2.41	15.72	9.00

Source: Crop and pasture areas are from the UN Food and Agriculture Organization (1991) and apply to years around 1957.

Table 6.10   Data on Population, Land, and GDP, 1990

Country or Area	Share of Population	Share of Crop Area	Share of Crop + Pasture	Share of GDP	GDP ÷ Population (1)	GDP ÷ Crop (2)	GDP ÷ (Crop + Pasture) (3)
India	0.161	0.117	0.037	0.054	0.34	0.46	1.45
China	0.215	0.067	0.102	0.076	0.35	1.13	0.74
United Kingdom	0.011	0.005	0.004	0.38	3.52	8.30	10.39
Rest of Europe	0.068	0.072	0.033	0.206	3.03	2.87	6.28
Austria	0.001	0.001	0.001	0.005	3.38	4.74	6.84
Belgium	0.002	0.001	0.000	0.007	3.52	11.73	21.63
Bulgaria	0.002	0.003	0.001	0.003	1.65	0.98	2.21
Denmark	0.001	0.002	0.001	0.004	3.70	2.03	6.27
Finland	0.001	0.002	0.001	0.004	3.74	2.10	6.70
France	0.011	0.013	0.006	0.040	3.70	2.98	6.29
Germany	0.012	0.005	0.002	0.046	3.89	8.81	18.67
Greece	0.002	0.003	0.002	0.003	1.80	1.27	1.82
Hungary	0.002	0.004	0.001	0.003	1.43	0.78	2.13
Ireland	0.001	0.001	0.001	0.002	2.47	2.51	1.41
Italy	0.011	0.008	0.003	0.036	3.32	4.34	10.39
The Netherlands	0.003	0.001	0.000	0.010	3.47	15.25	23.50
Norway	0.001	0.001	0.000	0.003	3.97	5.33	15.83
Portugal	0.002	0.002	0.001	0.004	1.99	1.69	4.48
Spain	0.007	0.014	0.006	0.019	2.55	1.34	2.99
Sweden	0.002	0.002	0.001	0.006	3.93	3.26	9.13
Switzerland	0.001	0.000	0.000	0.006	4.39	19.58	13.39

Sources: Crop and pasture areas are from the UN Food and Agriculture Organization (1991); GDP is from the Penn World Tables (5.6).

Table 6.11   Implied Efficiency of Labor and Land, 1910 and 1990

India Relative to Other Country	Efficiency of Labor (upper bound) (1)	Efficiency of Cropland (lower bound) (2)	Efficiency of Cropland + Pasture (lower bound) (3)	Efficiency of Cropland ÷ Labor (lower bound) (4)[a]	Efficiency of (Cropland + Pasture) ÷ Labor (lower bound) (5)[b]
Results for 1910 (using population)					
United Kingdom	0.13	0.04	0.11	0.33	0.85
Finland	0.22	0.38	0.39	1.69	1.75
Germany	0.15	0.06	0.08	0.41	0.58
Sweden	0.16	0.21	0.23	1.27	1.41
Results for 1990 (using population)					
United Kingdom	0.10	0.06	0.14	0.58	1.46
Finland	0.09	0.22	0.22	2.45	2.41
Germany	0.09	0.05	0.08	0.61	0.90
Sweden	0.09	0.14	0.16	1.66	1.85
Results for 1990 (using workers)					
United Kingdom	0.12	0.06	0.14	0.46	1.15
Finland	0.12	0.22	0.22	1.87	1.83
Germany	0.11	0.05	0.08	0.49	0.72
Sweden	0.11	0.14	0.16	1.25	1.39

Sources: Columns (1)–(3) for 1910 (using population) are computed by dividing data in the like-numbered columns for India and each comparison country, from table 6.9. Columns (1)–(3) for 1990 (using population) are computed by dividing data in the like-numbered columns for India and each comparison country, from table 6.10. Columns (1)–(3) for 1990 (using workers) are recomputed from table 6.10 but use the number of workers in each country rather than the population.

Notes: The bounds shown in columns (4) and (5) are valid only if the comparison country is a net importer of land and a net exporter of labor (as embodied in goods). The countries listed above satisfy this for 1910 and 1990, with the exception being the United Kingdom, which is an importer of both land and labor.

[a]Column (2)/column (1).
[b]Columns (3)/column (1).

India relative to the United Kingdom. They give a value of 0.04 or 0.11, implying that a hectare of land in India is *at least* 4 percent as productive (11 percent for crop land) as that in the United Kingdom. Putting together these estimates for labor and land, we obtain the final columns in table 6.11, which show that the efficiency of crop land relative to labor is *at least* 0.33 in India relative to the United Kingdom (or 0.85 for crop plus pasture). Because these values are less than unity, we do not find evidence of factor-specific productivity differences. That is, the trade patterns for India and the United Kingdom, as measured by signs of their factor-content of trade, are consistent with *generalized inefficiency* within India.

One explanation for this finding is the extremely small size of the British Isles, so that when measured relative to population, the United Kingdom is scarce in land compared to India. Another explanation, though, is that the United Kingdom may not have the opposite sign pattern of trade as India, in which case the inequalities in equation (10) do not apply. In fact, using the data of Estevadeordal and Taylor (2001, 2002) circa 1910 and Trefler (1993, 1995) for 1983, it turns out that the United Kingdom is a net importer of *both* land and labor, whereas we presume that India is a net exporter of land and importer of labor. So it makes sense to work with some other European countries that have the opposite sign pattern of trade from India.

Using Estevadeordal and Taylor's (2002a, b) data, we find that there are only three countries that have the opposite sign pattern of trade as India in 1910, being net importers of land (measured by renewable resources) and net exporters of labor: Finland, Germany, and Sweden. These three countries were still net importers of crop land and net exporters of (nonagricultural) labor in 1983, according to the data from Trefler (1993, 1995). Trefler does not report the factor-content of trade for India, but he does include Pakistan, which is a net exporter of crop land and importer of (nonagricultural) labor; we presume that the same sign patterns holds for India. Accordingly, we report results for these three comparison countries in the rest of table 6.11.

Using Finland as the comparison country, we see that the implied efficiency of crop land relative to labor is at least 1.69 in 1910, and that this lower bound has risen to 2.45 in 1990. In this case, there is evidence of *biased technological change,* with land in India becoming increasingly productive relative to labor. To understand where this result is coming from, we note that the ratio of population to crop land in India, relative to the world, has changed little in the century, falling from 1.5 in 1910 to 1.4 in 1990.[11] In contrast, Finland has experienced a larger fall in this ratio, from 0.9 in 1910 to 0.6 in 1990. With fewer persons per acre in Finland, the fact that it re-

---

11. These ratios can be computed by dividing the population and cropland columns within tables 6.9 and 6.10.

mains a *net importer* of land indicates that the productivity of its workers relative to land must be enhanced over time; conversely, the productivity of Indian workers must be falling relative to land.

The results of comparing India to Sweden are similar to those for Finland and indicate that land is more productive than labor in India, and that this differential has been increasing over time. Again, this result can be understood by noting that the ratio of population to crop land in Sweden, relative to the world, has fallen from 1.2 in 1910 to 0.8 in 1990. Despite this, Sweden has remained a net importer of land and net exporter of labor, with the opposite trade pattern in India, so the productivity of Indian workers must be falling relative to land. When using Germany as a comparison country, however, we do not obtain bounds that are tight enough to indicate any factor-specific technological differences with India.

Unfortunately, there are no other countries we can use that have the opposite trade pattern from India. However, to check the robustness of our results, there is one other calculation we can do, at least for 1990: Namely, we can use the number of *workers* in each country, rather than total population, to measure the labor endowment. This is done at the bottom of table 6.11, which can be compared to the results immediately above it.

We can see that using workers rather than population generally reduces our lower-bound estimates of the efficiency of land relative to labor, in columns (4) and (5) of table 6.11. The reason for this is that only about 40 percent of the population in India is economically active workers, whereas this percentage varies around 50 percent for Finland, Germany, Sweden, and other European countries. Recalling that columns (4) and (5) are computed as labor relative to land area, in India compared to each country, we expect these ratios to fall when workers rather than population are used. Nevertheless, it remains true that land is more productive than labor in India relative to either Finland or Sweden. This supports our hypothesis that the unusual trade pattern of India and Pakistan, whereby they are net exporters of land-intensive products both historically and today, is explained by a lower efficiency of labor relative to land in those countries.

6.8   Conclusions

We have shown above that the fundamental cause of the divergence of income per capita experienced since the Industrial Revolution is a difference in the ability of countries to employ the same technology at equal levels of efficiency. Improvements in the mobility of goods and capital fall into relative unimportance when compared to the effects of differences in TFP, both in historical periods and today.

The source of these differences in TFP remains mysterious. In this paper we explore potential methods of testing whether these were generalized efficiency differences, such as would be caused by a lack of knowledge, or managerial ability in poor countries, or whether they were more specifically linked to problems with the efficiency of labor in poor economies. The data we have assembled so far support the hypothesis that labor in India has a lower efficiency than land, with each measured relative to countries with the opposite sign pattern of trade. By comparing countries with opposite trade patterns, both in 1910 and 1990, we ended up with a very small sample: India or Pakistan relative to Finland, Germany, and Sweden. There are two directions our research could go to enlarge this sample and gain more confidence in the results.

First, we could obtain further evidence on relative productivities by using the *magnitude* of trade, rather than just its sign pattern. For modern times these data are available from Trefler (1993, 1995). Indeed, we have utilized the factor-efficiency reported by Trefler to compare Pakistan to a wider range of other countries and to confirm the results reported in table 6.11: For most comparison European countries, Pakistan has a lower efficiency of labor relative to land. This exercise is incomplete, however, without the equivalent comparison for historical periods, and here the data are much harder to obtain. Estevadeordal and Taylor (2002a, b) do not include India (or any other developing country) in their data circa 1910, and in addition, their units of resource endowments are incommensurate with their units for resources embodied in trade. Thus, we have not been able to utilize data on the *magnitude* of trade to estimate factor productivities for historical periods.

A second direction for research is to extend the HOV model we have outlined to incorporate nonhomothetic tastes (some progress along these lines is made by Trefler 1995). The fact that India is a net exporter of land is all the more surprising when we consider that this factor is needed to grow food, which figures so prominently in the budgets of its poorest citizens. In other words, the effective endowment of land is lower than it appears once we subtract that amount that is essential for its large population to survive. This observation can be formalized in the context of the HOV model, to obtain effective endowments of land (and other factors) that adjust for nonhomothetic tastes. We expect that the implied factor productivities that would come out of the resulting HOV equations would show an even *lower* efficiency of labor in India than we have obtained. This would reinforce our conclusion that it is the inefficiency of technology in its use, rather than in its availability, that appears to limit the prospects of poorer countries.

References

Acemoglu, Daron, Simon Johnson, and James A. Robinson. 2001. Reversal of fortune: Geography and institution in the making of the modern world income distribution. MIT, Sloan School of Management, Department of Economics, and University of California–Berkeley, Department of Political Science. Mimeograph.

Boag, George L. 1912. *Manual of railway statistics*. London: Railway Gazette.

Brecher, Richard A., and Ehsan U. Choudhri. 1982. The Leontief paradox, continued. *Journal of Political Economy* 90 (4): 820–23.

Bruland, Kristine. 1989. *British technology and European industrialization: The Norwegian textile industry in the mid-nineteenth century*. Cambridge: Cambridge University Press.

Bureau of Railway Economics. 1915. *Comparative railway statistics: United States and foreign countries, 1912*. Washington, D.C.: Bureau of Railway Economics.

Clark, Gregory. 1987. Why isn't the whole world developed? Lessons from the cotton mills. *Journal of Economic History* 47 (March): 141–73.

De Long, J. Bradford, and Lawrence H. Summers. 1991. Equipment investment and economic growth. *Quarterly Journal of Economics* 106:445–502.

Easterly, William, and Ross Levine. 2000. What have we learned from a decade of empirical research on growth? It's not factor accumulation: Stylized facts and growth models. *World Bank Economic Review* 15:177–219.

Edelstein, Michael. 1982. *Overseas investment in the age of high imperialism: The United Kingdom, 1850–1914*. New York: Columbia University Press.

Estevadeordal, Antoni and Alan M. Taylor. 2002a. A century of missing trade? *American Economic Review*, 92 (1): 383–93.

———. 2002b. Testing trade theory in Ohlin's time. In *Bertil Ohlin: A centennial celebration, 1899–1999*, ed. R. Findlay, L. Jonung, and M. Lundahl. Cambridge: MIT Press, 463–93.

Headrick, Daniel. 1988. *The tentacles of progress: Technology transfer in the age of imperialism, 1850–1940*. Oxford: Oxford University Press.

Homer, Sidney, and Richard Sylla. 1996. *A history of interest rates*. New Brunswick, N.J.: Rutgers University Press.

Investor's India Yearbook. Various years. Calcutta: Siddons and Gough.

Jones, Charles I. 1994. Economic growth and the relative price of capital. *Journal of Monetary Economics* 34 (3): 359–82.

Jones, Charles I., and Robert E. Hall. 1999. Why do some countries produce so much more output per worker than others? *Quarterly Journal of Economics* 116 (1): 83–116.

Lancashire Records Office. Platt Records, DDPSL/1/42/7-25.

Maddison, Angus. 1989. *The world economy in the twentieth century*. Paris: Organization for Economic Cooperation and Development.

Mauro, Paolo, Nathan Sussman, and Y. Yafeh. 2001. Emerging market spreads: Then versus now. Working Paper, Hebrew University.

Morris, Morris David, and Clyde B. Dudley. 1975. Selected railway statistics for the Indian subcontinent (India, Pakistan, and Bangladesh), 1853–1946/7. *Artha Vijnana* 17 (3).

Oliver, Douglas L. 1974. *Ancient Tahitian society*. Vol. 1, *Ethnography*. Honolulu: University Press of Hawaii.

Pamuk, Sevket. 1987. *The Ottoman Empire and European capitalism, 1820–1913: Trade, investment, and production*. Cambridge: Cambridge University Press.

Pomeranz, Kenneth. 2000. *The great divergence: Europe, China, and the making of the modern world economy*. Princeton, N.J.: Princeton University Press.

Prados de la Escosura, Leandro. 2000. International comparisons of real product, 1820–1990: An alternative data set. *Explorations in Economic History* 37 (1): 1–41.

Sachs, Jeffrey D. 2001. Tropical underdevelopment. NBER Working Paper no. 8119. Cambridge, Mass.: National Bureau of Economic Research.

Trefler, Daniel. 1993. International factor price differences: Leontief was right! *Journal of Political Economy* 101 (6): 961–87.

———. 1995. The case of the missing trade and other mysteries. *American Economic Review* 85 (5): 1029–46.

United Nations, Food and Agriculture Organization. 1991. *Production yearbook.* Rome: UN Food and Agriculture Organization.

U.S. Department of Commerce, Bureau of Foreign and Domestic Commerce. 1915. *Special consular reports, no. 72: British India.* Washington, D.C.: GPO.

U.S. House of Representatives. 1912. *Report of the tariff board: Cotton manufactures.* Washington, D.C.: GPO.

Wolcott, Susan, and Gregory Clark. 1999. Why nations fail: Managerial decisions and performance in Indian cotton textiles, 1890–1938. *Journal of Economic History* 59 (2): 397–423.

Comment   Joel Mokyr

The sixty-four-thousand-dollar question is why the West grew rich and the countries that were somehow not like the West did not. Clark and Feenstra document that much of this divergence occurred after 1800. Not enough is known about incomes to be sure if *all* of it occurred after 1800, although in other papers Gregory Clark (2001) has suggested that income in Great Britain at least was already quite high in 1800 and rose little until 1860, which suggests that he may not quite subscribe to the "California School" led by Pomeranz (2000) and Goldstone (2001). These scholars maintain that the great divergence between West and "rest" was a fairly recent phenomenon and that by 1800 incomes were still comparable, at least between western Europe and the Yang-Zi delta. In any case, Clark and Feenstra attribute the difference between Europeans and non-Europeans to differences in productivity, and specifically labor productivity.

This paper is thus yet another installment in the Clarkian search for the Holy Grail of productivity differences. Clark's interpretation of the history of productivity as he has delineated it in a string of brilliant and provocative papers (starting with Clark 1987) is that advanced countries and poor countries faced basically the same kind of technology and had access to the same equipment and capital goods, and that institutions and culture mattered not one whit. And yet, for some reason, labor productivity in these poor countries was only a fraction of what it was in the richer countries. The difference is this mysterious substance that I shall call in his honor "factor C," the nature of which has never been specified. Clark has insisted that the data indicate that there are deep and fundamental differences in TFP be-

Joel Mokyr is Robert H. Strotz Professor of Arts and Sciences and professor of economics and history at Northwestern University, and a member of the board of directors of the National Bureau of Economic Research.

tween different economies, but he refuses even to speculate what the deeper causes might be.

Meanwhile, here is what the paper does: Clark and Feenstra demonstrate, using an array of techniques and data sources, that the poor countries of today were already poor and backward in 1910. Yet, they argue, they were not poor because their capital-labor ratios were lower than they should have been. In fact, the paper assumes that capital markets were efficient enough to roughly equalize rates of return between different countries. Whether that assumption actually holds up or not (their own data seem to cast some doubt on it), I think there is probably good reason to think that capital scarcity was not the *main* reason that the underdeveloped countries of 1910 were poor.

Clark and Feenstra estimate a set of Cobb-Douglas aggregate production functions in which they calculate TFP in a world in which equalized rates of return on capital are imposed as a constraint. In that case the *amount* of capital employed would depend entirely on the efficiency of the economy (since the rate of return is exogenous), and hence differences in capital-labor ratios between poor and rich countries are not a *cause* of poverty but its effect. What this means, of course, is that TFP is the sole determinant of differences in income per capita. In fact, the story as they see it is that capital is proportional to output. Low-productivity countries get punished twice: They get lower labor productivity *and* lower capital-labor ratios. The paradigmatic industry Clark and Feenstra have in mind for their observations in 1910 is railroads, on which they spend quite a bit of time. Measuring capital in terms of railway line per GDP in 1910, they find an approximate proportionality, as they do for more encompassing measures in 1990.

The differences in TFP, the authors argue, are not due to differences in *access to* technology either. It is easier to copy technology and to employ it than to develop it de novo, and they find it hard to believe that lack of access to it could block productivity from increasing. The use of fertilizers, the exploitation of railroads, or the spinning of coarse cotton were all techniques that required little knowledge to be applied, apart from investment in them, and thus could be readily deployed anywhere in the world. The well-documented globalization of the pre-1914 world was instrumental in making this technology more accessible. While Europe and the United States protected themselves by tariffs, the poorer parts were dominated by free-trade-minded imperialist governments and had no such choice. Clark and Feenstra document in some detail the improvement in transportation and communication, and this material is well known and uncontroversial.

Where the paper gets really interesting is where Clark and Feenstra try to measure "efficiency in the *use* of technology." It is not entirely clear what is meant by that, but in some sense it is the mother of all residuals: Once you have accounted for all factors of production *and* for differences in access to technology, this difference in TFP is what is left to explain. For 1910, their test case is the efficiency of railroad transport, presumably a technology that was wholly shared among poor and developed nations. Table 6.5 gives us railroad operating efficiency, an interesting variable, measured as railroad output per worker, per track mile and "overall efficiency" (presumably a weighted average of the two). By the logic of this table, however, not only India had a problem: Austria and Switzerland, hardly third world countries even in 1910, are only half as efficient as the United States and barely better than Japan, and in terms of overall efficiency China actually beats Sweden.

More perplexing, Clark and Feenstra point out that in India, whose railroads are the doormat of this efficiency contest, railroads were run and operated mostly by British engineers and experts. They conclude that "the problem of operating Western technology efficiently in poor countries like India was the main barrier to the spread of this technology." This variable called "operating a technology efficiently," factor C if you will, remains mysterious in nature and leaves the reader dissatisfied. Once or twice they raise the issue of whether the paradox could be caused by some greater failure of "managerial ability." But this, too, remains unresolved.

Instead, they embark on an exercise to see which of the factors of production is responsible for the lower efficiency by examining the relative factor-content of traded goods. India, they point out, is more densely populated than Europe in terms of population per cultivable land, yet it is exporting land-intensive goods. This exercise follows Dan Trefler's technique of elaborating on the Leontief paradox literature, trying to find factor-specific differences in productivity based on the factor-contents of tradables. This discussion is not very easy to follow, in part because the discussion moves somewhat quickly from a three-factor to a two-factor world (presumably because capital is assumed to be equally efficient worldwide, although I wonder why this assumption does not get tested here) and in part because of the need to examine countries that have opposite trade patterns (in terms of their factor-content) from India. These countries both turn out to be Scandinavian. Clark and Feenstra find that Indian land is more productive than Indian labor relative to these countries, and that this gap got worse over the twentieth century. This is, in some sense, a demonstration of comparative advantage, but it also raises the classical Leontief issue of why countries export goods intensive in factors in which they are ostensibly poorly endowed. Clark and Feenstra argue that India had lots of labor, and its labor force was cheap. But that labor force lacked sadly in factor C, which made it so unproductive as to actually make India look like a country relatively rich in land. The source of the differences in TFP, which is to blame for everything, as the authors say, "remains mysterious." It seems fair to say that they obviously spent more ingenuity in posing the issue than in giving us a clue as to how it may be resolved.

I should say from the outset that I do not know the answer either, and that the best one can do is to suggest to the authors where to look a bit more closely. Despite the careful research in compiling and analyzing their data, the paper conveys the impression that the authors decided to ignore the literature on virtually every one of the subtopics they deal with, and just start with a fresh mind. Such a strategy, in some cases, makes sense and I am sure that there are examples in the history of science in which a major breakthrough was attained by a sharp and unbiased mind who did not let the existing literature that was denying the very possibility of the discovery confuse him. Ignoring what has been done before does, of course, mean that there is a certain danger of reinventing a few wheels and providing an audience with a sense of dèja vu, as well as a danger of missing clues that others have noticed.

For instance, there are a few pages in Grossman and Helpman (1991), not cited in this paper, that deal with the issue of the international diffusion of knowledge. They point out that a country gains access to the body of knowledge that has accumulated in the outside world through trade contacts, and that this is how integration into the world economy can promote innovation and growth. They speculate that this access is a function of the *level* of trade, which would be testable given the TFPs computed by Clark and Feenstra. I am not entirely sure that I would really expect the level of trade to be a good proxy for the amount of contact that makes the use of foreign technology more effective, but it seems worth a look.

There is, of course, a large literature on the Leontief paradox. Whether the introduction of human capital into the story resolved the mystery there to his satisfaction or not, I do not know. But the words *human capital* and *skill* do not appear in this paper, which is rather odd. Perhaps education, and the kind of culture that workers get imbued with in some countries to make them work harder and be more conscientious on the job, is a complete canard in the view of the authors, but they need to dismiss it on the basis of more evidence than is supplied here.

Moreover, in the literature there is one publication much similar to this project, namely a small paper published by Bob Lucas (1990). Much like Clark, Lucas has the marvelous ability to pose a very naive and elementary-sounding question to an audience of economists, and then force them to admit that they do not know the answer even though they instinctively feel that they should. Unlike Clark, however, Lucas does have the tendency to suggest answers to these conundrums, and although they are not always convincing to everyone, they seem to be sufficiently so to account for his influence. In this paper Lucas asked a simple question, namely, "Why doesn't capital flow from rich to poor countries?" The dilemma is posed in a similar way to Clark and Feenstra: Start from a simple C-D production function, plug in some stylized numbers, and take a step back: presto, a paradox.

Lucas figured that, given that U.S. output per worker was 15 times that of India, the rate of return to capital should be 15 to the power of the reciprocal of the elasticity of the capital-labor ratio, which comes to 58 times higher in India than it is in the United States. In other words, Lucas asked the same question as Clark and Feenstra with the exactly reversed assumption: Assume TFP is the same between the two countries, and let the entire difference be in the rates of return. If this were even remotely true, capital should flow like mad from rich to poor countries even if the rates of return do not end up being wholly equalized. In fact, Lucas pointed out that there should be no investment in rich countries at all—every penny of investment should flow to poor countries.

Of course, Lucas could have stopped right there and said, well, that's not happening, so there must be a mysterious difference in the productivity coefficient and that's it. But in fact he proceeded in that paper and elsewhere to discuss the quality of labor and human capital, not only in the sense that more educated and better trained workers are more efficient, but also in the sense of cross–labor force externalities by which more educated workers make other workers more efficient. Lucas also worried more about international capital markets than Clark and Feenstra. He pointed out that before 1945, with much of the recipients of capital controlled by imperialist powers, one might have expected the colonialists to behave more like labor-market monopsonists and therefore underinvest in poor countries to keep wages low and reap a rent. He claimed that there is no reason why such monopsonistic power disappeared after 1945, even if it switched from foreigners to locals, but that political independence may have exacerbated capital market imperfections by producing risks of repudiation. Lucas then tried to compute how much of the original gap is explained by these various modifications, and while I cannot say that his methods are less oversimplified than Clark and Feenstra's, his paper does leave less of an aftertaste of "un-resolvedness."

My point, then, is not to argue that Lucas's approach is superior to the one here, but rather that if they had gone back and compared their methodology with his, they might have nuanced and qualified some statements and perhaps left us with a few more clues as to where the resolution might lie. This is also true, mutatis mutandis, for another piece of recent scholarship, although one using a very different methodology, namely Amsden (2001). There are some ideas in that book that might suggest to the authors where some of the clues to their riddle might lie. In a chapter alliteratively entitled "Tribulations of Technology Transfer," Amsden details the many complexities in adopting Western technology, the many things that can go wrong, and why seemingly similar forces could lead to very different productivity outcomes. By pointing to the important implicit or "tacit" component of technology, she is actually suggesting a new and important role for human capital and a possible clue to what factor C may be. Here Clark and Feenstra could do worse than to read more in the work of historians of technology. One of those, Rachel Laudan (1984, 6–7), points out that technological knowledge is tacit knowledge, that rules of performance cannot be fully spelled out, and that effective transmission requires personal contact. In her view, this can go a long way toward explaining why technology transfer from inventor to follower country so often fails. To be sure, the tacit component in technology has been declining as codifiability has increased, but because many techniques have become more complex, the total amount of tacit knowledge may not have been. To understand codified knowledge, one needs a "book of codes," and even if the book of codes is explicit, one needs a higher order code to read that one, and so on (Cowan and Foray 1997).

Such tacit knowledge transfers poorly from society to society, certainly more poorly than cotton-spinning equipment, railroad cars, or bags of synthetic fertilizer. Even if the British ran much of the Indian railroads, their local unskilled workers and small station managers were still obviously at an early stage of learning to decode English technology and management. Hence, perhaps, the appalling productivity performance of Indian railroads. Yet some of these firms were essentially Western enclaves managed by westerners, and thus in some sense they should have performed well. One wonders if a study of productivity by firms would yield that foreign-managed firms performed better than native-managed. In 1913, out of 162 Indian cotton factories, 30 were managed by Europeans and 132 by Indians. Did this make a difference to productivity? If not, the role of human capital is of course amplified, and the fact that an Indian worker in 1950 had 1.4 years of schooling as opposed to about 11 years for their U.K. and U.S. counterparts has a lot to account for.

I have never fully understood what schools *precisely* did that made people more productive. Lucas sighs that we "need a more refined view of human capital than one in which five day-laborers equal one engineer" or, I would add (if Clark and Feenstra are correct), in which five Indians equal one Briton. I would suggest that we distinguish between the *education,* the *training,* and the *drilling* aspect of child conditioning. It seems that insofar as schools educated people to think for themselves and to appreciate cultural matters, we may discount their importance for productivity. This kind of education, after all, leads to the creation of independent thinking, perhaps the emergence of novel ideas, but the benefits of those were soon spread to the entire world. Training was more important, since it taught people to decode technical information and thus facilitated their learning in the arena where most of the training took place, which was of course on the job. Drilling and social conditioning may have been more important than either one of those, since they directly affected the absorption of tacit knowledge. In the end, they may have had the largest impact on productivity. Even Amsden does not explicitly make this point, yet the existence of a motivated, disciplined, and punctual labor force may be one of those bridges between culture and measurable productivity that does not collapse the moment you set foot on it.

At the end of the day, the authors will ultimately have to agree that the knowledge to operate and maintain equipment does not move freely and effortlessly across boundaries, even if the capital goods themselves do. There is a deep difference between the knowledge needed to invent or design a new machine and the knowledge required to build it on a routine basis. These are in turn different from operating and maintaining it. Thus there is a very different knowledge base required to design a bicycle, to repair one, and to ride one. To actually carry out a technique, a firm needs something we might call "competence" to set it apart from the concept of "knowledge," which is used to invent or design a technique. This competence, the literature in management science tells us, is neither free nor uniformly distributed.

Clark and Feenstra do not have much time for the notion that *institutions* had an important impact on the outcome of this game. In the Clark-Feenstra world, law and order rule, property rights are enforced, contracts are honored, and governments do nothing at best. Eventually, however, economists will come around to recognizing that institutions do more than just that: They actually help determine the motivation and loyalty of workers, the honesty of managers and bureaucrats, the reliability of consultants and experts, and the willingness of the labor force to submit itself to whatever it takes to get to the productivity levels attained elsewhere. An interesting attempt in this direction was provided recently by Parente and Prescott (2000).

Without considering institutions, Clark and Feenstra's paper faces a deep problem. After all, Mexican or Indian workers migrating to high-productivity economies do not bring their factor C with them. They leave it behind at home. That suggests that it is neither cultural nor racial, but something deeply embedded in the societies whence they come. That, perhaps, is what we mean by institutions.

References

Amsden, Alice. 2001. *The rise of the "rest": Challenges to the West from late-industrializing economies.* New York: Oxford University Press.

Clark, Gregory. 1987. Why isn't the whole world developed? Lessons from the cotton mills. *Journal of Economic History* 47:141–73.

———. 2001. The secret history of the Industrial Revolution. University of California–Davis, Department of Economics. Manuscript.

Cowan, Robin, and Dominique Foray. 1997. The economics of codification and the diffusion of knowledge. *Industrial and Corporate Change* 6 (3): 595–622.

Goldstone, Jack A. 2002. Efflorescences and economic growth in world history: Rethinking the "rise of the West" and the Industrial Revolution. *Journal of World History,* 13 (2): 323–89.

Grossman, Gene, and Elhanan Helpman. 1991. *Innovation and growth in the global economy.* Cambridge: MIT Press.

Laudan, Rachel, ed. 1984. *The nature of technological knowledge: Are models of scientific change relevant?* Dordrecht, the Netherlands: D. Reidel.

Lucas, Robert E. 1990. Why doesn't capital flow from rich to poor countries? (The "new" growth theory). *American Economic Review* 92 (May): 92–97.

Parente, Stephen L., and Prescott, Edward C. 2000. *Barrier to riches.* Cambridge: MIT Press.

Pomeranz, Kenneth. 2000. *The great divergence: China, Europe, and the making of the modern world economy.* Princeton, N.J.: Princeton University Press.

Globalization in History
A Geographical Perspective

Nicholas Crafts and Anthony J. Venables

7.1 Introduction

Globalization is about the changing costs of economic interactions across distance and the effects of these changes on the geographical distribution of economic activity. Technical change has been driving the costs of interactions steadily downward for many centuries, although policy interventions have sometimes raised them. Changes in the economic geography of the world economy have been more complex. There have been periods when activity has become more unevenly distributed across space, and periods when these spatial differences have narrowed as activity has spread from established centers into other regions and countries.

The mechanisms driving these changes were, among other things, easier movement of people, capital, and goods—"globalization." But why did the location of economic activity evolve in the way it has? Why did the world not develop some quite different economic geography, with different centers of production, or with activity more evenly distributed? Many factors are important, but in this chapter we highlight the role of geography. This includes the "first-nature" geography of oceans, rivers, mountains, and endowments, although our focus will be mainly on the "second-nature" geography of the spatial interaction between economic agents. The essence of globalization is that it changes these spatial interactions.

Most traditional analyses are based on economic models in which there are diminishing returns to most activities. Thus, migration tends to reduce

Nicholas Crafts is professor of economic history at the London School of Economics. Anthony J. Venables is professor of international economics at the London School of Economics.

The authors thank the conference participants, particularly Richard Baldwin and Jeff Williamson.

the wage in the host country, and an increase in manufacturing output encounters increasing costs. We argue in this paper that it is not possible to interpret several of the most important aspects of economic development in such a framework. An alternative is provided by models of "new trade theory" and "new economic geography" in which market imperfections at the micro level can give rise to increasing returns at a more aggregate level. The balance between increasing and decreasing returns in these models depends crucially on spatial interactions (determining, for example, the extent of the market) and changes in these interactions can have major effects. Globalization can trigger cumulative causation processes that cause uneven development to occur at a variety of different spatial levels—urban, regional, and international.

Our objective in this paper is to apply this new approach to several aspects of the historical experience of globalization. We proceed in three stages. First we sketch out some of the facts about the changing location of activity and the way that spatial interactions between economic agents changed over time. There were dramatic falls in the costs of moving goods, people, and information, occurring particularly from the 1870s onward. The falling costs were associated with large increases in trade relative to income, narrowing of international price gaps, and increases in migration flows. Second, we outline theoretical approaches to thinking about the consequences of these changes. One approach is the neoclassical model of production and trade, in which production is determined by factor endowments, technological differences, and the freeness of trade. We contrast this with a new economic geography approach, in which locations derive some of their comparative advantage from scale, and ability to exploit scale is in turn limited by the extent of the market. In this approach firms seeking profitable locations will be drawn to locations with good market access and proximity to clusters of related activities, as well as locations with appropriate factor endowments. We show that this alternative view provides a broad-brush picture that, in many respects, seems consistent with the historical record.

We then turn to look in more detail at several historical episodes. From the nineteenth century we focus on the rise of New World economies and the development of urbanization. We confront the central issue of early twentieth-century economic history, namely how the United States came to overtake other regions, and argue that insights from new economic geography can shed important light on this change. From the late twentieth century we revisit the East Asian "miracle," the most spectacular shift of the center of gravity in the world economy since the rise of the United States.

In pursuing the theme that geography matters for economic development we are consciously swimming against the tide of recent work both in economic history and in growth economics. Economic historians, notably in the new institutional economic history (North 1990), have stressed the impact of incentive structures on investment and innovation and have argued that divergence stems from the path dependency of institutional arrangements. Endogenous growth models also tend to underline the centrality of microeconomic foundations for growth outcomes (Aghion and Howitt 1998), whereas neoclassical growth economists still believe in ultimate (twenty-first-century) convergence, following a post–Industrial Revolution interlude of divergence due to lags in the diffusion of best practice institutions, policies, and technology (Lucas 2000). Our position is that these conventional wisdoms are significantly modified by taking into account the way that changing costs of distance interact with economies of scale to shape the economic geography of the world.

A stylized version of this alternative perspective can be outlined as follows. If trade costs are very high then economic activity must be dispersed, whereas if trade costs are very low then firms will not care whether they are close to markets and suppliers. At intermediate levels of trade costs, however, the likelihood of agglomeration is high. Agglomeration forces operating through linkages across a wide range of activities will cause the world to divide into an industrialized rich center and deindustrialized poor periphery even if there are no differences in institutional quality or economic policy. Over time a number of mechanisms, including falling trade costs and growing world demand for manufactures, will make a new location outside the center become competitive, so industry moves there and it now benefits from agglomeration effects. Following the initial agglomeration phase, development therefore takes the form of enlargement of the set of countries in the center. This is not a process of steady convergence of poor countries to rich ones but rather the rapid transition of selected countries (close to or with good transport links to the center) from the poor to the rich club.

7.2   Location and Trade Costs: The Historical Record

In 1750 more than 50 percent of the world's industrial output was produced in China and India, compared to some 18 percent in Western Europe. The following eighty years saw the Industrial Revolution, with western Europe's industrial output more than doubling and that of the United Kingdom increasing by a factor of 7. Over the same period, industrial production in China and India continued to increase (by around 20 percent). It is not our purpose to analyze the origins of the Industrial Revolution but instead to study the changing economic geography of the world from this point on. The technological changes that resulted from the industrial revolution, notably in the form of the harnessing of steam power, not only raised European industrial output but also facilitated large reductions in both inland and ocean transport costs associated with the coming of the railroad and the steamship.

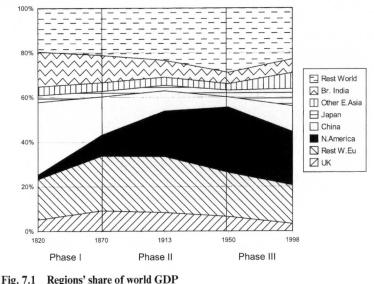

Fig. 7.1   Regions' share of world GDP
Source: Maddison (2001).

7.2.1   Location of Production: The Three Phases

Figure 7.1 shows the shares of world gross domestic product (GDP) attributable to major regions of the world economy at selected dates from 1820 onward, and figure 7.2 gives shares of industrial production for the same regions from 1750 on. Three main phases are apparent in both figures, although they are more pronounced for industrial production than for GDP as a whole. The first phase is the rise of the United Kingdom and western Europe as a whole and the dramatic collapse of China and India from these start dates through to the latter part of the nineteenth century. This period saw not only a decline of industrial production in China and India relative to the rest of the world but also an absolute fall such that 1830s levels were not regained until the 1930s (Bairoch 1982). The second phase is the rise of North America. Its share of world GDP and industrial output increased most rapidly from the American Civil War to the start of the Great Depression, peaking shortly after World War II. The third phase is revealed in the data for 1998 but has its origins in the postwar "golden age" of growth, namely, the large and rapid increase in the shares of Japan, China, and other East Asian countries in world GDP and industrial output.[1]

These phases correspond first to a concentration of activity in the United Kingdom and northwestern Europe (phase I), and then to two different

---

1. A complementary perspective on geographic aspects of catch-up and convergence is set out in Dowrick and DeLong, chapter 4 in this volume.

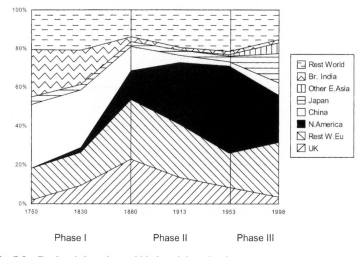

Phase I   Phase II   Phase III
Fig. 7.2   Regions' share in world industrial production
Sources: Bairoch (1982); UN (1965); UNIDO (2001).

phases of dispersion, first to North America (phase II), and then to parts of Asia (phase III). Figure 7.3, which reports shares of world population, underlines the tendencies toward concentration, especially in industrial production, which became apparent during and after the nineteenth century. Whereas in the 1820s China and India accounted for a little over half the world's population and a little under half of world GDP and industrial production, by 1913 western Europe and North America, with about one-fifth of the world's population, produced over half of world GDP and nearly three-quarters of world industrial output. By 1998, with a rather smaller share of world population, these countries still accounted for well over half of world industrial output, whereas China and India, with over 40 percent of world population, produced only about 8 percent of industrial output.

Figure 7.4 reports manufacturing exports (from 1876–80 onward). Here there is evidence of even more concentrated activity. In the late nineteenth century the United Kingdom looms very large with over a third of all exports, even though only representing about 2.5 percent of world population. It was then superseded as the world's leading exporter by the rise of North America, which accounted for over a quarter of manufactured exports in 1955 with only about 6 percent of world population. (Europe looks large in the figure relative to the United States, essentially because intra-European trade is reported, in contrast to intra-U.S. trade). The remarkable feature of the last decades of the twentieth century was the rise of Chinese, Japanese, and other East Asian manufactured exports, representing a real breakthrough for newly industrializing countries.

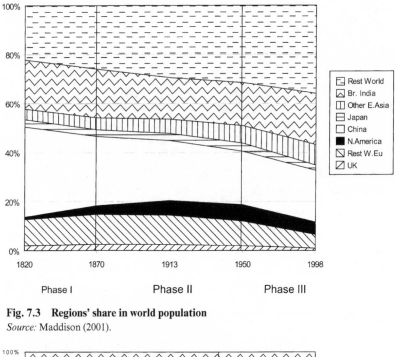

Fig. 7.3 Regions' share in world population
Source: Maddison (2001).

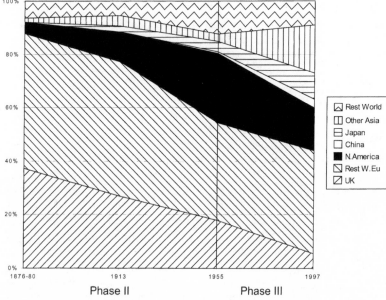

Fig. 7.4 Regions' share in world manufactured exports
Sources: UNCTAD (1983, 2000); Yates (1959).

Table 7.1   **Real Costs of Ocean Shipping (1910 = 100)**

Year	Cost
1750	298
1790	376
1830	287
1870	196
1910	100
1930	107
1960	47
1990	51

Sources: Derived using Dollar (2001), Harley (1988), and Isserlis (1938).

7.2.2   The History of Transport Costs

Although distance remains a barrier even at the start of the twenty-first century, the continuing communications revolution has been one of the most outstanding features of the last 200 years. Table 7.1 reports on the cost of ocean shipping for selected years since 1750. The period between 1830 and 1910 emerges as the era of very substantial decreases, and by the late twentieth century ocean shipping rates in real terms were about one-sixth of the level of the early nineteenth century.[2]

Ocean shipping is only a small part of the story, however, especially for the nineteenth century. This was also a period of spectacular declines in inland transport costs, which between 1800 and 1910 fell by over 90 percent (Bairoch 1990, 142). After World War II, however, new modes of transport became important, and by 1980 the real costs of airfreight had fallen to about a quarter of its level on the eve of World War II (Dollar 2001).

Trends in barriers to trade created by policymakers also need to be taken into account. Here the broad trends are well known even though details are sometimes elusive. The estimate of the unweighted world average tariff rate given by Clemens and Williamson (2001) and illustrated in figure 7.5 rises from about 12 percent in 1865 to 17 percent in 1910. In the interwar period, at a time when transport costs had ceased falling, trade wars pushed the Clemens-Williamson tariff rate up to 25 percent at its 1930s peak, and, in addition, quantitative trade restrictions proliferated, affecting perhaps 50 percent of world trade (Gordon 1941). After World War II, the Clemens-Williamson tariff rate is in the 12–15 percent range, where it remains until the 1970s, after which it falls to a low of 7–8 percent in the late 1990s. The quantitative restrictions of the 1930s and 1940s among the Organization for Economic Cooperation and Development (OECD) countries were largely removed in the postwar liberalization phase, and despite a revival in the era of voluntary export restraints in the 1970s and 1980s, post–Uruguay Round

2. A much more detailed account of this phenomenon can be found in Findlay and O'Rourke, chapter 1 in this volume.

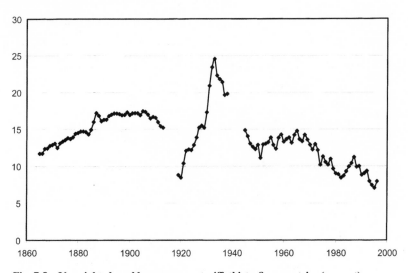

Fig. 7.5   Unweighted world average own tariff, thirty-five countries (percent)
Source: Clemens and Williamson (2001).

Table 7.2   Ratio of World Merchandise Exports to World GDP (%)

Year	Ratio
1820	1.0
1870	4.6
1913	7.9
1929	9.0
1950	5.5
1973	10.5
1998	17.2

Source: Maddison (2001).

these are probably as low as at any time since World War I (Daly and Kuwa-hara 1998).

Concurrent with these changes in trade costs and tariffs have been changes in ratio of foreign trade to world GDP, reported in table 7.2. In the early nineteenth century trade costs are so high and trade volumes so low (around 1 percent of GDP) that, of necessity, most production is located close to local markets. This constraint becomes relaxed through the nineteenth century, permitting the agglomeration of manufacturing to occur. After the reverses of the interwar period, the growth of trade relative to income resumes, again allowing new economic geographies to develop.

Nevertheless, at the beginning of the twenty-first century distance is still a powerful barrier to economic interaction. Gravity modelling finds that,

Table 7.3   Economic Interactions and Distance (flows relative their magnitude at
                    1,000 km)

	Trade	Equity Flows	FDI	Technology
1,000 km	1.00	1.00	1.00	1.00
2,000 km	0.42	0.55	0.75	0.65
4,000 km	0.18	0.31	0.56	0.28
8,000 km	0.07	0.17	0.42	0.05

Sources: See text.

controlling for the economic mass of the countries concerned, trade between them falls off steeply with distance. The elasticity of trade flows with respect to distance is typically estimated to be between –0.9 and –1.5, and the implications of this for trade volumes are given in the first column of table 7.3, which expresses trade volumes at different distances relative to their value at 1,000 km. With an elasticity of –1.25, trade volumes at 4,000 km are down by 82 percent, and by 8,000 km they are down by 93 percent. Similar methodologies have been used to study other sorts of economic interactions, and some results are summarized in remaining columns of table 7.3. Portes and Rey (1999) study cross-border equity transactions (using data for fourteen countries accounting for around 87 percent of global equity market capitalization, 1989–96), and their baseline specification gives an elasticity of transactions with respect to distance of –0.85, so that flows at 8,000 km are less than one-fifth those at 1,000 km. Foreign direct investment (FDI) flows are studied by Di Mauro (2000), who finds an elasticity with respect to distance of –0.42. The effect of distance on technology flows has been studied by Keller (2000) who looks at the dependence of total factor productivity on research and development (R&D) stocks for twelve industries in the Group of Seven (G7) countries, 1971–95. The R&D stocks include both the own-country stock and foreign country stocks weighted by distance.[3] Both own- and foreign-country stocks are significant determinants of each country's productivity, and so too is the distance effect, with R&D stocks in distant economies having much weaker effects on productivity than do R&D stocks in closer economies, so that the effect at 8,000 km is only 5 percent of its effect at 1,000 km.

7.3   Location and Trade Costs: Theory

How have the changing costs of spatial interactions shaped the geography of world economic activity? In this section we show how theory suggests that declining costs can explain the observed phases of concentration and of dispersion.

---

3. Distance weighting according to $\exp(-\theta \, \text{distance}_{ij})$.

7.3.1 The Location of Activity

Two sorts of considerations determine the structure of production and level of income of a country or region. One is its internal capacity, its endowment of stocks of factors of production, skills, knowledge, and social infrastructure. The other is its relationship with other countries or regions—its geography, meaning the access that it has to world markets and to external supplies of goods, factors, and knowledge.

Traditional trade theory's analysis of location focuses heavily on the endowments of primary factors of production. Special cases of the approach are the Heckscher-Ohlin trade model (with equal numbers of goods and factors) and the specific factors or Ricardo-Viner model, with more factors than goods. Both models show how, given world prices, the production structure and income of each country are determined, with countries tending to export goods intensive in their abundant factors. What are the predictions of these models about the effects of globalization? The first is that goods trade liberalization allows countries to exploit their comparative advantage more fully that we expect to see land-abundant countries becoming increasingly specialized in agricultural products, and so on. The second prediction derives from the fact that factor mobility and goods trade are, in general, substitutes. This means that goods trade liberalization reduces factor price differences between countries and thereby reduces the incentives for migration and capital movements.[4] Conversely, factor mobility will in general reduce trade flows, as factors flow to countries where they are relatively scarce, and thereby reduce the cross-country endowment differences that are the basis of trade.

The traditional approach is based on constant returns to scale in production, whereas new trade theory and new economic geography are based on increasing returns within the firm, and possibly in the economy more widely. The analysis focuses on the location decisions of firms and workers. Drawing on developments made in trade theory in the 1970s and 1980s, manufacturing production is modeled as distinct increasing returns to scale firms operating in imperfectly competitive markets (usually monopolistically competitive). There is intraindustry trade, as firms—subject to transport costs and trade barriers—sell their products into each market. What determines whether a country is profitable place for a firm to locate? As in traditional theory, factor prices and factor supplies matter. So too does geography, because firms seek to locate close to large markets and to good sources of intermediate input supply. The fact that locations with good market access are particularly attractive means that these locations will typi-

---

4. See Markusen (1983) and Venables (1999) for discussion of the issue of whether trade liberalization and factor mobility are substitutes or complements.

cally have a disproportionately large share of manufacturing firms and can support substantially higher wages than remote regions.[5] Two implications follow from this. The first is that size matters: A location with a large market will tend to draw in manufacturing activity, possibly bidding up the wage in the location. The second implication follows from combining this with labor mobility. If labor is mobile between locations, then the higher wage will attract labor inflow, enlarging the market still further. This interaction between firms wanting to locate in large markets and demand from their workers enlarging the market provides the basis for a process of cumulative causation leading to spatial concentration of activity. Krugman (1991b) shows how, if transport costs are low enough, mobile factors will agglomerate in just one location.

Although labor mobility can provide a basis for agglomeration of activity, it is not a necessary condition for it to occur. Much of the demand for firms' output comes not from final consumers but from other firms that purchase intermediate goods and services. Thus, as downstream firms move to a location they enlarge the market for upstream firms, and as upstream firms move they increase the supply and lower the price of intermediate goods. This interaction can create cumulative causation and clustering of linked industrial activities in a location (Venables 1996). The process is no more than the interaction of forward and backward linkages that received so much attention in the development literature of the 1960s, and whose origins date back (at least) to Marshall (1920), in whose words

> Subsidiary trades grow up in the neighbourhood, supplying it with implements and materials, organising its traffic, and in many ways conducing to the economy of its material . . . [T]he economic use of expensive machinery can sometimes be attained in a very high degree in a district in which there is large aggregate production of the same kind. . . . [S]ubsidiary industries devoting themselves each to one small branch of the process of production, and working it for a great many of their neighbours, are able to keep in constant use machinery of the most highly specialised character, and to make it pay its expenses.

The contributions of the new literature are to identify circumstances under which these linkages will lead to clustering of activity and the extent to which they support wage differences between locations. As we will see, outcomes depend critically on the level of trade costs, so clustering occurs at some levels of trade costs, and dispersion at other levels.

Other forces too can give rise to spatial clustering of activity, and we note

5. The implications of good market potential for production are sometimes called the "home market effect." Davis and Weinstein (1997) find considerable empirical support for it. Wage implications of market access are studied in Redding and Venables (2000). The advantages of coastal regions and other geographical factors in developing countries are documented in Gallup, Sachs, and Mellinger (1999).

just two further mechanisms, drawing on Marshall's treatment. His second clustering force is a thick labor market:

A localized industry gains a great advantage from the fact that it offers a constant market for skill. Employers are apt to resort to any place where they are likely to find a good choice of workers with the special skill which they require; while men seeking employment naturally go to places where there are many employers who need such skill as theirs and where therefore it is likely to find a good market. The owner of an isolated factory, even if he has good access to a plentiful supply of general labour, is often put to great shifts for want of some special skilled labour; and a skilled workman, when thrown out of employment in it, has no easy refuge.

This—while undoubtedly important—has received much less attention in the modern literature, although see Krugman (1991a) for a rudimentary model.

The third mechanism is geographically concentrated technological externalities:

The mysteries of the trade become no mystery; but are as it were in the air. . . . Good work is rightly appreciated, inventions and improvements in machinery, in processes and the general organisation of the business have their merits promptly discussed; if one man starts a new idea, it is taken up by others and combined with suggestions of their own; and thus it becomes the source of further new ideas.

This idea is applied in much of the regional and urban literature (see, e.g., Henderson 1974), as well as in some older trade literature (Ethier 1979). It is perhaps best viewed as a black box for a variety of difficult-to-model yet important proximity benefits.

7.3.2   History of the World?

Once these clustering forces are put in a full general equilibrium model of trade and location, what happens, and what predictions are derived for the effects of globalization? A sweeping view of world history is provided by the model by Krugman and Venables (1995) that studies the effects of falling trade costs on industrial location and income levels. Their model has just two countries (N and S), endowed with the same quantities of internationally immobile labor. There are two production sectors: perfectly competitive agriculture, and manufacturing. Manufacturing has increasing returns (modeled as monopolistic competition) and forward and backward linkages (modeled as firms using manufactured products as well as labor to produce output for use by other firms as well as for final consumption).

The Krugman and Venables story is summarized in figure 7.6, which has trade costs on the horizontal axis and real wages in N and S on the vertical axis. At very high trade costs the two economies have the same wage rates

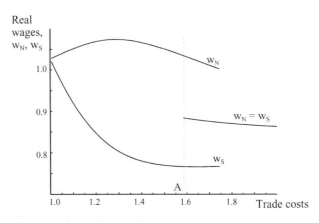

Fig. 7.6   History of the world

($w_N = w_S$), reflecting the fact that they are identical in all respects. The linkages between manufacturing firms create a force for agglomeration, but when trade costs are high these are dominated by the need for firms to operate in each country to supply local consumers. As trade costs fall (moving left on the figure), so the possibility of supplying consumption through trade rather than local production develops, and clustering forces become relatively more important. At point A clustering forces come to dominate, and the equilibrium with equal amounts of manufacturing in each country becomes unstable; if one firm relocates from S to N then it *raises* the profitability of firms in N and *reduces* the profitability of firms in S, causing further firms to follow. Four forces are at work. By moving to N the firm raises wages in N and increases supply to N consumers, both effects tending to reduce profitability in N. But against this it increases the size of the N market (the backward linkage, creating a demand for intermediates) and reduces the costs of intermediates in N (the forward linkage, offering a supply of intermediates). The last two effects come to dominate, and we see agglomeration of industry in one country, which raises wages in the country with industry, as illustrated.[6]

For a range of trade costs below A, the world necessarily has a dichotomous structure. Wages are lower in S, but it does not profit any firm to move to S because to do so would be to forgo the clustering benefits of large markets and the proximity to suppliers that are found in N. However, as trade costs fall it becomes cheaper to ship intermediate goods; linkages matter less, so the location of manufacturing becomes more sensitive to factor

6. There is a range in which agglomeration (with $w_N > w_S$) and dispersion (with $w_N = w_S$) are both stable equilibriums. See Fujita, Krugman, and Venables (1999) for details.

price differences. Manufacturing therefore starts to move to S and the equilibrium wage gap narrows. In this model, wage gap goes all the way to factor price equalization when trade is perfectly free—the "death of distance."

The relationship between the model and our earlier discussion of the changing spatial patterns of industrial location is apparent. Falling trade costs combined with industrial linkages offer an explanation of both the concentration of manufacturing activity and its dispersion. As trade costs go from very high to somewhat lower levels there is deindustrialization of some regions and widening income gaps—the first phase of concentration of activity. At lower levels of trade costs, industry starts to spread out of established centers to some lower-cost regions.

Of course, the model is stylized, and many extensions are needed if it is to be convincingly linked to the historical record. We discuss some of these extensions in detail in following sections, and outline them here. Most obviously, figure 7.6 assumes international immobility of labor. Labor migration can be an additional force for agglomeration—at the city and regional level, as well as internationally—and was clearly important historically, notably in the nineteenth and early twentieth centuries. We return to this in section 7.4. Also, the story needs to be enriched to include many countries, many sectors, and other clustering mechanisms. If there are many countries then the convergence phase is no longer smooth; it involves an increasing number of locations with industry, rather than steady industrialization of them all. Other clustering mechanisms may interact with trade costs in different ways from the linkages described above. For example, the strength of clustering forces arising from labor market skills is likely to be largely unaffected by trade costs. In sectors where this is important, falling trade costs will not bring about the death of distance, and clusters are likely to remain in place. We take up some of these issues in following sections, and formal analysis of them is undertaken in Fujita, Krugman, and Venables (1999).

7.4   The Nineteenth Century

We have already shown the potential that a geographical approach has for the explanation of one of the three phases highlighted in figures 7.1 and 7.2, namely, the decline—absolute as well as relative—of industrial activity outside the emerging core of northwestern Europe. In this section we want to pursue two further aspects of the nineteenth-century experience in greater detail. One is the rise of the New World, and the other is the growth of urbanization.

7.4.1   The Economic Development of the New World

Following the relative and absolute decline of the Asian economies, the other main change in the economic geography of the nineteenth-century world was the rise of the New World, and within this the particular dominance of the United States. By 1913, the United States was a leading industrial producer and a successful manufacturing exporter. Its industrialization, accomplished behind high tariff walls, was concentrated in the "manufacturing belt" of the northeast, a region with the highest GDP per person in the world. This had not seemed at all probable in 1860, when America's role in the world economy was apparently destined to be that of a large primary products exporter based on an abundant endowment of natural resources.

This prompts two obvious, related questions. First, why did the United States rather than Latin America become the area that overtook the United Kingdom and the rest of Europe in real GDP per person? Second, why did the United States also become the only non-European country to establish a position as a net manufactured exporter? In 1913, while Canada, Latin America, and Oceania had net imports of manufactures to the value of $525 million, $828 million, and $361 million, respectively, the United States had net exports of $368 million and already represented the third largest share in world manufactured exports (Yates 1959).

The contrast with the overall experience of Latin America was marked. The nineteenth century can be seen as a period when Latin America fell seriously behind, although by 1913 its most successful economy, Argentina, had experienced several decades of rapid growth and had an income level greater than many European countries. Even so, Argentina had failed to match the United States over the course of the nineteenth century from a position of near parity of incomes per head in 1800 (Coatsworth 1998). Latin America as a whole, which accounted for slightly more of world GDP than the United States in 1820, produced only 4.5 percent in 1913, compared with 19.1 percent for the United States and fell from a level of GDP per person of 52.9 percent that of the United States in 1820 to 28.5 percent in 1913.

Recent interpretations of these developments by economic historians have stressed the differing role of institutions and rent-seeking in North and South America and the political economy configurations from which they emerged. North, Summerhill, and Weingast (2000) pointed to the unfortunate legacy of the ending of Spanish colonialism and an associated failure to establish secure political foundations for economic growth in Latin America; they contrasted this outcome with the aftermath of British rule in the United States, which resulted in a constitution with strong protection of property rights. They see this as the crucial difference: "No deus ex machina translates endowments into political outcomes. If that were so, Argentina would be as rich as the United States" (2000, 19).

Engerman and Sokoloff (1997) also argued that institutions made all the difference to development outcomes between Latin and North America but placed their emphasis on the role of initial factor endowments in creating institutional divergence that exhibited path-dependent tendencies. Interestingly, one of the ways in which their story plays out is through different implications for labor inflow with small family farms in North America conducive to good institutions and greater equality of wealth and political power which underwrote both rapid growth and high immigration.

Similarly, David and Wright (1997) have pointed to several highly favorable aspects of American institutions and policies for the exploitation of abundant resources that led to American primacy in the minerals-based, resource-intensive technology that was central to technological progress in the early twentieth century. These included promoting education and scientific research in relevant disciplines, subsidizing transportation, and organizing geological surveys and sustaining minerals property rights but without claiming government entitlement to royalties. Organized thus, American endowments promoted a technological trajectory that no European country could emulate.

We have no wish to dispute these claims, but we do suggest that it is important that they are placed more firmly in a geographic context. In particular, we believe that size and increasing returns to scale mattered. Table 7.4 displays some information on the size of the United States compared with other leading New World economies and the United Kingdom. In addition, we disaggregate the United States into the northeast and other regions. It is clear that, by 1870, when international transport costs began to fall rapidly, the United States was already a very large economy.

Indeed, at that time, the United States had almost matched the United Kingdom in terms of total GDP, and its population was nearly a third larger. The population of the United States by then already exceeded that of the whole Latin American and Caribbean area defined by Maddison (2001), and its GDP was well over three times larger. Relative to the other individual economies of the New World the United States was in a completely different league in terms of the size of its economy. This was also true, however, for the northeast, which taken separately matched the United Kingdom in terms of GDP per person around 1880 and for population by about 1900. This region already had 29.5 percent of the labor force in manufacturing in 1870, rising to 38.7 percent by 1910 (Perloff et al. 1960), far ahead of any New World country and approaching British levels of industrialization.

The growth of the New World economies was boosted by massive factor flows from the Old World. Declining costs of transport, together with rising incomes in a world relatively free of immigration restrictions, encouraged large international migration. Between 1870 and 1910 this augmented the New World labor force by 40 percent while at the same time reducing the Old World labor force by 13 percent. The impacts on labor force size in some individual countries were much larger—for example, an increase of 86 percent in Argentina and a fall of 45 percent in Ireland—while the U.S. inflow amounted to 24 percent and Great Britain's outflow to 11 percent of the 1910 labor force (Taylor and Williamson 1997). The ratio of foreign as-

Table 7.4   **Population, GDP, and GDP per person, 1870 and 1913**

	1870	1913
Population (in thousands)		
Argentina	1,796	7,653
Australia	1,770	4,821
Canada	3,781	7,852
United States	40,241	97,606
Northeast	21,609	49,193
Rest of country	18,632	48,413
United Kingdom	31,393	45,649
GDP (in millions of 1990 international dollars)		
Argentina	2,354	29,058
Australia	6,452	27,552
Canada	6,407	34,916
United States	98,374	517,383
Northeast	65,615	320,004
Rest of country	32,759	197,379
United Kingdom	100,179	224,618
GDP per person (in 1990 international dollars)		
Argentina	1,311	3,797
Australia	3,645	5,715
Canada	1,695	4,447
United States	2,445	5,301
Northeast	3,036	6,505
Rest of country	1,758	4,077
United Kingdom	3,191	4,921
Real Wages		
Argentina	86	101
Australia	169	127
Canada	147	200
United States	165	160
United Kingdom	100	100

Source: Maddison (2001); U.S. regional figures approximated using the data in Perloff et al. (1960) and their definition of the northeast, which comprises the New England, Middle Atlantic, and Great Lakes regions. Real wage comparisons from Williamson (1995, 1998).

sets to world GDP grew from 7 percent in 1870 to 18 percent in 1914, about the same level as in 1980 (Obstfeld and Taylor, chapter 3 in this volume). The United Kingdom was the principal capital exporter, and outflows averaged almost 5 percent of GDP; 34 percent of all British foreign investment went to North America, compared with 17 percent to Latin America (Simon 1968). Further discussion of Old World–New World factor flows from a neoclassical perspective can be found in Lindert and Williamson, chapter 5 in this volume.

7.4.2   Modeling Migration and Development

If we take the drivers of change to be falling transport costs of goods and factor mobility (in particular labor migrations, facilitated by falling costs of moving people), the challenge for a model is to explain the following stylized facts: the continuing wage advantage of North America relative to the United Kingdom and to other New World economies, despite migration flows; the rise of manufacturing in the United States, overturning its apparent comparative advantage in agricultural products; and the failure of manufacturing to develop in other New World economies.

The overtaking of Great Britain by the United States used to be explained in terms of various kinds of market failure in the former. Briefly, these arguments claimed that inefficiencies in the capital market encouraged excessive foreign and inadequate domestic investment, while conservative British firms were slow to adopt new techniques and to diversify into new industries. These claims have, however, failed to stand up to the scrutiny of economic historians using neoclassical economics because it is now recognized that foreign investment was justified in terms of its returns, diversification into new lines of activity was not impeded by the capital market, and choices of technique were rational given British factor costs (Crafts 2002a).

Given the successful use of neoclassical economics to debunk crude claims of British failure it is perhaps not surprising to find that existing studies modeling the development of North-Atlantic economy have been built largely on a comparative advantage trade model. Applications of the Heckscher-Ohlin model are said to have performed well (Hutchinson 2000; Wright 1990). In this tradition, O'Rourke and Williamson (1994) concluded that a calibrated computable general equilibrium (CGE) model of this type allowed a good explanation of trends toward Anglo-American factor price convergence, driven by commodity market integration in the face of falling transport costs and by labor migration. General equilibrium modeling in this tradition by O'Rourke and Williamson (as summarized by O'Rourke 1996) found that over the period 1870–1910 and initial wage gap of 71.2 percent between the United States and the United Kingdom would have been reduced by 34.8 percentage points by migration but raised by 13.7 percentage points by capital flows. The net impact of factor flows would therefore have reduced the gap by 24 percentage points, to which commodity market integration would have added a further 28.5 percentage points. Interestingly, however, instead of narrowing sharply (by 52.5 percentage points) the U.S.-U.K. wage gap decreased by just 5 percentage points (table 7.4).[7]

This last points to American access to sources of productivity improvement not available to the United Kingdom and consequently reveals a serious problem with the neoclassical exoneration of the late Victorian British economy, namely, that it does not have an adequate explanation for American overtaking. Indeed, it might be argued that this is a general difficulty with neoclassical growth economics; in principle, it can readily embrace catching-up and convergence but not changing leadership in a Solovian

7. Or possibly actually widened, depending on data sources used.

world of constant returns to scale and common technology. There are two ways to address this issue in the context of the North-Atlantic economy. The first is to drop the assumption of common technology and argue that the United States developed its own technology (based on cheap raw materials and mass markets) that was not transferable to Europe at this time (Abramovitz and David 1996). This has historical plausibility but may not be the whole story, however. The second, relatively neglected, is to focus on the role that geography played through scale economies and agglomeration benefits. While accepting that localized technical change also mattered, we explore this by undertaking some rather simple formal modeling to draw out the differences between a comparative advantage approach and a new economic geography approach, and to argue that the latter does much better at explaining both the factor-price and the quantity side.

Before developing the models, it is worth recording other voices that have suggested that the traditional neoclassical framework does not encompass an important part of the picture in that economies of scale in manufacturing are ignored. Although this may be entirely reasonable for the pre–Civil War American economy, it is much less appropriate for the later nineteenth century. Both the traditional business history literature (Chandler 1977) and the cliometricians (Cain and Paterson 1986; James 1983) agree that economies of scale in manufacturing between 1870 and 1913 were substantial and pervasive. These were associated with labor-saving and materials-using biases in technological change and were exploited in the context of a large and rapidly expanding domestic market. Moreover, a closer look at trade flows also reveals some limitations of analyses of the Heckscher-Ohlin type. There was already a considerable amount of intraindustry trade prior to World War I, and this was associated with scale economies in labor and materials use (Hutchinson 2000).

Turning to the modeling, let us start with a stylized model of how people and activity relocate between world regions. We suppose that there are three regions, each having the same endowment of land and the same spatial relationship to each other (they are located at vertices of an equilateral triangle). The model is intended to be suggestive of the location of activity between Europe, the United States, and the rest of the New World, but we impose symmetry in order to get to the heart of the economic forces at work. We assume that there are two production sectors, agriculture and manufacturing. The output of both these sectors is tradable, although both are subject to transport costs. Production in agriculture uses labor and land, and manufacturing uses labor and manufactures (as an intermediate good). Sales of agriculture all go to final consumption, but sales of manufacturing go both to final consumption and to meet the derived demand for manufactures from manufacturing industry. The structure of the model is similar to Krugman and Venables (1995) and is set out formally in the appendix.

The experiment that we undertake is to start with an initial position in

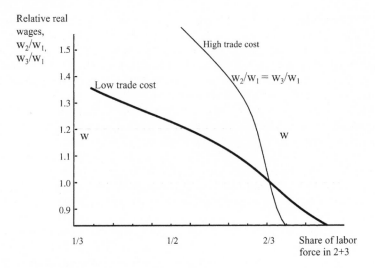

Fig. 7.7   Relative wages in competitive model

which most of the labor force is in region 1 (Europe) and to look at the effects of moving labor out of this region. As it moves we shall assume that it goes to regions 2 and 3 in a way that equalizes real wages in 2 and 3. The idea we seek to capture is that there is out-migration from 1 that is costly, but (in the spirit of our symmetry assumption) the same migration costs are incurred in going to either of the other regions. In the exposition that follows we will talk as if out-migration from region 1 is exogenous. However, we keep track of the real wage gap between region 1 and other regions, so inverting the relationship between the distribution of population and the wage gap shows how a given wage gap (equal to the migration cost) is consistent with a level of population movement.[8]

Globalization and Geography: The Competitive Model

We start with a perfectly competitive variant of the model, in which production in all sectors takes place under constant returns and comparative advantage is determined entirely by factor endowments. The proportion of the world labor force in regions 2 and 3 combined is measured on the horizontal axis of figure 7.7, so that migration is measured by a movement to the right along the figure. On the vertical axis we measure the real wages in regions 2 and 3 relative to region 1 ($w_2/w_1 = w_3/w_1$). The light line is for a case when goods trade costs are high (both agriculture and manufacture face an iceberg transport cost factor of 1.7), and the heavy line corresponds to a lower transport cost factor of 1.25.

8. Migration plays a central role in our story. Further analysis of the economic impact of migration in this period can be found in Chiswick and Hatton, chapter 2 in this volume.

The information contained in the figure is in line with expectations. We see that as long as region 1 is labor abundant (regions 2 and 3 combined have less than two-thirds of the world labor force although each region has one-third of the land), then the wage in regions 2 and 3 exceeds the wage in region 1. Migration narrows the wage gap, as does a reduction in the cost of shipping goods (as in O'Rourke and Williamson 1994). At a given level of migration costs, indicated by the horizontal line *ww*, migration flows are smaller the lower are trade costs, indicating that factor mobility and goods trade are substitutes.

Figure 7.7 is the benchmark case, demonstrating how either factor flows or goods trade liberalization causes factor price convergence. However, in this competitive variant neither region 1 nor region 2 can become a net exporter of manufactures. These regions expand their share of manufacturing only by attracting labor inflow and attract labor inflow only by being land abundant, and hence net importers of manufactures. This means that there is no mechanism in this model by which an economy that initially has a comparative advantage in agriculture can overturn this and become a net exporter of manufacturing. Furthermore, regions 2 and 3 are, in this model, bound to follow identical development paths. Given symmetry in technology, preferences, and endowments, the two regions must have the same outcomes.

Globalization and Geography: The Monopolistic Competition Model

The second variant of the model makes manufacturing monopolistically competitive, containing firms that operate under increasing returns and are subject to forward and backward linkages.[9] The model now predicts a quite different development path, for two main reasons. The first is that market size (as well as factor prices) becomes an important determinant of where manufacturing locates; as we have already seen, if two locations differ only in market size then disproportionately many firms will locate in the larger market. The second reason for the different development path is the propensity of manufacturing to agglomerate, arising because of forward and backward linkages and reinforced by the mobility of labor.[10]

Panels A and B of figure 7.8 give the case when trade costs are relatively high. Like figure 7.7, the horizontal axis measures the combined population of regions 2 and 3. On the vertical axis, panel A of figure 7.8 has relative real wages and panel B has the share of world manufacturing activity in region 2 and in region 3. We see that when the combined population of regions 2 and 3 is small all manufacturing is agglomerated in region 1. The wage in regions 2 and 3 is quite high because of high land-labor ratios, and adding

9. As outlined in the appendix. This is the same structure as in section 7.3.2, except that there are three regions, labor migration is studied, and agriculture, as well as industry, has transport costs and product differentiation.

10. This input-output structure was also present in the perfectly competitive variant of figure 7.6, but the linkages are important only when combined with increasing returns.

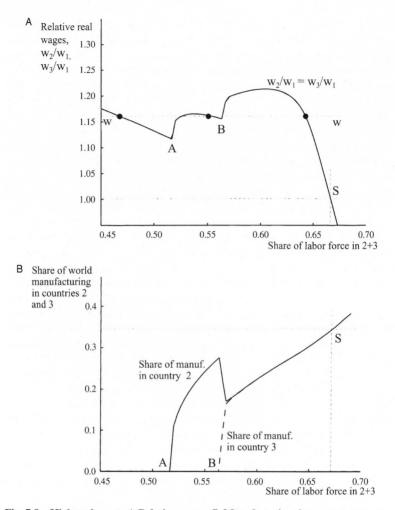

Fig. 7.8   High trade cost: *A,* Relative wages; *B,* Manufacturing shares

more labor reduces the wage gap (like in fig. 7.7). However, as the labor force of regions 2 and 3 increases, the combination of lower wages and larger market size makes it profitable for manufacturing activity to start in these regions (at point A). Industrialization in both simultaneously is, however, unstable, because if one region got just slightly ahead then agglomeration benefits would make it more profitable, attracting more manufacturing and more labor inflow. If the regions are identical it is a matter of chance which one industrializes, and we suppose that it is region 2, as indicated in panel B. The effect of this is to increase wages, as labor in region 2 is drawn off the land and into manufacturing.

Further labor outflow from region 1 will go predominantly to region 2, but after some point the additional labor in these regions starts to reduce wages again, as well as further enlarging market size. Region 3 then industrializes (at point B), catching up with region 2, and resulting in another increase in relative wages. The relative wage path illustrated in panel A of figure 7.8 can then be understood in terms of labor inflow tending to depress wages as land-labor ratios fall, punctuated by industrialization episodes raising labor demand and wages. We can also use panel A of figure 7.8 to analyze the endogenous migration story. If migration were perfectly free to respond to any wage differential, however small, then labor flows would move the world economy to point S, at which all three regions are identical with the same economic structures and factor price equalization. Alternatively, if we contrive migration costs to be just sufficient to support a wage gap illustrated by the line *ww*, then there are three stable migrational equilibriums (as well as two unstable), as marked by the solid circles. Thus, the equilibriums of industry in just region 1, in regions 1 and 2, or in regions 1, 2, and 3 are all stable equilibriums. However, at this level of migration costs, simple dynamics starting with population concentrated in region 1 would leave the world in the first of these equilibriums, with regions 2 and 3 remaining agricultural.

Panels A and B of figure 7.9 are analogous, but computed for a lower value of trade costs. There are three main differences. First, manufacturing commences in region 2 only when more population has moved to regions 2 and 3; this is because a larger market size is required to offset the effects of more intense import competition from region 1. Second, manufacturing never takes off in region 3—again, because of the more intense import competition it faces; essentially, at this level of transport costs world demand for manufactures can be met from just one or two clusters. Region 2 therefore develops a different economic structure from region 3, with a larger population and higher share of world income. Third, region 2 becomes a net exporter of manufactures, and this occurs at the point at which its share of world production of manufactures exceeds its share of world income (see panel B).

Lower trade costs have the effect of decreasing wages in labor-abundant economies (as in the competitive case, fig. 7.7), and the wage path is illustrated by the heavy line *aa* on figure 7.9, panel A. There is a kink in this curve at the point at which industrialization in region 2 commences, but in the case illustrated this kink occurs when real wages are lower in regions 2 and 3 than in region 1, suggesting that migration would not bring about sufficient labor movement to reach the point at which manufacturing develops. Thus, product market integration has the effect of locking the manufacturing agglomeration into an established center and also, because of the labor demand this creates, of reducing the incentive for out-migration from this center.

The higher wage curves in panel A figure 7.9 offer some responses to this dilemma. The first of these, *bb*, is computed allowing transport costs to fall

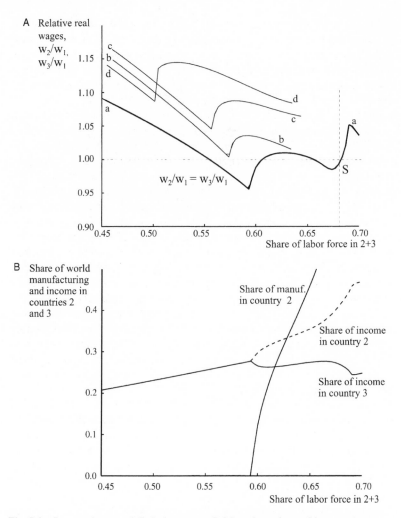

Fig. 7.9   Low trade cost: *A,* Relative wages; *B,* Manufacturing and income shares

concurrently with the movement of labor. Higher trade costs mean higher wages in regions 2 and 3 relative to region 1, thus increasing migration flows and creating a migration path that supports industrialization by region 2 although not by region 3. Thus, the model is able to explain both the asymmetric development of ex ante identical countries and the way in which an economy with initial comparative advantage in agriculture can industrialize and become a net exporter of manufactures.

The next curve, *cc,* introduces (additionally) an asymmetry between regions, letting region 2 have 20 percent greater land endowment than regions

1 and 3. This raises wages and increases the population and market size of region 2, thereby bringing forward the industrialization of region 2, as indicated by the position of the kink in this wage schedule. The final curve, *dd*, illustrates the effect of a region 2 import tariff on manufactures of 10 percent (on top of the different land endowment). When region 2 has no industry this reduces real wages, for the usual reasons of welfare loss associated with tariffs. However, the tariff brings forward industrialization, which in turn raises wages and accelerates the growth of population of the region.

Although these are very stylized exercises, we think that viewing the development of the New World through this lens can offer important insights. As we have seen, it offers an explanation of how one region can industrialize while another does not; of how this region can have its relative wages increase despite population inflow; and of how it can become a net exporter of manufactures despite its initial comparative advantage. The importance of scale effects suggests that open-access migration policies may have mattered much more than is generally acknowledged, and it indicates a potentially more powerful and different role for tariff policies than traditional analyses would allow (Irwin 2000). Given the interrelationship between migration and trade costs, the model also highlights the importance of the timing of the transport improvements that came when migration into the American economy was already substantial and when manufacturing production functions were being transformed. None of this should be taken to negate the insights of those economic historians who have rightly pointed to the role of institutions in growth outcomes, but it might suggest that undue emphasis on property rights is to be avoided.

Finally, in related research, Crafts and Venables (2001) have simulated the development of the North Atlantic economy using a computable general equilibrium model, calibrated to 1870 and 1913 data. This gives results that are consistent with the approach set out here. The competitive variant of the model cannot replicate the large growth of American manufacturing and predicts a large decline in the U.S.-U.K. real wage gap, whereas incorporating increasing returns and linkages in the manufacturing sector largely rectifies these deficiencies. Comparison of results with and without the high American tariffs of the period shows that these had a substantial positive effect on industrialization based on the positive feedbacks associated with the migration that it induced. In nineteenth-century conditions, these results suggest that the United States, starting with an "empty country," gained from employing the opposite of the current OECD policy norm of blocking migration from poorer countries and freeing up trade.

7.4.3   Urbanization

The implications of declining trade costs are felt at the subnational level as well as internationally, and, just as they facilitated concentration of world manufacturing, so they also promoted the development of urban agglom-

Table 7.5   Urbanization Levels (% population, criterion of 5,000 for urban population)

	1800	1850	1910	1980
England	23	45	75	79
France	12	19	38	69
Germany	9	15	49	75
Europe	12	19	41	66
United States	5	14	42	65
Australia	—	8	42	80
Latin America	14	18	22	63
Third world	9	9	10	32

Source: Bairoch (1988, tables 13.4, 29.1).
Note: Dash indicates data are not available.

erations. Urbanization is one of the most dramatic changes in economic geography that occurred during the decades before World War I, and its impact on the location of the labor force far outweighed that of international migration. Whereas about 34 million people emigrated from European countries between 1851 and 1910 (Ferenczi and Willcox 1929), the increase in urban population in Europe and North America totalled 145 million in the same period. Moreover, the number of large cities grew disproportionately: Whereas in 1800 there were 24 cities in the developed world with a population over 100,000, by 1914 this had risen to 281 (Bairoch 1988). Table 7.5 reports the rapid increase in urbanization rates in these countries that contrast with an unchanged urban proportion in the third world.

The hypothesis underlying the growth of urban centers is simple: The division of labor is limited by the extent of the market, and improved transport technologies overcome this, enabling production to take place on a larger scale (and with more division of labor) and enabling cities to form and reap the agglomeration benefits outlined above.

Until recently, there has been surprisingly little formal economic analysis of this hypothesis. The central-place theory of Losch (1954) puts forward the trade-off between returns to scale and transport costs, but its focus is on the optimal lattice of market areas, rather than the equilibrium size and structure of cities. Henderson (1974) broke with these traditions and modeled city size on the basis of technological externalities within industries. But at the same time, he took a strangely aspatial approach, saying nothing about where cities are located, the spatial nature of economic interactions, or the role of transport and communications technologies in enabling city formation. Fujita (1989) developed both an explicit geography and microfoundations for returns to scale.[11] The trade-off between transport costs

---

11. Fujita, Krugman, and Venables (1999) extend this approach. See also Puga (1998) for the interaction of scale economies and transport costs.

and increasing returns means that the real wage that can be paid in a city is a function of its size, and there is in general a unique city size that gives the maximum wage. This wage-maximizing city size depends on transport costs; as transport costs fall, cities will become larger.

In Great Britain, this process became really apparent during the canal era of the late eighteenth century and is epitomized by the growth of Birmingham (Turnbull 1987). Detailed simulation of British experience during the Industrial Revolution reveals that cities were underpinned by an elastic supply of agricultural imports from the rest of the world contingent on the development of an improved commercial and transport infrastructure (Harley and Crafts 2000; Crafts and Harley 2002). For nineteenth-century Europe, regression analysis shows that the major influences on the pace of urbanization across countries were the growth of industrialization, international trade, and agricultural productivity (Bairoch and Goertz 1986). Lowered transport costs and, in particular, new rail facilities facilitated the growth of large cities in nineteenth-century America and gave rise to agglomeration benefits as the costs of moving goods fell. The division of labor was enhanced by increased market size (Ades and Glaeser 1999). Small-scale producers in regions like the midwest were disadvantaged, and manufacturing activities became increasingly spatially concentrated. By 1890, over 25 percent of value added in American manufacturing originated in New York, Philadelphia, and Chicago (Pred 1977).

Although clustering of activities promotes development of cities, there has been debate about the extent to which clustering forces are industry specific or broader. If they are industry specific, then the process of city growth will be accompanied by specialization. High degrees of specialization were indeed an important feature of nineteenth-century cities. In 46 of the largest 100 American cities in 1880, one or two industries accounted for more than 50 percent of manufacturing employment (Kim 2000). In the second half of the nineteenth century large cities were increasingly industrial, and spatial concentration of manufacturing in already large cities was a prominent feature of the industrialization experience.

David's (1989) study of Chicago confirmed that its phenomenal growth was founded on agglomeration effects rather than internal economies of scale. Chicago's success, however, stemmed from a diversified industrial base that suggests that interindustry knowledge spillovers may also have been important, as hypothesized by Jacobs (1969). This is also a strong theme in the account of late nineteenth-century European urbanization by Hohenberg and Lees (1985), who stressed an explosion of knowledge-centered economic growth, and it appears to be borne out by the econometric investigation of English city growth performed by Simon and Nardinelli (1996).

In fact, it appears likely that both industry-specific (Henderson-type) and Jacobs-type external economies of scale were operative in Victorian cities and could be of substantial importance. This is the conclusion reached by Broadberry and Marrison (2002) in an analysis of the British cotton textiles industry on the eve of World War I. They found that both types of external-scale economies were critical to the industry's ability to withstand foreign competition from relatively low-wage producers.

Thus, although we usually think of globalization as occurring at the international level, its driving forces are also important at the subnational level. They promoted the urbanization of the nineteenth-century world, thereby facilitating the division of labor and exploitation of returns to scale associated with industrialization. In addition, it is clear that the experience of nineteenth-century urbanization bears out the value of the new economic geography approach to explaining the location of production.

7.5   The Late Twentieth Century

The interwar period is well known to have been a period of globalization backlash in which there was disintegration of the world economy. This was an epoch of trade wars and international capital controls, and also a time when transport costs ceased to fall. The reconstruction of the world economy after World War II involved a successful liberalization of international trade in manufactures under the General Agreement on Tariffs and Trade (GATT) and a resurgence in international capital mobility, notably from the breakdown in the Bretton Woods fixed exchange rate system in the early 1970s. As table 7.2 reported, the ratio of world merchandise exports to world GDP, which had fallen to 5.5 percent in 1950, rose to 10.5 percent by 1973 and to 17.2 percent in 1998. Foreign assets as a proportion of world GDP, which had fallen to 5 percent in 1945, regained the 1914 level of 18 percent in 1980 and by 1995 had surged to 57 percent (Obstfeld and Taylor, chapter 3 in this volume).

Falling transport and communications costs continued to be a driver of globalization, as table 7.1 suggests. A decline in shipping costs was augmented by several other important developments. One was the development of new information and communications technologies (ICT), the implications of which we discuss in section 7.5.3. Another was the reduction in transit times associated with the development of air travel (and airfreight) and the development of containerization, bringing both faster port handling and faster ocean shipping. The importance of time in transit has been estimated in recent work by Hummels (2000), who finds that the cost of an extra day's travel is (for imports as a whole) around 0.3 percent of the value shipped. For manufacturing sectors, the number goes up to 0.5 percent, costs that are around 30 times larger than the interest charge on the value of the goods. One implication of these figures is that transport costs have fallen much more through time than is suggested by looking at freight charges alone. The share of U.S. imports going by airfreight rose from zero to 30 percent between 1950 and 1998, and containerization approximately doubled the speed of ocean shipping. Together these innovations give a reduction in average shipping time of twenty-six days, equivalent to a shipping cost reduction worth 12–13 percent of the value of goods traded.

The growing value of trade only tells part of the story, because there were also new types of trade developing. The growth of international production networks is reflected in growing volumes of trade in parts and components. Yeats (1998) estimates that 30 percent of world trade in manufactures is trade in components rather than final products. Hummels, Ishii, and Yi (2001) chart trade flows that cross borders multiple times, as when a country imports a component and then re-exports it embodied in some downstream product. They find that (for ten OECD countries) the share of imported value added in exports rose by one-third between 1970 and 1990, reaching 21 percent of export value.

Finally, the period saw the growing role of FDI. Although the world FDI stock showed virtually no growth between 1938 and 1960 (Jones and Schroter 1983) after that it rose rapidly from 5.4 percent of world GDP in 1980 to 14.1 percent in 1998 (World Bank 2000). The vast majority of this capital was in Europe and North America—about 68 percent in 1980 and 63 percent in 1999—but East Asia, not including China or Japan, had 10 percent already by 1980, and China's share had grown to over 6 percent by 1999.

7.5.1 Divergence, Big Time

Traditional neoclassical theories of economic growth predict convergence of incomes based on the catch-up of countries with initially low levels of (broad) capital and output per worker in a world of universally available technology. The empirical application of these ideas has usually been phrased in terms of conditional convergence allowing some role for differences in rates of factor accumulation (Barro and Sala-i-Martin 1995). The actual experience of the world in the twentieth century has, however, been described recently as "divergence, big time" (Pritchett 1997) which is not surprising given the trends reported in table 7.6. Whereas in 1870 income per head in Africa was about one-eighth that in the leading country, by 1998 the ratio was about one-twentieth (Maddison 2001). In 1998, as table 7.6 shows, many of the world's population lived in countries where income levels were a lower percentage of the U.S. level than in 1950. Western Europe and East Asia gained ground relatively, while other countries fell back. This is the pattern of "twin peaks" highlighted by Quah (1997).

A variant on the neoclassical perspective is provided in Lucas (2000). He argues that the divergence of the twentieth century will be reversed because sooner or later every country will join the industrial revolution as best-practice policies and institutions are imitated in hitherto unsuccessful countries and thus the Solovian assumption of "universal technology" be-

Table 7.6   Real GDP per Person Gaps with the United States (United States = 100)

	1950	1998
Western Europe	48.0	65.6
Eastern Europe	22.2	20.0
China	4.6	11.4
Japan	20.1	74.7
Other East Asia	9.6	20.1
British India	6.4	6.1
Latin America	26.7	21.2
Africa	8.9	5.0

Source: Maddison (2001).
Note: In each year the income level is expressed as a percentage of the U.S. level. Regions defined as in figure 7.1.

comes valid: "The restoration of inter-society income equality will be one of the major economic events of the century to come" (Lucas, 166). He bases his prediction on a simple model in which new entrants to the growth process start at $(2 + 2.5n)$ percent per year, where n is the number of fifty-year periods to have elapsed since 1800; thus, a country experiencing take-off in the early twenty-first century will grow initially at 12 percent per year, compared with 7 percent for the 1900 entrant. All countries have an equal chance of joining the growth club with a hazard rate evolving from .01 to .03 over time. This last assumption is clearly contrary to the predictions of the geography school as well as the new institutional economic history.

The new institutional economic historian's perspective provided by North (1990) sees institutions as the key stumbling block. In this view there are no Coasian bargains available to ensure that bad institutions are replaced; rather, the world is one of path dependency, where network externalities, vested interests spawned by the existing arrangements, and informal constraints, embodied in customs, traditions, and codes of conduct that are impervious to deliberate policy reform, hold sway. The economic geography perspective argues that agglomeration benefits dominate the development process such that size and distance matter, as set out in section 7.3.

The evidence of growth regressions certainly suggests that institutions have a strong effect on growth outcomes (Knack and Keefer 1995) and bad institutions remain unreformed in many countries (Kaufmann, Kraay, and Zoido-Lobaton 1999). But recent experience also shows that institutional reform in the third world has delivered a good deal less than followers of growth regressions might have expected (Easterly 2001). This last study found that, taking into account standard conditioning variables, third world growth is strongly influenced by growth in the country's main OECD trading partner. It is also typically the case either that regional dummy variables (East Asia, positive; Africa and Latin America, negative) show up strongly or that justifying their omission requires the inclusion of explicit geographic variables (Gallup, Sachs, and Mellinger 1999). And when income levels are related to measures of market and supplier access, about 70 percent of the variance can be explained in this way (Redding and Venables 2000).

Thus, the world may not be quite the level playing field that the Lucas model supposes. Both institutional and geographic variables affect catch-up growth prospects. The chances of joining the fast growth club appear to be quite uneven. East Asia has succeeded, however. According to conventional wisdom this has been the result of good institutions and policy that have underpinned high rates of capital accumulation and strong productivity performance (World Bank 1993). What does a geographic perspective have to add?

7.5.2   The Spread of Industry

At the heart of East Asian success has been prowess in manufacturing. In section 7.2 we established the growing spread of industry out of established centers and pointed out how exceptional East Asian performance had been, especially in growth of manufactured exports and production.

Conventional treatments suggest that Japan and then the Tigers and China established institutions and policies that were conducive to strong investment in both human and physical capital and facilitated technology transfer. In most cases "developmental states" were involved in jump-starting the development process and in creating institutions that lowered transactions costs in imperfect markets, thus implementing a Gerschenkronian escape from economic backwardness (Crafts 2002b). In particular, these economies were committed to an outwardly oriented growth process in which competition to succeed in world markets held rent-seeking in check (World Bank 1993).

These arguments are well taken, but they are not the whole story. As the development process evolved, aspects consistent with what would be expected from the geographical approach previously outlined play an increasingly important role. If we add many countries to the Krugman-Venables story of figure 7.1, the approach predicts that during phase III convergence will not be uniform but will instead take the form of countries, in sequence, making a relatively rapid transit from the "poor club" to the "rich club." For example, Puga and Venables (1996) modeled a situation of a large number of identical countries, with manufacturing initially agglomerated in just one of them. They considered a steady (exogenous) growth in demand for manufactures, which had the effect of bidding up the wage in the country with the agglomeration. At some point the wage gap between this country and others becomes too large to be sustainable, and industry starts to move to other countries. However, moving to all other countries is unstable, as in figures 7.8 and 7.9; if one country gets just slightly ahead, then cumulative causation causes this one to take off and the others to fall back. The model therefore predicts rapid transit by one country from the poor club to the rich club. Continuing demand growth (as well as falling transport costs) then makes the cycle repeat itself: Industry once again spills out, and another country makes a rapid transit to the rich club. The model was intended to be suggestive of the industrialization experience in Asia, which is illustrated in figure 7.10. The vertical axis of this figure is the share of manufacturing in GDP in selected Asian countries, and the story is very much as predicted by the theory.

In this perspective, the initial success of Japan adds to the development prospects of the rest of East Asia much as the so-called "flying geese" model suggests. As Japanese wage costs rose, particularly from the 1980s, domestic manufacturing investment was discouraged and FDI flowed out to other parts of the region; "hollowing out" of Japanese industry became a noticeable feature (Cowling and Tomlinson 2000). In 1991–95 Japanese investment in Asian manufacturing totalled $22.9 billion, compared with $7.6 billion in 1951–85 (Legewie 1999). East Asian wage costs typically were low relative both to other parts of the world and to the labor productivity gap with the established centers. Thus, even in the mid–1980s labor costs in Korea and Taiwan were only around 10 percent of the American (20 percent of the Japanese level; Jacobs 2000) when manufacturing labor productivity was close to 20 percent of the American level (Timmer 1999) and at a time when African wages were, in most cases, 15 to 25 percent of those in the United States.

The costs of regional transactions fell sharply. As one recent survey put it, both the hardware and software of East Asian linkages improved rapidly; better communications and networks of overseas Chinese both played an important part (Petri 1995). As new economic geography models predict, clustering became apparent (e.g., microcomputers in Taiwan, electronics in Malaysia), and external economies of scale from agglomeration accrued. In a detailed study of Korea, Henderson, Lee, and Lee (2001) found that in the period 1983–93 these were comparable to U.S. experience and that a doubling of an industry's size in a particular city implied a productivity increase of about 6 percent. Japanese FDI has tended to cluster, which also underlines the importance of agglomeration benefits (Head, Ries, and Swenson 1995).

The manufacturing export performance of the newly industrializing Asian countries has been impressive. It cannot be explained, however, within the confines of the traditional Hecksher-Ohlin model, as Lall (1998) showed. The pattern of exports with its strong achievement in high-technology sectors has relied on external economies of scale which accrue from learning and labor market pooling. Undoubtedly, this has been the result in part of good policy, in terms of addressing market failures (for example) through public-private partnerships although not through intersectoral transfers of resources (Crafts 1999); but it seems clear that intra-

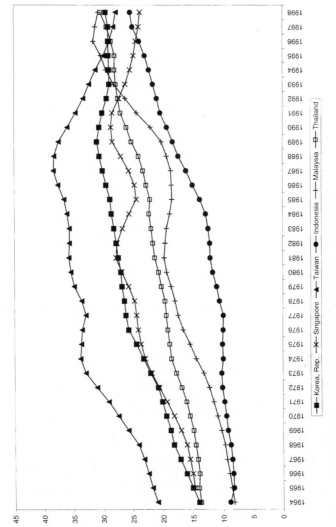

Fig. 7.10   Manufacturing VA share of GDP, five-year moving average
Source: World Bank (2001).

sectoral productivity improvement based on agglomeration benefits has been central to the achievement (Hobday 1995).

7.5.3 New Technologies: The Death of Distance?

We conclude with some remarks about the implications of new technologies for the likely future economic geography of the world. Although the continuing spread of industry—through lower trade costs, easier remote management, and the development of production networks—seems likely, what are the prospects for a more radical change, a "death of distance" whereby technologies will enable suitably qualified countries to operate "as though geography has no meaning" (Cairncross 2001)? Evidently, some activities can now be fully digitized and located and transmitted around the world at essentially zero cost. The best examples are the ICT-enabled services, such as transcription of medical records or cartoon film drawings, that now (with other software services) make up around 10 percent of India's total exports. Although these activities have brought prosperity to some developing regions, it seems unlikely that more than a few percent of world GDP is likely to fall in this category. Activities that become digitizable fall rapidly in price and are likely to be fully automated in time (e.g., by voice recognition software or computer graphics).

Other activities remain tied to markets, or retain a propensity to cluster. Some technical changes seem to increase the value of proximity—for example, the improved stock control and information flows that support just-in-time technologies, and the consequent clustering of suppliers around assembly plants. The importance of access to pools of skilled or specialist labor (one of Marshall's agglomeration forces) is not likely to be significantly diminished, nor the mobility of this labor significantly increased, by new technologies. Indeed, the microfoundations of agglomeration economies for U.S. manufacturing industries now, unlike in the nineteenth century, seem to rest more than any other single factor on labor market pooling (Rosenthal and Strange 2001). The role of cities in reducing transport costs for goods is much less important now, whereas the role that cities play in eliminating the distance between people appears to be growing as time costs increase (Glaeser 1998).

It is quite probable that the growing use of e-commerce will in some cases increase the attractiveness of market transactions relative to vertically integrated production; that is, it will change the optimal boundaries of the firm—for example, by raising the effective number of suppliers of intermediates and reducing the scope for opportunism in the presence of asset specificity. Thus, the classic historical example of vertical integration, the takeover of Fisher Body by General Motors in the 1920s, was reversed in 1999 when the parts division of General Motors became a separate company, Delphi Automotive Systems (Lucking-Reiley and Spulber 2001).

But in an increasingly information-based economy, much information seems to be too complex to be codifiable, so face-to-face contact remains important. Sometimes this is because of the inherent complexity of the information (as in R&D and coauthorship), and sometimes because of incomplete contracting, which requires face-to-face contact for monitoring and for building trust (Leamer and Storper 2001). Indeed, the possibility of spatially separating these activities from more routine parts of the supply process will likely enhance their concentration. For example, in financial services, once the backroom operations can be separated from the front room, then the agglomeration forces on the latter become overwhelming and the attractions of London, New York, and Tokyo are no longer diluted by the expense of office space for clerical activities.

What this suggests, then, is that agglomeration forces—and consequent inequalities in the location of activity and in income levels—are likely to remain important. However, the basis of these forces might change, from the nineteenth-century model of high transport costs for goods and agglomeration of heavy industries, to the twenty-first-century model of agglomeration of information-based activities—in finance, R&D, and entertainment—in cities with pools of highly specialized labor.

7.6   Conclusions

Our aim in this paper has been to show that placing the economic history of the past two centuries in a geographical perspective can add to our understanding of the past experience of economic development and thus to future prospects for income convergence following a long phase of divergence. We have argued that agglomeration has mattered a great deal and will continue to be important. Modeling of the shifting international location of industry is enhanced by including scale economies and linkage effects.

A historical episode in which this approach offers major new insights is the performance of the United States relative both to Great Britain and to Latin America. This cannot readily be encompassed in a traditional neoclassical framework and is not wholly explained by the quality of American institutions. Our analysis highlights the roles played by migration and tariff policies in promoting the industrialization of the United States.

For today's world, recognizing the importance of agglomeration in economic development implies that size and location will continue strongly to influence future relative income levels. Predictions of the death of distance in the new economy based on ICT are premature. However, there are several distinct sources of agglomeration benefits, and in the twenty-first century these are likely to revolve much more around complexities of information and pools of skilled labor than the costs of transporting manufactured goods.

With regard to the issues of catch-up and convergence in economic growth, we have stressed that both the neoclassical growth and the new institutional economic history schools are missing an important dimension. We do not share the optimism of Lucas (2000) that the present century will be one in which international income inequality is eliminated, and we believe that current fashions in economic history are in danger of exaggerating the role played by institutional quality in development outcomes. A geographical perspective suggests that in economic development the playing field is far from level and that recognition of this casts a different light on both past performance and future prospects.

Obviously, this paper is no more than a preliminary analysis. Nevertheless, we hope that it may help to establish a research agenda that can enrich the study of comparative economic development in an imperfectly integrated world economy.

Appendix
The Three-Country Model

There are three countries, and country-specific variables are denoted by subscripts. The two sectors are manufacturing and agriculture, indicated by superscripts. Proportion μ of consumers' expenditure goes on manufacturing, the remainder on agriculture. Within each sector there are differentiated products, and demands are derived from a subutility function (or price index) taking the forms

$$G_j^M = \left[\sum_i n_i^M (p_i^M t^M)^{1-\sigma^M}\right]^{1/(1-\sigma^M)}, \qquad G_j^A = \left[\sum_i (p_i^A t^A)^{1-\sigma^A}\right]^{1/(1-\sigma^A)}$$

where n_i^M is the number of industrial products and each country produces a single agricultural variety; p_i^M and p_i^A are the prices; and t^M and t^A the iceberg transport costs. Values of demand for a product produced in country i and sold in country j are

$$p_i^M x_{ij}^M = \left(\frac{p_i^M t^M}{G_j^M}\right)^{1-\sigma^M} E_j^M, \qquad p_i^A x_{ij}^A = \left(\frac{p_i^A t^A}{G_j^A}\right)^{1-\sigma^A} E_j^A$$

Agriculture is produced by a Cobb-Douglas production function using each country's endowment of land (set equal to 1), and an amount of labor. The labor share in the production function is θ. If L_i and L_i^M denote the total labor force and labor employed in manufacturing, respectively, then agricultural output and the wage are

$$x_i^A = (L_i - L_i^M)^\theta, \qquad w_i = \theta(L_i - L_i^M)^{\theta-1}$$

Manufacturing firms use labor and manufacturing to produce output, with manufacturing share γ. They therefore have price equal to

$$p_i^M = (w_i)^{1-\alpha}(G_i^M)^\alpha.$$

Input demands can be found by Shephard's lemma. In the perfect competition case n_i^M is exogenous, and quantities of each variety are given by demand. In the monopolistic competition case n_i^M is endogenous and adjusts so that each firm makes zero profits. Given an increasing returns-to-scale technology, this occurs when it reaches a certain level of output, x, so we have the additional equation

$$x = \sum_j x_{ij}^M.$$

Expenditure levels come from income (wage income and agricultural rent) and from derived demands, according to

$$E_i^M = \mu[w_i l_i^M + p_i^A(L_i - L_i^M)^\theta] + \alpha n_i^M p_i^M x,$$

$$E_i^A = (1 - \mu)[w_i l_i^M + p_i^A(L_i - L_i^M)^\theta].$$

Real wages are nominal wages deflated by the price index, $(G_i^A)^{1-\mu}(G_i^M)^\mu$.

Results are presented for $\theta = 0.1$, $\mu = 0.3$ and $\alpha = 0.35$, and $\sigma^A = 20$ and $\sigma^M = 20$ (perfect competition) or $\sigma^M = 6$ (monopolistic competition). Trade costs in the two sectors are equal, and the high level of the iceberg factor is 1.8, and the low level 1.475.

References

Abramovitz, Moses, and Paul David. 1996. Convergence and delayed catch-up: Productivity leadership and the waning of American exceptionalism. In *The mosaic of economic growth,* ed. Ralph Landau, Timothy Taylor, and Gavin Wright, 21–62. Stanford: Stanford University Press.

Ades, Alberto F., and Edward L. Glaeser. 1999. Evidence on growth, increasing returns, and the extent of the market. *Quarterly Journal of Economics* 114:1025–45.

Aghion, Philippe, and Peter Howitt. 1998. *Endogenous growth theory.* Cambridge: MIT Press.

Bairoch, Paul. 1982. International industrialization levels from 1750 to 1980. *Journal of European Economic History* 11:269–331.

———. 1988. *Cities and economic development: From the dawn of history to the present.* Chicago: University of Chicago Press.

———. 1990. The impact of crop yields, agricultural productivity, and transport costs on urban growth between 1800 and 1910. In *Urbanization in history,* ed. A. D. van der Woude, A. Hayami, and J. de Vries, 134–51. Oxford, U.K.: Clarendon Press.

Bairoch, Paul, and Gary Goertz. 1986. Factors of urbanization in the nineteenth century developed countries: A descriptive and econometric analysis. *Urban Studies* 23:285–305.

Barro, Robert J., and Xavier Sala-i-Martin. 1995. *Economic growth.* New York: McGraw-Hill.

Broadberry, Stephen N., and Andrew Marrison. 2002. External economies of scale in the Lancashire cotton industry, 1900–1950. *Economic History Review* 55:51–77.

Cain, Louis P., and Donald G. Paterson. 1986. Biased technical change, scale, and factor substitution in American industry, 1850–1919. *Journal of Economic History* 46:153–64.

Cairncross, Frances. 2001. *The death of distance.* Boston: Harvard Business School Press.

Chandler, Alfred D. 1977. *The visible hand.* Cambridge, Mass.: Belknap.

Chiswick, Barry, and Timothy Hatton. 2001. International migration and the integration of labor markets. Paper presented at the National Bureau of Economic Research conference Globalization in Historical Perspective, 4–5 May, Santa Barbara, Calif.

Clemens, Michael A., and Jeffrey G. Williamson. 2001. A tariff-growth paradox? Protection's impact the world around 1875–1997. NBER Working Paper no. 8459. Cambridge, Mass.: National Bureau of Economic Research, September.

Coatsworth, John H. 1998. Economic and institutional trajectories in nineteenth century Latin America. In *Latin America and the world economy since 1800,* ed. John H. Coatsworth and Alan M. Taylor, 23–54. Cambridge: Harvard University Press.

Cowling, Keith, and Philip R. Tomlinson. 2000. The Japanese crisis: A case of strategic failure. *Economic Journal* 110:F358–F381.

Crafts, Nicholas. 1999. East Asian growth before and after the crisis. *IMF Staff Papers* 46:139–66.

———. 2002a. *Britain's relative economic decline 1870–1999.* London: Institute of Economic Affairs.

———. 2002b. The East Asian escape from backwardness: Retrospect and prospect. In *Economic challenges of the twenty first century in historical perspective,* ed. Paul David and Mark Thomas. Oxford: Oxford University Press (forthcoming).

Crafts, Nicholas F. R., and C. Knick Harley. 2002. Precocious British industrialization: A general equilibrium perspective. Working Papers in Economic History no. 67. London: London School of Economics, August.

Crafts, Nicholas F. R., and Anthony J. Venables. 2001. Globalization and geography in historical perspective. Paper presented at the National Bureau of Economic Research Globalization in Historical Perspective. 4–5 May, Santa Barbara, Calif.

Daly, M., and H. Kuwahara. 1998. The impact of the Uruguay Round on tariff and non-tariff barriers to trade. *The World Economy* 21:207–34.

David, Paul A. 1989. The Marshallian dynamics of industrial localization: Chicago, 1850–1890. Stanford University. Mimeograph.

David, Paul A., and Gavin Wright. 1997. Increasing returns and the genesis of American resource abundance. *Industrial and Corporate Change* 6:203–45.

Davis, Donald R., and David E. Weinstein. 1997. Does economic geography matter for international specialisation? NBER Working Paper no. 5706 (revision). Cambridge, Mass.: National Bureau of Economic Research.

Di Mauro, Francesca. 2000. The impact of economic integration on FDI and exports: A gravity approach. CEPS Working Document no. 156. Brussels: Center for European Policy Studies.

Dollar, David. 2001. Globalization, inequality, and poverty since 1980. Washington, D.C.: World Bank. Mimeograph.

Dowrick, Steven, and J. Bradford DeLong. 2001. Globalization and convergence.

Paper presented at the National Bureau of Economic Research conference Globalization in Historical Perspective, 4–5 May, Santa Barbara, Calif.

Easterly, William. 2001. The lost decades: Developing countries' stagnation in spite of policy reform, 1980–1998. *Journal of Economic Growth* 6:135–67.

Engerman, Stanley L., and Kenneth L. Sokoloff. 1997. Factor endowments, institutions, and differential paths of growth among new world economies. In *How Latin America fell behind,* ed. Stephen Haber, 260–304. Stanford, Calif.: Stanford University Press.

Ethier, Wilfred J. 1979. Internationally decreasing costs and world trade. *Journal of International Economics* 9:1–24.

Ferenczi, Imre, and Walter F. Willcox. 1929. *International migrations.* New York: National Bureau of Economic Research.

Findlay, Ronald, and Kevin O'Rourke. 2001. Commodity market integration, 1500–2000. Paper presented at the National Bureau of Economic Research Globalization in Historical Perspective, 4–5 May, Santa Barbara, Calif.

Fujita, Masahisa. 1989. *Urban economic theory: Land use and city size.* Cambridge: Cambridge University Press.

Fujita, Masahisa, Paul R. Krugman, and Anthony J. Venables. 1999. *The spatial economy: Cities, regions, and international trade.* Cambridge: MIT Press.

Gallup, John L., Jeffrey D. Sachs, and Andrew D. Mellinger. 1999. Geography and economic development. *International Regional Science Review* 22:179–232.

Glaeser, Edward L. 1998. Are cities dying? *Journal of Economic Perspectives* 12(2): 139–60.

Gordon, Margaret. 1941. *Barriers to world trade.* New York: Macmillan.

Harley, C. Knick. 1988. Ocean freight rates and productivity, 1740–1913: The primacy of mechanical invention reaffirmed. *Journal of Economic History* 48:851–76.

Harley, C. Knick, and Nicholas F. R. Crafts. 2000. Simulating the two views of the Industrial Revolution. *Journal of Economic History* 60:819–41.

Head, Keith, John Ries, and Deborah Swenson. 1995. Agglomeration benefits and location choice: Evidence from Japanese manufacturing investments in the United States. *Journal of International Economics* 38:223–47.

Henderson, J. Vernon. 1974. The sizes and types of cities. *American Economic Review* 64:640–56.

Henderson, Vernon, Todd Lee, and Yung Joon Lee. 2001. Scale externalities in Korea. *Journal of Urban Economics* 49:479–504.

Hobday, Michael. 1995. *Innovation in East Asia.* Cheltenham, U.K.: Edward Elgar.

Hohenberg, Paul M., and Lynn H. Lees. 1985. *The making of urban Europe.* Cambridge: Harvard University Press.

Hummels, David J. 2000. Time as a trade barrier. Purdue University. Mimeograph.

Hummels, David J., Jun Ishii, and Kei-Mu Yi. 2001. The nature and growth of vertical specialization in world trade. *Journal of International Economics* 54:75–96.

Hutchinson, William K. 2000. United States international trade: Proximate causes, 1870–1910. Paper presented at the American Social Science Association meetings, 7–9 January, Boston.

Irwin, Douglas A. 2000. Tariffs and growth in late nineteenth century America. NBER Working Paper no. 7639. Cambridge, Mass.: National Bureau of Economic Research.

Isserlis, Leon. 1938. Tramp shipping cargoes and freights. *Journal of the Royal Statistical Society* 101:53–146.

Jacobs, Eva. 2000. *Handbook of U.S. labor statistics.* Lanham, Md.: Bernan.

Jacobs, Jane. 1969. *The economy of cities.* New York: Vintage Books.

James, John A. 1983. Structural change in American manufacturing, 1850–1890. *Journal of Economic History* 43:433–59.

Jones, Geoffrey, and H. G. Schroter. 1983. Continental European multinationals, 1850–1992. In *The rise of multinationals in continental Europe,* ed. Geoffrey Jones and H. G. Scroter, 3–27. Aldershot, U.K.: Edward Elgar.

Kaufmann, Daniel, Aart Kraay, and Pablo Zoido-Lobaton. 1999. Governance matters. World Bank Policy Research Working Paper no. 2196. Washington, D.C.: World Bank.

Keller, Wolfgang. 2000. Geographic location of international technology diffusion. *American Economic Review* 92:120–42.

Kim, Sukkoo. 2000. Urban development in the United States, 1690–1990. *Southern Economic Journal* 66:855–80.

Knack, Stephen, and Philip Keefer. 1995. Institutions and economic performance: Cross-country tests using alternative institutional measures. *Economics and Politics* 7:207–27.

Krugman, Paul R. 1991a. *Geography and trade.* Cambridge: MIT Press.

———. 1991b. Increasing returns and economic geography. *Journal of Political Economy* 49:137–50.

Krugman, Paul R., and Anthony J. Venables. 1995. Globalization and the inequality of Nations. *Quarterly Journal of Economics* 110:857–80.

Lall, Sanjaya. 1998. Exports of manufactures by developing countries: Emerging patterns of trade and location. *Oxford Review of Economic Policy* 14 (2): 54–73.

Leamer, Edward E., and Michael Storper. 2001. The economic geography of the Internet age. NBER Working Paper no. 8450. Cambridge, Mass.: National Bureau of Economic Research.

Legewie, Jochen. 1999. The impact of FDI on domestic employment: The phenomenon of industrial hollowing out in Japan. In *Foreign direct investment and the global economy,* ed. Nicholas A. Phelps, 179–99. London: Stationery Office.

Lindert, Peter H., and Jeffrey G. Williamson. 2001. Does globalization make the world more unequal? Paper presented at the National Bureau of Economic Research conference Globalization in Historical Perspective, 4–5 May, Santa Barbara, Calif.

Losch, A. 1954. Reprint. *The economics of location.* English translation. New Haven, Conn.: Yale University Press. Original edition, Jena, Germany, 1940.

Lucas, Robert E. 2000. Some macroeconomics for the twenty-first century. *Journal of Economic Perspectives* 14 (1): 159–68.

Lucking-Reiley, David, and Daniel F. Spulber. 2001. Business-to-business electronic commerce. *Journal of Economic Perspectives* 14 (4): 3–22.

Maddison, Angus. 2001. *The world economy: A millennial perspective.* Paris: Organization for Economic Cooperation and Development.

Markusen, James R. 1983. Factor movements and commodity trade as complements. *Journal of International Economics* 13:341–56.

Marshall, Alfred. 1920. *Principles of economics.* 1890. 8th ed., London: Macmillan.

North, Douglass C. 1990. *Institutions, institutional change, and economic performance.* Cambridge: Cambridge University Press.

North, Douglass C., William R. Summerhill, and Barry R. Weingast. 2000. Order, disorder, and economic change: Latin America vs. North America. In *Governing for prosperity,* ed. Bruce Bueno de Mesquita and Hilton L. Root, 17–58. New Haven, Conn.: Yale University Press.

Obstfeld, Maurice, and Alan M. Taylor. 2001. Globalization and capital markets. Paper presented at the National Bureau of Economic Research conference Globalization in Historical Perspective, 4–5 May, Santa Barbara, Calif.

O'Rourke, Kevin. 1996. Trade, migration, and convergence: An historical perspective. CEPR Discussion Paper no. 1319. London: Center for Economic Policy Research.

O'Rourke, Kevin, and Jeffrey G. Williamson. 1994. Late nineteenth century Anglo-American factor-price convergence: Were Hecksher and Ohlin right? *Journal of Economic History* 54:892–916.

Perloff, Harvey S., Edgar S. Dunn Jr., Eric E. Lampard, and Richard F. Muth. 1960. *Regions, resources, and economic growth.* Baltimore: Johns Hopkins University Press.

Petri, Peter A. 1995. The interdependence of trade and investment in the Pacific. In *Corporate links and foreign direct investment in Asia and the Pacific,* ed. Edward K. Y. Chen and Peter Drysdale, 29–55. New York: Harper Educational.

Portes, Richard, and Helene Rey. 1999. The determinants of cross-border equity flows. NBER Working Paper no. 7336. Cambridge, Mass.: National Bureau of Economic Research, September.

Pred, Allan C. 1977. *City-systems in advanced economies.* New York: Wiley.

Pritchett, Lant. 1997. Divergence, big time. *Journal of Economic Perspectives* 11 (3): 3–17.

Puga, Diego. 1998. Urbanisation patterns: European vs. less developed countries. *Journal of Regional Science* 38:231–52.

Puga, Diego, and Anthony J. Venables. 1996. The spread of industry: Agglomeration in economic development. *Journal of the Japanese and International Economies* 10:440–64.

Quah, Danny T. 1997. Empirics for growth and distribution: Stratification, polarization, and convergence clubs. *Journal of Economic Growth* 2:27–60.

Redding, Stephen J., and Anthony J. Venables. 2000. Economic geography and international inequality. CEPR Discussion Paper no. 2568. London: Center for Economic Policy Research.

Rosenthal, Stuart S., and William C. Strange. 2001. The determinants of agglomeration. *Journal of Urban Economics* 50:191–229.

Simon, Curtis J., and Clark Nardinelli. 1996. The talk of the town: Human capital, information, and the growth of English cities, 1861 to 1961. *Explorations in Economic History* 33:384–413.

Simon, Matthew. 1968. The pattern of New British portfolio foreign investment, 1865–1914. In *The export of capital from Britain 1870–1914,* ed. A. R. Hall, 15–44. London: Methuen.

Taylor, Alan M., and Jeffrey G. Williamson. 1997. Convergence in the age of mass migration. *European Review of Economic History* 1:27–63.

Timmer, Marcel. 1999. *The dynamics of Asian manufacturing.* Eindhoven, The Netherlands: Centre for Innovation Studies.

Turnbull, Gerard L. 1987. Canals, coal, and regional growth during the Industrial Revolution. *Economic History Review* 40:537–60.

United Nations. 1965. *The growth of world industry, 1938–1961.* New York: UN.

United Nations Conference on Trade and Development. 1983. *Handbook of international trade and development statistics.* New York: UN.

———. 2000. *UNCTAD handbook of statistics.* New York: UN.

United Nations Industrial Development Organization. 2001. *International yearbook of industrial statistics.* Cheltenham, U.K.: Edward Elgar.

Venables, Anthony J. 1996. Equilibrium locations of vertically linked industries. *International Economic Review* 37:341–59.

———. 1999. Trade liberalization and factor mobility: An overview. In *Migration: The controversies and the evidence,* ed. Riccardo Faini, Jaime de Melo, and Klaus F. Zimmerman, 23–48. Cambridge: Cambridge University Press.

Williamson, Jeffrey G. 1995. The evolution of global labor markets since 1830:

Background evidence and hypotheses. *Explorations in Economic History* 32:141–96.

———. 1998. Real wages and relative factor prices in the third world before 1940: What do they tell us about the sources of growth? Discussion Paper no. 1855. Harvard Institute of Economic Research.

World Bank. 1993. *The East Asian miracle.* Washington, D.C.: World Bank.

———. 2000. *World investment report.* Washington, D.C.: World Bank.

———. 2001. *World development indicators.* Washington, D.C.: World Bank.

Wright, Gavin. 1990. The origins of American industrial success. *American Economic Review* 80:651–68.

Yates, P. Lamartine. 1959. *Forty years of foreign trade.* London: Allen and Unwin.

Yeats, Alexander J. 1998. Just how big is global production sharing? Policy Research Paper no. 1871. Washington, D.C.: World Bank.

Comment   Richard E. Baldwin

Linking economic geography to the history of globalization is a good and an old idea. Kuznets, Myrdal, and Rostow gave geography and agglomeration forces center stage in their theories, but they lacked tools to formalize the links.[1] These were provided in the early 1990s with the emergence of the so-called new economic geography. This paper by Crafts and Venables applies this new approach to several aspects of the historical experience of globalization. Although this effort is welcome, the outcome falls short of what one could have hoped for given the towering contributions of the authors to economic history on the one hand and economic geography on the other.

In the mid-1990s, Paul Krugman and Tony Venables *formally* showed that "new" economic geography models provided a sweeping account of how falling trade costs and agglomeration forces could explain the broad outline of two centuries of global economic developments (the working title of their paper was "History of the World: Part I"). The basic logic of the Krugman-Venables story sparked great interest, but many found its mapping to historical data disturbingly vague. Crafts and Venables would be the perfect team to shore up its historical underpinnings, but here their paper disappoints; what we get are a few cursory and well-known facts on transport costs and, separately, on global economic activity since the early nineteenth century.

Moreover, the authors focus a good deal of attention on the way economic geography explains how the United States came to overtake other regions in terms of income and output. They note that "following the relative

Richard E. Baldwin is professor of international economics at the Graduate Institute of International Studies, Geneva, and a research associate of the National Bureau of Economic Research.

1. For example, when it comes to Rostow's famous "growth take-off," he writes that it "may come about through a technological (including transport) innovation which sets in motion a chain of secondary expansion in modern sectors and has powerful potential external economy effects which the society exploits" (1960, 36).

and absolute decline of the Asian economies, the other main change in the economic geography of the nineteenth-century world was the rise of the New World, and within this the particular dominance of the United States." This focus on how the United States shouldered the United Kingdom out of the number one spot, combined with a resolute disregard of continental Europe, seems to reflect a very British view of the world.

The nineteenth-century rise of the United States' economy was caused by, and indeed could not have happened without, a growth take-off, so the issue the authors are addressing is really the timing of growth take-offs. Geography clearly has a role to play in explaining the spread of modern growth, but the U.S. experience must be seen in a broader context. The emergence of modern growth, which is intimately associated with industrialization, first occurred in Great Britain in the late eighteenth century (Crafts 1995). After a significant delay of a few decades, modern growth began in a series of other economies—all of which are close to the United Kingdom in terms of transport costs. Belgium, France, and the United States experienced industrialization and modern growth in the 1830s and 1840s, with Germany, Sweden, Austria, Italy, Russia, and Canada joining in the mid- to late 1800s. Keeping in mind that sea transport was much more efficient than land transport for much of this period, the centrality of geography in this nineteenth-century saga just leaps off the page. The authors' concentration on why the United States rather than Latin America became the area that overtook the United Kingdom looks distinctly odd. Indeed, Puga and Venables (1996) have a nice model of the spread of industrialization, which could have—with the straightforward addition of knowledge spillovers and endogenous growth—been usefully applied to study the role of geography in this key growth/industrialization question. This is just one example of the contributions that this pair of authors could have made.

Grand Unified Theory of Globalization and Geography

Perhaps the biggest missed opportunity in this paper concerns what might be called the grand unified theory of globalization and geography. All the elements are lying around in the literature; Crafts and Venables would have been the perfect pair to put them together. Before sketching out what this might have looked like, allow me to stylize the main facts of globalization since the mid-nineteenth century.

Globalization's Five Famous Facts

The world has seen two waves of globalization: one from roughly 1850 to 1914, and one from the 1960s to the present. At a high level of abstraction the key facts are as follows:[2]

---

2. This section draws on Baldwin and Martin (2000), available as an NBER working paper or at [http://heiwww.unige.ch/~baldwin/].

- *Industrialization/deindustrialization.* In the first wave, the "North" (Western Europe and the United States) industrialized while the South (especially India and China) deindustrialized. In the second wave, the South (East Asia) industrializes while the North deindustrializes.
- *Divergence.* The first wave saw North and South incomes diverge massively, whereas the second wave witnesses a convergence, at least between the North and the industrializing South.
- *Trade.* International trade in goods and factors (labor migration and long-term capital flows) exploded in the first wave. After being shut down by two world wars, a surge of protectionism, and the Great Depression, the second wave has been marked by a return of trade and capital flows to levels that have recently topped those seen in Victorian England. Mass international migration, however, remains small by the standards of the first wave.
- *Growth take-off.* Some time before the first globalization wave kicked in, the Industrial Revolution triggered modern growth in the North, but the South continued to stagnate in per capita terms. Modern growth—that is, a self-sustained growth process whereby output per hour worked rises steadily year by year—began in the United Kingdom but spreads to western Europe and the United States around the middle of the nineteenth century. Of course, this is not independent of the income divergence since big differences in income levels come from sustained differences in growth rates—not from one-time shifts of the location of industry. Moreover, the limited income convergence in the second wave is linked to spectacular growth in the industrializing South and a moderate slowdown in the North.
- *Urbanization.* Whereas some of the largest cities in the world were in the South prior to the nineteenth century, the first globalization wave is accompanied by a rapid and historically unprecedented urbanization in the North. Northern urbanization continued during the second wave, but cities grew even more rapidly in the South.

Accounting for the Facts: Economic Geography's Say

The Krugman-Venables history of the world sews together the first three of the five facts. Here it is. In 1750 or so, the world's economic geography was quite homogenous—that is, poor and agrarian. With domestic and international trade costs nearly prohibitive, each village essentially had to make all its own goods; this meant manufactured goods were dear and the available range of varieties limited. As trade costs fell, both inside and between nations, specialization became feasible, and this triggered a process of what Myrdal (1939) called "cumulative causality." Modeling this circular-causality process is the heart of the new economic geography's contribution, so an aside is in order. Migration of firms or workers dehomogenizes the world, turning it into economically big and small regions (markets). When industries are imperfectly competitive and trade is costly,

Krugman's "home market effect" favors the location of industry in large regions, but since industries are marked by increasing returns, getting a disproportionate share of industry means a region's labor is disproportionately productive, and this in turn results in higher real wages, a higher return to capital, or both. The circle is closed by noting that capital and labor are attracted to the region with higher rewards, and their migration makes the big region bigger and the small region smaller.

According to Krugman and Venables, advances in transport technology in the early nineteenth century triggered this dehomogenization of the world's economic geography, and, as history would have it, the North won at the South's expense. This single event is the root cause of the first three facts: Northern industrialization and Southern deindustrialization, the rapid expansion of international trade (England becomes the world's workshop, providing cheap and varied manufactured goods in exchange for raw materials, and this specialization both fosters trade and is fostered by it), and income divergence (due to increasing returns in industry and decreasing returns in other sectors, a high share of industry in GDP means high labor productivity and thus high incomes).

One problem with this story is that the magnitudes just do not fit. One-time concentrations of industry just cannot account for the observed income gaps. Here is the argument. Krugman and Venables ignore endogenous technological progress, assuming that physical technology is identical in the North and South. Thus, in the Krugman-Venables story, the difference in incomes between the United Kingdom and India must be due to the difference in industry's share in the U.K. and Indian output mix and the productivity gap between industry and traditional sectors. If the United Kingdom's per capita income was 100 in 1850, India's was 23 according to Maddison (1995, tables C16 and D1), so the income gap to be explained is 77. Moreover, Crafts (1989, 417) tells us that in 1840, 47 percent of the U.K. workforce was in industry, and Bairoch (1982, table 9) tells us that India was only 4.7 percent as industrialized as the United Kingdom in 1860, so (ignoring the mismatch in dates) we can conclude that the static allocation of industry can only account for the income difference if industrial workers are 171 times (i.e., 17,100 percent) more productive than workers in the traditional sector.

This just cannot be right. Plainly, the real story must lie elsewhere, and growth is the obvious suspect. Indeed, since the headline story in the nineteenth century was the spread of modern growth, the Krugman-Venables story is a bit like Hamlet with the Prince. Clearly, one has to add endogenous growth to the Krugman-Venables story to account for the facts on income divergence and convergence as well as on growth take-offs.

Adding Endogenous Growth to Economic Geography Models

Fortunately, the literature combining economic geography and growth models is fairly well developed (see, e.g., Baldwin and Forslid 1997; Martin and Ottaviano; 1999; and Baldwin 1999). Indeed, Baldwin, Martin, and Ottaviano (2001) have used this combination of geography and growth to account for the first four of globalization's five famous facts.

The basic idea is quite simple and turns on the fact that transporting ideas—as well as goods—is expensive, so that learning spillovers tend to be localized geographically. Starting in the Krugman-Venables phase I, where transporting goods is expensive and industry is thinly spread, growth does not occur because the dispersion of industry prohibits a virtuous learning and innovation cycle from starting. As the transport cost of goods falls, industry—and thus learning—gets geographically concentrated. Due to localized technological spillovers, industrial agglomeration in the North implies that the South has no incentive to invest and innovate, while the incentive to innovate in the North increases. In this way, industrial agglomeration not only generates industrialization and a growth take-off in the North, but it also produces a massive income divergence.

Now, as we move on to the second wave of globalization, we presume that the cost of transporting goods asymptotes toward some natural limit, but additionally, and importantly, we assume that the cost of trading ideas decreases. At some point, this generates a rapid industrialization in the South because the South is more easily able to benefit from historical innovation in the North and more easily able to access Northern markets. The emergence of southern industry slows global growth somewhat (since it disperses learning) and forces a relative deindustrialization in the North.

The only facts left unaccounted for concern urbanization. To get this into the story, one would have to allow internal geography in the regions considered (Baldwin, Martin, and Ottaviano follow Krugman and Venables in assuming that regions are just points in space), but once the technical difficulties were mastered, the economics would be straightforward. In the first wave of globalization, economic activity characterized by localized spillovers is concentrating in the North. It would not therefore be too surprising that urbanization proceeded faster in the North than in the South during this era. Likewise, in the second wave of globalization, the industrialization of the South (emergence of the Asian tigers, etc.) strengthens the forces that foster within-South concentration of economic activity (i.e., urbanization), while the deindustrialization of the North does the opposite.

These comments have, I hope, illustrated that the Crafts-Venables paper is a small first step in what should prove a very fruitful direction for research.

References

Bairoch, P. 1982. International industrialization levels from 1750 to 1980. *Journal of European Economic History* 2: 268–333.

Baldwin, R. 1999. Agglomeration and endogenous capital. *European Economic Review* 43 (2): 253–80.

Baldwin, R., and R. Forslid. 1997. The core-periphery model and endogenous growth: Stablising and de-stablising integration. *Economica* 67 (3): 307–24.

Baldwin, R., and P. Martin. 2000. Two waves of globalisation: Superficial similarities and fundamental differences. In *Globalisation and labour,* ed. H. Siebert, 3–59. Tubingen, Germany: Mohr.

Baldwin, R., P. Martin, and G. Ottaviano. 2001. Global income divergence, trade, and industrialization: The geography of growth take-offs. *Journal of Economic Growth* 6 (1): 5–37.

Crafts, N. 1989. British industrialization in an international context. *Journal of Interdisciplinary History* 19 (3): 415–28.

———. 1995. Exogenous or endogenous growth? The Industrial Revolution reconsidered. *Journal of Economic History* 55 (4): 745–72.

Krugman, P., and A. Venables. 1995. Globalisation and inequality of nations. *Quarterly Journal of Economics* 60: 857–80.

Maddison, A. 1995. *The world economy: 1820–1992.* Paris: OECD Development Centre.

Martin, P., and G. Ottaviano. 1999. Growing locations: Industry location in a model of endogenous growth. *European Economic Review* 43 (2): 281–302.

———. 2000. Growth and agglomeration. *International Economic Review* 42 (4): 947–68.

Myrdal, G. 1939. *Monetary equilibrium.* London: Hodge.

Puga, D., and A. J. Venables. 1996. The spread of industry: Spatial agglomeration in economic development. *Journal of the Japanese and International Economies* 10 (4): 440–64.

Rostow, W. W. 1960. *The stages of economic growth: A non-communist manifesto.* Cambridge: Cambridge University Press.

III

Financial Institutions, Regimes, and Crises

8

Financial Systems, Economic Growth, and Globalization

Peter L. Rousseau and Richard Sylla

What is the relationship between a country's financial development and its economic growth? And how do a country's financial development and economic growth relate to the extent of its participation in the global economy? In particular, is there a relationship between domestic financial development and participation in global capital markets? Few would doubt that countries with highly developed financial systems might well export capital to other countries. But are there conditions under which having such a system might also promote imports of capital? These are the broad questions that motivate our paper.

To address the questions and attempt to answer them, we draw on insights from two bodies of research that have developed independently of one another, but that in our view are quite related. One includes the work of economic historians on the development of financial systems—especially banking systems—in various countries, and the impact of financial developments on economic growth within those countries. Also included in this historical work is a vast body of literature on aspects of globalization: cross-border financing and capital flows, international banking and financial crises, and the integration of the world's money and capital markets. Among economic historians, these two strands of literature, one dealing with domestic and the other with international developments, are not al-

Peter L. Rousseau is associate professor of economics at Vanderbilt University and a research associate of the National Bureau of Economic Research. Richard Sylla is the Henry Kaufman Professor of the History of Financial Institutions and Markets, professor of economics at the Leonard N. Stern School of Business at New York University, and a research associate of the National Bureau of Economic Research.

The authors thank Michael Bordo, Charles Calomiris, and conference participants for their helpful comments and suggestions.

ways related to one another. Both, however, are elements of the story of financial globalization.

The other body of research on which we draw is the work of contemporary economists on the relationship between measures of financial development and such variables as the growth of real per capita income and investment. Typically these are cross-country analyses based on models of the finance-growth nexus for the postwar period, when broadly consistent data for a large number of countries at varying levels of economic development became available. They are the economists' equivalent of the economic historians' comparative studies of national financial and banking systems and their relationship to economic growth. They do not say much about financial globalization.

Our goal here is to integrate and extend these two bodies of existing research, the historical and the economic, in a longer-term investigation of financial globalization during the past two centuries. Our operating hypothesis is that countries with well-functioning financial systems have one of the conditions, perhaps a key one, conducive to economic growth *and also* a set of institutions that give confidence to foreign investors and thus promote financial globalization by allocating the world's capital more efficiently.

We begin with a discussion of what we mean by a good or well-functioning financial system (section 8.1). Next (section 8.2) we develop several historical case studies of countries that built such systems early in their modern economic histories: the Netherlands, Great Britain, the United States, France, Germany, and Japan. For each case, we consider when and how a modern financial system emerged, how it contributed to economic growth, and what relationship it had to the country's participation in international finance. With some lessons of financial history drawn from the cases in mind, we then investigate, in the context of a larger set of countries for which we have data covering the period from the middle of the nineteenth century to the present, the finance-growth nexus, and the finance-growth-globalization nexus. This one-and-a-half-century period encompasses two eras of economic globalization that others have identified, that of the late nineteenth and early twentieth centuries, and that of the late twentieth century extending now into the twenty-first century. After discussing data sources and methodological considerations (section 8.3), we present and discuss our econometric results (section 8.4), and conclude (section 8.5).

8.1   What is a Good Financial System?

History appears to indicate that a good financial system is one that has five key components. These components are (a) sound public finances and public debt management; (b) stable monetary arrangements; (c) a variety of banks, some with domestic and others with international orientations, and perhaps some with both orientations; (d) a central bank to stabilize domestic finances and manage international financial relations; and (e) well-functioning securities markets.[1] Such an articulated financial system, once it is in place and functioning, can mobilize capital domestically and thereby promote a country's economic development and growth. In a financial globalization context, it can also serve, either directly by the facilities it offers or indirectly by enhancing growth prospects, to attract the interest of foreign investors.

To place our vantage point here in perspective, we make two comments. First, academic specialization being what it is, contemporary scholars and those of previous generations often focus their attention on one or a subset of the components. Some economists are public finance experts, whereas others study money, banking, and central banking. Securities markets and company finance are usually the provinces of finance departments in business schools. Even economic historians, who often take a longer and broader view of economic development than economists and finance specialists, tend to concentrate on one component—usually banking—or a subset of them. Our view is that in a well-functioning financial system, there are numerous interactions among all of our five components. Hence, we think that the unit of observation for studying finance's role in economic modernization should be the financial system as a whole, and not just one or two of its components.

Second, whenever one peels back the layers of the great onion of history and stops at a layer that seems important for later developments, the question inevitably arises, "But what made that layer possible?" In our case, what makes a good financial system possible? What are its prerequisites? Without going into detail, we would say that the prerequisites would likely include a combination of good government, including representative political institutions, an independent judiciary or court system, clearly defined and secure property rights, and financial savvy on the part of leaders—finance ministers, central bankers, and so on—among the components of a good system.

We place sound *public finance* first in our list of financial-system components largely for historical reasons. In modern history, good financial systems emerged out of the needs of the nation-state for financing, often to

1. Insurance might well be added to our list, as a sixth component. We leave it out here, in part because it involves a function—risk management—similar to that in which another component, banking, engages, and in part because, in a global historical context, it could be and often was supplied by insurers in other countries. Nonetheless, we recognize that the leading economies to be discussed in section 8.2 did develop the insurance component of their financial systems early in their financial and economic modernizations. Insurance is a financial product, and insurance companies invested the premiums they received in other financial assets such as securities. In the context of modern financial systems, it may be useful to think of the bank as the paragon of the institutional lender and the insurance company as the paragon of the institutional investor.

fight its wars with other nation-states.[2] Sound public finance includes setting and controlling public expenditure priorities, raising revenues adequate to fund them efficiently, and if—as is often the case—that involves issuing public debt, then provision must be made for servicing the debt to gain and keep the confidence of the investors who purchase it.

The historical primacy of public finance in the development of financial systems, to be documented below, serves another purpose. It reminds us that much of finance, historically and now, and especially when finance has global dimensions, is inextricably bound up with politics. It is both naive and a misreading of history to assume that capital moved throughout the world solely, or even mostly, in search of the highest available return commensurate with the risks taken. It is equally naive to assume that capital usually moved in response to the demands of users who wanted to make productive economic investments. In a world without governments and foreign policies, that might have been the case. But ours is not such a world. This is a reality that needs to be kept in mind in any discussion of economic globalization. Nonetheless, it should also be kept in mind that the needs of governments to raise and deploy funds internationally for reasons of state (typically, wars) resulted in the creation of financial systems that could mobilize capital and deploy it for productive economic purposes (Ferguson 2001).

Stable money is desirable for the usual textbook reasons. Money is useful as a medium of exchange, a store of value, and a standard of deferred payments. All three uses, but especially the latter two, are harmed if money fluctuates and depreciates in value in unpredictable ways. *Banks and banking* have played large roles in modern economies. Once a monetary base is specified, banks of deposit, discount, and note issue amplify it into a money stock that consists largely of bank money convertible into the monetary base. They do this by granting credit to entrepreneurs and other users of funds. The credit-granting function turns banks into risk managers, the essence of their role as financial intermediaries. A lot of the risk that banks manage arises from borrowing short and lending long. Individual banks and banking systems become troubled, even fail, when recipients of bank credit are unwilling or unable to repay on schedule (illiquidity and default problems) or at all (insolvency and repudiation problems). If depositors, the holders of bank money from whom the banks borrow short, learn of such problems, they may compound them by attempting en masse to convert their bank money to base money.

Central banks, the fourth of our key components of a modern financial

2. Unless one subscribes to an economic theory of war, the importance of war in shaping financial systems in modern history argues for treating the origins of modern financial systems as economically exogenous rather than endogenous. Later in the chapter, we discuss the debate between those who say real-sector economic changes lead to financial-developmental responses and those who, like us, would give more primacy to financial development as leading to real-sector development.

system, can prevent such problems from arising, or at least alleviate them when they do arise. They do this by monitoring and regulating the operations of individual banks in a banking system with the goal of preventing problems. And they do it to alleviate problems when they do arise by acting as lenders of last resort. Central banks also act in the areas of other financial-system components. For example, they often serve as the government's bank—that is, as an adjunct of public finance. And they act to stabilize the value of a country's money, both domestically and internationally.

Securities markets, the last component, facilitate the issuance of public and private debt securities and private equity securities. Specialized banks—investment or merchant banks—serve here as financial intermediaries between the borrowers/issuers (governments and business enterprises) of bonds, stocks, and other forms of securities, and the lenders/investors who purchase securities. Once securities are issued, trading markets provide them with transferability and liquidity that enhance their appeal to investors, be they domestic or foreign.

One could arrive at the above list of key financial-system components as an inference from observing the financial systems of highly developed national economies today. Such financial systems are one of the characteristics of these countries that distinguish them from the far larger number of less developed economies. In that connection, our chapter relates to that of Bordo and Flandreau (ch. 9 in this volume). They argue that core countries with developed economies and mature financial systems, including the wide and deep financial markets as well as sound fiscal and monetary arrangements that are among the components we identify, are now able to function within a framework of flexible exchange rates between countries. In contrast, peripheral developing economies with immature financial systems have a well-justified "fear of floating" and therefore often find it useful, in order to access international capital markets, to anchor their currencies to those of core countries.

Our chapter also is related to that of Obstfeld and Taylor (ch. 3 in this volume). They find, for example, that in the globalization of a century and more ago capital flowed more freely from the core countries to the periphery than it has in the more recent revival of capital-market globalization. Now core countries invest relatively more of the total international flow of capital in each other and relatively less in the periphery than they did a century ago. In our view, this illustrates the importance of mature national financial systems in attracting capital from foreign investors, and the disadvantages of immature systems in doing the same. A century ago, as Obstfeld and Taylor hint, many of the periphery countries were parts of core-country empires. Therefore, the immaturity of their domestic financial systems, which were overseen by imperial authorities, mattered less than it does in today's world of independent nations.

We turn now to a more detailed account of the historical origins of modern, mature financial systems.

8.2   Good Financial Systems in History: Case Studies

The foregoing discussion of a good financial system in terms of its key components and their connections to one another raises several questions. When, where, and how did such articulated financial systems appear in modern economic history? And did it matter for the countries concerned in terms of their economic growth and their participation and status in the world economy?

Our reading of modern economic history is that countries that developed such good financial systems early in their histories grew rapidly thereafter and often attracted foreign capital inflows that served to enhance their growth. The Netherlands, Great Britain, and the United States are leading examples. In succession, these three countries after their financial emergence went on to become *the* economic leaders of the past four centuries and also leaders in the export of capital.

The Dutch Republic was the first country to develop such a system, early in the seventeenth century. Despite its small size, the country became a leading political and economic power of the seventeenth century, and its economic leadership continued into the eighteenth century.

Great Britain developed such a system at the end of the seventeenth century and in the first decades of the eighteenth century. It went on to have the first industrial revolution later in the century, to build a worldwide empire, and to succeed the Dutch Republic as the leading world economy during the eighteenth and much of the nineteenth century.

At the end of the eighteenth century, the newly independent United States also developed such a system. It was then a small country on the periphery of a world system dominated by Europe, with about half a percent of the world's population. A century later, with about 5 percent of world population, the United States had become the world's largest economy, a position it maintains after the elapse of another century.

In each of these three cases, financial innovation led to economic leadership, and then to the Dutch, the British, and the Americans successively becoming world leaders in the export of capital to other countries.

During the second half of the nineteenth century, France and Germany in Europe, and Japan in Asia also became financial innovators, with beneficial results for their economic growth and their ability to become major exporters of capital. In 1914, at the end of the first era of globalization, the four European countries and the United States accounted for about 90 percent of the world's capital exports. Together with Japan, now the world's second largest economy, their share in the second era of globalization at the end of the twentieth century has not changed much from what it was nine decades earlier. Even peculiarities of the earlier era remain, with the United States again—as in 1914—being a net importer of capital even as it exports a great deal of it.

We now examine these countries' early financial development in more detail. There are many similarities among them, but also some differences. The United States and Japan are of special interest because their financial revolutions were far separated in time and space from the European home ground of modern finance and because they have become the two largest national economies.

8.2.1   The Dutch Republic

The Republic or United Provinces was born late in the sixteenth century when the northern provinces of the Spanish Netherlands revolted against Spanish Habsburg rule and, over several decades of protracted warfare extending well into the seventeenth century, established independence from Spain. Even before Dutch independence, provincial governments in the Spanish Netherlands developed a permanent public debt market, likely the world's first, when annuities were issued as a means of lightening tax burdens in response to the revenue demands of Spanish overlords (Tracy 1985). This would now be termed tax smoothing. At roughly the same time, the Spanish Netherlands perfected a continuing market in negotiable international bills of exchange to finance trade without necessitating large movements of hard money across borders (Van der Wee 1963; Neal 1990).

The Dutch revolt maintained the public-debt and money-market innovations in the United Provinces. When coupled with the new republic's tolerance of minorities in the southern Netherlands, the revolt also led to an inflow of both capital and financial expertise to Dutch cities, particularly Amsterdam (De Vries and Woude 1997, 669). In 1609 came two additional and major financial innovations. One was the *Wisselbank*, or Bank of Amsterdam, an exchange bank for merchants and the government whose bank money was better than gold, or at least better than the motley collection of gold and silver coins then in circulation. Similar banks were established in other Dutch cities, as were local private banks (*kassiers*) and, somewhat later, merchant banks. The other innovation of 1609 was the common stock, created when the Dutch East India Company decided to make its capital permanent and issued dividend-paying, tradable shares to its owners instead of liquidating each of its trading expeditions at its conclusion and distributing all of the proceeds to the owners. As warfare with Spain wound down in the early decades of the seventeenth century, and with the aid and example of *Wisselbank* money, the Dutch guilder became stable in value and remained so until the end of the eighteenth century (Neal 1990; Hart, Jonker, and van Zanden 1997; De Vries and Woude 1997).

Thus, by the early seventeenth century, the Dutch Republic had established a version of each of the key components of a modern financial system: strong public finances, stable money, banks, a central bank of sorts, and bond and stock markets. There followed an era of great development and prosperity variously described as "the first modern economy" (De

Vries and Woude 1997), "the golden age," and "the embarrassment of riches" (Schama 1988). The republic could not long keep the dominating political power that by the mid-seventeenth century it had derived from its strong economy. It was too small a country and too decentralized a state to accomplish such a feat in a world increasingly dominated by larger, more centralized states. But Dutch wealth continued to accumulate, Dutch capital sought returns all over the world, and Dutch financial expertise was exported to other countries.

8.2.2 Great Britain

Dutch expertise in finance was introduced directly to England after the Glorious Revolution of 1688, when the Dutch *stadhouder*, Willem of Orange, was invited to become King William III of England. After generations of erratic financial behavior of previous monarchs, the British, envious of Dutch economic and financial power and hoping to surpass it, passed control of their country's finances and monetary system from the king to Parliament.

Adopting Dutch finance, the British also improved upon it. The Bank of England was formed in 1694 as a bank of discount, deposit, and note issue capitalized by public debt, and was thus closer to the modern concept of a central bank than the Amsterdam Wisselbank. The metallic currency was recoined, and paper issues such as bank notes were made convertible into the metallic base. England thus achieved a stable money (Capie 2001a, b). In subsequent decades the public finances were also stabilized, in part by the introduction of standardized perpetual annuities that became the basis for a liquid public debt market. A domestic money market in bills of exchange appeared. Even earlier, the British East India Company followed its Dutch counterpart by making its capital permanent and issuing tradable shares against it, and an active equity market in company shares was present by the 1690s (Neal 1990; Chancellor 1998). These developments have been described as an English "financial revolution" (Dickson 1967) and as "the sinews of power" that enabled the British state to win wars and build an empire (Brewer 1990).

After the mid-eighteenth century, note-issuing country banks began to dot the English and Welsh countryside, joining the long-existing private bankers of London and the Bank of England. The banking system was knit together via the London money market, through which capital surpluses of English agriculture could be recycled to finance the capital deficits of areas industrializing in the first industrial revolution (Pressnell 1956). In Scotland, large banking co-partnerships with branches and freedom of note issue joined several corporations chartered with banking privileges earlier in the century (Cameron et al. 1967; Checkland 1975).

Larry Neal's (1990) study of the eighteenth-century London and Amsterdam capital markets documents the manner in which these developments promoted a flow of capital to England, mainly from the Dutch Republic but also from other continental financial centers. Foreign holdings of shares in leading British companies (East India, South Sea, and the Bank of England) reached nearly 20 percent of the total by midcentury, and foreigners also held about 14 percent of the English national debt. Neal also demonstrates that the two markets across the North Sea from each other were remarkably integrated, with nearly equivalent prices and price changes for the same securities. Even the famous French and English bubbles of 1720 were synchronized in ways that were probably orchestrated by Dutch investors (Neal 1990, 101–15, 147). At the end of the century, during the French Revolution and the Napoleonic Wars, Neal argues that the ability of these markets and institutions to transfer flight capital from the continent to England enabled the industrial revolution there to proceed. Because of international capital market integration, heavy British government borrowing to finance war efforts did not crowd out private investment.

If one is willing to consider northwestern Europe as the world, the eighteenth century surely was the first era of financial globalization. It was the result of two modern financial systems, most likely the only two such systems existing then, linking up with each other across the North Sea, to the advantage of borrowers and investors in both the Dutch Republic and Great Britain. These systems had a version of each of the five key components of a good financial system.

8.2.3   The United States

If one thinks that true financial globalization must link continents separated perhaps by an ocean, and not merely two countries separated by the North Sea, history does not stand in the way with much of a delay. That is because the United States in the early 1790s engineered a financial revolution quite like the earlier ones of the Dutch Republic and Great Britain (Sylla 1999b). The engineer was Alexander Hamilton, first secretary of the treasury (1789–95) of the new federal government that assembled in 1789 under the Constitution. Hamilton's earlier writings indicate that he had absorbed many of the key lessons of Dutch, English, and French financial history. In office, with the backing of the president, Congress, and the private sector, he applied them.

First, Hamilton set up a federal revenue collection system based on import tariffs and domestic excise taxes authorized by Congress, as well as hoped-for revenues from land sales that were slow to materialize. While proceeding with that, Hamilton in 1790 proposed and Congress adopted a plan for restructuring the par value of the national debt from the American Revolution. The debt included state debts assumed by the new federal government and arrears of interest on it that the previous government had been unable to pay. The restructuring took the form of three new issues of new federal securities with varying interest rate terms. The new securities were payable, principal and interest, in hard-money dollars to be collected by the revenue system. These provisions applied to the domestic debt of some $65 million; an additional $12 million owed to foreigners, mainly the French government and Dutch investors, was rolled over with fresh loans from Dutch bankers (Perkins 1994).

Also in 1790, Hamilton proposed a Bank of the United States modeled on the Bank of England, but with several innovative features including a large capital ($10 million), the possibility of branches, and partial (20 percent) government ownership. Like the Bank of England, it was to be the government's bank and it could also engage in private-sector banking. There were only three other banks, small state institutions, in the country at the time. Congress enacted the bank proposal early in 1791. The bank had its initial public offering in July of that year; it was quickly oversubscribed. The bank opened in Philadelphia at the end of 1791, and branches were established in other cities starting in 1792. Fearing that the federal bank with its branches would dominate U.S. banking, the states moved quickly in the 1790s to charter more banks of their own. A country with no banks prior to 1782 became one a decade later with a rapidly expanding banking system, and one that by 1802 had thirty-five chartered banks (Fenstermaker 1965, 111).

With the bank proposal enacted, Hamilton next produced a report on a mint, which defined a new U.S. dollar in terms of both gold and silver (i.e., a bimetallic monetary base) and proposed establishing a mint to make a variety of coins based on the decimal system, also an innovation, albeit one earlier proposed by Hamilton's cabinet colleague, Thomas Jefferson. Banknotes convertible into a specie base gradually replaced the early fiat paper issues of state governments.

The new federal debt securities appeared late in 1790, followed by the stock of the bank in mid-1791. So many new and putatively high-quality securities energized the informal trading markets of Philadelphia, New York, and Boston. Trading was vigorous, speculative spirits were unleashed, and new private issues joined those of the government. Government debts that had sold at 15 cents on the dollar in 1789 reached par in 1791, and 120 percent of par in early 1792, just before Wall Street's first crash knocked 20 percent off their value in two months. New York State enacted a law to end speculation in the streets, causing brokers to meet under a buttonwood tree in Wall Street in May 1792 and draw up an agreement to trade indoors. This was the origin of the New York Stock Exchange.

In roughly three years, from 1789 to 1792, the United States was transformed from a bankrupt country with a primitive financial system to a country servicing its debts and equipped with a modern financial system like the ones that the Dutch and the British had developed earlier over many decades. What were the effects of that system? In keeping with the general approach of our paper, we discuss them under growth and globalization.

In an earlier paper (Rousseau and Sylla 1999), we analyzed relationships between financial developments and real growth in the period 1790 to 1850. Although good data do not become available until late in this period (and show the U.S. economy growing at modern rates), it is the consensus of economic historians that real growth, total and per capita, accelerated over the six-decade period. Our work developed several annual time series measures of financial development (money stock, bank numbers and capital, and the number of securities listed in major securities markets), and measures of real growth and development (investment, imports, and an index of the cumulative stock of business corporations chartered, which we regard as a measure of entrepreneurial activity). A set of vector autoregressive (VAR) models indicated that in general causality ran from the financial to the real variables, with an occasional feedback effect of real developments on finance. These results led us to conjecture that the acceleration of U.S. growth that occurred in the 1790–1850 period was "finance led."

What does "finance led" mean? The discussion above suggests the possibility that Dutch and British economic growth may also have had roots in financial development. In the Dutch case, a modern financial system was in place before the Golden Age and the rise of the Dutch economy to seventeenth-century preeminence. In the British case, a modern financial system was in place before the first industrial revolution and the rise of the English economy to eighteenth-century preeminence. In the U.S. case, a modern financial system was in place before the U.S. industrial and transportation revolutions and the westward movement of the nineteenth century, by the end of which the United States was the preeminent economy. We see a pattern emerging in this history.

What about globalization? Does having a good financial system mean that foreign capital is more likely to flow to that country? Although residuals from balance-of-payments data indicate only modest net capital inflows during the period from 1790 to 1812 (Davis and Cull 1994, 2000), more detailed data on foreign holdings of U.S. securities tell a different story. Benchmark estimates of such holdings in 1789 and 1803, a period encompassing the financial revolution of the Hamiltonian Federalists, indicate that foreign investors increased their holdings by $48–52 million from a 1789 base of $17–18 million, the majority of which consisted of Revolutionary War debts owed to France and the Dutch (Wilkins 1989, table 3.1, p. 50). The inflow of portfolio capital implied by Wilkins's data is fairly consistent with U.S. Treasury and other records for 1803 on total U.S. securities issuance and the amounts in domestic and foreign hands. Foreign investors held 53 percent of the U.S. national debt in 1803, and 62 percent of the stock of the Bank of the United States. With shares of state banks, insurance, and transportation companies added in, there was a grand total of $122 million in public and private securities issued, almost all after 1789 as state chartering of corporations took off. Foreign investors held nearly half of these securities, or $59 million (Sylla, Wilson, and Wright 1997, tables 4 and 5).

The modern concept of an emerging market involves the generation of confidence among foreign investors. The ingredients of confidence include fiscally responsible governments, stable money, and sound domestic financial institutions, markets, and instruments. Confidence in a country's securities increases, we think, when there are domestic stock and bond markets to enhance their liquidity. Two centuries ago the United States was such an emerging market, and, with an occasional slip, it has remained a Mecca for foreign investors ever since. A century earlier, Dutch and other foreign investors saw something similarly attractive in England. A century before that, foreign investors saw it in the Dutch Republic. Emerging markets are not new in history.

8.2.4   France and Germany

After Great Britain, France and Germany were the leading foreign lenders in the era of globalization during the late nineteenth and early twentieth centuries. Even then, however, these two large and relatively prosperous European countries lagged well behind Great Britain, another large country, in international lending, and, on a per capita basis, even behind the Netherlands. Moreover, the Dutch and the British became foreign lenders and international investors long before the French and the Germans. This raises two questions. What accounts for the French and German lag? And why did the two countries then play major roles in the financial globalization of the late nineteenth century?

We would answer both questions by saying that until the middle of the nineteenth century neither France nor Germany had developed all of the components of a good financial system that the Netherlands developed two centuries earlier, Great Britain a century earlier, and the United States half a century earlier. In the case of France, while England was having its financial revolution in the decades around 1700, the country's public finances were chaotic, and the collapse of John Law's scheme in 1720 made the French public suspicious of paper money and banking for a century or more (White 2001; Murphy 1997). Nonetheless, after the end of the Napoleonic Wars in 1815, France's public finances and currency were stabilized, and the central Bank of France had been present since 1800. There were also a variety of bankers, but nothing like the extensive banking systems that existed in the United States and Great Britain. Paris had a stock exchange, but it listed just a few securities, mostly government debt. France's relative financial backwardness during the early nineteenth century resulted from the state's strict controls on, and limitations of, banking and securities market development (Cameron et al. 1967). Kindleberger (1984, 114–15) provides an extensive list of reasons for concluding that "France lagged a hundred years behind Britain in money, banking, and finance. . . . [T]his was both a reflection and a cause of its economic retardation." More recent research drawing attention to loan-market substitutes, such as loans arranged by notaries that France developed to compensate for its lag, serves to confirm the country's relative backwardness in financial development (Hoffman, Postel-Vinay, and Rosenthal 2000). The substitutes gradually gave way to modern forms of finance in the nineteenth century.

In the case of Germany, the country was of course not unified in fact until the middle of the nineteenth century, or in law until 1871. When the United States began its financial revolution in 1790, there were hundreds of separate German states, each with its own ruler. By the early nineteenth century (if not before), the major German states had stable public finances and stable money, but in other financial-system components respects they lagged even behind France. The Prussian Bank, forerunner of the central Reichsbank that came in 1875, was not founded until 1846. There were a variety of private bankers, including such famous houses as the Rothschilds, that began in Germany, and other public and private financial institutions. But as in France, state controls limited banking development. Securities markets were slow to develop, and those of the early decades of the nineteenth century were more adjuncts of the private bankers' businesses than independent sources of finance.

In both France and Germany financial systems began to take on a more modern form around 1850. The capital needs of large enterprises such as railways, and the growing perception that the two countries were lagging behind Great Britain, provided reasons for change. Change came in more liberal state approaches to banking development; in particular the innovation (for these countries, although it had existed in the United States for six to seven decades and in England for two to three decades) was joint-stock banking. The French leader Louis Bonaparte, after declaring himself Emperor Napoleon III in 1851, sought to justify his authoritarian regime by fostering rapid economic development. With his backing, the joint-stock Credit Mobilier bank was formed in 1852; it combined commercial and investment banking. Although the Credit Mobilier failed in 1868, it had an impact in and outside of France. With the French Credit Mobilier as an example, the Germans founded similar institutions (Landes 1965; Cameron et al. 1967; Born 1983; Kindleberger 1984). During the middle decades of the nineteenth century, France and Germany thus added missing elements of a good financial system. As their financial systems mobilized capital more effectively, the two economies grew faster and their financiers began to invest large sums of capital in other countries.

8.2.5 Japan

Japan until the 1850s was almost totally out of the loop of western economic development. Yet it quickly became a major economic and political power during the era of globalization a century ago, and then within a century became the world's second largest national economy. That makes Japan perhaps the most interesting of the cases studied here. How did it happen?

Among the important reasons is that Japan, like the other cases here but unlike so many of the world's countries, had a financial revolution that resulted in a good financial system. After the Meiji revolution toppled the isolationist shogun regime in 1868, there were in the 1870s both bold initiatives and false starts in building a modern financial system. The bold initiative included commuting feudal dues paid in rice to government bonds paid in money. This created a securities market, and the Tokyo and Osaka stock exchanges formed in 1878 to trade the new issues. The false starts included excessive issues of fiat currency and an attempt to copy the U.S. national banking system with bank notes backed by government bonds. The banks purchased large amounts of government bonds and issued large amounts of bank notes against them, without much attention to the specie reserves they were supposed to maintain. Fiat money and bank-created money led to rampant inflation from 1876 to 1881 (Tamaki 1995).

Financially, Japan turned the corner during the 1880s. The Yokohama Specie Bank was founded in 1880 and given the task of accumulating specie through financing the country's exports so that a currency convertible to specie could in time be established. The alternative of gaining specie by means of a foreign loan was rejected on grounds that foreign lenders could not be trusted or given influence in Japanese affairs. The Specie Bank's operations were clever. It paid Japanese exporters in Japanese currency advanced from the government when goods were exported, then drew bills of exchange collectible in specie on the foreign purchasers and collected them at branches it established in foreign cities, and finally remitted the specie to the government to repay the government's advance (Tamaki 1995; Sylla 1999a). Financial innovation thus encouraged exports and the government's accumulation of specie.

In 1881, Masayoshi Matsukata became Japan's finance minister, an office he held for many years. Matsukata played a role in Japan's financial revolution comparable to that of Hamilton in the United States (Rosovsky 1966; Sylla 1999a). In 1882, he established the central Bank of Japan. He also instituted a regime of fiscal austerity and deflation to end the inflationary excesses of the 1870s. By 1885, paper money circulation was reduced enough, and the government's specie accumulations had increased enough, for the Bank of Japan to introduce silver-convertible bank notes. Private bank note issue rights were taken away in 1883, and the government's fiat issues were gradually retired. Bank of Japan notes were 2 percent of Japan's note circulation when they were introduced in 1885; by 1897 they had increased to 75 percent. Along with these changes, Matsukata instituted reforms of Japan's banking system (Sylla 1999a).

With fiscal and currency stability achieved by the mid-1880s, Japan recovered quickly from the deflation of the decade's first years. Company formation tripled between 1885 and 1890. During a credit crisis in 1889, the Bank of Japan found a way to aid these companies and the Japanese securities markets. The bylaws of the bank forbade lending on securities, but it could increase market liquidity by "special discounting" of bills covered by high-quality public and private securities. The innovation allowed companies to repay the banks during the credit crunch, and it thus cemented ties between companies, banks, and the Bank of Japan by encouraging the banks to hold company shares (Morikawa 1992). Although this might seem to indicate the origins of modern Japan's strong bank-firm relationships, we now know that securities markets and equity finance were important independent sources of firm financing from the 1880s to the 1920s (Miwa and Ramseyer 2000a,b, 2001).

In 1897, aided by an indemnity in gold paid by China after the Sino-Japanese War of 1894–95, Japan adopted the gold standard and started the system of long-term credit banks. These banks were joint stock companies, although under the supervision of the ministry of finance. Issuing debentures, most of which were purchased by the ministry with surplus government funds and postal savings deposits, the new banks invested the proceeds in infrastructure and other investments (Cameron et al. 1967).

Once on the gold standard maintained by the world's leading economies, Japan lost its earlier aversion to borrowing abroad and quickly became an emerging market for foreign investors. Ten Japanese government loans totaling more than 80 million British pounds were raised on the London capital market between 1897 and 1910; a similar total was raised in the markets of Paris, New York, and Germany in these years (Suzuki 1994; Tamaki 1995). Sussman and Yafeh (2000) show that adoption of the gold standard dramatically improved the terms on which Japan could borrow in foreign markets. Our interpretation of this gain is that it was Japan's financial (and economic) development during the three decades prior to 1897 that made the adoption of the gold standard possible, and successful.

It is often wondered why, of all the possible candidates, Japan was the one non-Western country to modernize its economy and join the ranks of the wealthy Western countries. We think an important part of the answer, and one supported by Rousseau (1999) with time series evidence, is that early in its history, during the Meiji era, Japan developed a sophisticated financial system like that of the Western leaders. As in the other cases essayed here, that financial system included stable public finances, sound money, banks, a central bank, and securities markets. It enabled Japan, a poor and relatively isolated country in 1870, to become an emerging market and a rapidly growing economic and political power by the early twentieth century. As Herbert Feis long ago put it,

> Japan, of all the countries of the Orient, proved itself capable of using to good advantage the capital of Europe. Its government succeeded in the threefold task of promoting internal industrial development, extending and reinforcing Japanese economic interests in Korea and China, and adjusting its plans to the political rivalries of the European continent. . . .

The growing strength obtained from the use of that capital made Japan a better credit risk for investors and a more important ally. By 1914 the small island empire had become a great power in its own right and might. (Feis 1965, 429)

Japan had learned an important lesson of history, namely that financial development can be the basis of economic growth and participation as a major player in the global economy. With all the elements of a good financial system in place before the twentieth century, Japan's economic success seems less an exception to the rule of West-dominated economic modernization and more a confirmation the key role of financial development in promoting economic modernization.

8.3   Data and Methodology

8.3.1   Overview

In section 8.2, we identify a well-functioning financial system as central to the economic growth of five Atlantic economies and Japan at various times over the past three centuries. We next ask whether the available data support a leading role for finance in the growth of incomes for a broader set of countries, and whether financial development promoted globalization by facilitating trade and reducing international dispersion in long-term interest rates. We do this using the cross-country regression framework of Barro (1991), with the availability of appropriate data over a long historical period limiting our sample to seventeen countries from 1850 to the present. The study is to our knowledge the first to apply recent cross-country regression techniques in a systematic study of the finance-growth nexus that includes the period before 1960.[3] The results, which we describe later, support the view that finance affects growth most emphatically in the earlier stages of economic development. In this respect, they are consistent with Cameron et al. (1967) and Rousseau and Wachtel (1998), who conducted comparative analyses on smaller sets of countries. We also find a role for both financial development and trade in reducing interest rates and promoting their convergence across the Atlantic economies in the pre-1914 period.

Before presenting these findings, however, we observe that macroeconomic theory has made much progress over the past decade in laying the analytical foundations for scientific discussion of the finance-growth nexus.[4] Greenwood and Jovanovic (1990) and King and Levine (1993b), for example, formulate general equilibrium models in which banks and other financial intermediaries arise endogenously to improve the allocation of

3. This part of our study can thus be viewed as the historical analogue to the cross-country analysis of King and Levine (1993a).
4. Earlier, more descriptive studies of the relationship between financial factors and growth include, among others, Gurley and Shaw (1955), Goldsmith (1969), and McKinnon (1973).

available credit. This so-called total factor productivity (or TFP) channel thus operates through the selection and funding of projects with high private and social returns. Other models, such as those of Bencivenga and Smith (1991) and Rousseau (1998), emphasize "debt accumulation" or the ability of a well-functioning financial system to mobilize resources for projects that would otherwise have remained in the drawer. Empirical investigations, including Levine and Zervos (1998) and Bell and Rousseau (2001), offer evidence on the TFP and debt accumulation channels, respectively, with the latter suggesting accumulation as even a precondition for improved allocation in developing countries. If this is indeed the case, the confidence of potential market participants, as enhanced by the first four characteristics of a good financial system that we describe in section 8.2, is critical to achieving a threshold level of lending activity from which a fuller menu of financial institutions can emerge.

Our study does not distinguish empirically between these complementary yet distinct channels of finance-led growth due to the limited nature of measures of financial development that are available over the past century and a half for the broad set of countries that we consider. Since emerging financial institutions are likely to have affected both the accumulation and the allocation of resources in the economies that we study, however, we do not view our joint tests for both channels as particularly limiting.

Finance, some would argue, perhaps should not be considered a truly exogenous component in the growth process. Indeed, the consensus view of economists some fifty years ago, and which to some degree persists, can be summarized by Joan Robinson's (1952) assertion that "By and large, . . . where enterprise leads, finance follows." In the long run, increases in economic activity will undoubtedly generate demand for financial services and lead to a larger intermediating sector. This channel might be important in the later stages of development when financial systems have matured, and possibly in providing one of the impulses needed to develop a financial system in the first place.[5] In contrast, the TFP and debt accumulation channels are likely to operate most emphatically in the early to middle stages of a country's economic modernization, with the TFP channel retaining importance as the economy matures. In the formal analysis, we will address the endogeneity of financial institutions by using instruments and predetermined variables in our cross-country regression models.

8.3.2   The Data

To study relationships between the financial and real sectors, we first identify measures of financial development, outward orientation, and real-sector performance that can be constructed with the available historical

---

5. Our historical survey of financial system development in section 8.2 indicates that the politics of war, if anything, was more important than the economics of enterprise and growth as an impulse for financial modernization.

data. To this end, we build a panel using annual data for 1850–1997 from three main sources. From 1960, we use the World Bank's *World Development Indicators* database. For earlier years we use data from worksheets underlying Bordo and Jonung (1987, 2001) and Obstfeld and Taylor (2000), and supplement with financial, trade, and public-sector aggregates from Mitchell's (1998a-c) volumes of *International Historical Statistics*. The resulting data set includes seventeen countries. The appendix describes the sources in detail.

Table 8.1 lists the seventeen countries along with their average annual growth rates of real per capita income and financial depth (as measured by the ratio of the broadest available monetary aggregate to output) for the 1850–89, 1890–1929, and 1945–94 periods.[6] It also includes the level of real per capita income measured in 1960 U.S. dollars at the midpoints of these periods (i.e., 1870, 1910, and 1970).[7] The remarkable feature of the table is the growth in the ratios of the broad money stock to gross domestic product (GDP) in all but three of the seventeen economies between the 1850–89 and 1890–1929 periods, with the ratio rising by more than 50 percent in nine of the countries. In contrast, financial depth grew in only ten of our countries between the 1890–1929 and 1945–94 periods, and only three countries experienced growth in the ratio of more than 50 percent.

Bordo and Jonung (1987) examine the behavior of the velocity of circulation, which is roughly the inverse of our measure of financial depth, for five of the countries in our study (Canada, Norway, Sweden, the United Kingdom, and the United States) and observe a U-shaped pattern from 1870 to 1975.[8] They then show that the downward portion of the U-curve can be explained by financial development in the form of monetization, as measured by the changes in the agricultural/industrial mix of the economy and the ratio of financial assets to total assets, and that the upward portion may reflect an availability of substitutes for money as an asset. The evidence in table 8.1 is consistent with this interpretation for our broader sample in the pre-1930 period. The ratio of the money stock to output may thus be a

6. The starting years of the averages that appear in table 8.1 under the column headings "1850–1889" are as follows: Argentina, 1884; Australia GDP growth, 1870; Australia money/GDP, 1880; Brazil, 1880; Canada, 1870; Denmark, 1850; Finland, 1860; France, 1850; Germany, 1850; Italy GDP growth, 1862; Italy money/GDP, 1872; Japan, 1878; the Netherlands, 1850; Norway, 1865; Portugal, 1880; Sweden GDP growth, 1861; Spain GDP growth, 1858; Spain money/GDP, 1875; Sweden money/GDP, 1870; United Kingdom GDP growth, 1850; United Kingdom money/GDP, 1870; United States, 1850. Data from 1914–24 and 1945–48 are unavailable for Germany and thus are not included in the relevant averages. The same applies to France for 1914–20 and 1945–48.

7. When computing output growth rates, we use GDP in real local currency units. When computing levels in 1960 U.S. dollars, we use the U.S. dollar equivalents from the *World Development Indicators* database for 1960–1997. For earlier years, we use official exchange rates to convert local currency output into U.S. dollars and then deflate the result using the U.S. implicit price deflator.

8. Bordo and Jonung extend their study of velocity to more than eighty countries after 1950.

Table 8.1   Selected Macroeconomic Indicators

	Per Capita Income (1960 US$)			% Growth Real per Capita Income			Broad Money (% of GDP)		
	1870	1910	1970	1850–89	1890–1929	1945–97	1850–89	1890–1929	1945–94
Argentina	n.a.	516	977	5.79	1.08	1.42	49.2	32.0	30.0
Australia	684	1,067	2,284	1.65	0.42	2.06	38.1	45.0	60.6
Brazil	n.a.	93	529	0.52	2.58	3.63	42.2	30.1	38.3
Canada	417	976	2,427	1.50	2.25	1.58	20.7	40.0	56.0
Denmark	319	608	1,953	1.90	1.74	3.02	34.8	76.8	53.5
Finland	274	368	1,751	1.37	1.83	3.20	41.3	96.9	47.5
France	388	560	2,062	1.20	3.37	3.22	28.8	43.3	60.2
Germany	98	176	4,474	1.63	1.57	3.89	18.2	47.6	33.7
Italy	207	236	1,285	-0.22	1.34	4.20	34.3	50.1	72.3
Japan	n.a.	156	1,152	6.11	1.75	5.48	30.1	60.7	121.7
The Netherlands	280	451	1,501	1.39	2.02	2.94	30.7	62.3	76.8
Norway	170	273	2,022	1.12	1.88	3.14	35.1	82.4	57.3
Portugal	n.a.	153	582	3.05	0.99	3.95	21.6	19.6	86.0
Spain	188	243	689	0.83	0.76	3.41	8.7	26.5	74.9
Sweden	203	486	2,759	1.82	2.57	2.62	62.6	77.8	61.5
United Kingdom	607	747	1,725	1.04	0.51	2.41	48.7	56.2	43.8
United States	413	1,087	3,641	1.91	1.82	1.66	30.1	60.3	70.4

Source: See appendix.

Notes: Per capita incomes are reported for 1870, 1910, and 1970. Income growth rates and the ratio of broad money to GDP are averages of the available annual observations over the 1850–89, 1890–1929, and 1945–97 periods. n.a. = not available.

particularly useful proxy for financial development in the earlier decades of our study in that it reflects industrialization as well as an increased use of financial assets.

Turning to the potential real effects of finance, for which we are most interested, we observe that among the nine countries in table 8.1 that saw financial depth rise by 50 percent or more, six of them saw real per capita GDP also rise by more than 50 percent. Interestingly, all three of the countries that saw financial depth rise by more than 50 percent in the postwar period also had income growth of more than 50 percent. The data thus indicate wide disparities in the growth experiences of the economies in our sample but also suggest a correlation between financial depth and real incomes. We now proceed to investigate these relationships more formally.

8.3.3   Methodology

Our examination of links between financial development, trade, and income focuses on the broad implications that can arise in a cross-country framework. This type of analysis has become a near tradition in the empirical study of growth and its determinants since Barro (1991) isolated key variables, such as education and political stability, as members of a benchmark set of robust correlates. Given that most studies of financial factors in growth are extensions of this framework (see, e.g., King and Levine 1993a and Levine and Zervos 1998), we begin by exploring partial correlations between growth and the ratios of broadly defined money and international trade to output from 1850 to the present and over two subperiods covering 1850–1929 and 1945–94.

The ratio of the liquid liabilities to output is a common measure of the size and possibly the sophistication of the financial sector in an individual country, yet it is imprecise because of nonbank intermediaries such as insurance and investment companies, whose liabilities do not wind up in the broad money aggregate. These omissions are likely to be far less important in the prewar period, but quite substantial in recent years. Further, a financial system should be characterized by all of the institutions that promote the accumulation of capital, including securities markets. Rousseau and Sylla (1999) show that securities markets played an important role in early U.S. growth presumably because they attracted foreign capital, whereas Levine and Zervos (1998) and Rousseau and Wachtel (2000) present evidence of their importance in cross-country models that use recent data. Unfortunately, we do not yet know the extent of securities market development in the prewar period for most of the countries in our sample, and so to conduct an analysis that allows for consistent comparisons across time periods we must for now be satisfied with the ratio of broad money to GDP.

A reasonable way to measure economic performance is through growth in real per capita incomes. Although such a measure ignores the impact of the distribution of income on welfare, it nevertheless provides a convenient summary of economic conditions in a given country and has the important advantage of being readily available for a fairly large set of countries as far back as the mid-nineteenth century. We use it here as the primary measure of economic outcomes.

Measures of economic "globalization" are even more difficult to identify for a large set of countries. It is clear, however, that the degree to which a country has an "outward orientation" is related to the extent of its integration with other markets, and trade data are readily available for most of the counties in our sample—in most cases even farther back in time than output. To participate in trade arrangements, short-term finance is critical, and much of this financing is provided through the banking sector in the form of credits and acceptances. When seen in this light, banks can contribute to economic globalization by providing the credits needed to promote trade. To examine the importance of these effects, we also consider models in which the ratio of trade (the sum of imports and exports) to GDP enters either as a regressor or as the dependent variable.

Existing empirical studies of the relationship between trade and growth have reached mixed conclusions, presumably because most measures of openness are themselves endogenous and influenced by nonpolicy factors (see Edwards 1998 for a useful survey). This has led to sensitivity of trade effects in cross-country regressions to the choice of conditioning variables. Frankel and Romer (1999) have recently shown, however, that geographic characteristics are good instruments for isolating the impact of the predetermined component of trade on the level of real income, and that this effect is large but not always significant statistically. Such an effect is likely to be more elusive in our study, where the focus is on growth rather than levels. We nevertheless attempt to extract the predetermined component of the ratio of trade to output with instruments and then examine its explanatory power when added to our cross-country specifications.

The tendency for real interest rates to converge in the Atlantic economies before 1914 and again more recently is documented by Obstfeld and Taylor (1998) and has been interpreted by them as an indicator of the extent of economic integration. What remains unstudied is the role of financial institutions, and primarily banks, in promoting interest rate convergence. Since Homer and Sylla (1996) and Obstfeld and Taylor (2000) together make annual interest rate series for long-term debt available for twelve of the countries in our study well into the nineteenth century, we conclude by examining the roles of finance and trade in the process of convergence in the pre-1914 period.

8.4   Results and Discussion

8.4.1   Finance, Trade, and Growth

Our first set of specifications uses decadal average growth rates of real per capita GDP from 1850 to 1997 as the dependent variable and conditions

Table 8.2   Cross-Country OLS Growth Regressions, 1850–1997

	Dependent Variable: % Growth of Per Capita Real GDP			
	(1)	(2)	(3)	(4)
Constant	6.113**	6.279**	7.463**	7.542**
	(1.434)	(1.471)	(1.500)	(1.507)
Log of initial real per capita GDP	−0.672**	−0.699*	−0.706**	−0.718**
	(0.178)	(0.183)	(0.179)	(0.180)
Initial ratio of broad money to GDP	1.293**	1.245**	0.949*	0.899*
	(0.557)	(0.567)	(0.541)	(0.547)
Initial ratio of trade to GDP		0.161		0.213
		(0.330)		(0.318)
Initial ratio of government expenditure to GDP			−5.280**	−5.591**
			(2.299)	(2.349)
R^2	0.336	0.339	0.359	0.361
N	214	211	200	200

Notes: The table reports coefficients from OLS regressions with standard errors in parentheses. The dependent variable is the growth rate of real per capita GDP averaged for each decade from 1850 to the 1990s. Initial values are taken from the first year of each decade. Decade dummies are included in the regression but are not reported.
**Significant at the 5 percent level.
*Significant at the 10 percent level.

on the level of real per capita income (in 1960 U.S. dollars) at the start of each decade.[9] The "convergence" or "catch-up" effect, as manifested by a negative sign for the coefficient on initial income, has been shown to be quite strong in cross-country regressions for the post-1960 period. By including initial income in our baseline specification, we can determine if it is important in the pre-Depression period as well. Placing the ratio of broad money to GDP on the right-hand side allows us to evaluate the role, if any, that finance plays in the conditional growth process. Since the levels variables are trending in nature and we would like to control for other business-cycle related effects, we include (but do not report coefficients on) dummy variables for each decade.

Table 8.2 presents the regressions, which use the first observations of each decade as regressors to ameliorate the impact of possible reverse causality from growth to additional finance. This technique cannot fully eliminate the simultaneity problem due to autocorrelation in the time series for financial depth, but it does ensure that all regressors are predetermined and thus plausible determinants of *subsequent* growth. The first column of table 8.2 presents our baseline, which includes only initial income, financial

9. We compute a "decadal" average for a country in any decade for which observations are available for seven or more years. When we divide the sample and work with five-year subperiods, observations must be available in at least three years before we compute a five-year average.

Table 8.3   Cross-Country Instrumental Variables Growth Regressions, 1850–1997

	Dependent Variable: % Growth of Per Capita Real GDP			
	(1)	(2)	(3)	(4)
Constant	6.424**	6.427**	6.776**	6.821**
	(1.457)	(1.462)	(1.477)	(1.985)
Log of initial real per capita GDP	–0.697**	–0.700**	–0.603**	–0.610**
	(0.179)	(0.180)	(0.179)	(0.180)
Ratio of broad money to GDP	1.056**	1.042**	0.956*	0.903*
	(0.542)	(0.549)	(0.540)	(0.548)
Ratio of trade to GDP		0.071		0.234
		(0.364)		(0.368)
Ratio of government			–5.915**	–6.286**
expenditure to GDP			(2.583)	(2.658)
R^2	0.355	0.355	0.372	0.370
N	199	199	197	197

Notes: The table reports coefficients from two-stage least squares regressions with standard errors in parentheses. All data items are decadal averages covering the 1850s through the 1990s. Instruments include initial values of the full set of regressors as well as the inflation rate, with initial values taken as the first observation of each decade. Decade dummies are included in all regressions but are not reported.
**Significant at the 5 percent level.
*Significant at the 10 percent level.

depth, and time effects on the right-hand side, while columns (2)–(4) report results for specifications with the ratios of international trade and/or government expenditure to GDP as additional conditioning variables. We include the ratio of trade to output to control for direct effects of international trade on growth that do not operate indirectly through finance. We include the government expenditure variable because it is likely that the resource requirements associated with large public expenditure crowd out private investment and lead to less efficient resource allocations than the private sector might be able to provide.

A strong convergence effect, as indicated by negative and significant coefficients on initial income, and a positive and significant role of financial depth in subsequent growth are common to all four regressions that we report in table 8.2. When included with financial depth on the right-hand side, trade is not significant, and government expenditure, as expected, is negative and significant. The inclusion of the conditioning variables in equations (2)–(4) tends to reduce the measured effect of finance on growth, yet significance of the broad financial aggregate persists. The R^2 from the regressions suggests that a large portion of the cross-sectional variation in output growth can be explained by our simple models.

Table 8.3 presents a similar set of specifications, but instead of using initial values of the data in each period as regressors, we use contemporaneous averages and control for simultaneity with instruments. By including the initial values of the complete set of regressors as well as initial inflation as instruments, these two-stage least squares regressions extract the predetermined (i.e., explainable through information in the initial information set for each period) components of the right-hand-side variables and use them in place of the actual regressors in the estimation. This alternative yields results that are quantitatively very similar to those presented in table 8.2. As a group, the regressions reported in tables 8.2 and 8.3 are thus consistent with a leading role for financial factors in growth for our seventeen-country sample over a 150-year period.[10]

Tables 8.4 and 8.5 evaluate the robustness of the ordinary least squares (OLS) and instrumental variables (IV) results in subperiods covering 1850–1929 and 1945–94. To make more observations available for each estimation, we work with five-year rather than decadal averages of the data. In the pre-1929 period, we note again the significance of the convergence and finance effects on growth and the robustness of the results to the choice of estimation technique. Government expenditure remains negative but less significant in the pre-Depression period, perhaps because the government, in the absence of a less sophisticated financial system, must play a more central role in delivering resources to productive projects.

A less prominent role for finance in the postwar period is the striking feature of table 8.5. Financial depth retains significance when appearing alone on the right-hand side, but this effect vanishes when trade is included in the regressions either explicitly or in the instrument set. King and Levine (1993a) find the effects of finance on growth robust to the inclusion of trade using post-1960 data for a wider group of industrialized and emerging economies, and that the trade variable itself is not statistically significant. We attribute this difference to the industrialized nature of nearly all of the countries in our sample by 1960. Indeed, the rise of money substitutes in more mature economies weakens the effectiveness of broad money to GDP as a measure of financial sophistication.

It is difficult to draw strong conclusions about the nonrobustness of the

---

10. Our findings are consistent with growth being "finance-led" but do not preclude the possibility that growth may also be promoting further financial development. In fact, when we momentarily set the relevant growth theory aside by moving finance to the left-hand side of our regressions and placing the growth rate of output on the right, we find that output growth enters with a positive and significant sign in the pre-1930 period, though not over the full sample or in the postwar period. This result is consistent with, though not overwhelmingly supportive of, the priors of generations of economists who have stressed what we would call "reverse causality" in the finance-growth nexus. Indeed, in time series analyses of five countries in our sample (Canada, Norway, Sweden, the United Kingdom, and the United States) from 1870 to 1929, Rousseau and Wachtel (1998) do not find a role for growth in promoting additional finance in the short to medium term. Our main cross-sectional results, which reduce simultaneity problems by using initial values of finance as regressors in OLS specifications and as instruments in IV specifications, are meant to suggest that finance plays an important leading role in the growth process—a role that is likely to be central.

Table 8.4   **Cross-Country Growth Regressions, 1850–1929**

	Dependent Variable: % Growth of Per Capita Real GDP			
	OLS (initial values)		IV	
	(1)	(2)	(3)	(4)
Constant	4.829**	6.506**	4.804**	6.342**
	(1.728)	(2.060)	(1.821)	(2.059)
Log of initial real per capita GDP	–0.587**	–0.755**	–0.568*	–0.737**
	(0.275)	(0.311)	(0.289)	(0.307)
Ratio of broad money to GDP	2.593**	2.158*	2.273**	2.113*
	(1.067)	(1.104)	(1.048)	(1.070)
Ratio of trade to GDP		0.113		0.120
		(0.386)		(0.403)
Ratio of government expenditure to GDP		–6.713*		–6.595
		(3.919)		(4.216)
R^2	0.136	0.136	0.124	0.147
N	208	185	185	185

Notes: The dependent variable is the growth rate of real per capita GDP averaged for each five-year period from 1850–54 through 1925–29. Initial values are taken from the first year of each five-year period. Standard errors are reported in parentheses. Period dummies are included in the regressions but not reported. The left panel of the table reports coefficients and standard errors from OLS regressions using initial values as regressors. The right panel reports coefficients and standard errors from two-stage least squares regressions. The IV regressions use the five-year averages of the data as regressors. Instruments include initial values of the full set of regressors as well as the inflation rate.
**Significant at the 5 percent level.
*Significant at the 10 percent level.

result of financial development on growth in the postwar period once trade is added to the specification or the instrument set due to potential problems of collinearity between trade and the other regressors. For example, it is also possible that the trade aggregate in recent decades has proxied for a concept much broader than trading volume, namely the degree to which an economy is integrated internationally. In mature economies, a banking system, which is the essence of our financial development measure, may be a less important factor in such integration.

We move toward disentangling these effects by exploring the degree to which finance affects trading volume across sample periods in table 8.6. In these regressions, the ratio of trade to output serves as dependent variable, and we again control for initial income. The financial variables are significant over the full sample and the 1850–1929 period but are not significant in the postwar period. These results suggest that financial systems do play a role in promoting trade in the earlier stages of financial and economic development. To the extent that trade in turn also promoted growth, finance may be even more important to long-run growth than our regressions suggest.

Table 8.5　　　　　**Cross-Country Growth Regressions, 1945–94**

	Dependent Variable: % Growth of Per Capita Real GDP			
	OLS (initial values)		IV	
	(1)	(2)	(3)	(4)
Constant	9.941**	9.275**	10.064**	9.366**
	(2.316)	(1.821)	(1.738)	(1.861)
Log of initial real per capita GDP	−1.404**	−0.968**	−1.153**	−0.961**
	(0.283)	(0.247)	(0.211)	(0.269)
Ratio of liquid liabilities (M3) to GDP	3.570**	0.372	0.321	0.299
	(0.663)	(0.591)	(0.578)	(0.587)
Ratio of trade to GDP		−0.089		−0.045
		(0.723)		(0.765)
Ratio of government		−3.794		−4.348
expenditure to GDP		(2.860)		(4.108)
R^2	0.416	0.370	0.362	0.361
N	166	162	162	162

Notes: See notes for table 8.4. The dependent variable is the growth rate of real per capita GDP averaged for each five-year period from 1945–49 through 1990–94.

Table 8.6　　　　　**Cross-Country Trade Regressions**

	Dependent Variable: Ratio of Trade to GDP			
	OLS 1850–1997	IV 1850–1997	IV 1850–1929	IV 1945–94
Constant	−0.077	−0.054	0.100	−0.102
	(0.291)	(0.316)	(0.360)	(0.203)
Log of initial real per	0.050	0.049	0.004	0.064**
capita GDP	(0.036)	(0.039)	(0.057)	(0.025)
Ratio of broad money	0.247**	0.214*	0.605**	0.096
to GDP	(0.111)	(0.118)	(0.207)	(0.071)
R^2	0.100	0.093	0.055	0.128
N	211	199	185	164

Notes: The dependent variable is ratio of trade (exports plus imports) to gross domestic product averaged for decades from the 1850s through the 1990s (cols. [1] and [2]) and for five-year periods for 1850–1929 (col. [3]) and 1945–94 (col. [4]). Initial values are from the first year of each period. Period dummies are included in the regressions but not reported. Standard errors are in parentheses. The first column reports results from OLS regressions that use initial values as regressors. The others report results from two-stage least squares regressions that use the periodic data averages as regressors. Instruments include initial values of the ratio of government expenditure to output, the inflation rate, and the full set of regressors.

**Significant at the 5 percent level.
*Significant at the 10 percent level.

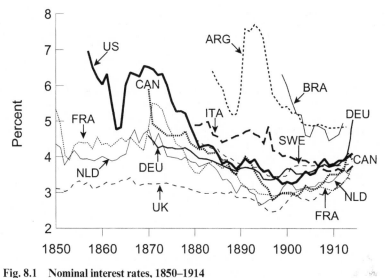

Fig. 8.1   Nominal interest rates, 1850–1914
Sources: Homer and Sylla (1996) and Obstfeld and Taylor (2000).

8.4.2   Finance and Interest-Rate Convergence

In this section, we examine the possible roles of finance and international trade in promoting the decline and convergence of long-term interest rates among the economies in our sample over the 1850–1914 period. Figure 8.1, which presents nominal interest rates for ten of the truly "Atlantic" economies in our sample, indicates that decline and convergence is indeed the general pattern of long-term rates.[11] The convergence is most striking among the European and North American countries, whose capital flows as a share of GDP over this period exceeded those achieved at any point in the postwar period,[12] and for which financial deepening over the period was particularly vigorous. To examine more explicitly whether these factors contributed importantly to the pattern in figure 8.1, we turn again to cross-country regression analysis.

In our first specification, for which we report results in table 8.7, the dependent variable is the nominal interest rate averaged over five-year periods for each country. Such a regression allows us to test for the role of finance and openness in one of the characteristics that is clear from figure 8.1, namely the decline in interest rates. To control for Fisher-type effects, we include current period inflation on the right-hand side. Since economic the-

11. Figure 8.1 includes interest rates for ten countries, including Argentina 1884–1913, Brazil 1899–1912, Canada 1870–1914, Germany 1870–1914, France 1850–1914, Italy 1880–1914, the Netherlands 1850–1914, Sweden 1880–1914, the United Kingdom 1850–1914, and the United States 1857–1914.
12. See Obstfeld and Taylor (1998, 359–60).

Table 8.7   Interest Rate Regressions, 1850–1914

	Dependent Variable: Long-Term Interest Rate					
	12 Countries			Exclude Australia and Japan		
	OLS	IV	IV	OLS	IV	IV
Constant	4.401**	4.665**	4.665**	6.724**	7.162**	7.358**
	(0.862)	(0.962)	(0.958)	(0.936)	(0.974)	(0.940)
Log of initial real per	0.059	0.041	0.038	−0.297*	−0.353**	−0.390**
capita GDP	(0.137)	(0.154)	(0.154)	(0.152)	(0.159)	(0.154)
Ratio of broad money	−2.138**	−2.437**	−2.147**	−2.290**	−2.512**	−1.971**
to GDP	(0.815)	(0.885)	(0.913)	(0.775)	(0.810)	(0.808)
Ratio of trade to GDP			−0.192			−0.343**
			(0.158)			(0.137)
Inflation rate	0.023	0.020	0.017	0.053	0.055*	0.052*
	(0.033)	(0.034)	(0.034)	(0.033)	(0.033)	(0.031)
R^2	0.268	0.294	0.309	0.355	0.394	0.447
N	101	93	93	87	84	84

Notes: The dependent variable is the average nominal long-term interest rate over a five-year period. Period dummies are included in the regressions but not reported. Standard errors are in parentheses. The OLS regressions use initial values in each five-year period as regressors. The IV regressions use the periodic data averages as regressors, and the initial values of the ratio of government expenditure to output and the full set of regressors (except inflation, which enters as a period average) as instruments.
**Significant at the 5 percent level.
*Significant at the 10 percent level.

ory also suggests a long-run link between the growth rate of the economy and the real rate of interest, we include, as in cross-country growth regressions, the initial log level of per capita real GDP on the right-hand side. The left panel of table 8.7 presents regression results for all twelve countries for which we have interest rate data (i.e., the ten countries from figure 8.1 plus Japan and Australia), while the right panel excludes the non-"Atlantic" economies. We use initial values of financial development as regressors for the OLS regressions, and contemporaneous averages of finance and trade for the IV models, with initial values of all regressors and the ratio of government expenditure to output as instruments.

The results indicate a negative partial correlation between initial financial depth and subsequent interest rates, but the results for trade and initial income (right panel) are larger when we exclude Japan and Australia. These countries were far more isolated both economically and geographically from the others, and it is thus likely that convergence would have been slower for them. The regressions in the right-hand panel seem to fit the conditional convergence model more snugly, with initial income entering with the expected negative and significant coefficient, and inflation entering with an expected positive coefficient that is significant at the 10 percent level. The

Table 8.8   Interest Rate Convergence Regressions, 1850–1914

| | Dependent Variable: Absolute Value of Long-Term Interest Rate Less Cross-Country Average | | | | | |
| | 12 Countries | | | Exclude Australia and Japan | | |
	OLS	IV	IV	OLS	IV	IV
Constant	1.818**	1.914**	1.913**	0.381	0.633	0.626
	(0.610)	(0.671)	(0.672)	(0.686)	(0.712)	(0.720)
Log of initial real per	−0.145	−0.151	−0.152	0.091	0.060	0.061
capita GDP	(0.097)	(0.107)	(0.108)	(0.111)	(0.116)	(0.118)
Ratio of broad money	−1.022*	−1.136*	−0.985	−1.145**	−1.273**	−1.292**
to GDP	(0.577)	(0.617)	(0.641)	(0.568)	(0.592)	(0.619)
Ratio of trade to GDP			−0.100			0.013
			(0.111)			(0.105)
Inflation rate	0.030	0.027	0.025	0.026	0.026	0.026
	(0.023)	(0.024)	(0.024)	(0.024)	(0.024)	(0.024)
R^2	0.122	0.156	0.164	0.147	0.191	0.191
N	101	93	93	87	84	84

Notes: The dependent variable is the absolute value of the difference of the average nominal long-term interest rate for a country over a five-year period and the cross-country average for that period. Period dummies are included in the regressions but not reported. Standard errors are in parentheses. The OLS regressions use initial values in each five-year period as regressors. The IV regressions use the periodic data averages as regressors, and the initial values of the ratio of government expenditure to output and the full set of regressors (except inflation, which enters as a periodic average) as instruments.
**Significant at the 5 percent level.
*Significant at the 10 percent level.

final IV specification reveals a partial correlation between trade and subsequent interest rates that is negative and significant at the 5 percent level. These results are consistent with roles for finance and trade in the regressions, and it is likely that they also reflect a combination of decreasing returns to capital as globalization succeeded in directing resources to the most productive uses and reductions in risk premiums that were made possible by the improved risk-sharing arrangements that accompany increasingly sophisticated financial systems.

In table 8.8, we present regressions that examine the other key feature of figure 8.1—absolute convergence in nominal long-term rates. To do this, we subtract the mean of the average interest rates of countries with observations in a given five-year period from the individual country average, and use it as the dependent variable. The right-hand sides, estimation techniques, instrument sets, and country samples are the same as in table 8.7. These results show that, controlling for time, initial income, and inflation, countries with greater financial depth at the start of a five-year period had long-term interest rates over that period that were closer to the periodic mean of the sample than those that were less financially developed by our measure. Trade effects, though important in reducing the level of interest rates, do not appear to contribute to their convergence over the 1850–1914 period.

8.5 Conclusion

Our paper brings together two strands of the economic literature—that on the finance-growth nexus and that on capital market integration—and explores the key issues surrounding each strand through both institutional or country histories and formal quantitative analysis. We find a robust correlation between financial factors and economic growth that is consistent with a leading role for finance in a broad cross-section of seventeen economies over the 1850–1997 period, with the effects of finance strongest prior to the Great Depression. This result suggests that our earlier findings for the United States between 1790 and 1850 (Rousseau and Sylla 1999) may have broader implications in other parts of the nineteenth- and early twentieth-century world.

We next showed that countries with more sophisticated financial systems engage in more trade and appear to be better integrated with other economies by econometrically identifying roles for both finance and trade in the absolute convergence in long-term interest rates that is observed among the Atlantic economies between 1850 and the start of the First World War. The results, when combined with the evidence presented from historical case studies of the Dutch Republic, England, the United States, France, Germany, and Japan over the past three centuries, suggest that the economic growth and increasing globalization of the Atlantic economies might indeed have been finance-led. In short, our reading of the evidence is that domestic financial development promotes the capital inflows from abroad that are associated with emerging markets and capital-market globalization. The two are complementary. For short historical periods, inflows of foreign capital may seem to substitute for domestic financial development. Absent the latter, however, they come to an end, usually in what are termed "financial crises." For the flow of foreign capital to be sustained over long periods, a country needs to have what we have described as a good domestic financial system.

Our broad view of such a financial system, encompassing public finance, money, banking, a central bank, and securities markets, can incorporate within it a number of issues of financial history. Did adoption and adherence to the gold standard give credibility to a country's commitments and make it easier to access international capital markets? Most likely it did, but adoption of the gold standard itself depended on other financial-system components' functioning well. Did banking promote industrialization and economic modernization? It often did, but not always all by itself. The issue is sometimes phrased in terms of whether banks made long-term loans to industrial companies. Whether that was important might depend on the presence or absence of securities markets. Moreover, the presence of securities markets is a definite advantage for banks, particularly joint stock and incorporated banks, in raising their own capitals and providing market instruments of varying degrees of liquidity in which banks could invest funds not employed in traditional bank lending. Are central banks necessary? Do they do more harm than good? These issues are complicated by the fact that most central banks evolved from public or national banks that were originally founded to serve as adjuncts of public finance. The lender of last resort and other modern central banking functions emerged later in time. So issues involving the utility of central banks cannot be separated from issues of public finance, money, banking, and even securities markets.

These issues, and others like them, indicate that one can get only so far by studying individual components of a financial system without relating them to the larger system of which they are a part and in which they function. Context matters when we study banking, central banking, money (and exchange rate regimes), securities markets, and public finance.

Questions raised by our work here remain to be explored. Are there cases in history, or in the world today, where ostensibly good financial systems did not lead to economic growth and globalization? Or are there cases in which one or both of these occurred in the absence of good financial systems? We tend to doubt it, but we recognize that more investigation is needed before we can be highly confident that good financial systems are a key ingredient of both sustained economic growth and effective participation in the global economy.

Appendix
Data Sources

In this section, we list the data sources for the series used in our regression analysis. The data draw from six sources: World Bank's *World Development Indicators 1999* database, worksheets underlying Obstfeld and Taylor (2000), Bordo and Jonung (1987), Rousseau and Wachtel (1998), and Rousseau (1999), and published interest rates from Homer and Sylla (1996). Of course, these sources themselves draw upon a vast body of government documents and the collective work of generations of economic historians whose efforts have made it possible to consolidate key macroeconomic and financial aggregates into a database that covers the Atlantic economies for the past century and a half. We do not list the primary sources here, but refer the interested reader to the materials listed above for details.

In nearly all cases, data for a given series are from more than one source. Further, the definitions across sources of a given data item are not always consistent. For example, we use the broad M3 aggregate as a measure of financial development for the later years of our sample, but in many cases have only a narrower aggregate such as M2 for earlier years. When the data are obtained from multiple sources and differ in value at the point of joining, we always use the most recent data as they appear and adjust earlier data with a ratio-splice.

We present the data sources below by country.

Argentina, 1884–1997

GDP, GDP deflator, population, money stock. 1960–97 from *World Development Indicators;* 1884–1959 from worksheets underlying Obstfeld and Taylor (2000).

Imports, exports. 1960–97 from *World Development Indicators;* 1884–1959 from Mitchell (1998b), table El, pp. 442–52.

Government expenditure. 1960–97 from *World Development Indicators;* 1884–1959 from Mitchell (1998b), table G5, pp. 670–78.

Long-term interest rate. 1884–1913 from worksheets underlying Obstfeld and Taylor (2000).

Australia, 1870–1997

GDP, GDP deflator, population. 1960–97 from *World Development Indicators;* 1870–1959 from worksheets underlying Obstfeld and Taylor (2000).

Money stock. 1960–97 is M3 from *World Development Indicators;* 1870–1959 is M2 from worksheets underlying Bordo and Jonung (1987).

Imports, exports. 1960–97 from *World Development Indicators;* 1870–1959 from Mitchell (1998a), table E1, pp. 551-58.

Government expenditure. 1960–97 from *World Development Indicators;* 1870–1959 from Mitchell (1998a), table G5, pp. 905–06.

Long-term interest rate. 1870–1914 from worksheets underlying Obstfeld and Taylor (2000).

Brazil, 1880–1997

GDP, GDP deflator, population, money stock. 1960–97 from *World Development Indicators;* 1880–1959 from worksheets underlying Obstfeld and Taylor (2000).

Imports, exports. 1960–97 from *World Development Indicators;* 1880–1959 from Mitchell (1998b), table E1, pp. 442–52.

Government expenditure. 1960–97 from *World Development Indicators;* 1880–1959 from Mitchell (1998b), table G5, pp. 670–78.

Long-term interest rate. 1899–1912 from worksheets underlying Obstfeld and Taylor (2000).

Canada, 1870–1997

GDP, GDP deflator, population. 1960–97 from *World Development Indicators;* 1870–1959 from worksheets underlying Obstfeld and Taylor (2000).
Money stock. 1960–97 is M3 from *World Development Indicators;* 1870–1959 is M2 from worksheets underlying Bordo and Jonung (1987).
Imports, exports. 1960–97 from *World Development Indicators;* 1870–1959 from Mitchell (1998b), table E1, pp. 429–41.
Government expenditure. 1960–97 from *World Development Indicators;* 1870–1959 from Mitchell (1998b), table G5, pp. 664–69.
Long-term interest rate. 1870–1914 from worksheets underlying Obstfeld and Taylor (2000).

Denmark, 1850–1997

GDP, GDP deflator, population. 1960–97 from *World Development Indicators;* 1850–1959 from worksheets underlying Obstfeld and Taylor (2000).
Money stock. 1960–97 is M3 from *World Development Indicators;* 1880–1959 is M2 from worksheets underlying Bordo and Jonung (1987); 1850–79 is liquid liabilities of the banking system from worksheets underlying Obstfeld and Taylor (2000).
Imports, exports. 1960–97 from *World Development Indicators;* 1870–1959 from Mitchell (1998c), table E1, pp. 571–86.
Government expenditure. 1960–97 from *World Development Indicators;* 1854–1959 from Mitchell (1998c), table G5, pp. 816–24.

France, 1850–1997

GDP, GDP deflator. 1960–97 from *World Development Indicators;* 1850–1913, 1921–38, 1949–59 from worksheets underlying Obstfeld and Taylor (2000).
Population. 1960–89 from *World Development Indicators;* 1850–1959 from worksheets underlying Obstfeld and Taylor (2000).
Money stock. 1960–97 is M3 from *World Development Indicators;* 1900–59 is the sum of banknote circulation from Mitchell (1998c), table G1, pp. 788–92, commercial bank deposits from Mitchell, table G2, pp. 793–99, and savings bank deposits from Mitchell, table G3, pp. 800–10; 1880–99 is banknote circulation from Mitchell, savings bank deposits from Mitchell, and M1 less circulation in the hands of the public from worksheets underlying Bordo and Jonung (1987); 1850–79 is the sum of banknote circulation and savings deposits from Mitchell.
Imports, exports. 1960–97 from *World Development Indicators;* 1850–1959 from Mitchell (1998c), table E1, pp. 571–86.
Government expenditure. 1960–97 from *World Development Indicators;* 1854–1959 from Mitchell (1998c), table G5, pp. 816–24.

Long-term interest rate. 1880–1914 from worksheets underlying Obstfeld and Taylor (2000); 1850–79 from Homer and Sylla (1996) table 25, pp. 222–23.

Finland, 1862–1997

GDP, GDP deflator. 1960–97 from *World Development Indicators;* 1862–1959 from worksheets underlying Obstfeld and Taylor (2000).

Money stock. 1960–97 from *World Development Indicators;* 1862–1959 from worksheets underlying Obstfeld and Taylor (2000).

Imports, exports. 1960–97 from *World Development Indicators;* 1862–1959 from Mitchell (1998c), table E1, pp. 571–86.

Government expenditure. 1960–97 from *World Development Indicators;* 1882–1959 from Mitchell (1998c), table G5, pp. 816–24.

Germany, 1850–1989

GDP, GDP deflator. 1960–89 from *World Development Indicators;* 1850–1913, 1925–38, 1950–59 from worksheets underlying Obstfeld and Taylor (2000).

Population. 1960–89 from *World Development Indicators;* 1880–1959 from worksheets underlying Obstfeld and Taylor (2000); 1850–79 from Mitchell (1998c), table A5, pp. 79–91.

Money stock. 1960–97 is M3 from *World Development Indicators;* 1850–1944, 1948–59 is liquid liabilities in the financial system from worksheets underlying Obstfeld and Taylor (2000).

Imports, exports. 1960–97 from *World Development Indicators;* 1880–1959 from Mitchell (1998c), table E1, pp. 571–86.

Government expenditure. 1960–97 from *World Development Indicators;* 1872–1959 from Mitchell (1998c), table G5, pp. 816–24.

Long-term interest rate. 1870–1914 from worksheets underlying Obstfeld and Taylor (2000).

Italy, 1862–1997

GDP, GDP deflator. 1960–97 from *World Development Indicators;* 1862–1959 from worksheets underlying Obstfeld and Taylor (2000).

Population. 1960–97 from *World Development Indicators;* 1880–1959 from worksheets underlying Obstfeld and Taylor (2000), 1862–79 from Mitchell (1998c), table A5, pp. 79–91.

Money stock. 1962–97 is M3 from *World Development Indicators;* 1880–1961 is M2 from worksheets underlying Bordo and Jonung (1987); 1872–79 is the sum of banknote circulation from Mitchell (1998c), table G1, pp. 788–92, commercial bank deposits from Mitchell, table G2, pp. 793–99, and savings bank deposits from Mitchell, table G3, pp. 800–10.

Imports, exports. 1960–97 from *World Development Indicators;* 1862–1959 from Mitchell (1998c), table E1, pp. 571–86.

Government expenditure. 1960–97 from *World Development Indicators;* 1862–1959 from Mitchell (1998c), table G5, pp. 816–24.

Long-term interest rate. 1880–1914 from worksheets underlying Obstfeld and Taylor (2000).

Japan, 1885–1997

GDP. 1960–97 from *World Development Indicators;* 1945–59 from Mitchell (1998a) table J1, pp. 1025–38; 1885–1944 from worksheets underlying Rousseau (1999).

GDP deflator. 1960–97 from *World Development Indicators;* 1945–59 from Mitchell (1998a) table J1, pp. 1025–38 constructed as quotient of nominal GDP and GDP in constant 1934–36 units; 1885–1944 from worksheets underlying Rousseau (1999).

Population. 1960–97 from *World Development Indicators;* 1945–59 from Mitchell (1998a) table A5, pp. 57–63; 1885–1944 from worksheets underlying Rousseau (1999).

Money stock. 1960–97 is M3 from *World Development Indicators;* 1945–59 is the sum of banknote circulation from Mitchell (1998a), table G1, pp. 830–37, commercial bank deposits from Mitchell, table G2, pp. 848–56, and savings bank deposits from Mitchell, table G3, pp. 864–68; 1878–1944 from worksheets underlying Rousseau (1999).

Imports, exports. 1960–97 from *World Development Indicators;* 1860–1959 from Mitchell (1998a), table E1, pp. 538–50.

Government expenditure. 1960–97 from *World Development Indicators;* 1860–1959 from Mitchell (1998a), table G5, pp. 898–904.

Long-term interest rate. 1880–1914 from worksheets underlying Obstfeld and Taylor (2000).

The Netherlands, 1850–1997

GDP, GDP deflator, population. 1960–97 from *World Development Indicators;* 1850–1959 from worksheets underlying Obstfeld and Taylor (2000).

Money stock. 1960–97 is M3 from *World Development Indicators;* 1918–59 is the sum of circulation in the hands of the public from Mitchell (1998c), table G1, pp. 788–92, commercial bank deposits from Mitchell, table G2, pp. 793–99, and savings bank deposits from Mitchell, table G3, pp. 800–10. 1900–17 is circulation and savings deposits from Mitchell; 1850–99 is defined as in 1918–59, with commercial bank deposits interpolated under a constant growth assumption between five-year benchmarks for 1850–74.

Imports, exports. 1960–97 from *World Development Indicators;* 1850–1959 from Mitchell (1998c), table E1, pp. 571–86.

Government expenditure. 1960–97 from *World Development Indicators;* 1850–1959 from Mitchell (1998c), table G5, pp. 816–24.

Long-term interest rate. 1850–1914 from worksheets underlying Obstfeld and Taylor (2000).

Norway, 1865–1997

GDP, GDP deflator, population. 1960–97 from *World Development Indicators;* 1865–1959 from worksheets underlying Rousseau and Wachtel (1998).

Money stock. 1960–97 is M3 from *World Development Indicators;* 1865–1959 is the sum of circulation in the hands of the public from Mitchell (1998c), table G1, pp. 788–92, commercial bank deposits from Mitchell, table G2, pp. 793–99, and savings bank deposits from Mitchell, table G3, pp. 800–10. Commercial and savings bank deposits were interpolated under a constant growth assumption between five-year benchmarks for 1865–74.

Imports, exports. 1960–97 from *World Development Indicators;* 1865–1959 from Mitchell (1998c), table E1, pp. 571–86.

Government expenditure. 1960–97 from *World Development Indicators;* 1865–1959 from Mitchell (1998c), table G5, pp. 816–24.

Portugal, 1880–1997

GDP, GDP deflator, population. 1960–97 from *World Development Indicators;* 1880–1959 from worksheets underlying Obstfeld and Taylor (2000).

Money stock. 1960–97 is M3 from *World Development Indicators;* 1880–1959 from worksheets underlying Obstfeld and Taylor (2000).

Imports, exports. 1960–97 from *World Development Indicators;* 1880–1959 from Mitchell (1998c), table E1, pp. 571–86.

Government expenditure. 1960–97 from *World Development Indicators;* 1880–1959 from Mitchell (1998c), table G5, pp. 816–24.

Spain, 1850–1997

GDP, GDP deflator, population. 1960–97 from *World Development Indicators;* 1875–1959 from worksheets underlying Obstfeld and Taylor (2000).

Money stock. 1960–97 is M3 from *World Development Indicators;* 1875–1959 is the sum of banknote circulation from Mitchell (1998c), table G1, pp. 788–92, commercial bank deposits from Mitchell, table G2, pp. 793–99, and savings bank deposits from Mitchell, table G3, pp. 800–10.

Imports, exports. 1960–97 from *World Development Indicators;* 1875–1959 from Mitchell (1998c), table E1, pp. 571–86.

Government expenditure. 1960–97 from *World Development Indicators;* 1875–1959 from Mitchell (1998c), table G5, pp. 816–24.

Sweden, 1861–1997

GDP, GDP deflator, population. 1960–97 from *World Development Indicators;* 1861–1959 from worksheets underlying Obstfeld and Taylor (2000).

Money stock. 1960–97 is M3 from *World Development Indicators;* 1870–1959 is the sum of banknote circulation from Mitchell (1998c), table G1,

pp. 788–92, commercial bank deposits from Mitchell, table G2, pp. 793–99, and savings bank deposits from Mitchell, table G3, pp. 800–10.
Imports, exports. 1960–97 from *World Development Indicators;* 1870–1959 from Mitchell (1998c), table E1, pp. 571–86.
Government expenditure. 1960–97 from *World Development Indicators;* 1870–1959 from Mitchell (1998c), table G5, pp. 816–24.

United Kingdom, 1850–1997

GDP, GDP deflator. 1960–97 from *World Development Indicators;* 1850–1959 from worksheets underlying Obstfeld and Taylor (2000).
Population. 1960–97 from *World Development Indicators;* 1870–1959 from worksheets underlying Obstfeld and Taylor (2000); 1850–79 from Mitchell (1998c), table A5, pp. 79–91.
Money stock. 1994–97 is M2 from *World Development Indicators;* 1870–1993 is M2 from worksheets underlying Obstfeld and Taylor (2000).
Imports, exports. 1960–97 from *World Development Indicators;* 1850–1959 from Mitchell (1998c), table E1, pp. 571–86.
Government expenditure. 1960–97 from *World Development Indicators;* 1850–1959 from Mitchell (1998c), table G5, pp. 816–24.
Long-term interest rate. 1870–1914 from worksheets underlying Obstfeld and Taylor (2000).

United States, 1870–1997

GDP. 1960–97 from *World Development Indicators;* 1870–1959 from worksheets underlying Obstfeld and Taylor (2000), 1850–69 from Berry (1988), table 3, pp. 18–20.
GDP deflator. 1960–97 from *World Development Indicators;* 1870–1959 from worksheets underlying Obstfeld and Taylor (2000), 1850–1869 derived as quotient of nominal and real GNP from Berry (1988), table 3, pp. 18–20, and table 7, p. 23.
Population. 1960–97 from *World Development Indicators;* 1870–1959 from worksheets underlying Obstfeld and Taylor (2000), 1850–69 from Berry (1988), table 6, p. 22.
Money stock. 1960–97 is M3 from *World Development Indicators;* 1870–1959 is M2 from worksheets underlying Wachtel and Rousseau (1995); 1850–69 from worksheets underlying Obstfeld and Taylor (2000).
Imports, exports. 1960–97 from *World Development Indicators;* 1850–1959 from Mitchell (1998b), table E1, pp. 429–41.
Government expenditure. 1960–97 from *World Development Indicators;* 1850–1959 from Mitchell (1998a), table G5, pp. 664–9.
Long-term interest rate. 1870–1914 from worksheets underlying Obstfeld and Taylor (2000), 1860–69 are high-grade railroad bond yields from Homer and Sylla (1996), table 42, pp. 309–10.

References

Barro, Robert J. 1991. Economic growth in a cross section of countries. *Quarterly Journal of Economics* 56:407–43.

Bell, Clive, and Peter L. Rousseau. 2001. Post-independence India: A case of finance-led industrialization? *Journal of Development Economics* 65 (2): 153–75.

Bencivenga, Valerie R., and Bruce D. Smith. 1991. Financial intermediation and endogenous growth. *Review of Economic Studies* 58:195–209.

Berry, Thomas Senior. 1988. Production and population since 1789: Revised GNP series in constant dollars. Bostwick Paper no. 6. Richmond, Va.: Bostwick Press.

Bordo, Michael D., and Lars Jonung. 1987. *The long-run behavior of the velocity of circulation*. New York: Cambridge University Press.

———. 2001. A return to the convertibility principal? Monetary and fiscal regimes in historical perspective, ed. Axel Leijonhufvud. In *Monetary theory as a basis for monetary policy*. London: Macmillan. In press.

Born, K. E. 1983. *International banking in the nineteenth and twentieth centuries*. New York: St. Martin's.

Brewer, J. 1990. *The sinews of power: War, money, and the English state, 1688–1783.* Cambridge: Harvard University Press.

Cameron, Rondo, with O. Crisp, Hugh T. Patrick, and Richard Tilly. 1967. *Banking in the early stages of industrialization: A study in comparative economic history.* New York: Oxford University Press.

Capie, Forrest H. 2001a. The monetary dimension in eighteenth-century England. Working paper. Forthcoming in *Festschrift for Patrick O'Brien.*

———. 2001b. The origins and development of stable fiscal and monetary institutions in England. In *The legacy of Western European fiscal and monetary institutions for the New World,* ed. Michael D. Bordo and Roberto Cortes Conde, 19–58. Cambridge: Cambridge University Press.

Chancellor, Edward. 1998. *Devil take the hindmost: A history of financial speculation.* New York: Farrar, Straus, and Giroux.

Checkland, S. G. 1975. *Scottish banking: A history, 1695–1973.* Glasgow: Collins.

Davis, Lance E., and Robert J. Cull. 1994. *International capital markets and American economic growth, 1820–1914.* Cambridge: Cambridge University Press.

———. 2000. International capital movements, domestic capital markets, and American economic growth, 1820–1914. In *The Cambridge economic history of the United States.* Vol. 2, *The long nineteenth century,* ed. Stanley L. Engerman and Robert E. Gallman, 733–812. Cambridge: Cambridge University Press.

de Vries, Jan, and A. van der Woude. 1997. *The first modern economy: Success, failure, and perseverance of the Dutch economy, 1500–1815.* Cambridge: Cambridge University Press.

Dickson, P. G. M. 1967. *The financial revolution in England: A study in the development of public credit, 1688–1756.* London: Macmillan.

Edwards, Sebastian. 1998. Openness, productivity, and growth: What do we really know? *Economic Journal* 108 (477): 383–98.

Feis, H. 1965. *Europe, the world's banker, 1870–1914.* 1930. Reprint, New York: Norton.

Fenstermaker, J. Van. 1965. *The development of American commercial banking: 1782–1837.* Kent, Ohio: Kent State University Press.

Ferguson, Niall. 2001. *The cash nexus: Money and power in the world, 1700–2000.* New York: Basic Books.

Frankel, Jeffrey A., and David Romer. 1999. Does trade cause growth? *American Economic Review* 89 (3): 379–99.

Goldsmith, Raymond W. 1969. *Financial structure and development.* New Haven, Conn.: Yale University Press.

Greenwood, Jeremy, and Boyan Jovanovic. 1990. Financial development, growth, and the distribution of income. *Journal of Political Economy* 98:1076–107.

Gurley, John G., and Edward S. Shaw. 1955. Financial aspects of economic development. *American Economic Review* 45 (2): 515–38.

Hart, M., J. Jonker, and J. L. van Zanden. 1997. *A financial history of the Netherlands.* Cambridge: Cambridge University Press.

Hoffman, Philip T., Gilles Postel-Vinay, and Jean-Laurent Rosenthal. 2000. *Priceless markets: The political economy of credit in Paris, 1660–1870.* Chicago: University of Chicago Press.

Homer, Sydney, and Richard Sylla. 1996. *A history of interest rates.* 3rd ed., rev. New Brunswick, N.J.: Rutgers University Press.

Kindleberger, Charles P. 1984. *A financial history of Western Europe.* London: George Allen and Unwin.

King, Robert G., and Ross Levine. 1993a. Finance and growth: Schumpeter might be right. *Quarterly Journal of Economics* 108:717–37.

———. 1993b. Finance, entrepreneurship, and growth: Theory and evidence. *Journal of Monetary Economics* 32 (3): 513–42.

Landes, D. 1965. Technological change and development in Western Europe, 1750–1914. In *The Cambridge economic history of Europe.* Vol. 6, *The industrial revolutions and after: Incomes, population, and technological change,* ed. H. J. Habakkuh and M. Postan, 274–601. Cambridge: Cambridge University Press.

Levine, Ross, and Sara Zervos. 1998. Stock markets, banks, and economic growth. *American Economic Review* 88:537–58.

McKinnon, Ronald I. 1973. *Money and capital in economic development.* Washington, D.C.: Brookings Institution.

Mitchell, Brian R. 1998a. *International historical statistics: Africa, Asia, and Oceania, 1750–1993.* 4th ed. New York: Stockton.

———. 1998b. *International historical statistics: The Americas, 1750–1993.* 4th ed. New York: Stockton.

———. 1998c. *International historical statistics: Europe, 1750–1993.* 4th ed. New York: Stockton.

Miwa, Yoshiro, and J. Mark Ramseyer. 2000a. Banks and economic growth: Implications from Japanese history. Discussion Paper no. 289. Cambridge, Mass.: Harvard Law School, John M. Olin Center for Law, Economics, and Business, August.

———. 2000b. Corporate governance in transitional economies: Lessons from the pre-war Japanese cotton textile industry. *Journal of Legal Studies* 29:171–204.

———. 2001. Property rights and indigenous tradition among early twentieth-century Japanese firms. Discussion Paper no. 311. Cambridge, Mass.: Harvard Law School, John M. Olin Center for Law, Economics, and Business, February.

Morikawa, H. 1992. *Zaibatsu: The rise and fall of family enterprise groups in Japan.* Tokyo: University of Tokyo Press.

Murphy, Antoin E. 1997. *John Law: Economic theorist and policy-maker.* Oxford, U.K.: Clarendon.

Neal, Larry. 1990. *The rise of financial capitalism: International capital markets in the age of reason.* Cambridge: Cambridge University Press.

Obstfeld, Maurice, and Alan M. Taylor. 1998. The Great Depression as a watershed: International capital mobility over the long run. In *The defining moment: The Great Depression and the American economy in the twentieth century,* ed. Michael D. Bordo, Claudia Goldin, and Eugene N. White, 353–402. Chicago: University of Chicago Press.

————. 2000. *Global capital markets: Integration, crises, and growth.* Japan-U.S. Center Sanwa Monographs on International Financial Markets. Cambridge: Cambridge University Press.

Perkins, Edwin J. 1994. *American public finance and financial services, 1700–1815.* Columbus: Ohio State University Press.

Pressnell, L. S. 1956. *Country banking in the industrial revolution.* Oxford, U.K.: Clarendon.

Robinson, Joan. 1952. *The rate of interest and other essays.* London: Macmillan.

Rosovsky, Henry. 1966. Japan's transition to modern economic growth, 1868–1885. In *Industrialization in two systems: Essays in honor of Alexander Gerschenkron,* ed. Henry Rosovsky, 91–139. New York: Wiley.

Rousseau, Peter L. 1998. The permanent effects of innovation on financial depth: Theory and U.S. historical evidence from unobservable components models. *Journal of Monetary Economics* 42 (2): 387–425.

————. 1999. Finance, investment, and growth in Meiji-era Japan. *Japan and the World Economy* 11 (2): 185–98.

Rousseau, Peter L., and Richard Sylla. 1999. Emerging financial markets and early U.S. growth. NBER Working Paper no. 7528. Cambridge, Mass.: National Bureau of Economic Research.

Rousseau, Peter L., and Paul Wachtel. 1998. Financial intermediation and economic performance: Historical evidence from five industrialized countries. *Journal of Money, Credit, and Banking* 30 (4): 657–78.

————. 2000. Equity markets and growth: Cross country evidence on timing and outcomes. *Journal of Banking and Finance* 24 (12): 1933–57.

Schama, S. 1988. *The embarrassment of riches: An interpretation of the Dutch culture of the golden age.* New York: Knopf.

Sussman, Nathan, and Yishay Yafeh. 2000. Institutions, reforms, and country risk: Lessons from Japanese government debt in the Meiji era. *Journal of Economic History* 60 (2): 442–67.

Suzuki, T. 1994. *Japanese government loan issues on the London capital market, 1870–1913.* London: Athlone.

Sylla, Richard. 1999a. Emerging markets in history: The United States, Japan, and Argentina. In *Global competition and integration,* ed. Ryuzo Sato et al., 427–46. Boston: Kluwer Academic Publishers.

————. 1999b. Shaping the U.S. financial system, 1690–1913. In *The state, the financial system, and economic modernization,* ed. Richard Sylla, R. Tilly, and G. Tortella, 249–70. Cambridge: Cambridge University Press.

Sylla, Richard, Jack W. Wilson, and Robert E. Wright. 1997. America's first securities markets, 1790–1830: Emergence, development, and integration. Paper presented at the Cliometrics Conference, 16–18 May, Toronto, Canada.

Tamaki, N. 1995. *Japanese banking: A history, 1859–1959.* Cambridge: Cambridge University Press.

Tracy, J. D. 1985. *A financial revolution in the Habsburg Netherlands: Renten and renteniers in the country of Holland, 1515–1565.* Berkeley: University of California Press.

van der Wee, H. 1963. *The growth of the Antwerp market.* 3 vols. The Hague: Nijhoff.

Wachtel, Paul, and Peter L. Rousseau. 1995. Financial intermediation and economic growth: A historical comparison of the United States, the United Kingdom, and Canada. In *Anglo-American financial systems: Institutions and markets in the twentieth century,* ed. Michael D. Bordo and R. Sylla, 329–81. Homewood, Ill.: Business One Irwin.

White, Eugene N. 2001. France and the failure to modernize macroeconomic institutions. In *The legacy of western European fiscal and monetary institutions for the*

New World, ed. Michael D. Bordo and Roberto Cortes Conde, 59–99. Cambridge: Cambridge University Press.
Wilkins, Mira. 1989. *The history of foreign investment in the United States to 1914.* Cambridge, Mass.: Harvard University Press.
World Bank. 1999. *World development indicators.* Washington, D.C.: World Bank.

Comment   Charles W. Calomiris

Do good financial institutions promote economic growth? To what extent are the gains from international linkages contingent on the prior establishment of a robust domestic financial system? These questions, posed by Rousseau and Sylla, are important, and the contributions they make toward answering them are significant. In no other paper of which I am aware have the methodologies of narrative economic history and econometrics been combined so well to analyze the nexus among finance, growth, and international openness over a long stretch of time for so many countries. The careful assembly and use of pertinent data is impressive. The empirical evidence and narrative lend support to the authors' working hypotheses that (a) a robust domestic financial system is conducive to growth, and (b) a robust domestic financial system attracts foreign capital, thus magnifying both the gains from good domestic financial institutions and the gains from participating in global commodity and factor markets.

The authors begin by defining what constitutes a good domestic financial system. They provide narrative historical case studies of the development of such systems in Great Britain, the Netherlands, the United States, France, Germany, and Japan, and show that the development of a good financial system, in each of these important cases, predates periods of rapid economic growth. In the formal econometric analysis in the paper, the authors show, more generally, that the establishment of a proper domestic financial system (indicated by the ratio of M3 to GDP) predates growth in per capita income, growth in trade, and interest rate convergence to the international norm. The case studies are authoritative and fairly convincing, and the cases are historically important, involving large countries and important turning points in global economic development. The stories are told well. The regression evidence is new and interesting, and is consistent with a growing empirical literature that suggests strong causal links from domestic finance to economic growth in the post–World War II era (for reviews, see Beim and Calomiris 2001, ch. 2–4, and World Bank 2001).

Not surprisingly in a paper of this scope, the analysis raises interesting

Charles W. Calomiris is the Paul M. Montrone Professor of Finance and Economics at the Columbia University Graduate School of Business and a research associate of the National Bureau of Economic Research.

questions that the paper does not fully answer. Two of the most important questions that arise in the paper are (a) can one be sure that the statistical measures of financial progress are exogenous with respect to economic growth, and (b) which element of domestic financial progress is most important for producing economic growth?

A convincing econometric demonstration of exogeneity of M3-GDP would require the identification of instruments—variables that are clearly correlated with financial development and not with economic development. Lagged M3-GDP or lagged inflation (which the authors employ) are not satisfactory in this regard, since both are endogenous to economic growth, which is itself serially correlated. Of course, part of the appeal to combining historical case studies and statistical evidence is that the case studies help to establish the exogeneity of financial institutions by describing the importance of historical forces other than prior economic growth in establishing good financial institutions.

Another empirical question relevant for determining the direction of causality is whether M3-GDP proxies for investment (because bank credit responds passively to investment-related demands for funds), given that investment is not included in the system of equations. In other words, one could argue that M3-GDP plays a passive role in economic growth but appears to be important in causing growth because of the exclusion of investment from the system of equations.

Even if one accepts the causal interpretation of the authors—that a good financial system promotes growth—there is still the intractable problem of determining which element of financial development discussed by the authors matters most for promoting economic growth, trade, and financial integration. I am not very troubled by the authors' choice of M3-GDP as a measure of financial development, despite the exclusion of securities market depth from the measurement of financial development. In a single number M3-GDP captures reasonably well the two basic building blocks of any financial system—a transacting system and a credit system—because M3 combines currency (whether provided by banks or the government) with bank deposits (an indicator of bank credit and liquidity). Liquidity and credit are crucial prerequisites to the development of securities markets. Indeed, banking system depth and securities market depth tend to be positively correlated across countries precisely because the two go hand in hand. This should not be surprising. Bank lending is an early form of finance for firms that eventually move to securities markets, and banks provide important sources of credit to securities market dealers.

Despite M3's appeal as a measure of financial system activity, the M3 aggregate does not distinguish among the various aspects of financial development. Good monetary policy raises money demand, which can raise M3 and contribute to economic growth. By establishing a reliable hard money standard, a country may encourage foreign capital inflows (what Bordo and

Rockoff [1996] have termed the "Good Housekeeping Seal of Approval" from adopting the gold standard), which can also raise M3 and promote growth. Good banking policy can increase private bank chartering, which can raise credit supply, which is also reflected in M3, and which also can contribute to growth. Which is the more important influence, sound money or abundant bank credit?

Nor does the M3 measure distinguish between the activities of private and public banks, both of which contribute to deposit and credit creation. The authors' stories revolve mainly, but not entirely, around the role of private bank finance in domestic economic development, but they also recognize the importance of stable money and of developed public financial institutions (central banks or public banks). In some of the early episodes of financial development the authors discuss (the early British and Dutch experiences) it is even difficult to separate the private from the public character of banking enterprises. Was government policy (e.g., empire building via the creation of joint stock companies, including banks) more or less important than the supply of domestic credit for spurring Dutch and British growth? Was the effect of banks on the fiscal health of the government relatively important or unimportant? All these influences—private credit supply, fiscal health, stable money, mercantilist financing of empire—are mixed in the "black box" of M3.

In summary, the excellent paper by Rousseau and Sylla charts an ambitious course and, not surprisingly, poses more questions than it resolves. We can look forward to future work by these and other authors that will investigate further the directions of causation between real and financial growth, and the relative importance of the various parts of financial development for economic development.

References

Beim, David O., and Charles W. Calomiris. 2001. *Emerging financial markets.* New York: Irwin/McGraw-Hill.

Bordo, Michael D., and Hugh Rockoff. 1996. The gold standard as a "Good Housekeeping Seal of Approval." *Journal of Economic History* 56 (2): 389–429.

World Bank. 2001. *Finance for growth.* Washington, D.C.: World Bank.

9

Core, Periphery, Exchange Rate Regimes, and Globalization

Michael D. Bordo and Marc Flandreau

9.1 Introduction

Historians know the crucial importance played by the boundary that separated the core of the Roman Empire from its periphery—a boundary known as the *Limes*. In addition to being a line of military defense, it was a locus of cross-influences. While the core contributed to shaping the "barbarous" lands located beyond its walls, the periphery shaped the inner areas, since protection from the dangers of military conflict involved providing for such outcomes. And for reasons that are hard to understand, the long survival of this frontier extended long after the fall of the Roman Empire: More than ten centuries after its collapse, the former *Limes* surprisingly coincided with the line that separated Christians during the religious wars, into Protestants and Roman Catholics.

In comparison with this very long-run phenomenon, the experience of the international monetary system is that of a toddler. And yet the recent turmoil in international financial markets has forced economists and policymakers to come to grips with something similar. The recent discussions on the exchange rate regimes that are advisable in order to cope with finan-

Michael D. Bordo is professor of economics at Rutgers University and a research associate of the National Bureau of Economic Research. Marc Flandreau is professor of economics at the Institut d'Etudes Politiques de Paris.

We are grateful to Ignacio Briones, Dhiman Das, Sonal Dhingra, Juan Flores, and David Khoudour-Casteras for excellent research assistance. They thank Larry Neal, Marc Weidenmeir, Antu Murshid, Ugo Pannizza, and Anne Jansen for providing data. Comments from our discussants Anna Schwartz, Charlie Calomiris, Angela Redish, Chris Meissner, and especially Alan Taylor, and conference participants are gratefully acknowledged. Discussions with Frédéric Zumer proved very useful to foster thinking on the Feldstein-Horioka regressions. Bordo gratefully acknowledges the financial support of the NBER and the National Science Foundation.

cial instability rest on the observation that the challenges of globalization are not quite the same depending on whether we focus on developing countries and emerging markets or developed ones. Whereas the latter are free to go their exchange rate way, the former are said to face the dilemma of either anchoring themselves to core countries with extra strong glue, or remaining out of the *Limes* of modern integration with a volatile exchange rate.

As a recent literature has argued, there is a certain "fear of floating" among modern developing countries. But this is obviously *nihil novi sub sole* for economic historians familiar with that other major experience of globalization, namely that of the late nineteenth century. For then, already, there was a core that followed the high road of more or less complete gold convertibility, and an infamous periphery that had trouble pegging but resented floating. And it is striking that the list of "peripheral" nations has not changed that much over the course of the century: Today, like yesterday, it includes Latin American countries, Central Europe, Russia, and to some extent Asia—among the latter, Japan was already standing out as an exception.[1]

This persistence nonetheless conceals a profound transformation of the international monetary system—a transformation that has occurred at the core of the global exchange rate system. Today, flexible exchange rates have superseded, in advanced countries (with the notable exception of Europe) the nineteenth-century system of fixed exchange rates known as the gold standard. In other words, "globalization" appears to mean surprisingly consistent things in the periphery, but radically opposite things in the core. This may in fact sound somewhat paradoxical: In the late nineteenth century globalization was in the popular mind associated with the gold standard, and most academics concurred (Kemmerer 1916). Yet after the collapse of the Bretton Woods system in the early 1970s the heart of the global monetary system is based on floating exchange rates. How do we interpret this? On the surface, this would seem to suggest that the exchange rate system is quite irrelevant to the process of globalization: Nature finds its ways. At the same time, how do we make sense of the serious concerns that academics and policymakers have over the problem of the appropriate exchange rate system for the emerging countries? Why should there be different recipes for the advanced and the emergers?

The theoretical literature pertaining to the links between integration and

1. We use the distinction *core* versus *periphery* for the pre-1914 period following a well-established tradition in economic history. For the recent period we use the terminology *advanced* versus *emerging* countries. The difference between the two demarcations is largely geographical (the core before 1914 meant Western Europe and after 1900 the United States, whereas the periphery was everyone else). Today advanced countries are in every region. The key unifying theme for both demarcations, as pointed out by our discussant Anna Schwartz, is that (core) advanced countries are generally capital rich and the (periphery) emerging countries are generally capital poor.

exchange rate regimes generally overlooks this problem. Two opposite views may be identified. Both assume some kind of market imperfection, because in a perfectly rational and frictionless world, fixed and flexible systems should deliver identical outcomes and the question of the links between exchange rate regimes and integration would be irrelevant (Helpman 1981).

The "transaction costs" view on the one hand assumes that floating exchange rates are a risk that cannot be diversified away and thus tantamount to a distortion preventing full specialization. From this perspective a fixed exchange rate may deliver both a higher level of integration and superior economic performance. This view is very old and originates in nineteenth-century classical economics.

On the other hand, the "policy view" rests on the notion that, due to the existence of nominal rigidities and factor immobility, flexible exchange rates might be advisable to smooth out the international adjustment process: Exchange rate flexibility, from this perspective, is not an enemy to international integration. This view is traditionally associated with Robert Mundell, and Padoa-Schioppa's trilemma. It has been put to work by Barry Eichengreen to explain the (according to the recent literature, partial) trend toward fluctuating exchange rates. The expansion of democracy, by calling for an increase in income smoothing, has led more and more countries to float their way into globalization—again with the notable exception of Europe.

None of these views, however, takes seriously into account the dichotomy between core and peripheral countries. And yet the quite distinct dynamics of exchange rate regimes depending on whether we focus on the center or on the periphery suggests that different stories may have to be told for each. At the same time, as the comparison with the Roman Empire suggests, the record of the center cannot be understood without reference to the periphery, and vice versa. Systems are tested on their margins.

In this paper we seek to provide an interpretation of both the presence of "fear of floating" in the periphery and the transition to flexible exchange rates in the center. Our argument rests on the role of technological progress in money and finance. In the nineteenth century, adherence to gold provided a stable environment that contributed to the development of deep and liquid money markets. At the same time, gold convertibility was a constraint on monetary policies because it implied currency bands within which core nations sought to obtain as much room to maneuver as they could. By the 1970s, financial maturity allowed the core countries to float. In a sense in the current floating regime countries, by learning to follow a domestic nominal anchor, have been able to eliminate the credibility bands of the classical gold standard, which in its time granted the core countries only a modicum of the policy independence they have today.

By contrast to the core, many peripheral countries in the pre-1914 period lacked what we suggest calling the "financial maturity" to successfully adhere to gold. The alternative of floating was fraught with danger because they were forced to obtain the foreign capital crucial to their development by borrowing in terms of sterling (or other core-country currencies) or else having gold clauses.

In times of financial crises, then as now, devaluations led to debt crises. Thus, we argue that peripheral countries then, as now, were forced to adopt super-hard fixed exchange rates (currency boards or close to 100 percent gold reserves then, currency boards or dollarization now) because they had not developed the financial maturity to float, or else they had to restrict foreign borrowing. Thus, the link between globalization and the exchange rate regime turns out to depend on financial maturity:[2] That is, "Tell us how financially mature you are, and we will tell you what exchange rate regime you'll end up with through globalization!"

The remainder of the paper is organized as follows. In section 9.2, we set the stage by considering the evidence on global financial integration from 1880 to 1997, using the well-known Feldstein-Horioka approach. The contribution of our work is that it combines both cross-section and time series dimensions with an extended sample of emerging countries to show a number of disturbing facts that suggest that financial globalization varies a lot depending on the type of country—core (advanced) or periphery (emerging)—and the type of regime (floating, fixed) we consider. This leads to the conclusion that financial integration today is primarily an advanced country phenomenon, while the link with the exchange rate regime is a complex one.

Section 9.3 lays out the financial maturity hypothesis and presents narrative evidence for the pre-1914 period of the different experiences of the core and peripheral countries in adhering to the gold standard.

Section 9.4 presents some empirical evidence on the link between financial depth and the exchange rate regime for core (advanced) and peripheral (emerging) countries 1880–1913 and today.

Section 9.5 summarizes our findings and suggests some lessons from history.

9.2   Financial Integration, Exchange Rate Regimes, and Hollowing Out

In this section, we use saving-investment correlation tests (Feldstein and Horioka 1980). Saving-investment (S-I) tests seek to measure the degree of

2. The main focus of our study is the exchange rate arrangements of the two periods of globalization (i.e., of open capital markets and relatively open trade). We do not take a stand on why the global system collapsed after 1918 (or, more correctly, after 1931) and was not reattained until the 1980s. We are sympathetic to the view that the deglobalization of the middle two quarters of the twentieth century had a lot to do with the disruptive "second thirty years' war" that began in 1914 and only really ended with the end of the cold war. We are agnostic on the views of those who see the breakdown of the global system as related to flaws of the gold standard and to those who see it as a backlash to the excesses of the earlier age of globalization.

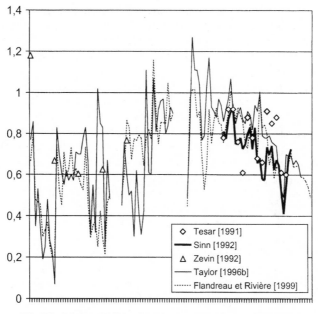

1880 1888 1896 1904 1912 1920 1928 1936 1944 1952 1960 1968 1976 1984 1992

Fig. 9.1   The inverted U-shaped pattern of financial integration
Source: Flandreau and Rivière (1999).

financial integration by examining the relationship between saving and investment. Integration is high if the correlation of a regression of investment on saving is low and vice versa: In the latter case investment is constrained by domestic savings, whereas it is not in the former case. Feldstein-Horioka's analysis sparked a considerable research effort. One important area of research was the analysis of the historical behavior of correlation coefficients in order to document the historical progress of international financial integration. Standard references in this field are Bayoumi (1990), Tesar (1991), Zevin (1992), Eichengreen (1992), Obstfeld (1995), Jones and Obstfeld (1997), Bayoumi (1997), and Obstfeld and Taylor (1998).[3] These works outline the now famous inverted U-shaped pattern of financial integration, which is obtained when one plots the results from a series of annual cross-section regressions for the period 1880–1995 (fig. 9.1).[4] The message

3. See Flandreau and Rivière (1999) for a survey.
4. The countries were Argentina, Australia, Austria, Belgium, Canada, Denmark, Finland, France, Germany, Greece, Ireland, Iceland, Italy, Japan, Luxembourg, Norway, New Zealand, the Netherlands, Portugal, Russia, Spain, Sweden, Switzerland, the United Kingdom, and the United States. For data sources see appendix to Flandreau and Rivière (1999), available on request.

seems to be that, after the interruption of the interwar years, the world is heading toward reglobalization that recalls nineteenth-century patterns. We refer to this as the "folk view."

9.2.1   Taking Panel Econometrics Seriously

We seek to show that this wisdom is too simple and conceals a number of finer phenomena. This is done by extending existing analyses in two critical directions. First, we supplement the traditional cross-section regressions by panel estimates. Second, when this can be done (i.e., for the post-1973 period) we supplement the traditional group, of primarily advanced countries that researchers have been looking at, with a large sample of emerging countries.

The importance of panel econometrics for analyzing S-I correlation was emphasized by Krol (1996), Coiteux and Simon (2000), and Flandreau and Rivière (1999). Panel data such as those used in Feldstein-Horioka (FH) regressions have two dimensions. Research on the long-run behavior of S-I regressions has focused on the interindividual dimension, computing cross-section regressions either on annual data on or individual averages for given periods. These latter estimates are known as between-estimates. They may be thought of as generalizations of pointwise cross-section regressions.

One problem with between-estimates, though, is that they introduce a number of biases in the estimation technique. For instance, they tend to overestimate "true" disintegration when current accounts experience frequent reversals, because averaging wipes out those reversals. This is why "within"-estimates are in our view a much sounder measure, because they highlight an essential dynamic dimension of financial integration by focusing on the ability of countries to finance *changes* in their current account position. Indeed, within estimates measure whether increases in investment above average can occur without running into an investment constraint. A third possible estimate, known as "pooling," gives equal weight to the time and individual dimensions.

Figure 9.2 shows the results of computing triplets of estimates (pooling, within, between) for the standard subperiods people have focused on and for the typical group of countries for which such estimates have been computed before. As can be seen, while the popular inverted U-shaped pattern is discernible, the precise picture depends on the estimator used.

Although the three estimates give a similar picture for the pre-1914 period, within-estimates suggest that the interwar was less closed than has been assumed, probably because the frequency of current account reversals during those years tends to average out the countries' short-term ability to use foreign capital. Moreover, we observe huge discrepancies among the various estimates for the period after 1973. This suggests that although some countries have dramatically increased their ability to use the foreign capital market, the sample's ability at financing current account imbalances has increased much less. In what follows we shall accordingly give special

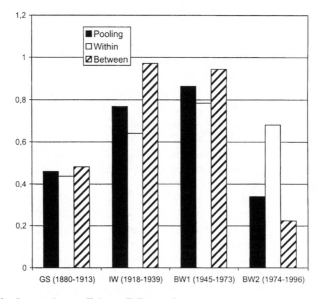

Fig. 9.2   Integration coefficients: Folk sample

weight to the within-estimates, which might sound as a better measure,[5] although for the sake of completeness, we will report all three measures.

9.2.2   Regimes of Financial Integration

Having emphasized the importance of panel estimates, our strategy is the following: Using a sample similar to the one previous scholars have worked with, we replicate benchmark estimates of S-I correlation by subperiods and compare these with the estimates one obtains for subgroupings that we think may be relevant, because they were characterized by arrangements implying exchange rate stability.[6]

In this fashion, we identify (a) gold countries before 1914; (b) gold countries, gold bloc members, and sterling area members in the interwar; (c) countries that pegged to the dollar under the fixed Bretton Woods era;[7] and (d) members of the European exchange rate mechanism (ERM) after 1979.[8]

---

5. As will be seen, the standard errors of between-estimates are always larger than those of the two alternative estimators.

6. Our sample only differs from the existing one in that some corrections were made. For instance, the sample used by Eichengreen, Taylor, and others has France importing capital before 1914; whereas Lévy-Leboyer shows that it was exporting. See Flandreau and Rivière (1999) for a discussion of alternative samples.

7. We identified the arrangements using data from Bordo and Schwartz (1996), Bordo (1993), and Ghosh et al. (1995).

8. We compute this restriction rather than a restriction to fixed exchange rate regimes because of problems with identifying these regimes to which we return to below.

Our goal is to see whether these groupings succeeded in achieving significantly higher levels of integration than the sample at large. The intuition is that, if exchange rate stability is an instrument meant to unlock participating countries' current account constraints, then we should observe lower betas for subgroupings than for the sample at large (see fig. 9.2).

Table 9.1 displays the results.[9] They show that for the pre–World War I period, countries that strictly adhered to gold do not seem to have been able to achieve a significantly greater degree of financial openness than those who did not. The estimated beta for both the entire population and the restricted sample shows figures that are very close to each other so that it is impossible to reject the null that they are the same.

The interwar years reveal an interesting pattern: We see that countries that adhered to gold, as well as members of the sterling zone, actually achieved less integration than the international average reported in table 9.3. The straightforward interpretation of this is probably that members of the interwar gold standard could only retain membership through capital controls, thus actually achieving less integration than the sample at large. A similar result is in fact obtained for the Bretton Woods period, probably for the very same reason.

Finally, moving to the recent experience, we see that ERM membership did succeed in reducing the beta parameters compared to the entire sample.[10] At the same time, since we know that the making of the euro was accompanied by a companion capital movement liberalization within European countries, it is not clear whether the greater integration is due to exchange rate stability or to lower controls.

At this stage, one forceful conclusion that emerges is that fixed exchange rate regimes were not in the nineteenth century an instrument for financial integration. Financial integration has been directly related to the presence or absence of capital controls, and these controls have been used in periods of both fixed and flexible exchange rates. The pre-1914 period stands out as one that was exceptionally free from these controls rather than one whose globalization was related to exchange rate stability since, as observed, the restriction of the integration coefficient to those countries that did not float is not higher than the one obtained by the entire sample. In fact, it is quite striking to see that even with fixed exchange rates, even with no capital controls at all, the degree of integration achieved was not perfect. We think that these findings are consistent with the notion that globalization in the nineteenth century caused the adoption of the gold standard, rather than the

9. Similar results can be found in Flandreau and Rivière. The only difference comes from minor updates in the database.

10. In this part, we use the folk sample. The very low pooling and between-estimates come from the inclusion of Luxembourg. Results without Luxembourg are respectively P: 0.700, W: 0.521, B: 0.819, and for the restriction to Europe P: 0.551, W: 0.502, B: 0.664. As can be seen, the within-estimates are much more robust than the between and pooling.

Table 9.1   Financial Integration: Benchmark Estimates and Fixed Exchange Rates Restrictions (folk sample)

	Classical Gold Standard (1880–1913)	Interwar (1918–1939)	Bretton Woods 1: Gold Dollar (1945–1973)	Bretton Woods 2: Float (1974–1996)
Benchmark estimates	P: 0.460 (0.030) *W: 0.437 (0.030)* B: 0.482 (0.184)	P: 0.768 (0.027) *W: 0.641 (0.030)* B: 0.971 (0.082)	P: 0.863 (0.019) *W: 0.784 (0.022)* B: 0.944 (0.090)	P: 0.339 (0.026) *W: 0.681 (0.106)* B: 0.224 (0.035)
Restriction to gold standard	P: 0.445 (0.038) *W: 0.475 (0.037)* B: 0.459 (0.211) N = 433 (15 countries)	P: 1.015 (0.066) *W: 0.876 (0.082)* B: 1.082 (0.096) N = 59 (10 countries)		
Restriction to sterling zone		P: 0.808 (0.048) *W: 0.804 (0.088)* B: 0.854 (0.110) N = 63 (8 countries)		
Restriction to gold standard + gold bloc		P: 0.943 (0.049) *W: 0.864 (0.056)* B: 1.002 (0.106) N = 82 (11 countries)		
Restriction to gold bloc		P: 0.693 (0.055) *W: 0.676 (0.060)* B: 0.677 (0.216) N = 19 (3 countries)		
Restriction to dollar standard (IMF data)			P: 0.932 (0.025) *W: 0.809 (0.030)* B: 1.042 (0.088) N = 372 (17 countries) P: 0.089 (0.028)	
Restriction to exchange rate mechanism				*W: 0.316 (0.057)* B: 0.0944 (0.099) N = 196 (13 countries)

Source: Authors' computations (see text).

other way round, and the remainder of the paper shall seek to develop this intuition.

9.2.3   Expanding the Horizon: Developed and Emerging Integration since 1973

In order to go beyond these findings, we extend existing analyses in a second direction. We seek to expand the folk sample used in the literature (essentially, developed countries plus Argentina) to include for the more recent period a large number of emerging countries in Asia and Latin America. Although data availability limits the number of emerging countries that can be identified during the late nineteenth century (and thus the significance of tests conducted on more limited samples), such is not the case for the more recent period. This enables us to make systematic comparisons between performances in the core (advanced) and in the periphery (emerging).[11] For this purpose we constructed an expanded database comprising forty-six countries and spanning the period 1973–98. The folk database is embedded in this broader set.[12] To document the properties of the expanded sample, we run cross-section regressions for the period after 1973. As can be seen in figure 9.3, the trend toward greater financial integration after 1973 captured by estimates based on the folk sample (the right part of the inverted U) mostly reflects the properties of the sample itself. In other words, it shows that there was indeed a process of financial integration, but this process varied a lot along the individual dimension, as illustrated by the increase in the cross-section correlation for emerging countries in the second half of the 1980s. Moreover, extracting from the sample countries belonging to the European Union shows that the trend toward greater integration that many authors have emphasized is truly a story about European integration. The disproportionate share of European nations in the sample has led scholars—unknowingly—to eurocentric conclusions.

In line with the previous discussion, however, it is obvious that one cannot restrict one's attention to these cross-section estimates, as telling as they are. In a second stage, we thus use our new sample to compute benchmark estimates and test in a second stage whether restrictions to given exchange rate regimes are associated with higher or lower levels of integration.

The identification of exchange rate regimes is more complex today than it was one century ago when the choice was between paper and gold. We decided to rely on the Masson and Levy-Yeyati and Sturzenegger (LYS) clas-

---

11. Earlier exercises in Flandreau and Rivière (1999) based on the Folk's sample plus five emergers suggested that the record of peripheral countries might be different from that of developed ones.

12. The additional countries are Brazil, Chile, China, Colombia, Egypt, Hong Kong, Hungary, India, Indonesia, Israel, Malaysia, Mexico, Peru, the Philippines, Poland, the Czech Republic, Russia, Singapore, South Africa, South Korea, Thailand, Turkey, Uruguay, and Venezuela. For data sources, see data appendix to Flandreau and Rivière (1999), available on request, and the IMF's *International Financial Statistics*.

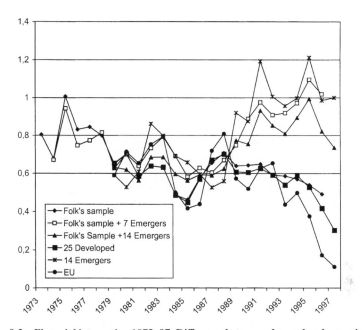

Fig. 9.3   Financial integration 1973–97: Difference between advanced and emerging countries

sifications of countries by type of exchange rate regime (Masson 2001; LYS 2001). Both provide country classifications that recognize that modern exchange rate regimes can be of the fixed, floating, or intermediary category. Since one needs to cross the information available in our sample and that available in either the Masson or LYS databases, one is bound to lose some countries or observations in the process. We end up with two restricted databases of forty-two (Masson) or thirty-five (LYS) countries, whose properties, when one considers both samples in their entirety, are almost identical.[13]

The Masson classification works with the International Monetary Fund (IMF) categories but follows an earlier IMF study by Ghosh et al. (1995) which demarcated the IMF's twenty-six categories into just three (flexible, intermediate, and floating).[14] Masson rearranges the Ghosh categories by defining *flexible* as strictly independent floats and *fixed* as hard pegs (currency boards and announced pegs with no change in parity), with the remainder classified as intermediate. As a result Masson has a much smaller

13. We checked this by running pooling-within-, and between-estimates. Results (available upon request) are virtually identical, a result of the broad overlap between the two samples.
14. Flexible arrangements included crawling pegs, target zones, managed floats, and independent floats. Pegged arrangements include single currencies, special drawing rights (SDR) pegs, other official basket pegs, and secret pegs.

number of truly fixed or truly flexible regimes, with the bulk of the sample being made of intermediate regimes.

The LYS indicators use measures of the volatility of exchange rates and international reserves and cluster analysis to classify countries into four groups (floating, dirty floating, crawling pegs, and fixed).[15] The classification is based on the theoretical prior that countries that really float should have greater exchange rate volatility and smaller international reserve movements than those that do not. We further classified the LYS classification into three by combining dirty floats and crawling arrangements into an intermediate category. Thus, our rearrangement of the LYS classification gives much weight to the tails.

The results we get from these exercises are documented in table 9.2. First, it appears that there are several patterns of financial integration. We find important distinctions among emergers, and also among regimes. In practice, whereas Asian countries are less financially open than the average, Latin American nations are more open for both the Masson and LYS databases.

The effects of alternative exchange rate regimes on financial integration are also interesting. Developed countries are more integrated when they fix, but to a certain extent also when they float, at least according to LYS. This is interesting because floating developed countries are typically made of large mature economies with sophisticated financial systems, such as Great Britain or the United States, whereas fixing developed countries typically include small open economies such as Austria.

We take these results as illustrating how financially deep economies, while floating, can nonetheless achieve high levels of financial integration that can compare with nineteenth-century gold standard records. On the other hand, smaller countries may find themselves opting for a fixed exchange rate regime because they are very open rather than being open because they have a fixed exchange rate system.

Emerging countries face varied experiences: As can be seen from the Masson database, emerging Latin countries are highly integrated at both ends of the exchange rate regime spectrum, with intermediate regimes being less integrated. Something similar is also perceptible in the LYS database, especially if we recall the greater significance we attach to the within-estimates. For Asian countries, by contrast, the opposite is obtained: There, intermediary regimes correspond to comparatively higher, not lower, levels of integration than extreme floats or fixed regimes. However, even for the intermediate category the degree of integration achieved is very low.

This certainly gives support to Fischer's view that developing countries, which are not very exposed to international capital flows, have the opportunity to adopt intermediate exchange rate options (Fischer 2001). To us,

---

15. They also have another category, called "inconclusive," which results from the statistical technique employed, and which we omit in our classification scheme.

Table 9.2 The World According to Masson and Levy-Yeyati and Sturzenegger

	Total	Fixed	Intermediate	Floating
		A. Masson (1973–97)		
Total sample	P: 0.703 (0.018) W: 0.527 (0.025) B: 0.812 (0.053) N = 1017 (42 countries)	P: 0.441 (0.128) W: -0.102 (0.220) B: 0.672 (0.164) N = 42 (5 countries)	P: 0.747 (0.021) W: 0.511 (0.029) B: 0.866 (0.056) N = 774 (39 countries)	P: 0.625 (0.034) W: 0.584 (0.057) B: 0.654 (0.117) N = 198 (countries)
Developed	P: 0.718 (0.027) W: 0.737 (0.036) B: 0.704 (0.101) N = 550	P: -0.251 (0.202) W: 0.295 (0.228) B: n.a. N = 21 (2 countries: 3 et13)	P: 0.736 (0.038) W: 0.654 (0.045) B: 0.837 (0.104) N = 377 (19 countries)	P: 0.661 (0.031) W: 0.648 (0.059) B: 0.711 (0.110) N = 150
Total emerging	P: 0.793 (0.032) W: 0.615 (0.044) B: 0.911 (0.095) N = 341	P: 0.446 (0.198) W: -0.153 (0.344) B: 0.676 (0.237) N = 19 (3 countries: 25.36.46)	P: 0.838 (0.031) W: 0.615 (0.046) B: 0.929 (0.096) N = 278 (16 countries)	P: 0.294 (0.149) W: 0.454 (0.141) B: -0.146 (0.404) N = 43 (5 countries)
Emerging Asia	P: 0.833 (0.060) W: 0.850 (0.080) B: 0.814 (0.146) N = 107	n.a.	P: 0.757 (0.079) W: 0.826 (0.085) B: 0.610 (0.128) N = 87 (5 countries)	P: 1.621 (0.037) W: 1.621 (0.370) B: impossible N = 18 (1 country)
Emerging Latin America	P: 0.521 (0.046) W: 0.478 (0.057) B: 0.603 (0.159) N = 176	P: 0.455 (0.209) W: -0.311 (0.357) B: n.a. N = 15 (2 countries: 25, 46)	P: 0.573 (0.049) W: 0.516 (0.052) B: 0.623 (0.210) N = 150 (8 countries)	P: -0.277 (0.097) W: -0.411 (0.107) B: -0.061 (0.152) N = 10 (3 countries)

(continued)

Table 9.2 (continued)

	Total	Fixed	Intermediate	Floating
		B. Levy-Yeyati and Sturzenegger (1973–97)		
Total sample	P: 0.727 (0.021)	P: 0.542 (0.069)	P: 0.766 (0.037)	P: 0.625 (0.035)
	W: 0.617 (0.028)	W: 0.196 (0.091)	W: 0.481 (0.058)	W: 0.395 (0.058)
	B: 0.808 (0.071)	B: 0.766 (0.137)	B: 0.810 (0.080)	B: 0.652 (0.091)
	N = 848 (35 countries)	N = 129 (16 countries)	N = 386 (29 countries)	N = 393 (31 countries)
Developed	P: 0.685 (0.029)	P: 0.487 (0.113)	P: 0.526 (0.057)	P: 0.636 (0.040)
	W: 0.699 (0.038)	W: 0.164 (0.119)	W: 0.615 (0.097)	W: 0.413 (0.074)
	B: 0.676 (0.119)	B: 0.743 (0.283)	B: 0.578 (0.096)	B: 0.583 (0.119)
	N = 467 (18 countries)	N = 84 (9 countries)	N = 83 (10 countries)	N = 238 (16 countries)
Total emerging	P: 0.756 (0.031)	P: 0.476 (0.097)	P: 0.794 (0.043)	P: 0.801 (0.055)
	W: 0.562 (0.043)	W: 0.224 (0.148)	W: 0.463 (0.071)	W: 0.552 (0.078)
	B: 0.884 (0.086)	B: 0.658 (0.128)	B: 0.869 (0.100)	B: 0.958 (0.128)
	N = 357 (16 countries)	N = 45 (7 countries)	N = 168 (16 countries)	N = 135 (14 countries)
Emerging Asia	P: 0.723 (0.065)	P: 0.704 (0.072)	P: 0.698 (0.087)	P: 0.856 (0.192)
	W: 0.850 (0.080)	W: 0.895 (0.128)	W: 0.507 (0.123)	W: 0.932 (0.255)
	B: 0.791 (0.130)	B: 0.630 (0.099)	B: 0.877 (0.161)	B: 0.774 (0.096)
	N = 112 (5 countries)	N = 17 (3 countries)	N = 69 (5 countries)	N = 23 (3 countries)
Emerging Latin America	P: 0.523 (0.046)	P: 0.440 (0.149)	P: 0.339 (0.064)	P: 0.603 (0.079)
	W: 0.480 (0.055)	W: 0.168 (0.217)	W: 0.454 (0.081)	W: 0.406 (0.074)
	B: 0.611 (0.168)	B: 0.652 (0.049)	B: 0.376 (0.159)	B: 0.917 (0.279)
	N = 184 (8 countries)	N = 22 (3 countries)	N = 77 (8 countries)	N = 82 (8 countries)

Source: Authors' computations.

Note: n.a. = not available.

these results clearly support the notion that more open countries will end up either in a fixed exchange rate system or in a flexible one.

To sum up, we found that a large part of the extensive integration that the advanced countries have achieved has to do with European integration that has been able to drive Europe over and beyond what has been achieved elsewhere under both fixed and flexible exchange rates. We think that this should be seen as a result of the liberalization of financial services, which Europe has implemented, rather than as a result of the exchange rate regime per se. A number of advanced floaters have in effect been quite good at implementing financial openness: Although a fixed exchange rate regime in advanced countries often goes with higher integration, a flexible one might do quite well too.

Moreover, our results support the hollowing-out hypothesis for emerging countries, since they show that the trend toward greater integration has split Latin America into two groups, where financial integration has in turn forced the adoption of either floating or fixed exchange rate regimes. By contrast, Asia has been able to retain intermediate and both fixed and floating exchange rate regimes because it has remained on average more financially closed than the rest of the world.

In other words, the exchange rate regime is a product of globalization, and globalization has caused a polarization between floating and fixed exchange rates—a process known as hollowing out. Only those who have maintained a degree of financial insulation have been able to postpone the choice. Again, globalization appears to have been the driving force.

9.3   Brave New World: Is Financial Vulnerability a Discovery of the 1990s?

The previous section has suggested that causality goes from globalization to the exchange rate regime.[16] In this section, we carry on with this line of analysis. We survey the recent literature on exchange rate regimes and financial crises and argue that it has a lot to say about nineteenth-century macroeconomic problems.

9.3.1   Exchange Rate Regimes and Financial Crises: The Modern Literature

The experience of both advanced and emerging countries on financial crises teaches us that pegged exchange rates invariably succumb to speculative attacks. From a theoretical point of view, this can be explained as a re-

---

16. In a previous draft of this paper we used gravity equations to analyze the relationship between trade integration and the exchange rate regime. Our results for the 1880–1919 period complement those presented above for financial integration and the exchange rate regime. We found, among other things, that exchange rate volatility did not significantly hinder bilateral trade, and although adhering to gold was associated with greater trade, it seems as if this is explained by deeper institutional forces at work.

sult of growing tensions between the peg and domestic economic conditions (Krugman 1979; Obstfeld 1984). The general lesson seems to be that the only alternatives in the face of mobile capital are floating or a hard fix such as a currency board, dollarization, or membership in a monetary union.

Thus, the "corner solutions" literature has developed on the notion that emerging countries (and to a certain extent developed ones as well) must choose between fixed and floating regimes, but cannot durably remain in any intermediary system. More fundamentally, the flexible corner has come under further attack in the "fear of floating" literature—according to which seemingly flexible countries do not truly float, because in effect, such a policy is for them both inefficient and dangerous. The argument runs as follows: In principle, a country that experiences a shock can adjust by lowering the exchange rate. This is supposed to enable that country to enjoy transitorily lower interest rates so that output may recover. But according to Hausmann et al., (1999), this aspirin, although it may have been good medicine for European nations in the 1990s, in effect gives headaches to Latin American countries. According to this view, the record for Latin American countries is that letting the exchange rate go forces an increase in interest rates and causes a major decline of output.

This is because exchange rate depreciation in turn triggers a capital flight, perhaps because that country relies heavily on foreign capital (so that exchange rate depreciation signals serious problems ahead). Another mechanism goes through the share of external debt that is denominated in a foreign currency. Today, only a very limited number of about twenty-five countries can issue debt in their own currency. As a result, exchange crises may cause a debt crisis. In such a setting, emerging markets would be better off pegging, even if rampant "peso" problems imply for them that pegging, whatever the amount of glue they use, does not automatically buy lower interest rates. At least, the argument goes, countries doing so would be protected from short-term external disturbances, which they would not have to shore up against.

9.3.2   Credibility, Interest Rates, and Monetary Policy

For students of the gold standard, it is striking how familiar the modern view sounds, if only we look carefully at the record. The European aspirin, on the one hand, closely resembles what a large body of literature has described as the normal state of affairs for core members of the gold standard. Because exchange depreciation (be it the result of suspended convertibility or a widening of the gold bands through the well-known "gold devices") was not expected to last,[17] these nations, often also the more developed ones, enjoyed a measure of short-term policy flexibility that enabled them

---

17. This is the logic of what Bordo and Kydland (1995) refer to as the gold standard as a contingent rule.

to buffer transitory shocks, very much in the same fashion modern developed floaters can: Exchange rate depreciation did not induce capital flight.

Recent tests have suggested that in effect, support was provided by the market itself, which took bets on the eventual reappreciation of the currency, thus enabling monetary authorities to lower interest rates and thus compensate for declining output; in other words, the gold points served as a credible target zone (Hallwood, MacDonald, and Marsh 1996; Bordo and MacDonald 1997). Working with data from the Vienna forward market, Flandreau and Komlos (2001) have shown that modern target zone theory was in fact invented and successfully applied in Austria-Hungary in the early twentieth century, once it had stabilized its currency. In the case of large foreign shocks (such as during the crisis of 1907) Austria-Hungary would let its exchange rate go. This triggered stabilizing expectations that enabled the monetary authorities to keep a lower interest rate than abroad, with speculators taking bets on an eventual reappreciation.

Thus, to a certain extent, the current trend toward floating in advanced countries has some resemblance to a classical gold standard in which the fluctuation margins have been, in line with Keynes' (1931, 314–31) proposal, widened to give more flexibility. The key difference between then and now is that the nominal anchor—gold parity, around which the target zone operated—has been jettisoned and a domestic nominal anchor has been substituted in its place, which allows exchange rate flexibility without the constraints of a target zone. Thus if the degree of flexibility compared to the gold standard is greater, the spirit is the same, a point to which we will come back later.[18]

This possibility for the core countries of the classical gold standard era to actually manage the money supply despite the gold constraints is in sharp contrast with what countries in the European periphery, in Asia, or in Latin and Central America could do.

On the one hand, floating did not create much room for them to conduct active monetary policies. Exchange depreciation often triggered expectations of further depreciation rather than expectations of eventual stabilization. For instance, Flandreau and Komlos (2001) show that, intriguingly enough, it was the stabilization of the Austro-Hungarian currency that opened the door to active monetary policies. During the infamous period of exchange rate gyrations that extended until the mid-1890s, exchange depreciation was not usually followed by expectations of an eventual recov-

---

18. Thus, we are not arguing that monetary authorities are following a target zone approach, as advocated by (for example) Bergsten and Williamson (1983). Rather, we are arguing that the credibility of adhering to gold convertibility gave the core countries before 1914 the flexibility to conduct discretionary policy within the gold points as if they were operating in a target zone à la Krugman (1991) and Svensson (1994), whereas today the credibility attached to following monetary rules such as inflation targeting gives the monetary authorities the freedom to operate with much greater flexibility without the bands of a target zone.

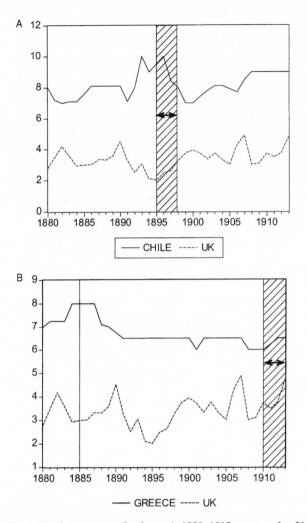

Fig. 9.4   Short-term interest rates (bank rates), 1880–1913, compared to United Kingdom: *A,* **Chile;** *B,* **Greece;** *C,* **Portugal;** *D,* **Russia;** *E,* **Italy**
Source: See appendix.
Note: Shaded areas represent periods when each country was on the gold standard.

ery—unlike what would happen when the country regained credibility after joining the gold standard in 1896.

On the other hand, going onto gold did not buy immediate credibility, as
illustrated by the levels of short-term interest rates in a number of typical
members of the periphery. Figure 9.4 shows that the weaker members of the
gold club faced higher short-term interest rates *even when on gold* than is

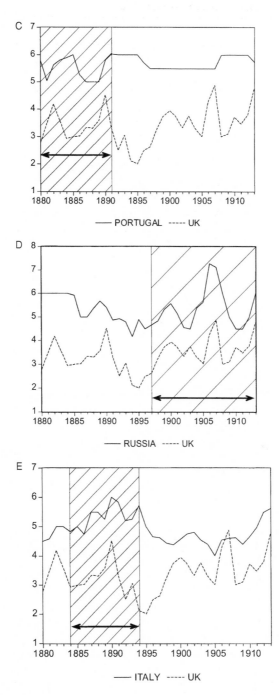

Fig. 9.4 (continued)

consistent with their actual exchange rate record. This suggests some kind of peso problem. The high short-term rates faced by Chile, Greece, Portugal, Italy, or Russia during their more or less extended flirt with gold suggest that the problems that the modern periphery has with pegging have nineteenth-century precedents. The fact that even when on gold these countries could face high short-term interest rates might explain why some of them ended up floating. An interesting case from that perspective is Chile, whose attempt at returning onto gold in 1895–98 involved both a sharp increase in interest rates—because that decision was not credible—and a substantial fall in the rate of inflation, with the result that the stabilization was associated with huge real interest rates, recession, and a quick reversal to floating exchange rates (Subercaseaux 1926). *Plus ça change . . .*

9.3.3 Fear of Floating, Nineteenth-Century Style: A New View of the Gold Standard

If going on gold was so costly for the periphery, one may wonder why a number of countries nonetheless sought to stick to gold. We argue that this choice rested on something quite similar to the current fear-of-floating dilemma. If fixing was quite painful under the gold standard for many of the peripheral countries, floating could be just as deadly as today. This was due to pervasive problems of currency mismatch arising from the inability, for underdeveloped borrowing countries, to issue foreign debts in their own currency.

It is well known from the works of historians that the financial markets of the less developed countries were very backward.[19] This led governments of the European or Latin American periphery to issue their debts in the large financial markets of the core countries, such as London, Amsterdam, Paris, or later Berlin, which by contrast had developed early on (Neal 1990). In effect, the investors in peripheral countries developed the habit of holding that part of their wealth which they invested in domestic bonds in the large markets of the core countries (Broder 1975; Lévy-Leboyer 1976; De Cecco 1990).

Borrowing abroad also implied borrowing in foreign currencies. Today, many emerging countries find it impossible to borrow abroad in their own currency. Ricardo Hausmann and various co-authors[20] refer to these nations as suffering from "original sin." Something similar existed one century ago. According to John Francis (1859), exchange rate guarantees in international bond issues were an innovation that had been pioneered by the London Rothschilds.[21] The guarantees were widely used during the boom

19. See Rousseau and Sylla (ch. 8 in this volume).
20. See Hausmann et al. (1999), Hausmann, Pannizza and Stein (2000), Fernandez-Arias and Hausmann (2000), and Eichengreen and Hausmann (1999).
21. Previous to the advent of Mr. Rothschild, foreign loans were somewhat unpopular in England, as the interest receivable abroad, subject to the rate of exchange, liable to foreign caprice, and payable in foreign coin. He introduced the payment of the dividends in England, and fixed it in sterling money, one great cause of the success of these loans in 1825" (298–99). See also Ferguson (1998, 132–34).

of Latin American bond issues of the 1820s (Fodor 2000). As foreign investment soared, this practice became widespread. Prior to the advent of the gold standard, countries were alternatively tied to gold, silver, or bimetallic currencies depending on the market they were tapping. With the spread of the gold standard in Western Europe, gold clauses generalized.[22]

Fully comprehending the logic of these gold clauses is a theoretical challenge that is beyond the scope of this paper. It is not clear, for instance, why investors should have preferred a lower exchange rate risk—but with a greater default risk when exchange rate crises occurred—to a higher exchange rate risk but a lower risk of default.

One possible answer is that, in a system where instruments to hedge against long-run exchange rate risks were not available, the clauses enabled foreign investors to pass on the costs of exchange risk to issuing governments or corporations.[23] This was one way contemporaries rationalized this practice, emphasizing that it was motivated by the risk aversion of foreign investors.[24] But this would imply that contemporaries were more willing to run default risk than exchange rate risks.

Second, this practice might be understood as the solution to a commitment problem. While local issues could be easily inflated away, foreign issues with gold clauses provided safeguards, precisely because they in turn induced governments to be on their guard (Missale and Blanchard 1990).

22. Flandreau (2002) argues that this contributed to tying countries to the monetary system of the financial center on which they depended, thus contributing to the emergence of regional groupings such as the Latin Union.

23. There were forward exchange markets, but only for a small number of currencies, and only for short horizons (Einzig 1937). We are not aware of swap contracts that would have involved long-term cover against exchange rate risk. The only kind of protection against exchange rate volatility would have been diversification, which by definition does not provide full insurance.

24. On Russia see de Block, (1889, 214): "Pour décider ces capitalistes à engager leurs fonds dans une entreprise dont l'avenir pour eux état incertain, il fallut leur garantir un minimum normal de revenu annuel sur les actions et obligations de chemins de fer russes, en fixant ce minimum sur l'étalon métallique" (In order to convince capitalists to put their money in projects whose success was for them uncertain, it was necessary to provide them with a guaranteed minimum revenue on their railway bonds and stocks and to index this minimum on a metallic standard). On Spain, Austria, and Hungary see Lévy (1901, 6): "Chez nous surtout où les rentiers quelque peu timorés et mal au courant des questions de change ont marqué de tout temps une grande répugnance à admettre dans leur portefeuille des titres don't le revenu ne fût pas stable; la première condition de cette fixité du coupon étant celle de la monnaie la conséquence naturelle de cette exigence légitime de notre public a été la création de monbreaux titres étrangers stipulés payables en francs ou en or. L'un des premiers a été la rente espagnole extérieure 3% depuis transformée en 4%; puis sont venues les rentes autrichiennes 4% or, la rente hongroise 6% or" (In our country where rentiers are risk averse and not very conversant in exchange matters and have always been reluctant to take in their portfolio bonds whose income is variable [and a necessary condition for revenue stability is the stability of the currency], francs or gold clauses emerged as a natural requirement in many bond issues. One of the first was the Spanish rente 3 percent, then came the Austrian 4 percent, the Hungarian 6 percent). On the United States, see Wilkins (1989, 619): "Often sovereign investors insisted on gold clauses in railroad bonds. They wanted 'sound money' in America and worldwide. The US adherence to a gold standard (after 1879) was in part a consequence of America's desire to attract such investment."

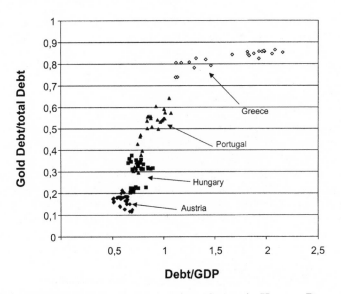

Fig. 9.5   Total indebtedness and currency mismatch: Austria, Hungary, Portugal, Greece, 1880–1913
Source: Crédit Lyonnais Archives as adapted by the authors.

Figure 9.5 gives some support to this view because it shows that the share of gold debt was an increasing function of total indebtedness for a number of peripheral countries. On the other hand, it is hard to determine the extent to which markets and governments were in a position to internalize the consequences of gold clauses plus exchange depreciation: In the politically unstable, revolution-driven Latin America, could precommitment actually work? Moreover, although commitment might explain why some debt would have been issued with gold clauses, it is not clear why all debt issued abroad should have included such clauses.

A final possibility rests in the motivations of international bankers whose syndicates arranged the loans. Because the bankers offered a number of services to cash-strapped government in periods of crisis, lending into arrears and helping them to muddle through financial trouble, they were also in a position to impose a lot of conditionality (Flandreau 2002). This asymmetry was often emphasized by contemporary observers: According to Lévy, "The creation of debts denominated in the currency of the lending country can be understood as resulting from the fact that it is the lending country that dictates its conditions to the borrowing part" (1901, 6). It must be that the bankers expected that the bonds they were prepared to guarantee would face a deeper and more willing demand as a result of the gold clauses, and they thus persuaded borrowers to issue their securities with fixed exchange rate clauses that tied the coupon to the unit of the market where the bonds were sold.[25] But then we are back to the question, why shouldn't the regular investor be willing to hold paper debts, provided he gets a return for it?

In any case, given the situation, the fixed exchange rate clauses drew a sharp line between those members of the core where there had been a long record of adherence to a convertible standard and those who did not. As one leading financial economist of the time explained, robust gold convertibility was an acceptable substitute for the gold clauses: "When it comes to the bonds of countries where the gold standard prevails, such as Great Britain, Sweden, Norway, Denmark or Canada, special clauses are not necessary, since the obligation to pay in gold results from the fact that bonds are denominated in the currency of that country" (Lévy 1901, 6).

This was certainly a reason why a number of countries became quite interested in trying to find ways to stabilize their currency in terms of gold. Yet the gold standard was definitely not a perfect substitute for gold clauses, since the club of countries that could issue abroad debts denominated in their own currency was much more selective than the gold club (as illustrated later, in table 9.5, which shows the list of "senior" sovereigns in London.[26] These data come from Burdett's Official Stock Exchange Intelligence.) Table 9.3 lists the bonds with various characteristics, including the currency in which it was issued and the currency in which the coupon was payable for ten major countries, eight of which issued bonds in their own currencies without fixed exchange rate clauses.[27] Other countries listed only showed bonds issued in some gold-tied unit.[28]

The borderline members of the list (i.e., those for which the currency denomination was ambiguous) provide interesting evidence that the mere stabilization of the currency in terms of gold was not enough. As can be seen, Austria-Hungary's position is ambiguous. And as a matter of fact, we found in separate French sources an interpretation of this problem: In the early 1890s, this country sought to stabilize its currency and defined a new unit, the crown, with a fixed gold parity. At first, market participants understood

25. The fixed exchange rate clause could come in various ways: either by denominating the currency in the foreign currency, by denominating it in a gold or silver domestic unit that thus had a fixed exchange rate with foreign gold or silver units, or by stating the fixed exchange rate at which the coupon would be paid to foreigners regardless of the actual exchange rate against paper money. From an economic point of view all these are equivalent.

26. The countries that could issue sovereign bonds in terms of their own currencies during the period 1880–1914 were the United States, the United Kingdom, France, Germany, the Netherlands, Belgium, Denmark, and Switzerland. Two additional countries included in the table that listed sovereign debt in their own currency were Austria, Hungary and Italy. However, there is ample evidence to suggest that these bonds bore gold clauses. See Tattara (1999) and Flandreau (2002).

27. For the United States, table 9.3 shows three bonds listed as payable in gold coin for the years 1895, 1898, and 1900. The previous bonds shown are listed as "payable in the coin standard of the United States." The changed status was a response to the silver uncertainty of the 1890s, to remove any ambiguity over which metallic coin was the standard. See Wilkins (1989) and Laughlin (1903).

28. These data are available on request.

Table 9.3   International Sovereign Securities Listed on the London Stock Exchange, 1880–1913, Selected Countries

	Name of Agents or Bankers	Year of Issue	Price of Issue (%)	Income (%)	IPO Yield	Year of Redemption	Currency	Total Amount	Interest	
									City/Country	Currency Payable
France										
3% rentes		1886–91					Francs or pounds	15,304,231,433	Paris	No fixed exchange
								612,169,256		
4% rentes							Francs	11,152,400		
4.5% rentes, old							Francs	831,855,666		
4.5% rentes of 1883		1883					Francs or pounds	6,789,783,906		
								271,466,397		
3% redeemable rentes		1878				1953	Francs or pounds	4,004,346,100	Paris	
		1881						160,173,844		
		1884								
Germany										
3.5% consols	Berlin, London						Marks	450,000,000	Germany	
3% imperial loan		1890	87	3	3.45		Marks	170,000,000	Germany, London	Marks; pounds: exchange of the day
		1891	84.4	3	3.55		Marks	200,000,000		
		1892	83.6	3	3.59		Marks	160,000,000		
		1893	86.8	3	3.46		Marks	160,000,000		
		1905	101.2	3.5	3.46		Marks	300,000,000		
3.5% bonds		1906	100.1	3.5	3.50		Marks	260,000,000		
		1909	95.6	3.5	3.66		Marks	160,000,000		
4% bonds		1909		4			Marks	940,000,000	Berlin, Frankfurt	
Bavaria										
Prussia										
Prussian consols (now 3.5%)							Marks	3,592,667,850	Berlin, chief Prussian towns	
4% consols							Pounds	84,500,000	Berlin, chief Prussian towns	
3% consolidated state loan		1890–1905					Marks	1,501,296,150	London, Germany	
4% bonds		1909		4			Marks	1,260,000,000		
3.5% bonds		1906	100.1	3.5	3.50		Marks	6,090,675,900		

The Netherlands										
2.5%		1814					Florins	626,008,900	Holland	Florins
3.5% of 1830		1830					Florins	3,356,000	Holland	Florins
4%							Florins	182,075,900	Holland	Florins; twelve guilders to the pound
3%	Barings	1844,1896,1898					Florins	468,175,300	Holland	Florins
State railway stock		1870					Florins	2,719,693	Holland	
State railway stock		1876					Florins	294,000	Holland	
3.5%		1886					Florins	11,250,000	Amsterdam, London, Paris Frankfurt, Berlin	
4%		1878	98.375	4	4.07	1936	Florins	43,000,000	Holland	Florins
							Pounds	3,583,333		
4% of 1883		1883	98.75	4	4.05	1939	Florins	609,000,000	Amsterdam	Florins
							Pounds	5,075,000		
3.5% of 1891		1892	100.5	3.5	3.48		Florins	44,700,000	Amsterdam	Florins; at the exchange of the day
3.5% loan, 1911		1911		3.5					Amsterdam; London, Paris, Berlin Hamburg, Frankfurt	
United States										
4.5% funded		1876				1891	Dollars	300,000,000	America	
4% funded		1877				1907	Dollars	1,000,000,000	America	
3%		1882					Dollars	274,937,250	America	
4.5% loan of 1891							Dollars	25,364,500		Gold coin
4% loan		1895				1925	Dollars	162,315,400	United States	Gold coin
3% loan		1898				1908	Dollars	198,792,660	United States	Gold coin
2% thirty-year bonds		1900				1930	Dollars	646,250,150	United States	Gold coin
Belgium										
2.5%	Rothschilds	1842					Francs	389,271,000	Belgium Paris	Belgium Paris
4%							Francs	731,287,900		
							Francs	134,719,000		
4% loan of 1883		1883	104.28	4	3.84		Francs	164,796,000	Belgium, Paris	Belgium, Paris
3.5% debt		1886					Francs	1,296,935,757	Belgium, Paris	Belgium, Paris

(continued)

Table 9.3 (continued)

Name of Agents or Bankers		Year of Issue	Price of Issue (%)	Income (%)	IPO Yield	Year of Redemption	Currency	Total Amount	Interest City/Country	Interest Currency Payable
3% bonds (first series)		1895					Francs	544,956,275		
		1897					Francs	208,046,500		
		1898					Francs	195,993,800		
3% bonds (second series)	Barings	1873–1912					Francs	1,912,520,800	Belgium, Paris, London	Francs pound: 25 francs 25 cents (fixed)
	Cashier of state Rothschilds	1895					Francs	960,489,882		
3% bonds (third series)	Cashier of state	1895					Francs	200,040,000	Belgium	Francs; pound: 25 francs 25 cents (fixed)
	Rothschilds	1895			3		Francs	59,856,600	Paris	
3% conversion loan							Francs	1,301,446,057	Belgium, Paris	
Denmark										
4% 1850	Hambros	1850–61	90	4	4.44		Pounds	400,000		
4% 1862	Hambros	1862	91	4	4.40		Pounds	660,000		
4% state loan	Hambros	1880					Kronen	26,339,700	London	
							Pound	93,525		
3.5% internal debt loan	Hambros	1887	98.5	3.5	3.55		Kronen	155,000,000	Copenhagen, London	Current exchange rate
3.5% amortisable loan	Crédit Lyonnais	1900	94.75	3.5	3.69				Copenhagen, London, Paris, Berlin Hamburg, Brussels	
3% gold loan of 1894	Hambros	1894	96.375	3	3.11	1914	Kronen	66,306,000	London, Paris	Exchange of the day; 10.50 francs per 500 kronen
3% gold loan of 1897	Hambros	1897	99.125	3	3.03		or pounds	3,684,777	Copenhagen, London, Paris	

	Issuer	Date	Price	Rate	Yield	Redemption	Currency	Amount	Where payable	Exchange basis
4% loan of 1912	Hambros	1912	97	4	4.12		Pounds	2,500,000	London, Paris, Copenhagen Hamburg, Amsterdam	Sterling; 25.20 francs; 1816 kronen 20.43 reichsmarks, 12.10 florins
Switzerland 3.5% loan		1903–07					Francs	500,000,000	Switzerland London	
Austria Austrian 5% silver rentes		1868–					Florins	1,005,757,895	Vienna	Silver
Austrian 5% paper rentes		1868–					Florins	1,483,387,487	Vienna	Paper
Austrian 4% gold rentes		1876–					Florins	490,850,200	Vienna; Berlin, Stuttgart, Frankfort Brussels, Amsterdam, Paris	Gold; marks, 20.25 marks per 10 florins. Francs, 25 francs per 10 florins
Paper rentes		1881					Florins	238,877,100	Vienna	Paper
Austrian 4% converted rentes		1903					Kronen	3,614,486,820	Brussels, Amsterdam, Paris, Bale, Zurig	25 francs per 10 florins
Austrian 4% kronen rentes		1901–12					Kronen	2,265,844,500	Vienna, Amsterdam, Germany	
Austrian 3.5% rentes		1897					Kronen or florins	116,901,000 58,450,500		
Hungary Hungarian loan	London & County	1868	71.66	5	6.98	1917	Pounds	8,512,560		
5% 1871	Raphaels	1872	81	5	6.17	1904	Pounds	300,000	Paris, Frankfort-on-the-Main, Amsterdam Vienna, Budapest	
5% of 1873	Raphaels	1873	80	5	6.25	1904	Pounds	5,400,000	Paris, Frankfort-on-the-Main, Amsterdam Vienna, Budapest	
4% gold rentes	Rothschilds	1881–88	75.5	4	5.30		Pounds	62,200,000	London, Paris, Frankfurt, Amsterdam Vienna, Budapest	

(continued)

Table 9.3 (continued)

	Name of Agents or Bankers	Year of Issue	Price of Issue (%)	Income (%)	IPO Yield	Year of Redemption	Currency	Total Amount	Interest City/Country	Interest Currency Payable
4.5% state railways bonds		1889					Florins (gold)	52,000,000	Budapest, Vienna, Berlin, Frankfurt, Paris	
3% state gold loan	Lloyds	1895	87	3	3.45		Pounds	1,875,000	London, Budapest, Vienna, Berlin Frankfurt, Amsterdam	
4% rentes		1892					Kronen	1,062,000,000	Budapest, Vienna, Berlin, Frankfurt, Amsterdam	
		1900					Kronen	120,000,000	Hamburg	
		1902					Kronen	1,087,470,000		
4.5% treasury bonds		1910	99.4	4.5	4.53	1913–14	Crowns	250,000,000	Budapest, Vienna	
Italy										
Sardinian 5%	Hambros	1851	85	5	5.88		Pounds	3,600,000	London	
5% rentes	Rothschilds Barings Hambros	1861–		5			Lire	8,025,000,000	Italian treasuries, Rome; Paris, London	
Maremmana railway loan	Hambros	1862	74	5	6.76	1960	Pounds	1,782,000	Italian treasuries, London	
3% rentes	Rothschilds	1863					Lire	160,600,000		
Irrigation canal company	Hambros	1863 onward		6		1915	Pounds	2,700,000	London, Paris, Italy	
4% rentes		1895							Paris, Berlin, Vienna, London	
3% railway bonds	Barings Hambros	1887–96		3		1986	Pounds	48,914,000		
3.5% (net) rentes	Rothschilds	1902	96	3.5	3.65		Lire	33,013,293		
Credit communal and provincial bonds	Hambros	1904		3.75		1964	Lire	152,582,000		Lire (home); gold (abroad)
3.5% rentes	Rothschilds	1911		3.5			Lire	283,448,336	Also in Paris, Berlin, Vienna, London	Fixed by government

Source: The *Official Stock Exchange Intelligence* (1880–1913).

that since the crown "only exists as gold unit, and there are no paper crowns" a crown-denominated debt had to be understood as a gold debt with an exchange rate "worth 1.05 French francs."[29] However, once the Austro-Hungarian currency was stabilized and the crown became in 1900 the actual unit of account, it was realized that Austria's and Hungary's crowns debts were "without fixed parities in terms of foreign currencies, [because] Austria's monetary regime is a paper regime. In the event of a crisis, the value of the Austrian crown might experience depreciation."[30] This shows that having a gold parity that was credible over the short run was not a perfect substitute for a very long-term commitment to exchange rate stability.

Having a large gold debt and experiencing an exchange rate crisis could have devastating consequences. When a country embarked on a spending spree and public debt increased, the share of gold-denominated debt increased in its turn. This created an explosive mismatch. The crises of the early 1890s—very much like those of the 1990s—provided evidence of the mechanism at work. Argentina opened the dance: There, the expansion of the gold debt (*cedulas*), accompanied by paper money issue, pushed the level of the debt burden to unsustainable heights.[31] The interruption of capital exports that resulted increased the needs of a number of financially weak peripheral countries whose currencies depreciated in turn. As argued in Flandreau (2002), the public debt crises in Portugal and Greece (in 1892 and 1893 respectively) both resulted from the depreciation of the exchange rate that had brought these countries' public debts to unsustainable levels.

The responses to these problems induced by high debts and financial vulnerability were also surprisingly modern. Some countries, such as Spain or Portugal, continued to float but minimized their exposure by limiting their borrowings abroad. Some others, such as Russia or Greece, developed de facto currency boards. They accumulated gold reserves beyond what was statutorily necessary and in effect adopted stabilization cover ratios that were consistently above 100 percent. Yesterday, like today, the response to financial vulnerability has been either a float with reduced exposure to the foreign capital market, or super-strong pegs. Hollowing out is a very old thing.

This discussion should shed a new light on the abundant quotes that one finds in the old literature regarding the importance of the gold standard as a way to foster integration and which have so often been analyzed in the recent literature as evidence of the ideology or "spirit" of the time.[32] There might in fact have been a lot more economic motivations behind these recommendations than is commonly acknowledged. Clearly, in view of the

29. Crédit Lyonnais Archives, date 1893.
30. Crédit Lyonnais Archives. The date of this statement, certainly not incidentally, is 1 May 1914.
31. See, for example, Eichengreen (1997).
32. See, for example, Gallarotti (1995) and Eichengreen and Temin (1997).

narrow list of countries that were able to float debts in their own currency, much of the emerging world was bound to face problematic currency mismatches.[33]

From this point of view, gold adherence became for those willing to protect themselves against international financial disturbances a second-best solution. It is not that a gold standard immediately bought credibility. Rather, it served as an insurance mechanism and in this sense fostered globalization. In other words, the spread of the gold standard in the periphery was an endogenous response to the gold clauses: As soon as the price of this insurance decreased (as was the case during the gold inflation of 1896–1914), the gold standard expanded, as more and more countries found it less dangerous to borrow with gold clauses since the risk of being tipped off gold declined.[34]

9.3.4   Exchange Rate Regimes and the Financial Maturity Hypothesis

A consequence of the analysis developed here is that logically, pre-1914 core countries that had developed strong money and financial markets before WWI and were thus able to issue foreign debts in their own currency ought to have floated—which they did not. At first sight, this seems to be a serious challenge to our view and may require a word of explanation. However, the evidence reported above, that core countries pioneered the use of exchange rate adjustments within the gold points in a target zone fashion, suggests that core countries were nonetheless exploiting to the fullest possible extent whatever flexibility they had. In a sense, the seeds of a floating exchange rate system were sown at the center.

The question still arises: Why did advanced countries before 1914 that were financially mature not float as advanced countries do today? Possible answers include the protection that gold gave to bond holders against inflation risk and the path dependency of gold as money.

Indeed, historians have emphasized that the rise of a large and liquid market for government debt in the eighteenth and nineteenth century has been the hallmark of financial development. But this meant that at the beginning of the process, domestic residents saving for their retirement had their money mostly in the fixed income portion of the market and would

33. This was likely to become a serious problem for governments in the periphery, given the role government undertakings had in the process of catching up in the late nineteenth century (Gerschenkron 1962).

34. This explanation is not a mutually exclusive one. An alternative reason why periphery countries may have favored gold standard adherence is that the gold standard served as a "Good Housekeeping Seal of Approval"—a signal to lenders in the core that peripheral countries followed sound financial policies. See Bordo and Rockoff (1996) for evidence that sovereign debt spreads on London were lower for emerging countries that adhered strongly to gold relative to those whose adherence was less conscientious and those on paper standards. Also see Obstfeld and Taylor (ch. 3 in this volume). Flandreau, Le Cacheux, and Zumer (1998) stress the role of gold inflation after 1896 as reducing the burdens of public debt for European peripheral countries and hence making their adherence to the gold standard more sustainable.

take a beating if governments inflated away.[35] Thus the response, as in the well-known British case, was to develop powerful parliaments that took the power over money out of the hands of sovereigns and linked the domestic unit to a weight of gold. But once this was done, this created strong constituencies that resisted the devaluation of the unit in terms of gold.

This domestic mechanism was supplemented by an international one, since in practice no single country could easily take the lead and move away from the system and widen the fluctuation bands, without raising the suspicion that it truly wanted to depreciate. In the end, core countries were locked onto gold, and peripheral countries had either to float or to lock onto core countries. To give way, the gold standard needed some easily identifiable external shock such as WWI. It took another six decades for a universal floating exchange rate system based on a credible domestic nominal anchor to be established (although earlier successful efforts prevailed in the United Kingdom and Sweden in the 1930s and in Canada in the 1950s).[36]

The history of the international monetary system for the advanced countries in the twentieth century has been well documented (Bordo and Schwartz 1999; Redish 1996; Eichengreen 1996). The path dependency of gold seen in adherence to some form of gold convertibility prevailed until 1971. The golden nominal anchor was stretched with the use of international reserves in the interwar exchange standard and even more under the Bretton Woods system, while monetary policies became increasingly geared toward domestic goals.[37] Ultimately the gold-based system became unworkable, and it collapsed in 1971. The full shift to a credible domestic nominal anchor and floating exchange rates in the 1970s and 1980s required the development of deep and mature financial markets discussed here and in Rousseau and Sylla (ch. 8 in this volume) as well as the adoption of monetary rules that in many ways echoed the functions of the gold standard convertibility rule.

Thus today by contrast, the more financially developed part of the world has finally been able to exploit to its fullest possible extent its ability to float. As a matter of fact, the generalization today of floating in the developed countries virtually encompasses the list of countries that can issue international securities in their own currency, as we will discuss in section 9.4.

35. In today's world, where price indexes are systematically constructed by generally careful institutions and are thus fairly consensual, the issue of determining the reasons why governments scarcely issue indexed bonds might be addressed (see, however, the mid-1990s controversies on the inflation measurement problem in the presence of rapid technological progress). But at the time the distrust of index numbers was not even a question.

36. The case for generalized floating was made clearly by Gottfried Haberler in the 1930s but was rejected by the consensus view of the time that floating was destabilizing, see Bordo and James (2001).

37. According to Bordo and Eichengreen (1998), had the Great Depression not intervened, the gold exchange standard would have prevailed until the late 1950s.

9.4   Financial Depth and the Exchange Rate Regime

The interpretation of the seemingly opposite nature of global exchange rate regimes in the two big eras of globalization (fixed exchange rates back then, floating ones today) has put at the center of the picture the role of financial vulnerability and financial crises. To some extent, the Baring crisis yesterday played a role similar to the crises of the late 1990s in reminding floaters about the dangers of an impervious flexible exchange rate. As a result, whereas developed countries have always had the temptation and ability to float (with floating restricted yesterday by path dependency and the difficulty of creating domestic institutions that could create a domestic nominal anchor), the periphery has always faced serious difficulties in floating, viewing the gold standard yesterday, and hard pegs today, as a second-best solution.

The change in the dominant form of regime has implications as to where we should find greater financial depth: In the pre-1914 era, when the gold standard was the dominant monetary arrangement, we would expect countries adhering to *gold* to have greater financial depth than those that did not. In the post-1973 period, in which floating is the dominant regime, we would expect by contrast that countries that can *successfully* operate *pure floats* would also be more financially developed than those that could not. However, those emerging countries that could not, or for other reasons—such as considerable openness or close trading linkages to a large country—choose not to float and instead adhered to hard pegs (e.g., Hong Kong and Singapore), would also have greater financial depth than countries following intermediate regimes.

In this section we seek to investigate this prediction by looking at the record of both the periods 1880–1914 and 1973–97 and attempting to identify the effects of alternative exchange rate regimes on financial depth, which we proxy before 1914 by the ratio of a broad monetary aggregate (M2) to gross domestic product (GDP) and after 1973 by similar variables plus other broader measures, to be discussed below. These variables can in turn be viewed as indicators of a set of factors that come under the rubric of financial maturity.[38]

9.4.1   The Classical Gold Standard, 1880–1913

Because of its biblical simplicity, the 1880–1913 period is an ideal testing ground for our hypothesis that the dominant exchange rate regime, by

---

38. Rousseau and Sylla (ch. 8 in this volume) list five attributes of a good financial system, which overlap our meaning of financial maturity: sound public finance and debt management; stable money; a sound banking system; a central bank to act as a lender of last resort and to manage international financial arrangements; and a well-functioning securities market. They employ the same measure of financial depth we do both as a determinant of economic growth and as a determinant of international financial integration.

which we mean the more technically advanced, is associated with greater financial sophistication. Case studies of financial development in the nineteenth century have emphasized that those countries which adhered to gold in the 1880s, 1890s, and 1900s, such as France, Great Britain, and Germany, were also the more financially developed. This cross-section evidence is supplemented by time series analysis such as in Gregory (1995) and Komlos (1987), according to whom the Russian and Austro-Hungarian stabilizations in the 1890s were both associated with a considerable expansion of the monetary base. In line with these earlier studies, we believe that the expansion of real broad money would be a good proxy for financial depth before 1914 because this was an era in which monetization (the spread of the money economy) proliferated across the world, as did the growth of banking systems (Bordo and Jonung 1987).

To test systematically for the link between the exchange rate regime and financial development, we assembled a panel of data for twenty-three countries for 1880–1913.[39] The panel includes both advanced (core) and less developed (periphery) countries.[40] The strategy followed is to run panel regressions of the log of M/Y (money to income ratio) on a number of controls to see whether a dummy capturing the years in which a country adhered to gold or did not, and another one capturing whether a country had international sovereign bonds listed in terms of its own currency on the London Stock Exchange in 1913, had positive and significant effects.[41] Other things being equal, we would expect that our measures of financial depth would be higher under the gold standard than under paper money, and for a country that can issue foreign bonds denominated in its own currency than for another that cannot.

To test this, it is necessary to control for other effects. The first is per capita real income. From the literature on money demand, other things being equal, we would expect the elasticity of M/Y with respect to real per capita income to be zero (Friedman 1959).[42] However, in the situation where money balances are a luxury good and the income elasticity of money de-

39. The data sources are listed in the appendix.

40. The advanced countries, demarcated both by income and by the fact that they were capital exporters (with the principal exception of the United States before 1900) were Belgium, France, Germany, the Netherlands, the United Kingdom, the United States, and Switzerland. The emergers were Argentina, Australia, Austria-Hungary, Brazil, Canada, Denmark, Chile, Finland, Greece, Italy, Japan, Norway, Portugal, Russia, Spain, and Sweden.

41. Gold standard adherence dates come from Bordo and Schwartz (1996) and Eichengreen and Flandreau (1996). We did not distinguish between countries that left and returned to gold at the same parities and those that altered their parities. The domestic currency bond dummy is derived from information in table 9.5. We also ran the regressions using the log of real per capita money balances as our measure of financial depth. This, of course, is the traditional measure of demand for money. The results are very similar to the ones we report below.

42. Real per capita income was expressed in 1913 U.S. dollars. The purchasing power parity–adjusted data are from Maddison (1995). We also tried the unadjusted data in the regressions below.

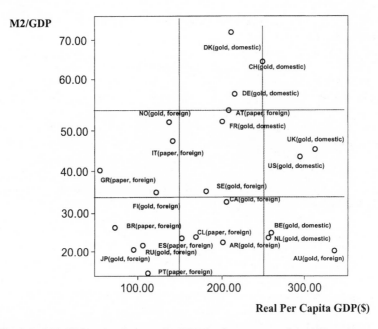

Fig. 9.6   M2-GDP and real per capita GDP (exchange rate regime, debt currency denomination), 1880–1913

mand is greater than one, as evidenced in Friedman and Bordo and Jonung (1987) for a number of our countries for the pre-1914 period, then real income per capita would be positively associated with our measure of financial depth. Thus, we would expect countries with high per capita income before 1914 to have greater financial depth. Such countries would also more likely be on the gold standard and would be able to issue bonds in terms of their own currencies.

Figure 9.6 presents a scatter plot of M/Y and real per capita income showing this relationship nicely.[43] In the left-hand corner we see mainly paper currency countries with low financial depth that borrowed abroad in sterling or had gold clauses. In the upper right-hand corner we observe high-income countries with high M/Y who were on gold and could issue bonds in their own currency, with the anomalies being easily explained.[44] Similar figures for 1880–96 and 1897–1914 (not shown) nicely trace out the

43. A similar pattern is observed comparing real per capita cash balances and real per capita income.
44. Belgium and the Netherlands, with high per capita income but low financial depth. This reflects the fact that broad money data are unavailable for these countries before 1913 and we had to use M1.

Table 9.4   **Panel Estimates: Regressions with Fixed Effects 1880–1913, Twenty-
                    Three Countries**

Independent Variable	Dependent Variable log M2-GDP			
	(1)	(2)	(3)	(4)
Gold standard	**0.082**		**0.102**	**0.099**
	[20.8]		[26.6]	[25.5]
	(5.134)		(5.686)	(5.409)
Domestic currency bonds		**0.102**		**0.083**
		[26.4]		[21.1]
		(4.632)		(3.833)
Real per capita GDP (log)			**0.266**	**0.263**
			(4.753)	(4.684)
Short-term interest rate (log)			**−0.089**	**−0.089**
			(−3.780)	(−3.887)
N	782	782	782	782

Notes: Generalized least squares (GLS) with cross-section weights; country dummies, and a time trend (not shown in the table); *t*-values in parentheses; response percent in brackets.

transition from paper to gold by a large number of emerging countries as their incomes and financial development progressed.[45]

As controls in the regression we used the traditional determinants of the demand for money: real per capita income (discussed above) and a short-term interest rate. We would expect the short-term interest rate, representing the opportunity cost of holding money balances, as well as the presence and spread of financial assets as substitutes for money, to be negative.[46] Other controls tried in the regressions (but not presented in the results below) were the (log of the) consumer price index (CPI) inflation rate, to measure the opportunity cost of holding money relative to goods, and the fiscal balance, because a tendency to run a deficit might signal eventual attempts to predate the financial sector, thus causing, in line with our earlier discussion, a persistence of domestic financial underdevelopment as people continue to hold their balances abroad.

Table 9.4 shows log linear panel regressions for twenty-three countries for M2-GDP including country (fixed effects) and a time trend. In column (1) the gold adherence dummy is significantly associated with a higher ratio of M2 to GDP. Going from paper to gold is associated with a 21 percent higher M2-GDP ratio (the response indicated in brackets).[47] Countries that

45. See Eichengreen and Flandreau (1996) for other factors explaining the transition.
46. For the short-term interest rate in most countries we used the official discount rate. For the core countries (United States, United Kingdom, France, Germany, and the Netherlands) we used open market rates. For several countries where data on short-term interest rates are unavailable we used long-term interest rates.
47. Calculated as in Halvorsen and Palmquist (1980).

could issue sovereign debt in terms of their own currencies also had higher ratios of M2-GDP by 26 percent (column [2]). The addition of real per capita income and short-term interest rates to the regression with the gold dummy (column [3]) shows significant coefficients for all regressors with signs suggested by theory, the positive and greater than one coefficient on real per capita income agrees with earlier evidence in Bordo and Jonung (1987). Finally, and quite importantly, the addition of the Bond dummy is also significant (column [4]).

In sum, these results suggest that countries that could adhere to gold were financially more developed. Also financially developed countries were those that could issue sovereign debt in terms of their own currency.[48]

9.4.2   1973–97

In this section, we conduct similar exercises for the current regime of open capital markets and generalized floating. Our assumption is that to-day, as in the previous era of globalized financial markets, we would expect that advanced countries would have greater financial depth than emerging ones and (ceteris paribus) would float. Moreover, as emerging countries moved toward advanced country status they would adopt the monetary regime of the advanced countries. Thus we would expect to find that, across both advanced and emerging countries, financial depth would be positively associated with adherence to freely floating regimes relative to adherence to other regimes.

A number of reasons, however, suggest that the clean results we reported in the previous section might not be so easy to replicate in today's world. And since these affect the regression strategy, it seems necessary to spend a while discussing them. One reason is that the expansion of the real broad money supply might not be as good a measure for today as it was for the late nineteenth century, especially for the advanced countries because of the development of other financial assets as substitutes for money bal-

48. As a sensitivity test, we ran a panel probit regression taking the choice of exchange rate (adherence to gold or not) as the dependent variable and M2-GDP and the other controls from table 9.4 as the independent variables. In the regressions the M2-GDP ratio was positive and significant but the bond dummy was insignificant. The coefficient on M2-GDP suggests that a 1 percent increase in financial depth would increase the probability of a country adhering to gold by 6.5 percent. This result, compared to the coefficient of the exchange rate variable shown in the regression in table 9.4, raises the tricky issue of causality between financial depth and the exchange rate regime.

On the one hand, Rousseau and Sylla's (ch. 8 in this volume) evidence that financial development is a key determinant of the earlier growth of today's advanced countries and Eichengreen and Flandreau's (1996) findings that growth is a determinant of pre-1914 gold standard adherence suggest that financial development may explain the ability to adhere to gold. On the other hand, adherence to the specie standard in Europe long predated modern growth, and England's switch to gold de facto in 1717 also preceded both modern economic growth and much of England's financial development. Thus arguments for causality between the exchange rate regime and financial depth can go both ways.

ances, as well as technological innovation, which economizes on cash balances.[49]

A second reason is that the simple menu of alternatives to floating that prevailed in the late nineteenth century (peg to gold) has been replaced by a more complex one: peg to the dollar, peg to the mark, peg to the euro, peg to a basket, not to mention various intermediate arrangements ranging from dirty floats and adjustable pegs to crawling pegs. These latter arrangements purport to maintain some of the advantages of floating—monetary independence and insulation from external shocks—with the advantages of pegging.

A third reason is that, as a number of recent papers have argued, the IMF classification of exchange rate regimes, which is based on information provided by the member countries, may not reflect the true underlying regime. Thus, Calvo and Reinhart (2000a,b) present evidence to the effect that countries that say they are floating show little variation in their exchange rates but substantial variation in their international reserves and interest rates and hence act more like peggers.

What we argue here is that the dose of "nineteenth-centurism," which according to us has survived in the periphery, implies that for those emerging countries that are unable to successfully float because a substantial portion of their outstanding financial obligations are denominated in dollars or other advanced countries currencies, pegging would mean financial deepening—in a nineteenth-century fashion. This follows because the alternative of volatile exchange rates could have serious consequences for the private sector's balance sheet and hence for the real economy—manifest by their inability to sell their debt denominated in their own currency in international markets. These countries would be better off, it is argued, if they dollarized.

For these emerging markets, especially those of Latin America, Hausmann, Panizza, and Stein (2000) argue that greater financial depth would be associated with fixed exchange rate arrangements (i.e., to peg as second best).[50] Thus we may expect to see a bipolar pattern wherein advanced countries and some emergers that can emulate them have greater financial depth associated with floating, and others who cannot float—or because of their greater openness choose not to—have greater depth associated with fixing.

In our empirical work, we use a panel of forty-four countries with data from Bordo et al. (2001): twenty-two advanced countries and twenty-two emerging countries.[51] Exchange rate regimes are identified with dummies

---

49. Thus, velocity (the inverse of M2-GDP) displays a U-shaped pattern over the past century and across countries by levels of development (Bordo and Jonung 1987).

50. Also see Eichengreen and Hausmann (1999).

51. The twenty-two advanced countries are Australia, Austria-Hungary, Belgium, Canada, Denmark, Finland, France, Germany, Greece, Iceland, Ireland, Italy, Japan, the Netherlands,

constructed using the two exchange rate definitions discussed in section 9.2 (Masson 2001 and Levy-Yeyati and Sturzenegger 2001). To measure financial depth, as we did for the 1880–1913 period, we used the M2-GDP ratio. However, as argued above, we might expect that this measure may not be as good a proxy for financial depth today as it was a century ago. As alternative measures of financial depth we use three measures developed for the World Bank by Beck, Demirguc-Kunt, and Levine (1999): FD1, defined as the ratio of private credit to GDP; FD2, defined as private credit plus stock market valuation to GDP; and FD3, defined as FD2 plus private and public bond market capitalization as a share of GDP.[52]

To account for the domestic currency denomination of international bonds we used two databases. The first is the Bank for International Settlements (BIS) data used by Hausmann, Pannizza, and Stein (2000), which contain all international securities and bank loans by currency and issuer, but only for the period 1993–97. Countries that issued international securities in terms of their own currency consisted of most of the Organization for Economic Cooperation and Development (OECD) countries and in our sample only four emergers: Hong Kong, Singapore, South Africa, and Taiwan. The second measure is all international bonds from data supplied by the IMF. These data cover the period 1980–97 and again consist mostly of OECD countries, plus seven emergers: Argentina, China, Hong Kong, Singapore, Korea, the Philippines, and South Africa. We defined a dummy as equal to one if a country could issue such securities.[53]

Finally, as in the 1880–1913 period, we used as controls in the regression: per capita real GDP in U.S. dollars, short-term interest rates (open market rates where available, otherwise deposit rates), the ratio of fiscal deficit to GDP, and the log of the CPI inflation rate. All these data come from IFS.

9.4.3   Results: All Advanced and Emerging Countries

We present tables similar to those for the pre-1914 period. Table 9.5 shows the coefficients of regressions of the log of M2-GDP on the Masson and LYS floating exchange rate dummies, a dummy for the IMF indicator of the issue of international bonds in domestic currency, and, as a control, the short-term interest rate.[54]

New Zealand, Norway, Portugal, Spain, Sweden, Switzerland, United Kingdom, and the United States. The twenty-two emerging countries are Argentina, Brazil, Chile, China, Colombia, Ecuador, Hong Kong, Indonesia, Israel, Korea, Malaysia, Mexico, Paraguay, Peru, the Philippines, Singapore, South Africa, Taiwan, Thailand, Turkey, Uruguay, and Venezuela.

52. See Khan and Senhadji (2000) for an earlier use of these measures to explain the pattern of growth across emerging countries.

53. The dummy starts the year that the listings begin.

54. We also used the Bank for International Settlements (BIS) measure of bonds issued in domestic currency. The results were usually similar, so because the data for these bonds only cover five years we do not report them unless otherwise indicated. As an alternative to the log of short-term interest rates we use the log of the inflation rate. The results using this variable were almost identical to those using the log of interest rates, so we do not report them here. We

Table 9.5   **Panel Estimates: Regressions with Fixed Effects 1973–97, All Countries**

	Dependent Variable log M2-GDP					
	All Countries		Advanced Countries		Emerging Countries	
Independent Variable	(1)	(2)	(3)	(4)	(5)	(6)
Masson float	**0.094**		**0.108**		**0.070**	
	[24.1]		[28.1]		[17.5]	
	(3.614)		(3.433)		(1.677)	
Levy-Yeyati-		**0.020**		**0.031**		**0.021**
Sturzenegger float		[4.8]		[7.4]		[5.1]
		(2.010)		(1.987)		(1.592)
Domestic currency	**0.081**	**0.087**	−**0.024**	**0.059**	**0.184**	**0.456**
boards	[20.5]	[22.3]	[−5.4]	[14.7]	[52.6]	[186]
	(6.424)	(5.101)	(−1.539)	(3.167)	(5.251)	(4.199)
Short-term interest	−**0.067**	−**0.074**	−**0.060**	−**0.049**	−**0.064**	−**0.093**
rate (log)	(−6.933)	(−7.048)	(−5.153)	(−3.433)	(−4.294)	(−5.952)
N	1,025	1,008	500	504	525	504

Notes: GLS with cross-section weights; country dummies, and a time trend (not shown in the table); *t*-values in parentheses; response percent in brackets. For columns (2), (4), and (6) we used the BIS bond dummy.

As in the 1880–1913 regressions we include country fixed effects and a time trend. We exclude real per capita income from the regressions shown because the estimated income elasticity was close to zero (the income elasticity with respect to real cash balances close to one). Indeed, the specification of the M2-GDP ratio we present is similar to the one first used by Latane (1954) and by Lucas (1988).

In table 9.5 we present the results for all countries and then separately for advanced and emerging countries. As can be seen in columns (1) and (2) for all countries, all three independent variables are significant. Financial depth increases on average when countries float—according to the Masson definition, by 24 percent; for the LYS, by 5 percent. When they can issue bonds in terms of their own currencies, financial depth increases by slightly over 20 percent.[55]

For the advanced countries (see columns [3] and [4]), as in the case of all countries, both floating exchange rate indicators are positive and significant, as is the bond variable in column (4).[56] For the emerging countries (see columns [5] and [6]), the Masson dummy is positive and significant at conventional levels, whereas the LYS dummy is barely significant at the 10 per-

---

also do not report results for regressions including the fiscal deficit–GDP ratio. That ratio was often insignificant.

55. In the regressions in column (2) we used the BIS measure of local currency bonds because the IMF measure was not significant.

56. Again, in column (4) we used the BIS bond dummy.

Table 9.6   **Panel Estimates: Regressions with Fixed Effects 1973–97**

	Dependent Variable log M2-GDP					
	All Countries		Advanced Countries		Emerging Countries	
Independent Variable	(1)	(2)	(3)	(4)	(5)	(6)
Masson fixed	**–0.110**		**–0.079**		**–0.268**	
	[–22.4]		[–16.7]		[–46.1]	
	(–3.959)		(–2.723)		(–2.802)	
Levy-Yeyati-		**–0.039**		**–0.026**		**–0.018**
Sturzenegger fixed		[–8.6]		[–5.8]		[–4.0]
		(–1.943)		(–1.183)		(–0.601)
Domestic currency	**–0.065**	**–0.111**	**–0.060**	**–0.049**	**–0.077**	**–0.081**
rate (log)	(–6.807)	(–11.696)	(–5.007)	(–3.477)	(–5.351)	(–5.326)
N	1,025	504	500	504	525	504

Notes: GLS with cross-section weights: country dummies, and a time trend (not shown in the table); *t*-values in parentheses; response percent i brackets. For column (4) we used the BIS bond dummy.

cent level. Also, the bond variable is significant and positive in both specifications.

We then ran similar regressions to those in the above tables but substituted the Masson and LYS fixed exchange rate dummies for the floats used in table 9.5; see table 9.6. For all countries both fixed exchange rate dummies were significant and negative in a regression including the bond dummy and the interest rate.

The same result obtained for the advanced countries using the Masson dummy, with the LYS exchange rate indicator insignificant. Finally, for the emerging countries, the Masson fixed exchange rate dummy was negative and significant in all the regressions, whereas the LYS dummy was always insignificant.[57]

In sum, the results from tables 9.5 and 9.6 for the 1973–97 period when floating was the dominant exchange rate regime seem to be consistent with those of the pre-1914 era in table 9.4, when gold was the dominant regime. For advanced countries and, to a lesser extent, emerging countries, greater financial depth both as measured by M2-GDP and the ability to issue international bonds in domestic currency is associated with floating.

57. As for the pre-1914 sample, we also reran the regressions above as panel probits with the exchange rate regime dummies as dependent variable. Taking the floating exchange rates as dependent variables we found that M2-GDP was generally positive and significant for all the country classifications using both the Masson and LYS indicators. Similar results obtained for the bond dummies. Taking the fixed exchange rate regime as dependent variable, M2-GDP was generally negative and the bond dummy was insignificant. As was the case for the pre-1914 period gold standard, the question of causality between financial depth and the exchange rate regime is difficult to sort out. A deeper analysis of the circumstances of each country is likely required.

9.4.4   Latin America and Asia

The results from table 9.6 for a sample of emergers across the world suggest that hard fixers on average had lower financial depth than others. These results seem to contradict evidence presented in Hausmann, Panizza, and Stein (2000) for Latin America suggesting that fixers had greater financial depth. However, they may also be explained by the fact that emergers who could float were less financially integrated than the advanced countries, as seen in section 9.2, and by the aggregation of very different categories of emerging countries.

To correct for this, in table 9.7 we split the emerging sample of countries into Latin America and Asia, presenting only the significant results. For Latin America we find that the Masson float dummy is positive and significant when introduced alone (but is insignificant with the addition of the interest rate control), whereas the LYS floating dummy is negative and significant in the regressions with controls. At the same time, the Masson fixed exchange rate dummy is negative and significant. Both bond dummies for Latin America are always insignificant.

The LYS results that Latin American countries that float do not have greater financial depth may be consistent with the evidence from the Feldstein-Horioka regressions in section 9.2 that Latin America is relatively financially open. The LYS results, which are based on the economic characteristics of the regime, rather than on information supplied by the reporting countries that lie behind the Masson dummies, may be more telling.

For Asia, we find both floating indicators to be associated with greater financial depth, as is the domestic currency bond indicator, evidence that some Asian countries may be able to emulate the advanced countries. However, the evidence from section 9.2 that financial integration in Asia is less than in Latin America may also explain why some Asian countries could successfully float. At the same time, the LYS fixed exchange rate dummy is also positive and significant in column (9). This last result seems consistent with the hollowing-out hypothesis.

In sum, for the emergers, the case is mixed. Although there is some evidence for the group as a whole that floating was associated with greater financial depth and the ability to issue bonds denominated in domestic currency, we also find when we disaggregate the emerging countries into Latin America and Asia that, although some Latin American countries may have had deeper financial markets associated with floating, there was quite strong evidence that Asian countries with floating exchange rates had greater financial depth than other countries, and moreover they seem to be more mature than their Latin counterparts in terms of the ability to issue international bonds denominated in their own currency (although, again, they may have been able to achieve this because they were less open than other countries). The evidence at the same time that some Asian countries

Table 9.7   Panel Estimates: Regressions with Fixed Effects 1973–97

	Dependent Variable log M2-GDP								
	Latin America					Asia			
Independent Variable	(1)	(2)	(3)	(4)	(5)	(6)	(7)	(8)	(9)
Masson float	**0.129** [34.5] (2.700)					**0.15** [43] (3.009)			
Levy-Yeyati-Sturzenegger float			**−0.09** [−18] (−2.044)				**0.08** [19] (2.700)	**0.05** [11] (1.735)	
Masson fixed		**−0.198** [−37] (−3.811)		**−0.43** [−63] (−2.005)					
Levy-Yeyati Sturzenegger fixed									**0.06** [15] (1.759)
Domestic currency bonds					**0.022** [66] (6.443)			**0.18** [53] (5.140)	**0.11** [29] (3.094)
Short-term interest rate (log)			**−0.06** (−4.975)	**−0.098** (−4.812)				**−0.05** (−1.848)	**−0.02** (−0.792)
N	250	250	240	240	264	300	288	264	264

Notes: GLS with cross-section weights; country dummies, and a time trend (not shown in the table); *t*-values in parentheses; response percent in brackets.

with fixed rates had greater financial depth is consistent with both the hollowing-out and "original sin" hypotheses.

9.4.5 An Alternative Measure of Financial Development

Finally, we experimented with regressions similar to those displayed in the two previous subsections but taking as dependent variable the alternative measures of financial development produced by the World Bank: FD1, private credit to GDP; FD2, private credit plus stock market valuation to GDP; and FD3, FD2 plus bond market capitalization to GDP.

The most significant results were for FD2 and FD3, which were quite similar. We show selected results taking the log of FD3 as dependent variable for advanced and emerging countries, Latin America, and Asia in table 9.8. The results for the advanced countries are almost identical to those in table 9.5. For advanced countries greater financial depth is associated positively and significantly with floating and the ability to issue securities in domestic currency. This evidence may be important, because these measures of financial development, unlike M2-GDP, account for

Table 9.8   **Panel Estimates: Regressions with Fixed Effects 1973–97**

| | Dependent Variable log FD3 | | | | | |
| | Advanced Countries | | Emerging Countries | | Latin America | |
Independent Variables	(1)	(2)	(3)	(4)	(5)	(6)
Masson float	**0.128** [34.4] (3.697)					
Levy-Yeyati-Sturzenegger float		**0.025** [6.0] (1.634)				
Masson fixed			**0.200** [58.5] (3.41)		**0.546** [251.3] (4.145)	
Levy-Yeyati-Sturzenegger fixed				**0.271** [86.7] (4.725)		**0.344** [120.6] (4.619)
Domestic currency bonds	**0.55** [13.6] (1.915)	**0.063** [15.5] (2.304)				**−0.196** [−36.3] (−3.737)
Short-term interest rate (log)	**0.072** (3.615)	**0.025** (1.748)	**−0.025** (−1.45)			**−0.010** (−2.900)
N	440	440	462	462	210	242

Notes: GLS with cross-section weights; country dummies, and a time trend (not shown in the table); *t*-values in parentheses; response percent in brackets. For column (2) we used the BIS bond dummy.

the substitution away from money once an economy becomes fully monetized.[58]

For the emerging countries the evidence unequivocally suggests that greater financial depth is associated with fixed exchange rates. In addition to the fixed exchange rate results presented here, the various floating exchange rate indicators are negative. Similar evidence obtains for both Latin America and Asia. Also of interest, the bond dummy is insignificant in most of the regressions except for Asia, where it is negative and insignificant.[59] These results seem much more in accord with Hausmann's "original sin" hypothesis.

The question then arises: Which measure of financial depth should we pay more attention to, M2-GDP or FD3? For the advanced countries the broader measure should surely be superior to M2-GDP, but this may not be the case for the emergers because the stock and bond markets in these countries may still be in a nascent state, at least compared to the advanced countries.

9.4.6 Summary

In conclusion, the evidence presented in this section for the two eras of globalization suggests some remarkable similarities. In general, countries with greater financial development followed the dominant regime—gold before 1914, floating after 1973. Also, countries that issued international bonds in terms of their own currencies could successfully follow the dominant regime. The exchange rate experience of the advanced countries exactly fits this pattern.

The case of the emerging countries is, however, less clear. Before 1914 emergers went to great lengths to join the gold standard, and the financial performance of those who could not adhere was clearly worse. Today the incidence of emergers who float and who have greater financial depth is less than the pre-1914 incidence of emergers who adhered to gold. Those who cannot float but need access to international capital according to the "original sin" theory must adhere to hard fixes.

The evidence for the recent period is mixed on who has greater financial depth. According to the M2-GDP results, it is floaters based on the Masson exchange rate indicator, although this is not evident from the LYS results, which may be the more economically meaningful. But the FD3 (and FD2) results see hard fixers (especially those in Asia) as more financially developed. In addition, the evidence for Asia that associates some countries' floating experience with greater financial depth may also be reflecting the

---

58. This substitution process may also explain the positive coefficient on the short-term interest rate for the advanced countries.

59. Panel probit regression of the exchange rate regime dummies on FD3 revealed a pattern of coefficients similar to that in table 9.10, again raising the issue of causality.

fact that Asia is less financially open than Latin America so that it may be capital controls (hidden or otherwise) that allow these regimes to be viable.

Thus we conclude that our empirical results for the emerging countries today are in general consistent with both the hollowing-out and "original sin" hypotheses. More research is clearly needed.

Finally, an important fact that emerges from the evidence in this section is that the number of countries that could issue bonds in terms of their own currencies has not increased all that much over the past century. Before 1914, it was eight. Today, it is about twenty-five. Virtually all of the expansion is by countries like Canada, Italy, and Sweden who graduated to advanced status after WWI. There are very few emerging countries today in either of the lists of bonds that we had access to, and most of them only entered in late in the past decade. The question as to how countries graduate from junior to senior country status in the bond markets is also a subject for further research.

9.5 Conclusion: Financial Maturity—The Holy Grail

The traditional view is that fixed exchange rate regimes are best for the globalization of financial markets. This view is based on the stellar performance of the classical gold standard. Yet today we are in another era of globalization as pervasive as the earlier one, and now the dominant regime is floating. This paradox suggests at first glance that globalization, rather than being determined by the exchange rate regime, occurs independent of the exchange rate regime. However, as we argue in this paper, although this may be the case for advanced countries, it is not for emergers, whose regime choice is in large measure driven by international financial integration.

In this paper we focus on the different historical regime experiences of the core and the periphery. Before 1914, advanced countries adhered to gold and periphery countries tried to emulate the core, especially when they were concerned with attracting foreign capital. Because of their extensive external debt obligations denominated in core-country currencies, peripheral countries were especially vulnerable to financial crises and debt default. This made devaluations difficult for them, leaving them with the difficult choice of floating but restricting external borrowing or devoting considerable resources to maintaining an extra-hard peg. Today, whereas advanced countries can successfully float, emergers must also borrow abroad in terms of advanced country currencies and are afraid to float for the same reason as their nineteenth-century forebears. To maintain access to foreign capital they may need a hard peg to the core-country currencies.

Thus the key distinction between core and periphery countries, both then and now, that we emphasize in this paper is financial maturity. It is evidenced in the ability to issue international securities denominated in domestic currency, or what Ricardo Hausmann refers to as the absence of original sin. Indeed, our hypothesis is that countries that are financially developed, in a world of open capital markets, should be able to float as advanced countries do today. Evidence for the core countries that the classical gold standard operated as a target zone with the gold points serving as bands in which credible floating could occur and external shocks could be buffered is a presage of the regime followed today. Today's floating is a product of financial maturity and the development of the technological and institutional structures and constraints that allow policymakers to follow stable money and fiscal policy without adhering to an external nominal anchor.

We present several strands of evidence for our hypothesis that globalization is largely independent of the regime for advanced countries but drives the exchange rate regime for the periphery. First, evidence from Feldstein-Horioka tests over the period since 1880 agrees with the folk wisdom that financial integration was high before 1914, as it is today. But the evidence suggests that it was not the exchange rate regime followed that mattered, but the presence of capital controls. Moreover, a comparison between advanced and emerging countries today suggests that although there is considerable financial integration among the advanced countries, most of whom can float, this is not the case for the emergers, and indeed those that float may do so because they are not financially open.

Second, in section 9.3 we elaborate on the financial vulnerability hypothesis, which is related to the recent literature on original sin. Descriptive material from the pre-1914 history of the periphery paints a very familiar picture of financially "backward" countries required to borrow abroad in sterling, francs, or marks, or with gold clauses, being hammered by the crises of the 1890s, forced to devalue and default, and then devoting considerable resources to obtain the gold reserves needed to adhere to gold as if on a currency board (Russia, Greece) or floating but restricting foreign borrowing (Spain, Portugal)—hollowing-out déjà vu. Future research will have to explain the reasons for the inability many countries have faced, and most probably will continue to face, when borrowing abroad.

Finally, in section 9.4 we present some empirical findings for the pre-1914 period showing a clear connection between the ability to borrow abroad in domestic currency, gold adherence, and financial depth. Extending our methodology to the post-1973 era led to identical results for the advanced countries whose dominant exchange rate regime is now floating (with the exception of the European experiment with a monetary union).

For the emerging countries, however, it appears as if those that are financially open, especially the Latin American countries, have difficulty floating because they do suffer from original sin as evidenced in their inability to borrow abroad in domestic currencies. They tend to have greater financial depth when they have fixed rates. For Asia, floating exchange rates are associated with one measure of greater financial depth, but this may be because it is less financially open. For another measure fixed rates and financial depth go hand in hand, similar to the experiences of Latin America.

In conclusion, the dynamics of the international monetary system and the evolution of the exchange rate regime can be understood as being complex, involving both the financial development of countries and international financial integration. Financial crises such as those in the 1890s and the 1990s are the defining moments that reveal the regime fault lines between advanced and emerging countries. The evolution from the gold standard to floating by the advanced countries required achieving financial maturity, and the same will ultimately be required for the rest of the world. In the interim, the panoply of intermediate arrangements with varying forms of government intervention, including impediments to the free flow of capital, will prevail. Financial crises as occurred in the 1890s and the 1990s will also continue to be an important part of the process of regime evolution as an ultimate structuring force.

Appendix
Data Sources

1880–1913

M2. Data appendix to Bordo et al. (2001; available on request) for all countries except the following: Austria, Komlos (1987); Chile, Bordo and Rockoff (1996); Greece, Kostelenos (1995); the Netherlands and Norway, Bordo and Jonung (2001); Portugal, Bordo and Schwartz (1996); Russia, Drummond (1976).

Nominal GDP, real GDP, implicit price deflator, and CPI. Data appendix to Bordo et al. (2001) for all countries except the following: Austria, Komlos (1987); Chile, Bordo and Rockoff (1996); Greece, Kostelenos (1995); Russia, Drummond (1976).

Population. Data appendix to Bordo et al. (2001) for all countries except the following: Austria, Crédit Lyonnais economic studies; the Netherlands, Russia and Switzerland, Mitchell (1992).

Short-term interest rates. Argentina, data provided by Alan Taylor from Obstfeld and Taylor (ch. 3 in this volume); Austria, *The Economist;* Australia, Bordo and Rockoff (1996); Belgium, Mitchell (1992); Brazil, Global Financial Data; Canada, Bordo and Jonung (1987; we substituted long-term interest rates for short-term interest rates); Chile, Subercaseaux (1926); Denmark and Finland, constructed by Marc Flandreau from a variety of national official sources; France and Germany, Bordo (1993); Greece, data provided by Olga Charodonlakis; Italy, *The Economist;* Japan, Bordo; the Netherlands, Bordo and Jonung (1995); Norway, Flandreau;

Portugal, *The Economist;* Russia, *The Economist;* Spain, Sweden, and Switzerland, Flandreau; United Kingdom, Bordo; United States, Bordo. *Government finance (expenditures and tax receipts).* Argentina and Austria, Mitchell (1992); Australia, David Pope (ANU); Belgium, Bordo and Jonung (2001); Brazil, Mitchell (1993); Canada, Bordo and Jonung; Chile, Mitchell (1993); Denmark, Finland, France, and Germany, Bordo and Jonung; Greece, Mitchell (1992); Italy, Japan, the Netherlands, and Norway, Bordo and Jonung; Portugal, Russia, and Spain, Mitchell (1992); Sweden, Switzerland, the United Kingdom, and the United States, Bordo and Jonung.

1973–1997

M2, nominal GDP, real GDP, population, implicit price deflator and CPI, and government expenditures and tax receipts. Forty-four countries, twenty-two advanced countries, and twenty-two emerging countries: See data appendix to Bordo et al. (2001).

References

Bayoumi, Tamin. 1990. Saving-investment correlations, immobile capital, government policy, or endogenous behavior. *IMF Staff Papers* 37 (2): 360–87.
———. 1997. *Financial integration and real activity.* Studies in macroeconomics series. Manchester, U.K.: Manchester University Press.
Beck, Thorsten, Asli Demirguc-Kunt, and Ross Levine. 1999. A new database on financial development and structure. World Bank Working Paper. Washington, D.C.: World Bank.
Bergsten, C. Fred, and John Williamson. 1983. Exchange rates and trade policy. In *Trade policy in the 1980s,* ed. William R. Cline. Washington, D.C.: Institute for International Economics.
Bini-Smaghi, Lorenzo. 1991. Exchange rate variability and trade: Why is it so difficult to find any empirical relationship? *Applied Economics* 23 (5): 927–35.
Bordo, Michael D. 1993. The Bretton Woods international monetary system: A historical overview. In *A retrospective on the Bretton Woods system: Lessons for international monetary reform,* ed. Michael D. Bordo and Barry Eichengreen, 3–98. Chicago: University of Chicago Press.
Bordo, Michael D., and Barry Eichengreen. 1998. Implications of the Great Depression for the development of the international monetary system. In *The defining moment: The Great Depression and the American economy in the twentieth century,* ed. Michael D. Bordo, Claudia Goldin, and Eugene White, 403–53. Chicago: University of Chicago Press.
Bordo, Michael D., Barry Eichengreen, Daniela Klingebiel, and Soledad Martinez-Peria. 2001. Is the crisis problem growing more severe? *Economic Policy* 32:51–82.
Bordo, Michael D., and Harold James. 2002. The Adam Klug memorial lecture: Haberler versus Nurkse: The case for floating exchange rates as an alternative to Bretton Woods. In *The open economy macromodel: Past and future,* ed. Arie Arnon and Warren Young, 161–82. Boston: Kluwer Academic.

Bordo, Michael D., and Lars Jonung. 1987. *The long-run behavior of the velocity of circulation: The international evidence.* New York: Cambridge University Press.

———. 1995. Monetary regimes, inflation, and monetary reform: An essay in honor of Axel Leijonhuvhud. In *Inflation, institutions, and information: Essays in honor of Axel Leijonhuvhud,* ed. D. E. Vaz and K. Vellupillai, 157–244. London: Macmillan.

———. 2001. A return to the convertibility principle? Monetary and fiscal regimes in historical perspective. In *Monetary theory as a basis for monetary policy,* ed. Axel Leijonhuvhud, 225–83. London: Macmillan.

Bordo, Michael D., and Finn Kydland. 1995. The gold standard as a rule: An essay in exploration. *Explorations in Economic History* 32 (October): 423–69.

Bordo, Michael D., and Ronald MacDonald. 1997. Violations of the "rules of the game" and the credibility of the classical gold standard, 1880–1914. NBER Working Paper no. 6111. Cambridge, Mass.: National Bureau of Economic Research, July.

Bordo, Michael D., and Hugh Rockoff. 1996. The gold standard as a "Good Housekeeping Seal of Approval." *Journal of Economic History* 56 (2): 389–428.

Bordo, Michael D., and Anna J. Schwartz. 1996. The operation of the specie standard: Evidence for core and peripheral countries, 1880–1990. In *Currency convertibility: The gold standard and beyond,* ed. Jorge Braga de Macedo, Barry Eichengreen, and Jaime Reis, 11–83. London: Routledge.

———. 1999. Monetary policy regimes and economic performance: The historical record. In *Handbook of macroeconomics,* ed. John Taylor and Michael Woodford, 149–234. New York: North Holland.

Broder, Labert. 1975. *Le role des intérêts économiques étrengers dans la croissance de l'espagne au 19ᵉ siècle, 1797–1984.* Lille, France: ANRT.

Calvo, Guillermo, and Carmen Reinhart. 2000a. Fear of floating. NBER Working Paper no. 7993. Cambridge, Mass.: National Bureau of Economic Research.

———. 2000b. Fixing for your life. NBER Working Paper no. 8001. Cambridge, Mass.: National Bureau of Economic Research, November.

Coiteux, Martin, and Olivier Simon. 2000. The saving retention coefficient over the long and short run: Evidence from panel regressions. *Journal of International Money and Finance* 19 (4): 535–48.

de Block. 1889. *Les finances de la Russie.* Paris: Dupont.

De Cecco, Marcello. 1990. Introduction. In *L'italia nell sistema finanziaro internazionale 1861–1914,* ed. De Cecco, 3–54. Rome: Laterza.

Drummond, I. M. 1976. The Russian gold standard 1897–1914. *Journal of Economic History* 36:633–88.

Eichengreen, Barry. 1992. Trends and cycles in foreign lending. In *Capital flows in the world economy,* ed. Horst Siebert. Tübingen, Germany: Mohr.

———. 1996. *Globalizing capital: A history of the international monetary system.* Princeton, N.J.: Princeton University Press.

———. 1997. The Baring crisis in a Mexican mirror. University of California–Berkeley, Department of Economics. Mimeograph.

Eichengreen, Barry, and Marc Flandreau. 1996. The geography of the gold standard. In *Currency convertibility: The gold standard and beyond,* ed. Jorge Braga de Macedo, Barry Eichengreen, and Jaime Reis, 111–43. New York: Routledge.

Eichengreen, Barry, and Ricardo Hausmann. 1999. Exchange rates and financial fragility. In *New challenges for monetary policy,* 329–68. Kansas City: Federal Reserve Bank of Kansas City.

Eichengreen, Barry, and Peter Temin. 1997. The gold standard and the Great Depression. NBER Working Paper no. 6060. Cambridge, Mass.: National Bureau of Economic Research, June.

Einzig, Paul. 1937. *The theory of forward exchange.* London.

Feldstein, Martin, and Charles Horioka. 1980. Domestic saving and international capital flows. *The Economic Journal* 90 (June): 314–29.

Ferguson, Niall. 1998. *The world's banker: The history of the House of Rothschild.* London.

Fernandez-Arias, Eduardo, and Ricardo Hausmann. 2000. Is FDI a safer form of financing? IADB Working Paper no. 416. Washington, D.C.: Inter-American Development Bank.

Fischer, Stanley. 2001. Is the bipolar view correct? *Journal of Economic Perspectives* 15 (2): 3–24.

Flandreau, Marc. 2002. Crises and punishment: Moral hazard and the pre-1914 international financial architecture. Centre for Economic Policy Research Working Paper.

Flandreau, Marc, and John Komlos. 2001. How to run a target zone? Age old lessons from an Austro-Hungarian experiment (1896–1914). University of Munich, Center for Economic Studies. Working Paper.

Flandreau, Marc, J. Le Cacheux, and F. Zumer. 1998. Stability without a pact? Lessons from the European gold standard, 1880–1913. *Economic Policy* 26:117–62.

Flandreau, Marc, and C. Rivière. 1999. La grande retransformation? L'intégration financière internationale et controles de capitaux 1880–1996. *Economie Internationale* 78:11–58.

Fodor, Giorgio. 2000. The boom that never was? Latin American loans in London, 1822–25. Università di Trento, Department of Economics. Mimeograph.

Francis, John. 1859. *Chronicles and characters of the Stock Exchange.* London: Willoughby.

Friedman, Milton. 1959. The demand for money: Some theoretical and empirical results. *Journal of Political Economy* 67 (4): 327–51.

Gallarotti, Giulio M. 1995. *The anatomy of an international monetary regime: The classical gold standard 1880–1914.* New York: Oxford University Press.

Gerschenkron, Alexander. 1962. *Economic backwardness in historical perspective.* Cambridge, Mass.: Harvard University Press.

Ghosh, Attish R., Anna Marie Gulde, Jonathan Ostry, and Holger Wolf. 1995. Does the nominal exchange rate regime matter? IMF Working Paper no. WP/95/121. Washington, D.C.: International Monetary Fund.

Gregory, Paul. 1995. *Before command: An economic history of Russia from emancipation to the first five-year plan.* Princeton, N.J.: Princeton University Press.

Hallwood, C. Paul, Ronald MacDonald, and Ian W. Marsh. 1996. Credibility and fundamentals: Were the classical and interwar gold standards well behaved target zones? In *Modern perspectives on the gold standard,* ed. Tamim Bayoumi, Barry Eichengreen, and Mark P. Taylor, 129–61. New York: Cambridge University Press.

Halvorsen, Robert, and Raymond Palmquist. 1980. The interpretation of dummy variables in semilogarithmic equations. *American Economic Review* 70 (3): 474–75.

Hausmann, Ricardo, and Eduardo Fernandez-Arias. 2000. Foreign direct investment: Good cholesterol? IADB Working Paper no. 417. Washington, D.C.: Inter-American Development Bank.

Hausmann, Ricardo, Michael Gavin, Carmen Pages, and Ernesto Stein. 1999. Financial turmoil and the crises of exchange rate regime. IADB Working Paper no. 400. Washington, D.C.: Inter-American Development Bank.

Hausmann, Ricardo, Ugo Panizza, and Ernesto Stein. 2000. Why do countries float the way they float? IADB Working Paper no. 418. Washington, D.C.: Inter-American Development Bank.

Helpman, Ellhanon. 1981. An exploration in the theory of exchange rate regimes. *Journal of Political Economy* 89 (October): 865–90.

Jones, M. T., and Maurice Obstfeld. 1997. Saving, investment, and gold: A reassessment of historical current account data. NBER Working Paper no. 6103. Cambridge, Mass.: National Bureau of Economic Research, July.

Kahn, Mohsin, and Abdelhak Senhadji. 2000. Financial development and economic growth: An overview. IMF Working Paper no. WP/00/209. Washington, D.C.: International Monetary Fund.

Kemmerer, Edwin Walter. 1916. *Modern currency reforms.* New York: Macmillan.

Keynes, John M. 1931. *A treatise on money.* Vol. 2. London: Macmillan.

Komlos, John. 1987. Financial innovation and the demand for money in Austria-Hungary, 1867–1913. *Journal of European Economic History* 16:587–606.

Kostelenos, G. C. 1995. *Money and output in modern Greece 1858–1938.* Athens: Center of Planning and Economic Research.

Krol, R. 1996. International capital mobility: Evidence from panel data. *Journal of International Money and Finance* 15 (3): 467–74.

Krugman, Paul. 1979. A model of balance of payments crises. *Journal of Money, Credit, and Banking* 11:311–25.

———. 1991. Target zones and exchange rate dynamics. *Quarterly Journal of Economics* 106 (3): 669–82.

Latane, Henry. 1954. Cash balances and the interest rate: A pragmatic approach. *Review of Economics and Statistics* 36 (November): 456–60.

Laughlin, J. Laurence. 1903. *The principles of money.* New York: C. Scribner's Sons.

Lévy, Raphael-Georges. 1901. Le role des valeurs mobilieres dans le commerce international et dans les reglements financiers internationaux. In *Congrès International des valeurs mobilières,* 23 pp. Paris: Dupont.

Lévy-Leboyer, Maurice. 1976. *La position internationale de la France* (The international position of France). Paris: Presse de L'ecole des Hautes Etudes en Sciences Sociales.

Levy-Yeyati, Eduardo, and Federico Sturzenegger. 2001. Exchange rate regimes and economic performance. *IMF Staff Papers* (forthcoming).

Lucas, Robert E. 1988. Money demand in the United States: A quantitative review. *Carnegie Rochester Conference Series on Public Policy* 29:137–68.

Maddison, Angus. 1995. *Monitoring the world economy 1920–92.* Paris: Organization for Economic Cooperation and Development.

Masson, Paul. 2001. Exchange rate regime transitions. *Journal of Development Economics* 64 (January): 571–86.

Missale, Alessandro, and Olivier Jean Blanchard. 1994. The debt burden and debt maturity. *American Economic Review* 84 (1): 309–19.

Mitchell, Brian R. 1992. *International historical statistics.* New York: Macmillan.

Neal, Larry. 1990. *The rise of financial capitalism: International capital markets in the age of reason.* New York: Cambridge University Press.

Obstfeld, Maurice. 1984. The logic of currency crises. NBER Working Paper no. 4640. Cambridge, Mass.: National Bureau of Economic Research.

———. 1995. International capital mobility in the 90s. In *Understanding interdependence: The macroeconomics of the open economy,* ed. Peter B. Kenen, 201–61. Princeton, N.J.: Princeton University Press.

Obstfeld, Maurice, and Alan M. Taylor. 1998. The Great Depression as a watershed: International capital mobility over the long run. In *The defining moment: The Great Depression and the American economy in the twentieth century,* ed.

Michael D. Bordo, Claudia Goldin, and Eugene White, 353–402. Chicago: University of Chicago Press.

Redish, Angela. 1996. Anchors aweigh: The transition from commodity money to fiat money in Western economies. *Canadian Journal of Economics* 26 (November): 777–95.

Subercaseaux, Guillermo. 1926. *Monetary and banking policy of Chile.* New York: Carnegie Endowment.

Svennson, Lars E. O. 1994. Why exchange rates bands? *Journal of Monetary Economics* 33:157–99.

Tattara, Guiseppe. 1999. A paper money but a gold debt: Italy under the gold standard. University of Venice, Department of Economics. Mimeograph.

Tesar, Linda L. 1991. Saving, investment, and international capital flows. *Journal of International Economics* 31:55–78.

Wilkins, Myra. 1989. *The history of foreign investment in the United States to 1914.* Cambridge, Mass.: Harvard University Press.

Zevin, Robert B. 1992. Are world financial markets more open? If so, why and with what effects? In *Financial openness and national autonomy: Opportunities and constraints,* ed. T. Banuri and J. B. Schor, 43–83. Oxford, U.K.: Clarendon.

Comment   Anna J. Schwartz

The question the paper is designed to answer is how to account for the different exchange rate regimes that countries adopted during the era of globalization before the First World War and during the second era of globalization post–Bretton Woods. The authors offer three different approaches to answer the question: They provide correlation tests between saving and investment panel data; they discuss financial immaturity before 1914 in terms of the need by capital-poor countries to include gold clauses in debt instruments and denote the ability to borrow abroad in domestic currency as a hallmark of gold adherence and financial depth; and they estimate money demand equations to test the difference in financial depth between capital-rich and –poor.

Let me note why I prefer a distinction between capital-rich and capital-poor rather than core and periphery, the authors' choice. The core-peripheral classification seems an apt one applied to the gold standard world. For this paper, which concerns globalization, a better choice for classifying the two sets of countries would have been capital-rich and capital-poor. Foreign direct investment flows not only from the capital-rich to the capital-poor, which is often discussed in globalization studies, but in the current era increasingly from one capital-rich country to other capital-rich countries.

The focus of the paper is on why the capital-rich countries adopted fixed

Anna J. Schwartz is adjunct professor of economics at the Graduate Center of the City University of New York and a research associate of the National Bureau of Economic Research.

exchange rates during the first era of globalization and, during the second era of globalization, except for the European Union (hardly as minor an exception as the paper implies), adopted the radically opposite system of floating exchange rates. The capital-poor countries, on the other hand, the authors say, have been "surprisingly consistent"; they tried unsuccessfully to adhere to the gold standard during the first era of globalization and ended up with currency boards, close to 100 percent gold reserves, or floating exchange rates and, in the second era, have had trouble maintaining floating rates and have pegged to capital-rich-country currencies. The "consistency" must refer to the variety of exchange rate system choices in both eras of globalization by capital-poor countries. I doubt the reference to currency boards during the first era. Colonial countries then had currency boards, dictated by the imperial country. Colonial countries had no voice in the choice.

The explanation the paper offers for the differential exchange rate arrangements of the two classes of countries in the two eras hinges on the attainment of financial maturity. Financial maturity encompasses the development of wide and deep financial markets and sound fiscal and monetary arrangements. For the capital-rich countries, reaching that nirvana allowed them to float in the second era. I do not accept this explanation for their decision to float post–Bretton Woods. What seems more likely is that these countries fixed their exchange rates before the First World War because that seemed the only way to avoid inflation, but they later learned that floating freed monetary policy and that it was possible to avoid inflation if monetary policy was conducted to that end.

The authors regard the current episode of floating as proof of financial maturity and the exchange rate regime to which all countries should aspire. Barely twenty years ago, floating rates were held to be temporary arrangements that would be succeeded by fixed rates in the absence of shocks. It is premature for economic historians to describe the brief experience of floating free of inflation since the 1990s as a durable system. History is a record of repeated reversals between fixed and floating.

Financial immaturity may be an adequate explanation for the failure of capital-poor countries to adhere to the gold standard in the first era. When they then floated and devalued, they suffered losses imposed on them as borrowers in the international capital market because interest payments and principal were denominated in the currencies of capital-rich countries. That experience clarified the advantage of adopting the gold standard, but failed monetary and fiscal policies undermined their adherence. Financial immaturity may also explain why capital-poor countries that tried fixing had to shift to floating rates of exchange in the current era of globalization and learned that floating was no panacea. Financial immaturity may be a euphemism for misguided monetary and fiscal policies.

Section 9.2 uses correlation tests between saving and investment panel data to measure the degree of financial integration. The pre-1914 subgroup of gold standard countries did not achieve greater financial openness than the entire complement of countries. In the interwar years, gold standard and sterling area countries were less financially integrated than the entire complement of countries. The paper attributes this result to the presence of capital controls that reduced integration. All in all, the paper concludes that because the pre-1914 sample with fixed exchange rates and no capital controls was only imperfectly integrated, the gold standard was not the reason globalization occurred. Globalization was the reason the gold standard was adopted. Small differences in the correlation results are the basis for this conclusion.

For 1973–97, the paper presents saving and investment correlation estimates for a sample, subgrouped into developed, total emerging, emerging Asia, and emerging Latin American countries, classified as participating in one of three types of exchange rate regime (fixed, intermediate, or floating) associated with higher or lower levels of integration. Asian countries are less open than the average, Latin American countries more open. With respect to alternative exchange rate regimes, developed countries are more integrated whether they fix or float, with the fixers tending to be smaller countries.

The conclusion the paper reaches in section 9.2 is that European integration in the second era of globalization is a result of liberalization of financial services rather than a result of the exchange rate regime. Whether fixed or floating, capital-rich countries have implemented financial openness. Financial integration in Latin American countries, however, according to the paper, has forced the adoption of either fixed or floating rate regimes. The authors find that Asia has retained all three exchange rate regimes because it has remained more financially closed than the rest of the world. The exchange rate regime is a product of globalization. The authors believe that globalization has polarized the choice of exchange rate regimes between floating and fixing—a result known as hollowing out. In fact, an exchange rate regime does not exist in a vacuum. Whatever the choice, it can succeed only if a country's policy decisions are sound and its institutions—labor markets, fiscal arrangements, legal framework—function well.

Section 9.3 provides a discussion of exchange rate regimes, financial crises, and financial maturity. The paper inquires whether exchange rate problems today differ from nineteenth-century problems, and answers no. The capital-poor adopted the gold standard before 1914 as an insurance mechanism against international financial disturbances. The gold standard for them was an endogenous response to gold clauses. For the capital-rich which had developed strong money and financial markets before 1914 and could issue debt in their own currency, however, floating should have been preferred, but they did not float. The explanation, according to the paper, is that the capital-rich, by using exchange rate adjustments within the gold points, were as flexible as possible. In the second era of globalization, they have finally been able to exploit their ability to float.

It used to be said that there was leeway under the gold standard in the short term for monetary authorities to delay adjustment. However, the leeway is explained differently by the authors, who describe it in terms of the fluctuation bands between the gold export point and the gold import point, within which bands monetary authorities could buffer transitory shocks. The gold standard bands thus served as a conceptual target zone. On this view, there is less of a difference between the degree of flexibility of the pre-1914 gold standard and the post–Bretton Woods floating rate that capital-rich countries have favored. In any event, although I believe that there was a degree of short-term flexibility under the gold standard, it was far from the flexibility of a float. The paper makes too much of this supposed similarity. Moreover, there is no justification for the authors' belief that there should be such a similarity.

Capital-poor countries had trouble pegging before 1914 because of current account and terms-of-trade shocks, and were especially vulnerable to world deflation during 1873–96. Adopting gold did not immediately win them credibility and lower short-term interest rates. Their interest rates were persistently higher before 1914 than discount rates of the capital-rich countries. Pegging was a problem for the capital-poor during both the first and second globalization eras. If fixing posed problems before 1914 for the capital-poor, and floating did the same in the current era, one common reason was that they borrowed from the capital-rich in the latter's currencies. Early on, the capital-poor had to issue securities with a fixed exchange rate clause that tied the coupon to the currency of the market where they were sold. When the gold standard became widespread, this practice became gold clauses. Exchange risk was assumed by capital-poor issuers, whether governments or corporations. Mere linking of the local currency to gold was not enough to enable a country to issue obligations in its own currency. Only a narrow list of countries could issue debt in their own currency.

The paper argues that before 1914 this condition prevented the capital-poor from developing well-organized domestic financial markets. They could not attract foreign bank deposits, but were dependent on bank loans from merchant banks in capital-rich countries that were denominated in the currencies of the capital-rich. For this reason the capital-poor countries were vulnerable to financial crises. If their spending increased, the share of debt denominated in gold rose in relation to the debt-GDP ratio. The mismatch between the currency in which debt was denominated and the local currency aggravated the debt burden when the local currency depreciated.

This explanation of financial crises before and since 1914 provides a lesson that the capital-poor countries should learn. The paper refers to the response of Spain and Portugal that floated but minimized their exposure by avoiding borrowing abroad.

In section 9.4, the paper compares the effects of alternative exchange rate regimes in 1880–1914 and 1973–97 on financial depth, proxied by the ratio of broad money to GDP.

The paper concludes that the key difference between capital-rich and capital-poor countries is that the former enjoy financial maturity, manifested in open and domestic financial markets, stable money, and fiscal probity. The capital-rich can issue debt denominated in domestic currency. Countries that are financially mature in a world of open capital markets should be able to float as do capital-rich countries.

I ask the authors: If you believe that globalization isn't conditional on any particular exchange rate regime, and it was feasible before 1914 with a predominantly gold standard, and has been feasible since the mid-1970s with a predominantly floating rate regime, why are you so eager to portray the gold standard as really not so different from a floating rate regime?

Also, you claim that we will know that the capital-poor are financially mature when they successfully adopt floating. I believe that we will know that they are financially mature when they adopt sound monetary and fiscal policies with the appropriate institutional infrastructure. Whatever exchange rate financially mature capital-poor countries adopt will then work well.

Crises in the Global Economy from Tulips to Today
Contagion and Consequences

Larry Neal and Marc Weidenmier

10.1 Introduction

As the global financial system has evolved since 1971, financial historians have become increasingly struck by similarities between the stresses and setbacks that have occurred in international financial markets and those that plagued earlier attempts at creating a global financial system. The decade of the 1990s was beset by exchange rate crises in Asia and meltdowns of emerging markets in the former centrally planned economies. Likewise, the decade of the 1890s a century earlier saw a series of financial crises that threatened to become systemic at times. Just as the booming U.S. capital markets in the late 1990s seemed to help stabilize the international financial system at the time, so did the flurry of new activity in the London Stock Exchange promote a rise of international liquidity in the late 1890s. Just as leading commentators on the state of financial markets at the end of the twentieth century argued that the provision of liquidity to financial markets by the actions of the U.S. Federal Reserve System only made the dangers of financial fragility more serious when the markets inevitably collapsed, so did serious analysts, especially R. H. Palgrave (1903), criticize the actions of the Bank of England in the 1890s.

The similarity between the financial pressures and varied responses of participating countries to the emergence of global capital markets in the 1890s and 1990s has not gone unnoticed by economic historians. Bordo and Eichengreen (1999) look systematically at the characteristics of crises par-

Larry Neal is professor of economics at the University of Illinois at Urbana-Champaign and a research associate of the National Bureau of Economic Research. Marc Weidenmier is assistant professor of economics at Claremont McKenna College and a faculty research fellow of the National Bureau of Economic Research.

ticularly in the gold standard period to determine the extent to which infer-ences may be drawn about the roles of capital mobility, fixed exchange rates, and financial regulation in those earlier crises. Bordo and Schwartz (1999) have made a useful catalog of crises, distinguishing between banking crises that interrupt the internal payments system and currency crises that disrupt the external payments relations. Kindleberger (2000)[1] has provided a check-list of financial crises going back to the tulip mania of 1636 in Holland and up to the Asian crisis of 1997 and the subsequent Russian and Brazilian crises in 1998.

The interpretations placed on these historical experiences of interna-tional financial crises by the respective authors reflect, ultimately, their judgments whether today's global financial market needs an international lender of last resort (Kindleberger) or a time-consistent set of monetary rules among the participating countries (Bordo). If contagion, the spread of a financial crisis from the country of origin to innocent trading partners or geographical neighbors whose financial fundamentals are sound, is a frequent consequence of a financial crisis, then surely a lender of last resort is a good idea. Injection of liquidity at the appropriate time in the center of the crisis could forestall scrambles for liquidity from trading partners or al-lies. If, on the other hand, crises spread mainly because trading partners have either weak currencies or fragile banking systems, then credible com-mitments to a sound currency and conservative banking practices need to be acquired by countries participating in a global financial system. Lurking behind each viewpoint is a historical judgment call: Either the conse-quences of financial crises are so dire they should be averted when at all pos-sible, or they provide useful learning experiences that can lead to ever sounder financial and monetary systems. Relying on a lender of last resort to bail out one's unwise or risky loans, by contrast, removes the incentives for developing either sound financial institutions or monetary arrange-ments.

The classic account of financial contagions, Kindleberger's *Manias, Pan-ics, and Crashes* (2000), presents a standard pattern in which speculative fevers are caused by the appearance of new, unusually profitable investment opportunities. Often, the new opportunities accompany movements to-ward globalization as new markets or technologies appear that can be ex-ploited by a given country or by an economic sector in several countries. Prices of the new assets that are created in response to the new opportunity are driven to unsustainable heights; panic eventually occurs and investors then scramble to withdraw their funds, not only from the original market but also from any other market that resembles it. The renewed possibilities of contagion in the global capital markets of the twenty-first century have

---

1. Reflecting the renewed interest in financial crises and contagion, this work came out in its fourth edition in November 2000.

created concerns for national policymakers and for international organizations charged with maintaining order in the international marketplaces (e.g., Baig and Goldfajn 1999; Classens and Forbes 2001).

Countering these concerns with contagion in financial markets, academic economists have distinguished between "contagion" and "interdependence." Propagation of a financial shock from the origin economy to one or more host economies may occur through the channels of short-term credit flows if the economies are interdependent by virtue of substantial trade with each other and substantial investments in each other (Frankel and Rose 1998). Contagion, however, should not be restricted to economies that are relatively insular, as even normally interdependent economies with substantial flows of trade and factor movements with each other may be subject to contagion—if propagation of the financial shock is more rapid and widespread than reactions to normal fluctuations in trade and capital movements. Noting that recent financial crises in the late 1990s created increased turbulence in related markets, they ask whether the increase in correlation among, say, bond prices or stock market indices that accompanied the Asian financial crisis starting in July 1997 was due simply to the statistical effect that an increase in variance of two variables will raise their measured correlation. If, after adjusting for the effect on correlation of increased variance, there is no increase in correlation among the financial markets after a crisis, the case for contagion disappears (Forbes and Rigobon 1999). All that remains, then, is the normal responses to each other's difficulties that will arise among interdependent economies. So also, presumably, the case for a lender of last resort would disappear. The force of this argument depends on whether one thinks that prior interdependence was a good thing, enlarging the country's production possibilities, rather than a bad thing, simply setting it up for a fallout from a crisis in any of its trading partners. If a good thing originally, then common lessons learned should be beneficial as well and not averted. Another possibility is that interconnected countries are struck by a system-wide shock that has similar effects on each country—for example, the oil shocks of the 1970s on the oil-importing countries. Whether a lender of last resort would have coped better with the Organization of Petroleum Exporting Countries (OPEC) cartel than the learning experience that actually occurred depends on one's appraisal of the consequences of the crisis and then of the lessons learned.

Below, we consider Kindleberger's historical examples of international crises and contagion in chronological sequence, asking in each case (a) what is the evidence for contagion, judged by the standards set by analysts of the crises of the 1990s, and (b) what were the consequences of the crisis for the evolution of financial and monetary systems? The crises considered are the tulip mania of 1637, the Mississippi and South Sea bubbles of 1719–20, the Latin American debt crisis of 1825, the international crisis of 1873, the Barings crisis of 1890, the stock market crises of 1893, the panic of 1907, the

Wall Street crashes of 1929 and 1987, and the Asian crises of 1997. Kindleberger picks on the crises of 1720, 1873, 1890, and 1929 as cases of international financial crises whose consequences were especially severe and there was no lender of last resort (Kindleberger, 2000, 207).[2] We deal with other, minor episodes in passing, but pay special attention to the crises of 1873, 1890, 1893, and 1907 using new, high-frequency data from a wide range of financial markets in those years of the classic gold standard. These also happen to be the same international financial crises identified by Goodhart and Delargy (1998) as yielding analogies to today's financial crises. As we shall see, the evidence for contagion is mixed, as is the evidence for learning. Historical circumstances count for a great deal, today as in the past, but we insist that learning has occurred and can continue to occur. Implementation of the institutional reforms required to avert financial crises in the future, however, depends upon the political will and sense of common peril among policymakers.

10.2   The Tulip Mania of 1636–37

The first financial crisis of note after the European "discoveries" of the trading and exploitation possibilities in the rest of the world—especially the West Indies, the East Indies, and Africa—was the tulip mania in Holland, 1637 (Garber 2000). Despite the attention paid to this episode by the chroniclers of human folly, Garber's analysis of this dramatic episode reduces it to a month's worth of idle speculation by burgers confined to bars in the city of Haarlem at the height of the Thirty Years' War during an outbreak of the plague. These individuals, short of capital and long on leisure, knowingly made unenforceable bargains on common tulips for delivery in six months. In fact, their bargains were not enforced, save at 3.5 to 10.0 percent of the original amount, for those traders wishing to continue in the tulip business afterward. Such capital as was bound up in these futures contracts, however, was seen by the authorities as a diversion from more useful investments in government bonds to continue financing the Dutch war effort. The government's hostility to such private uses of funds during wartime accounts for the negative press that the tulip mania received at the time, which has been continued by generations of historians ever since.

In Garber's economic analysis, however, the prices usually quoted as examples of speculative excess were, indeed, normal for first-generation bulbs of unusual beauty that could be used to reproduce generations of subsequent blooms, which naturally fell sharply in price as production grew. Later markets for bulbs in normal times, whether for tulips or hyacinths, show similar high prices for the originals and rapid declines afterward.

---

2. Kindleberger also points to the domestic crises of 1882 in France and 1921 in Britain where no lender of last resort acted, but these were limited to the country of origin.

Furthermore, there seems to have been no contagion to other financial centers from the tulip speculation as such, although the financial demands of the Thirty Years' War upon the commercial cities and towns of the European continent created disruptions as well.

While Kindleberger leads off his chapter on "Domestic Contagion" with a critique of Garber's analysis (Kindleberger 2000, 109–10), the evidence he cites from other secondary works emphasizes the general prosperity of the Dutch republic after the mania had passed and prices had collapsed. The inference he draws implicitly is that building canals and luxury residences were also silly speculations by the Dutch. Most historians, and contemporaries, however, attribute the prosperity of the Dutch in this "golden age" to the profits they extracted as an entrepôt for Protestant forces in northern Europe during the Thirty Years' War, 1618–48. Especially beneficial was their monopoly of the Baltic trade as they circumvented the Spanish blockade to the Mediterranean and even established trading colonies in the West Indies (Israel 1995). The closest thing to contagion was speculation in other commodity derivatives in the summer of 1636 in other Dutch towns, but these, like the tulip mania in Haarlem, are attributed to the outbreaks of plague and the quarantines imposed by municipal authorities on traveling merchants (de Vries and van der Woude 1997, 150–51).

The main outcome of the financial crises attending the Thirty Years' War, however, was the promotion of lasting financial innovations, creating perpetual or life annuities that could be easily transferred to third parties. These were issued by individual cities in northern Europe that were forced to pay *kontributionen* to warlords maintaining armies in their vicinity (Redlich 1959). When the armies moved on, leaving the structures of the town intact if the payment had sufficed, the town's debts remained but were serviced indefinitely from the local tax base. Eventually, these were marketed to citizens in adjacent towns and cities as well, laying the basis for the "financial revolution" in public finance of the later seventeenth century (Tracy 1985). The lessons learned by the Dutch were evident in their emphasis on promoting overseas trade by maintaining a joint stock company for the Asian trade (the Dutch East India Company), unifying the mint standards of the provinces, facilitating merchant payments through a public exchange bank in Amsterdam, and assigning specific excise taxes for the service of government debts issued mainly by the individual cities and provinces (Neal 2000). The golden age of the Dutch Republic ensued, the contagion of the tulip mania safely contained.

10.3   The Mississippi and South Sea Bubbles of 1719–20

Nearly a century after the tulip mania in Holland, the French and British governments created the Mississippi and South Sea bubbles, stock market schemes designed to reduce the burden of debt service, given weak governments that lacked the authority to raise taxes. Both governments sought to swap the bulk of their outstanding debt for equity in large joint-stock trading companies with monopoly privileges—the Mississippi Company (*Compagnie des Indes*) in France and the South Sea Company in Great Britain. Both efforts had the full support of the government currently in power, and both were successful ultimately in reducing the respective debt burdens, at the expense of debt holders who delayed converting their debt holdings or who failed to sell out their equity holdings before the crash. The two schemes were connected through international capital movements, as investors from both the Netherlands and Great Britain were first attracted to John Law's investment opportunities in France from July to December 1719, and then to the rising stock markets in London from March to September 1720. By October 1720, however, both schemes had collapsed, thanks mainly to the total disruption of the European payments system in the summer of 1720. This was caused mostly by Law's efforts to rescue his system from the dangers of capital flight (by letting the French currency depreciate rapidly, he hoped to induce speculative inflows in anticipation of the revaluation that would follow), but complicated by the last outbreak of the plague on the European continent and the quarantines imposed by municipal authorities.

Much has been made of the supposed contagion of irrational speculation that swept across northern Europe in these two years (Kindleberger 2000, 77–78, 122–29; Chancellor 1999, chap. 3), but recent work by economists has reduced both to essentially rational, if premature, schemes to relieve pressure on government finances (Neal 1990; Murphy 1997; Carswell 1993). The lesson of history is not that contagion occurred, but that the two countries suffered a common shock—the excessive debt created by the enormous expenses of the War of the Spanish Succession.

The aftermath of the bubbles, however, laid the basis for the rise of an international capital market, increasingly centered in the city of London. Most important for the future success of the capital markets in Great Britain, the huge mass of illiquid "Irredeemable Ninety-nine Year Annuities" that had constituted the major part of British national debt in 1719 had been largely converted by 1723 into liquid, easily tradable, and transparently priced South Sea annuities. This greatly enlarged mass of tradable financial assets in the secondary market for securities in London preserved an active stock market in London, more than offsetting the effects of the Bubble Act of 1720.

The Bubble Act eliminated dealing in a welter of bubble companies that had sprung up in the previous speculative boom, but does not seem to have eliminated continued use of the joint-stock company for financing the continued expansion of British infrastructure—turnpikes, canals, docks, and waterworks (Harris 2000). The basic outlines of the Anglo-American structure of finance were set by 1723—a complementary set of private commercial and merchant banks all enjoying continuous access to an active, liquid secondary market for financial assets, especially government debt. The South Sea Bubble proved to be the "big bang" for financial capitalism in England. In 1726, even the Bank of England had to acknowledge the success of the South Sea Company's 3 percent perpetual annuity when it issued its own "Three Per Cent Annuity."

Unfortunately for France, the collapse of the Mississippi Bubble there in 1720 proved to be the end of secondary markets for financial assets in that country (Hoffman, Postel-Vinay, and Rosenthal 2000). In the inflation that had accompanied Law's efforts to create a market for the Mississippi Company shares, French debtors had repaid their bonds in depreciated currency, inflicting large and long-lasting losses on French creditors. Only a limited market for private debt arose after the currency reform of 1726, and that was a primary market mediated by the public notaries in Paris (Hoffman and Rosenthal 1995). Amsterdam's capital market survived the collapse of the minibubbles that had popped up there at the end of 1720, but continued to be fragmented among the various bonds issued by the Generalitet of the United Provinces and the individual cities and provinces. Only the shares of the new marine insurance company created in response to the financial innovations in Paris and London remained as a new investment opportunity for Dutch savers. For the most part, they focused first on the increasing issues of national debt created by the British government (Dickson 1967) and then on bonds issued by various European governments after mid-century (Riley 1980). The British, French, and Dutch governments learned different lessons from the first international financial crisis.

10.4   After the Bubbles

Financial crises in the remainder of the eighteenth century were caused by shocks from the aftermath of war finance, but usually had quite different effects among the financial centers of London, Amsterdam, and Paris. During the Seven Years' War (1756–63), which caused bankruptcies among the public notaries in Paris and put an end to the efforts of the most enterprising to become de facto bankers, the most spectacular military victories won by the British were in India. The territorial gains there and rewards by grateful Indian princes yielded the promise of greatly increased profits for the East India Company. Speculation could be financed in Amsterdam by drawing bills of exchange on the basis of credits expected from the Bank of England as it remitted bills payable in Amsterdam to support its mercenary troops on the Continent, as well as the troops of Frederick the Great. This led to *wisselruiterij,* a Dutch version of check-kiting (writing checks on a demand deposit before the check has cleared for the original deposit), that came to a sudden and widely embarrassing halt in 1763. A chain of bankruptcies then occurred in Amsterdam and Hamburg, where the British subsidies had been directed. According to Wilson (1941, 168–69), however, the crisis was short-lived and focused on the least reputable bankers. London bankers, who had not been involved in *wisselsruiterij,* perhaps due to a lack of opportunity or in sophistication in the use of the Wisselbank's facilities, sent large shipments of specie to their most reliable correspondents. The London bankers and the Bank of England also temporarily suspended requests for payment of their bills in Amsterdam. The connections between the sources of public credit for the British government and the instruments of private credit for foreign trade between London and Amsterdam were thereby sustained and even strengthened.

A similar liquidity crisis, however, occurred again in 1772, also the result of speculation on East India Company stock. But the only response in the Amsterdam financial sector this time was to patch together a Loan Bank to serve as a form of deposit insurance by helping to recapitalize merchant banks that were temporarily illiquid. Even the connections with the London capital market were weakened as Dutch rentiers withdrew their holdings of British national debt in favor of seeking placements in other European government debt (Riley 1980).

The learning experience of these first stock market bubbles and crashes varied, then, depending whether we take Great Britain, France, or the Netherlands as our object of study. While Kindleberger asserts that the consequences were prolonged and destructive to all three economies, economic historians remark that the following quarter-century was one of remarkable prosperity for all three countries, chiefly due to the absence of major war until the War of the Austrian Succession (Tracy 1990). The French financial system was weakened permanently, however, while the British benefited from the creation of a liquid secondary market for successive issues of its national debt and the Dutch connection with London benefited both (Neal 2000). The case for a lender of last resort is strongest in the French experience, weakest in the British, unless one thinks of the reorganization of the South Sea Company in 1723 as a delayed action of a reluctant lender of last resort—the Bank of England acting under political duress from the administration of Robert Walpole.

10.5   The First Latin American Debt Crisis in 1825

After the disruptions to financial markets caused by the French Revolution and the wars that ensued until 1815, the London stock exchange emerged as the dominant capital market in the world. The first foray of British investors into international finance, however, ended in disaster with the crash of 1825. The origins of the 1825 crisis began with the withdrawal of foreigners from the British national debt after the war. Following the final defeat of Napoleon at Waterloo in 1815, capital flowed back to the European continent from Great Britain. Foreign holdings of British debt diminished rapidly, the price of consols rose as the supply diminished, and prices of Bank of England and East India stock rose in tandem. British investors, used to safe returns ranging between 4 and 6 percent for the past twenty years now, found their options limited to yields between 3.5 and 4.5 percent. The opportunities for investment in new issues of French 5 percent rentes were more attractive than continuing their holdings in consols. Indeed, the rentes maintained a steady return over 5 percent throughout the crisis period and offered a stable alternative to the British funds.

Baring Brothers and Co., by its successful finance of Wellington's army in 1815, had established itself as the dominant merchant bank in England. By undertaking the flotation of the first two issues of French rentes sold to pay the reparations and support Wellington's occupation forces, Barings became the "Sixth Power" in Europe, according to the Duc de Richelieu (Jenks 1927, 36).[3] From February to July 1817, Barings disposed of three loans, the first two at a net price of 53 for 100 million francs each and the third at 65 which raised 115 million francs. Yet, according to the historian of the Baring firm, no disturbance in the British trade balance or in French reserves seems to have occurred—the inflow of capital to France from Great Britain from the issue of rentes seems to have been offset by indemnity payments and army contracts from France to Great Britain (Jenks, 37). (What the historian has missed, of course, is the fall in the exchange rate of the British pound that occurred at the time; the pound was still floating after the suspension of convertibility in February 1797.) From this success for British investors in foreign investment with the French rentes, it has traditionally been argued, came increased enthusiasm for other forms of investment, first in the bonds issued by the new government of Spain established in 1820, and then in the bonds issued by the new states emerging in Latin America.[4]

The collapse of Spanish control over its American empire during the Napoleonic Wars led to the formation of a variety of independent states from the former colonies by 1820. Battling one another for control over strategic transport routes, mainly rivers and ports, and over state enterprises, mainly mines, each appealed to foreign investors as a source of government finance and as a means to substitute foreign expertise and technology for the vanquished Spanish. Their government bonds and their mining shares found a ready market in the London Stock Exchange, which had become the dominant marketplace for finance capital in the world during the Napoleonic Wars. The loan bubble of 1822–25 ensued, eventually

---

3. See also Ziegler 1990, 100–11.

4. While the focus for foreign loans was mostly on Spain and Spanish America, literature buffs may be forgiven for thinking instead of Greece, which received a loan and much-needed publicity for its then-premature efforts to break away from Turkish rule. Over fifty years later, when the Greek government was attempting to assure the international community it would go on a gold standard, part of its commitment was to resume payment on these initial bonds!

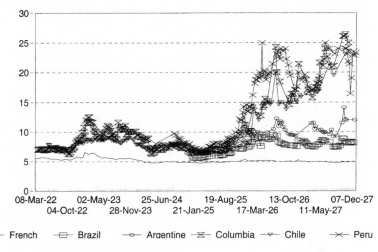

French —⊟— Brazil —⊖— Argentine —✕— Columbia —▽— Chile —✕— Peru

Fig. 10.1   Yields of Latin bonds, 1822–27

giving British foreign bondholders their first experience with defaults by sovereign states. None of the new Latin American states emerging from the remains of the Spanish empire (Brazil remained part of the Portuguese empire) found the means, whether by exports or taxes, to service the debts they had incurred in London. Meanwhile, they dissipated rapidly in military conflicts with neighboring states the net proceeds they received after the bonds were sold at discount and they had paid large commissions up front to the London investment houses.[5]

From 1822, when both Chile and Colombia floated bond issues with London agents, an increasing number of Latin American governments tried to find the means for financing their transition to independence from the flush pockets of British investors. The bonds they issued, in terms of the amounts actually paid up, as distinguished from the amounts actually received by the governments, were the largest single category of new investment in the London capital market in this period (Gayer, Schwartz, and Rostow 1975, 189). It is true, even so, that the amount was small relative to the remaining sum of the British government's funded debt—£43 million compared to £820 million.[6]

Figure 10.1 compares the prices of several bond issues of the emerging

5. Dawson (1990) provides a readable account of this episode, but Marichal (1989) puts it into a longer run Latin American perspective. Brazilians point with pride that their bonds never went into default, which is why their prices remained the highest among the Latin American bonds in the late 1820s. The Brazilian bonds, in fact, were the only ones issued by the Rothschilds. None of their government bond issues for Austria, Belgium, Naples, Prussia, or Russia defaulted in this period. (Doubleday, 1847, 281).

6. Gayer, Rostow, and Schwartz (vol. 1, p. 408n. 8) and Mitchell (1962, 402). These are nominal values in each case, but government debt was then trading at close to par, so its market value was roughly the same.

Table 10.1   **Stock Market Crisis of 1825**

	Correlation Coefficient	
	Precrisis	Postcrisis
Index	0.794	0.521
French rentes	0.848	−0.197
Colombia 6%	0.881	0.328
Chile 6%	0.910	0.190
U.K. var		
Precrisis	12.740	
Postcrisis	4.031	

	Adjusted Correlation Coefficient		Contagion		
	Precrisis	Postcrisis	SE Precrisis	SE Postcrisis	Test
Index	0.914	0.724	0.166	0.282	−0.423 NC
French rentes	0.940	−0.327	0.139	0.386	−2.411 NC
Colombia 6%	0.955	0.513	0.122	0.350	−0.936 NC
Chile 6%	0.967	0.316	0.105	0.387	−1.323 NC

South American states, as given in James Wetenhall's semiweekly *Course of the Exchange.* At the peak of the stock market boom, there was surprising convergence in the prices of all the Latin American bonds. It was only in the ensuing two years that information on the fiscal capacity of the individual governments and their respective economic bases enabled the London market to distinguish among them. Mexico and the Andean countries were clearly marked to be disaster cases by the end of 1828, while already Argentina and Brazil were demonstrating their attractiveness to British investors, an allure that would increase until the Barings crisis of 1890.

To see if this early financial crisis is properly another example of contagion, we have analyzed the cross-correlations of various asset prices in the London Stock Exchange during the first Latin American debt crisis in the 1820s, which led to the financial crisis of December 1825. Using the prices of the Three Percent Consol as the reference security, table 10.1 shows that correlations were quite high before the crisis between the price of consols, a general index of stock market prices, the price of French rentes (a seasoned foreign security), and the first Latin American bonds issued by Colombia and Chile. After the crisis, correlations broke down and, contrary to the recent stock market crises, the variance of the reference asset in this case actually declined. Consequently, adjusting for heteroscedasticity actually increases the likelihood of finding evidence of contagion, but even so, the hypothesis of contagion from the collapse of Latin American bond prices to the stock market index, or mature bond markets, is resoundingly rejected.

The lesson learned by the British government in this case was to make major changes in the financial structure of Great Britain, reforming the bankruptcy law, repealing the Bubble Act of 1720, and forcing the Bank of England to open branches in the major commercial and industrial cities, while maintaining the gold standard and avoiding most Latin American involvements for another quarter-century. If the Bank of England acted as a lender of last resort, it was erratic, belated, and ultimately inadequate.[7] In the view of modern economic historians, however, this set the stage for the true industrial revolution in the British economy—the beginning of sustained increases in per capita income, increases sustained to the present day. It may be, then, that other reforms in the financial architecture of a country can compensate for the absence of an effective lender of last resort.

10.6   The Gold Standard Emerges

Meanwhile, European countries took note of the superiority of the British public financial system that Great Britain had conclusively demonstrated during the Napoleonic Wars from 1803 to 1815. The lesson was clear, but adapting the British system to Continental conditions was a slow and painful process, marked by numerous setbacks as European governments clung as long as possible to their traditional fiscal regimes, monetary standards, and financial institutions. Over the course of the nineteenth century, the individual European nation-states gradually moved as best they could toward an imitation of the obviously successful British system of public finance. Issuing perpetual annuities backed by the permanent taxing authority of an elected parliament was a key element in the British system, but the reigning monarchs of Europe only reluctantly ceded authority over taxation to their parliaments.

Constraining the growth of the money supply with a credible rule such as the gold standard was also important, not least to maintain the market value of the debt issued by a government. But no country was willing to follow the British example of a gold standard, set in 1821, until little Portugal adopted gold as its monetary standard in 1854. Then it took the Franco-Prussian War in 1870 to get united Germany to adopt a gold standard to replace the varieties of silver standards among the various German states. France, and its major trading partners in Europe, persisted with the bimetallic standard, maintaining a mint ratio of 15.5:1.0 of silver to gold until 1871. Then, the flood of German silver on the market as the German Empire replaced the silver coinage with either gold or token coins led France and the other members of the Latin Monetary Union to demonetize silver, effectively adopting the gold standard as well after 1879 (Flandreau 1996).

With the adoption by 1880 of a nearly universal regime of fixed exchange

7. Comments by Michael Bordo on Neal (1998).

rates within Europe, a truly Europe- (and Atlantic-) wide financial market arose quickly, which came to encompass much of Latin America (Argentina and Brazil) and Asia (India) as well as Australia (Gallarotti 1995). It served well to finance an impressive surge of international trade as well as labor and capital movements that remain benchmarks for today's global marketplace. The trade, labor, and capital movements of the period were clearly driven by technological revolutions in steam-driven transport, electrical communication, and agricultural mechanization (O'Rourke and Williamson 2000). All of these epochal changes placed immense new demands upon the international financial markets as well, which in turn expanded rapidly their depth and range of services.

While previous analysts have focused on either the bond market (Ferguson 2001; Bordo and Murshid 2000) as an indicator of long-term capital movements, or on exchange rates as an indicator of credible commitment to the gold standard (Bordo and MacDonald 1997), we have chosen to focus on the open market interest rates for three-month accommodation bills, which were reported weekly in *The Economist* newspaper. While the discount rates at the public banks of issue on the European continent remained sticky compared to the Bank of England, the open market rates were much more responsive to market conditions. Table 10.2 demonstrates dramatically how much more volatile were short-term interest rates on three-month trade bills than the long-term interest rates on the respective government bonds. For the five countries shown, the standard deviations of the short-term rates we use for our analysis of the transmission of financial crises were several times greater than the standard deviations of the long-term rates. In the cases of Great Britain and Germany, the difference was nearly 10 times. In the statistical analysis below, we concentrate on correlations of movements in interest rates in this short-term capital market. It was the short-term capital market that had the greatest volume of trading activity, financing not only the continually rising volume of domestic and foreign trade arising from the transportation revolution of the steam age, but also the temporary liquidity needs of financial intermediaries. This so-called "money market" was precisely where we expect pressures from liquidity de-

Table 10.2   **Interest Rate Volatility During the Classical Gold Standard Period, 1880–1914**

	Standard Deviation	
Country	Long-term Bonds	Short-term Market Bills
Austria	0.375	0.712
France	0.299	0.682
Germany	0.169	1.11
The Netherlands	0.317	0.917
United Kingdom	0.217	1.17

Table 10.3   "Contagious" Crises during the Classical Gold Standard Period

	Precrisis	Postcrisis
Panic of 1873	21 September 1872–13 September 1873	20 September 1873–12 September 1874
Barings crisis of 1890	5 October 1889–27 September 1890	4 October 1890–26 September 1891
U.S. Banking Crisis of 1893	8 October 1892–7 October 1893	13 October 1893–29 September 1894
Panic of 1907	22 October 1906–19 October 1907	26 October 1907–17 October 1908

mands by banks to be expressed, raising discount rates when demands for cash surged and lowering discount rates when the supply of cash was plentiful. Indeed, even Kindleberger notes that it was the short-term capital market that was the usual, and most effective, transmission mechanism for the examples of contagion he cites, which become exceptionally numerous in this period (Kindleberger 2000, chap. 8).

The analysis below draws upon the extensive data set we have compiled specifically for this study. The data set comprises weekly observations on prices of long-term government bonds and interest rates on three-month, prime-quality trade bills determined in national capital markets and the discount rates charged by their public banks for fourteen countries over the period 1 January 1870 through 27 June 1914 (see the appendix for a full description.) Including over 100,000 observations, this rich data set, now available to researchers, can be used for detailed analyses of the transmission process of financial disturbances in the world's first global financial market. We use it in this study to focus on the issue of whether contagion characterized the financial crises of the gold standard period. Table 10.3 show the dates of the crises and the periods we analyze pre- and postcrisis.

10.7   The Crisis of 1873

We begin with the 1873 crisis, which is considered to have started in Germany and Austria but was amplified by the repercussions in the United States, still in the greenback period. Table 10.4 shows the correlation coefficients between the market interest rates on call money in New York and, respectively, Paris, Berlin, Amsterdam, Brussels, Vienna, and Petersburg, and three-month bills in London.[8] Germany had just adopted the gold standard formally, but was still in the process of replacing the silver coinage. Paris, Amsterdam, Brussels, and Vienna were bimetallic but suffering the aftershock of Germany's switch from silver to gold and the flood of silver coming into their mints.

---

8. All interest rate data for the period 1873–1914 were deseasonalized using the ESMOOTH facility in RATS, which is based on the Holt-Winters exponential smoothing algorithm.

Table 10.4   **Crisis of 1873, Short-Term Capital Markets**

	Correlation Coefficient	
	Precrisis	Postcrisis
France	0.664	0.429
Germany	0.144	0.281
The Netherlands	−0.099	0.284
Belgium	−0.016	0.476
Austria	0.187	0.680
Russia	0.259	−0.235
United Kingdom	0.098	0.163
U.S. var		
Precrisis	−0.209	
Postcrisis	−0.824	

	Adjusted Correlation Coefficient		Contagion		
	Precrisis	Postcrisis	SE Precrisis	SE Postcrisis	Test
France	0.409	0.232	0.135	0.143	−0.635 NC
Germany	0.073	0.146	0.147	0.146	0.248 NC
The Netherlands	−0.050	0.147	0.147	0.146	0.674 NC
Belgium	−0.008	0.263	0.147	0.142	0.935 NC
Austria	0.095	0.423	0.147	0.134	1.168 NC
Russia	0.134	−0.121	0.146	0.146	−0.870 NC
United Kingdom	0.409	0.232	0.135	0.143	−0.635 NC

The last column in table 10.4 indicates whether there is evidence of contagion (C) or not (NC) between the London market rate and the market rate of the country in question. None of the seven cases show contagion on the Forbes and Rigobon criterion, after adjusting for heteroscedasticity, although Austria does increase its correlation considerably while failing the one-sided t-statistic test of $+1.65$. While we have taken the United States as the source of the crisis, Kindleberger might well argue that Austria was the source. It certainly was the weakest financial sector, with the Austro-Hungarian monarchy struggling with the aftermath of its defeat at the hands of Prussia in 1866 and the triumph of the German reich establishing a gold standard in 1871. Rather than a case of possible contagion, Austria's apparent response to the U.S. crisis can also be interpreted as a defensive reaction in common with the United States to maintain their gold stocks in response to German pressures.

These statistical measures of contagion are completely at odds with the standard story of the 1873 crisis. According to Kindleberger, the crisis was initiated by the speculative excesses in Germany resulting from the reparations payments extracted from France after its defeat in 1870; the German mania spilled over into Austria in 1871 and 1872. Both stock market bubbles collapsed in May 1873, with contagion spreading to Italy, Holland, and Belgium, eventually taking in the United States in September 1873 (Kindleberger 2000, 131–32). If that was a process of contagion, then we should have found the correlation of Austria and the United States falling after the collapse of Jay Cook's firm in September 1873, not rising as it did. The panic in the United States, which we take as the crisis point, was followed by a worldwide depression in trade and economic activity that lasted until 1879 and that encompassed France and Russia, neither of which shared in the initial euphoria and so were exempted from the crash.

The cases of Austria and the United States show that, even in the absence of a lender of last resort or any close substitute for the actions of such a lender, effective steps were taken to limit their correlations with the epicenter of the crisis, Germany in this case. Other unpleasant economic consequences followed from their respective resolves to hasten deflation and return to a fixed metallic standard (the United States in 1879 when the economy picked up again, and Austria not until the early 1900s when it was finally successful in shadowing the gold standard). Financial contagion, however, was not, on our reading of the statistical evidence in the short-term capital markets of the time, part of the picture, but the gold standard system was incomplete, still in its formative years.

10.8   The Crisis of 1890

The Barings crisis of 1890 forced Portugal and Argentina off the gold standard, while leaving Great Britain breathing a collective sigh of relief in the financial sector. Governor Lidderdale of the Bank of England coordinated a swap of equity for debt among the major banking houses of London so they could take over much of the Barings business while forestalling a run on them by their clients. But as he admitted freely, his efforts would likely have failed had it not been for the pledges of support by the Banque de France and the British government.[9] What seems surprising at first glance is that the gold centers experienced much more volatile market and bank rates through these three crisis years than did the smaller, more vulnerable trading centers such as Vienna, Madrid, and Genoa. Figure 10.2, panels A and B, highlights the contrast in performance by the respective money markets of the core and periphery countries in Europe. The much lower volatility of both the bank and market rates in the periphery countries compared to the bank and money rates in the core countries persisted right through the crisis year of 1890, the effects of which are impossible to discern in panel B.

The explanation of lower volatility in the periphery than the core cannot

9. Kindleberger (2000, 151–52, 184–85), drawing on the authoritative account of Pressnell (1968).

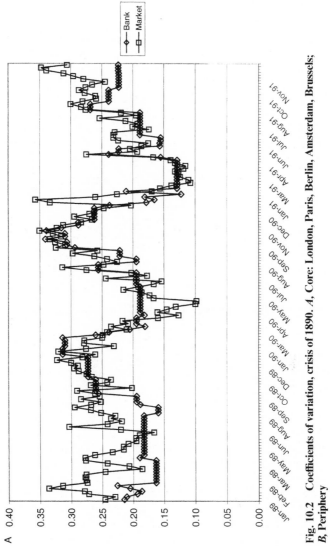

Fig. 10.2 Coefficients of variation, crisis of 1890. *A,* Core: London, Paris, Berlin, Amsterdam, Brussels; *B,* Periphery

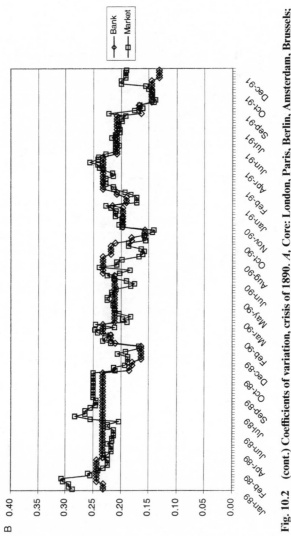

Fig. 10.2 (cont.) Coefficients of variation, crisis of 1890. *A*, Core: London, Paris, Berlin, Amsterdam, Brussels; *B*, Periphery

be that only the credit markets of the large industrial countries were affected by the crisis; trade intensity among the European continental countries was still rising in the 1880s despite signs of reversal in the free trade movement that had begun in the 1860s. It seems self-evident that the less advanced countries were using their public banks to limit access to trade credit through informal credit rationing. Their implicit capital controls were clearly effective, as their respective money markets mirrored faithfully both the stable levels and the low volatility of the very stable bank rates. Bloomfield (1959, 28) identified the variety of informal capital controls that central banks employed when under duress in the gold standard period, although he hesitated to draw any definite conclusions about the policy implications of his anecdotal evidence. Schumpeter, on the other hand, asserted that every commercial bank was assigned a ration and "such ration was cyclically varied as well as currently revised" (1939, 651). The question is whether the behavior of the periphery countries changed over time with experience or with changes in circumstance?

We have even more data on short-term interest rates with which to examine the possibility of contagion from the financial crisis of 1890, which may have started with a banking crisis in the United States in October, leading to exacerbation of Barings' difficulties with Argentina in November of that year. Table 10.5 gives the results for twelve trading partners, most of whom were on the gold standard at this point, the main exception being Portugal, which left the gold standard in 1890. The only two cases of possible contagion are Russia and the United States, but again this may be interpreted as a defensive reaction as in the earlier crisis of 1873. Russia did not formally commit to a gold standard until the reforms of Sergei Witte in 1896. The correlations of short-term interest rates in these gold standard markets with the London market were higher, typically, than in 1873 both before and after the crisis of 1890, reflecting the increase in short-term capital flows that accompanied the spread of the gold standard.

Our results can be compared with those reported by Bordo and Murshid (2000), who analyzed the correlation patterns on government bond prices for eight countries before and after the first crisis in April 1890 when the Banco de la Nacion stopped dividend payments, provoking a run on all Argentine banks, and then before and after the November failure of Baring Brothers. Only in the case of Argentine and British bonds did they find an increase in correlations and then only after the April crisis within Argentina, suggesting the unlikely case that contagion spread from Argentina to Great Britain, or that Argentine bonds became absorbed by the reorganized and recapitalized Barings firm. Both their results and ours indicate that the actions of the governor of the Bank of England in reorganizing Barings while supporting its depositors limited the fallout from this crisis to the English banking establishment in the short run. It may have had

Table 10.5   Crisis of 1890, Short-Term Capital Markets

	Correlation Coefficient	
	Precrisis	Postcrisis
France	0.211	0.546
Germany	0.442	0.698
The Netherlands	−0.164	0.280
Belgium	0.646	0.769
Italy	0.366	0.688
Austria	0.578	0.608
Portugal	0.647	0.462
Russia	0.052	0.711
United States	0.336	0.837
Denmark	0.047	0.275
Australia	−0.162	−0.489
India	−0.302	0.095
U.K. var		
Precrisis	0.547	
Postcrisis	1.513	

	Adjusted Correlation Coefficient		Contagion		
	Precrisis	Postcrisis	SE Precrisis	SE Postcrisis	Test
France	0.129	0.365	0.146	0.137	0.833 NC
Germany	0.284	0.506	0.141	0.127	0.825 NC
The Netherlands	−0.099	0.173	0.147	0.145	0.932 NC
Belgium	0.454	0.586	0.131	0.119	0.528 NC
Italy	0.230	0.495	0.143	0.128	0.976 NC
Austria	0.392	0.418	0.136	0.134	0.098 NC
Portugal	0.454	0.299	0.131	0.141	−0.572 NC
Russia	0.031	0.519	0.147	0.126	1.786 C
United States	0.210	0.677	0.144	0.109	1.849 C
Denmark	0.028	0.169	0.147	0.145	0.482 NC
Australia	−0.098	−0.319	0.147	0.140	−0.722 NC
India	−0.187	0.057	0.145	0.147	0.837 NC

more widespread influences, however, in the medium and long run, due to the interconnections of the various money markets that had arisen.

10.9   The Crisis of 1893

To see the longer term effects of the 1890 experience we are fortunate that another, more serious, more widespread financial crisis struck in 1893. Panels A and B of figure 10.3 show how the short-term credit markets in Europe responded to this crisis. The volatility of bank rates among the core gold standard countries was nearly as stable during this crisis as in the periphery

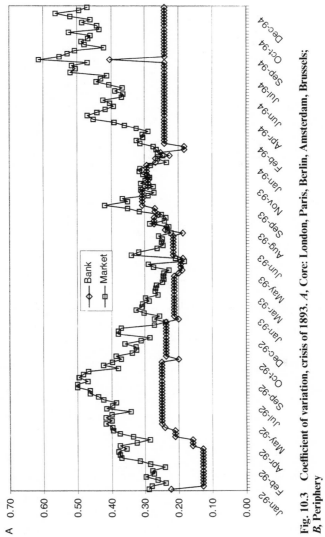

Fig. 10.3 Coefficient of variation, crisis of 1893. *A*, Core: London, Paris, Berlin, Amsterdam, Brussels; *B*, Periphery

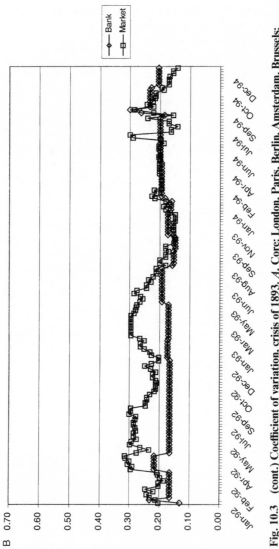

Fig. 10.3 (cont.) Coefficient of variation, crisis of 1893. *A*, Core: London, Paris, Berlin, Amsterdam, Brussels; *B*, Periphery

countries, most of whom were merely shadowing the gold standard at this time. Portugal had abandoned it, Russia and Austria had not yet adopted it, Italy was about to drop it, and Spain would never adopt it formally. The real contrast in this crisis came in the open market rates, which, as in the previous crisis of 1890, were much more volatile in the core countries than in the periphery. We take this again as evidence that credit rationing was effectively administered in the periphery countries, implying de facto capital controls in the periphery, but exposure to external market pressures in the core.

Additional evidence in support of our interpretation of the contrasting results for core and periphery countries in Europe comes from the Australian case in 1893. For Australian economic development, the crisis of 1893 has been interpreted as a major turning point. The large number of branch banks that had financed Australia's "long boom" over the preceding quarter-century had to suspend payments for varying periods during the year 1893 and to consolidate services when they resumed. Despite the internal turmoil that was occurring in the domestic payments system, the discount rates in Melbourne, Sydney, and Adelaide remained rock solid throughout that year and the following years. Indeed, the only sign of trouble that we can pick up in our financial data from *The Economist* is that it stopped reporting the Australian data altogether in 1894. It was in London's bill market, where most of the Australian banks had their headquarters, that the action occurred.

The crisis of 1893, originating in the United States with a banking crisis combined with a currency crisis created by the Silver Purchase Act of 1893, included Australia, Italy, and Germany in its extent, according to Bordo and Eichengreen (1999). In the short-term capital markets, however, it appears to have created contagion in only three of the twelve cases analyzed in table 10.6. Only the Netherlands, Belgium, and Switzerland, apparently, were affected. All three small countries had essentially no correlation at all with the very volatile call money rates of the United States before the crisis, unlike Italy, France, and Austria. But after the crisis, their correlation with U.S. call money rates shot up significantly. The odd thing about this crisis, however, is that the variance of the central capital market actually fell during the crisis period compared to the precrisis period—from 0.442 to 0.255. If we were to take the London three-month bill rate as the epicenter of the crisis instead, we would still have the same problem—a decline in variance so that the adjustment of the correlation coefficient for increased variance should actually be reversed, reducing the precrisis correlation. The same conclusion, nevertheless, would emerge—somehow the crisis of 1893 increased the interdependence of the short-term capital markets in the Atlantic trading world for three of the smaller, but very open, economies in Europe while decreasing it for the major economies of France, Italy, and Great Britain.

Table 10.6   Crisis of 1893, Short-Term Capital Markets

	Correlation Coefficient	
	Precrisis	Postcrisis
France	0.475	−0.339
Germany	0.234	0.234
The Netherlands	−0.144	0.895
Belgium	0.098	0.706
Italy	0.549	−0.656
Austria	0.438	−0.792
Portugal	0.228	0.150
Russia	−0.077	−0.717
Switzerland	0.045	0.573
Australia	−0.084	0.097
India	−0.187	−0.715
United Kingdom	−0.170	−0.523
U.S. var		
Precrisis	0.442	
Postcrisis	0.255	

	Adjusted Correlation Coefficient		Contagion		
	Precrisis	Postcrisis	SE Precrisis	SE Postcrisis	Test
France	0.579	−0.429	0.120	0.133	−3.977 NC
Germany	0.302	0.303	0.141	0.141	0.002 NC
The Netherlands	−0.188	0.935	0.145	0.052	5.702 C
Belgium	0.129	0.795	0.146	0.089	2.831 C
Italy	0.654	−0.753	0.112	0.097	−6.747 NC
Austria	0.540	−0.863	0.124	0.075	−7.063 NC
Portugal	0.295	0.196	0.141	0.145	−0.346 NC
Russia	−0.101	−0.804	0.147	0.088	−3.002 NC
Switzerland	0.059	0.677	0.166	0.123	2.138 C
Australia	−0.110	0.127	0.147	0.146	0.811 NC
India	−0.243	−0.803	0.143	0.088	−2.424 NC
United Kingdom	−0.221	−0.638	0.144	0.115	−1.574 NC

We believe this may again be a defensive reaction limited to the smaller countries with smaller gold reserves at their disposal, compared to the major countries. This may be a further demonstration that the pressures upon the gold standard's viability as an international monetary system were becoming extreme by that time as the American and German economies expanded rapidly and increased their holdings of monetary gold. While the discovery of new sources of gold in South Africa and Alaska in the following years eased the pressures overall from 1897 to the outbreak of World War I, the financial techniques developed by continental bankers in imitation of the British example were also important. We return to this point in our conclusion after examining the case, or not, for contagion in the following international financial crises, starting with the one major international financial crisis during the period of gold inflation, 1897–1914.

10.10   The Crisis of 1907

After 1897, gold inflation relieved the pressures imposed upon monetary authorities committed either formally or informally to fixed exchange rates under the gold standard system. Not only did currency crises remain on the sideline, but the frequency of banking crises diminished as well. The crisis of 1907, however, was very serious and its effects widespread, extending from the United States to Germany and Italy. Panels A and B of figure 10.4 contrast the results for the core and now a much expanded membership in the periphery. Even with the greater numbers of centers reporting to *The Economist* by this time, however, the same stability of bank rates and corresponding market rates in the periphery countries remains in sharp contrast to the volatility of market rates in the core countries. Moreover, bank rates were more responsive in the 1907 crisis as more central banks began either to imitate the practices of the Bank of England, or to take defensive measures in response to the bank's frequent changes of discount rate.

In the midst of the gold inflation period, from 1897 to 1914, occurred the most severe and widespread financial crisis before World War I. No doubt that its origin was the United States, but the financial interdependence already developed within the gold standard area meant that its effects were quickly transmitted abroad. While the crisis that caught everyone's attention was the banking crisis with the failure of the Knickerbocker Trust Company of New York in October 1907, the ultimate cause of the crisis was likely the San Francisco earthquake in April 1906.[10] Naturally, the physical destruction caused by the earthquake put immediate demands upon the financial resources of first the Californian and then the U.S. economy. It was not until October 1906, however, that these pressures were transmitted to London, but then the pressures were sudden and overwhelming as over £50 million of gold were shipped in that month from London to the United States. The cause was the reluctant decisions by British insurance companies to pay out on the claims lodged by their San Francisco insurees. While the insurance companies had initially claimed that the losses of property in San Francisco were caused by the earthquake, and not by the fires that followed immediately, so they were not liable for payments, they realized that U.S. courts would certainly rule against them. They began payments in October, dealing with six months of accumulated claims.

The effect was twofold: First, the Bank of England raised the discount rate sharply; and second, when it lowered the discount rate in January 1907,

---

10. This paragraph draws on Odell and Weidenmier (2001).

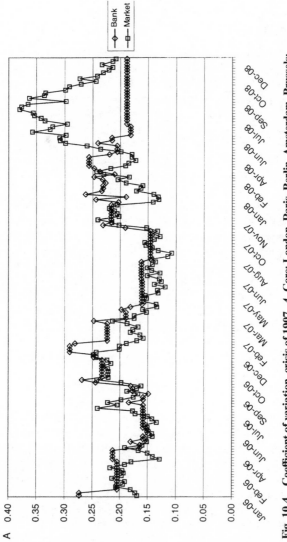

Fig. 10.4   Coefficient of variation, crisis of 1907. *A*, Core: London, Paris, Berlin, Amsterdam, Brussels; *B*, Periphery

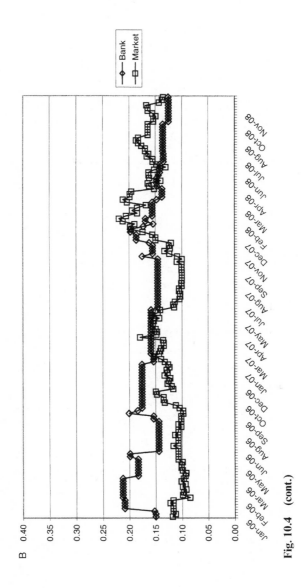

Fig. 10.4   (cont.)

it refused to discount any bills originating from the United States. Ultimately, this cut off New York trust companies from their usual source of
funds for financing liquidity demands in the fall. The fall of 1907 saw another large outflow of gold from London to the United States, and this time
the response was felt throughout the capital market, transmitting quickly to
Germany, France, and Italy.

Table 10.7 shows how dramatic this final episode of the gold standard was
for the global financial system of the time. The increase in variance of short-
term interest rates in the London market was the greatest experienced in the
entire gold standard period. The evidence of contagion is nearly universal

Table 10.7	Crisis of 1907, Short-Term Capital Markets, Seasonal Adjusted Data				
	Correlation Coefficient				
	Precrisis	Postcrisis			
France	−0.708	0.915			
Germany	0.750	0.956			
The Netherlands	0.065	0.955			
Belgium	−0.229	0.963			
Italy	0.511	0.941			
Austria	−0.144	0.921			
Switzerland	0.615	0.961			
United States	0.788	0.952			
India	0.393	0.173			
Sweden	0.602	0.791			
Denmark	0.746	0.744			
Spain	0.460	0.595			
U.K. var					
Precrisis	0.723				
Postcrisis	3.158				
	Adjusted Correlation Coefficient		Contagion		
	Precrisis	Postcrisis	SE Precrisis	SE Postcrisis	Test
France	−0.432	0.735	0.133	0.100	5.014 C
Germany	0.477	0.842	0.130	0.080	1.744 C
The Netherlands	0.031	0.839	0.147	0.080	3.547 C
Belgium	−0.112	0.863	0.147	0.074	4.412 C
Italy	0.274	0.799	0.142	0.089	2.282 C
Austria	−0.069	0.749	0.147	0.098	3.345 C
Switzerland	0.350	0.857	0.138	0.076	2.369 C
United States	0.522	0.830	0.125	0.082	1.480 NC
India	0.200	0.084	0.144	0.147	−0.400 NC
Sweden	0.339	0.526	0.139	0.125	0.707 NC
Denmark	0.472	0.470	0.130	0.130	−0.009 NC
Spain	0.241	0.334	0.143	0.139	0.331 NC

in Europe—only the Scandinavian gold bloc remained impervious, along with the United States, India, and Spain. Forbes and Rigobon (1999) might classify these results for 1907 as less an example of contagion, however, than of an aggregate shock affecting all the financial centers of the gold standard. The problem with that explanation, of course, is the anomalous case of the United States, the very epicenter of the crisis. But this may be another case where our statistical test is too rigorous, as the t-statistic of 1.48 is even closer to the critical value of 1.65 than the case of Austria in 1873. If the U.S. financial market was subjected to special discrimination in this crisis, excluded from the London discount market precisely in the year before the crisis of October 1907, the U.S. anomaly is explained. Effectively, the U.K. interest rate against the U.S. bills of exchange was infinity.

We have, then, a historical example of what can happen when a country is excluded from an interdependent financial system precisely when its financial needs are greatest, as is always the case when a major, unexpected, and unpredictable "bolt from the blue" hits an economy. When interdependence is already high, attempts to shelter the rest of the international system from an idiosyncratic shock in one financial center are likely to prove fruitless. With the benefit of hindsight, we can see that the European centers might have been better off if they had come to the aid of San Francisco, or their own insurance companies, promptly. Of course, if all the governments concerned were nursing their reserves of gold in case a major war were to break out, their actual reaction is understandable.

10.11   The Greatest Financial Crisis of All: 1929–33

The issues touched on in our discussion of historical crises are motivated, of course, by our awareness of the tragic consequences of the Great Depression of 1929–33, which all analysts agree was initiated by a truly international financial crisis and most acknowledge that the consequences—economic, political, and social—were long-lasting and dire. Here is where Kindleberger's argument for a lender of last resort has its greatest force. Thanks to cooperation between Montagu Norman, governor of the Bank of England, and Benjamin Strong, governor of the Federal Reserve Bank of New York, a working version of the pre–World War I gold standard had been built up over the years 1924–28. While it worked, this "gold exchange standard" provided the financial basis for an expansion of international trade and rapid economic recovery in the major industrial economies. But when a liquidity crisis struck—basically because world agricultural prices fell, making it impossible for farmers from the plains of Nebraska to the pampas of Argentina to the steppes of Hungary to make payments on the debts they had incurred—there was no lender of last resort around. The Bank of England was willing, but incapable with its limited resources, to serve in this role. The Federal Reserve System of the United States was capable, but unwilling to play that role, given its dysfunctional internal decision-making procedures.[11]

Our view of this terminal crisis of the gold standard era is that the entire period from the outbreak of World War I in late July 1914 until the collapse of the Bretton Woods system of fixed exchange rates in mid-August 1971 was the antithesis of globalization. The work of Jeffrey Williamson (1995) on convergence of real wages, which made substantial progress in the gold standard years and came to halt in the 1914–45 period, confirms this view. The study of capital movements and the various measures of capital market integration by Maurice Obstfeld and Alan Taylor (1998) identifies this period as one of "de-globalization" as well. Only the brief interlude of 1924–28, which W. A. Lewis (1949) called "the five good years" in his history of the interwar period, had any resemblance to the global economy and its methods of operation that had arisen in the half-century before World War I—and that was based on a flawed financial structure that could not have endured.[12]

From this perspective, which we share with Kindleberger, the key financial crisis was not the Wall Street panic in October 1929, but the failure of the Kreditanstalt Bank in Austria, announced on 11 May 1931. The contagion effects in this crisis were the worst possible for globalization as they consisted of payment defaults that led to a widening circle of exchange controls and a downward spiral of international trade. But in terms of our indicators of contagion, there would be little or no effect, much as we found for the crisis of 1873, at the beginning of the gold standard era.

Indeed, Bordo and Murshid (2000) find a similar outcome in their analysis of correlations of bond prices for twenty-one countries before and after each of three crises they identify in the 1929–33 period. These are the Wall Street crash in October 1929, Britain's departure from the gold standard in September 1931, and the U.S. law passed in May 1933 that allowed devaluation of the U.S. dollar. In general, they find little evidence of contagion, especially after adjusting for the increase in volatility of the British bond prices after September 1931. The only cases that seem to show contagion are Greece and Finland after the U.S. devaluation in 1933, but these may reflect more the importance of U.S. holdings of Greek and Finnish bonds than Kindleberger-style scramble for liquidity.

10.12   Lessons Learned from Deglobalization

Nevertheless, the lessons learned are still being discussed today. The idea that the periphery countries always suffer relative to the core countries, a

11. We hope this capsule summary captures the essence of Kindleberger's (1986) argument, expressed in his *World in Depression, 1929–1939,* as well as in *Manias, Panics, and Crashes* (2000) and many other places.
12. Eichengreen (1992) is the classic analysis of the plight of the gold exchange standard.

hint of which comes from the Bordo-Murshid (2000) findings, was articulated most effectively by Mihail Manoilescu, a Romanian economist appalled by the damage Romania suffered as it tried to follow French advice by staying on the gold standard as long as possible while rejecting offers of markets for its oil from Nazi Germany. Manoilescu's ideas found a receptive audience in Argentina, where Raul Prebisch, a young economist in the central bank of Argentina, was similarly appalled at the damage to Argentina's export economy caused by following British advice. Prebisch's ideas persisted long afterward, thanks to his influence in the Economic Commission of Latin America (Love 1996).

After the failure of the World Economic Conference in 1933, the world divided up into mutually exclusive trading blocs: the sterling area, with its imperial preference; the reichsmark bloc, based on bilateral exchange agreements; the Japanese-led "Asian co-prosperity sphere"; and the autarkic economies of the Soviet Union and fascist Spain, Italy, and Portugal. These assorted regional trading blocs and the attempts by Nazi Germany and imperial Japan to expand their regions to become entirely self-sufficient were important elements in the economic background conditions that set the stage for the tragedies of World War II. Whether all this could have been avoided by a lender of last resort acting at the critical crisis (Wall Street crash? Kreditanstalt collapse? Britain leaving gold? U.S. devaluation?) seems doubtful.

What was needed, in Kindleberger's view, was an economic and political hegemon, a role willingly adopted by the United States after World War II as it took the lead in establishing the Bretton Woods system, based on the institutions of the International Monetary Fund (IMF) and the World Bank, with increasing efforts to make the patchwork General Agreement on Tariffs and Trade become effective, eventually turning into the World Trade Organization. The results of the Bretton Woods era, essentially 1958–71 when it was fully functioning as planned, were remarkably good, as shown by Bordo (1993). In particular, financial crises were limited to the occasional currency crisis when a country, usually Great Britain, could no longer sustain its dollar peg, but thanks to capital controls these were confined to the country of origin, so there was never an issue of contagion. But the monetary basis of the Bretton Woods system—the dollar exchange standard with the dollar fixed in price relative to gold—was also fatally flawed, essentially because the costs of maintaining political hegemony for the United States undermined its ability to act as economic hegemon. After its sudden collapse in 1971, the disintermediation created by the worldwide inflation that followed led to the rise once again of international capital markets, this time in a world of fiat currencies and floating exchange rates, leading to a new series of international financial crises that began to emerge in the late 1980s as capital controls were increasingly lifted.

10.13   The New Financial Crises: 1987, 1994, 1997

The Asian crises started in July 1997 with the collapse of the Thai currency, the baht, as the Bank of Thailand ran out of dollar reserves needed to maintain its peg with the dollar. They quickly spread to other East Asian countries including Malaysia, Indonesia, the Philippines, and, with a lag, South Korea, making a strong case for financial contagion in the global capital market. *IMF Staff Papers* and the *World Economic Outlook* have repeatedly referred to the Asian crisis as a prime example of "contagion." IMF loans made to Argentina and Turkey in 2001 were given credit for preventing contagion's spread from the financial difficulties in those countries. Further, recovery has been slow, complicated by political difficulties in each country, although the sharp devaluations of each currency have moderated the fall in gross domestic product.

The most powerful statistical evidence in support of the contagion hypothesis is Baig and Goldfajn (1999). They use the criterion that if correlations among countries' financial markets increase significantly after a crisis, contagion has occurred. Analyzing the correlations among the five afflicted countries for foreign exchange rates, equity market indexes, interest rates, and prices of government bonds, both before and after the crisis, they find strong evidence of contagion in the currency and government bond markets. They find mixed evidence of contagion in the equity markets, until they control for country-specific events and other fundamentals, whereupon contagion appears to have occurred. Certainly, the financial press drew similar conclusions and it may be that managers of emerging market mutual funds decided to cut back their exposures to all Asian markets, anticipating contagion in a self-fulfilling action.

Another argument, however, could be that all five countries were victims of a common shock, namely the sharp rise in the value of the U.S. dollar relative to the Japanese yen, a rise that began in 1996. All five countries had pegged their currencies to the dollar and in the early 1990s, when the dollar was falling relative to the yen, all five had profited by expanding their exports into markets previously dominated by the Japanese. Several also gained from Japanese investment in their economies as Japanese firms relocated production facilities into Thailand and Malaysia. These advantages turned to disadvantages when the dollar began to rise sharply against the yen and the European currencies. This would not have caused a crisis by itself—Singapore, Taiwan, and Hong Kong also had pegged their currencies to the U.S. dollar—but the five crisis countries also had incredibly weak banking systems caused by financing long-term property investments with short-term loans denominated in dollars.

A more substantive objection to the contagion scenario is due to the work of Forbes and Rigobon (1999), who examine the cases of the U.S. stock market crash in October 1987, the Mexican peso crisis in 1994, and the East Asian crises in 1997. Unlike Baig and Goldfajn (1999), however, Forbes and Rigobon adjust their postcrisis correlations for the increase in volatility that also occurred and that upwardly biases standard measures of correlation. Making the appropriate adjustment for heteroscedasticity in their correlation measures, they conclude that for stock market indices, at least, interdependence was already high before the crises in question and remained high afterward, showing that contagion did not appear to have been a factor even in these cases. If it had existed, the degree of correlation among the stock markets would have increased after the crisis, independent of the increase in variance. Moreover, they find that when correlations among stock market indices are adjusted for heteroscedasticity in the previous crises of 1987 and 1994, contagion does not appear to have been a factor then, either.

For example, calculating correlation coefficients between indexes of stock market values in twenty-seven countries during the East Asian crisis of 1997, they find evidence of contagion in fifteen of the cases. Adjusting for the increase in variance that occurred in the various markets after July 1997, however, they eliminate the evidence of contagion in all but one case: Italy. And that case is more likely due to Italy's reentry into the European Monetary System in November 1996, reducing exchange risk with the rest of European stock markets, than to any psychological fears overtaking Italian investors.

Performing the same adjustment on correlation coefficients among stock market indices before and after two other major financial crises—the October 1987 collapse of the New York Stock Exchange and the collapse of the Mexican peso in late 1994—Forbes and Rigobon systematically eliminate statistical evidence of contagion. Their conclusion is that "contagion is not simply a high cross-market correlation after a shock. It is a significant increase in this correlation after the shock. The high levels of co-movement across many stock markets during these three tumultuous periods reflects a continuation of strong cross-market linkages, and not a significant shift in these linkages" (1999, 35). As they find high levels of correlation before each crisis as well as after, they direct our attention to the causes of interdependence across international equity markets even in periods of relative stability. These cross-market linkages, they suggest, make today's financial markets especially vulnerable to shocks. Kindleberger should approve of this conclusion, although he might shy away from substituting "interdependence" for "contagion" in future writings.

Bordo and Murshid (2000) also examine the behavior of long-term government bonds for the Mexican peso crisis in 1994 and the Asian banking and currency crisis of 1997. Like Forbes and Rigobon (1999), they find little evidence of increased correlation in government bond markets after each crisis. The only case of increased correlation with the Thai government bonds after July 1997 turns out to be Brazilian bonds and U.S. bonds

(Bordo and Murshid, table 5B). Nevertheless, they do find some evidence that correlations with emerging market government bonds do increase relative to correlations with developed-country government bonds after both the Mexican and Asian crises (tables 6A and 6B). As the current debate over the IMF's role as a potential lender of last resort continues, we are obviously still extracting lessons from current experiences. What insight, then, might be taken from our findings from the gold standard period when changes in contagion occurred as the monetary environment changed from mild deflation to mild inflation?

10.14   Conclusion: Crisis Connections or Contagions?

Our formal analysis, above, of the correlations among the market short-term interest rates before and after the three major crises of the gold standard period leads us to doubt that contagion was an important feature then, even under a regime of fixed exchange rates and open capital markets. Rather, we conclude that different rules of the game were appropriate for different players. Countries that had weak specie reserves and governments prone to budget deficits were well advised not to follow the example of the Bank of England during crisis episodes. Rather than lend freely at a penalty rate when the international markets were roiled by a credit crunch somewhere else in the world, they were better off maintaining their previous discount rates so they could lend judiciously with side conditions to only the most solvent of their customers. This surely inhibited risk-taking by the local banking establishment, and probably retarded economic growth, but it did preserve stability in the political sphere while coping with wrenching structural changes in their economies. It also meant that financial crises, rather than increasing correlations among capital markets, actually tended to decrease them.

Policymakers acting through the maintenance of discount rates established by their respective public banks, therefore, had different concerns, which varied from country to country. Comparing the responses of the several countries that eventually formed the basis for the first global financial market to the systemic crises that struck from time to time, contagion appeared less likely (1890) when the short-term capital markets had been allowed to operate in an interdependent, well-integrated manner before the crisis. Only when differences in interest rate patterns were attempted by countries before a crisis by whatever means—different monetary regimes, informal capital controls, support of fiduciary issues—then an especially severe crisis made common responses more likely to a common shock (1893 and 1907).

Appendix

Country	Description	Data Availability
Bank discount rates		
Austria		1 January 1870–27 June 1914
Belgium		1 January 1870–27 June 1914
Denmark		10 May 1884–27 June 1914
France		1 January 1870–27 June 1914
Germany	Berlin bank rate	1 January 1870–27 June 1914
Italy	Genoa bank rate	24 January 1885–27 June 1914
The Netherlands		1 January 1870–27 June 1914
Norway		6 January 1894–27 June 1914
Portugal		24 January 1885–27 June 1914
Russia	St. Petersburg	1 January 1870–27 June 1914
Spain		6 January 1885–27 June 1914
Sweden		17 December 1892–27 June 1914
Switzerland		17 December 1892–27 June 1892
United Kingdom		1 January 1870–27 June 1914
Open market rates (three-month bills)		
Austria		1 January 1870–27 June 1914
Australia	Discount rate for Australian banks operating in London	10 May 1884–30 December 1893
Belgium		1 January 1870–27 June 1914
Denmark		10 May 1884–27 June 1914
France		1 January 1870–27 June 1914
Germany	Berlin open market rate	1 January 1870–27 June 1914
India	Bombay bank rate	10 May 1884–27 June 1914
Italy	Genoa open market rate	24 January 1885–27 June 1914
The Netherlands		1 January 1870–27 June 1914
Norway		6 January 1894–27 June 1914
Portugal		24 January 1885–27 June 1914
Russia	St. Petersburg open market rate	4 February 1871–27 June 1914
Spain		6 January 1885–27 June 1914
Sweden		17 December 1892–27 June 1914
Switzerland		17 December 1892–27 June 1914
United Kingdom		1 January 1870–27 June 1914
United States	Call money rate in New York City	27 November 1880–27 June 1914
Long term bond rates		
Austria	5% silver rentes	2 January 1880–29 December 1899
	4% gold rentes	2 January 1880–December 1913
Belgium	3% rentes	16 January 1885–21 October 1898
France	3% rentes	2 January 1880–31 July 1914
Germany	Prussian consols (4% converted to 3.5% 22 April 1898)	31 December 1880–31 December 1909
	3% imperial	24 August 1894–26 December 1913
	4% imperial	23 November 1894–26 December 1913
Italy	4%	2 January 1880–26 December 1913
The Netherlands	3%	25 August 1882–26 December 1913
Russia	5%	2 January 1880–31 July 1914
United Kingdom	3%/2.75% consols	2 January 1880–31 July 1914
United States	4%	2 January 1880–9 August 1907
	4% (due 1925)	6 January 1905–31 July 1914

References

Baig, Taimur, and Ilan Goldfajn. 1999. Financial market contagion in the Asian crisis. *IMF Staff Papers* 46 (June): 167–95.

Bloomfield, Arthur I. 1959. *Monetary policy under the international gold standard, 1880–1914.* New York: Federal Reserve Bank of New York.

Bordo, Michael D. 1993. The Bretton Woods international monetary system: A historical overview. In *A retrospective on the Bretton Woods system: Lessons for international monetary reform,* ed. Michael Bordo and Barry Eichengreen, 3–98. Chicago: University of Chicago Press.

Bordo, Michael D., and Barry Eichengreen. 1999. Is our current international economic environment unusually crisis prone? Unpublished working paper, August.

Bordo, Michael D., and Ronald MacDonald. 1997. Violations of the rules of the game and the credibility of the classical gold standard, 1880–1914. NBER Working Paper no. 6115. Cambridge, Mass.: National Bureau of Economic Research, July.

Bordo, Michael D., and Antu Panini Murshid. 2000. Are financial crises becoming increasingly more contagious? NBER Working Paper no. 7900. Cambridge, Mass.: National Bureau of Economic Research, September.

Bordo, Michael D., and Anna J. Schwartz. 1999. The operation of the specie standard: Evidence for core and peripheral countries, 1880–1990. In *The gold standard and related regimes: Collected essays,* ed. Michael D. Bordo, 238–317. New York: Cambridge University Press.

Carswell, John. 1993. *The South Sea Bubble.* Rev. ed. London: Alan Sutton.

Chancellor, Edward. 1999. *Devil take the hindmost: A history of financial speculation.* New York: Farrar, Straus, and Girous.

Classens, Stijn, and Kristin Forbes, eds. 2001. *International financial contagion.* New York: Kluwer.

Dawson, Frank G. 1990. *The first Latin American debt crisis: The city of London and the 1822–25 loan bubble.* New Haven, Conn.: Yale University Press.

de Vries, Jan, and Ad van der Woude. 1997. *The first modern economy: Success, failure, and perseverance of the Dutch economy, 1500–1815.* Cambridge: Cambridge University Press.

Dickson, P. G. M. 1967. *The financial revolution in England: A study in the development of public credit, 1688–1756.* London: Macmillan.

Doubleday, Thomas. 1847. *A financial, monetary, and statistical history of England from the Revolution of 1688 to the present time.* London: Effingham Wilson.

Eichengreen, Barry. 1992. *Golden fetters: The gold standard and the Great Depression, 1919–1939.* New York: Oxford University Press.

Ferguson, Niall. 2001. *The cash nexus: Money and power in the modern world, 1700–2000.* New York: Basic Books.

Flandreau, Marc. 1995. *L'or du monde: La France et la stabilité du système monétaire international, 1848–1914* (The gold of the world: France and the stability of the international monetary system.) Paris: L'Harmattan.

———. 1996. The French crime of 1873: An essay on the emergence of the international gold standard. *Journal of Economic History* 56:849–72.

Forbes, Kristin, and Roberto Rigobon. 1999. No contagion, only interdependence: Measuring stock market co-movements. NBER Working Paper no. 7267. Cambridge, Mass.: National Bureau of Economic Research, July.

Frankel, Jeffrey, and Andrew K. Rose. 1998. The endogeneity of the optimum currency area criteria. *Economic Journal* 108 (July): 1009–25.

Gallarotti, Giulio M. 1995. *The anatomy of an international monetary regime: The classical gold standard, 1880–1914.* New York: Oxford University Press.

Garber, Peter M. 2000. *Famous first bubbles: The fundamentals of early manias.* Cambridge: MIT Press.

Gayer, Arthur D., Anna Jacobson Schwartz, and W. W. Rostow. 1975. *The growth and fluctuation of the British economy, 1790–1850.* 2 vols. New York: Barnes and Noble Books.

Goodhart, C. A. E., and P. J. R. Delargy. 1998. Financial crises: Plus ça change, plus c'est la meme chose. *International Finance* 1 (2): 261–87.

Harris, Ronald. 2000. *Industrializing English law: Entrepreneurship and business organization, 1720–1844.* New York: Cambridge University Press.

Hoffman, Philip T., Gilles Postel-Vinay, and Jean-Laurent Rosenthal. 2000. *Priceless markets: The political economy of credit in Paris, 1660–1870.* Chicago: University of Chicago Press.

Hoffman, Philip, and Jean-Laurent Rosenthal. 1995. Redistribution and long-term private debt in Paris, 1660–1726. *Journal of Economic History* 55 (June): 256–84.

Homer, Sidney, and Richard Sylla. 1991. *A history of interest rates.* 3rd ed. New Brunswick, N.J.: Rutgers University Press.

Israel, Jonathan. 1995. *The Dutch Republic: Its rise, greatness, and fall, 1477–1806.* Oxford, U.K.: Clarendon.

Jenks, Leland H. 1927. *The migration of British capital to 1875.* New York: Knopf.

Kindleberger, Charles P. 1986. *The world in depression, 1919–1939.* Rev. ed. Berkeley, Calif.: University of California Press.

———. 1987. *International capital movements.* New York: Cambridge University Press.

———. 2000. *Manias, panics, and crashes.* 4th ed. New York: Wiley.

Lewis, W. Arthur. 1949. *Economic survey, 1919–1939.* London: Allen and Unwin.

Love, Joseph. 1996. *Crafting the third world: Theorizing underdevelopment in Rumania and Brazil.* Stanford, Calif.: Stanford University Press.

Marichal, Carlos. 1989. *A century of debt crises in Latin America: From independence to the Great Depression, 1820–1930.* Princeton, N.J.: Princeton University Press.

Mitchell, B. R. 1962. *Abstract of British historical statistics.* Cambridge: Cambridge University Press.

Murphy, Antoine. 1997. *John Law: Economic theorist and policy-maker.* Oxford, U.K.: Clarendon.

Neal, Larry. 1990. *The rise of financial capitalism: International capital markets in the Age of Reason.* New York: Cambridge University Press.

———. 1998. The financial crisis of 1825 and the restructuring of the British financial system. *Federal Reserve Bank of St. Louis Review* 80 (May–June): 53–76.

———. 2000. How it all began: The monetary and financial architecture of Europe during the first global capital markets, 1648–1815. *Financial History Review* 7:117–40.

Obstfeld, Maurice, and Alan M. Taylor. 1998. The Great Depression as a watershed: International capital mobility over the long run. In *The defining moment: The Great Depression and the American economy in the twentieth century,* ed. Michael D. Bordo, Claudia Goldin, and Eugene N. White, 353–402. Chicago: University of Chicago Press.

Odell, Kerry, and Marc D. Weidenmier. 2001. Real shock, monetary aftershock: The 1906 San Francisco earthquake and the panic of 1907. Claremont Colleges Working Paper no. 2001–07. NBER Working Paper no. 9176. Cambridge, Mass.: National Bureau of Economic Research.

O'Rourke, Kevin, and Jeffrey G. Williamson. 2000. *Globalization and history: The evolution of a nineteenth century Atlantic economy.* Cambridge: MIT Press.

Palgrave, Robert Harry Inglis. 1903. *Bank rate and the money market in England, France, Germany, Holland, and Belgium, 1844–1900.* London: J. Murray.

Pressnell, Leslie. 1968. Gold reserves, banking reserves, and the Baring crisis of 1890. In *Essays in money and banking in honour of R. S. Sayers,* ed. C. R. Whittlesey and J. S. G. Wilson, 167–228. Oxford, U.K.: Clarendon.

Redlich, Fritz. 1959. Contributions in the Thirty Years' War. *Economic History Review* 12 (December): 247–54.

Riley, James C. 1980. *International government finance and the Amsterdam capital market.* Cambridge: Cambridge University Press.

Schumpeter, Joseph A. 1939. *Business cycles: A theoretical, historical, and statistical analysis of the capitalist processes.* New York: McGraw-Hill.

Tracy, James. 1985. *A financial revolution in the Habsburg Netherlands.* Berkeley: University of California Press.

———, ed. 1990. *The rise of merchant empires, 1500–1800.* Cambridge: Cambridge University Press.

Williamson, Jeffrey G. 1995. The evolution of global labor markets since 1830: Background evidence and hypotheses. *Explorations in Economic History* 32 (April): 141–96.

Wilson, Charles. 1941. *Anglo-Dutch commerce and finance in the eighteenth century.* Cambridge: Cambridge University Press.

Ziegler, Dieter. 1990. *Central bank, peripheral industry: The Bank of England in the provinces, 1826–1913.* Leicester, U.K.: Leicester University Press.

Comment   Mark P. Taylor

The last decade of the twentieth century witnessed a spate of international financial and exchange rate crises, including the domino collapse of the European exchange rate mechanism in 1992–93, the 1994 Mexican "tequila hangover," the Asian "flu" of 1997–98, and the turmoil in emerging and global financial markets following the August 1998 Russian crisis.

Not surprisingly, this highly dramatic sequence of events led to the rapid expansion of economics research into exchange rate and financial crises. Part of this research has been concerned with examining the nature of financial crises and developing methods for anticipating them and understanding the channels through which they tend to spread. Another, related strand of research has tracked the policy debate that naturally followed, concerning how best to deal with crises and their transmission at a policy level and, in particular, the role of the International Monetary Fund (IMF)—whether it should act as a lender of last resort and add liquidity in times of crisis or whether its role is more to police sound macroeconomic and financial structural reform.

Mark P. Taylor is professor of macroeconomics at the University of Warwick.

Some, for example, would argue that the IMF seriously exacerbated the 1997–98 crisis in East Asia by calling for extensive structural reforms before making adequate official funding available, thereby delaying the restoration of investor confidence, allowing the collapse of the Asian currencies, and—by insisting on a tightening of monetary policy—exacerbating the effects of the crisis by generating domestic credit crunches. On the other hand, those advocating structural reform above all else might argue that this was a perfectly correct judgment call, since without structural reform official funding would have been simply wasted—the IMF was just the unfortunate messenger of some economic home truths.

On the sound principle that those who ignore the lessons of history are condemned to repeat the mistakes of the past, Neal and Weidenmier provide in their paper a wide-ranging discussion of a set of well-known financial crises over the past three and a half centuries, ranging from the Dutch tulip mania of the seventeenth century through the Mississippi and South Sea bubbles of the eighteenth century, the first Latin American debt crisis of 1825, the 1873 crisis, and three crises of the international gold standard period, before focusing their analysis on twentieth century episodes—first the Crash of 1929 and then some of the more recent crises mentioned in the opening paragraph of this comment. They pay special attention to three major crises that sprung up in the gold standard period of 1880–1913, which they divide into an initial period of mild gold deflation from 1880 to 1896 and a subsequent period of mild gold inflation from 1897 to 1913.

They conclude that countries with weak fundamentals were well advised not to follow the example of the Bank of England during crisis episodes, in terms of lending at penalty rates of interest, but rather to pursue a policy of "credit rationing" whereby they carried on lending at their previous discount rates but only to their most solvent customers.

The paper is an impressive display of scholarship, although I do have some misgivings about the clarity of the hypotheses tested in the paper. In part, this results from the surprisingly slippery nature of the term *contagion*. The authors define this early on as "the spread of a financial crisis from the country of origin to innocent trading partners or geographical neighbors whose financial fundamentals are sound." In fact, however, contagion has proved hard to pin down (see, e.g., Masson 1999; Edwards 2000; Corsetti, Pericoli, and Sbracia 2002). Pericoli and Sbracia (2001), for example, list no fewer than five definitions of contagion current in the literature.

In their empirical work, however, Neal and Weidenmier implicitly use a definition based on the work of Forbes and Rigobon (2002). This can be set out briefly as follows. Let r_{it} be the return on an asset at time t for the ith country and let n_{it} be a country-specific, or national, component. Then Forbes and Rigobon assume a linear relationship between returns in the ith country and returns in the reference country j of the form

(1) $$r_{it} = \beta_i r_{jt} + n_{it}, \qquad i = 1, 2, \ldots m; i \neq j,$$

where $E(r_{it} n_{it}) = 0$ and the variance of idiosyncratic national shocks, $\mathrm{var}(n_{it})$, is assumed to be constant across tranquil and crisis periods. The country-specific coefficients β^i may be taken to measure the strength of a country's interconnection to country j. Thus we have

(2) $$\mathrm{var}(r_{it}) = \beta_i^2 \mathrm{var}(r_{jt}) + \mathrm{var}(n_{it}),$$

and

(3) $$\mathrm{cov}(r_{it}, r_{jt}) = \beta_i \mathrm{var}(r_{jt})$$

so that

(4) $$\mathrm{corr}(r_{it}, r_{jt}) = \beta_i \sqrt{\frac{\mathrm{var}(r_{jt})}{\beta_i^2 \mathrm{var}(r_{jt}) + \mathrm{var}(n_{it})}}.$$

From equation (4), however, we can see that the correlation of the two asset returns is increasing in the variance of the reference-country asset returns. Thus, in times of increased volatility, correlations will rise. If this is the case and the coefficient β_i has remained constant, Forbes and Rigobon define this as interdependence, rather than contagion. If, however, there has been a shift in this structural parameter brought about by the crisis—perhaps due to herding or other effects that force a disconnect—then this is taken as evidence of contagion. In order to test whether the increase in correlation is due to such a structural shift (contagion) or is due simply to a common rise in volatility with the underlying structural link (1) constant (interdependence), Forbes and Rigobon thus suggest a measure of correlation that adjusts for shifts in volatility of this kind. In their empirical work, the result is to downgrade a number of international crises from instances of contagion to instances of interdependence (i.e., a nonzero but stable β_i).

Corsetti, Pericoli, and Sbracia (2002), however, argue that the results in these papers reflect restrictive assumptions (restrictions on the country-specific effects) and that a more general specification leads to a finding of greater contagion. Drawing on the finance literature, they suggest a single-factor model for r_{it} and r_{jt} of the form

(5) $$r_{it} = \gamma_i \kappa_t + n_{it}, \qquad i = 1, 2, \ldots m, i \neq j$$

(6) $$r_{jt} = \gamma_j \kappa_t + n_{jt},$$

where κ_t is the unobserved factor common to all of the countries under consideration and γ_i is the country-specific factor loading. The terms n_{it} and n_{jt} again represent idiosyncratic national components. Substituting out for the common factor in equation (5) using equation (6), we have

(7) $$r_{it} = \beta_i' r_{jt} + n_{it}', i = 1, 2, \ldots m,$$

where

(8)
$$\beta_{it}^i = \frac{\gamma_i}{\gamma_j}, \; n_{it}' = \left(n_{it} - \frac{\gamma_i}{\gamma_j} n_{jt} \right).$$

Now, although equation (7) is superficially of the form of equation (1), the only case where this more general model collapses to the Forbes-Rigobon setup is under the unrealistic assumption that the idiosyncratic national component in the reference country is identically equal to zero, so that the asset return in the reference country effectively becomes identical to the international common factor. Otherwise, at least two of the conditions that are crucial to the results derived by Forbes and Rigobon are violated. First, $E(r_{it}n_{it}') \neq 0$, and second, insofar as the reference country experiences increased volatility at the time of the crisis, $\text{var}(n_{it}')$ will not be constant across tranquil and crisis periods. Both of these violations will tend to induce a bias in the Forbes-Rigobon statistic, and although bias from the first source is difficult to sign, bias from the second source will tend to bias the statistic toward nonrejection of the null hypothesis of no structural shift (i.e., no contagion; see Corsetti, Pericoli, and Sbracia 2002 for further details).

The implication, alas, is that unless one is willing to make quite stringent assumptions about the factors driving international asset returns, the Forbes-Rigobon statistic may well be biased, and probably toward nonrejection of the null hypothesis. Hence, some of the empirical results derived in Neal and Weidenmier's paper may be brought into question.

While this is a shortcoming of the paper, it is not, in the present author's opinion, fatal, and it is one for which the authors should be exonerated—at press time for this volume, Forbes and Rigobon (2002) had literally just been published. Moreover, the verbal argument and the wealth of analysis contained in the Neal and Weidenmier paper remain an impressive *tour de force* and contribution to scholarship. Neal and Weidenmier have, moreover, put together an important database for the gold standard period and further empirical analysis therefore seems both warranted and possible.

Although the present author is clearly partisan, one way in which they might fruitfully address the issues of interest is through the common-vulnerabilities approach suggested by Mody and Taylor (2002). These authors begin with a common factor model of the kind of equations (5) and (6) and estimate the unobservable common factor using Kalman filtering techniques.[1] As a step to understanding what movements in this common factor are due to underlying macroeconomic and financial similarities across a region (the "common vulnerability") and what part is unanticipated during a crisis (contagion) they then extract the "expected" changes by relating the common factor to a vector of underlying (regional) macroeconomic and financial indicators. As a result, they are able to assess the

---

1. Mody and Taylor are in fact concerned with modeling movements in the exchange market pressure index during the East Asian crisis, although their approach could be applied equally to asset returns.

underlying factors driving common vulnerability across a region. Since Neal and Weidenmier are concerned with whether the countries they examine were prone to the spread of crisis due to weakness in the underlying fundamentals, this may be a useful way to proceed with further analysis.

References

Corsetti, Giancarlo, Marcello Pericoli, and Massimo Sbracia. 2002. Some contagion, some interdependence: More pitfalls in the tests of financial contagion. Yale University, Department of Economics. Mimeograph.

Edwards, Sebastian. 2000. Contagion. *World Economy* 23:873–900.

Forbes, Kristin J., and Roberto Rigobon. 2002. No contagion, only interdependence: Measuring stock market co-movement. *Journal of Finance* 57 (5): 2223–61.

Masson, Paul. 1999. Contagion: Monsoonal effects, spillovers, and jumps between multiple equilibria. In *The Asian financial crisis,* ed. P. R. Agénor, M. Miller, D. Vines, and A. Weber, 265–80. New York: Cambridge University Press.

Mody, Ashoka, and Mark P. Taylor. 2002. Common vulnerabilities. International Monetary Fund, Research Department. Mimeograph.

Pericoli, Marcello, and Massimo Sbracia. 2001. A primer on financial contagion. Banca d'Italia. Mimeograph.

11

Monetary and Financial Reform in Two Eras of Globalization

Barry Eichengreen and Harold James

This paper reviews the history of successes and failures in international monetary and financial reform in two eras of globalization, the late nineteenth century and the late twentieth century, and in the period in between. That history is rich, varied, and difficult to summarize compactly. We therefore organize our narrative around a specific hypothesis.

That hypothesis is that a consensus on the need for monetary and financial reform is likely to develop when such reform is seen as essential for the defense of the global trading system. Typically the international monetary and financial system evolves in a gradual and decentralized manner in response to market forces. The shift toward greater exchange rate flexibility and capital account convertibility since 1973 is the most recent and therefore obvious illustration of what is a more general point. Large-scale and discontinuous reform at a more centralized level—that is, reforms agreed to and implemented by groups of governments—tend to occur only when problems in the monetary and financial system are seen as placing the global trading system at risk. Throughout the period we consider, there has existed a deep and abiding faith in the advantages of trade for economic growth, the principal exception being the unusual circumstances of the 1930s, when trade and prosperity came to be seen as at odds. Consequently, priority has been attached to reform in precisely those periods when monetary and financial problems are perceived as posing a threat to the global trading system and hence to growth and prosperity generally. In contrast,

Barry Eichengreen is the George C. Pardee and Helen N. Pardee Professor of Economics and Political Science at the University of California, Berkeley and a research associate of the National Bureau of Economic Research. Harold James is professor of history at Princeton University.

We thank Michael Bordo and Peter Kenen for helpful comments.

there has never existed a comparable consensus on the benefits of open international capital markets for stability, efficiency, and growth.[1] It follows that disruptions to capital markets that do not also threaten the trading system have had less of a tendency to catalyze reform. We test this hypothesis by confronting it with evidence from major attempts—successful and unsuccessful—to reform the international monetary system.

Changes in the balance of opinion regarding the operation of capital markets also help to explain the form that successive reform efforts have taken. In the nineteenth century, capital markets were viewed as benign. The role of governments was limited to providing a framework for their operation; the principal constituents of that framework were the gold standard, which provided stable exchange rates, and the national central bank, which provided a uniform and elastic currency. International economic policy, such as it was, was limited to supporting this regime in times of crisis.

When, in response to policy inconsistencies between countries, capital markets malfunctioned in the 1930s, controls were slapped on their operation. Financial markets were suppressed, and banks became the agents of governments' industrial policies. The role of policy became to supersede rather than to support the markets. Mostly policy was formulated solely with regard to a national context. After 1945, when internationalism revived, policy at the international level largely meant coordinating the financial restrictions imposed by governments and in addition supplying the international financial services that immobilized markets could not.

As memories of the Great Depression faded and the inefficiencies of financial repression became evident, the notion that the allocation of financial resources was a task for the market, familiar from the nineteenth century, enjoyed a rebirth. The task for policy again came to be seen as providing a framework within which markets could operate. But how to do so was controversial. Whether the efforts of national governments and multilateral institutions (the International Monetary Fund [IMF] in particular) to structure and stabilize the operation of international financial markets have helped by diminishing the incidence and severity of crises or hurt by aggravating moral hazard thus became the topic of the day.

The result has been a wide-ranging debate over how to reform the IMF, the Group of Seven (G7) and the "international financial architecture" generally.[2] As we read it, the key conclusions of this debate are the need to limit the frequency and magnitude of IMF rescue loans in order to contain moral hazard, and the need to encourage adherence to international standards for

---

1. However, the official community may have come near to such a consensus on the eve of the 1997 Asia crisis, when there appeared to be general agreement on the need to add a code for capital market liberalization to the IMF's Articles of Agreement, a decision from which it revealingly stepped back subsequently.

2. Williamson (2000) and Goldstein (2001) provide two overviews of the key contributions to this debate.

sound financial practice as a way of stabilizing and strengthening financial markets. An historical perspective suggests that these foci are logical consequences of the move back to a more market-based financial system; they reflect the world economy's return to a more nineteenth-century-style international financial system following an extended rupture. That nineteenth-century system featured limited lender-of-last-resort-type facilities at the domestic and international levels. In addition, international standards—specifically, the international gold standard—provided the basis for organizing the operation of nineteenth-century financial markets. Not coincidentally, the focus of the current debate on the role of official lending and international standards in structuring and stabilizing the operation of international financial markets has a pervasive "back-to-the-future" flavor about it.

11.1 The Nineteenth Century

The first notable nineteenth-century attempt to reform the international monetary and financial system was in 1867 at a conference in Paris called by Emperor Napoleon III. There was substantial agreement about the desirability of a common monetary standard. Some of the participants went a step further, advocating standardized coinage.

Two aspects of this initiative are worth emphasizing. First, the impulse to coordinate monetary arrangements reflected not threats to financial stability but rather the desire for monetary standardization as a way of promoting international trade, which was uniformly regarded as a high priority. Second, the call for monetary standardization was a manifestation of the broader desire for economic standardization in an era when technology and policy were drawing national economies more closely together. Trade expanded enormously following France and Britain's negotiation of the Cobden-Chevalier Treaty in 1860 and its extension to other countries. The railway and the telegraph had already begun to link national markets more tightly (O'Rourke and Williamson 1999). As a result, the 1860s and 1870s were marked by an unprecedented drive for international standards and harmonized regulation. An International Postal Congress met in Paris in 1863, and an International Statistical Congress convened in Berlin later that same year. The First Geneva Convention on the Treatment of Wounded Soldiers was signed and the International Committee of the Red Cross established in 1864. In 1868 Heinrich von Stephan launched an initiative for an International Postal Union, and the Mannheim Rhine Shipping Agreement made possible large-scale navigation on Europe's largest inland waterway. Standardization was all the rage.

Money was an obvious area where standardization promised major benefits. In 1866 the U.S. Congressional Coinage Committee concluded that "The only interest of any nation that could possibly be injuriously affected by the establishment of this uniformity is that of the money-changers—an interest which contributes little to the public welfare" (Russell 1898, 35). At the end of the Paris conference, the diplomat in charge of the Emperor's currency program, de Parieu, concluded that the meeting had laid "siege to the citadel of monetary diversity, the fall of which you would like to behold, or, at least, to gradually destroy its walls, for the benefit of the daily increasing commerce and exchanges of every description among the different members of the human family" (U.S. Senate 1879, 875–70).

There was, however, less agreement on the monetary arrangement around which this standardization should take place. Whereas Great Britain was wedded to the gold standard, France was committed to bimetallism. There was little urgency to the proceedings apart from the Emperor's search for a bolster to his waning prestige. There was no sense of crisis: Trade was growing, monetary harmonization or not. The outcome of the deliberations was thus some additional sentiment in favor of gold-based currencies but no specific plan (Einaudi 2000).[3]

There being no pressing need for action, the international monetary and financial system evolved on the basis not of intergovernmental negotiations but of its own momentum.[4] That the leading economic and financial power, Great Britain, had adopted the gold standard encouraged other countries to do the same in order to be able to better access British markets. By joining the gold standard, countries were better able to borrow abroad (Bordo and Flandreau, chap. 9 in this volume), which in this period primarily meant borrowing from Britain, while going onto the gold standard lent additional stimulus to trade with other gold-standard countries (Lopez-Cordoba and Meissner 2000). Thus, market forces more than negotiations among governments provided the impetus for monetary standardization. It did not go unnoticed that the first country to experience an industrial revolution had also been first to adopt the gold standard. On the European continent, the desire to emulate the first industrial nation thus provided additional motivation for joining the gold standard club. Once Germany went onto the gold standard, the attractions for other countries were heightened.[5] The United States chose gold rather than bimetallism in 1873 and 1879 as a way of restoring credibility in the disordered postbellum circum-

---

3. Subsequent conferences were no more successful (Reti 1998). Agreement even on cooperation limited to the standardization and intercirculation of coinage was limited to cases like the members of the Scandinavian Union, who had already developed unusually close ties over a number of years.

4. This is the theme of Gallarotti (1995).

5. Germany emerged from Franco-Prussian War as Great Britain's leading industrial rival, was flush with reparations, and derived no trading advantages from the use of silver currency as the result of the Russian and Austro-Hungarian empires' reliance on inconvertible paper. For all these reasons it found going over to gold attractive, which made it attractive for other countries to follow. The importance of these network effects is a theme of Eichengreen (1996). See Meissner (2000) for evidence.

stances. With the three major industrial countries on gold, a new world order was born.

The other element of the prewar institutional framework was the national central bank. It was precisely in the second half of the nineteenth century that central banks developed their distinctive profiles and responsibilities, first as bankers to the government and then as stewards of the financial system. This was when Walter Bagehot articulated their role as lenders of last resort and specified rules for the extension of those services. The new central banks—in particular the German Reichsbank and the U.S. Federal Reserve System—were also intended to deal with internationally transmitted developments. The development of this institutional capacity can again be interpreted as a functionalist response to industrialization and financial deepening.

The stability of this regime should not be overstated. Banking crises and forced suspensions of convertibility were recurrent problems, as attested to by the vast literature on the subject. Bordo et al. (2001) show that, compared to today, banking and currency crises were only slightly less frequent, and their impact on output was every bit as severe. But no ambitious international reforms were tabled to address these problems.

There is some controversy about the cooperative management of this international system. Eichengreen (1992) argues that support operations by the Bank of France, the Bank of England, the State Bank of Russia, and other central banks and governments, while sporadic and ad hoc, were critical for regime maintenance when the stability of the system was under threat. Flandreau (1997) and Mouré (2002) have argued that this overstates the extent of cooperation prior to the Great War. Central bank cooperation—whether frequent or not, whether critical or not—was, however, increasingly recognized as a way of contending with threats to stability. It follows that, when it came time to reconstruct the international monetary and financial system after the Great War, discussions centered on the scope for regularizing and institutionalizing the practice.

11.2   From World War I to the Great Depression

The first reform efforts of the interwar years were at international conferences in Brussels in 1920 and Genoa in 1922. The overarching goal of these meetings was the "reconstruction of Europe," but the most pressing political-economic issues, reparations and war debts, could not be touched. The worst threat came from countries that experienced exchange rate depreciation and noticed benefits for exports and, more important politically, for employment. Many of the war-devastated European countries in this way came more or less openly to regard inflation and competitive devaluation as devices for securing employment and political stabilization. Their "exchange dumping" was not happily received abroad. The United Kingdom, Canada, and the United States sought a response in antidumping legislation, of which the culmination came with the U.S. Fordner-McCumber Tariff Act of 1922.

For a country such as Great Britain, which had been at the center of the prewar trading system, this was devastating. Consequently, the leading British figure at Genoa, the charismatic wartime prime minister David Lloyd George, made the trade motivation for currency agreements the center of the British strategy. As Lloyd George explained to parliament before leaving for Genoa, "The machinery of commerce, on whose sweet and steady working England depends more than any country in the world, has been shattered. . . . At the beginning of 1922 England's international trade was about fifty percent of its pre-war figure. Two million of her artisans were workless and wageless, and dependent on a vast and ruinous provision of outdoor relief." On his return from the conference, the prime minister explained further: "If Genoa were to fail, the condition of Europe would indeed be tragic. The channels of international trade would become hopelessly clogged by restrictions and difficulties, artificial and otherwise. Countries would stagnate in the poisonous national swamps of insolvency. There would be quarrels, suspicions and feuds between nations, ending in who knows what great conflict" (Mills 1922, 11, 313).

Although the recommendations of the Genoa experts included measures to simplify customs procedures and reduce transport costs, their main thrust was monetary—they were directed at stopping currency depreciation. They recommended the restoration of gold convertibility, the creation of independent central banks, fiscal discipline, financial assistance for weak-currency countries, and cooperative central bank management. It will be evident from our description of the prewar system that none of these elements was entirely new. Gold convertibility and an independent central bank to reconcile its maintenance with the fluctuating financial needs of industry and trade (by providing "an elastic currency," in the phrase that featured in discussions of the establishment of the Federal Reserve System) had been centerpieces of the prewar system, and there was agreement at Brussels and Genoa on the desirability of putting them back in place.[6] Regime-preserving cooperation had already brought several of those banks of issue into closer, more regular contact. Even the form of that cooperation, assistance for countries with financial problems, suggested a mechanism through which the incentives to rejoin the international system might now be sharpened.

In all these respects, then, the appropriate metaphor for the development of the international monetary and financial system was evolution rather

6. About the gold standard there was no question. And, as the delegates to the Brussels Conference concluded, "Banks and especially Banks of Issue should be free from political pressure and should be conducted only on lines of prudent finance" (Bank of England, OC50/6, 13 December, 1933, per Jacobsson, "Notes on a Conversation with Sir Otto Niemeyer").

than revolution. Absent threats to the global trading system and hence to growth and recovery, neither Brussels nor Genoa generated reform proposals that departed significantly from the prewar status quo.

The consequences were mixed. Genoa was a successful negotiation to the limited extent that it produced a workable short-term solution to the problems of the postwar international monetary system, but it did nothing to address the underlying weaknesses of the gold-exchange standard, something that became painfully evident once the Great Depression struck. At a more fundamental level, it failed to achieve policymakers' goal of rebuilding the international trading system.

Genoa was basically a monetary agreement, although discussions touched on a number of other issues. The international standard to which parties to the Genoa Agreement were held was the international gold standard. But at Genoa we also see a first hint of a trend that would become increasingly evident as the century progressed: that full participation in the international system, and in particular the ability to derive the full benefits of open, multilateral trade, required adherence to standards for policy and behavior beyond the strictly monetary. This tendency manifested itself at Genoa in the recognition that fiscal policy was a matter of common concern. All countries that participated actively in the international system, the delegates agreed, should strive for balanced budgets and fiscal transparency. Fiscal discipline had acquired prominence when the budgets of the countries that had been engaged in World War I fell into deficit and postwar societies, confronting a changed balance of political pressures, found it impossible to produce the consensus needed to restore fiscal balance. As hyperinflation in Central and Eastern Europe revealed, chronic budget deficits could wreak havoc with financial stability, exchange rate stability, and the reconstruction of international trade. As a result of these political changes, monetary and financial stability, and the reconstruction of international trade, now required more than simply adoption of a particular monetary standard. Specifically, the fiscal prerequisites for the maintenance of that monetary standard also had to be met.

Unfortunately, the parties to this agreement lacked a mechanism for encouraging adherence to this standard. Conditional financial assistance was a potential carrot, but not all countries sought or obtained such assistance, although a limited number of stabilization loans were extended through the League of Nations, notably in the cases of Austria and Hungary, and by national governments (Santaella 1992). Just as IMF conditionality cannot affect behavior when countries are reluctant to come to the IMF, fiscal discipline could not be required as a condition of official assistance in the 1920s when official assistance was provided only sporadically.

The major drawback of the League system was that there existed no multilateral organization with the requisite capacity, absent U.S. membership. The establishment of the Bank for International Settlements (BIS) can be seen as a response to this problem. The effort to establish the first "world bank" (as contemporaries referred to the BIS) originated in the effort to use technocratic means to solve the postwar dispute over reparations and interallied debt payments that pitted Germany against France, France against Great Britain and the United States, and Great Britain against the United States, and to prevent that dispute from derailing efforts to reconstruct the international trading system.[7] But the BIS was intended as more than a reparations bank; its founders saw it as a way of providing technical solutions to economic problems, of cultivating cooperation among central banks, and ultimately of stabilizing the world trading system.[8]

The constitution of the BIS reflected the political circumstances in which it had been established.[9] All of South and Central America, Africa, Great Britain's overseas dominions, and Asia were excluded, with the exception of Japan, which owed its inclusion to its status as a reparations creditor.[10] While Spain was left out, the United States was brought in, although its representation was unofficial because the Federal Reserve System was forbidden to participate.[11]

7. In 1929, a new reparations scheme, the Young Plan, was adopted at the Paris Experts' Conference. Previously, under the Dawes Plan, the agent-general had been responsible for converting the marks paid by the German government into foreign currency and judging whether the foreign exchange market would allow such a large transaction. Now, Germany was to instead pay her reparation marks to a new institution, the BIS, which replaced the transfer protection mechanism of the Dawes Plan. Whereas the agent general had possessed the discretionary power to reinvest reparation payments in German securities and thus to limit the pressure on the exchange rate, now the transfer would be automatic, but the national central bankers who comprised the new institution's board would collaborate in offsetting any adverse consequences for the foreign exchange market. The bank also acted as the fiscal agent for the Dawes and Young loans, as well as other international loans.

8. Sir Charles Addis, a member of the committee established at the 1929 Hague Conference to design the new bank, wrote: "It was hoped by this plan to fulfill the dream of Genoa by the gradual development of the BIS into a cooperative society of Central Banks" (Bank of England, G1/1, 28 July 1929, Addis to Leith-Ross [British Treasury]). Others described the object of the BIS as collaboration to "evolve a common body of monetary doctrine" and to "smooth out the business cycle, and to contribute toward a greater equilibrium in the general level of economic activity" (*Fifth Annual Report,* also quoted in Eichengreen 1992, 263).

9. Disputes among the Paris experts, at the Hague conferences, and within the Organization Committee left the BIS "vague, obscure, badly arranged and sometimes inconsistent," in the words of one of its directors. (Bank of England, G1/1, Otto Niemeyer memorandum).

10. One is reminded of the fact that fully a third of the executive directors on today's IMF board are European, while only two out of twenty-four are African, reflecting political imperatives when this successor to the BIS was created in 1944.

11. Reflecting the risk of involving the United States officially in the reparations quagmire. As a consequence, the BIS held its dollar deposits at two leading private New York banks. Moreover, the bank was not situated in a major financial center: The choice of site initially lay between the small countries of Europe, Belgium, the Netherlands, and Switzerland, with France advocating a Belgian location and Great Britain and Germany militantly opposed. In Switzerland, the eventual choice, Zürich, was rejected because, although a major financial center, it was too German; Geneva implied too much of an entanglement with the League of Nations; and thus the choice fell on Basel. Staffing followed the principal of national representation. The first president, Gates McGarrah, was an American, but the general manager in charge of operations was a young Banque de France official, Pierre Quesnay. Protests from

It was difficult after the deliberations of the organization committee to avoid the conclusion drawn by a later British director of the Bank, Sir Otto Niemeyer, that "No one who started out to construct a Super Bank for world cooperative purposes could conceivably have hit on the constitution proposed for the BIS."[12] The BIS was not permitted to make medium- or long-term investments (outside Germany) that might have been useful for stabilization purposes. Its capital was a mere 500 million gold francs suisses, subscribed by central banks or (in the case of Japan and the United States) banking groups.[13] It had only 1,800 million Swiss francs in deposits, of which SF 300 million were reinvested in Germany, SF 650 million were short-term deposits by reparations creditors that had not yet transferred their annuities, and SF 800 million represented other central bank deposits. These resources were already exhausted by August 1930, three months after the bank opened for business.[14]

The BIS was then confronted by a world financial crisis of unimagined proportions. Should it provide emergency credits to central banks? This seemed logical, given that the BIS was a central banker's bank, but French objections to a proposed Austro-German customs union and to German rearmament, both of which were prohibited under the Versailles Treaty, blocked the Bank from providing early and generous assistance in response to requests for Germany and Austria. Should it attempt new forms of lending? The need arose out of the world depression and financial crisis immobilizing bank loans, including loans and credits from foreign banks denominated not in domestic currency but in dollars and sterling. This was where an international lender might have done what national central banks, constrained by fixed exchange rates and unable to print dollars, could not.

In the autumn of 1930 a BIS subcommittee launched an inquiry into how

---

Reichsbank president Hjalmar Schacht that Quesnay had been the figure responsible for organizing a speculative attack on the mark in the spring of 1929 were ignored. Quesnay had powerful claim to his new position: Owen Young, the architect of the new reparations plan, hailed the thirty-six-year-old economist as the principal author of both the Young Plan and the Bank. (Neue Zürcher Zeitung, no. 185, 30 January 1930, "Bank für internationalen Zahlungsausgleich"). Quesnay's deputy was Ernst Hülse from the Reichsbank, a blinkered and unimaginative bureaucrat more intent on warding off invasions of his administrative turf than on rescuing the international financial system (e.g., Bank of England G1/4, 2 November 1931, Rodd to Siepmann). The result would have been deadlock or a descent into routine and trivial business had Quesnay not possessed rather more imagination and initiative.

12. Bank of England, G1/1, Otto Niemeyer memorandum.

13. See Auboin (1955). This was a mere 0.1 percent of 1930 U.S. gross national product (GNP), whereas the capital of the IMF was 4.0 percent of U.S. GNP in 1945.

14. Bank of England, G1/2, 12 July 1930, Siepmann memorandum on phone conversation with Rodd (BIS). One of its staff came to the conclusion that "if things continue to take their present course, the Bank will be in a completely frozen position within a month and unable to meet its liabilities without borrowing" (Bank of England, G1/2, 10 August 1930, HAS Note on telephone conversation with Rodd). The BIS's sole operation of systematic significance in its first year of existence was a stabilization credit of £3 million in April 1931 designed to allow Spain to return to the gold standard, a goal that the global depression prevented from being achieved.

the Bank might address these problems.[15] To thaw Central European credit, it recommended that a sum equivalent to the BIS's capital, plus its deposits, be placed in medium-term bills bought from banks. A more ambitious proposal was tabled in February 1931 by the Bank of England and became known as the Kindersley (or Norman-Kindersley) scheme. (Montagu Norman was the influential governor of the Bank of England, and Sir Robert Kindersley was a director of both the Bank of England and the BIS.) This was a response to the collapse of international bond markets, on which new issues had been rendered impossible by the implosion of security prices. Kindersley and Norman recommended the creation of an international corporation with a capital of £25–50 million empowered to issue bonds up to three times its capital on behalf of national governments, municipalities, mortgage banks, harbor boards, railways, and public utility companies.[16]

Although their scheme won the support of Germany, where the danger of financial collapse was acute, other countries feared the inflationary consequences. The governor of the Banque de France argued that BIS participation in the Kindersley scheme would be contrary to the Bank's statutes.[17] American financiers were similarly skeptical. The Bank's first president, an American, Gates McGarrah, warned the leading New York bank, J. P. Morgan, that the scheme was impractical and that it would be better to organize new loans through private banking channels.[18] The proposal thus languished. As Norman noted sadly, the BIS was "already slipping to the bottom of a ditch and in that position seems likely to do no more than helpfully perform a number of routine and Central Banking operations."[19]

A more modest but in some ways more interesting idea submitted by the Belgian banker Emile Francqui to the medium-term credit subcommittee fared little better. Reflecting worries that rescue efforts relying on central banks and official institutions would fail owing to their limited financial and political resources, Francqui proposed to supplement official contributions by catalyzing private-sector lending (to use modern IMF parlance). The BIS, he proposed, should rediscount up to £10 million of commercial paper in order to reinvigorate financial markets and pave the way for Ivar Kreuger, the charismatic Swedish speculator and financier, to underwrite

15. Bank of England, OV4/84, 29 October 1930, Quesnay to Siepmann, attaching memorandum by Dr. Simon.
16. Bank of England, OV4/34, 2 February 1931, memorandum "Kindersley scheme."
17. Moreover, where French banks were supposed to subscribe most of the bonds, there was no readiness to offer them "means of controlling the use of the funds furnished" (27 February 1931, Moret communication to McGarrah).
18. The Morgan bankers agreed. (Federal Reserve Bank of New York, 797.3; BIS, 18 March 1931, McGarrah cable for Lamont and Gilbert).
19. 3 March 1931, Norman to Harrison.

new issues. But Francqui's initiative was not well received by the two hostile camps in the BIS. The British and Germans regarded the idea as inadequate, while the French dismissed it as "utopian."[20]

In sum, the BIS lacked the finances and leadership to cope with a crisis of such enormity. There was no consensus regarding its role and a reluctance on the part of the creditor countries to finance its operations. Its shareholders were divided, and no country had the capacity to impose a coherent vision. The BIS therefore retreated into the safer world of data dissemination. It failed to do anything to prevent a major crisis and was out of its depth in dealing with the consequences.

11.3 The 1930s

While this attempt to manage the crisis failed, there was still hope that the international community would draw constructive lessons from it. The first opportunity to demonstrate that it had was the London Conference. A World Economic Conference had long been suggested by American diplomats as a way of bringing Europe to its senses and as a way of limiting retaliation against the Smoot-Hawley tariff. Here, then, we see the role of threats to the trading system in galvanizing reform. Great Britain took up the idea in October 1930 and passed it on to Germany. The Germans, for their part, thought it might open a way to make the United States interested in the financial side of economic questions and in particular in the end of reparations. The German foreign minister then urged his ambassadors to sell the plan to the Americans as a potential platform for Hoover's reelection campaign.[21]

As the conference approached, governments realized that a large meeting would not produce results unless adequate groundwork was laid. The meetings of preliminary commissions and committees that began in late 1932 under the auspices of the League of Nations represented the last major attempt to deal with the policy questions of the Depression era in an international framework. Separate monetary and trade subcommittees met to define the respective agendas. Unfortunately, each saw the design of its deliberations as hinging on its counterpart's. Speakers at the Financial Sub-Committee agreed that "freer trade was a prerequisite of a return to normal

20. Bank of England, OV4/84, 7 May 1931, report of Francqui subcommittee; 22 April 1931, McGarrah to Norman; 18 May 1931, BIS board meeting. This pessimism was not unjustified, since the BIS meeting at which Francqui and Kindersley plans were killed off took place just a week after the collapse of the Vienna Creditanstalt. The crisis quickly infected much of the European continent and moved over to England and the United States. Less than a year after he was supposed to have organized a scheme that might rescue the international financial system, Ivar Kreuger killed himself in a Paris hotel room.

21. Politisches Archive des Auswartigen Amtes, W21A, 20 December 1930, Hoesch cable; 29 December 1930, Curtius to Hoesch.

economic conditions and of a return to the gold standard."[22] In the Economic (i.e., trade) Sub-Committee, financial normalization was seen as a precondition for rebuilding trade. No progress was made in breaking this logjam.

The second attempt at preparation involved politicians rather than technocrats in April-May 1933. The newly inaugurated U.S. president, Franklin Roosevelt, offered a tariff truce for the duration of the conference. The debt issue was widened by the German central bank president's attempt to win consent for a German moratorium on servicing long-term private foreign debt. And the monetary issue was raised in acute form by the announcement of the U.S. gold embargo while British Prime Minister Ramsay Mac-Donald and his chief financial adviser, Sir Frederick Leith-Ross, were still en route to a preliminary meeting in Washington, D.C.

By the time the conference finally met, on 12 June 1933 at the London Geological Museum, there were too many parties interested in killing it off for there to be much chance of success. The conference resembled nothing so much as an Agatha Christie novel in which there are too many suspects, all with plausible motives and dubious alibis. Great Britain's insistence on war debt reduction, which it believed to be the original raison d'être of the conference, meant that it did not want discussions to widen. Chancellor of the Exchequer Neville Chamberlain stressed that the conference would not be successful if it did not resolve the war debt issue. But Roosevelt's instructions to the U.S. delegation excluded either formal or informal discussion of war debts as well as disarmament.[23]

The currency stabilization goals of the conference were fatally undermined by President Roosevelt's "bombshell message" that the United States had no intention of stabilizing the dollar. The U.S. administration was determined that national stability should have priority over internationalism. Rebuilding trade was desirable as a way of giving impetus to U.S. exports, but there was little immediate scope for this in the depressed conditions of the 1930s, with much of Central Europe having come under German domination and Latin America having turned to import substitution. Roosevelt's unilateral monetary initiative was thus a desperate effort to stimulate recovery at home regardless of the consequences for the international monetary and trading systems. By the fifth week, delegates realized that the position was hopeless. On 27 July, the conference went into recess, and the free-trading U.S. Secretary of State Cordell Hull delivered a mournful closing speech.[24]

22. League of Nations, R2672, 1 November 1932, second meeting of monetary subcommittee.
23. Foreign Relations of the United States, 1933 I, p. 621.
24. "A reasonable combination of the practicable phases of both economic nationalism and economic internationalism—avoiding the extremes of each—should be our objective," he modestly concluded. In practice, the participants ignored even the tariff truce: Great Britain

The reasons for this failure are not hard to see. The Roosevelt administration recognized the desirability of rebuilding world trade but, in the absence of international cooperation, saw domestic stability and trade reconstruction as at loggerheads. It saw itself as having no choice but to put this aspiration on hold until currency depreciation and monetary reflation had succeeded in initiating recovery. In any case, rebuilding world trade was the last thing that appealed to a Germany intent on expanding its influence in Central and Eastern Europe. Support for protectionist measures was also strong in France, where farmers were now feeling the brunt of the depression. Thus, proposals for monetary and financial stabilization as a way of rebuilding world trade met with limited support.

11.4   Bretton Woods

From this experience the British economist John Maynard Keynes drew the conclusion that multilateral negotiations among governments of roughly comparable influence could not be expected to succeed and that a workable plan could only be realized at the insistence of "a single power or like-minded group of powers" (Skidelsky 1992, 482). Keynes's insight provides the obvious explanation for the greater success of the next conference. Although there were forty-four or forty-five nations represented at Bretton Woods (depending on one's view of the status of the Danish delegation), only the United States and the United Kingdom played significant roles.[25] Plans for the IMF and the World Bank had already emerged from earlier Anglo-American discussions, which the other participants had no choice but to accept. Although there was negotiation over the Bretton Woods Agreement, that negotiation was fundamentally bilateral.

Moreover, it was lopsided bilateralism: the United States had a preponderance of power, whereas the United Kingdom was financially and economically strapped. This imbalance shaped the negotiations, in which Keynes's vision (which would have placed much greater obligations to adjust on the surplus country or countries) was defeated and the America's White Plan was adopted with only minor modification.

In addition, there was now more of a consensus regarding the economic basis of the new world order. Capital flows were destabilizing, competitive devaluations a threat, discriminatory trade policies a danger.[26] Some scholars trace the making of the postwar settlement to the emergence of what

---

raised schedules on fifty items, claiming that it had made applications for these before the truce came into effect on 12 May. In September, the Netherlands and Sweden, and then in November Great Britain, withdrew from the truce. This was the end of the last major attempt at international cooperation on trade and financial issues.

25. Although it is sometimes claimed that in-between powers, in particular Canada and France, played a role in brokering between the British and American delegations.

26. And associated with the politically discredited systems of Germany and Japan.

they term an "epistemic community" of policy experts who trusted one other and shared a vision of managed internationalism (Ikenberry 1993). Intellectual consensus there was, but this does not suffice to explain the success of Bretton Woods; there had been a similar consensus in the 1920s regarding the desirability of returning to the gold standard and of central bank cooperation. Montagu Norman, Hjalmar Schacht, and Benjamin Strong had been on terms of great intimacy, in other words; although they spoke a common intellectual language, and evolved a sort of international solidarity of central banks, they nonetheless proved incapable of mounting an institutionalized response to global financial problems.

Why, then, when they failed did their successors at Bretton Woods succeed? To start with, the context for Bretton Woods was different. Although there was no immediate crisis, there was significant pressure to produce a settlement. The conference met just after the Allied landings in Normandy, which created the possibility of an early end to the European war.[27] The timetable was further tightened by the need to act before the November U.S. elections.[28]

Moreover, the participants structured and ordered the Bretton Woods negotiations by attaching priority to the reconstruction of trade. In the 1920s nationalism had subverted the efforts of internationalists to restore a free and open trade regime; the new nations of Central and Eastern Europe depended on tariffs for public-sector revenues and for easing the adjustment to their new economic and political circumstances. The tariff truce conferences convened by the League of Nations consequently elicited little enthusiasm. In 1933 attitudes toward trade liberalization had been mixed; whereas some governments attached priority to reconstructing trade, others preferred to suppress it.[29] What sort of monetary and financial order might be tailored to such a world was unclear. In 1944, in contrast, there was no doubt about the U.S. commitment to trade liberalization and therefore about its preference for a monetary system that mandated exchange rate stability and current-account convertibility as a way of creating a trade-friendly financial environment.[30] U.S. export interests could be enlisted to push for congressional ratification of the Bretton Woods Agreement. And given America's preponderance of power, other countries had no choice but

27. The conference took place before the Allied disaster at Arnhem.

28. As Morgenthau candidly told a strategy meeting preparing for Bretton Woods, "we felt that it was good for the world, good for the nation, and good for the Democratic Party, for us to move" (Blum 1967, 248). White was equally insistent that the meetings had to take place before the American party political conventions (Interdepartmental meetings, 1 April 1944).

29. As noted above, the attitude of the U.S. government was somewhat ambivalent (Cordell Hull felt much more strongly about liberalization than many of his colleagues), and other countries, whether they saw protection and discrimination as a means of cultivating self-sufficiency (as in Germany) or supporting agriculture (as in France and Italy), were strongly opposed.

30. Capital account convertibility, being less essential to trade, was a different story.

to go along. They might push for concessions on the margin, insisting that pegged exchange rates should also be adjustable, by arguing that there should be a five-year transitional period before current account convertibility was required, and by seeking to maximize the financial resources of the IMF and the World Bank. But with memories of trade warfare in the 1930s still fresh, they fundamentally shared the U.S. priority of establishing a trade-friendly monetary and financial environment.

11.5 After Bretton Woods

That this vision took time to be realized reminds us that monetary and financial reform is rarely swift. Even in Western Europe, the restoration of current account convertibility took longer than envisaged, until December 1958.[31] Japan accepted the obligations of Article VIII of the IMF agreement on current account convertibility in 1964. Most developing countries retained current account restrictions until the 1980s and 1990s.

Two stories can be told about the disintegration of Bretton Woods. According to one, the breakdown was a Triffinite consequence of a buildup of claims on the United States that were needed for the liquidity of the system but could be converted in a panic. According to the other, the breakdown was a result of U.S. action in response to a worsening trade position, in which the country's most aggressive trade partner, Japan, refused to consider any revaluation that might stem the tide of exports. Since foreign competition, and especially the competition of Japanese manufactured goods (at that time the greatest attention was given to textiles) was a major political issue, action by the administration was needed to tackle the trade problem. The Nixon package of 15 August 1971, which by closing the gold window (through which gold had been made available at $35 an ounce) ended the par value system, limited the import surcharge to 10 percent. By this interpretation, a modification of the monetary order was needed to prevent a trade war.

The new system of parities calculated at the Smithsonian in December 1971 held for just over a year. The renewed collapse is best explained in terms of an expansive U.S. monetary policy leading to larger U.S. trade deficits and thus to the reemergence of the same problems that had caused the breakdown of August 1971 in the first place. Allowing the international monetary system to break down was thus seen as the alternative to a vicious descent into protectionism and trade warfare. Alternatives they were, but not mutually exclusive ones: As it was, the 1970s witnessed a dramatic expansion in the "new protectionism" of voluntary export restraints, dubious

---

31. It was achieved not so much through the IMF as with the bilateral support of the United States through the Marshall Plan to the European Payments Union (although the attainment of convertibility was preceded by a surge of IMF credit in 1956–57).

consumer safety standards, and similar devices to circumvent General Agreement on Tariffs and Trade (GATT) rules.

Following the collapse of the par value system, calls were heard for a new Bretton Woods. But there was never a systematic redesign of international monetary and financial arrangements. The international monetary system (or "non-system" as it was dubbed by John Williamson) evolved through a series of patchwork reforms. The agency of this process, the Committee of Twenty (C20), faced no particular time pressure and broke down in the face of the 1973–74 oil shock. France and Japan preferred the restoration of fixed exchange rates but in the context of a system that imposed firmer constraints on the United States. German policymakers were divided, British policymakers weak and confused. The United States, for its part, did not want the dollar to be placed again in the impossible position of the 1960s. U.S. Treasury Secretary George Shultz and his undersecretary, Paul Volcker, were prepared to contemplate pegged rates only if the bands around them were wide and a mechanism was created to force surplus countries to adjust. With lack of agreement on the latter, they reluctantly concluded that floating rates were the only option. And this was not acceptable to America's C20 partners.

Bilateral discussions between U.S. and French Treasury officials, rather than the more multilateral C20 approach, produced the formula that reconciled prevailing institutions with the new reality. Instead of a "system of stable rates," countries committed to maintaining a "stable system of rates."[32] This was a minimalist approach to reform but probably the only one practicable at the time. It acknowledged the shift by a growing number of countries toward more flexible exchange rates, which was already a fait accompli. Beyond that, it committed them to little.

The failure of more radical reforms reflected the absence of a consensus on the direction that they should take. There was no overwhelming threat to world trade from the increased variability of exchange rates, contrary to warnings sounded following the collapse of Bretton Woods. In part this reflected the large number of small countries that continued to peg their currencies to that of a larger trading partner. In addition it reflected the ample supply of credit provided by the process of petro-dollar recycling.

Where fears for the continued expansion of trade were greatest was where trade mattered most: namely, in Europe. In response, Germany and France devised for themselves a mini–Bretton Woods (the Snake and then the European Monetary System). Initially, negotiations proceeded on a tripartite basis, with the United Kingdom (now a member of the European Community) playing an active part. This produced few results, but the scheme developed quickly when only German and French negotiators were involved.

---

32. This Franco-American compromise was discussed at the Rambouillet Summit (by the five leading Western industrial countries) and institutionalized in the Second Amendment of the Articles of Agreement, which obliged countries to promote stable exchange rates by fostering orderly economic conditions while empowering the Fund to conduct "firm surveillance" of those policies.

The most active phase of monetary and exchange rate coordination in the post–Bretton Woods years was the mid-1980s. Again, governments were prompted to act by threats to the trading system, specifically the appreciation of the dollar and the threat of a protectionist response by the U.S. Congress. In the spring of 1985, the Senate unanimously voted a resolution calling for retaliation against Japanese imports, and a bill was then introduced providing for surcharges on the products of those countries with large surpluses against the United States. The obvious response that might defuse domestic pressure in the United States without threatening the international trading system was exchange rate realignment. Formally the venue was the regular meetings of Group of Five (G5) or G7 finance ministers (probably the central locus of financial cooperation between the major industrial countries), although critical momentum was gained in bilateral discussions between Japan and the United States. The United States had a preponderance of influence insofar as Japan was vulnerable to U.S. protectionism. Trade issues lent monetary discussions substantial urgency and made the Japanese willing to accept a deal. The outcome was agreement by the G5 finance ministers and central bank governors meeting at the Plaza Hotel in New York in September 1985 to reduce the value of the dollar in an "orderly" way through concerted intervention and, more importantly, the adoption of stimulative policies by Japan.[33] The Plaza Agreement was followed in 1987 by a new negotiation at a meeting of the finance ministers (now the Group of Six, or G6) at the Louvre, with the aim of stabilizing exchange rates and again of stimulating growth in Japan (Funabashi 1998).

None of these discussions tackled what appears in retrospect to be the most important new development of the post–Bretton Woods years, namely, the explosive growth of capital flows.[34] This oversight was rudely

33. Though it should be noted that the dollar was already declining on foreign exchange markets.

34. In the international system as it was emerging in the 1970s, with strong private-sector lending solving the problem of petro-dollar recycling, it actually looked as if the Bretton Woods institutions were redundant. The IMF's attempt to remain at the center of the system through a new approach to the reserve problem, in which a "substitution account" would replace national currencies with SDRs, was never realized. The private sector handled the imbalances and liquidity problems of the 1970s sufficiently well that many commentators concluded that the IMF and the World Bank would lead a more and more marginal existence, catering only to poor countries excluded from the world's capital markets. We are aware of similar arguments made about the diminished role of the multilaterals at the beginning of the twenty-first century and choose our language in order to bring out the parallels. Irving Friedman put it then, "because they depend upon full and prompt servicing of their loans for their financial profitability and viability, private banks (in contrast to the Fund and the Bank) understandably tend to focus their attention upon the best managed countries, and, within these countries, the best managed firms in the most advanced sectors of the economy" (Friedman 1977, 119). Another prominent banker, Rimmer de Vries of Morgan Guaranty, in April 1982 described the new private-sector consensus in the following terms: "in recent years Fund and commercial bank lending have evolved in different directions." They had distinct and separate spheres of operation, and "thus the Fund must not be viewed as a protective umbrella under which the international banking community can find shelter in times of trouble" (de Vries 1982, 10).

brought to the world's attention in the summer of 1982 by threats of default by Mexico and Argentina. Dealing with what became the Latin American debt crisis required new money from official as well as private sources. The most difficult task was to involve the private sector—as had been attempted in 1931 when the BIS called on Ivar Kreuger. Initially, efforts to do so were led not by the multilateral institutions but by national central banks, especially in the major financial centers, which promptly and even brutally pressed commercial banks to put in new funds. The BIS offered bridge loans while the crisis countries awaited IMF assistance. Although the IMF eventually came to play a central role, linking its conditionality to bank assistance, the cumbersome structure of its decision making precluded an immediate response of the sort needed in times of crisis.[35]

This solution removed the threat of default at a time when the money-center banks were heavily exposed. Thus, 1982 did not join 1873, 1890, or 1931, when crises at the periphery spread to the center. It did less to solve the problems of the debtor countries. In the end, it was initiatives by private financial institutions to write down nonperforming debt that prompted U.S. Treasury Secretary Nicholas Brady to embrace a scheme that would reduce rather than pile up debt and enable developing countries to regain market access.

Given how rapidly the crisis unfolded and the consequent lack of time to redesign the system, it is not surprising that existing institutions and mechanisms (national central banks, the BIS, the IMF) were stretched beyond their original (some might say proper) purposes. In any case, the climate was inhospitable for radical redesign. It should be recalled that this was a time of tension between the major industrial countries over economic and monetary policy, when the Europeans attacked the United States for what German Chancellor Helmut Schmidt called the "highest interest rates since Jesus Christ," and in which many U.S. policymakers (notably Treasury Secretary Donald Regan) had a thinly veiled contempt for any kind of internationalism.

The financial crisis of the early 1980s was a shock to international trade. The dollar value of world trade only reached its 1980 level again in 1986, and Western Hemisphere trade again matched its 1980 level only in 1988. Nevertheless the form of crisis resolution, which obliged Latin American countries to export in order to service debt, meant that there was little room for 1930s-style experiments in trade restriction. Ultimately, the global trading system was not jeopardized. Hence, these events did not prompt fundamental monetary and financial reform.

The end of the 1980s is as good a point as any at which to take stock of the situation on the eve of the events that provide the context for current de-

---

35. In critical cases, the managing director in fact regularly agreed on measures ahead of formal executive board votes (James 1996, ch. 12).

bates. Although much had changed in the course of preceding decades, the extent of continuity is also striking. International monetary stability and exchange rate stability were still regarded as largely synonymous. But exchange rate stability was valued less for its own sake than as a way of supporting a stable and expanding network of trade. There was nothing new about this. It is one way of interpreting the enthusiasm for the International Monetary Conference of 1867, the Brussels Conference in 1920, and the Genoa Conference in 1922. The absence of a comparable commitment to free and open trade explains the failure to agree on an agenda for monetary reform at the London Conference of 1933. The desire to rebuild the network of international trade, thereby providing foreign markets for U.S. exports and solidifying intra-European links, was a prime motivation of U.S. negotiators at Bretton Woods. And the concern of U.S. and Japanese officials over protectionist threats was a motivation for the Plaza and Louvre Accords.

11.6   The 1990s

Globalization was the byword of the 1990s, reflecting the rapid growth of international financial transactions, the integration of developing countries into the world economy, and the information and communications revolution that brought satellite television, the cell phone, and the Internet to remote corners of the world. Capital flows rose exponentially, enabling countries to finance their development needs abroad but also applying more intense pressure—in the form of capital flight—if things went wrong.

Influencing this market was no easy task. In the debt crisis of the 1980s, large banks could be counted on to coordinate their smaller counterparts, and the IMF could simply communicate with the large intermediaries. By the time of the next debt crisis in 1994–95, the progress of securitization meant that the investor base was larger and more heterogeneous: It now included hedge funds, pension funds, and mutual funds as well as legions of individual investors. Getting such a large number of creditors to recognize their collective interest (sometimes even to determine their identity) was no easy task. This explains the dilemma facing the IMF of how to ameliorate the severity of a crisis without at the same time bailing out investors (who may have a collective interest in staying in but an individual interest in getting out) and aggravating moral hazard.

An inadvertent effect of these capital flows was to highlight weaknesses in domestic financial systems. Capital-account liberalization allowed banks and corporations to fund themselves offshore and currency mismatches to develop on their balance sheets. It facilitated gambling where corporate governance was weak, supervision and regulation were underdeveloped, and the financial safety net was unconditional. This environment proved a fertile seedbed for banking crises. And the same factors limited the capacity of central banks and governments, unable to print dollars and worried that re-regulating flows would damage their credibility, to intervene in stabilizing ways. They meant that IMF intervention to contain the consequences might require unprecedented quantities of finance.

Moreover, just as the recovery of capital mobility in the quarter century following World War II had undermined the pegged-but-adjustable exchange rates of Bretton Woods, the further growth of capital flows now complicated efforts to operate crawling bands and exchange rate target zones. If doubts arose about the sustainability of an exchange rate, market participants could take positions against it. These dynamics played themselves out in the series of crises that ricocheted through Europe, Latin America, and Asia. The result was steady erosion in the share of IMF member countries operating soft currency pegs, which were abandoned in favor of currency boards (and, in Europe, monetary union) on the one hand and more freely floating exchange rates on the other.[36]

This left the IMF in search of an anchor for macroeconomic policy and a focus for its advice. Should it advocate currency boards and dollarization? Should it urge its members to float their currencies and target inflation? Should it discourage intermediate regimes as crisis prone, or was any exchange rate arrangement still viable so long as domestic macroeconomic policies were brought into conformance with its dictates? Disagreements over these issues among the Fund's shareholders, staff, and management (reflecting equally deep divisions in the scholarly literature) prevented the institution from offering clear and coherent advice, which did not enhance its credibility in the eyes of the markets or its members (assisting in exchange rate management having been the IMF's original raison d'être and intellectual bread and butter). Floating rates appeared to many developing-country governments as presenting too great a risk to domestic financial systems, which might be exposed to a mismatch between liabilities (in dollars or other foreign currencies) and domestic currency assets. Pegging the exchange rate, adopting a currency board, or dollarizing (in the late-1990s variant) were still regarded as valid devices where the crisis was extreme, but there was an understandable reluctance to endorse policies that were tantamount to locking the door and throwing away the key.[37]

One way of understanding the expanding scope of IMF conditionality is as a search for new sources of credibility for national policy. The Fund might condition its assistance on agreement to make the central bank independent, to empower the prime minister or the finance minister to veto the spending decisions of subcentral governments, or to make budgeting more transparent, all as ways of enhancing the credibility of policy. These in-

---

36. See Fischer (2001) for an overview of these trends.
37. This was the well-known inability to articulate an exit strategy from these rigid monetary-cum-exchange-rate regimes, analyzed in Eichengreen et al. (1998).

stances of what the critics of the IMF dismissed as the Fund's excessively intrusive structural conditions were justified by the institution and its champions as attempts to enhance credibility by strengthening policy-making institutions, as opposed to extracting incredible promises of intent.[38]

None of these justifications prevented the IMF from being roundly and widely criticized for its structural interventions (Feldstsein 1998). The Fund attached more than fifty structural policy conditions to the typical three-year loan disbursed through its Extended Fund Facility in the 1990s and nine to fifteen structural conditions to its typical one-year standby arrangement. Their scale and scope were unlike anything in the institution's prior history. The IMF moved into areas like corporate governance, accounting methods and principles, attacks on corruption, and even at times the desirability of democratization, unprecedented issues for what was a financial institution.

Mexico in 1994–95 was the first test of this new approach.[39] The Mexican crisis was a debt crisis, but it was also a banking crisis, as a result of the balance sheet mismatches described above, and a confidence crisis, reflecting turmoil in the political system (the Colosio assassination in the run-up to the presidential election).[40] The Fund conditioned its assistance on reform of the banking system as well as on the standard macroeconomic measures. Moreover, the scale of the assistance received by Mexico was unprecedented, reflecting the explosive growth of international financial markets and the need for large amounts of liquidity if default and restructuring were to be headed off.

The Fund's actions were consonant with the preferences of its principal shareholder. The mid-1990s may have been the peak of U.S. Treasury influence over the IMF, matched only by the first fragile decade of the Fund's existence. Europe's Maastricht-minded countries were busy tending their gardens, and Japan was in the throes of its financial crisis. The emerging markets had only begun asserting themselves. Although it is easy to exaggerate the intimacy of the IMF–U.S. Treasury connection, it is hard to offer another equally convincing explanation for the extraordinary pressure for

38. In addition, this new emphasis on structural reform is impossible to understand except in the context of transition in Eastern Europe and the former Soviet Union. Transition was the dominant event of the 1990s. As such, it dominated the IMF's attention. And it was fundamentally a problem of structural transformation. It is hard to imagine approach to multilateral support for this process that would have not emphasized structural reform, in other words, or focused on privatizing public enterprise, building regulatory institutions, and developing administrative capacity. This preoccupation shifted the focus of IMF staff and management from macroeconomic surveillance to a host of new structural policy issues. For better or for worse (opinions differ), the IMF grew accustomed to attaching structural policy conditions to its loans and did so whether the recipient was a Latin American reformer or an Asian tiger.

39. The European currency crisis of 1992–93 had been handled internally and involved IMF only as an observer.

40. Thus, some authors (Sachs, Tornell, and Velasco 1995) have been led to characterize the Mexican episode as purely a crisis of investor confidence.

capital account liberalization placed on emerging markets by the Fund and other multilaterals in this period.

The Asian crisis of 1997–98 and its repercussions in Brazil and globally (with Russia's default and the all-but-failure of Long-Term Capital Management) brought these issues to a head. Suffice it to say that virtually every aspect of IMF intervention was called into question.[41] Yet there is a paradox. At the same time the IMF was so universally excoriated, it came to be seen as more vital that ever to the operation of the global financial system. The obvious manifestation of this was the increase in the fund's resources from 146 billion in special drawing rights (SDR) to SDR 212 billion in the 1998–99 quota review. Until the Asian crisis threatened to become a global crisis, the review had been stalled because of the reluctance of the U.S. Congress to agree to an increase.[42] But once the crisis threatened to reach U.S. shores, debate quickly gave way to action.

11.7 Reform for the Future

At the same time, there is little consensus on desirable directions for reform. In part this reflects disagreement and confusion over the nature of recent crises. The events surrounding the devaluation of the Thai baht on 2 July 1997 could be regarded as a conventional crisis of a sort to which the IMF was accustomed.[43] But the consequences, not only for Thailand but for its neighbors, were unexpectedly severe. Indeed, it was the international spread of the crisis that was particularly perplexing. Growth rates in other

41. The fund was criticized for failing to anticipate the crisis, for paying inadequate attention to the hedge-fund problem, and for inadequately monitoring financial markets. It was attacked for creating moral hazard. Its conditionality was impugned on the grounds that the Asian countries had not entered their crises with monetary and fiscal problems (Thailand to the contrary notwithstanding). Its exchange rate advice was rejected by the champions of currency boards and collective pegs. Demands that insolvent financial intermediaries be closed and the financial system restructured were faulted for damaging confidence in the midst of the crisis. The fund's structural conditions were criticized for exceeding the institution's competence and as poorly attuned to Asian economies' distinctive development model. Its deliberations were criticized as opaque and unrepresentative. About the only feature of the institution that remained free of criticism was the food in the staff cafeteria.

42. Congress was blocking the increase by threatening to attach to the increase in the U.S. quota demands on IMF conditionality of very dubious relevance to the IMF's mission (limitations on government funding of family planning, labor, and environmental issues). Its veto was binding, since members holding over 85 percent of the IMF's quotas had to agree.

43. The baht was overvalued (Chinn and Dooley 1998). The growth of Thailand's export markets (and those of most other Asian countries) had already begun to slow in the second half of 1995. Real estate and other asset valuations had already declined significantly, presaging slower economic growth and problems in the banking system. The current account deficit had ballooned to 8 percent of GDP, presaging serious problems if investors pulled the plug. The IMF saw this problem coming and warned the Thai authorities before the fact. And its program—financial assistance to moderate the demand compression required to close the capital account, conditioned on policy reforms to constrain the rate of growth of domestic credit—was cut from familiar cloth.

Asian countries had slowed at most modestly in 1995–96. No one was warning of unsustainable external positions. The force with which turbulence hit the rest of the region thus constituted a surprise. Asia's plight could not be dismissed as comeuppance for governments that had run unsustainable policies fueled by excessive credit expansion and manifested in dangerously overvalued exchange rates.

In the absence of another diagnosis with clear policy implications, the IMF instinctively prescribed the standard course of treatment. It recommended narrowing budget deficits, hiking interest rates, and closing insolvent financial institutions to restore confidence and attract back flight capital. When these steps failed to calm the markets, the Fund was forced to acknowledge that they had been ineffectual (IMF 1999).

Even with benefit of hindsight, it is not clear what alternative course of treatment would have been better. Two schools emerged, one that attributed the crisis to connected lending, excessive reliance on debt finance, and poor prudential supervision and regulation, which together undermined the resilience of the financial system (Goldstein 1998), and another that ascribed it to investor panic, compounded by the IMF's insistence on pointing to structural problems (Radelet and Sachs 1998; Furman and Stiglitz 1998). With the passage of time there has emerged a synthesis of these views to which most observers now subscribe. However, the weight attached to the components continues to differ. U.S. and European officials, who embrace the view that the Asian crisis was a product of flawed domestic financial systems and drew the lesson that such problems can put global stability at risk, have placed at the top of the international agenda measures to upgrade financial-market governance and supervision.

The vehicles for doing so are international financial codes and standards for everything from auditing and accounting to bankruptcy, insolvency, and corporate governance. To be sure, some emerging markets, in Asia in particular, view these standards as an effort to foist upon them Western modes of corporate and financial governance ill suited to an "Asian model" of high debt gearing and close public-private collaboration. Low-income countries fear that they will be denied market access and multilateral assistance if they are unable to meet the standards of the international community. But there remains no other coherent approach to strengthening financial systems.[44] The most difficult task for the multilaterals is to monitor compliance

44. In principle, it continues in a way that is attuned to the worries of Asian and emerging-market economies. That the Financial Stability Forum includes a number of emerging economies, the BIS (whose Committee of Banking Supervisors is responsible for revision of the Basel international capital standards) has expanded into Asia, and private-sector organizations like the International Accounting Standards Committee include representatives of emerging markets and have subcommittees dedicated to their problems go some way toward meeting their objections.

and publicize their findings in a way that strengthens market discipline without running the risk of precipitating a crisis.[45] Whether the IMF is sufficiently nimble to walk this line remains to be seen.

Group of Seven summiteers, finance ministers, and the governors of the IMF drew the further lesson that the Fund must strengthen its surveillance, of capital markets in particular, in order to better anticipate and avert future crises. This is no easy adaptation for staff schooled in the principles of macroeconomic management but not accounting or corporate governance. This leaves the Fund no alternative but to access the relevant expertise externally.[46]

Asian governments, including Japan's, understandably resist the idea that Asia is a hotbed of "crony capitalism," preferring the interpretation of the crisis that blames the overreaction of investors. This has led them to call for tighter regulation of capital flows, to be achieved by forcing over-the-counter forward currency transactions into organized exchanges, taking steps to prevent large traders from manipulating markets, and cracking down on hedge funds. Unfortunately, it is not clear how these goals can be achieved short of the reimposition of capital and exchange controls and the re-regulation of financial markets. While the over-the-counter market can be taxed, it can move offshore.[47] Hedge funds can be regulated, but they can disguise their transactions. Hong Kong could intervene in the Hang Seng to squeeze speculators, but it is not clear that other governments can do so without casting doubt on their commitment to the market.

The same constraint shapes the debate over the functions of the international financial institutions. The World Bank has taken on board the critique that its role should be to subsidize investments in global public goods like health and environment that, standard economic arguments suggest, private markets undersupply, now that the growth of private capital markets has reduced the need for official sources of development finance.[48] The IMF has accepted that its members should draw on its facilities mainly in times of crisis and not borrow for extended periods. There is agreement that market-based debt restructuring should be relied on more, financial rescues less. Why is there consensus on these points but not on so many others? Simply put, these conclusions reflect the recognition that the role of international financial cooperation is now conceived, as it was once before, in the nineteenth century, as supporting rather than superseding the markets.

---

45. The IMF has taken its first tentative attempts in this direction by releasing several experimental Reviews of Standards and Codes (ROSCs).

46. This is the approach being taken to gathering and analyzing the information needed for the ROSCs that the IMF now proposes to issue for its members, and in the IMF's and World Bank's joint Financial Sector Assessment Programs.

47. From Kuala Lumpur to Singapore, for example.

48. As for whether it will actually curtail its development lending, we will have to see.

11.8   Conclusion

In this essay we have characterized the development of the institutions of international monetary and financial cooperation in evolutionary terms. We have shown that large-scale, comprehensive reform like that which took place in 1944 is extremely rare; it is the exception to the rule. The 1944 reforms were a response to circumstances so unusual (the breakdown of the international monetary and trade regimes in the 1930s, and the world war) that they are unlikely to be repeated. The normal process of change is different. As with many evolutionary processes, punctuated equilibrium seems an appropriate metaphor for its pace and character.

What then determines the nature of the equilibrium and the location of the punctuation marks? We have argued that concerted monetary and financial reform is most likely when there is a consensus on the benefits of free and open trade and when monetary and financial problems are seen as threatening the stability of the global trading system. To take two examples, at Bretton Woods the desire to construct a free and open trading system, and the fear that financial dislocations placed this goal at risk, helped to set the stage for monetary and financial reform; in the 1930s, in contrast, there was no comparable consensus regarding the benefits of free and open trade, and as a result there was no significant reform of the international monetary system.

This insight sheds light on the mixed success of recent efforts to strengthen the international financial architecture. The most durable component of the late-twentieth-century liberal consensus is, once again, the benefits of free and open trade. The fear that monetary disorder might provoke a protectionist backlash consequently provides powerful impetus for reform at the regional level, where trade matters most. When in the early 1990s the crisis in the European Monetary System (EMS) threatened to unleash "competitive devaluations" and jeopardize political support for the single market, Europe accelerated its forced march to monetary union. And when exchange rate volatility disrupted Asian trade following the onset of the region's crisis in 1997–98, Asian policymakers displayed a surprisingly readiness to contemplate ambitious reform initiatives such as swap arrangements, collective pegs, and even a regional monetary fund.

Yet the trading system has proven surprisingly resilient to these financial body blows. Notwithstanding the financial disruptions of the most recent decade, trade has continued to expand.[49] To argue that far-reaching monetary and financial reforms are needed to shield the global trading system

---

49. There have been casualties, to be sure, such as the U.S. president's fast-track authority, efforts to quickly expand the North American Free Trade Agreement into a free trade area for the Americas, and a new round of global trade talks. But it is hard to argue that the global trading system has been seriously placed at risk.

from a destructive protectionist backlash would be a stretch. Absent this threat, it has been difficult to develop a consensus for radical reform of the international monetary and financial system.

To be sure, this is only one of several reasons why nations have not been able to agree on far-reaching changes in international financial institutions and arrangements. No country today possesses the financial power and political leverage of the United States in 1944. The number of consequential players in international negotiations is larger than ever before. Their circumstances and outlooks are more varied. The complexity of negotiations is correspondingly greater. It follows that a nonnegligible portion of progress on monetary and financial reform has been at the regional level, where numbers are smaller, outlooks are more uniform, and exceptional institutions or concentrations of power limit transactions costs. Suffice it to say that no monocausal explanation for the success or failure of particular negotiations (including our own) can be fully adequate. Unfortunately, multifactor explanations (like those hinted at in this paper and summarized in table 11.1) are impossible to test formally, given the small size of the sample.

Still, to the extent that monetary spillovers and financial flows are global and not just regional, there continue to be calls for a global response. Clearly, there will be no global regulatory agency with the power to override national financial policies because there is no appetite for global government.[50] Rather, the response of the international policy community is to embrace international standards as a way of simulating some of the functions of a global regulator.

This agenda for reforming the international monetary and financial system is frequently characterized as historically unprecedented—as demanding of countries that wish to participate in international capital markets a commitment to institutional harmonization unlike anything required of their predecessors. This is the view of both the champions of the standard-centered agenda and of its critics, who see it as intrusive, subversive of national sovereignty, and insensitive to the needs and circumstances of developing countries. Our review of the historical evidence suggests that the initiative is in fact neither as novel nor as unprecedented as these interpretations suggest. In the nineteenth century, as now, reform efforts were centered on international standards designed to stabilize and stimulate international transactions. The difference then was that the pressure for institutional reform and harmonization in the interest of trade expansion and financial stability focused on the monetary standard narrowly defined (and on the gold standard in particular). After World War II the standard

---

50. Although the experience of European Union suggests that there may exist a feasible halfway house, the reaction again the intrusions of European Union regulation, evident in the September 2000 Danish referendum and in British political discourse, suggests that resistance to the construction of institutions of global governance, with significant enforcement powers of their own, will not be easily subdued.

Table 11.1   **International Reform Negotiations: Preconditions and Outcomes**

	Consensus	Time Pressure	Power Politics	Outcome
1867 Paris	Yes	No	Cooperative multilateral	None
1922 Genoa	Yes	No	multilateral	Restored gold standard, central bank cooperation
1929 Paris/the Hague	Yes	No	Antagonistic multilateral	Weak and small international bank
1933 London	No	No	Highly antagonistic multilateral	None
1944 Bretton Woods	Yes	Yes	Bilateral/preponderance United States/United Kingdom	Fixed but adjustable exchange rates, convertibility requirement, rules on deficits, support facilities (IMF)
1970s C20	No	No	Bilateral/preponderance United States/France	Exchange rate choice, IMF remains in existence
1979 EMS	Yes	Yes	Bilateral/preponderance Germany/France	Fixed but adjustable exchange rates, limited intervention requirements
1982 Latin American debt	No	Yes	Unsettled multilateral	New tasks for IMF
1985–87 Plaza/Louvre	No	Yes	Bilateral/preponderance United States/Japan	Intervention, monetary policy coordination
1994–95 Mexico	No	Yes	Weak cooperative	
1997–98 East Asia	No	Yes	Weak cooperative	

to which countries were held was the Articles of the Agreement of the International Monetary Fund, which detailed commitments to current account convertibility and pegged exchange rates. Now the range of monetary and financial standards to which countries are expected to conform is greater: These include not just IMF codes of conduct for monetary and fiscal policies but a lengthy list of international financial standards covering everything from auditing and accounting to bankruptcy and insolvency procedures, prudential supervision and regulation, and corporate governance. This is obviously a response to the rapid internationalization of business activity. Although the scope of these commitments is unprecedented, their nature is not: The new approach is a throwback to the nineteenth century insofar as the markets rather than the multilaterals are the ultimate arbitrators of countries' compliance.

What then accounts for what is new and novel, namely, the scope and ambition of the agenda? Whereas in the nineteenth century adherence to the gold standard was regarded as both necessary and sufficient for a country to be active on international financial markets, adherence to a particular monetary standard is now seen as insufficient. The change reflects the unprecedented extent of financial integration, reflecting technology as well as policy, which has erased the line between domestic and international financial markets and led to the recognition that measures to strengthen and stabilize domestic financial markets are prerequisites for international financial stability.[51] Absent a U-turn away from financial integration, which we think is unlikely, this approach to buttressing financial stability, organized around standards for areas extending well beyond the monetary, is likely to remain the focus of reform efforts for the foreseeable future.

References

Auboin, Roger. 1955. The Bank for International Settlements 1930–1955. Princeton Essays in International Finance no. 22. Princeton University, Department of Economics, International Finance Section.

Blum, John Morton. 1967. From the Morgenthau diaries. Boston: Houghton Mifflin.

Bordo, Michael, Barry Eichengreen, and Douglas Irwin. 1999. Is globalization today really different from globalization a hundred years ago? In Brookings trade forum 1999, ed. Susan M. Collins and Robert Z. Lawrence, 1–72. Washington, D.C.: Brookings Institution Press.

Bordo, Michael D., Barry Eichengreen, Daniela Klingebiel, and Soledad Maria Martinez-Peria. 2001. Is the crisis problem growing more severe? Economic Policy 32:51–82.

Chinn, Menzie, and Michael Dooley. 1998. Monetary policy in Japan, Germany,

---

51. Bordo, Eichengreen, and Irwin (1999) make the case that financial integration today is deeper, wider, and in an economic sense more profound than a hundred years ago.

and the United States: Does one size fit all? NBER Working Paper no. 6092. Cambridge, Mass.: National Bureau of Economic Research, July.

de Vries, Rimmer. 1982. The limited role of the IMF. *World Financial Markets,* April, p. 10.

Eichengreen, Barry. 1992. Golden fetters: The gold standard and the Great Depression 1919–1939. New York: Oxford University Press.

——. 1996. *Globalizing capital: A history of the international monetary system.* Princeton: Princeton University Press.

Eichengreen, Barry, and Paul Masson, with Hugh Bredenkamp, Barry Johnston, Javier Hausmann, Esteban Jadresic, and Inci Otker. 1998. Exit strategies: Policy options for countries seeking greater exchange rate flexibility. IMF Occasional Paper no. 168. Washington, D.C.: International Monetary Fund, August.

Einaudi, Luigi. 2000. From the franc to the "Europe": The attempted transformation of the Latin Monetary Union into a European Monetary Union, 1865–1873. *Economic History Review* 53:284–308.

Feldstein, Martin. 1998. Summary. In *Maintaining financial stability in a global economy,* Federal Reserve Bank of Kansas City, 319–29. Kansas City, Mo.: Federal Reserve Bank of Kansas City.

Fischer, Stanley. 2001. Exchange rate regimes: Is the bipolar view correct? *Journal of Economic Perspectives* 15:3–24.

Flandreau, Marc. 1997. Central bank cooperation in historical perspective: A skeptical view. *Economic History Review* 50:765–63.

Friedman, Irving S. 1977. Evaluation of risk in international lending: A lender's perspective. Boston: Federal Reserve Bank of Boston.

Funabashi, Yoichi. 1998. *Managing the dollar: From the plaza to the Louvre.* Washington, D.C.: Institute for International Economics.

Furman, Jason, and Joseph Stiglitz. 1998. Economic crises: Evidence and insights from East Asia. *Brookings Papers on Economic Activity,* Issue no. 2:1–135. Washington, D.C.: Brookings Institution.

Gallarotti, Giulio. 1995. *The anatomy of an international monetary regime: The classical gold standard, 1880–1914.* New York: Oxford University Press.

Goldstein, Morris. 1998. *The Asian financial crisis.* Washington, D.C.: Institute of International Economics.

——. 2001. An evaluation of proposals to reform the international financial architecture. Washington, D.C.: Institute for International Economics. Unpublished manuscript.

Ikenberry, G. John. 1993. A world economy restored: Expert consensus and the Anglo-American postwar settlement. *International Organization* 46 (1): 155–200.

International Monetary Fund (IMF). 1999. Lessons of the Asian crisis. Washington, D.C.: IMF. Unpublished manuscript.

James, Harold. 1996. *International monetary cooperation since Bretton Woods.* New York: Oxford University Press.

Lopez-Cordoba, José, and Chris Meissner. 2000. Exchange-rate regimes and international trade: Evidence from the classical gold standard era. Working Paper no. COO-118. University of California–Berkeley, Center for International and Developmental Economics Research (CIDER).

Meissner, Chris. 2000. A new world order: Explaining the emergence of the classical gold standard. University of California, Berkeley. Unpublished manuscript.

Mills, J. Saxon. 1922. *The Genoa Conference.* New York: Houghton Mifflin.

Mouré, Kenneth. 2002. *The gold standard illusion: The Bank of France and the international gold standard, 1914–1939.* New York: Oxford University Press.

O'Rourke, Kevin H., and Jeffrey G. Williamson. 1999. *Globalization and history: The evolution of a nineteenth century Atlantic economy.* Cambridge: MIT Press.

Radelet, Steven, and Jeffrey Sachs. 1998. The East Asian financial crisis: Diagnosis, remedies, prospects. *Brookings Papers on Economic Activity,* Issue no. 1:1–174. Washington, D.C.: Brookings Institution.

Reti, Steven. 1998. *Silver and gold: The political economy of international monetary conferences, 1867–1892.* Westport, Conn.: Greenwood Press.

Russell, Henry B. 1898. *International monetary conferences: Their purposes, character, and results.* New York: Harper.

Sachs, Jeffrey, Aaron Tornell, and Andrés Velasco. 1995. Financial crises in emerging markets: The lessons from 1995. *Brookings Papers on Economic Activity,* Issue no. 1:147–215. Washington, D.C.: Brookings Institution.

Santaella, Julio A. 1992. Stabilization programs and external enforcement: Experience from the 1920s. *IMF Staff Papers* 40 (3): 584–621.

Skidelsky, Robert. 1992. *John Maynard Keynes: The economist as savior.* London: Macmillan.

U.S. Senate. 1879. *International Monetary Conference of 1878.* 45th Cong., 3rd sess.

Williamson, John. 2000. Modernizing the international financial architecture. Washington, D.C.: Institute of International Economics. Unpublished manuscript. Available at [http://www.iie.com/paperswilliamson0900-1.htm].

Comment   Peter B. Kenen

The title of this paper led me to expect that Eichengreen and James would concentrate on ways in which globalization influenced the evolution of the monetary and financial system during the last part of the nineteenth century and the last part of the twentieth century. In fact, they take on a much larger task: asking why some reform efforts failed and others succeeded. They set out their hypothesis right away: "That hypothesis is that a consensus on the need for monetary and financial reform is likely to develop when such reform is seen as essential for the defense of the global trading system." In most periods, they say, the monetary and financial system evolves in a gradual manner, largely in response to market forces. Discontinuous reform, by contrast, occurs only when problems in the monetary and financial system are seen as putting the global trading system at risk. This is, they say, a result of the fact that, throughout most of the period under study, there was "deep and abiding faith in the advantages of trade for economic growth" but no "comparable consensus on the benefits of open international capital markets for stability, efficiency, and growth."

This way of interpreting the history of monetary reform has much to commend it. Reforms *do* occur discontinuously. So do other forms of international monetary cooperation. I made the same point several years ago (Kenen 1989), when I said that the episodic nature of policy coordination among the major industrial countries calls into question the way that econ-

Peter B. Kenen is the Walker Professor of Economics and International Finance at Princeton University.

omists usually model policy coordination. It can best be viewed, I said, as a sporadic regime-preserving process, not a continuous policy-optimizing process. I was therefore pleased to note that Eichengreen and James use the same phrase to characterize the episodes studied in their paper.

Nevertheless, I have reservations about the strong form of the hypothesis set out in their paper—one that attaches *exclusive* importance to the preservation of the trading system and little or no intrinsic importance to the preservation of open capital markets or to the influence of the monetary system on the ability of national governments to maintain domestic economic stability.

On several occasions, Eichengreen and James demonstrate clearly that the defense of the trading system *was* indeed the dominant objective of some or all of the governments involved in a particular episode. They quote, for example, the statement by David Lloyd George about the importance of the Genoa Conference for the preservation of the trading system. Soon thereafter, however, they appear to contradict him. They say that the Genoa Conference failed to generate significant reforms because the impending return to the prewar monetary system did not appear to pose a threat to the trading system.

At times, moreover, Eichengreen and James adopt a somewhat dubious strategy. They argue, plausibly enough, that failure to reform the monetary and financial system *would* have done damage to the trading system, and they therefore conclude that defense of the trading system was the rationale for the particular reform at issue. Remember, however, the wording of their own hypothesis. Reform of the monetary and financial system occurs when it "is *seen* as essential" to defend the trading system. To say that the trading system might have been harmed in the absence of monetary reform is different and less compelling than adducing evidence to show that those involved in a particular reform effort were fully cognizant of that possibility.

This brings me to my second reservation about the paper. Some reforms of the monetary and financial system have been trade-regime preserving. The Plaza and Louvre agreements come to mind immediately—although they should perhaps be viewed as examples of ad hoc cooperation rather than examples of full-fledged reform. The dollar crisis of 1971 is another example; although the prevailing exchange rate regime was not seen as a threat to the trading system, the tactics employed by the United States to achieve an exchange rate realignment were widely seen as a serious threat to the trading system.

Consider, however, some other episodes, starting with the Bretton Woods conference of 1944, which was the most comprehensive reform of the international monetary system. No one would deny that the attempt to stabilize exchange rates in the postwar world reflected the common belief that the resort to tariffs and quotas in the 1930s was due in part to the disintegration of the monetary system. Furthermore, the Bretton Woods system attached very little importance to the revival of private capital flows. In other words, trade trumped finance. But Eichengreen and James pay no attention to the other important aim of those who designed the Bretton Woods system—maintaining domestic prosperity in the postwar world. Nor do they pay enough attention to domestic matters in their account of reform—or its absence—during the nineteenth century. The failure of the 1867 Paris Conference to produce a meaningful reform of the monetary system was not, I believe, due mainly to the absence of any grave threat to the trading system. It appears to have reflected lack of agreement about the best way to achieve domestic monetary stability.

Leaping forward once again, this time to the 1980s, the reforms or ad hoc arrangements—call them what you will—adopted to cope with the Latin American debt crisis reflected concerns about the vulnerability of the U.S. banking system. They had very little to do with trade, except in the tautological sense that, left to themselves, the crisis-stricken countries might have imposed import controls that would have been marginally disruptive of the trading system. (The paper notes that trade contracted in the early 1980s when measured in nominal terms, but that was due to the recession and subsequent stagflation in the industrial countries and to the fall in the price of oil, not to major trade-policy changes or the debt crisis itself.)

Coming at last to the 1990s, I am not persuaded that the steps taken to deal with the Asian crisis, whatever their merits or defects, reflected deep worries about the effects of the crisis on the trading system. By that time, if not earlier, the official community was strongly committed to the integrity of an international financial system friendly to private capital flows, as well as the liberalization of trade in financial services. How else can one explain the ill-fated push for capital account convertibility on the eve of the Asian crisis? How else can one explain the importance attached to financial-sector reform in the crisis-stricken countries and the ongoing attempt to foster compliance with international codes and standards defining "best practice" in the public, financial, and corporate sectors?

Eichengreen and James rightly observe that the commitment to an open trading system has been an "abiding" commitment, whereas the commitment to open capital markets has waxed and waned. This fact by itself, however, should not cause us to minimize the importance of the sporadic commitment to open capital markets when we interpret attempts to reform the international monetary system.

Before turning to the last part of the paper, let me draw attention to a monetary reform—the move to European monetary union—that does support the thesis of this paper. Eichengreen and James mention it only in passing, because they limit themselves to reform of the global monetary system. Yet the move to European monetary union was in part the consequence of a perceived threat to the trading system. The timing of the move owes much to the adoption of the Single European Act, which required the rapid elimination of all controls on intra-European capital movements and thus posed a threat to the viability of the EMS. Padoa-Schioppa (1988) laid out the implications. If the EMS was not replaced by a full-fledged monetary union, it would succumb eventually to an exchange rate crisis and give way to greater exchange rate flexibility within the European Community. But large exchange rate changes would threaten the integrity of the single market by generating pressures for covert protection—and that is what actually happened during the EMS crisis of 1992–93 (see, e.g., Eichengreen 1996). In short, the move to monetary union cannot be explained without citing the threat to the trading system posed by the removal of capital controls.

In the last part of their paper, Eichengreen and James make some intriguing statements about the current attempt to reform the international financial system.

One of those statements pertains to the role of international standards and codes in promoting domestic adaptation to the integration of financial markets. Eichengreen and James are right to point out that the scope of this effort is unprecedented, but they go on to argue that the strategy is not new—that it is a throwback to the nineteenth century because it involves global standardization and "insofar as the markets rather than the multilaterals are the ultimate arbitrators of countries' compliance." If that proves to be true, however, it will be because the various standards and codes have been poorly designed for the purpose at hand. They attempt to define "best practice" rather than minimally acceptable practice. As a result, developing countries have insisted that they be judged by the progress they make, not the level of compliance they achieve, and they have thus far blocked any attempt by the official sector to devise and apply incentives and penalties designed to promote compliance with the new standards and codes.[1] But markets don't care very much about progress; they are—and should be—interested in absolute compliance. Therefore, they are not likely to make much sense or much use of the ongoing official assessments of compliance, which also emphasize progress.

The second statement pertains to the role of the IMF. "There is," we are told, "agreement that market-based debt restructuring should be relied on more, financial rescues less." This is true but says very little. The official community has used similar language ever since the Mexican crisis but has continued to engage in financial rescues. A seemingly innocuous sentence in a communiqué of the IMF's International Monetary and Financial Committee points to the unresolved problem. It "reaffirms the exceptional character of financing beyond normal access limits, and repeats that reliance on

---

1. For evidence to this effect, compare two documents, the *Issue Paper of the Task Force on Implementation of Standards* (Financial Stability Forum 2000a), which contains a long list of incentives and penalties that might be employed by the official sector, and the *Report of the Follow-Up Group on Incentives to Foster Implementation of Standards* (Financial Stability Forum 2000b), which backs away from most of them.

the catalytic approach at high levels of access must presume substantial justification" (IMF 2001). Let me translate that from fundspeak into ordinary English. Up to now, the committee is saying, official financing has been regarded as best way to catalyze voluntary private-sector involvement in crisis resolution. If we limit official financing to "ordinary" levels, can we expect to catalyze that sort of involvement, or will we have to rely more heavily on other, "concerted" ways of involving the private sector? There is, to be sure, little enthusiasm for large-scale official financing, partly because of concern about moral hazard. But there is less than full agreement on the best way to do without it.

References

Eichengreen, Barry. 1996. *A more perfect union? The logic of economic integration.* Essays in International Finance no. 198. Princeton University, Department of Economics. International Finance Section.
Financial Stability Forum. 2000a. Issue paper of the Task Force on Implementation of Standards, 15 March. Basel, Switzerland: Financial Stability Forum.
———. 2000b. Report of the Follow-Up Group on Incentives to Foster Implementation of Standards, 31 August. Basel, Switzerland: Financial Stability Forum.
International Monetary Fund. 2001. Communiqué of the International Monetary and Financial Committee of the Board of Governors, 29 April. Washington, D.C.: IMF.
Kenen, Peter B. 1989. *Exchange rates and policy coordination.* Manchester, U.K.: Manchester University Press.
Padoa-Schioppa, Tommaso. 1988. The European Monetary System: A long-term view. In *The European Monetary System,* ed. F. Giavazzi, S. Micossi, and M. Miller, 369–84. Cambridge: Cambridge University Press.

Globalization in Interdisciplinary Perspective
A Panel

Clive Crook
Gerardo della Paolera
Niall Ferguson
Anne O. Krueger
Ronald Rogowski

Clive Crook

History has shown us that globalization is reversible. It was in fact cata-strophically reversed after 1914, and the earlier trend toward international economic integration was not then reestablished until after 1945. Two world wars and a Great Depression in between is thankfully an extreme scenario. What history does not tell us very clearly is whether something less than a cataclysm of that magnitude is capable of reversing globalization—in particular, whether globalization might be interrupted and set back by the action of democratic politics, at a time of comparative peace and prosperity.

Certainly globalization has a powerful economic momentum of its own. Technological progress, left to its own devices, promotes integration. And there is more to it than that, because integration tends to undermine certain kinds of economic regulation. In finance, which has globalized as much as any industry one can think of, technology and deregulation (sometimes reluctant deregulation) have created a self-reinforcing mechanism pushing strongly in that direction. Integration seems in many ways a natural economic process, which can only be reversed, if at all, when policies are deliberately framed to that end.

But political support for just such policies is on the rise. The antiglobalization protests in Seattle marked a dramatic escalation. But what is most striking, and most worrying, about that protest and the others that have followed it is the measure of tacit support that the protesters command among ordinary citizens. The view that globalization hurts workers and keeps poor

Clive Crook is deputy editor of *The Economist*.

countries poor is widely shared. Opinion polls on globalization and on trade agreements such as the North American Free Trade Agreement (NAFTA) show lukewarm support, at best. And politicians, even those supposedly committed to liberal trade, are beginning to respond to voters' anxieties.

Bill Clinton said he wanted to see the Seattle protesters inside the meeting, not out on the street. At the April 2001 Summit of the Americas meeting in Quebec City, George Bush, making his first appearance on the world stage, said that "Our commitment to open trade must be matched by a strong commitment to protecting our environment and improving labor standards." Lori Wallach of Public Citizen, an antiglobalist group, said, "You could have dialed 911 when I heard what Bush said. I needed to be resuscitated. When we started organizing and educating on trade in the early '90s, no one but a handful of progressive Democrats understood what we were talking about. And now comes Mr. Trade-uber-alles Bush, saying we need to respect labor and environmental concerns. It shows the political shift. Now we've got to see the policy shift" (Paul Blustein, "Protests a Success of Sorts: Labor, Environment on Leaders' Agenda," *Washington Post,* 22 April 2001, p. A11).

If it comes, it will be because governments have responded so inadequately to voters' fears. I count seven main worries about globalization, most of them already touched on in earlier remarks. First is the fear that wages of low-skill workers will fall in markets that face cheap imports. Second, that economic insecurity will increase for almost everyone: As economic change speeds up, nobody has a job for life. Third, that patterns of existing income support and other forms of subsidy will become more explicit, and therefore harder to sustain (farm support in the European Union would be one example). Fourth, that poverty in developing countries gets worse because of "unbalanced growth." Fifth, that social spending falls under pressure of "international competitiveness." Sixth, another kind of race to the bottom, that environmental standards come under pressure. Seventh, that much international trade is "unfair" because it is based on exploitation.

To varying degrees, fears four through seven are misconceived, on my reading of the evidence—yet, far from saying so, governments and international institutions either endorse them or, at best, ignore them. What President Bush said in Quebec City, for instance, endorses the view that globalization, unless carefully managed, poses a threat to the environment. That is why Wallach was right to be pleased. Fears one through three, on the other hand, have some basis in reality. In these cases, the right response from governments would be policies aimed at mitigating the problems: better training policies, say, more generous wage-insurance policies, or mechanisms for buying out interest groups that have acquired a kind of property right over subsidy. None of this gets much attention.

Politically this is the worst of all worlds. Governments bolster rather than repudiate the false antiglobalization arguments, and fail to respond to the ones that have some force. And if all that were not bad enough, they also deploy false arguments of their own to support the case in favor—for instance, the argument that trade liberalization creates jobs. People are suspicious of that argument, and they are right to be, of course, because it is wrong. Really there can be very little mystery about weak popular support for globalization.

How far, if at all, does globalization require our big social goals to be traded off against each other? Dani Rodrik has argued that the question can be seen as involving a "trilemma," somewhat like the well-known exchange rate trilemma. Just as countries must choose only two from capital mobility, exchange rate stability, and monetary independence, so they are constrained to choose just two from economic integration, the social contract (meaning high levels of social spending), and national sovereignty. If you choose national sovereignty and high social spending, you must take steps to impede integration (otherwise, for instance, tax competition kicks in). This is the antiglobalists' choice. If you choose sovereignty and integration, you must scale down your ambitions for social provision. Judging by their own policy announcements, this is a choice that many Western governments have often made. Finally, if you choose integration and high social spending, avoiding the race to the bottom requires you to embark on closer international economic cooperation (level playing fields of labor-market regulation, tax harmonization in Europe, and so on), thus inhibiting your sovereignty.

As I have said, though, the "race to the bottom" argument is flawed—and just plain wrong when applied to social spending. This plausible-seeming trilemma is much more about perceived political constraints than economic constraints. Integration and sovereignty can happily coexist with high levels of social spending—as indeed they do. Come to Europe. High-income countries can choose and sustain high levels of social protection, redistribution, and regulation if they wish to. Tax competition, even on corporate taxes (where you might expect it to be intense), has had only limited effects. The European model of social provision is not, so far as one can tell, being crushed under the pressure of global competition.

Despite this, the trilemma seems to sum up the political options, at least as implied by what governments tell their voters. The argument for political integration within Europe is put to citizens as though the trilemma were true. You could argue that the case for bringing labor and environmental standards within the jurisdiction of the World Trade Organization (a case that President Bush, at any rate, is willing to entertain) points the same way. And the recent vogue for free-trade areas such as NAFTA may also owe something to the idea that a balance involving less sovereignty (or less integration?) is needed to defend the rich countries' economic settlement.

Globalization, on this view, poses difficult choices—choices perhaps best avoided altogether. This view is wrong, on the evidence, but governments are failing to say so. The case for integration is strong, but nobody is making it. The case against integration is weak, but leaders are implicitly conceding it. Given all this, the possibility is surely real that opposition to integration might one day succeed in slowing or even reversing globalization, despite its extraordinary benefits over the past fifty years.

Gerardo della Paolera

This conference offered a wonderful menu of papers written by the best minds in economic history and economics to tackle a perennial, but still unresolved, issue: globalization. A "dream team" was assembled to take up the challenge of grasping the issues of globalization: its causes, historical roots, and welfare consequences. To use Woody Allen's expression, everything you always wanted to know about globalization and history, but did not dare to ask, could be found in this conference.

Or almost everything. Maybe you thought you would leave the conference with a definitive handbook on globalization, but you ended up with still more questions and a vast agenda for future research. I believe most of us are thankful for standing on the shoulders of Jeffrey Williamson's (1996) pathbreaking work on globalization and history, which he began long before globalization became a buzzword. This and subsequent works have opened up new directions to our understanding of the globalization process and its impact on the welfare and attitudes of the many heterogeneous actors that participate in the world economy.

Before jumping to some reflections on the view of globalization from my own viewpoint in a persistently peripheral country, Argentina, let me reframe some of the main questions that were asked here.

- Are globalization and convergence connected?
- What are the transmission mechanisms that spur a global economy, and how strong are their interrelationships? For example, the movement of goods and services (purchasing power parity or arbitrage conditions are a long-run "must" in an integrated world economy), money (interest rate parity), and people and capital, technology, geography, and so on?
- In support of the convergence and globalization process, which institutions take center stage, and which are in the wings?

Here I offer some reflections on these questions, as far as I could distill answers from the output of this impressive conference.

Gerardo della Paolera is president and professor of economics at the American University of Paris and visiting fellow at Fundacion Pent in Buenos Aires, Argentina.

First, taking the very long view, it looks as if convergence—and hence globalization—is a temporary though recurrent phenomenon. This transpires clearly from the DeLong-Dowrick and Eichengreen-James papers. If this is the case, it is particularly important for the developing and emerging-market countries, some of which are eternal candidates to join the ranks of the "truly" integrated nations. To explain the nonmonotonic aspects of this process, pure and simple economic models are not sufficient. Certainly it is always the case that a developing economic ethos can unleash strong forces: Under grotesque economic distortions even slight improvements will set in motion dynamics for more integration and growth. Still, how long will this process last? The existence of dramatic reversals of fortune in historical experience, most spectacularly the divergence of Argentina, is a phenomenon that calls for more than what conventional unadorned neoclassical models can offer. For example, the historical and institutional facts presented by Eichengreen and James for interwar Europe are crucial to our understanding of the contemporary tensions between the developed and the developing world.

Second, an important aspect in explaining divergences and reversals is to relate the globalization process to the transition economies. I was very surprised by Anne Krueger's statement that globalization and transition are two entirely different issues: They are not for a developing society. Transition economies are generally classified relative to a benchmark that uses as a reference the set of institutions and policies adopted by the core societies. In this perspective, to understand developing countries' stop-and-go cycles in the convergence process (for example, the jumps in income distribution described in the Williamson-Lindert paper) will require much closer attention to the degree of institutional development and the political-economy process. To give an example, in the very good textbook on transition economies by Roland (2000), I was surprised to see that, even though the author is dealing almost entirely with open economies, the word *globalization* is not quoted in the index. Scholars should talk to each other!

Third, we must recognize the importance of truncated political-economy reforms—which many times will produce true and perceived reversals in the globalization cost-benefit calculus for a peripheral economy. In dynamic terms this is precisely a manifestation of the second-best theorem: When an economy is trapped with one or more big distortions, after a while the remaining Pareto improvements are not attainable, and under stress they may become less and less desirable. Thus, if you cannot engineer a well-behaved take-off toward integration with the world economy, the engines of modernization might stop and crash, and a reversal is likely to occur. Argentina is the most remarkable—and for me, most sad—historical and contemporaneous example.

Fourth, if the frequency of stop-and-go cycles in the integration of emerging-market societies is very high, wherein failure is the norm, the citizenry may finally adopt more credible foreign institutions. Argentina again is a good case in point, the most notable example being the Argentines' demand for an American institution, by their de facto (if not yet de jure) adoption of the U.S. dollar, now almost the only money of use after successive governments abused the inflation tax. This reality, where a group or subgroup can start importing institutions (again we might think of responses by the "losers" and "winners") is a striking new element that demands attention in any analysis of globalization and how it can ultimately constrain the voracity of politicians and rent-seekers.

Therefore, I think we take away from this conference an extraordinary panorama of what happened to the world economy in the last two or more centuries. It is now well understood that, at the end of the day, an enlargement of global integration was a world-welfare-improving development—but then, how can we account for all those incredible stop-and-go stages? One explanation, à la Patrick O'Brien, might eventually be constructed around a very difficult metanarrative, engaging a variety of factors from hypocrisy to incompetence. However, the introduction of the dynamics of institutions as causing particular economic outcomes seems essential. The unbalanced speed of reforms among those who want to join the "convergence club" is the main cause for political-economy design failures. The nature of human capital, and its specificity, also raises the question as to how one can cope with or undo such social or human capital obsolescence.

To sum up, I basically came to envisage the intimate linkages that I have discussed here because they came to the fore during the heat of debate during the conference, thanks to the extraordinary crowd of scholars that only Jeff, Mike, and Alan could have gathered here in globalized Santa Barbara.

References

Roland, Gerard. 2000. *Transition and economics: Politics, markets, and firms.* Cambridge: MIT Press.
Williamson, Jeffrey G. 1996. Globalization, convergence, and history. *Journal of Economic History* 56 (2): 277–310.

Niall Ferguson

What would a universal society be like which would have no particular country, which would be neither French nor English, nor German, nor Spanish, nor Portuguese, nor Italian, nor Russian, nor Tartar, nor Turkish, nor Persian, nor Indian, nor Chinese, nor American, or rather which would be all of these societies at the same time? . . . Under what similar rule, under what single law would this society exist? (François René, vicomte de Chateaubriand, 1841[1])

Niall Ferguson is professor of political and financial history at Jesus College, University of Oxford.
1. Quoted by Emma Rothschild (1999).

In many ways, the conference that produced this volume was itself a metaphor for globalization. A majority of the participants—65 percent—were employed by American institutions, though I suspect that not much more than half were American-born. (This could be taken as evidence either that the global market for intellectual capital is not perfectly integrated and that some "home bias" operated in the selection of contributors, or that flows of intellectual capital, both inherited and acquired, have for some time been disproportionately toward the United States.) As one of the minority of non-American participants, I found it very easy, in the space of just a few days, to travel from Oxford to Santa Barbara and back again: a journey which, if my great grandfather had made it a hundred years ago, would have been once-in-a-lifetime and one-way. David Lodge's satire of academic globalization *Small World* was published in 1984. That world is even smaller today. On the second day of our conference, I was able to read—in the international edition of the London *Financial Times*—this exemplary vignette: "A man thought to be the eldest son and heir-apparent of Kim Jong-il, the North Korean leader, arrived in China yesterday after having been deported from Tokyo for trying to enter Japan on a fake passport to visit Disneyland. . . . His companions carried Louis Vuitton suitcases" (Gillian Tett, "Japan Deports North Korean Leader's Son to China," *Financial Times,* 5/6 May 2001). The fact that globalization applies to politics as well as economics is one of the messages of table 1, which offers a simple schema of globalization. The first column lists what can be regarded as "givens" about the globe we inhabit; the second lists those things that can flow around that globe; the third lists the mechanisms that facilitate such flows; the fourth lists the policies that allow those mechanisms to operate.

I have highlighted in bold type the aspects of globalization that, with a few exceptions, the main chapters in this volume neglect. Economists and

Table 1   **Globalization: An Overview**

Given (more or less)	Flows	Mechanism	Policy
Laws of physics: gravity, second law of thermodynamics, etc.	Goods	Transport technology	Free trade
Human biology	Capital	Communications technology	Free capital flows
Climate	Labor	Financial markets and institutions	Free migration
Topography	Technology	Nongovernmental organizations	Free information flows
Resource endowment	Services	Government	The rule of law
	Institutions		Monetary standards
	Knowledge		Fiscal transparency
	Crises		Coercion
	Crime		Conquest
	Disease		

economic historians alike tend to focus their attention on flows of commodities, capital, and labor when trying quantify and periodize the process
of globalization. However, there are other flows that are susceptible to globalization: Flows of technology and services have been discussed, though in
less detail, but relatively little has been said about flows of disease, institutions, knowledge, culture, and "crises" (the process whereby a particular
event like a revolution or a financial crisis is transmitted by a kind of mime-
sis around the world).[2] The history of the fourteenth century would be in-
comprehensible without the globalization of the bubonic plague, just as the
conquest of the Americas by Europeans would not have happened so easily without the export of infectious diseases, which decimated native populations. As well as infections, the conquistadors and colonists brought institutions and ideas: the Church and Christianity in the first place (witness
the old Spanish Mission at Santa Barbara, which existed to convert the indigenous Chumash people), later the idea of representative government
and democracy. Slow and erratic though it has been, the process of global
democratization since the 1770s illustrates the way both institutions and
ideas can be spread internationally as readily as goods can be traded across
borders or money invested abroad. And the phenomenon of contagion, familiar to students of international money and capital markets, has its political counterpart in the international revolutionary waves after 1789, 1848,
1917, and 1989.

Economic historians also tend to pay more attention to the ways government can facilitate globalization by various kinds of deregulation (the first
four items in the last column of the table) than to the ways it can promote
globalization more actively. It is only relatively recently that we have come
to understand the importance of political institutions—the rule of law,
credible monetary systems, and transparent fiscal systems—in encouraging
cross-border capital flows. Little work, by contrast, has been done on the
way globalization can be imposed by the use of force. "Empire" is the concept that seems to lurk between the lines of a number of the preceding chapters, which have perhaps discussed the economic globalization of the eighteenth and nineteenth centuries with too little regard for the remarkable
political globalization brought about by the European empires in the same
period.

Before discussing these issues further I would like to sketch the methodological problems that seem to me to arise when we attempt to historicize a
modern concept like globalization. There is something very alluring about
the story implied by the "U" shape visible in some charts depicting long-run
levels of capital mobility. In this narrative, we find ourselves at the right-
hand side of the U, where international capital flows have resumed a rela-

---

2. For a useful introduction to the noneconomic facets of globalization see Held et al.
(1999).

tive importance not seen since the 1900s. The notion captured by the U—that there have therefore been two eras of globalization—makes sense if we are interested only in flows of commodities, people, and capital. But it makes much less sense if we are talking about flows of culture or disease.[3] A further question is whether or not we regard our model of globalization as "closed." Are certain things exogenous—for example, wars, so often caricatured by economists as "exogenous shocks"? Within the model, what is the direction of causation? Does it run from trade to capital flows or migration, from the development of the financial system to industrialization, or from globalization to international monetary systems?

A simpler question to ask might be: How much distance does a flow have to cover to qualify as global? Or does it just have to cross an international border? If so, we must ask ourselves why that particular criterion has been chosen, given the enormous variety in the sizes and longevity of nation-states. And in a similar vein, why privilege transoceanic flows of goods, capital, and labor? Was the trans-Siberian railway not as much a part of nineteenth-century globalization as the transatlantic steamship routes?

A further set of questions relates to the nature of the flows themselves. Are long-term flows more important than short-term flows? The question is usually asked with respect to capital flows, but one could also pose the question about movements of people: Is tourism less important than permanent migration? Are we more interested in gross flows than net flows? As Obstfeld and Taylor show in chapter 3 in this volume, this can make a big difference to our assessment of the scale of recent financial globalization, which looks much less impressive when net flows are measured. Does it matter if globalization is even or uneven? An important difference between the world of 1901 and the world of 2001 is that a much higher proportion of commodity trade and capital flows goes on within the developed economies, to the exclusion of the rest of the world. Around 63 percent of foreign direct investment in 1913 went to developing countries, whereas in 1996 the proportion was just 28 percent (Baldwin and Martin 1999, 20). In many respects, it appears, modern globalization is not really global at all. Finally, does competition matter? Or, to put it differently, are we mainly interested in the extent to which market forces are free? This is an important question to address, since the advance guard of globalization in the eighteenth century was made up of aggressive monopolistic trading companies like the East India Company, whereas in the twentieth century the Soviet system had considerable success in continentalizing, if not globalizing, the system of the planned economy in the greater part of what used to be called the "Eurasian land mass."

Each pair of authors has given a different implicit answer to these questions. To my mind, however, our most serious omission is that there is no

---

3. See Diamond (1997).

chapter in this book about "political globalization," with the partial exception of Eichengreen and James's chapter on global financial architecture. That there is a political dimension to the phenomenon is clear from almost every contribution. Crafts and Venables suggest that, given the geographical unevenness of industrial and urban development, there may still be a role for tariffs in modern policy; Chiswick and Hatton emphasize the importance of forced migration (slavery) and immigration restrictions in long-run trends in convergence and divergence; Lindert and Williamson point to the importance of bad government in limiting the benign effects of economic globalization; and Rousseau and Sylla demonstrate the linkage from warfare to financial innovation. Even Bordo and Flandreau's idea of "original sin"—the lack of which allows a country to issue bonds in its own currency—alludes implicitly to the enduring importance of political events, since most historic "sins" of currency depreciation were consequences of unsuccessful warfare. There is a general assumption that, in the periodization of globalization, the year 1914 was a watershed, a date whose significance is, needless to say, primarily political. Yet on what seems to me the most important aspect of political globalization—the role of *empires*—there is an uneasy silence, apart from an aside in Clark and Feenstra to the effect that their role is not important compared with the mysterious "factor C" that accounts for differences in total factor productivity.

That empires did not (and do not) matter in globalization seems implausible. Perhaps the most striking political fact about the period from around 1880 until 1939 was that a small number of European countries governed an inordinately large amount of the rest of the world. On the eve of the First World War, Great Britain, France, Belgium, Holland, and Germany—which between them accounted for around 0.9 percent of the world's land surface and 7.5 percent of its population—ruled in the region of 33 percent of the rest of the world's area and 27 percent of its people (Townsend 1941, 19). All of Australasia, nearly all of Polynesia, 90 percent of Africa, and 56 percent of Asia were under some form of European rule. And although only 27 percent of the American continent—mainly Canada—found itself in the same condition, nearly all the rest had been ruled from Europe at one time or another in the seventeenth and eighteenth centuries.

The economic implications hardly need to be spelled out. The history of the integration of international commodity markets in the seventeenth and eighteenth centuries is inseparable from the process of imperial competition between Portugal, Spain, Holland, France, and Great Britain. The spread of free trade and the internationalization of capital markets in the nineteenth century are both inseparable from the expansion of British imperial, and especially naval, power. Is it really conceivable that there would have been so much migration as well as capital export from Western Europe to the less developed economies of the world—and hence so much global convergence before 1914—without the encouragements and reassurances of empire? By the same token, the eclipse of globalization in the middle of the twentieth century was in large measure a consequence of the immensely costly and destructive challenge to British hegemony mounted by Germany between 1914 and 1918. Nothing did more than the First World War to promote alternative models of economic organization to that of the international free market. War was actively waged against seaborne trade. Yet, according to Taylor's earlier figures, the years 1914 to 1919 also saw the pre-1990s peak of international capital flows measured by the size of current account deficits and surpluses in relation to gross domestic product (GDP) (Taylor 1996). In the same way, it was the various wartime experiments with the control of trade and foreign exchange, the centralized allocation of raw materials, and the rationing of consumption, that provided the inspiration for later theories of economic planning in the Soviet Union and elsewhere.

Trying to conceive of the history of empire as a chapter in the history of globalization raises some fascinating questions. The British Empire in the nineteenth century, for example, can be understood in part as an agency for imposing free trade and the rule of law directly on about a quarter of the world's land surface and indirectly on a great many other places, to say nothing of the world's oceans. If we believe that economic openness is good, then, by extension, one might have expected some global benefit to result from this immense undertaking. (Interestingly, this is not the way most British economic historians have tended to approach the question: The debate has almost always been about the costs and the benefits of the empire to Great Britain.) Yet there is a paradox. India, more than any other major economy, had free trade and Western commercial norms imposed upon it. Yet the result was deindustrialization and economic stagnation. The United States, by contrast, threw off British rule and adopted the kind of protectionist tariff rates—averaging 44 percent on imported manufactures—that we would now condemn in a developing economy (Bairoch 1989). The result? By the end of the nineteenth century the United States overtook the United Kingdom by most measures of economic performance (see fig. 1). Clark's figures for labor productivity in the cotton industry are even more startling: In 1944 an American textile worker could doff 606 spindles per hour, compared with 354 for a British worker and just 124 for an Indian.

Conversely, the globalization of warfare in the twentieth century must bear a large share of the responsibility for the breakdown of international trade, capital flows, and migration. The wars of the eighteenth and nineteenth centuries had already ranged over a huge area, of course: Think only of the global character of the Seven Years' War. But these imperial wars were circumscribed by the available military technology and the limited coercive powers of government. At most, even the French Revolutionary and Napoleonic wars put together accounted for the lives of 0.3 percent of the world's population. It was only in the twentieth century that it became pos-

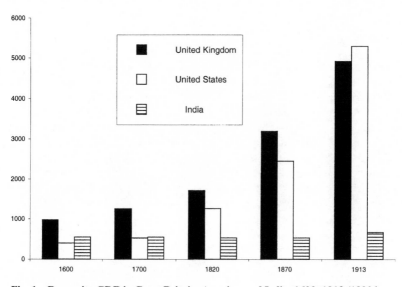

Fig. 1   Per capita GDP in Great Britain, America, and India, 1600–1913 (1990 international dollars)
Source: Maddison (2001, p. 264, table B-21).

sible to mobilize men—and kill men, women, and children—in millions. The total death toll of the Second World War was in the region of 57 million, around 2.4 percent of the world's population.[4]

More cheering, though no less remarkable, has been the globalization of democracy as a political institution. According to some estimates, more than half the world's countries were democracies in the 1990s, for the first time in history (see fig. 2). In part, democratization has been a consequence of decolonization, but it is also the fulfillment of "that irresistible revolution," which de Tocqueville detected already in the 1830s, "which has advanced for centuries in spite of every obstacle and which is still advancing in the midst of the ruins it has caused" (de Tocqueville [1835] 1945, 3, 7).

What is the relationship between the globalization of democracy and the globalization of the market? There are those who would like to think of the two processes as self-reinforcing. Yet the evidence on this point is ambiguous. To cite just one example, one phenomenon associated with (and perhaps fomented by) democratization has been political fragmentation. As democracy has spread, so the number of recognized states has risen from 74 in 1946 to 192 fifty years later. According to Alesina, Spolaore, and Wacziarg (1997), this process may impose some costs in terms of economic inefficiency (1, 23). It certainly imposes costs if secession is accompanied, as it often has been, by civil war. A striking paradox, in short, is that

---

4. My own calculations: for details see Ferguson (2001, appendix 1).

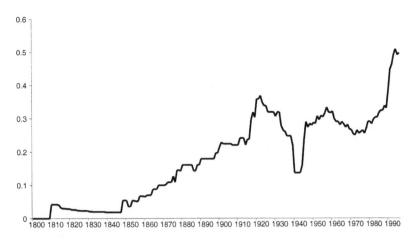

Fig. 2   Proportion of states in the world with a Polity III score of between 7 and 10 out of 10, 1880–1996
Source: Kristian S. Gleditsch and Michael D. Ward (adapted from the Polity III database)

nineteenth-century globalization coincided with political centralization, whereas today it seems to coincide with political fragmentation.

The evidence that economic openness raises living standards—or would, if the world economy were truly globalized—looks compelling, even if globalization will always have its losers, as hitherto privileged or protected social groups are exposed to international competition. But the principal barriers to an optimal allocation of labor, capital, and goods in the world are again in large measure political: On the one hand, civil wars and corrupt governments, which together (as Lindert and Williamson argue) have condemned so many countries in sub-Saharan Africa and parts of Asia to decades of immiserization; on the other, the reluctance of the United States and her allies to devote more than a trifling share of their vast resources to programs of economic aid, effective peacemaking, and the policing of "rogue" states. It is worth recalling that, at the time this conference took place, the conventional wisdom was that the new Republican administration should cut back America's military presence abroad.[5]

The events of 11 September 2001 put paid to such isolationist daydreams by demonstrating that political violence also has the potential to be globalized. It is a sobering thought that the very same planes that carried this book's contributors to their conference in May could have been used as weapons of mass murder just four months later. The dangers of neglecting the political dimensions of globalization have, regrettably, become much clearer since we met.

5. See O'Hanlon (2001).

References

Alesina, Alberto, Enrico Spolaore, and Romain Wacziarg. 1997. Economic integration and political disintegration. NBER Working Paper no. 6163. Cambridge, Mass.: National Bureau of Economic Research.

Bairoch, P. European trade policy, 1815–1914. 1989. In *The Cambridge economic history of Europe.* Vol. 8, ed. P. Mathias and S. Pollard, 1–160. Cambridge: Cambridge University Press.

Baldwin, Richard E., and Philippe Martin. 1999. Two waves of globalization: Superficial similarities, fundamental differences. NBER Working Paper no. 6904. Cambridge, Mass.: National Bureau of Economic Research, January.

Diamond, Jared. 1997. *Guns, germs, and steel: A short history of everybody for the last 13,000 years.* London: Jonathan Cape.

Ferguson, Niall. 2001. *The cash nexus: Money and power in the modern world, 1700–2000.* New York: Basic Books.

Held, David, Anthony McGrew, David Goldblatt, and Jonathan Perraton. 1999. *Global transformations: Politics, economics, and culture.* Cambridge, U.K.: Polity Press.

Lodge, David. 1984. *Small world: An academic romance.* London: Secker & Warburg.

Maddison, Angus. 2001. *The world economy: A millennial perspective.* Washington, D.C.: Organization for Economic Cooperation and Development.

O'Hanlon, Michael. 2001. Come partly home, America: How to downsize O.S. deployments abroad. *Foreign Affairs* (March/April): 2–8.

Rothschild, Emma. 1999. Globalization and the return of history. *Foreign Policy* (Summer): 106–16.

Taylor, Alan. 1996. International capital mobility in history: The savings-investment relationship. NBER Working Paper no. 5743. Cambridge, Mass.: National Bureau of Economic Research.

Tocqueville, Alexis de. 1945. *Democracy in America,* ed. Phillips Bowen, rev. by Francis Bowen, trans. Henry Reeve. Vol. 1. New York: Vintage Books.

Townsend, Mary Evelyn. 1941. *European colonial expansion since 1871.* Chicago: J. P. Lippincott Company.

Anne O. Krueger

There is a natural unease among economists and others about the current backlash against globalization. A large part of that unease originates from our understanding of the effects of globalization: In large measure, we believe that the evidence shows that the "ascent of man" has at a minimum been accelerated by, and at a maximum been enabled by, the phenomena that are now called "globalization" and that are under attack. But part of it stems from failure to recognize that there have always been opponents of change, and that there have always been opponents of the phenomena associated with globalization.

My comparative advantage lies in interpreting U.S. trade policy and in discussing the effects of globalization on the prospects for growth and

Anne O. Krueger is the first deputy managing director of the International Monetary Fund and a research associate of the National Bureau of Economic Research.

poverty reduction in developing countries. The change in tone in trade policy discussions, and the reactions of internationalists to it, probably reflects our failure to recognize the sources of change, and I will address that first. Thereafter, I will turn to the effects of globalization on developing countries' prospects for improved well-being, an instance where those protesting globalization seem to be largely ignorant of the facts.

Any economic historian can tell us that protectionist pressures, and resistance to freer trade, are not new. But those pressures have changed markedly over time, both in their political effectiveness and in their intensity. In the case of the United States, on which I shall concentrate, U.S. foreign trade policy was largely determined by Cold War considerations in the post–World War II era, supported by a coalition of humanitarians. The "realists"—that is, the Cold Warriors—wanted open trade and foreign aid in order to build alliances and support allies in the Cold War. The humanitarians wanted open trade and foreign aid because they wanted economic development in poor countries. This alliance between the realists and the idealists provided a fairly strong political support base for those policies that we would today associate with proglobalization. This included support for the international financial institutions (IFIs) and the regional development banks, the General Agreement on Tariffs and Trade (now the World Trade Organization), bilateral foreign aid, and successive rounds of very successful multilateral trade liberalization. The different motivations of the two groups led to a need for enormous political skills in forging a majority for internationalist objectives, as evidenced by the increasing constraints on foreign aid as various special interests achieved amendments requiring a multitude of actions.

What changed recently was the end of the Cold War as a driving force in international economic policy in the United States (and in other countries as well). That removed an important constituency from the pro–free trade coalition. It is not that most former Cold Warriors turned protectionist: It is that they failed to support trade liberalization with the same vigor as before.

At the same time, however, the humanitarians seem to have decided (erroneously, based on available evidence) that globalization is hurting poor countries. They have some genuine issues, and it is certainly true that globalization, or increasing economic integration with the rest of the world, is not a seamless process in which all benefit incrementally at the same rate. Addressing these issues is certainly important.

But there is also an irrational element. Part of that has always been there, as the quotation from Governor Clinton's letter made clear. There were warnings that train travel in excess of fifteen miles per hour would be hazardous to health; and that was resistance to change. In some cases, the concerns have a valid basis, such as with the environment, because as we get richer we can afford to address some of the side effects of having gotten there.

But in the present circumstances, I think there are some causes for concern. The first, already implicitly stated, is that those who perceive globalization to be harming the poor are in fact largely misinformed. Secondly, many of those people have formed nongovernmental organizations (NGOs) that have been very vocal in disproportion to their membership; those NGOs are not accountable as governments are and yet they demand voices at the table alongside governments. This is dangerous for a number of reasons, but since many of the NGOs are focused on globalization, the politicians seem to have been willing to "give those issues" to the NGOs, regardless of the merits of the case. The resulting international paralysis regarding international institutions and progress in addressing the genuine issues associated with globalization strikes me as potentially dangerous.

Let me turn now to policy with respect to developing countries. When most developing countries were very poor and almost entirely rural, the humanitarians could support giving them greater access to developed countries' markets and few special interests (including labor) in developed countries were concerned.

At the same time, the examples of East Asia clearly showed that very rapid development could be achieved with appropriate economic policies and open economies. Simultaneously, however, the newly industrializing countries (as they were then called) were gaining economic muscle, and it is often forgotten how very poor people were in countries such as Korea. With the competitive ability of the East Asian economies, and later others, greatly enhanced, protectionist pressures increased. Yet that runs the risk of greatly impairing the prospects for economic growth and poverty reduction in those countries that are now attempting economic policy reform. Even if governments in those countries are able to do the politically necessary (which is often painful and requires fighting vested interests there), they cannot achieve gains anywhere nearly as quickly as they could with less protection against their products in developed countries. To be sure, they can still achieve much more satisfactory results with appropriate policies, but given the depths of poverty and the degree of catch-up needed, less market access surely reduces the feasible rate of economic growth.

Let me finally turn to something more to the direct interest of economic historians. About fifteen years ago, I was asked to give a paper at a conference of economic historians. The question that I was asked to address was "what is different about twentieth-century globalization from nineteenth-century globalization, or in the catch-up process, to use the economic historians' term?" So I did some research. On that basis, I was confident that one could say that, at least for the East Asian countries that began their process of opening up in the late 1950s and 1960s, the opportunity to export enabled them to grow much more rapidly than they could have done had they had to rely on the domestic market, as nineteenth-century growth did. The difference in the twentieth century was that those who wanted to change policy regimes had achieved much bigger benefits than a similar policy switch could have done in the nineteenth century. This was partly due to lower transport and communications costs, but also partly due to lower tariff and other trade barriers. One statistic illustrates this: South Korea's per capita income growth in percentage terms over any single decade between 1960 and 1995 was greater than British per capita income growth over the entire nineteenth century!

There are reasons for this more rapid growth: a largely unskilled labor force (in the 1960s) could be employed to produce unskilled labor–intensive goods without encountering rapidly diminishing returns; competition from foreign producers is a major spur in countries with small domestic markets (as they necessarily are when people are very poor). There is also a role for importing technology and ideas, although in my judgment that is more important once countries have attained "middle income" status than it is for very poor countries.

And growth, and maintaining appropriate economic policies, is politically easier when growth is rapid: Losers lose less, and there are more new opportunities to shift into new and profitable activities. If one tries to identify those who lost absolutely in Korea in the 1960s or 1970s, there were relatively few factory closings, and the losers were largely older peasants, and even then their offspring often sent remittances from their urban jobs, so that rural living standards were rising rapidly. Urban employment grew 10 percent per year, while real wages were growing an average 8 percent. In those circumstances, there are few absolute losers. Even after 1997, all Koreans would agree that living standards had skyrocketed since the 1960s. That is not the same process as in the nineteenth century: Opportunities and living standards for the poor rose much more rapidly in the late twentieth century.

The countries that have not yet achieved the transition to more open economies, with their attendant supporting domestic policies, are having a hard time doing so. Political opposition is a major factor, and that gets intensified both by slower growth and by the rhetoric and reality of protection in developed countries.

How to get the antiglobalizers to recognize that the policies they advocate by and large achieve results opposite to those intended seems to me to be a major challenge for the international economic policy community.

Ronald Rogowski

I have taken seriously the brief to try to identify the cost and benefits, the winners and the losers, from easier trade in goods, factors, and services— from what is commonly called "globalization." That's obviously related to

Ronald Rogowski is professor of political science at the University of California—Los Angeles.

the question that Clive Crook raised, "Will this kind of globalization continue?" What are the odds that, exactly as happened in the waning nineteenth century, globalization will stall out or self-destruct because the costs are too high for too many people?

On one level we have a standard story of generalized benefits and localized costs. The benefits are clear for the world at large, and indeed for each individual country in what Dowrick and Delong called, in their paper for this conference, "the convergence club." From that standpoint, what we need is more globalization, not less; and we need to think more about the remaining barriers. Anna J. Schwartz raised the issue of migration, and there's a strong case to be made for much greater and possibly unlimited migration. As Niall Ferguson pointed out, increasing political fragmentation is also a concern, particularly in the light of an important literature—which somehow has hardly been mentioned here—about how high borders are. Even with relatively open policies, political fragmentation can significantly impede exchange of goods, services, and factors.

The costs of globalization get less discussion, but they are crucial. Following Williamson and Lindert's paper here, I'll discuss them under two headings: *within* countries and *between* countries. Both raise moral issues we haven't talked about and possibly are not well equipped to talk about. But in the crassest sense these costs have political consequences. That is most obviously the case *within* countries, particularly in powerful, advanced countries that could cause free trade to "stall out." Well, who are the losers within those advanced countries? The standard theory identifies them, and Lant Pritchett spoke eloquently about them in our discussions here: the unskilled workers.

Unskilled workers in today's developed countries are the counterpart of the European landowners and farmers of the nineteenth century, the ones who see themselves as most threatened by more open trade and are likeliest to turn against it. Just consider the aspect that is best documented, namely the growing *inequality* between the skilled and unskilled in the developed countries. The premium to a college education in lifetime earnings, which was below 40 percent as recently as the 1960s, is now hovering right around 70 percent. We have absolutely declining real wages; or, where wages are kept above market-clearing levels by restrictions on labor supply, as in much of Europe, high levels of unemployment. And we have growing insecurity, maybe affecting everybody, but surely most strongly affecting unskilled workers.

Now to be sure, some of this loss, maybe a lot of it, is due to technological change; but if our standard theories mean anything, globalization cannot be helping. Indeed, it should be harming unskilled workers in at least four ways:

- through classic Stolper-Samuelson effects, given that unskilled labor is the scarce factor within each of the advanced countries;

- by migration, which we know historically from Jeff Williamson's work has even more powerful effects (an important addendum is the finding from Hatton and Chiswick's paper here that, among the *illegal* immigrants, we find overwhelmingly unskilled people. The reason for that is clear once stated, namely that the unskilled aren't as easy to detect; but it also suggests that any attempt to crack down is going to fail most significantly among the unskilled);
- the possibility of capital flight, raised most notoriously in the Ross Perot line about the "giant sucking sound" from Mexico (this of course is the link to the between-countries story, the possibility that capital will move from the advanced to the less developed countries, entailing a further decline in advanced-country real wages. In fact, we've seen almost no capital flight; the big question remains the one Lucas asked a decade ago: why doesn't capital flow from rich to poor countries?); and
- greater exposure to exogenous shocks.

The political effects of growing inequality, some of it caused by globalization, some by technological change, seem to me already apparent. The most alarming is the xenophobic and protectionist movements that are now spreading like a rash around Europe. LePen, Haider, and the resurgent German Right draw heavily and I think predictably on unskilled, usually male, usually young, workers. The Austrian Socialist Party, notoriously, is simply losing its young people, its young unskilled workers, to the Haider movement.

Unions in the United States, of course, are also becoming more protectionist, and the more general story is to be found in the works, separately and collaboratively, of Ken Scheve and Matt Slaughter. Starting with the U.S. survey evidence, and extending now to France and the United Kingdom, they find consistently that the single best predictor of general support for free trade is *education*. The more educated the person is, the more human capital she possesses, the likelier she is to express generalized support for free trade; conversely, of course, it is the less educated who express generalized support for protection and isolation.

I don't think this is because of the great command of international economics that is being imparted by high schools and colleges. I think it's a shrewd assessment of self-interest. The more educated you are, the more likely you are to benefit from globalization and trade and the likelier you are to withstand relatively well the kinds of exogenous shocks that come from a more open economy. Now the good news is that in most of the advanced societies the median voter is skilled, which means—barring some sort of disaster—majority support for continued openness. The bad news is that the really unskilled, in particularly the ineducable, may become increasingly desperate and alienated losers; and the question then arises, what policy remedies if any can one adopt?

Redistribution is widely practiced in the advanced countries, and it's worth recalling that redistribution was quite explicitly advocated by Stolper and Samuelson in their landmark 1941 article. Since the aggregate gains from trade will always outweigh the losses, they said, one can always compensate the losers and come out ahead. But of course if you think on another level, redistribution simply impedes readjustment. It discourages people, for example, from acquiring the human capital that a more globalized market demands.

The second possibility, and particularly an answer to the volatility of a globalized economy, is some kind of social insurance. Not generalized redistribution, but something like the active labor market policies in Scandinavia that are supposed to help you through the transition. And we see of course in the empirical evidence of David Cameron and Dani Rodrik's work that this seems to happen: The more trade-exposed a country is, the more it relies on social insurance mechanisms. But Soskice and Iversen have begun to point out, in some more recent work, that extensive social insurance encourages a maladapted form of human capital, namely *highly specific* human capital. The more social insurance mechanisms a society has, the more rational it is for people to invest, not in generalized and transferable human capital, but in highly sector- or firm-specific kinds of human capital that turn out to be worthless if that sector or firm goes sour. So social insurance, too, doesn't look like a particularly good adaptation to the global market.

So the third and presumably best answer is more, and more suitable, human capital, and subsidies to its acquisition that to some extent internalize education's positive externalities. But that still leaves us with the moral and political issue of what to do with the "tail" of the distribution that is just not very educable, with the people whom nature has cut out to be pretty unskilled. I think we all see the dilemma, but the policy answer is by no means clear.

With that unresolved, let's turn to the question of gains and losses *between* countries. Lindert and Williamson rightly suggest that a lot more of the action is going on there than within countries. So why are some countries left behind, and why does investment not flow to poor countries? I shall of course resolve all of these very large issues in my remaining thirty seconds.

As I understand it—and the economists present will rush to correct me—four large classes of answers are proffered:

- *locational economies of scale,* represented at this meeting by the Venables and Crafts paper;
- *externalities to human capital,* the explanation associated with Romer and Lucas;
- *total factor productivity,* the explanation (or perhaps only description)

that goes back to Solow and was represented here by Greg Clark; and, finally,

- the neoclassical answer, namely *bad institutions and bad policies.*

I confess that I am drawn much more to the "bad institutions, bad policies" story, for much the same reason that Lant Prichett suggested yesterday, namely that these are the one thing that can explain the very rapid reversals that we observe, wherein a country suddenly moves from stagnation or decline to very rapid growth. (Anne O. Krueger mentioned the case of Korea as one of the most dramatic.) None of the other supposed explanations—local agglomerations of production, accumulation of human capital, learning by doing, or cultural shift—it seems to me, can change quickly enough to account for these sudden spurts.

But if this is right, why don't we just get universal convergence to good policies? It's frequently argued that we will, but so far there's little evidence in that direction. As I've tried to show in a recent paper, if you work through a pretty standard political economy model, assuming voters maximize a convex combination of policy per se and wages, what you come out with under completely mobile capital in a two-country Cournot equilibrium is *divergence:* As capital becomes more mobile, the countries that are already more capital-friendly become more so, the ones that were less capital-friendly become even less so, and therefore, surprisingly enough, more impoverished.

I think this is roughly what we see in the real world, most markedly in a place like sub-Saharan Africa, where real GDP per capita has steadily declined over twenty years in most countries. But that said, only a few countries, especially if they happen to be really big countries, need to get it right or even halfway right to have a major effect. If China becomes, as it has, a hospitable place for investment, then that can have a major effect on the developed world, leading to even greater pressure on the unskilled in the first world.

That brings us full circle back to the question, assuming that some of these countries are going to get it right and grow and export, and that this contributes both to future world welfare *and* to lower first world wages, then what do we do in terms of policy for the unskilled workers here? It's very much in our interest to figure that out, because if we don't the outcome could be very bad indeed.

Contributors

Richard E. Baldwin
Graduate Institute of International
    Studies
11A Ave de la Paix
CH-1202 Geneva
Switzerland

Michael D. Bordo
Department of Economics
New Jersey Hall
Rutgers University
New Brunswick, NJ 08901-1284

Charles W. Calomiris
Graduate School of Business
Columbia University
3022 Broadway Street, Uris Hall
New York, NY 10027

Barry R. Chiswick
Department of Economics
    (MC 144)
University of Illinois at Chicago
601 S. Morgan Street, Room
    2103 UH
Chicago, IL 60607-7121

Gregory Clark
Department of Economics
University of California, Davis
Davis, CA 95616

Nicholas Crafts
Department of Economic History
London School of Economics
Houghton Street
London WC2A 2AE
England

Clive Crook
The Economist
25 St. James's Street
London, SW1A 1HG
England

Gerardo della Paolera
The American University of Paris
6, rue du Colonel Combes
75007 Paris
France

J. Bradford DeLong
Department of Economics
601 Evans Hall
University of California, Berkeley
Berkeley, CA 94720-3880

Steve Dowrick
School of Economics (Building 26)
Faculty of Economics and Commerce
Australian National University
Canberra ACT 0200
Australia

Barry Eichengreen
Department of Economics
University of California, Berkeley
549 Evans Hall 3880
Berkeley, CA 94720-3880

Riccardo Faini
Ministero del Tesoro
Direzione I
Via XX Settembre 97
00187 Rome
Italy

Robert C. Feenstra
Department of Economics
University of California, Davis
Davis, CA 95616

Niall Ferguson
New York University
Leonard N. Stern School of
  Business
Henry Kaufman Management
  Center
44 West Fourth Street
New York, NY 10012

Ronald Findlay
Department of Economics
Columbia University
1022 International Affairs Building
420 West 118th Street
New York, NY 10027

Marc Flandreau
Economics Department
Institut d'Etudes Politiques, Paris
FNSP, 4, rue Michelet
75007 Paris
France

Timothy J. Hatton
Department of Economics
University of Essex
Wivenhoe Park
Colchester, Essex CO4 3SQ
England

Douglas A. Irwin
Department of Economics
Dartmouth College
Hanover, NH 03755

Harold James
History Department
218 Dickinson Hall
Princeton University
Princeton, NJ 08544-1017

Charles I. Jones
Department of Economics
University of California, Berkeley
549 Evans Hall, #3880
Berkeley, CA 94720-3880

Peter B. Kenen
Department of Economics
Fisher Hall
Princeton University
Princeton, NJ 08544

Anne O. Krueger
International Monetary Fund
700 19th Street, NW, Suite 12-300F
Washington, DC 20431

Peter H. Lindert
Department of Economics
University of California, Davis
Davis, CA 95616

Joel Mokyr
Department of Economics
Northwestern University
2003 Sheridan Road
Evanston, IL 60208

Larry Neal
328A David Kinley Hall
1407 W. Gregory Drive
University of Illinois at Urbana-
  Champaign
Urbana, IL 61801

Maurice Obstfeld
Department of Economics
University of California, Berkeley
549 Evans Hall #3880
Berkeley, CA 94720-3880

Kevin H. O'Rourke
Department of Economics
Trinity College
Dublin 2
Ireland

Richard Portes
London Business School
Regent's Park
London NW1 4SA
England

Lant Pritchett
Kennedy School of Government
Harvard University
79 John F. Kennedy Street
Cambridge, MA 02138

Ronald Rogowski
Department of Political Science
4289 Bunche Hall
University of California, Los Angeles
Los Angeles, CA 90095-1472

Peter L. Rousseau
Department of Economics
Vanderbilt University
Box 1819, Station B
Nashville, TN 37235

Anna J. Schwartz
National Bureau of Economic
    Research
365 Fifth Avenue, 5th Floor
New York, NY 10016-4309

Richard Sylla
Stern School of Business
New York University
44 West 4th Street
New York, NY 10012-1126

Alan M. Taylor
Department of Economics
University of California, Davis
One Shields Avenue
Davis, CA 95616

Mark P. Taylor
Department of Economics, Room
    S1.108
University of Warwick
Coventry CV4 7AL
England

Anthony J. Venables
Department of Economics
London School of Economics
Houghton Street
London WC2A 2AE
England

Marc Weidenmier
Department of Economics
Claremont McKenna College
Claremont, CA 91711

Jeffrey G. Williamson
Department of Economics
216 Littauer Center
Harvard University
Cambridge, MA 02138

Author Index

Subject Index

Made in the USA
Lexington, KY
11 January 2016